Bioinformatics: Principles and Analysis

Bioinformatics:
Principles and Analysis

Edited by **Gretchen Kenney**

SYRAWOOD
PUBLISHING HOUSE

New York

Published by Syrawood Publishing House,
750 Third Avenue, 9ᵗʰ Floor,
New York, NY 10017, USA
www.syrawoodpublishinghouse.com

Bioinformatics: Principles and Analysis
Edited by Gretchen Kenney

International Standard Book Number: 978-1-68286-291-9 (Hardback)

Printed in the United States of America.

Contents

Preface

This book aims to highlight the current researches and provides a platform to further the scope of innovations in this area. This book is a product of the combined efforts of many researchers and scientists from different parts of the world. The objective of this book is to provide the readers with the latest information in the field.

Bioinformatics is a dynamic field that emphasizes on the use of computational methods and tools to understand and analyze biological data. It has undergone rapid development over the past few decades. This book contains some path breaking studies in mapping and analysing DNA and RNA, genome annotation, gene identification, evolution modeling, etc. It includes contributions of experts and scientists from different parts of the world which will provide innovative insights into this field. The contents of this book will prove to be an invaluable resource for professionals, academicians and students, alike.

I would like to express my sincere thanks to the authors for their dedicated efforts in the completion of this book. I acknowledge the efforts of the publisher for providing constant support. Lastly, I would like to thank my family for their support in all academic endeavors.

Editor

A computational technique for prediction and visualization of promoter regions in long human genomic sequences

Q. M. Alfred[1]*, K. Bishayee[1], P. Roy[2] and T. Ghosh[3]

[1]University Institute of Technology, University of Burdwan, West Bengal, India 713104
[2]Department of Biotechnology, University of Burdwan, West Bengal, India, 713104
[3]Burdwan Medical College and Hospital, West Bengal, India.

This communication proposes a simple algorithm with high specificity and sensitivity for determining promoter regions in human genomic sequences. This method relies upon non-redundant and experimentally verified promoter data sets form Eukaryotic Promoter Database (EPD) as training parameters. This technique predicts and computationally satisfies the promoter regions in the NCBI annotated database around gene sequences.

Keywords: Promoter, CpG islands, transcription start site (TSS), discrete fourier transform/ fast fourier transform (DFT/FFT).

INTRODUCTION

Objective of human genome project is to correctly annotate the regulatory regions, transcription start and stop site, coding regions, exons and introns etc. Promoter is a fragment of DNA sequence centered on transcription-start-sites (TSS), is biologically responsible for the transcription from DNA to RNA sequence. Therefore reliable recognition of promoter region is essential for understanding the biological mechanism as well as helping the field of genetic engineering. As every gene is recognized by the features of promoter sequence and widely varies among species to species. Some promoter features are well reported in literatures, for example, TATA box which is sometimes located at -10 to -35 positions upstream of TSS (0 postion), CpG islands is another well known promoter feature mostly found in eukaryotic (human, mouse etc.) genomes but not in prokaryotes(*Escherichia coli* etc.). Till date, no feature is found which deterministically confirms the existence promoter sequence. The above mentioned feature in combine with some other features predicts the existence of promoter sequence in large genomes. Experimentally (biochemical method) finding a promoters form huge genome like human is

almost impossible for researchers. Hence, prediction of promoters by computational method is a highly regarded area of interest. Several research groups have developed techniques and algorithms for in-silico (in computer) promoter recognition. Among them, weight matrix model (Prestridge, 1995; Bucher, 1990), Hidden Markov Model (HMM) (Burge and Karlin, 1997; Kulp and Haussler, 1996), feature (signal/context) based model (TATA, CpG etc.) (Pedersen et al. 1998; Ponger and Mouchiroud 2002; Wu and Xie, 2007; Zhang, 1998a; Fickett and Hatzigeorgiou 1997), neural network model (Brunak et al., 1991; Pedersen and Engelbrecht 1995), graph based model (Matsuda et al., 2002) etc. But each method has its inherent advantage and disadvantage. Most of the models suffer from computational complexities and specificities in promoter prediction.

Motivated by the importance and presence of good research authors have proposed a simple but novel approach in promoter region identification as well as potential TSS prediction. Present method conceptually differs from the above well known techniques

METHOD

This method is highlighted by the following steps:

*Corresponding author. E-mail: quazi_alfred@yahoo.co.in.

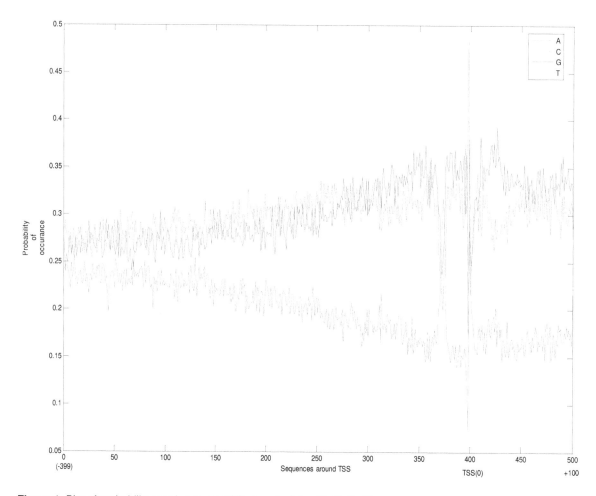

Figure 1. Plot of probability matrix around TSS of nucleotides (A, T, C, G).

Step-1:

First, more than 1500 Homo sapiens genes and their known promoter regions are gathered from SIB-EPD (Eukaryotic Promoter Database) database (Cavin et al., 1998). These data sets are selected as they are non-redundant, experimentally verified and filtered. Human promoter sequences in the region of -399 to +100(500 bp) around TSS are considered as testing data sets from these experimentally known genes.

From these data sets, a positional frequency matrix for four (4) nucleotides is derived at each 500 positions (4×500 matrix). As the number of promoter is very high, this frequency matrix may be approximated as positional probability matrix from the following relation.

$$P_{i<A,T,C,G>}=f_{i<A,T,C,G>}=\frac{n_{i\langle A,T,C,G\rangle}}{N}$$

Where;
i =-399,-398……..0(TSS).. 1, 2…..100
N=no. of promoters, n_i=no. of nucleotide at i^{th} positions

Step-2:

This 4×500 matrix signifies discrete probability distribution of four nucleotides at each 500 individual positions, is graphically plotted in

Figure 1. Unlike the weight matrix model, where a weight table is calculated in terms of background frequency ¼ (occurrence of any nucleotide), but here the probability at each position is exploited in the calculation of score.

Now, any unknown and long human genomic sequence is scanned by sliding window of length 500, which is then shifted by 1bp (may be shifted more for fast computation compromising error). Within each window, the scores are entered according to the occurrence of any of the four nucleotides with reference to the probability matrix. Total score is calculated by adding scores at each position within a window. This process is repeated by shifting the window by 1bp along the forward strand (5-3) direction.

Step -3:
Assuming background probability 0.25, the cut-off score is chosen as 125 for 500 positions.

During scanning any genomic sequence, when the total score in the sliding window exceeds 125, is selected as hit segment. Now, the scores and the positions of these hits are sorted out for further processing.

In each hit segment, probabilities during 371-420 positions are Fourier transformed (DFT), which will be used later.

Step-4:

Maximum occurrence value among four nucleotides are interpolated for all 500 positions in the probability matrix to generate a

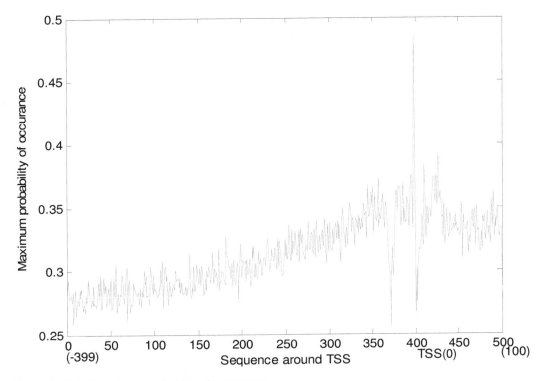

Figure 2. Plot of maximum probability of occurrence.

1×500 matrix, is plotted in Figure2. Then for 50 positions (-371 to +420) around transcription start site (TSS) are transformed (DFT) into frequency domain, shown in Figure 3. After DFT (FFT), the coefficients are obtained at 50 discrete frequency points. Among these, 0th coefficient (DC value) indicates sum of all max-values or global shape of the template but form 1st coefficient to the rest carries detailed feature of this template shape(shown in Figure 2).

Step-5:

It is found that, in eukaryotic genome the score is high (>130) in CpG rich regions whether the potential promoter exists or not. Therefore, to avoid false prediction rate (false positive), the probability score form position -29(371) to +20(420) duration is Fourier transformed for all hit positions (where score>125) at time of scanning a genomic sequences. First 20(1:20) DFT coefficients of each hit sequence (500 lengths) are compared with the template DFT (1:20) (Figure 3). When this yields minimum difference value, confirms the pattern matching with template, shown in Figure 2. Here, the objective is to consider those sequences as promoters which shows minimum error with the reference pattern of promoters

RESULTS

This algorithm is applied on the five moderately long genomic contigs of Homo sapiens chromosome 22 from NCBI's GenBank (Benson et al., 1998) of total length 3.65 Mbp and 41 TSSs in the forward strands. Table 1 shows the overview of these genomic sequences.

Earlier Xiomeng Li et al. (2008) and Lu et al. (2008) has compared the performance between four well known promoter prediction techniques in comprehensive manner.

Table 2 comparatively shows their performance in terms of specificity and sensitivity when checked with Chromosome-22 sequence annotated by Sanger institute (http://www.sanger.ac.uk/HGP/Chr22).

Among them, DragonGSF and HPR-PCA (Lu et al., 2008) are preferable for predicting promoter region for long genomic sequences. Table 3 details the performance comparison of this algorithm (designated as PR-DFT) along with DragonGSF and HPR-PCA.

To illustrate this algorithm with an example, Figure 4 graphically represents the score of matching when scanning the contig NT_037887 in chromosome-16. The peaks relative to the surroundings predicts potential promoter regions. Figure 5 confirms the result after matching the DFT coefficients to the reference shown in Figure 4. Lower the value of their difference (score) higher the probability of prediction.

From the figure it is obvious that it predicts eight (8) promoter (gene) regions in *NT_037887* between 140000 to 175000bp.

According to NCBI annotation this region consists of seven (7) promoters. The predicted TSS also satisfies the annotated site with acceptable accuracy.

This algorithm is implemented in Matlab® environment with SUN Ultra-40M2 workstations.

Data sets

Data sets used here as training data is taken from SIB-EPD promoter database. NCBI annotated human data-

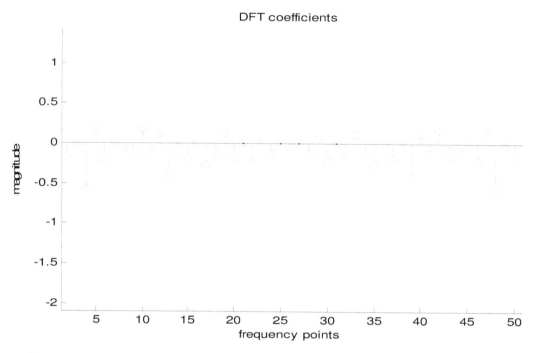

Figure 3. DFT coefficients for 50 frequency points (point 1 is not shown having magnitude 17).

Table 1. Description of large genomic sequence used as test set.

Contig	Description	Length	Number of TSS
NT_028395.3	Homo Sapiens	647850	9
NT_011521.4	Chromosome 22	830225	11
NT_011525.7	Genomic sequence	1384186	8
NT_019197.5		320440	5
NT_011526.6		464629	9
Total		3647330	41

Table 2. Performance of four prediction system (Source: Xiomeng Li et. al)

Systerm	TP	FP	S_e	S_P
DragonGSF	269	69	0.6844	0.7959
FirstEF	331	501	0.8422	0.3978
Eponin	199	79	0.5064	0.7158
HPR-PCA	301	65	0.7659	0.8224

database used for computational verification of the algorithm.

DISCUSSION

This communication presents a simple technique by visualizing promoter sequence. Identification of promoter regions demands some decision making by visualizing and comparing both the score plot as well as DFT diffe-rence plot.

Generally, peaks (high score) with respect to background (low score) can be decided as promoter sequence. But when there are high peaks along with background can be considered as high CG rich regions.

ACKNOWLEDGEMENT

This work is financially supported by AICTE, India under RPS grant.

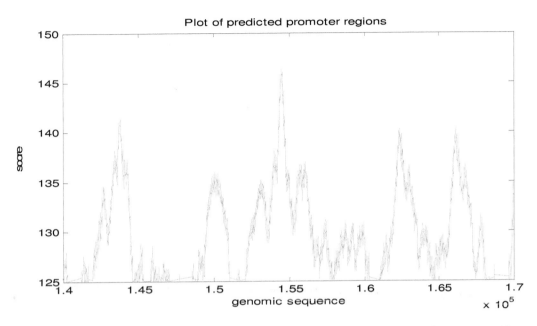

Figure 4. Plot of predicted promoter regions in NT_037887 (contig-1 14000-170000) of Chromosome-16.

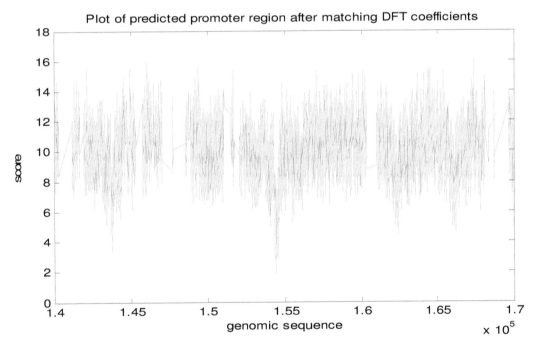

Figure 5. Plot of difference between DFT coefficients for Figure 4.

REFERENCES

Bucher P (1990). "Weight matrix descriptions of four eukaryotic RNA Polymerase II promoter elements derived from 502 unrelated promoter sequences. "Mol. Biol. 212: 563-589. Benson DA, Boguski MS, Lipman DJ, Ostell J, Ouellette BF, "Genebank", Nucleic Acids Res. 26(1):1-7.

Brunak S, Engelbrecht J, Knudsen S (1991). "Prediction of human mRNA donor and acceptor sites from the DNA sequence" J. Mol. Biol. 220: 49–65.

Burge C, Karlin S (1997). "Prediction of complete gene structures in human – 84- genomic DNA." J. Mol. Biol. 268: 78-94.

Cavin PR, Junier T, Bucher P (1998). 'Eukaryotic Promoter Database EPD", Nucleic Acids Res.26, 353-357.

Fickett JW Hatzigeorgiou AG (1997)."Eukaryotic Promoter Recognition." Genome Res. 7: 861-878.

http://www.sanger.ac.uk/HGP/Chr22

Kulp D, Haussler D (1996), "A generalized hidden Markov model for the recognition of human genes in DNA." Proc Int Cong Intell Syst. Mol. Biol. 4: 134-142.

Li XM, Zeng J, Yan H (2008). "PCA-HPR: A New Method of Human Promoter Recognition Based on Principle Component Analysis." Bioinformation 2(9): 373-378

Liu YM, Li XM, Yan H (2008). Codon Relation Analysis for Promoter Recognition Using Indepent Component Analysis", J. Inf Comput. Sci. 5(1): 33-39

Matsuda T, Motoda H, Washio T (2002) "Graph-based induction and applications," Advanced Engineering Informatics", 16:135-143.

Pedersen AG, Baldi P (1998). "DNA Structure in Human RNA polymerase II Promoters.", J. Mol. Biol. 281: 663-673.

Pedersen AG, Baldi P (1999). "The Biology of Eukaryotic Promoter Prediction —a Review.", Comput. Chem. 23(3): 191-207

Pedersen AG, Engelbrecht J (1995). "Investigations Escherichia coli promoter sequences with artificial neural networks: new signals discovered upstream of the transcriptional start point" , Proceedings, third international conference on intelligent systems for molecular biology (ISMB-95) 292–299.

Ponger L, Mouchiroud D (2002). "CpG ProD: identifying CpG islands associated with transcription start sites in large genomic mammalian sequences." Bioinformatics 18: 631-634.

Prestridge DS (1995). "Predicting Pol II promoter Sequences using Transcription -87- Factor Binding Sites." J. Mol. Biol. 249: 923-932.

Wu S, Xie X (2007). "Eukaryotic promoter prediction based on relative entropy and positional information.", Phys. Rev. E 75: 041908 1-7.

Zhang MQ (1998a). "A discrimination study of human core-promoters in silico.", Proc. Pacific Symp. Biocomputing 1998.

In silico effective inhibition of galtifloxacin on built Mtb-DNA gyrase

D. Gowsia[1,2], B. Babajan[1], M. Chaitanya[1], C. Rajasekhar[1], P. Madhusudana[1,2], C. M. Anuradha[1], G. Ramakrishna[3], K. R. S. Sambasiva Rao[2] and Chitta Suresh Kumar[1]

[1]DBT-Bioiformatics Facility Center, Department of Biochemistry, S.K. University, Anantapur-515055, India.
[2]Department of Biotechnology, Acharya Nagarjuna University, Guntur, India.
[3]Department of Microbiology, Government College (for Boys), Anantapur-515055, India.

Tuberculosis (TB) resurged in the late 1980s and now kills approximately 3 million people a year. The reemergence of tuberculosis as a public health threat has created a need to develop new anti-mycobacterial agents. The Mtb-DNA Gyrase is an attractive target for development of new drugs due to its indispensable role in catalyzing the negative supercoiling of DNA and is essential for efficient DNA replication, transcription and recombination. Fluoroquinolone families of inhibitors are developed against the Mtb-DNA gyrase which show the best inhibition with DNA gyrase in the past. Due to the development of Multi-drug resistant Mycobacterium tuberculosis strains, the drugs showed less efficiency on the targets, recently, a new flouroquinolone inhibitor was identified (Galtifloxacin), which shown best inhibition. In this study we carried out Homology model of 0 Mtb-DNA gyrase, secondary structure analysis and active site analysis. Docking studies were also carried out with the Galtifloxacin and Amifloxacin and are helpful for further studies on the development of novel drugs against Mtb-DNA gyrase.

Key words: Mycobacterium tuberculosis, DNA gyrase, galtifloxacin, amifloxacin, homology modeling, docking

INTRODUCTION

Tuberculosis (TB) is a contagious and deadly disease that spreads through the air, which has reached pandemic proportions. According to the World Health Organisation (WHO), in 2006 there were 9.2 million new cases and 1.7 million deaths from TB around the world (http://www.who.int/tb/en/). A significant proportion of these new cases and deaths occur in HIV-positive people. Owing to population growth, the number of new cases arising each year is increasing globally, posing a continued health and financial burden in various parts of the world, particularly Asia and Africa. TB is caused predominantly by Mycobacterium tuberculosis (Mtb), an obligate aerobic bacillum that divides at an extremely slow rate. The chemical composition of its cell wall includes peptidoglycans and complex lipids, in particular mycolic acids, which are a significant determinant of its virulence (Shah et al., 2007; Sylvain et al., 2007). The unique structure of the cell wall of Mtb allows it to lie dormant for many years as a latent infection, particularly as it can grow readily inside macrophages, hiding it from the host's immune system. The vast majority of TB infections are caused by Mtb, but other closely related mycobacteria (*Mycobacterium bovis* and *Mycobacterium africanum*) can also cause the disease (Ducati et al., 2006; Morcillo et al., 2007). When TB becomes active, it typically affects the lungs (pulmonary TB), but in around 25% of cases (immunosuppressed persons and young children), the bacteria enter the blood and infect other parts of the body, such as the pleura, the meninges, the lymphatic system, the genitourinary system and the bones and joints. Infection with HIV suppresses the immune system, rendering individuals more susceptible to TB infection, or allowing a latent infection to activate (Rosas-Taraco et al., 2006). Co-infection allows faster progress of both TB and HIV (Goletti et al., 1996) and also uncontrolled treatment, with rifampicin and isonizaid however, has led to rise of multi-drug-resistant TB inci-dence (MDR-TB: resistance to isonizaid and rifampicin and possibly other drugs), Poor compliance to the therapy

*Corresponding author. E-mail: chitta34c@gmail.com.

using these drugs combined with the second-line anti-tuberculotic (e.g. Pyrazinamide and ethambutol) resulted in extremely drug-resistant strains (XDR-TB: resistant to at least three of the available antituberculotics including rifampicin and isoniazid) (Babajan et al., 2009). The emergence of such strain urges the development of novel drug targets and drugs.

Most well known bacterial drug targets are the type II DNA topoisomerases, DNA Gyrase and topoisomerase IV. These ATP-dependent enzymes act by a transient double-stranded DNA break and cooperate to facilitate DNA replication and other key DNA transactions (Levine et al., 1998). DNA Gyrase is unique in catalyzing the negative supercoiling of DNA and is essential for efficient DNA replication, transcription and recombination, whereas topoisomerase IV has a specialized role in chromosome segregation. DNA Gyrase is a tetrameric A2B2 protein. The A subunit (90 to 100 kDa, depending on the bacterial species) carries the breakage-reunion active site, whereas the B subunit promotes ATP hydrolysis, needed for energy transduction. Mycobacterium tuberculosis genes encoding DNA Gyrase were identified from the genome analysis as a gyrB-gyrA contig in which gyrA and gyrB encode the A and B subunits, respectively (Madhusudan et al., 1994). Surprisingly, there is no evidence of the topoisomerase IV parC and parE gene homologs in the genome of Mycobacterium tuberculosis (Cole et al., 1998). It appears that DNA Gyrase is the sole topoisomerase drug target in Mycobacterium tuberculosis. The absence of a homologue in eukaryotic cells makes Mtb-DNA Gyrase an attractive target for small molecule inhibitors with the potential to have broad antibacterial activity. The Fluoroquinolone are a family of synthetic broad-spectrum antibiotics. They prevent bacterial DNA from unwinding and duplicating (Hooper et al., 2001). Since bacteria and humans unwind DNA with different enzymes, most of those enzymes (topoisomerases) in humans are not affected.

To the best of our knowledge, little attention has been paid to the theoretical study on the three-dimensional modeling of Mtb-DNA Gyrase to make a deeper understanding of Mtb-DNA Gyrase at molecular level, an attempt is made in this paper to build up a three-dimensional model of Mtb-MurB by the homology module of mod9v5 and structural characterization performed using different *in silico* approaches.

MATERIALS AND METHODS

All calculations were conducted on AMD-Athlon 64 bit, 3.4MHz, Dual processing machine. *In silico* analysis of the Mtb-DNA Gyrase structural model proceeded in three steps: sequence analysis, homology modeling and inhibitors docking and scoring. The procedures employed for each step are described below.

Molecular modeling

The amino acid sequence (15607148) of Mtb-DNA Gyrase was

obtained from National Center for Biotechnology Information (NCBI, http:// www.ncbi.nlm.nih.gov/). Homologous sequence identity was carrier out through the BLASTp server (Altschul et al., 1990), to search for short nearly exact matches and corrected the dataset to remove redundant sequences. Multiple sequence alignments for a series of Mtb-DNA Gyrase, were conducted using the ClustalW1.8 routine with default parameters (Chenna et al., 2003). They were grouped them based on sequence source (6 different sources). The alignment revealed functionally important conserved residues in all DNA Gyrase family of enzymes. Search of the PDB database using the sequence of Mtb-DNa Gyrase as the entry, structures of *Escherichia coli* DNA Gyrase (PDB code 1AB4) and *Staphylococcus aureus* topoisomerasae IV (PDB code 2INR) were used as templates to build a 3D model of Mtb-DNA Gyrase. A structural model of Mtb-DNA Gyrase was generated through homology modeling by the program Modeller9v5 (Sali et al., 2003). Total of 100 structures were generated, from which best one model were checked followed by optimization. Optimization of protein reduces the steric clashes of the side chains without modifying the backbone of the protein and it was able to solve bad contacts. And finally 1AB4, 2INR and Mtb-DNA Gyrase models were checked to assess the quality of the structure, resulting in the PROCHECK (Laskowski et al., 1993). To predict the secondary structure and active site amino acids of Mtb-DNA Gyrase 3D model was submitted to PDBSUM server (Laskowski et al., 2005).

Mtb-DNA gyrase docking with major fluoroquinolone inhibitors

For Docking with Autodock4, Galtifloxacin and Amifloxacin inhibitors were retrieved from pubchem (CID:5379, CID:55492) and were optimized using hyperchem program and AutoTors, as implemented in the Autodock tool kit (ADT) software program (Osterberg et al., 2002), which was used to define the torsional degrees of freedom to be considered during the docking process. The number of flexible torsions defined for L-CA and its derivative, was nineteen. Preparation of Mtb-DNA Gyrase enzyme with the AutoDock Tools software involved the addition of polar hydrogen atoms to the macromolecule, a necessary step for the correct calculation of partial atomic charges. Gasteiger charges were calculated for each atom of the macromolecule in AutoDock 4.0 instead of Kollman charges, which were used in the previous versions of this program. Histidine residues were maintained unprotonated as previously determined to be appropriate three-dimensional affinity grids of size 50 × 50 × 50 Å with 0.375 Å spacing were positioned around the active site. For every snapshot of protein, the center of the grid was set to the position of the neighborhood of the ASP145 cavity using the average coordinates of Cα atoms of Arg150 and Tyr206. During each docking experiment, 50 runs were carried out. The rest of the parameters were set as default values. At the end of a docking experiment with multiple runs, a cluster analysis was performed. Docking solutions with a inhibitors all-atom root mean square deviation (RMSD) within 0.1 nm of each other were clustered together and ranked by the lowest docking energy.

RESULTS AND DISCUSSION

3D model building

Figure 1 explains final alignment, which was modeled as Mtb-DNA Gyrase in Modeller 9v5. This alignment was obtained after manual adjustments of the initial alignment from the BLAST server. Four reference proteins, PDB, ID, 1AB4 and 2INR were used to model the structure of the Mtb-DNA Gyrase and homology scores comparing to target proteins were 60 and 59%, respectively. High level

```
Mtb-DNA   ---------MTDTTLPPD-----DSLDRIEPVDIEQEMQRSYIDYAMSVIVGRALPEVRDG   47
1AB4      ------------------------------------------------VGRALPDVRDG   11
2INR      MGSSHHHHHHSSGLVPRGSHMLEVSEIIQDLSLEDVLGDRFGRYSKYIIQERALPDVRDG   60
                                                          ****:.****

Mtb-DNA   LKPVHRRVLYAMFDSGFRPDRSHAKSARSVAETMGNYHPHGDASIYDSLVRMAQPWSLRY  107
1AB4      LKPVHRRVLYAMNVLGNDWNKAYKKSARVVGDVIGKYHPHGDSAVYDTIVRMAQPFSLRY   71
2INR      LKPVQRRILYAMYSSGNTHDKNFRKSAKTVGDVIGQYHPHGDSSVYEAMVRLSQDWKLRH  120
          ****:.**:.***** *    ::_   ***: *.:_.:.:*:*****:::*::**:.*  :.**;

Mtb-DNA   PLVDGQGNFGSPGNDPPAAMRYTEARLTPLAMEMLREIDEETVDFIPNYDGRVQEPTVLP  167
1AB4      MLVDGQGNFGSIDGDSAAAMRYTEIRLAKIAHELMADLEKETVDFVDNYDGTEKIPDVMP  131
2INR      VLIEMHGNNGSIDNDPPAAMRYTEAKLSLLAEELLRDINKETVSFIPNYDDTTLEPMVLP  180
           *::  :**  ** ..*.._.*******  :*: :.* *::  ::::***_.*: ***_.      * *:*

Mtb-DNA   SRFPNLLANGSGGIAVGMATNIPPHNLRELADAVFWALENHDADEEETLAAVMGRVKGPD  227
1AB4      TKIPNLLVNGSSGIAVGMATNIPPHNLTEVINGCLAYID----DEDISIEGLMEHIPGPD  187
2INR      SRFPNLLVNGSTGISAGYATDIPPHNLAEVIQATLKYID----NPDITVNQLMKYIKGPD  236
          :::.****.*** .*** ***:********  *:  .  :   ::     *  :*    ***

Mtb-DNA   FPTAGLIVGSQGTADAYKTGRGSIRMRGVVEVEEDSR-GRTSLVITELPYQVNHDNFITS  286
1AB4      FPTAAIINGRRGIEEAYRTGRGKVYIRARAEVEVDAKTGRETIIVHEIPYQVNKARLIEK  247
2INR      FPTGGIIQGIDGIKKAYESGKGRIIVRSKVEEETLRN-GRKQLIITEIPYEVNKSSLVKR  295
          ***..:.:* .:*  .::*:* :  . * :.   .* .  * :.::* **:*: ::     ::

Mtb-DNA   IAEQVRDGKLAGISNIEDQSSDRVGLRIVIEIKRDAVAKVVINNLYKHTQLQTSFGANML  346
1AB4      IAELVKEKRVEGISALRDS-DKDGMRIVEVKRDAVGEVVLNNLYSQTQLQVSFGINMV  306
2INR      IDELRADKKVDGIVEVRDET-DRTGLRIAIELKKDVNSESIKNYLYKNSDLQISYNFNMV  354
          * *   : :: **  :.*::  *: *:.*..*:*:.  .: :  *  **.::**  *:.  **:

Mtb-DNA   AIVDGVPRTLRLDQLIRYYVDHQLDVIVRRTTYRLRKANERAHILRGLVKALDALDEVIA  406
1AB4      ALHHGQPKIMNLKDIIAAFVRHRREVVTRRTIFELRKARDRAHILEALAVALANIDPIIE  366
2INR      AISDGRPKLMGIRQIIDSYLNHQIEVVANRTKFELDNAERKMHIVEGLIKALSILDKVIE  414
          *:.  .* *:.    : *  ::  *  **  *.*  *.*     *   :  .**  :.    *  :*

Mtb-DNA   LIRASETVDIARAGLIELLDIDEIQAQAILDMQLRRLAALERQRIIDDLAKIEAEIADLE  466
1AB4      LIRHAPTPAEAKT-----------------------------------------------  379
2INR      LIRSSKNKRDAKE-----------------------------------------------  427
          *** : .*

Mtb-DNA   DILAKPERQRGIVRDELAEIVDRHGDDRRTRIIAADGDVSDEDLIAREDVVVTITETGYA  526
1AB4      ALVANPWQLG-----NVAAMLERAGDD------AARPEWLEPEFGVRDG-----------  417
2INR      --------------NLIEVYE---------------------------------------  434
                          ::     : :

Mtb-DNA   KRTKTDLYRSQKRGGKGVQGAGLKQDDIVAHFFVCSTHDLILFFTTQGRVYRAKAYDLPE  586
1AB4      ------------------------------------------------------------
2INR      ------------------------------------------------------------

Mtb-DNA   ASRTARGQHVANLLAFQPEERIAQVIQIRGYIDAPYLVATRNGLVKKSKLTDFDSNRSG  646
1AB4      --------------LYYLTEQQAQAILDLR---------LQKLTGLEHEKLLDEYK-----  450
2INR      --------------FTEEQAEAIVMLQ---------LYRLTNTDIVALEGEHK-----  464
                        *:.  . .. ::      *

Mtb-DNA   GIVAVNLRDNDELVGAVLCSAGDDLLLVSANGQSIRFSATDEALRPMGRATSGVQGMRFN  706
1AB4      ---------ELL-------------------------DQIAELLRILGSADR--------  468
2INR      --------ELE-------------------------ALIKQLRHILDNHDA--------  482
                   .*                         :  :.:.

Mtb-DNA   IDDRLLSLNVVREGTYLLVATSGGYAKRTAIEEYPVQGRGGKGVLTVMYDRRRGRLVGAL  766
1AB4      -----LMEVIREELVREQFG-------------------------DKRRTEIT-----   493
2INR      ------LLNVIKEELNEIKKKFK-----------------------SERLSLIEAE   509
          ::: *::: *    :                               . *   :

Mtb-DNA   IVDDDSELYAVTSGGGVIRTAARQVRKAGRQTKGVRLMNLGEGDTLLAIARNAEESGDDN  826
1AB4      ------------------------------------------------------------
2INR      IEEIK-------------------------------------------------------  514

Mtb-DNA   AVDANGADQTGN  838
1AB4      ------------
2INR      ------------
```

Figure 1. Multiple sequence alignment of Mtb-DNA gyrase with crystal structure of *E. coli* topoisomerase (1AB4) and with topoisomerase of Streptococcus (2INR) the gap (-) represent the deleted regions, star (*) represents the conserved regions in the Figure.

of sequence identity could guarantee more accurate alignment between the target sequence and template structure. In order to define structurally conserved regions (SCRs) of the protein family, the multi-dimensional alignment based on the structural identity was used to superimpose four reference structures and 126 SCRs were determined (Figure 1). The Modeller program uses the spatial constraints, determined from the crystal structure of a template protein, to build a 3D model of the target protein with unknown tertiary structures, on the basis of amino acid sequence homology to the sequence alignment (Figure 2a). The Ramachandran plots reveal more than 95% of the amino acid residues in the favorable regions of the plot for the whole enzyme. The

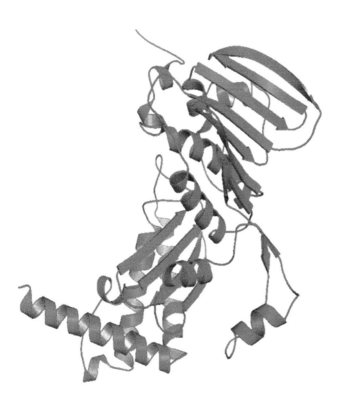

Figure 2a. Built 3 D model of Mtb-DNA Gyrase.

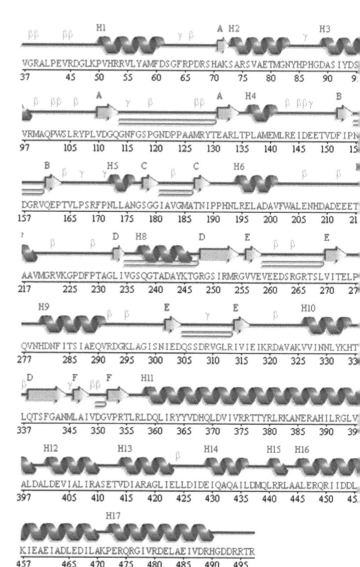

Figure 2b. Secondary structure of Mtb-DNA Gyrase.

main structural elements of the optimized Mtb-SHMT homology model as appeared are shown in Figure 3. In secondary structure, build model consists of three domains, the N-terminal domain, the second N-terminal domain and small domain, The N-terminal domain mediates inter subunit contacts and folds into two α-helices and one β-stand. The second N-terminal domain or large domain binds PLP, has most of the active site residues and folds into an α-β-α sandwich containing nine confirmations. The confirmation clearly appears as four beta sheets, three beta-alpha-beta motifs, four beta hairpins, one beta bulge, fifteen stands, , twenty two helices, thirty five helix-helix interactions, nineteen beta turns and three gamma turns (Figure 2b).

Active site analysis

The active site amino acids residues in built Mtb-DNA Gyrase model was accomplished based on its alignment to the templates 1AB4 and 2INR, which are shows 3 residues that is Arg65, Tyr100 and Asp160 (Figure 4a and 4b). Super position of the templates 1AB4 and 2INR on to Mtb-DNA Gyrase model shows structural similarity at actives site residues.

Inhibitors docking with Mtb-DNA gyrase

Most docked inhibitors interacted by the same mode of the inhibitors, Galtifloxacin and Amifloxacin within the Mtb-DNA Gyrase binding site. The different surface pocket for residue seems to be an important factor in determining the different mode of Galtifloxacin interaction with Mtb-DNA Gyrase of Arg[65] and Asp[160] amino acid residues (Figure 4a). Where the Amifloxacin shown interaction with amino acids Tyr[100] and Arg[65] (Figure 4b).

The energies of these residues were calculated based on their best docking scores (Table 1), that showed the binding free energies for Galtifloxin was -15.28 kcal/mol, RMSD of 0.08, inhibitory constant of $+1.43e^{-13}$ for rank one cluster. For Amifloxacin binding energies was -11.08 Kcal/mol, RMSD of 0.25, inhibitory constant of $+4.87e^{-8}$ for rank one cluster. It is revealed that energy difference and cluster runs of the Galtifloxacin, Amifloxacin with Mtb-DNA Gyrase, Galtifloxacin shown best interaction compare with Amifloxacin.

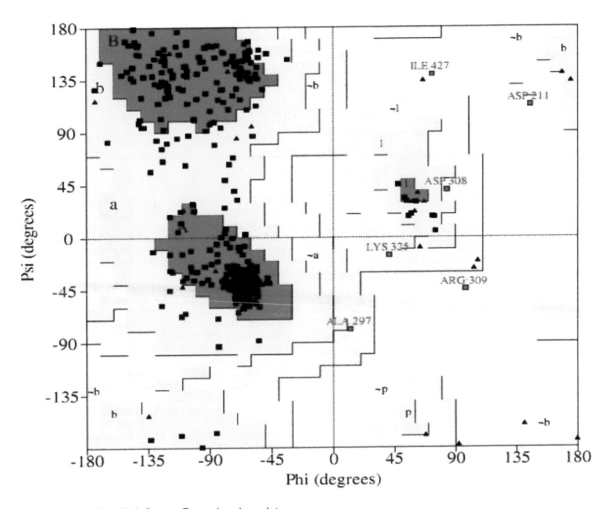

Figure 3. Built Mtb-DNA Gyrase Ramachandran plot.

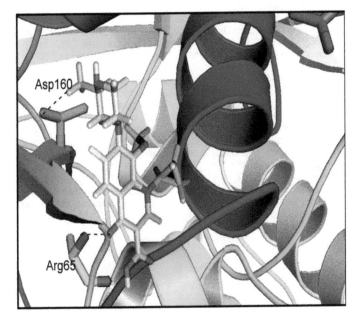

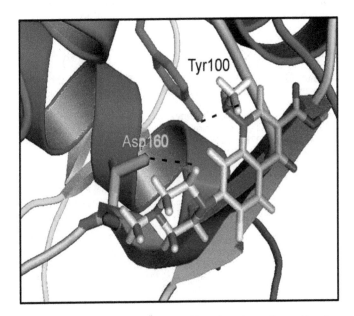

Figure 4a. Galtifloxin interaction with active site amino acids Mtb-DNA Gyrase Asp160 and Arg65.

Figure 4b. Amifloxacin interaction with active site amino acids of Mtb-DNA Gyrase Asp160, Tyr100.

Table 1. Docking score of Galtifloxacin and Amifloxacin with Mtb-DNA Gyrase.

Protein	Ligand	Cluster rank	RMSD	Lowest energy (Kcal/mol)	Free energy (ΔG)	Inhibition constant *Ki*
Mtb-DNA gyrase	Galtifloxacin	1	0.08	-15.28	-15.33	$+1.43e^{-08}$
		2	1.25	-11.03	-11.16	$+3.02e^{-08}$
		3	0.23	-10.78	-10.89	$+5.45e^{-08}$
		4	0.00	-10.43	-10.52	$+7.55e^{-08}$
	Amifloxacin	1	0.25	-11.08	-11.20	$+4.87e^{-08}$

Conclusion

In this study, we performed the homology modeling of Mtb-DNA Gyrase through the sequence similarity of 60% and we have adopted a stringent to measure the Mtb-DNA Gyrase enzyme which is not homologous to human (negligible similarity above the e-value threshold of 0.005). We also use the docking studies on Mtb-DNA Gyrase with currently market available drugs; Galtifloxacin and Amifloxacin. The docking studies explore the opportunities opened by the differences found for the interactions of Galtifloxacin and Amifloxacin and it was shown that the Galtifloxacin is a very good target for Mtb-DNA Gyrase compared to Amifloxacin. The results were satisfactory for development of more accurate Galtifloxacin derivative drugs against deadly Mycobacterium.

ACKNOWLEDGEMENTS

The authors are thankful to UGC and DBT, New Delhi for their financial assistance (UGC, New Delhi (F.No.33-222/2007-SR) and DBT, New Delhi (No.BT/BI/25/001/2006) to carry out this work and also to Prof. Chitta Suresh Kumar for providing a computer facility and valuable suggestion during Manuscript writing.

REFERENCES

Altschul SF, Gish W, Miller W, Myers EW, Lipman DJ (1990). GyraseBasic local alignment search tool.Gyrase J. Mol. Biol. 215(3): 403-10.

Babaja B, Anuradha CM, Chaitanya M, Gowsia D, Kumar CS (2009). Gyrase In silico structural characterization of Mycobacterium tuberculosis H37Rv UDP-N-acetylmuramate dehydrogenase. Gyrase Int. J. Integr. Biol. 6(1):12-16.

Chenna R, Sugawara H, Koike T, Lopez R, Gibson TJ, Higgins DG, Thompson JD (2003). GyraseMultiple sequence alignment with the Clustal series of programs.Gyrase Nucl. Acids Res. 31(13): 3497-500.

Cole ST, Brosch R, Parkhill J, Garnier T, Churcher C, Harris D, Gordon SV, Eiglmeier K Gas S, Barry CE, 3rd, Tekaia F, Badcock K, Basham D, Brown D, Chillingworth T, Connor R, Davies R, Devlin K, Feltwell T, Gentles S, Hamlin N, Holroyd S, Hornsby T, Jagels K, Krogh A, McLean J, Moule S, Murphy L, Oliver K, Osborne J, Quail MA, Rajandream MA, Rogers J, Rutter S, Seeger K, Skelton J, Squares R, Squares S, Sulston JE, Taylor K, Whitehead S, Barrell BG (1998). GyraseDeciphering the biology of Mycobacterium tuberculosis from the complete genome sequence. Gyrase Nat. 393(6685): 537-544.

Ducati RG, Ruffino-Netto A, Basso LA, Santos DS (2006). GyraseThe resumption of consumption -- a review on tuberculosis.Gyrase Mem. Inst. Oswaldo Cruz. 101(7): 697-714.

Goletti D, Weissman D, Jackson RW, Graham NM, Vlahov D, Klein RS, Munsiff SS, Ortona L, Cauda R, Fauci AS (1996). GyraseEffect of Mycobacterium tuberculosis on HIV replication. Role of immune activation.Gyrase J. Immunol. 157(3): 1271-8.

Hooper DC (2001). GyraseEmerging mechanisms of fluoroquinolone resistance.Gyrase Emerg, Infect, Dis. 7(2): 337-41.

Laskowski RA, Chistyakov VV, Thornton JM (2005) GyrasePDBsum more: new summaries and analyses of the known 3D structures of proteins and nucleic acids. Gyrase Nucl. Acids Res. 33 (Database issue): 266-268.

Laskowski RA, MacArthur MW, Moss DS (1993). GyrasePROCHECK a program to check the stereo chemical quality of protein structure. Gyrase J. Appl. Cryst. 26: 283-291.

Levine C, Hiasa H, Marians KJ (1998). GyraseDNA gyrase topoisomerase IV: biochemical activities, physiological roles during chromosome replication, and drug sensitivities.Gyrase Biochim Biophys Acta 1400(1-3): 29-43.

Madhusudan K, Ramesh V, Nagaraja V (1994). GyraseMolecular cloning of gyrA and gyrB genes of Mycobacterium tuberculosis: analysis of nucleotide sequence.Gyrase Biochem. Mol. Biol. Int. 33(4): 651-60.

Morcillo N, Zumarraga M, Imperiale B, Di Guiles B, Chirico C, Kuriger A, Alito A, Kremer K, Cataldi A (2007). GyraseTuberculosis transmission of predominant genotypes of Mycobacterium tuber-culosis in northern suburbs of Buenos Aires city region. Gyrase Rev. Argent. Microbiol. 39(3): 145-50.

Osterberg F, Morris GM, Sanner MF, Olson AJ, Goodsell DS (2002). Gyrase Automated docking to multiple target structures: incorporation of protein mobility and structural water heterogeneity in AutoDock. Gyrase Proteins 46(1): 34-40.

Rosas-Taraco AG, Arce-Mendoza AY, Caballero-Olin G, Salinas-Carmona MC (2006).GyraseMycobacterium tuberculosis upregulates co-receptors CCR5 and CXCR4 while HIV modulates CD14 favoring concurrent infection.Gyrase AIDS Res. Hum. Retroviruses 22(1): 45-51.

Sali A, Blundell TL (1993). GyraseComparative protein modelling by satisfaction of spatial restraints.Gyrase J. Mol. Biol. 234(3): 779-815.

Shah NS, Wright A, Bai GH, Barrera L, Boulahbal F, Martin-Casabona N, Drobniewski F, Gilpin C, Havelkova M, Lepe R, Lumb R, Metchock B, Portaels F, Rodrigues MF, Rusch-Gerdes S, Van Deun A, Vincent V, Laserson K, Wells C, Cegielski JP (2007). GyraseWorldwide emergence of extensively drug-resistant tuberculosis.Gyrase Emerg. Infect. Dis. 13(3): 380-7.

Sylvain G, Loubna T, Anne-Laure Bañuls (2007).GyrasePulmonary Tuberculosis and Mycobacterium Tuberculosis: Modern Molecular Epidemiology and Perspectives.Gyrase Encyclopedia of Infectious Diseases:Modern Methodologies, by M.Tibayrenc. 1-30.

## 3

Insights into the key enzymes of secondary metabolites biosynthesis in *Camellia sinensis*

Aditi Sharma, Ankita Punetha, Abhinav Grover and Durai Sundar*

Department of Biochemical Engineering and Biotechnology, Indian Institute of Technology (IIT) Delhi, Hauz Khas, New Delhi 110016, India.

Tea is one of the most popular beverages consumed throughout the world. It is a source of important secondary metabolites like monoterpenoids, carotenoids and catechins. Monoterpenoids and carotenoids are important constituents of tea aroma. The formation of tea aroma involves synthesis and release of volatile monoterpenoids and carotenoids. On the other hand, catechins are responsible for the beneficial health effects of tea. Detailed *in silico* analysis of enzymes: Phytoene Synthase (PSY), a key enzyme in the carotenoid biosynthetic pathway and β-primeverosidase (BPR), a diglycosidase responsible for release of bound volatile terpenoids, have been undertaken in this study. Similarly, to study catechin biosynthesis, key enzymes in the flavonoid pathway namely, flavanone-3-hydroxylase (F3H), dihydroflavonol-4-reductase (DFR) and leucoanthocyanidin reductase (LAR), have been identified and studied. The comparative sequence analysis of PSY, F3H, DFR and LAR was carried out to identify the consensus and conserved amino acids using multiple sequence alignment. Phylogenetic trees were created to understand the evolutionary relationship of these enzymes present in different species. The three dimensional model structures were obtained for PSY, BPR, F3H, DFR and LAR by homology modeling to gain insights into the structure function relationships of these enzymes. Multiple templates were used to generate more accurate models of the enzymes. The models were further improved by loop refining and energy minimization. Binding pocket analysis was also done to identify the putative substrate binding sites and understand the enzyme-substrate interactions of each of these enzymes. The computational analysis of these key enzymes, PSY, BPR, F3H, DFR and LAR, provided valuable insights into the mechanism of formation of tea aroma and the synthesis of bioactive secondary metabolites like catechins.

Key words: *Camellia sinensis*, catechin, modeller, phytoene synthase, β-primeverosidase, flavanone-3-hydroxylase, dihydroflavonol-4-reductase, leucoanthocyanidin reductase.

INTRODUCTION

Tea is one of the most widely consumed beverages in the world. India is among the major producers of tea. The commercial importance of the tea plant (*Camellia sinensis*) is due to its popularity as a refreshing health drink. It also has great value as a source of important secondary metabolites. The leaves of two varieties of *C. sinensis* are: *assamica* and *sinensis,* are used to manufacture tea. It is classified into three major categories according to the manufacturing process: green (unfermented) tea, oolong (partially fermented) tea, and black (fully fermented) tea.

Here, fermentation is the result of enzymatic action and exposure to atmospheric oxygen during the manufacturing process. The quality of tea can be assessed in terms of two main parameters, namely: flavour and colour of processed tea. Flavour comprises of taste and aroma. The non-volatile constituents are responsible for taste

---

*Corresponding author. E-mail: sundar@dbeb.iitd.ac.in.

Abbreviations: PSY, Phytoene synthase; **BPR,** β-primeverosidase; **F3H,** flavanone-3-hydroxylase; **DFR,** dihydroflavonol-4-reductase; **LAR,** leucoanthocyanidin reductase; **VFC,** volatile flavour compounds; **MEP,** methylerythritol phosphate; **GPP,** geranyl pyrophosphate; **GGPP,** geranylgeranyl pyrophosphate; **EGCG,** epigallocatechin gallate; **EGC,** epi-gallocatechin, **ECG,** epicatechin gallate; **EC,** epicatechin.

while aroma is due to the volatile constituents. A strong attractive aroma is the most important and desirable characteristic of good quality tea, since our sense of smell is much more highly developed than our sense of taste. In recent years, tea has attracted more and more attention because of its reported health benefits particularly as an antioxidant (Luczaj and Skrzydlewska, 2005) and anticarcinogenic (Way et al., 2009). The flavonoids of tea are generally believed to be responsible for these effects. An important class of these flavonoids is catechins which are predominant in black tea.

Tea aroma and tea catechins

Over 500 flavour compounds have been identified in tea (Rawat and Gulati, 2008). The aroma of tea is attributed to the Volatile Flavour Compounds (VFC) in tea. A significant number of these volatile compounds originate from large precursor molecules present in tea leaves. These precursor molecules include products of lipid breakdown, terpenoids and phenolics, which are present as bound glycosides in tea leaves and are released upon the action of enzymes like glucosidases (Rawat and Gulati, 2008).

Tea manufacturing process is known to enhance the release of volatile compounds from bound precursors. Besides the above, volatile compounds synthesised by oxidation of carotenoids are also present among the VFCs (Ravichandran and Parthiban, 1998). VFCs derived from terpenoid related compounds are important components of aroma because of their desirable sweet flowery aroma.

These VFCs include monoterpene alcohols like linalool and its oxides, geraniol and products of oxidation of carotenoids like α-ionone and β-ionone (Ravichandran and Parthiban, 1998). The precursors for the synthesis of monoterpenes and tetraterpenes like carotenoids are provided by the Methylerythritol Phosphate (MEP) pathway in the plastids.

The precursors for monoterpene and carotenoid synthesis are Geranyl Pyrophosphate (GPP) and Geranylgeranyl Pyrophosphate (GGPP) respectively. Tea catechins are, primarily, flavan-3-ols. The major catechins found in tea are epigallocatechin gallate (EGCG), epi-gallocatechin (EGC), epicatechin gallate (ECG) and epicatechin (EC). Catechins are colourless, water-soluble compounds which impart bitterness and astringency to tea. They have been reported to have antioxidative, anticarcinogenic, antiallergenic, anti-inflammatory, and vasodilatory properties. Catechins are synthesised by the flavonoid biosynthetic pathway starting with phenylalanine as the precursor. Almost all of the characteristics of manufactured tea, including its taste, colour and aroma, have been found to be associated directly or indirectly with catechins (Wang et al., 2000).

Key enzymes in aroma formation and catechin biosynthesis

Phytoene synthase (PSY) is a key enzyme in the biosynthetic pathway of carotenoids. Carotenoids are an important group of precursors of volatile flavour compounds present in tea aroma (Ravichandran, 2002). PSY catalyses the first step in the biosynthesis of carotenoids that is the head to head condensation of two GGPP molecules to produce phytoene (a colourless carotenoid). Phytoene thus formed is then converted, through a series of reaction steps, into the volatile carotenoids in tea aroma. Borthakur et al. (2008) studied the relationship of PSY gene expression to the accumulation of carotenoids in tea and found that the carotenoids accumulation showed a strong dependence on the expression of PSY gene (Borthakur et al., 2008). β-primeverosidase (EC 3.2.1.149) (BPR) is a disaccharide-specific glycosidase, which hydrolyzes aroma precursors of β-primeverosides (6-O-β-d-xylopyranosyl-β-d-glucopyranosides) to liberate various aroma compounds during the manufacturing process.

Monoterpene alcohols such as linalool and geraniol, and aromatic alcohols such as benzyl alcohol and 2-phenylethanol, are present as glycosidic precursors in fresh leaves of tea plants and are released by the action of BPR. It is known that amongst all the diglycosides present in tea, namely, β-primeverosides, β-acuminosides and β-D-gluconylpyranosides β-primeverosides are the most common that is most of the aroma precursors are present as β-primeverosides (Ijima et al., 1998; Ma et al., 2001).

Therefore, β-primeverosidase is an important enzyme involved the formation of tea aroma. Flavanone 3-hydroxylase (F3H) catalyzes an early step in flavonoid metabolism leading to the formation of dihydroflavonols from flavanones. These dihydroflavonols serve as intermediates for the biosynthesis of flavonols, flavan 3-ols and anthocyanidins. A strong correlation between the concentration of catechins and *CsF3H* expression indicating a critical role of F3H in catechin biosynthesis has been reported (Singh et al., 2008).

Dihydroflavonol 4-reductase (DFR) catalyzes the stereospecific reduction of dihydroflavonols to leucoanthocyanidins (flavan-3,4-diol) using NADPH as a cofactor. The expression of DFR has been reported to be closely related to the concentration of total catechins and polyphenols in various stages of leaf development (Singh et al., 2009). Leucoanthocyanidin reductase (LAR) catalyses the conversion of 3, 4-cis-leucocyanidin to catechin. In Camellia LAR is important in biosynthesis of catechin, epigallocatechin, and anthocyanidins in flavonoid metabolism in tea leaves. It has been reported that catechin accumulation in tea leaves is regulated by the mRNA accumulation of genes involved in their biosynthesis, which include LAR along with F3H and DFR (Eungwanichayapant and Popluechai, 2009).

Table 1. Templates used for basic modeling and multi-template modeling of BPR, PSY, F3H, DFR and LAR.

S.No.	Enzymes	Basic modeling templates	Multiple template modeling templates
1.	PSY	2ZCO:A	1EZF:A, 2ZCO:A
2.	BPR	1CBG:A	1CBG:A, 1H49:A, 1V02:A, 2JF7:A, 3GNP:A
3.	DFR	2C29:D	2C29:D, 2P4H:X
4.	F3H	2BRT:A	1W9Y:A, 1GP6:A
5.	LAR	1QYC:A	2GAS:A, 1QYC:A, 1QYD:A, 2QW8:A

MATERIALS AND METHODS

Comparative sequence analysis

The protein sequences were retrieved from Swissprot database (Stutz et al., 2006). The sequences were then submitted to BLASTP (Altschul et al., 1990). The database chosen for BLASTP was Non-Redundant Data Base (NRDB). The results were used to identify closely related species. Then multiple sequence alignments were performed by using CLUSTAL W web server (Thompson et al., 1994). The results were used to identify consensus and conserved amino acid residues. The output of the multiple sequence alignments were used to construct the phylogenetic trees using PhyloDraw (Choi et al., 2000) and study the relationships among the sequences.

Three dimensional structure prediction

Modeller 9v7 was used to generate basic three dimensional structure models of the enzymes (Eswar et al., 2008). Further, the advanced modeling feature of the Modeller 9v7 was used to improve the model structures. In this, multiple templates were used as opposed to a single template used in basic modelling. Firstly, the script salign.py is used to obtain the multiple sequences alignment of the templates with the target. The templates which were chosen for each of the enzymes have been listed in Table 1. After this, the target sequence was aligned to the template sequences using the align2d_mult.py script of Modeller (Figures 1, 2 and 3). The alignment thus obtained was used to generate the final model by using the model_mult.py script. This generated 5 models for each of the enzymes. The evaluate_model.py script was used to get the DOPE score for each of the models and the model with the lowest DOPE score was selected. Further, loop refinement was done to improve the loops/regions in the model structures with poor DOPE scores. The DOPE profile of the basic model and the multiple templates model were plotted and analyzed to identify such regions. The loop modeling feature was then used to refine the structure of these loops. This was done using the loop_refine.py script of modeller. This generated 10 models whose DOPE scores were then calculated by running the model_energies.py script. The model with the lowest DOPE score was selected and its profile was generated using the evaluate_model.py script. Discovery studio 2.1 was then used to perform energy minimization and stereo chemical quality checks to arrive at the best possible three dimensional structure of the protein. The force field applied was CHARMM and the energy minimization algorithm used was steepest descent with an RMS gradient of 0.1 using a maximum of 1000 steps.

Binding pocket analysis

The predicted three-dimensional structures were then used to locate the structural pockets and cavities in the structures. This helped in identification of the putative substrate binding sites. CASTp server was used to identify the putative binding pockets and protein substrate binding sites in the generated models (Binkowski et al., 2003). It uses the weighted Delaunay triangulation and the alpha complex for shape measurements, which provides identification and measurements of surface accessible pockets as well as interior inaccessible cavities for proteins. Identification of binding sites and active sites in an enzyme structure can give insights into enzyme-substrate and enzyme cofactor interaction.

RESULTS AND DISCUSSION

The number of amino acids present in PSY, BPR, F3H DFR and LAR sequences obtained from Swissprot database are 329, 507, 347, 342 and 368 respectively and their molecular weights are 37518.9, 57041.2, 41464.8, 38674.3 and 37517.9 Da respectively as calculated by ProtPram web server (Gasteiger et al., 2003).

Comparative sequence analysis and phylogenetic trees

Closely related sequences were identified by using the BLAST$_P$ (Altschul et al., 1990) against non-redundant protein sequence database (Tables 2, 3, 4 and 5). The multiple sequence alignment of these related sequences was done to identify the consensus sequences and conserved amino acid residues. These conserved domains were later compared to the results of the binding site analysis which was carried out using CAST$_P$. However, the BLAST$_P$ results for β-primeverosidase did not contain any result with this enzyme in other species. Therefore, due to lack of deposited data a comparative sequence analysis and phylogenetic analysis for β-primeverosidase could not be done.

Two major groups were obtained from phylogenetic analysis of phytoene synthase (Figure 4). Group 1 has one subgroup namely SG1 and two mono taxa: *Helianthus annus* and *Elaeagnus umbellate*. SG1 contains two clades, taxa *Diospyros kaki* and *Actinidia deliciosa* occur in clade A while *Coffea canephora* and *Gentiana lutea* occur in clade B. *C. sinensis* and *Solanum lycopersicum* exit as mono taxae in clade A and B respectively. Group 2 contains 1 clade which has *Carica*

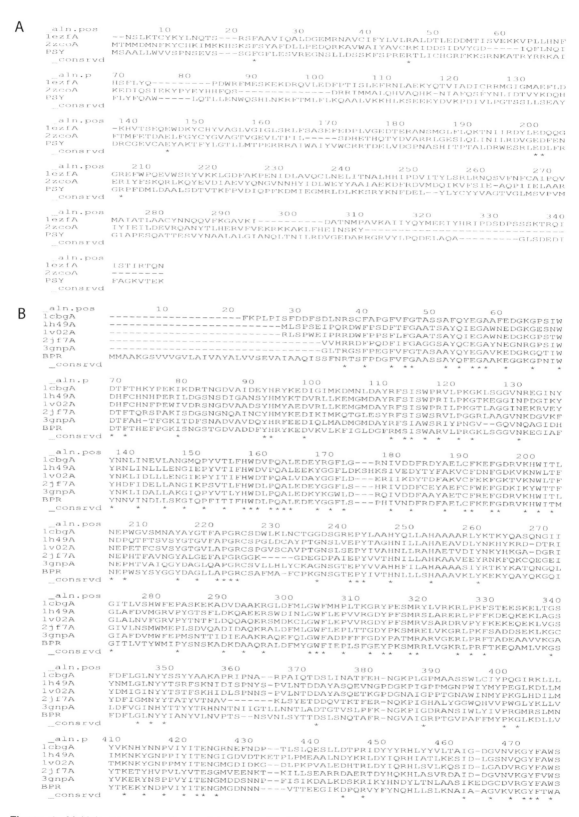

Figure 1. Multiple sequence alignment between (A) Phytoene synthase from *Camellia sinensis*, Squalene synthase from *Homo sapiens* (PDB Id - 1EZF:A) and Dehydrosqualene synthase from *Staphylococcus Aureus* (PDB Id – 2ZCO:A) (B) β-primeverosidase from *Camellia sinensis*, Cyanogenic Beta-glucosidase from *Trifolium repen* (PDB Id – 1CBG:A), Beta-glucosidase mutant from *Zea mays* (PDB Id – 1H49:A), Dhurrinase from *Sorghum bicolour* (PDB Id – 1V02:A), Strictosidine-o-beta-D-glucosidase from *Rauvolfia serpentine* (PDB Id – 2JF7:A) and Hydrolase from *Oryza sativa subsp. japonica* (PDB Id – 3GNP:A). "*" indicates a conserved region between two sequences and "-" indicates gaps.

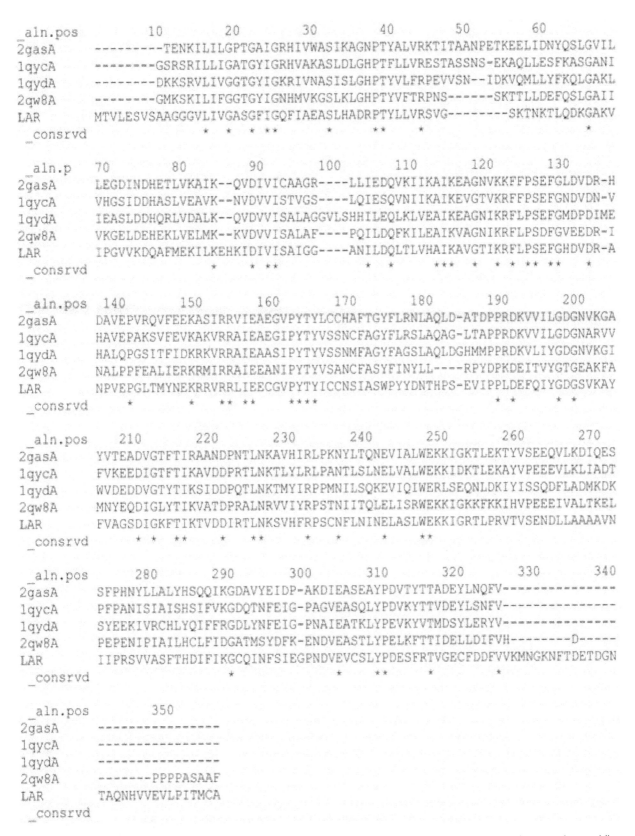

Figure 2. Multiple sequence alignment between (A) Flavanone-3-hydroxylase from *Camellia sinensis*, Leucoanthocyanidin dioxygenase from *Arabidopsis thaliana* (PDB Id - 1GP6:A) and 1-aminocyclopropane-1-carboxylate-oxidase 1 from *Petunia Hybrida* (PDB Id - 1W9Y:A) (B) Dihydroflavonol 4-reductase from *Camellia sinensis*, Dihydroflavonol 4-reductase from *Vitis Vinifera* (PDB Id - 2C29:A) and Chaperone from *Paracoccus denitrificans* pd1222. Hydrolase from *Actinomadura sp.r39* (PDB Id - 2P4H:X).

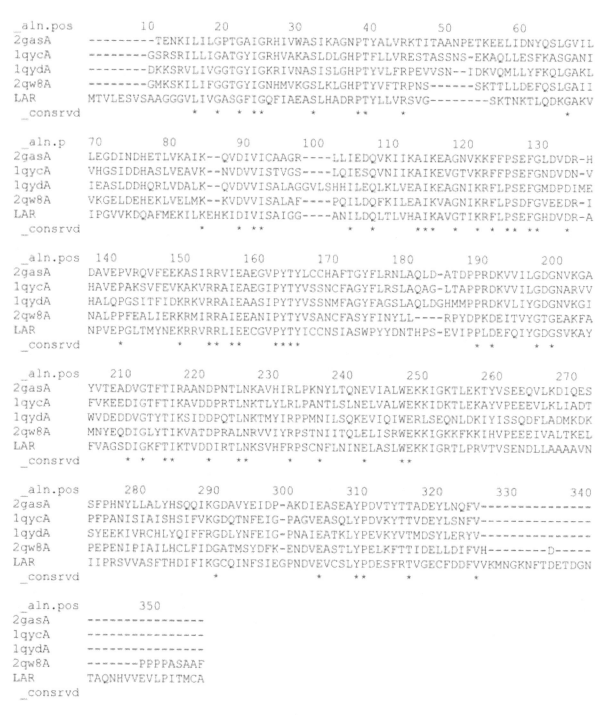

Figure 3. Multiple sequence alignment between Leucoanthocyanidin reductase from *Camellia sinensis, isoflavone reductase from Medicago sativa* (PDB Id - 2GAS:A), Phenylcoumaran benzylic ether reductase from *Pinus taeda* (PDB Id - 1QYC:A), pinoresinol-lariciresinol reductase from *Thuja plicata* (PDB Id - 1QYD:A) and Eugenol synthase 1 from *Osimum basilicum* (PDB Id - 2QW8:A).

papaya and *Citrus unshui* while *Momor charantia* exists as mono taxa in it. Phytoene Synthase from *C. sinensis* is closest to *D. kaki* and *A. deliciosa*. The most primitive forms of the enzyme include the ones in *Elaegnus umbellate* and *Momor charantia*.

The phylogenetic tree for flavanone-3-hydroxylase can be divided into 2 groups and one clade (Figure 5). The

clade contains *C. sinensis* and *Actinidia chinensis*. Group 1 has one clade which contains *Rubus coreanus* and *Pyrus communis* while *Epimedum sagittatum* exists as mono taxa near it. Group 2 contains 1 subgroup SG1 and clade which has *Gossypium hirsutum* and Dimocarpus longan. The subgroup contains *Solanum tuberosum* and *Nicotiana tabacum* in a clade while *Eustoma grandiflorum*

Table 2. Closely related protein sequences for PSY obtained using BLAST_P. The sequences with high identities with the target were used for multiple sequence alignment and phylogenetic analysis. The alignment score was obtained from multiple sequence alignment using ClustalW webserver and the distances were obtained using PhyloDraw by the neighbour joining method.

S.No	Accesssion number	Source	Identity (%)	Alignment score	Distance (s)
1	ACM44688	D. kaki	75	79	0.22
2	ACO53104	A. deliciosa	73	76	0.22
3	ABU40771	S. lycopersicum	73	75	0.25
4	ABA43898	Coffea canephora	70	74	0.25
5	ABG72805	C. papaya	70	73	0.26
6	AAF33237	C. unshiu	71	72	0.28
7	AAR86104	M. charantia var. abbreviate	72	71	0.27
8	ACU29637	E. umbellata	69	72	0.28
9	CAC27383	H. annuus	71	72	0.27
10	BAE45299	G. lutea	68	71	0.31

Table 3. Closely related protein sequences for flavanone-3-hydroxylase (F3H) obtained using BLAST_P which were used for comparative sequence analysis.

S.No	Accesssion number	Organism	Identity (%)	Alignment score	Distances
1	ACL54955	A. chinensis	89	89	0.1
2	ABW74548	R. coreanus	86	86	0.15
3	ABM64799	G. hirsutum	86	85	0.13
4	ABO48521	D. longan	86	86	0.13
5	BAD34459	E. grandiflorum	84	84	0.15
6	AAX89399	P.communis	84	85	0.16
7	Q7XZQ7	P. crispum	84	82	0.18
8	ABY63660	E. sagittatum	84	82	0.17
9	AAM48289	S. tuberosum	84	85	0.15
10	BAF96938	N. tabacum	83	82	0.15

Table 4. Closely related protein sequences for dihydroflavonol-4-reductase (DFR) obtained using BLAST_P.

S.No	Accesssion number	Organism	Identity (%)	Alignment score	Distances
1	CAC88859	R. simsii	88	87	0.13
2	ACK57789	C. maculosa	81	77	0.21
3	AAL89715	V.macrocarpon	85	79	0.2
4	ABU93477	H.annuus	80	76	0.23
5	ABQ97018	S. medusa	80	77	0.22
6	P14721	A. majus	77	74	0.25
7	ACB56920	H. pilosella	81	76	0.24
8	BAA12736	G. triflora	79	75	0.24
9	AAD56578	D. carota	79	73	0.27
10	ACN82380	V. amurensis	77	75	0.24

exists as mono taxa near this clade. *C. sinensis* is closest to *Actinidia chinensis*. The most primitive forms of the enzyme include *C. sinensis* and *A. chinensis*, which exit as an outgroup to Group 1 and 2, and *Petroselinum crispum* which exists as a segregated branch from Group 2.The molecular phylogenetic analysis of dihydroflavonol-4-reductase gave 2 groups (Figure 6). Group 1 has one subgroup namely SG1 and one clade which contains *Gentiana triflora* and *Antirrhinum majus*. SG1 contains 1 clade, taxa Rhododendron simsii and *Vaccinium macrocarpon* occur in it while *C. sinensis* exists as mono taxae near this clade. Group 2 contains 1 clade which

Table 5. Closely related protein sequences for leucoanthocyanidin reductase (LAR) obtained using BLAST$_P$.

S.No	Accession number	Organism	Identity (%)	Alignment score	Distances
1	CAI56319	*G. arboreum*	70	69	0.31
2	XP_002314885	*P. trichocarpa*	69	68	0.34
3	CAI56326	*Vi. shuttle worthii*	70	66	0.34
4	ABB77696	*P. communis*	66	64	0.33
5	ABC71328	*L. corniculatus*	65	63	0.35
6	CAI56327	*M.turcatula*	63	61	0.4
7	CAI56322	*P. coccineus*	63	61	0.39
8	CAI56328	*O.sativa*	60	56	0.43
9	CAI56320.1	*H. vulgare*	62	57	0.43
10	CAI56321	*P. taeda*	59	52	0.47

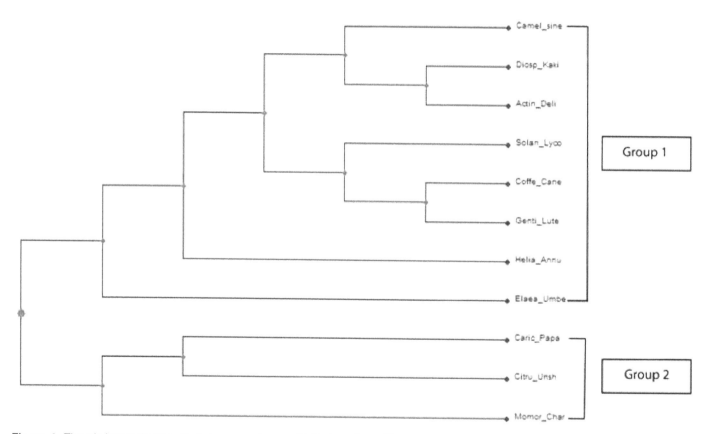

Figure 4. The phylogenetic tree of phytoene synthase with its homologs. The tree were constructed by neighbour joining method using PhyloDraw.

has *Centaurea maculosa* and *Saussurea medusa* while *Hieracium pilosella* exists as mono taxa near this clade. Group 2 also has *Helianthus annus*, *Daucus carota* and *Vitis amurensis* as mono taxae. DFR from *C. sinensis* is closest to *Rhododendron simsii* and *Vaccinium macrocarpon*. The most primitive branch is the enzyme from *Vitis amurensis*.

Two groups were obtained from the molecular phylogeny of LAR (Figure 7). Group 1 contains 1 clade and 1 subgroup. The clade has 2 taxae: *C. sinensis* and *Gossypium arboretum* while the subgroup contains *Oryza sativa* and *Hordeum vulgae* in 1 clade while *Pinus taeda* exists as a mono taxa near this clade. Group 2 contains two subgroups. Subgroup 1 contains a clade with *Populus trichocarpa* and *Pyrus communis* while *Vitis shuttleworthi* exists a mono taxa near it. Similarly subgroup 2 contains *Medicago truncatula* and *Phaseolus coccineus* in a clade with mono taxa *Lotus corniculatus* close to it. LAR from *C. sinensis* is closest to *G. arboretum* with which it shares the maximum identity.

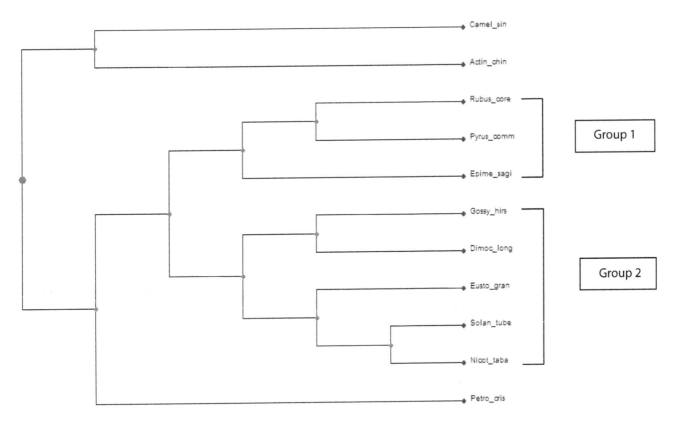

Figure 5. The phylogenetic tree of flavanone-3-hydroxylase with its homologs.

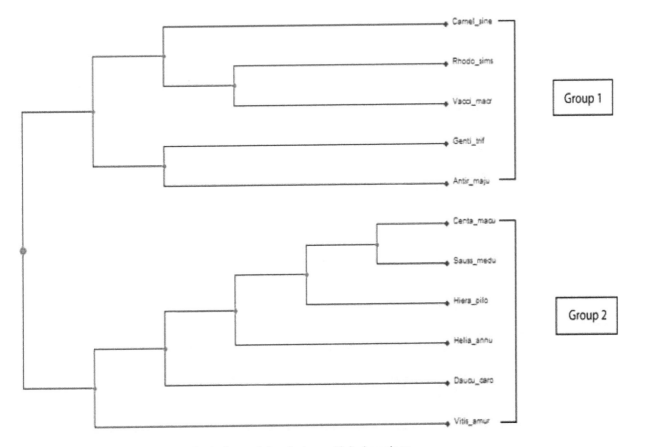

Figure 6. The phylogenetic tree of dihydroflavonol-4-reductase with its homologs.

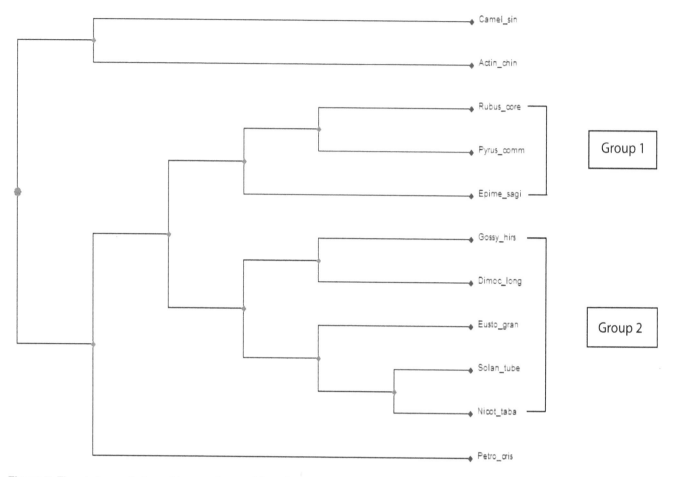

Figure 7. The phylogenetic tree of leucoanthocyanidin reductase with its homologs.

Table 6. Regions/loops of poor DOPE profile.

S.No.	Enzyme model	No. of regions	Residues
1	β-primeverosidase	2	418 to 428, 1 to 7
2	Phytoene Synthase	2	47 to 55, 103 to 108
3	Dihydroflavonol-4-reductase	3	73 to 77, 142 to 149, 161 to 167
4	Flavanone-3-hydroxylase	6	1 to 7, 22 to 28, 105 to 130, 220 to 220, 230 to 242, 340 to 345
5	Leucoanthocyanidin reductase	3	8 to 13, 308 to 321, 330 to 335

Prediction of homology models

The structures used as templates for the respective target enzymes to develop the basic and multiple-template models have been give in Table 1. The multiple templates were aligned using the align2d_mult.py script.

The models were generated using the model_mult.py script and the model with the lowest DOPE score was selected. The DOPE profiles of the basic models were plotted along with the multiple templates model using GNUPLOT (Figures 8 A, B, C and D). It can be seen that the plots for the improved models are better than the basic models.

Loop refining

The DOPE score profiles were used to identify the loops with poor DOPE score in the multiple template models. The regions/loops which were poorly modelled have been given in Table 6. The loop_refine.py script of Modeller 9v7 was used to improve the structure of these regions. This resulted in further decrease in the DOPE score. The DOPE scores of the models generated by basic modeling and advanced modeling as well as the final models obtained after loop refining have been given in Table 7.

We see that the model quality has improved by following the advanced modeling procedure followed by

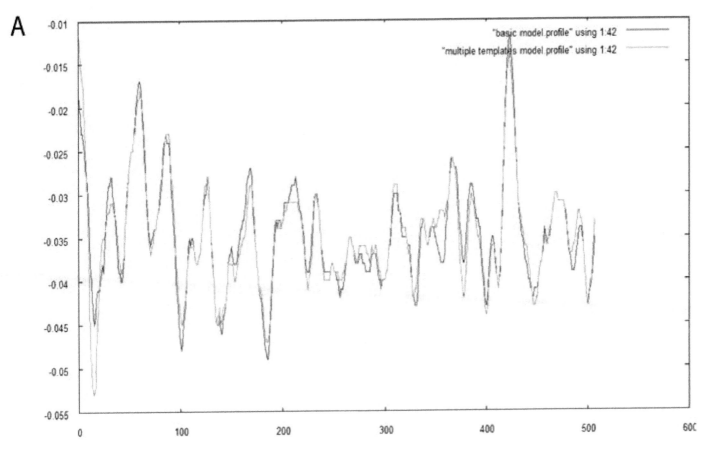

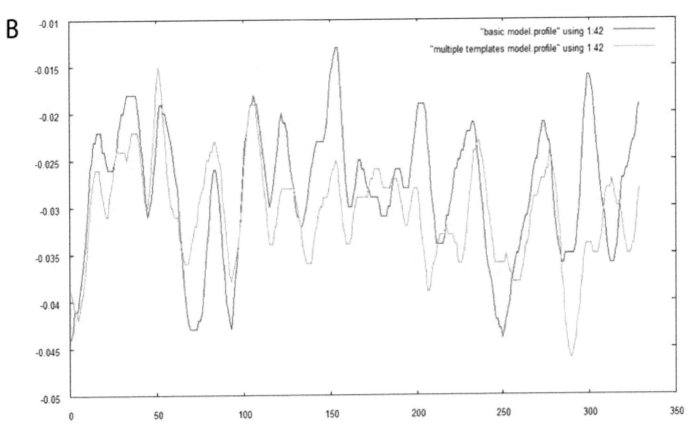

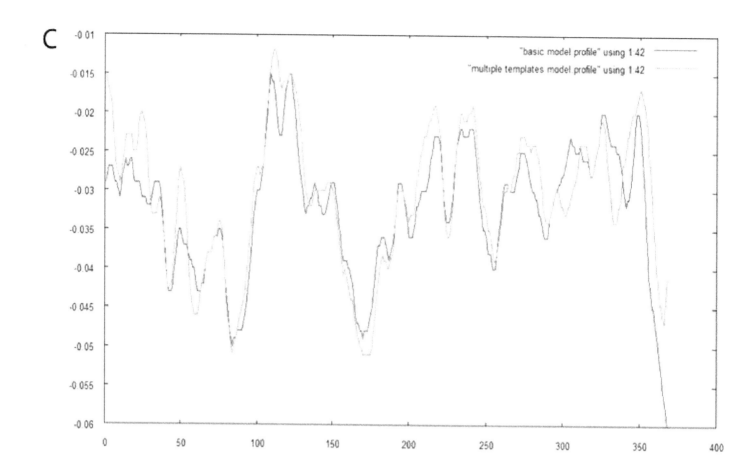

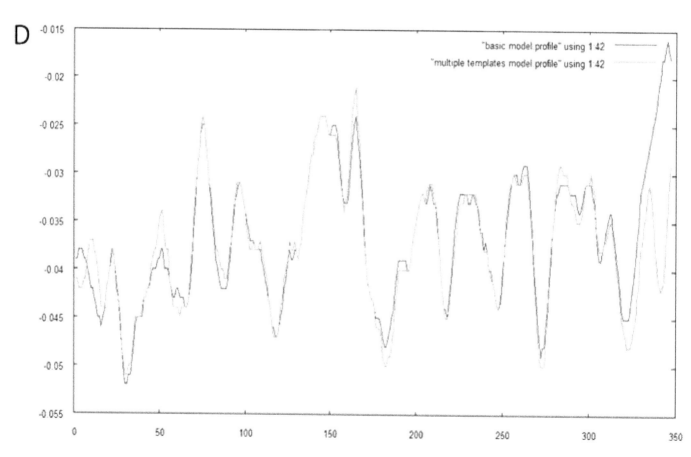

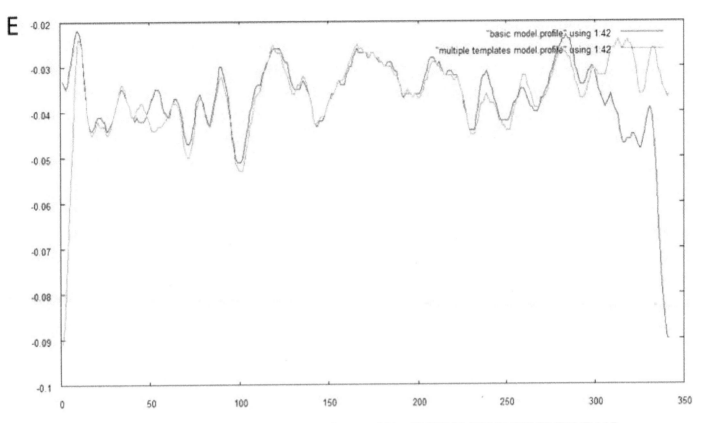

Figure 8. DOPE score profile of the basic model and multiple templates model for (A) BPR (B) PSY (C) DFR (D) F3H (E) LAR.

Table 7. DOPE score of basic models, multiple templates models and final models.

0	Enzyme model	Basic model DOPE score	Multiple templates model DOPE score	Final models DOPE score (after loop refining)
1	β-primeverosidase	-64611.58984	-66076.109375	-66212.117188
2	Phytoene Synthase	-30988.27148	-31887.291016	-32060.505859
3	Dihydroflavonol-4-reductase	-41902.91797	-41907.683594	-42024.601563
4	Flavanone-3-hydroxylase	-36218.65625	-36421.832031	-36973.710938
5	Leucoanthocyanidin reductase	-35788.60156	-38037.937500	-38435.492188

Table 8. Energy of models generated before and after minimization.

S.No.	Enzyme model	Initial potential energy (Kcal/mol)	Energy after minimization (Kcal/mol)
1	β-primeverosidase	1207309.9693	-29290.03714
2	Phytoene Synthase	715697.94340	-70384.83381
3	Dihydroflavonol-4-reductase	23983.39479	-19322.86169
4	Flavanone-3-hydroxylase	52848.11603	-20668.01549
5	Leucoanthocyanidin reductase	12939.21057	-18415.83381

loop refining. These improved final models were subjected to energy minimizations using discovery studio 2.1. The energy minimization results are shown in Table 8. The force field applied was CHARMM and the energy minimization algorithm used was Steepest Descent with an RMS gradient of 0.1 using a maximum of 1000 steps. The structures of the models obtained after energy minimization have been given in Figure 9.

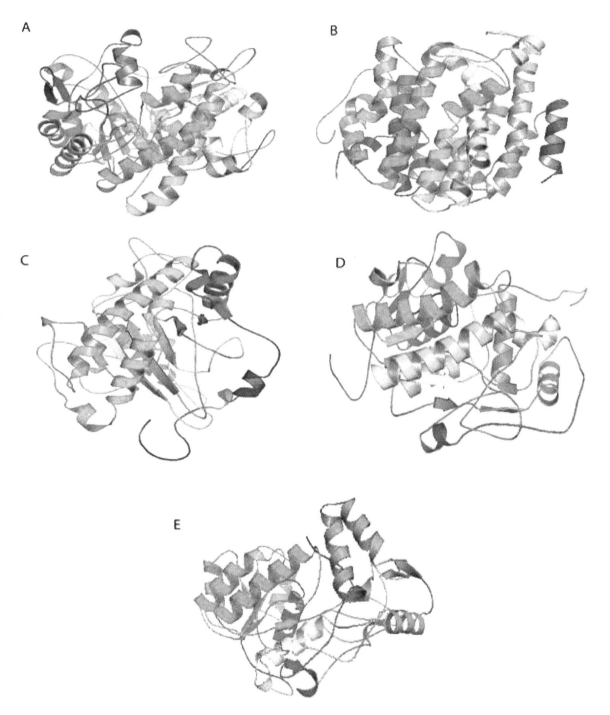

Figure 9. Models of (A) Phytoene synthase, (B) β-primeverosidase, (C) Flavanone-3-hydroxylase, (D) Dihydroflavonol 4-reductase, (E) Leucoanthocyanidin reductase.

Binding site analysis

CAST$_P$ server was used to locate the putative binding sites in each of the enzyme models with a probe radius of 1.4 A. The proposed binding sites have been shown in Figure 10. The binding site residues predicted by CAST$_P$ lie in the conserved regions obtained by the multiple sequence alignment of PSY, F3H, DFR and LAR. The binding site residues for phytoene synthase were: N12, V15, S16, S17, G18, F19, G20, L22, E23, F37, S38, P39, E41, R42, L44, I45, C46, H47, G48, R49, F50, K51, S53, R54, N55, T58, R62, N86, K87, R88, I115, V116, G119, L123, E126, A127, D129, T141, L144, G145, T146, L148, M149, R153, S177, H178, P181, T182, D185, R186, E188, S189, E192, R196, G197, R198, F200, L243, Y244, L245, Y248, L256, M257, V259, P260, V161,

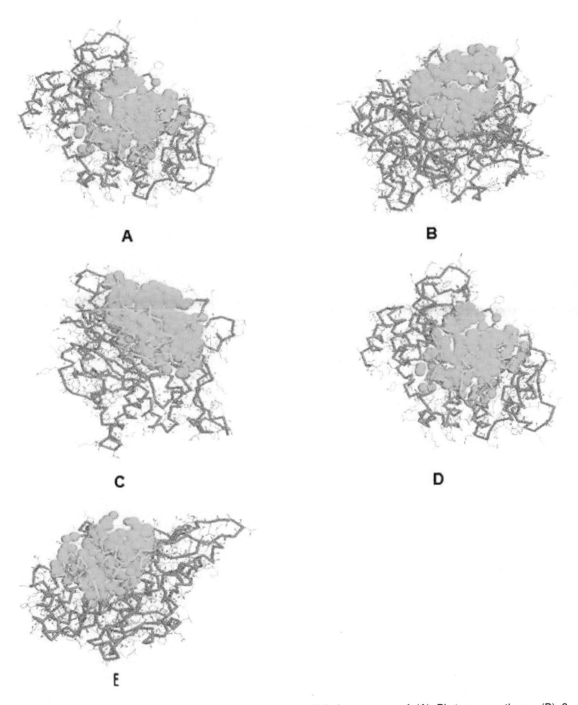

Figure 10. Potential substrate binding pocket for the modeled structures of (A) Phytoene synthase, (B) β-primeverosidase, (C) Flavanone-3-hydroxylase, (D) Dihydroflavonol 4-reductase, (E) Leucoanthocyanidin reductase

G263, I264, E267, A281, L282, G283, I284, N286, T289 and L292.

The binding site residues identified for β-prime-verosidase were: M1, M2, A3, K5, G6, S7. V8, V9, G11, V12, L13, A14, I15, V16, A17, Y18, A19, L20, V21, W276, M277, I278, P279, S281, N282, S283, K284, K287, D288, A290, Q291, L294, F307, R375, Y392, K394, K397, D398, V401, Y402, K404, E405, K406,

N408, A453 and V455.

The binding site residues for F3H were: M1, A2, P3, E12, E13, K14, S15, L16,Q17, Q18, K19, F20, F93, F94, P98, K101, L102, F104, D105, M106, S107, G108, G109, F114, I115, V116, S117, S118, H119, L120, Q121, G122, E123, A124, V125, Q126, D127, W128, R129, E130, I131, V132, T133, Y134, F135, S145, R146, D195, K197, V199, F202, P204, T212, L213, L215, K216, R217, H218,

T219, D220, P221, G222, R239, D261, Y265, Q277, F292, N294, P297, Y324, R326, M328, S329, D331, I332, E333, L334, A335, K336, K338, D352, I353, E354, K355, A356, L358, E359, I360, K361, S362, T363, E365, I366, F367 and A368.

The binding site residues for DFR were: T19, G20, A22, G23, F24, I25, G26, T43, V44, R45, K51, K52, A71, D72, L73, N74, F79, V92, A93, T94, P95, M96, F98, E99, T134, S135, S136, A137, G138, N141, V142, Q143, E144, Q146, F150, F160, K164, K165, M166, T167, Y171, F172, K175, P198, T199, L200, V201, M207, T209, P212, S213, I215, T216, R223, E225, G226, H227, Y228, S229, I230, I231, K232, Q233, G234, Q235, I268, P285, E287, F288, K289, I291, L295 and V298.

The binding site residues for LAR were: V17, G18, A19, S20, G21, F22, I23, L41, V42, R43, V45, S47, T49, N50, L53, G63, V64, V65, A86, I87, G88, G89, A90, N91, I92, D94, S114, E115, F116, G117, H118, V120, M132, Y133, K136, C155, N156, S157, I158, S160, W161, P162, Y164, D165, T167, P169, S170, E171, Q180, Y182, I197, L251, A254, A255, N258, P261, R262, S263, V264, V265, A266, F268, T269, I272, F273, P337, I338, T339, M340, C341 and A342.

Conclusion

Tea is an extremely important crop because of its popularity as a beverage and as a source of beneficial secondary metabolites. However, due to the long periods involved in conventional crop breeding, it is not really an option to improve crop varieties. So, computational studies of key biosynthetic enzymes in tea can provide valuable insights into the mechanism of action of these enzymes aiding in the ultimate aim of improving tea quality. The study of Volatile Flavour Compounds (VFC) and the enzymes involved in their synthesis and release is required to improve the quality of tea. Similarly, to enhance the beneficial health properties of tea the study of flavonoids like catechins is essential.

ACKNOWLEDGEMENTS

Research in the laboratory of DS is supported by grants from Department of Biotechnology (DBT), Department of Science and Technology (DST) and Department of Information Technology (DIT), Government of India, New Delhi, India.

REFERENCES

Altschul SF, Gish W, Mille W, Myers EW, Lipman DJ (1990). Basic local alignment search tool. J. Mol. Biol., 215(3): 403-410.

Binkowski TA, Naghibzadeh S, Liang J (2003). CASTp: Computed Atlas of Surface Topography of proteins. Nucleic Acids Res., 31(13): 3352-3355.

Borthakur D, Lu JL, Chen H, Lin C, Du YY, Liang YR (2008). Expression of phytoene synthase (psy) gene and its relation with accumulation of carotenoids in tea [Camellia sinensis (L) O Kuntze]. Afr. J. Biotechnol., 7(4): 434-438.

Choi JH, Jung HY, Kim HS, Cho HG (2000). PhyloDraw: a phylogenetic tree drawing system. Bioinformatics, 16(11): 1056-1058.

Eswar N, Eramian D, Webb B, Shen MY, Sali A (2008). Protein structure modeling with modeller. Methods Mol Biol 426145-159.

Eungwanichayapant PD, Popluechai S (2009). Accumulation of catechins in tea in relation to accumulation of mRNA from genes involved in catechin biosynthesis. Plant Physiol. Biochem., 47(2): 94-97.

Gasteiger E, Gattiker A, Hoogland C, Ivanyi I, Appel RD, Bairoch A (2003). ExPASy: the proteomics server for in-depth protein knowledge and analysis. Nucleic Acids Res., 31(13): 3784-3788.

Ijima Y, Ogawa K, Watanabe N, Usui T, Ohnishi-Kameyama M, Nagata T, Sakata K (1998). Characterization of beta-primeverosidase, being concerned with alcoholic aroma formation in tea leaves to be processed into black tea, and preliminary observations on its substrate specificity. J. Agric. Food Chem., 46(5): 1712-1718.

Luczaj W, Skrzydlewska E (2005). Antioxidative properties of black tea. Prev. Med., 40(6): 910-918.

Ma SJ, Mizutani M, Hiratake J, Hayashi K, Yagi K, Watanabe N, Sakata K (2001). Substrate specificity of beta-primeverosidase, a key enzyme in aroma formation during oolong tea and black tea manufacturing. Bioscience Biotechnology and Biochemistry 65(12): 2719-2729.

Ravichandran R (2002). Carotenoid composition, distribution and degradation to flavour volatiles during black tea manufacture and the effect of carotenoid supplementation on tea quality and aroma. Food Chem., 78(1): 23-28.

Ravichandran R, Parthiban R (1998). The impact of processing techniques on tea volatiles. Food Chem., 62(3): 347-353.

Rawat R, Gulati A (2008). Seasonal and clonal variations in some major glycosidic bound volatiles in Kangra tea (Camellia sinensis (L.) O. Kuntze). European Food Res. Technol., 226(6): 1241-1249.

Singh K, Kumar S, Yadav SK, Ahuja, P.S. (2009). Characterization of dihydroflavonol 4-reductase cDNA in tea [Camellia sinensis (L.) O. Kuntze]. Plant Biotechnol. Reports, 3(1): 95-101.

Singh K, Rani A, Kumar S, Sood P, Mahajan M, Yadav SK, Singh B, Ahuja PS (2008). An early gene of the flavonoid pathway, flavanone 3-hydroxylase, exhibits a positive relationship with the concentration of catechins in tea (Camellia sinensis). Tree Physiol., 28(9): 1349-1356.

Stutz A, Bairoch A, Estreicher A, Grp SP (2006). UniProtKB/Swiss-Prot: the protein sequence knowledgebase. Febs. J., 27362-62.

Thompson JD, Higgins DG, Gibson TJ (1994). CLUSTAL W: improving the sensitivity of progressive multiple sequence alignment through sequence weighting, position-specific gap penalties and weight matrix choice. Nucleic Acids Res. 22(22): 4673-4680.

Wang HF, Provan CJ, Helliwell K (2000). Tea flavonoids: their functions, utilisation and analysis. Trends Food Sci. Technol., 11(4-5): 152-160.

Way TD, Lin HY, Hua KT, Lee JC, Li WH, Lee MR, Shuang CH, Lin JK (2009). Beneficial effects of different tea flowers against human breast cancer MCF-7 cells. Food Chem., 114(4): 1231-1236.

## 4

Bioinfotracker: A novel system for advanced genome functional insight

Gopal Ramesh Kumar[1]*, Ganesan Aravindhan[1], Thankaswamy Kosalai Subazini[1] and Radhakrishnan Sathish Kumar[2]

[1]Bioinformatics Lab, AU-KBC Research Centre, MIT Campus, Anna University, Chennai-600 044, India.
[2]NRCFOSS, AU-KBC Research Centre, MIT Campus, Anna University, Chennai-600 044, India.

With the accelerated accumulation of genomic sequence data in the World Wide Web, it has become highly essential to understand the role of these sequences in the biological systems by incorporating various advanced research archetypes. The intricacy of handling such a huge dataset manually has increased the need to develop automated methods that can analyze enormous numbers of biological sequences and produce efficient results. This being the objective, a novel computational system, Bioinfotracker, has been developed for the purpose of carrying out large-scale protein annotations. Different online tools operating on different strategies have been integrated in Bioinfotracker so as reduce the overall processing time of these tools individually. Further, Bioinfotracker facilitates automatic parsing of the results from all the tools and produce them in an easily interpretable table format. This facility will, therefore, greatly lessen the burden of hectic human parsing. Moreover, AJAX (Asynchronous JavaScript and XML) is used as an interface within this tool that will greatly control the unwanted page refresh menace and bandwidth consumption. Thus, Bioinfotracker remains a well structured, species-independent, flexible and highly controlled functional analysis system for the protein sequences of any organism. The software is freely available at: http://biotool.nrcfosshelpline.in/.

Key words: Bioinfotracker, ajax, functional genomics, annotation, bandwidth, fasta.

INTRODUCTION

During the past decade, huge volumes of biological data have been generated and are deposited in the online repositories (Kim et al., 2003; Sasson et al., 2006). With this largely mounted data, it has become the most vital challenge for the research community to investigate these raw sequences and reveal their functions. Delineating the functions of the genome will facilitate a better insight into the biological systems (Rentzsch et al., 2009). In spite of various strategies for identifying the protein functions were carried out earlier, only 50 - 60% of genes have been identified with known functions in most of the completely sequenced genomes (Sivashankari et al., 2003). Therefore, the determination of protein functions has become the most focused research area of the post-genome era. The classical

approaches for the functional genomics use different types of high-throughput techniques to characterize the actual gene products. Though these traditional biochemical/molecular experiments can assign accurate functions for the genes, they consume a lot of chemicals, reagents and other materials and thus making them more cost ineffective (Diana, 2003). Above all, these methodologies involve much of the manpower and the man-hours. This demands the use of Bioinformatics automated systems to carry out sequence analysis with the perspective of functional prediction. Recent years have seen tremendous growth in the Bioinformatics tools and approaches in genome analysis. They help in investigating the large quantity of data available and propose biologically meaningful patterns for the genes. The general Bioinformatics-led approach for functional characterization of proteins involves the comparison of the unknown sequences against the known sequences in various databases using a variety of tools. These tools are supported by a number of algorithms and statistical

---

*Corresponding author. E-mail: gramesh@au-kbc.org.

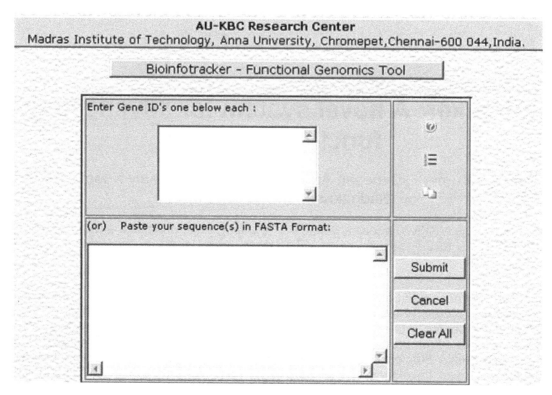

Figure 1. Homepage of Bioinfotracker which shows fields for entering GI number and sequences.

theories and predict the appropriate functions. In several cases, such predictions are proved to be efficient and this has led to the development of diverse Insilico protocols for the functional annotations of the proteins. Of various Insilico strategies, functional predictions using the tools that operate on the classification of proteins provide promising results. Presently, a number of different classification systems have been developed and deployed to categorize the functional annotations (Stuart et al., 2000) that include (i) BLAST (Altschul et al., 1990), a tool that helps in the sequence similarity searches (ii) Pfam (Bateman et al., 2004), a tool that is based on protein families (iii) COG (Tatusov et al., 2003) that represents phylogenetic classification of proteins (iv) Prodom, a tool that assists in protein domain searches (v) InterPro (Mulder et al., 2007), a tool integrated with different family classifications. Though functional predictions through computational programs have led to many scientific discoveries (Cathy et al., 2003), they tend to be complex as these applications are computationally intensive and time consuming. Moreover, a lot of human interventions are needed to carry out the analysis with these tools and to manually curate the results to identify potential functions. Although, there are a few tools like AIM-BLAST, Ajax Interfaced Multiple Sequence - BLAST (Aravindhan et al., 2009), that allows the users to analyse multiple sequences at an instance, their functional prediction is based on only one strategy. Hence, there is a pressing need to develop an advanced computational method that

will balance these limitations and handle functional annotations better.

METHODS

Progress in computational power and the advancements in Bioinformatics research permit the integration of the available information from various sources into single qualitative models, thus making the analysis simple (Ruepp et al., 2004; Lobley et al., 2008). Here, we have developed a simple and efficient tool, Bioinfotracker (Figure 1), for carrying out large-scale protein annotation. Bioinfotracker is a system that was developed by integrating different Bioinformatics tools such as Pfam (http://pfam.jouy.inra.fr/), BLAST (http://www.ebi.ac.uk/Tools/BLAST/), COG (http://www.ncbi.nlm.nih.gov/COG/) and InterproScan (http://www.ebi.ac.uk/Tools/InterProScan/). The front end of the tool was written using HTML/Java scripts whereas the server end of the tool is coded using Perl scripts. Moreover, AJAX (Paulson, 2005) was used as an interface in Bioinfotracker that will greatly reduce the unpleasing page refresh issue that is very common in other bioinformatics tools. Hence, Bioinfotracker will consume very low bandwidth but still performs effectively. This tool makes it possible to perform the annotation of an entire genome using four different annotation strategies with only a single submit. The input for this tool can either be protein sequences in FASTA format or GI numbers of the sequences. If the GI numbers are submitted, the tool will automatically search in the NCBI database (http://www.ncbi.nlm.nih.gov) and fetch the sequences corresponding to the GI numbers submitted and then starts the analysis. If sequences are submitted, then the processing starts immediately without any delay in time. The Sequences are individually submitted to different servers, such as BLAST, Pfam, COG and InterProScan, and the analyses are carried out in the respective servers. Once the

ID	Blast	InterProScan	PFam	COG	Time Taken
gi 15646184|NP_208368|ABC transporter, permease protein (yaeE) [Helicobacter pylori 26695].	ABC transporter, permease protein.	ABC transporter, permease protein.	Binding-protein-dependent transport system inner membrane component	Permease component of an uncharacterized ABC transporter	1:17
gi 15646188|NP_208372|methicillin resistance protein (llm) [Helicobacter pylori 26695].	Methicillin resistance protein (Llm).	Methicillin resistance protein (Llm).	Glycosyl transferase family 4	UDP-N-acetylmuramyl pentapeptide phosphotransferase/UDP-N-acetylglucosamine-1-phosphate transferase	1:33
gi 15646184|NP_208368|ABC transporter, permease protein (yaeE) [Helicobacter pylori 26695].	ABC transporter, permease protein.	ABC transporter, permease protein.	Binding-protein-dependent transport system inner membrane component	Permease component of an uncharacterized ABC transporter	1:06
gi 15646188|NP_208372|methicillin resistance protein (llm) [Helicobacter pylori 26695].	Methicillin resistance protein (Llm).	Methicillin resistance protein (Llm).	Glycosyl transferase family 4	UDP-N-acetylmuramyl pentapeptide phosphotransferase/UDP-N-acetylglucosamine-1-phosphate transferase	1:33

Figure 2. Sample result table in Bioinfotracker of BLAST, COG, Pfam and InterProScan output with time taken to get the result.

results of the analyses are available, Bioinfotracker will automatically parse them and filter out the appropriate function from each server and display them in a simple table, where the automatic parsing is based on the technical filtering process carried out by the tool which is explained in the efficiency part. Bioinfotracker utilizes the SOAP (Pillai et al., 2005) web services of EMBL-EBI, (European Molecular Biology Laboratory-European Bioinformatics Institute) to fetch the results from the BLAST server and the InterProScan Server. Whereas, LWP::Simple and HTML:: TreeBuilder:: Xpath modules are used to fetch the results from the Pfam server and COG Server. Thus in this tool, the results of the analyses will be produced in a simple and easily interpretable table format that displays the ID of the sequence submitted, the results from Pfam, COG, InterProScan , BLAST and the time taken for each analysis (Figure 2). There is also an option that comes with the tool to save the results of the analysis in the PDF format. With all these features, Bioinfotracker remains user-friendly.

Efficiency of bioinfotracker

Except for the BLAST program, parsing the output of all other tools is straightforward and simple. Although Bioinfotracker is found to be efficient in carrying out searches in all the tools integrated within the program, it is worth elaborating its strength in handling the BLAST output parsing. Since, searching a single sequence against a regular BLAST program (http://www.ebi.ac.uk/Tools/BLAST/), will itself generate large amount of results in terms of hits accompanied with varied parameters such as E-value, Percentage of Identity, Percentage of Similarity, BLAST score and sequence length. Interpreting, analyzing and filtering such a voluminous BLAST textual output manually to select an appropriate hit, remains a great problem with the scientific community (Aravindhan et al., 2009a, b).

To bypass such difficulties, Bioinfotracker is incorporated with some special filtering processes that can expertly handle the voluminous BLAST results of the sequences and select one best hit

for one sequence. The filtering process is performed in two parts. The first part of filtering is carried out to choose the BLAST hits that satisfy the values of all the parameters including BLAST score, the length and orientation of the hits, the percentage identity, percentage similarity and E-values. The second part of the process involves the further cleaning of the functions with any negative terms, functions that do not have any clear scientific evidence, such as predicted, putative, probable, hypothetical, conserved hypothetical and unknown. This filtering process of results, in Bioinfotracker, remains a powerful means of reducing the possibility of errors while choosing a single suitable function from mass of BLAST hits.

RESULTS AND DISCUSSION

The performance of the tool has been compared with the regular online tools using the Firefox Web browser. A sample set of sequences of varying length from *E. coli* were simultaneously submitted to Bioinfotracker and the four different tools Pfam, COG, BLAST and InterProScan. HttpFox, (https://addons.mozzilla.org/en-US /firefox/addon/6647), a Firefox add-on is operated at the backend to measure the loads of bytes transferred during the analyses. The amount of bytes sent and received for each sequence in Bioinfotracker and other tools is tabulated for comparison (Table 1). The results show that the online tools, in overall, consumed 103.87 kb of data transfer. Bioinfotracker, on the other hand, consumed only 7.38 kb of data transfer. Above all, the unwanted page refresh nuisance was completely absent when using the Bioinfotracker. Further, the results in this tool are displayed in a simple table thereby reducing human

Table 1. Comparison of bandwidth consumption between Bioinfotracker and other online tools.

Bioinfotracker		Online tools- individual analysis							
		COG		Pfam		BLAST		InterProScan	
Sent	Received	Sent	Received	Sent	Received	Sent	Received	Sent	Received
(In Bytes)		(In Bytes)		(In Bytes)		(In Bytes)		(In Bytes)	
1488	206	2195	453	2486	618	18135	176863	2195	732
850	206	2060	18564	1871	618	14742	176031	2060	453
1514	206	1221	453	2526	618	18737	176866	2526	618
1499	206	2739	732	2917	897	24206	178536	2917	618
997	206	1680	453	2409	897	16039	176532	2739	732
6348	1030	9895	20655	12209	3648	91859	884828	12437	3153
7378 [In Bytes]				1038684 [In Bytes]					

parsing. Hence, this tool prevails to be a novel system for the functional genomics research.

Conclusion

We present Bioinfotracker as one of the most appropriate and coordinated programs for performing functional annotation of the genes from any organism and for elucidating functions for unknown or hypothetical proteins. Henceforth, Bioinfotracker will be a useful tool for genomic research in the future.

ACKNOWLEDGEMENT

Ms. T.K. Subazini and Mr. G. Aravindhan, Junior Researchers were supported by the fundings provided by DIT.

REFERENCES

Altschul SF, Gish W, Miller W, Myers EW, Lipman DJ (1990) Basic local alignment search tool. J. Mol. Biol. 215 (3): 403–410.

Aravindhan G, Kumar GR, Kumar RS, Subha K (2009a). AIM-BLAST-AJAX Interfaced Multisequence Blast. Proteomics Insights 2:: 1-7.

Aravindhan G, Kumar RS, Subha K, Subazini TK, Dey A, Kant K, Kumar GR (2009b). Proteomics Insights 2: 9-13.

Bateman A, Coin L, Durbin R, Finn RD, Hollich V, Griffiths-Jones S, Khanna A, Marshall M, Moxon S, Sonnhammer EL, Studholme DJ, Yeats C, Eddy SR (2004). The Pfam protein families database Nucleic Acids Res.1: 32 D138-141.

Cathy HW, Hongzhan H, Lai-Su LY, Winona CB (2003). Protein family classification and functional annotation. Comput. Biol. Chem. 27(1): 37-47.

Diana MD (2003). Genomics and Bacterial Metabolism Curr. Issues Mol. Biol. 5(1): 17-25

Kim C, Matthew B (2003). MASV—Multiple (BLAST) Annotation System Viewer Bioinformatics 19 (17): 2313 –2315.

Lobley E, Nugent T, Orengo CA, Jones DT (2008). FFPred: an integrated feature-based function prediction server for vertebrate proteomes Nucleic Acids Res. 1-6.

Mulder NJ, Apweiler R, Attwood TK, Bairoch A, Bateman A, Binns D, Bork P, Buillard V, Cerutti L, Copley R, Courcelle E, Das U, Daugherty L, Dibley M, Finn R, Fleischmann W, Gough J, Haft D, Hulo N, Hunter S, Kahn D, Kanapin A, Kejariwal A, Labarga A, Langendijk-Genevaux PS, Lonsdale D, Lopez R, Letunic I, Madera M, Maslen J, McAnulla C, McDowall J, Mistry J, Mitchell A, Nikolskaya AN, Orchard S, Orengo C, Petryszak R, Selengut JD, Sigrist CJ, Thomas PD, Valentin F, Wilson D, Wu CH, Yeats C (2007) New developments in the InterPro database Nucleic Acids Res. 35: D224-8.

Paulson LD (2005). Building rich web applications with AJAX IEEE. 38: 14-17.

Pillai S, Silventoinen V, Kallio K, Senger M, Sobhany S, Tate J, Velankar S, Golovin A, Henrick K, Rice P, Stoehr P, Lopez R (2005) SOAP-based services provided by the European Bioinformatics Institute. Nucleic Acids Res. 33: W25-W28.

Rentzsch R, Orengo CA (2009). Protein function prediction - the power of multiplicity Trends Biotechnol. 27(4): 210.

Ruepp A, Zollner A, Maier D, Albermann K, Hani J, Mokrejs M, Tetko I, Güldener U, Mannhaupt G, Münsterkötter M, Mewes HW (2004). The FunCat, a functional annotation scheme for systematic classification of proteins from whole genomes Nucleic Acids Res. 14:32(18):5539-5545

Sasson O, Noam K, Michal L (2006) Functional annotation prediction: All for one and one for all. Protein Sci. 15(6): 1557.

Sivashankari S, Shanmughavel P (2003) Functional annotation of hypothetical proteins - Rev. Bioinformation 291(8): 335-358.

Stuart CG, Rison T, Charles H Janet M, Thornton J (2000) Comparison of functional annotation schemes for genomes, Funct. Integr. Genomics 1: 56–69.

Tatusov RL, Fedorova ND, Jackson JD, Jacobs AR, Kiryutin B, Koonin EV, Krylov DM, Mazumder R, Mekhedov SL, Nikolskaya AN, Rao BS, Smirnov S, Sverdlov AV, Vasudevan S, Wolf YI, Yin JJ, Natale DA (2003) The COG database: an updated version includes eukaryotes BMC Bioinformatics 11: 4-41

## 5

Avian influenza and micro RNA: Role of bioinformatics

Pankaj Koparde[1] and Shailza Singh[2]*

[1]Institute of Bioinformatics and Biotechnology, University of Pune, Pune -411007, India.
[2]National Centre for Cell Science, Pune University Campus, Pune -411007, India.

Avian influenza virus is a major cause of influenza all over the world. Influenza virus being a RNA virus shows high mutation rates, antigenic shift and drift. These phenomena contribute to ineffective chemotherapy against influenza viruses. Recent advances in the current therapy, drugs and vaccines are restricted with many factors such as toxicity, complexity, cost and resistance. New technologies particularly RNA interference (RNAi) mediated by microRNA (miRNA) have become more and more interesting and effective therapeutic entities to silence pathogenic gene products associated with viral infections. Today, RNAi technology is a leading technology in sequence specific therapeutics. The flexibility of miRNAs in function makes them good candidates for use in sequence specific therapeutics. Although, miRNAs have been shown to be useful in combating against viral infections, there are problems associated with miRNA prediction, designing and function. Following review focuses on avian influenza virus (H5N1), the role of miRNAs in its pathophysiology and the computational prediction of miRNAs as antiviral therapeutics.

Key words: Avian influenza, miRNA, sequence specific therapeutics.

INTRODUCTION

Influenza is a highly infectious, acute respiratory disease which affects all age groups and possesses potential to occur repeatedly in any individual. Avian Influenza, popularly known as "Bird Flu" is one of the most severe respiratory viral infectious diseases of this decade. Highly pathogenic avian influenza (HPAI) H5N1 virus has created industrial and economical problems in the affected countries; the most affected industry being the poultry industry (Elci, 2006). This has lead to the need to find out effective measures which can be applied to combat with or to eliminate influenza threat. The host range of avian influenza virus includes birds and mammals, but its natural hosts are wetland birds such as wild ducks, gulls, and shore-birds (Zambon, 1999). Avian influenza is recurrently been found to be present in poultry birds, because of the transmissibility of the virus within bird species. The causative agent of avian influenza is Influenza A virus H5N1 strains. H5N1 is Orthomyxoviridae family member, with negative sense, single stranded RNA genome. The genome of H5N1 is segmented with 8 RNA segments, coding for eleven recognized proteins in all. These are PB1, PB1-F, PB2, and PA polymerases, HA, NP, NA, M1, M2, NS1, and NS2 proteins (Cheung and Poon, 2007). Two proteins, Hemagglutinin (HA) and Neuraminidase (NA) are the major antigens of H5N1. Being a RNA virus with segmented genome, H5N1 shows high mutation rates, especially in the antigenic regions. The phenomena of antigenic shift and antigenic drift make H5N1, highly unpredictable for chemotherapeutic interventions. The most widely used protective agents against AI viruses are vaccines. Either inactivated influenza viruses or antiviral agents are used as anti-influenza vaccines (Suarez and Schultz-Cherry, 2000; Palese and García-Sastre, 2002).

A variety of drugs are already available and some are in the process of formulation against H5N1. Five classes of drugs are available today; these include: neuraminidase inhibitors, M2 ion channel blockers, IMP dehydrogenase inhibitors, interferon and siRNAs, RNA polymerase inhibitors (De Clercq and Neyts, 2007; Ludwig et al., 2003) (Table 1). Most of the available drugs fail to provide effective protection against H5N1 virus, because of the highly variable nature of the antigenic part of the virus. Inactivated influenza virus in the form of a

*Corresponding author. E-mail: shailza_iitd@yahoo.com.

Table 1. Available drugs against H5N1 virus and their modes of action.

Drug	Example	Mode of function
Neuraminidase Inhibitors	Zanamivir, Oseltamivir, Peramivir	Blocks the release of viral particles, prevents spread of viral particles
M2 Ion channel blockers	Amantadine, Rimantadine	Interferes with the viral uncoating process
IMP dehydrogenase inhibitors	Ribavirin, Viramidine	Interferes with the function of IMP dehydrogenase
Interferon and siRNAs	α-interferon	RNA interference, host antiviral pathway
RNA polymerase inhibitors	T705, flutimide	T705 is recognized as a nucleobase, which in turn inhibits viral polymerase

vaccine may not always provide active immunity against new pandemic strains of influenza (García-Sastre, 2002). According to Clercq et al. (2007), double-, triple-, quadruple- combinations of currently available anti-influenza drugs can be used potentially against H5N1 (De Clercq and Neyts, 2007). Such combinations, may lead to possible emergence of new influenza strains resistant to multiple drugs. This kind of treatment may also produce toxic side effects in host systems, if not properly implemented.

Interfering RNAs are one of the most reliable drugs which candidates can be used against H5N1 to achieve sequence specific inhibition of viral genes. Interfering RNAs work on the lines of RNA interference (RNAi). RNAi refers to post-transcriptional gene silencing mediated by either degradation or translation arrest of target RNA (Ryther et al., 2005). Many reports and research articles cite use of interfering RNAs as a potential drug candidate use against H5N1 (Bennink and Palmore, 2004; Zhou et al., 2007; Ge et al., 2003; Brahmachari et al., 2008; Tompkins et al., 2004). With the advent of bioinformatics, it has become easy to predict and design interfering RNAs against specific genes or gene products thereof. No doubt interfering RNAs can be used as a therapeutic against RNA viruses, there are certain discrepancies and problems related to *in silico* prediction of interfering RNAs and *in vivo* use of these compounds.

THE INFLUENZA VIRUSES

The influenza virus family *Orthomyxoviridae* includes four types of influenza viruses (A, B, C) and thogotovirus (influenza D). Among Influenza viruses A, B and C viruses can be distinguished by the differences in their antigenic proteins namely NP and M proteins. Influenza A viruses are further divided according to the antigenic nature of their HA and NA glycoproteins. All influenza viruses are enveloped viruses having single stranded, linear, segmented, negative sense RNA genome. Influenza viruses typically contain 8 segments of RNA,

except influenza C virus which contains 7 segments of RNA molecules (Lamb and Krug, 2001). All the 8 segments code for different proteins, encoding 11 proteins in all (Cheung and Poon, 2007). Thogotoviruses consists of 6 - 7 segments of RNA genome (Lamb and Krug,   2001; http://www.ncbi.nlm.nih.gov/ICTVdb/Ictv/index.htm). All the four groups of influenza viruses differ in their host preferences, antigenic nature, morphological features, and in their respective mechanisms of encoding proteins. Influenza A viruses, which are the major contributors to the influenza spread worldwide, are categorized into different subtypes, based on the nature of HA and NA glycoproteins. There are total of 16 HA and 9 NA subtypes known (Osterhaus et al., 2008). These subtypes are perpetuated in aquatic birds. This gene pool of AI viruses seems to be limited but it can evolve rapidly once it enters domestic avian or mammalian host. Some of the strains which can evolve rapidly into highly pathogenic strains are H5 and H7. H1, H2, H3 strains have previously caused pandemics and epidemics in humans. H5, H7 and H9 strains are transmissible to human through avian hosts. H5N1 is the only strain of avian influenza which has caused mortality in humans, so far (Webster and Hulse, 2004).

H5N1

Among all the proteins, encoded by H5N1 genome, HA and NA proteins are the major determinants of biology of H5N1. HA glycoprotein is responsible for attachment of virus to the host cell, while NA glycoprotein is responsible for release of virus from infected cell and consequently spreading the virus throughout the respiratory tract. HA protein attaches to the cell membrane glycoproteins via sialic acid linkage, triggering viral fusion with host cell membrane and entry into the cell (Proença-Módena et al., 2007). Table 2 shows the H5N1 proteins and their functions. The host cell preference for any influenza A viral strain depends on binding to cell surface receptor that consists of terminal sialic acid residues with a 2-3

Table 2. Functions of proteins coded by H5N1 genome segments.

Segment	Protein product	Function
1	PB2	Polymerase proteins
2	PB1, PB1-F	Polymerase proteins
3	PA	Polymerase proteins
4	HA	Attachment of viral particle to host cell, major antigen
5	NP	Major structural protein
6	NA	Integral membrane protein, major antigen, release and spread of mature virions
7	M1, M2	Matrix protein
8	NS1, NS2	NS1 counteracts with type I interferon antiviral pathway of the host, NS2 is Involved in nuclear transport and viral assembly

linkage [Neur Ac(α2-3)Gal] to a penultimate galactose residue of glycoproteins or glycolipids. The tracheal epithelia of birds and mammals express influenza A receptors with a 2-3 and 2-6 linkage of sialic acid, respectively, whereas pig tracheal epithelia expresses both 2-3 and 2-6 linkages of sialic acid. This has lead to the hypothesis of pig as a "mixing bowl" for influenza A strains.

Another mechanism suggested by Matrosovisch et al. (2004), states that H5N1 viruses may infect humans, by infecting ciliated respiratory epithelial cells, as these cells preferentially express receptors with 2-3 linkages of sialic acid in culture. Although, ciliated cells are minor constituents of human respiratory epithelia, they are significant in number. The other part of respiratory epithelia consists of nonciliated epithelial cells, which preferentially express receptors with 2-6 linkages of sialic acid in culture (Matrosovich and Matrosovich, 2004). Hence, it poses a possibility that recurrent infection with H5N1 in humans might lead to highly pathogenic strain with a preference to 2-6 linkage of sialic acid (Lewis, 2006). According to a recent review by Zhang (2009); the generalized view that α2-3 and α2-linked sialic acid residues are the sole receptors determining tissue and host tropism is not true. Other factors such as glycan topology, lipid raft microdomains, local density of sialic acid receptors, concentration of invading virus, coreceptors and sialic acid independent receptors, may also be important in determining tissue and host tropism of human, avian and animal influenza viruses (Hong, 2009).

Epidemiology of influenza A and H5N1

The occurrence of influenza viruses is widespread throughout the world. Influenza viruses are responsible for symptomatic and asymptomatic infections in many vertebrate species, lower animals and aquatic birds (Webster et al., 1992). Many articles (Brown, 2000; Trampuz et al., 2004; Peiris et al., 2007), cite that aquatic birds are the primary source of influenza viruses in other species. Over past 150 years, at least four pandemics of influenza occurred at irregular intervals (Table 3).

According to recent World Health Organization (WHO) reports (http://www.who.int/csr/disease/avian_influenza/en/), 471 cases of avian influenza in humans have been reported, with 282 deaths world-wide. The maximum numbers of cases (161) and deaths (134) are from Indonesia, since 2003. The current threat of swine influenza, the causative agent of which is H1N1 viral strain, is nothing but a H1N1 human-swine-avian reassortant strain (Zhang and Chen, 2009; Smith et al., 2009). From the first report of swine influenza 2009 in humans in April 2009 (Zhang and Chen, 2009) at least 13,554 deaths have been reported to WHO regional offices from more than 208 countries and overseas territories or communities.

Avian influenza viruses can be categorized into two groups: low pathogenic avian influenza (LPAI) and highly pathogenic avian influenza (HPAI). Avian influenza (AI) viruses are generally LPAI, but upon introduction of H5 or H7 subtypes into domestic poultry these viruses may change their virulence level and may turn into HPAI strains (Webster and Hulse, 2004). The first report of AI in humans was reported from (Hong Kong, 1997; Chan, 2002). The H5N1 virus has spread worldwide from Southeast Asia to Europe and Africa, with occasional infections in humans, and continues to spread across the world (De Clercq and Neyts, 2007; Yen et al., 2008). Southern China is considered as the hypothetical pandemic epicenter of influenza (Horimoto and Kawaoka, 2001). Three earlier pandemics of influenza in Asia and recent threat of swine influenza H1N1 virus suggests that the next flu pandemic is highly possible, the causative agent of which could be avian influenza H5N1 virus.

Modes of mutations of H5N1

The variable nature of influenza viruses is contributed by some of the characteristic phenomena shown by them, such as, antigenic drift, antigenic shift, and recombination.

Table 3. Influenza pandemics and their impact in terms of human deaths.

Pandemic	Date	Deaths	Virus subtype involved
Asian (Russian) Flu	1889 - 90	1 million	H2N2
Spanish Flu	1918 - 20	50 million	H1N1
Asian Flu	1957 - 58	1.5 - 2.0 million	H2N2
Hong Kong Flu	1968 - 69	1 million	H3N2
Swine Flu	April 2009 till December 2009	~7.880 - ~16.460*	H1N1

*Data Source: (http://www.cdc.gov/h1n1flu/estimates_2009_h1n1.htm).

These characteristics make them highly mutable. Antigenic drift occurs due to errors during replication, which are irreparable. These errors accumulate in the form of mutations in amino acid sequences within the viral genome, resulting in the existing strain being replaced by a new antigenic variant strain. The phenomenon of reassortment leads to exchange of RNA segments in two genotypically different influenza viruses infecting a single cell. This can result in the emergence of a novel strain and/or subtype. This phenomenon is known as antigenic shift; whereas recombination results in a single influenza RNA segment containing genetic material from two different sources. The current circulating swine influenza H1N1 virus is a reassortant of human, swine and avian influenza viruses, comprising of reassortant genomes of avian H1N1, H1N1 classical swine virus (Eurasian and North American) and H3N2 seasonal flu virus (Smith et al., 2009). The choice of mutations is most pronounced in HA and NA proteins, where selection is antibody mediated. Antigenic drift is common to all influenza viruses, but it is prominent in human influenza viruses as compared to AI viruses (Webster and Hulse, 2004) (Figure 1).

WHO FOOLED THE VACCINES?

A variety of vaccines and chemotherapeutic drugs are available which can act on H5N1 by inhibiting certain proteins or by interfering with viral metabolism. According to Clerq and Neyts (2007), five types of anti-influenza compounds are available and/or being evaluated for their anti-influenza properties. These include: neuraminidase inhibitors, M2 ion channel blockers, IMP dehydrogenase inhibitors, interferons and siRNAs, and RNA polymerase inhibitors (De Clercq and Neyts, 2007). Due to variable nature of viral antigens that is, HA and NA glycoproteins, neuraminidase inhibitors might not provide protection against all AI viruses (Bennink and Palmore, 2004; Fauci, 2005). Also, due to highly mutable nature of H5N1, other types of drugs might not provide protection at protein level. M2 ion channel inhibitors and neuraminidase inhibitors are also known to have side effects such as neurotoxicity (Brahmachari et al., 2008). According to Clerq and Neyts (2007), drug combinations can be used

as a plausible anti-influenza treatment (De Clercq and Neyts, 2007). This may lead to emergence of highly drug resistant viral strains, at the same time; it might produce severe side effects in human hosts. Also, expense, potential side effects, and the timing of delivery have lead to the limited use of these drugs in high risk populations (Bennink and Palmore, 2004). Drugs which can specifically interfere with viral replication machinery may prove to be effective as it is more difficult for the virus to adapt to missing cellular functions (Ludwig et al., 2003).

Interferons play an important role as antivirals in immune system in humans. The Mx protein of human innate defense mechanism inhibits virus replication at various levels; while influenza NS1 protein has been reported to inhibit IFN pathway at various levels (Katze et al., 2002). Studies by Seo et al. (2002) show that H5N1 virus escapes host anti-viral responses. The exact mechanism of NS1 action is not yet clear, which may mark the use of interferons as controversial. Sequence specific inhibition that is, use of molecules which can inhibit viral genome at mRNA level, is one of the most promising anti-influenza therapy. Recent advances in RNA interference (RNAi) therapy, has lead to the discovery of small interfering RNAs (siRNAs) as antiviral agents. RNAi is the phenol-menon of sequence specific gene regulation in which a double stranded (ds) RNA mediates sequence specific degradation of target mRNA. Small regulatory RNAs include siRNAs, micro RNAs (miRNAs), and Piwi-interacting RNAs (piRNAs). Many publications (Ryther et al., 2005; Bennink and Palmore, 2004; Zhou et al., 2007; Ge et al., 2003; Rayburn and Zhang, 2008; Cejka et al., 2006; Colbère-Garapin et al., 2005; Novina et al., 2002; Dorsett, 2004; Aagaard and Rossi, 2007), cite use small regulatory RNAs as antiviral and anti-influenza com-pounds. The potential advantage in the use of sequence specific therapeutics (SSTs) is that these agents might not require an intact, functional immune system (Bennink and Palmore, 2004).

SMALL REGULATORY RNAs

Small noncoding RNAs (ncRNAs) have vital role in regulating a wide range of cellular pathways, developmental processes and the protection of genome

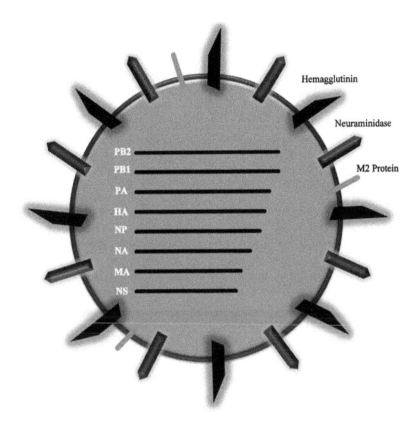

Figure 1. Diagram representing influenza virus. The eight segments of RNA code for eleven viral proteins.

against mobile genetic elements (Colbère-Garapin et al., 2005), such as viral genomes. In plants, siRNAs act as a conserved mechanism of antiviral immunity (Colbère-Garapin et al., 2005). Depending upon the type of ncRNAs, the mechanism of their biogenesis and action varies. The origin of miRNAs is endogenous while that of siRNAs is either endogenous or exogenous (Bushati and Cohen, 2007; Sontheimer and Carthew, 2005). The choice of type of ncRNA to be used in anti-influenza treatment is essential for achieving full-proof protection against the virus. There are conflicting views on efficacy of siRNA and miRNA as anti-viral therapeutics. Although, it is difficult to comment on the type of ncRNA to be used, as the treatment differs from virus to virus; miRNAs can be seen as promising ncRNA candidates; because of their flexibility in action.

miRNAs

miRNAs are generated by endogenous sources of nucleic acids. Most of the miRNAs are transcribed by RNA polymerase II, to generate pri-miRNAs, which are stem loop structures. Pri-miRNAs are processed by microprocessor, a multiprotein complex, consisting of RNase III enzyme Drosha and double stranded RNA-binding domain (dsRBD) protein DGCR8/Pasha. This complex cleaves pri-miRNA converting it into hairpin precursor pre-miRNA. The 2 nucleotide (nt) 3' overhangs produced by RNase III is recognized by Exportin-5, which transports pre-miRNA to cytoplasm via Ran-GTP-dependent mechanism. In the cytoplasm, pre-miRNA is cleaved to produce mature miRNA: miRNA* duplex by Dicer protein. Argonaute (Ago) proteins, together with Dicer form a trimeric complex, known as the RNA-induced silencing complex (RISC). The miRNA strand with lower stability is incorporated into RISC, whereas the other RNA molecule namely miRNA* is degraded. Once incorporated into RISC, the miRNA guides the complex to its target mRNA. Depending on the complementarities the target mRNA is either degraded, cleaved or the translation of the target is repressed (Bushati and Cohen, 2007; Gregory and Shiekhattar, 2005; Chang and Mendell, 2007; Esquela-Kerscher and Slack, 2006; Bartel, 2004). miRNAs can also be produced by drosha independent pathway (Ruby, 2007).

The size of miRNAs varies depending on the species and miRNA genes, but is found to be approximately 22 nt. The seed region (2-7 or 2-8 nt) of miRNA consists of 7-8 nucleotides at the 5' end of the miRNA. Seed region is the primary determinant of miRNA target specificity

(Bushati and Cohen, 2007; Chang and Mendell, 2007). Depending on the coding sequence miRNAs are categorized as exonic and intronic miRNAs. The intronic miRNA is similar structurally and functionally to the exonic miRNAs, only difference is in the requirement for RNA polymerase II and other RNA splicing components for biogenesis (Lin et al., 2006). miRNAs show phenolmena of multiplicity or redundancy and cooperativity. Multiplicity refers to the ability of a single miRNA to regulate many targets, whereas cooperativity refers to the ability of many miRNAs to possess a common target (Xiao and Rajewsky, 2009).

According to Bushati and Cohen (2007), miRNAs function as regulatory molecules using five different modes of functioning, acting as: developmental switches, fine tuners of developmental programs, a part of feedback loop, inducers of proliferation and/or apoptosis, and molecules which establish threshold levels (Bushati and Cohen, 2007). miRNAs possess roles in human diseases such as neurodegenerative diseases for example, Tourette's syndrome (Abelson et al., 2005). miRNAs also possess roles as oncogenes and tumor supressors. Some of the human miRNAs such as miR-15a, miR-16-1 and let-7 family possess tumor suppressor activity, whereas miR-155, miR-17 cluster, miR-21 possess oncogenic activity Esquela-Kerscher and Slack, 2006. According to Chang and Mendell (2007), miRNAs have role in fragile X syndrome and synaptic function (Chang and Mendell, 2007).

Viral miRNAs

Several viral groups especially DNA viruses encode miRNAs to regulate the viral and host cellular transcripts. These miRNAs play an important role in viral infection, latency and metabolism. The functions of viral miRNAs include: regulation of viral gene expression, induction of degradation of viral transcripts, regulation of viral transcripts with partial homology, and regulation of host gene expression (Scaria et al., 2007). It seems possible that virus encoded miRNAs possess role in the process of inhibiting antiviral responses of host cell (Cullen, 2006). Jopling (2008) cites that viruses can also use host cellular miRNAs for their own benefit (Jopling, 2008). This phenomenon suggests that viruses might also be able to interfere with host cellular miRNA biogenesis and functions (Sullivan and Ganem, 2005). It seems possible that viral miRNAs play a role in either cancer causing or tumor suppressing activity in host cell (Fujii, 2009). The use of miRNAs by viruses can be attributed to certain properties of miRNAs; such as their non-immunogenicity, hence they do not require much of genomic space, and that, they are powerful regulators of gene expression (Sullivan, 2008; Qi et al., 2006).

Most of the identified viral miRNAs show poor conservation. Poor conservation of viral miRNAs does not necessarily indicate that the identified miRNAs do not have similar expression patterns and/or functions. This diversity suggests that viral miRNAs and their viral targets may have coevolved. The other facet is that, viral miRNAs may lose the functions due to point mutations in the seed region; this might result due to either loss or gain of a large number of cellular or viral miRNA targets (Gottwein and Cullen, 2008). The other interesting characteristic of viral miRNAs is their lack of homology with cellular miRNAs. This makes sure that viral miRNAs are only involved in virus specific regulatory relations. Some viral miRNAs show seed homology with some of the cellular miRNAs; for example, Kaposi sarcoma associated herpesvirus (KSHV) miR-K12-11 is an ortholog of cellular miR-155, they show strong seed homology (Skalsky et al., 2007). Such orthologous miRNAs may share functions resulting into regulation of major metabolic pathways of host by viral miRNAs.

Why miRNAs?

There are numerous articles present on use of sequence specific inhibition as an antiviral means. Although, most of the researchers go for the use of siRNAs, recent researches show that miRNAs can be effectively used as antivirals. Certain pros and cons are related to use of any kind of sequence specific therapeutic agents; the differences between siRNA and miRNA might provide insights into it. Although, both miRNAs and siRNAs depend on similar kind of biogenesis machinery and its components, the most important distinction can be the flexibility in regulation provided by miRNAs. The mode of action of miRNAs depends on the extent of complementarities in miRNA and its target. Also, miRNA show redundancy and cooperativity in function (He and Hannon, 2004). siRNAs work in a highly sequence specific manner and even a single point mutation in siRNA sequence may abrogate siRNA mediated silencing. This leads to viral RNAi escape mutants (Das et al., 2004; Westerhout et al., 2005; Giltin and Andino, 2003), which might prove to be highly virulent than their parent strains. To avoid this, multiple sequences per target and multiple targets per viral genome are necessary to effectively inhibit the virus (Ryther et al., 2005), this might clog miRNA pathway of host as siRNA and miRNA use same pathway for biogenesis (Aagaard and Rossi, 2007). Also, not all viral sequences are accessible as targets, may be due to RNA binding proteins or because of their complex secondary structure (Ryther et al., 2005). Most of the miRNAs are constitutively expressed, while some are restricted in expression which is temporal in nature.

On the other hand, siRNAs are mostly inducted due to exogenous sources, which are not constitutive, and temporal (Hutavágner and Zamore, 2002). siRNAs are typically less conserved as compared to miRNAs and recognize targets with perfect complementarity, this is in accord with siRNAs being derived from the loci that they regulate or from the very closely related loci (Bartel, 2005). Endogenous siRNAs typically target same or similar loci, a phenomenon known as "auto-silencing", whereas miRNAs show "hetero-silencing" (Bartel, 2004). It is known that long dsRNA triggers interferon-I (IFN-I) response; siRNAs when introduced into the cell, might trigger IFN response. This is due to recognition of "pathogen associated molecular patterns" by innate immune system of host, which results due to exogenous nature of siRNAs (Sledz et al., 2003; Behlke, 2006; Tosi, 2005). Computational prediction of miRNAs is relatively easier as it has been observed that miRNAs possess higher adjusted minimum folding energy (adjusted MFE to avoid potential effect of nucleotide sequence length on MFE) and a higher base pair rate in their predicted secondary structures as compared to other coding and non-coding RNAs (Zhang, 2006; Loong and Mishra, 2007).

Although, theoretically siRNAs may not seem to be a good choice for sequence specific therapeutics, many articles report usefulness of siRNAs as antivirals (Novina et al., 2002; McCaffrey et al., 2003; Jacque et al., 2002). A review by Bennink and Palmer, (2004), suggests promising use of siRNAs against influenza viruses (Bennink and Palmore 2004). Researchers such as Zhou et al. (2007); Ge et al. (2003); and Tompkins et al. (2004) have shown the potential of siRNAs in the treatment of influenza. Brahmachari et al. (2008) have filed a patent on targets for human miRNAs in H5N1 genome.

WHEN PREDATOR BECOMES PREY

The innate immunity antiviral pathway that is, IFN pathway is the prime pathway which can detect viral genomes and/or fragments thereof and can efficiently inhibit them. Many viruses, especially plant viruses, code for viral suppressors of IFN pathway. In case of influenza A virus, NS1 protein coded by segment 8 of viral genome, seems to interfere with IFN pathway of host. The NS1 protein seems to be involved in many essential functions such as mRNA transport, splicing, polyadenylation and translation Katze et al., 2002. Studies by Geiss et al. (2002); Garcia-Sastre et al. (1998), have shown that influenza viruses lacking functional NS1 protein are susceptible to antiviral mechanism of host cell (Geiss et al., 2002; García-Sastre et al., 1998). Many articles cite ability of NS1 to inhibit host antiviral responses either by interfering with JNK pathway or by inhibiting synthesis of interferons (Bergmann et al., 2000; Wang et al., 2000; García-Sastre, 2001; Ludwig et al., 2002). This poses possibility of NS1 being the primary culprit in the Hong Kong H5N1 infection which lead to human deaths (Palese et al., 2002). Also, experiments in plants have proved that NS1

acts as viral suppressor of RNAi (Delgadillo et al., 2004).

The reports on NS1 attracted attention of our lab as a target for SSTs. We have predicted viral miRNAs which show homology with 3 of human miRNAs. Also, prediction of metazoan miRNAs for NS1 homologous proteins from humans was also carried out. This was done using Softberry findmiRNA, miReval, TargetScanS and DIANA microT web tools. The average length of the predicted miRNAs is 22nt and they show dominance of guanine (G) in the seed region. The predicted miRNAs show role in MAPK, insulin signaling and pathways leading to renal cell carcinoma, pancreatic cancer, melanoma and chronic myeloid leukemia. This suggests possible roles of predicted miRNAs in host pathways related to cancer. The interaction map of miRNAs and their target genes, constructed using Osprey network visualization platform (Breitkreutz et al., 2003), is shown in Figure 2. Analysis of pre-miRNA structures of predicted miRNA shows that guanine (G) and uracil (U) are dominating nucleotides in pre-miRNAs; out of which G dominates in metazoan pre-miRNAs whereas U dominates in viral pre-miRNAs. Analysis of binding site of target mRNA reveals that hsa-miR-138, hsa-mir-525-3p and hsa-miR-124 show maximum value of MFE inferring that these reactions are most stable (Unpublished results). The role of NS1 as an inhibitor of host antiviral pathways is not fully elucidated yet. NS1 might possess other roles in relation with RNAi silencing and viral replication. Also, it can be inferred that RNAi against influenza virus proteins may not be effective due to interference created by NS1 protein (Figure 3).

LIMITS OF SEQUENCE SPECIFIC THERAPEUTICS

Apart from advantages provided by sequence specific therapeutic agents, these agents might also pose some problems. RNA viruses show high rate of mutations, hence they show a high degree of sequence diversity between different genotypes. RNA viruses are rapidly evolving viruses particularly those with segmented genomes. This is problematic in case of sequence specific therapeutics, particularly siRNAs, which are highly, sequence specific in action (Colbère-Garapin et al., 2005). To avoid this problem, if a variety of siRNAs are incorporated into the host cell, the implication might be clogging of endogenous miRNA pathway, as shRNA and siRNA resemble miRNA precursors (Aagaard and Rossi, 2007). Viral suppressors of host RNAi pathway pose another problem (Li and Ding, 2001). This may be overcome by inhibiting viral suppressor proteins. In vivo use of SSTs is difficult due to problems such as, blood stability, delivery to infected tissue, poor intracellular uptake, and nonspecific immune stimulation (Leung and Whittakar, 2005).

Serum nucleases can degrade siRNAs (Dykxhoorn and Lieberman, 2005; Paroo and Corey, 2004); but this can

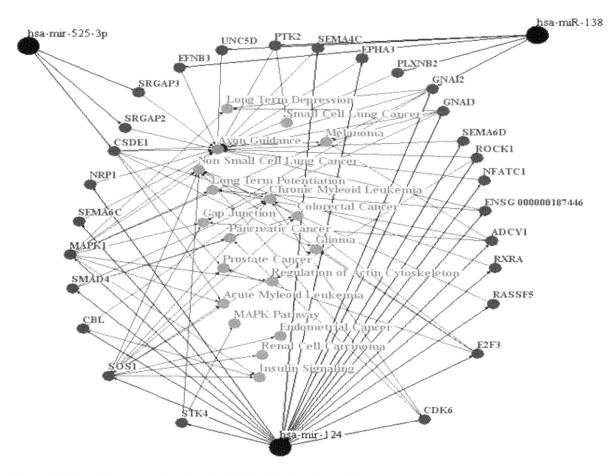

Figure 2. Interaction map of predicted miRNAs showing interrelationship between miRNA and their target genes. Predicted miRNAs show role in essential biochemical as well as cancer causing pathways of host cell.

be avoided to a certain extent by chemically modifying SSTs (Watts et al., 2008). Problematic delivery of SSTs to specific tissue types reduces efficacy of SSTs. Cationic polymers are usually applied to mediate delivery of SSTs into the host cell (Ge et al., 2003; Tompkins et al., 2004). SSTs should remain stable in the circulatory system, and should bind to blood proteins to a degree which should not be toxic (Dorsett, 2004). It has been suggested that the transfection agent may also contribute to the influence of expression independent of siRNA (Federov et al., 2005; Akhtar and Benter, 2007). Suppression off target presents another problem for SSTs. It has been observed that siRNA treated cells show off target gene silencing (Jackson et al., 2003; Jackson and Linsley, 2004; Couzin, 2004; Scacheri et al., 2004). Hence, it is of utmost importance to avoid off target gene silencing.

miRNA PREDICTION

Computational prediction of miRNAs is today's need for carrying out experiments related to or concerned with miRNAs. A variety of methods, protocols and online or offline web sources can be used and are in use for miRNA prediction. Table 4 shows the most popular web sources which are cited by most of the research articles. The computational prediction of miRNAs is based on the confirmed and known rules of miRNA and mRNA interactions (Wei et al., 2009). Several methods use evolutionary principles of miRNA sequence conservation, whereas recent methods have focused more on *ab initio* miRNA and target finding methods. Many methods use machine learning approaches (Legendre et al., 2005; Wang and Naqa, 2008). Although, machine learning approaches are efficient in prediction, the availability of data is less; this may affect efficiency of these methods (Lindow and Gorodkin, 2007). Biological properties of miRNA sequences are of great importance in computational prediction of miRNA and their respective targets. According to a review by Lindow and Gorodkin (2007), a variety of approaches can be applied for miRNA gene finding and for miRNA target prediction *in silico* (Lindow and Gorodkin, 2007). The miRNA gene finding takes into account approaches such as removal of exons and repeats, intergenomic matches, intragenomic matches, hairpin classification based on MFE values, rule

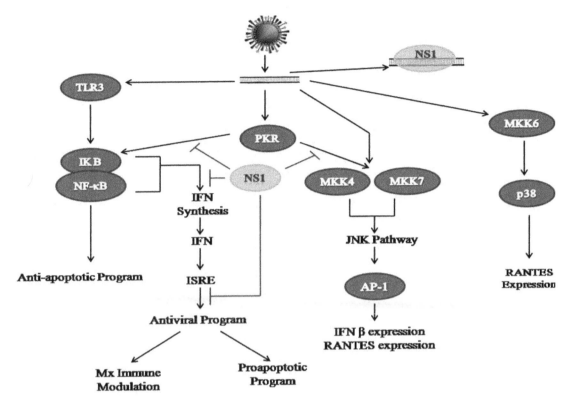

Figure 3. Involvement of NS1 protein of H5N1 in various cellular pathways leading to inhibition of IFN synthesis. Influenza virus infection activates a variety of chemokine and cytokine genes. H5N1 NS1 protein is found to be responsible for inhibition of antiviral mechanism of the host. This is mediated by inhibition of host proteins at different levels by NS1 as shown in the figure.

based classification of hairpins (Lindow and Gorodkin, 2007), and machine learning approach to classify hairpins (Lindow and Gorodkin, 2007; Xue et al., 2005). The miRNA target finding takes into account approaches such as conservation, use of target islands, seed matching. Target gene regulation by miRNAs and interrelationship between transcription factors and miRNAs can also be elucidated with the help of computational biology (Li et al., 2010).

Large scale genome analysis considering over 3853 reported miRNAs by Zhang et al. (2009) reveals that Uracil is the dominant nucleotide in the edges of seed region that is, at first and ninth position. This study also deduces the relationship between divergence in miRNA features and taxonomic level, inferring that as the taxonomic level increases diversity in miRNA features increases (Zhang et al., 2009). miRNA binding site location (3'UTR, coding sequence, 5'UTR), number of G: U wobble pairs in the seed region, and the kinetics and thermodynamics of miRNA and its target mRNA are some of the essential factors to be considered for computational miRNA prediction (Ghosh et al., 2007). The secondary structure prediction of miRNAs can be refined by eliminating pseudo knots, comparing with consensus structure, motif finding, statistical structure prediction and 2D structure prediction and comparison

(Hamilton et al., 2007).

Avian influenza genome was computationally screened for human miRNA targets by Brahmachari et al. (2008). Two miRNAs namely hsa-miR-136 and hsa-miR-507 show targets in HA and PB2 protein, respectively. This suggests need of integrated *in silico* and *in vitro* approaches (Brahmachari et al., 2008). A research article by Hevik et al. (2007) emphasizes on the role of Drosha processing sites in miRNA precursors, citing that hairpins should not be annotated as miRNAs unless they are verified by Drosha and Dicer substrates (Helvik et al., 200). Whereas, Grimson et al. (2007) cite the effect of factors other than seed pairing in the miRNA target specificity in mammals (Grimson et al., 2007). Hence, it seems plausible that computational miRNA prediction may involve several parameters and factors, than in use. Also, sensitivity and specificity of prediction differs according to the algorithm used (Martin et al., 2007). Computational miRNA prediction may fail due to availability of less data, diverse nature of miRNA sequences, and flexibility in functioning of miRNAs interms of multiplicity and cooperativity. This creates a need to experimentally validate the predicted miRNAs and their target study *in vivo* (Barbato et al., 2009). This can be achieved by experimentally studying miRNA effects on target mRNA co-expression, target protein and

Table 4. Available web-sources for prediction of miRNAs and their targets.

Web tool	Link	Functions/uses
miRBase	http://www.mirbase.org/index.shtml	Database of predicted and known miRNAs
TargetScanS	http://www.targetscan.org/	miRNA gene finding, conservation analysis
RNA22	http://cbcsrv.watson.ibm.com/rna22.html	miRNA target and precursor miRNA finding
mir viRDB	http://140.109.42.4/cgiandbin/miRNA/miRNA.cgi	Sequence match, secondary structure prediction
miRanda	http://www.microrna.org/microrna/home.do	Target finding based on sequence match and MFE values
RNAHybrid	http://bibiserv.techfak.uniandbielefeld.de/rnahybrid/	Target finding based on sequence match and MFEs
DIANA microT	http://diana.cslab.ece.ntua.gr/pathways/	Target finding, Pathway annotations
Softberry findmiRNA	http://www.softberry.com/	miRNA finding, Target finding, folding studies
miRRim	http://www.ncrna.org/software/miRRim	HMM, conservation and thermal stability
Mfold	http://www.bioinfo.rpi.edu/applications/mfold	Nucleic acid folding and hybridization prediction
Pita	http://genie.weizmann.ac.il/pubs/mir07	Incorporates the role of target-site accessibility within traditional seed finding procedures
ViTA	http://vita.mbc.nctu.edu.tw/	Prediction of host miRNAs targets on viruses

target biological function (Kuhn et al., 2008).

Many of the mechanistic factors of miRNA biogenesis, sequence functionality and mode of action are still unexplored. Hence, it may reflect in the computational prediction of miRNA as most of the tools are based on machine learning approaches which use experimentally available data. Similar to siRNAs, there are chances of emergence of escape mutants in the treatment of miRNAs. On the other hand, due to flexibility in function, miRNAs might target host proteins leading to nonspecific reactions. This process of nonspecific interactions and viral protein inhibition, if visualized, considering the rapid evolution rate of viruses, suggests that use of miRNAs may lead to stronger viral suppressors and/or emergence of novel mechanisms of host RNAi inhibition.

CONCLUSION

The need of SSTs as antivirals is increasing due to emergence of drug resistant strains of influenza viruses. Recent advances in computational biology and SST research has opened up new avenues for *in silico* prediction of SSTs and *in vitro* validation of SSTs. Although, SSTs can be applied as antivirals, there are some innate problems related with their use. Designing, delivery and stability in the host system are some of the major hurdles in developing SSTs against influenza viruses. miRNAs seem to be more effective as anti-influenza therapeutics compared to siRNAs, as they are flexible in action. This flexibility in function might prove advantageous to treat continuously varying sequences of AI viruses. On the other hand, SSTs may also function in

favour of viruses by nonspecifically inhibiting host metabolic pathways and/or proteins involved in essential metabolic pathways of the host. Computational prediction methods of miRNA prediction and miRNA target recognition have lead to easy and quick designing of SSTs. Although, there are certain discrepancies in different prediction methods applied by various algorithms; computational methods can be effectively used as a potential tool for further experimental validation of miRNAs.

REFERENCES

Aagaard L, Rossi JJ (2007). RNAi therapeutics: principles, prospects and challenges, Adv. Drug Delivery Rev., 59: 75-86.

Abelson JF, Kwan KY, O'Roak BJ, Baek DY, Stillman AA, Morgan TM, Mathews CA, Pauls DL, Rasin M, Gunel M, Davis NR, Ercan-Sencicek AG, Guez DH, Spertus JA, Leckman JF, Dure LS, Kurlan R, Singer HS, Gilbert DL, Farhi A (2005), Sequence variants in SLITRK1are associated with Tourette's syndrome, Science, 310: 317–320.

Akhtar S, Benter FI (2007). Nonviral delivery of synthetic siRNAs *in vivo*, J. Clin. Invest., 117(12): 3623-3632.

Barbato C, Arisi I, Frizzo ME, Brandi R, Sacco LD, Masotti A (2009). Computational challenges in miRNA target predictions: to be or not to be a true target? J. Biomed. Biotechnol., 2009: 1-9.

Bartel B (2005). MicroRNAs directing siRNA biogenesis, Nat. Struc. Mol. Biol., 12(7):569-571.

Bartel PD (2004). MicroRNAs: genomics, biogenesis, mechanism, and function, Cell., 116: 281-297.

Behlke AM (2006), Progress towards *in vivo* use of siRNAs, Molecular Therapy, 13(4): 644-670.

Bennink JR, Palmore TN (2004). The promise of siRNAs for the treatment of influenza, Trends Mol. Med., 10(12): 571-574.

Bergmann M, García-Sastre A, Carnero E, Pehamberger H, Wolff K, Palese P, Muster T (2000).Influenza virus NS1 protein counteracts PKR-mediated inhibition of replication, J. Virol., 74(13): 6203-6206.

Brahmachari SK, Hariharan M, Scaria V, Pillai B (2008). Targets for human microRNAs in avian influenza virus (H5N1) genome, US 2008/0045472.

Breitkreutz BJ, Stark C, Tyers M (2003). Osprey: a network visualization system, Genome Biol., 4(3): R22.

Brown HI (2000), The epidemiology and evolution of influenza viruses in pigs, Vet. Microbiol., 74: 29-46.

Bushati N (2007). Cohen MS, miRNA functions, Ann. Rev. Cell Dev. Biol., 23: 175-205.

Cejka D, Losert D, Wacheck V (2006). Short interfering RNA (siRNA): tool or therapeutic? Clin. Sci., 110:47-58.

Chan PKS (1997). Outbreak of avian influenza A (H5N1) virus infection in Hong Kong in. Clin. Infect. Dis., 34(suppl 2): 58-64, 2002.

Chang T, Mendell TJ (2007). microRNAs in vertebrate physiology and human disease, Ann. Rev. Genomics Hum. Genet., 8: 215-239.

Cheung KWT (2007), Poon LLM, Biology of influenza A virus, Ann. N.Y. Acad. Sci., 1102:1-25.

Colbère -Garapin F, Blondel B, Saulnier A, Pelletier I, Labadie K (2005). Colbère Silencing viruses by RNA interference, Microbes Infection., 7: 767-775.

Couzin J (2004). RNAi shows cracks in its armor, Science, 306(5699): 1124-1125.

Cullen RB (2006). Viruses and microRNAs, Nat. Genet. 38(suppl): 25-30.

Das TA, Brummelcamp TR, Westerhout EM, Vink M, Madiredjo M, Bernards R, Berkhout B (2004), Human Immunodeficiency virus type 1 escapes from RNA interference-mediated inhibition, J. Virol., 78(5): 2601-2605.

De Clercq E, Neyts J (2007). Avian influenza A (H5N1) infection: targets and strategies for chemotherapeutic intervention, Trends. Pharm. Sci., 28(6): 280-285.

Delgadillo MO, Sáenz P, García JA, Simón-Mateo C (2004). Human influenza virus NS1 protein enhances viral pathogenecity and acts as an RNA silencing suppressor in plants, J. Virol., 85: 993-999.

Dorsett Y (2004). Tuschl TsiRNAs, Applications in functional genomics and potential as therapeutics, Nat. Rev. Drug Discov., 3: 318-329.

Dykxhoorn MD, Lieberman J (2005). The silent revolution: RNA interference as basic biology, research tool, and therapeutic, Ann. Rev. Med., 56:401-423.

Elci C (2006). The impact of HPAI of the H5N1 strain on economies affected countries, In International Conference on Human and Economic Resources: Izmir. Natural Resources.

Esquela-Kerscher A, Slack JF (2006). Oncomirs-microRNAs with a role in cancer, Nat. Rev. Cancer., 6: 259-269.

Fauci SA (2005). Race against time. Nature, 435: 423-424.

Federov Y, King A, Anderson E, Karpilow J, Llsley D, Marshall W, Khvorova A (2005). Different delivery methods-different expression profiles, Nature Methods, 2(4): 241-252.

Fujii YR (2009). Oncoviruses and pathogenic microRNAs in humans, Open Virol. J., 3: 37-51.

García-Sastre A (1998), Influenza A virus lacking the NS1 gene replicates in interferon deficient systems, Virology, 252(2): 324-330.

García-Sastre A (2001). Inhibition of interferon-mediated antiviral responses by influenza A viruses and other negative strand RNA viruses, Virology, 279: 375-384.

Ge Q, McManus TM, Nguyen T, Shen S, Sharp PA, Eisen HA, Chen J (2003). RNA interference of influenza virus production by directly targeting mRNA for degradation and indirectly inhibiting all viral RNA transcription, Pro. Nat. Acad. Sci., 100(5): 2718-2723.

Geiss GK, Salvatore M, Tumpey TM, Carter VS, Wang X, Basler CF, Taubenberger JK, Bumgarner RE, Palese P, Katze MG, García-Sastre A (2002). Cellular transcriptional profiling in influenza A virus infected lung epithelial cells: the role of nonstructural NS1 protein in the evasion of the host innate defense and its potential contribution to pandemic influenza, Proc. Nat. Acad. Sci., 99(16): 10736-10741.

Ghosh Z, Chakrabarti J, Mallick B, miRNomics-The bioinformatics of microRNA genes, Biochem. Biophysic. Res. Comm., 363: 6-11, 2007.

Giltin L, Andino R (2003). Nucleic acid-based immune system: the antiviral potential of mammalian RNA silencing, J. Virol., 77(13): 7159-7165.

Gottwein E, Cullen RB (2008.). Viral and cellular microRNAs as determinants of viral pathogenesis and immunity, Cell Host Microbe

Rev., 3: 375-387.

Gregory RI (2005). Shiekhattar R, Micro RNA biogenesis and cancer, Cancer Research, 65(9):3509-3512.

Grimson A, Farth KK, Johnston WK, Garrett-Engele P, Lim LP, Bartel DP (2007). MicroRNA targeting specificity in mammals: determinants beyond seed pairing, Mole. Cell, 27: 91-105.

Hamilton SR, Davis I (2007). RNA localization signals: deciphering the message with bioinformatics, Seminars Cell Dev. Biol., 18: 178-185.

He L, Hannon JG (2004). MicroRNAs: small RNAs with a big role in gene regulation, Nat. Rev. Genet., 5: 522-531.

Helvik SA, Snøve Jr O, Sætrom P (2007). Reliable prediction of Drosha processing sites improves microRNA gene prediction. Bioinformatics, 23(2): 142-149.

Hong Z (2009). Tissue and host tropism of influenza viruses: importance of quantitative analysis. Science in China Series C: Life Sci., 52(12):1101-1110.

Horimoto T, KAWAOKA Y (2001). Pandemic threat posed by avian influenza A viruses. Clin. Microbiol. Rev., 14(1): 129-149.

http://www.who.int/csr/disease/avian_influenza/en/

Hutavágner G, Zamore DP (2002). RNAi: nature abhors a double strand, Curr. Opi. Genet. Dev., 12: 225-232.

ICTVdBManagement (http://www.ncbi.nlm.nih.gov/ICTVdb/Ictv/index.htm)

Jackson AL, Bartz SR, Schelter J, Kobayashi SV, Burchard J, Mao M, Li B, Cavet G, Linsley PS (2003). Expression profiling reveals off-target gene regulation by RNAi, Nat. Biotechnol., 21: 635-637.

Jackson AL, Linsley PS (2004). Noise amidst the silence: off-target effects of siRNAs? Trends in Genetics 20(11): 521-524.

Jacque J, Triques K, Stevenson M (2002). Modulation of HIV-1 replication by RNA interference, Nature, 418: 435-438.

Jopling LC (2008). Regulation of hepatitis C virus by microRNA-122, Biochem. Soc. Trans., 36(6): 1220-1223.

Katze GM, He Y, Gale Jr M, Viruses and Interferons: a fight for supremacy, Nat. Rev. Immunol., 2: 675-687, 2002.

Kuhn DE, Martin MM, Feldman DS, Terry Jr. AV, Nuovo GJ, Elton TS (2008). Experimental validation of miRNA targets, NIH Methods, 44(1): 47-54.

Lamb RA, Krug RM (2001), Orthomyxoviridae: the viruses and their replication, in Fields BN, Peter M, Howley MD, Griffin DE, Robert A, Lamb RA, Malcolm A, Martin MD, Roizman B, Straus MD, Knipe DM (eds.) Fields virology. Volume 1. 4th Edition. Lippincott Williams and Wilkins, pp. 1216-1253.

Legendre M, Lambert A, Gautheret D (2005), Profile based detection of microRNA precursors in animal genomes, Bioinformatics Discovery Note, 21(7): 841-845.

Leung RKM, Whittakar PA (2005). RNA interference: from gene silencing to gene specific therapeutics, Pharmacol. Therapeutics, 107: 222-239.

Lewis BD (2006). Avian flu to human influenza, Ann. Rev. Med., 57:139-154.

Li L, Xu J, Yang D, Tan X, Wang H (2010). Computational approaches for microRNA studies: a review, Mamm. Genome, 21: 1-12.

Li XW, Ding WS (2001). Viral suppressors of RNA silencing, Curr. Opin. Biotechnol., 12: 150-154.

Lin S, Miller JD, Ying S (2006). Intronic microRNA (miRNA), J. Biomed. Biotechnol., 2006:1-13.

Lindow M, Gorodkin J (2007). Principles and limitations of computational microRNA gene and target finding, DNA Cell Biol., 26(5): 339-351.

Loong KNS, Mishra SK (2007). Unique folding of precursor microRNAs: quantitative evidence and implications for de novo identification, RNA 13: 170-187.

Ludwig S, Planz O, Pleschka S, Wolff T (2003), Influenza-virus-induced signaling cascades: targets for antiviral therapy? Trends Mol. Med., 9(2): 46-52.

Ludwig S, Wang X, Ehrhardt C, Zheng H, Donelan N, Planz O, Pleschka S (2002). García-Sastre A, Heins G, Wolff T, The influenza A virus NS1 protein inhibits activation of Jun-N-terminal kinase and AP-1 transcription factors, J. Virol., 76(21): 11166-11171.

Martin G, Schouest K, Kovvuru P, Spillane C (2007). Prediction and validation of microRNA targets in animal genomes, J. Biosci., 32(6): 1049-1052.

Matrosovich NM, Matrosovich TY, Gray T, Roberts NA, Kenk H (2004). Human and avian influenza viruses target different cell types in cultures of human airway epithelium, Proc. Nat. Acad. Sci., 101(13): 4620-4624.

McCaffrey AP, Nakai H, Pandey K, Huang Z, Salazar FH, Xu H, Wieland SF, Marion PL, Kay MA (2003). Inhibition of hepatitis B virus in mice by RNA interference, Nat. Biotechnol., 21: 639-644.

Novina DC, Murray MF, Dykxhoorn DM, Beresford PJ, Riess J, Lee S, Collman RG, Lieberman J, Shankar P, Sharp PA (2002). siRNA-directed inhibition of HIV-1 infection, Nature Med., 8(7): 681-686.

Osterhaus DMEA, Munster JV, Fouchier RAM (2008). Epidemiology of avian influenza, in Klenk HD, Matrosovich MN, Stetch J (eds.), Monographs Virol., Karger Publishers, 27: 1-10.

Palese P, Basler CF, García-Sastre A (2002). The makings of a killer, Nature Med., 8(9): 927-928.

Palese P, García-Sastre A (2002). Influenza vaccines: present and future, J. Clin. Inv., 110(1): 9-13.

Paroo Z, Corey RD (2004), Challenges for RNAi in vivo, Trends in Biotechnol., 22(8): 390-394.

Peiris MJS, Jong MD, Guan Y (2007). Avian influenza virus (H5N1): a threat to human health, Clin. Microbiol. Rev., 20(2): 243-267.

Proença-Módena JL, Macedo IS, Arruda E (2007). H5N1 avian influenza virus: an overview, Braz. J. Infect. Dis., 11(1): 125-133.

Qi P, Han J, Lu Y, Wang C, Bu F (2006). Virus-encoded microRNAs: future therapeutics targets? Cell. Mol. Immunol., 3(6): 411-419.

Rayburn RE, Zhang R (2008). Antisense, RNAi, and gene silencing strategies for therapy: mission possible for impossible? Drug Discovery Today, 13(11/12): 513-521.

Ruby GJ (2007). Intronic microRNA precursors that bypass Drosha processing, Nature Lett., 448: 83-86.

Ryther RCC, Flynt AS, Philips III JA, Patton JG (2005). siRNA therapeutics: big potential from small RNAs, Gene Therapy, 12: 5-11.

Scacheri PC, Rosenblatt-Rosen O, Caplen NJ, Wolfsberg TG, Umayam L, Lee JC, Hughes CM, Shanmugam KS, Bhattacharjee A, Meyerson M, Collins FS (2004). Short interfering RNAs can induce unexpected and divergent changes in the levels of untargeted proteins in Mammalian cells, Pro. Nat. Acad. Sci., 101(7): 1892-1897.

Scaria V, Hariharan M, Pillai B, Maiti S, Brahmachari SK (2007). Host-virus genome interactions: macro roles of microRNAs, Cell. Microbiol., 9(12): 2784-2794.

Seo SH, Hoffmann E, Webster RG (2002). Lethal H5N1 influenza viruses escape host anti-viral cytokine responses, Nature Med., 8(9): 50-954.

Skalsky RL, Samols MA, Plaisance KB, Boss IW, Riva A, Lopez MC, Baker HV, Renne R (2007). Kaposi's sarcoma associated herpesvirus encodes an ortholog of miR-155, J. Virol., 81(23): 12836-12845.

Sledz CA, Holko M, Veer MJ, Silverman RH, Williams BRG (2003). Activation of interferon system by short-interfering RNAs, Nat. Cell Biol. 5(9): 834-839.

Smith GJD, Vijayakrishna D, Bahl J, Lycett SJ, Worobey M, Pybus OG, Ma SK, Cheung CL, Raghwani J, Bhatt S, Peiris JSM, Guan Y, Rambaut A (2009). Origin and evolutionary genomics of the 2009 swine-origin H1N1 influenza A epidemic, Nature, 459: 1122-1126.

Sontheimer EJ (2005). Carthew WR, Silence from within: endogenous siRNAs and miRNAs, Cell., 122: 9-12.

Suarez DL, Schultz-Cherry S (2000). Immunology of avian influenza virus: a review, Dev. Comparative Immunol., 24:269-283.

Sullivan CS (2008). New roles for large and small viral RNAs in evading host defenses, Nat. Rev. Genet., 9: 503-507.

Sullivan CS, Ganem D (2005). MicroRNAs and viral infection, Molecular Cell, 20: 3-7.

Tompkins SM, Lo C, Tumpey TM, Epstein SL (2004). Protection against lethal influenza virus challenge by RNA interference in vivo, Pro. Nat. Acad. Sci., 101(23): 8682-8686.

Tosi FM (2005). Innate immune responses to infection, J. Allergy Clin. Immunol., 116(2): 241-249.

Trampuz A, Rajesh MP, Smith TF (2004). Baddour LA, Avian influenza: a new pandemic threat? Mayo Clin. Proc., 79: 523-530.

Wang X, Li M, Zheng H, Muster T, Palese P, Beg AA, García-Sastre A (2000). Influenza A virus NS1 protein prevents activation of NF-κB and induction of alpha/beta interferon, J. Virol., 74(24): 11566-11573.

Wang X, Naqa EMI (2008). Prediction of both conserved and nonconserved microRNA targets in animals, Bioinformatics, 24(3): 325-332.

Watts JK, Deleavey GF, Damha MJ (2008). Chemically modified siRNA: tools and applications, Drug Discovery Today, 13(19/20): 842-855.

Webster RG, Bean WJ, Gorman OT, Chambers TM, Kawaoka Y (1992). Evolution and ecology of influenza A viruses, Microbiological Rev., 56(1): 152-179.

Webster RG, Hulse DJ (2004). Microbial adaptation and change: avian influenza, Rev. Sci. Tech. Off. Int. Epiz., 23(2): 453-465.

Wei X, GuoJan C, NingSheng S (2009). Progress in miRNA target prediction and identification. Science in China Series C: Life Sci., 52(12): 1123-1130.

Westerhout EM, Ooms M, Vink M, Das TA (2005). Berkhout B, HIV-1 can escape from RNA interference by evolving an alternative structure in its RNA genome, Nucleic Acids Res., 33(2): 796-804.

Xiao C, Rajewsky K (2009). MicroRNA control in the immune system: basic principles, Cell., 136: 26-36.

Xue C, Li F, He T, Liu G, Li Y, Zhang X (2005). Classification of real and pseudo microRNA precursors using local structure-sequence features and support vector machine, BMC Bioinformatics, 6: 310.

Yen H, Guan Y, Peiris M, Webster RG (2008). H5N1 in Asia, in Klenk HD, Matrosovich MN, Stetch J (eds.), Monographs Virol., Karger publishers, 27: 11-26.

Zambon MC (1999). Epidemiology and pathogenesis of influenza. J. Anti. Chem., 44(Topic B): 3-9.

Zhang B., Stellwag EJ, Pan X (2009). Large-scale genome analysis reveals unique features of microRNAs, Gene, 443: 100-109.

Zhang BH (2006). Evidence that miRNAs are different from other RNAs, Cell. Mol. Life Sci., 63: 246-254.

Zhang H, Chen L (2009), Possible origin of current influenza A H1N1 viruses. The Lancet 9: 456-457.

Zhou H, Jin M, Yu Z, Xu X, Peng Y, Wu H, Liu J, Cao S, Chen H (2007) Effective small interfering RNAs targeting matrix and nucleocapsid protein inhibit influenza A virus replication in cells and mice, Antivir. Res., 76:186–193.

## 6

Evolutionary analysis of gorilla, chimps and humans using sequence divergence

Vibhu Ranjan Prasad, Soumya Chaurasia and Rao Sethumadhavan*

School of Bioscience and Technology, Vellore Institute of Technology, Vellore, Tamil Nadu – 632014, India.

We have analyzed the sequence divergence amongst the three species that is, gorilla, chimpanzee and human varying from Hominidae and Pongidae. Apart from the genomic phylogeny, we compared the protein and rRNA phylogenies to increase the importance of phylogenetic analysis. The proteins selected are from the mitochondrial origin as mtDNA which codes for mitochondrial proteins, mutate at a higher rate compared to nuclear DNA, so as to give a more useful, magnified view of the diversity present in a population, and its history. The phylogenetic analysis of the mitochondrial genome, rRNA and proteins are done using parsimony, BIONJ and PHYML methods which $resulted into variable results. The proteins that were able to infer the already stated phylogeny between these members were ATP synthase subunit 6 and 8, cytochrome b, cytochrome oxidase subunit 1 and 3 and NADH dehydrogenase subunit 2, 3 and 5. Although BIONJ and PHYML methods predicted similar results most often parsimony was found to be predicting contradictory phylogeny with respect to above two methods. To verify the results as obtained from various methods and to further analyze the evolutionary relationship between these members, we applied the method of calculating sequence divergence using bioinformatics tools. Taking into account that local point mutations generate a considerable genetic variation and this variation being very high in mitochondrial DNA, we analyzed the sequence divergence between these three species using 0, ±1 and ±2 error in identical cut sites by different restriction enzymes. No identical site between chimpanzee-human clade at different errors indicated gorilla to be common ancestor of these two members. At ±2 error, an identical sequence divergence was obtained between the chimpanzee-gorilla and human-gorilla clades but overall results suggest chimpanzee to be a closer relative of gorilla than human.

Key words: Sequence divergence, in silico restriction digestion, phylogeny.

INTRODUCTION

The endless number of study related to the evolutionary analysis of the three species varying from Hominidae to Pongidae confirms the importance which these organisms hold in evolutionary analysis. One of the species among these, the *Homo sapiens* has also been studied widely in evolutionary and phylogenetic terms. Traditionally chimps are classified with other great apes, gorillas and orangutans in the family *Pongidae,* separated from the human family Hominidae, but at the level of DNA humans are so closely related to chimps that chimps

should not be part of the same taxonomic family, but also the same genus. Even the humans are also being called "the third chimpanzee" (Jeff, 2003). However, the close similarity in the nucleotides of two species does not mean that proteins coded by them are also the same. A recent study has proposed that 80% of the proteins between chimps and humans are different that leads to a considerable morphological difference between the two species (Galina et al., 2005). The molecular phylogeny using the complete sequences of mitochondrial DNAs for the evolution of prosimians is already being done (Atsushi et al., 2009). Moreover, taxonomic and phylogenetic analysis between great apes and humans has identified phylogentic relationship between these

---

*Corresponding author. E-mail: rsethumadhavan@vit.ac.in.

species as a never ending conflict (Galina et al., 2005). We have analyzed the phylogenetic relationship between the great apes, that is chimps and gorillas with humans using sequence divergence in their mitochondrial genome.

The paper deals with the use of novel bioinformatics tool in analyzing the phylogeny and stating some new points in the evolutionary relationship of chimpanzee, gorilla and human. The approach involves the use of parsimony, BIONJ and PHYML methods to analyze the phylogenetic relations between the mitochondrial DNA, 12s and 16s rRNA and mitochondrial proteins on which the life of animals are crucially dependent. The new method that we are using here is the analysis of sequence divergence between the mitochondrial genome of these organisms. Since mitochondria is found to be evolving much more rapidly than single-copy nuclear DNA in higher animals (Brown et al., 1979), the number of cut sites obtained after digesting the DNA with a variety of restriction enzymes were highly unlikely to be similar. We used a new approach considering the local point mutations to be one of the main causes of genetic variation among these sequences and obtained a result that can be used to state evolutionary relationship as well as the degree of separation between gorilla, chimpanzee and human. The results presented here may be further used in the evolutionary studies of Hominidae and great apes.

MATERIALS AND METHODS

Dataset

The mitochondrial genome, mitochondrial rRNA and mitochondrial proteins of *Pan troglodytes* (Chimpanzee), *Gorilla gorilla* (Gorilla) and *Homo sapiens* (humans) were taken from from Entrez Genome (available at http://www.ncbi.nlm.nih.gov/entrez) using the NCBI Sequence Viewer version 2. The details of the sequences taken and their accession numbers are depicted in Tables.

Multiple sequence alignment

The multiple sequence alignment of mitochondrial genome, mitochondrial rRNA and mitochondrial proteins was done using Clustal X 1.83 (Thompson et al., 1997). The program can align the sequences in both multiple alignment mode as well as Profile alignment mode. For the present work, we have used the multiple alignment mode to align the mitochondrial genome, mitochondrial rRNA and mitochondrial proteins of chimpanzee, gorilla and human.

Phylogenetic tree using parsimony

Phylogenetic tree using parsimony was calculated using PHYLIP's dnapars/protpars algorithm. The tool used for finding the tree is a standalone tool known as SeaView 4.0 (Galtier et al., 1996).

BioNJ tree

The distance based phylogenetic analysis of the mitochondrial

genome, mitochondrial rRNA and mitochondrial proteins of chimpanzee, gorilla and human was done using the BioNJ algorithm which is an improved version of NJ algorithm (Gascuel, 1997). The algorithm is well suited for distance estimation from DNA and protein sequences. BIONJ has better topological accuracy than NJ in all evolutionary conditions; its superiority becomes important when the substitution rates are high and varying among lineages.

PhyML tree

PhyML 3.0 program was used to estimate the phylogeny by maximum likelihood method (Thompson et al., 1997). The PhyML algorithm is a simple, fast and accurate algorithm to estimate the large phylogenies by maximum likelihood method. The tool used for calculating the PhyML tree is a standalone tool known as SeaView 4.0 (Galtier et al., 1996). The algorithm behind this program dramatically reduces time and can be used with much larger and more complex data sets.

In silico restriction digestion

The *in silico* restriction digestion of the mitochondrial genome, mitochondrial rRNA and mitochondrial protein was done using Webcutter 2.0 tool available at http://rna.lundberg.gu.se/cutter2. Webcutter 2.0 accesses the restriction enzymes from the Restriction Enzyme Database or REBASE available at http://rebase.neb.com (Gascuel, 1997). The mitochondrial genome was provided as a RAW input to the tool for restriction digestion analysis and the restriction digestion for chimpanzee, gorilla and human genomes are done separately. The selection of restriction enzymes was based upon the earlier works of Ferris et al. (1981). The 19 restriction enzymes used for the present work are Aval, BglII, BstEII, EcoRI, EcoRV, FaunDI, HincII, HindIII, HpaI, KpnI, PstI, PvuII, SacI, SalI, ScaI, SmaI, Xba I and XhoII with the exception of FaunDII. Since FaunDII is not available in the Webcutter 2.0, it was replaced by FaunDI for the present work.

RESULTS AND DISCUSSION

Nucleic acid phylogeny

Phylogenetic analysis of the mitochondrial genome, 12s rRNA and 16s rRNA of chimpanzee, gorilla and human was done and the trees are drawn in Table 2. BioNJ and PhyML phylogeny supported the already stated results of chimpanzee-human clade. However, the parsimony phylogeny using mitochondrial genome supported human-gorilla clade while using the 12s and 16s rRNA, phylogeny supported the chimpanzee-gorilla clade.

Protein phylogeny

Phylogenetic analysis of the mitochondrial proteins listed in Table 1 also gave variable results. Among the thirteen mitochondrial proteins selected for the analysis, cytochrome oxidase subunit 2 and NADH dehydrogenase subunit 1 and 4 were supporting the chimpanzee-gorilla clade and hence were considered faulty. ATP synthase

Table 1. Dataset of mitochondrial genome, rRNA and proteins.

mtDNA or proteins coded by mitochondria	Chimpanzee	Human	Gorilla
mt DNA	NC 001643	AC_000021	NC_011120
ATP synthase S6	NP_008191	AP_000644	YP_002120664
ATP synthase S8	NP_008190	AP_000643	YP_002120663
Cytochrome B	NP_008198	AP_000651	YP_002120670
Cytochrome ox S1	NP_008188	AP_000641	YP_002120661
Cytochrome ox S2	NP_008189	AP_000642	YP_002120662
Cytochrome ox S3	NP_008192	AP_000645	YP_002120665
NADH dehy sub 1	NP_008186	AP_000639	YP_002120659
NADH dehy sub 2	NP_008187	AP_000640	YP_002120660
NADH dehy sub 3	NP_008193	AP_000646	YP_002120666
NADH dehy sub 4	NP_008195	AP_000648	YP_002120667
NADH dehy sub 4L	NP_008194	AP_000647	YP_002117971
NADH dehy sub 5	NP_008196	AP_000649	YP_002120668
NADH dehy sub 6	NP_008197	AP_000650	YP_002120669

Table 2. BioNJ and PHYML trees for mitochondrial genome and 12s and 16s rRNA.

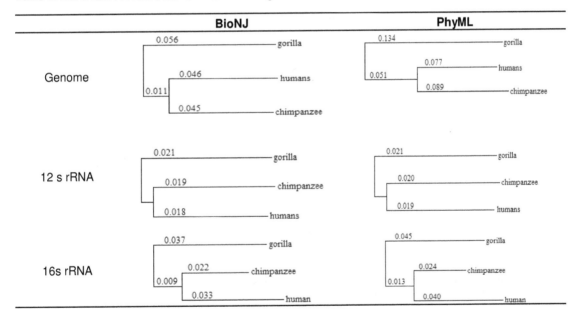

subunit 6 and 8, cytochrome b, cytochrome oxidase subunit 1 and 3, NADH dehydrogenase subunit 2, 3, 4 and 5 supported the chimpanzee-human clade. Mitochondiral protein phylogenetic analysis in these three organisms also indicated that the phylogenies predicted by parsimony method was contradictory to that obtained from BIONJ and PHYML methods.

In silico restriction digestion

As we know, most of the variation among genes in a gene family is caused by point mutations and positive selection (Xinli et al., 2006). *In silico* restriction digestion using Webcutter 2.0 and analysis of the number of sites shared between mitochondrial genome of chimpanzee, gorilla and human showed that there were no sites shared between the genome of chimpanzee-human and gorilla-human and the results are tabulated in Table 3. This could be due to the intense evolution that has resulted in a change in the position of restriction sites of the restriction enzymes. However, a total of 2 sites (PvuII454 and XbaI643) were found to be exactly common between chimpanzee-gorilla. This directly confers the strong similarity between these two and hence less sequence divergence during the course of evolution.

Table 3. Cut sites alongwith the restriction enzymes at increased level of error for gorilla, chimps and human mitochondrial genomic DNA.

Error	Chimpanzee	Gorilla	Human
0	PvuII 454	PvuII 454	-
	XbaI 643	XbaI 643	-
±1	EcoRI 3571	EcoRI 3570	-
	EcoRI 4724	EcoRI 4723	-
	HincII 1874	HincII 1873	-
	HincII 5143	HincII 5142	-
	HpaI 1874	HpaI 1873	-
	HpaI 5143	HpaI 5142	-
	PvuII 4416	PvuII 4415	-
	KpnI 2028	KpnI 2027	-
±2	-	AvaI 19	AvaI 17
	-	PstI 30	PstI 28
	-	SmaI 21	SmaI 19
	-	XbaI 18	XbaI 16
	-	XhoI 21	XhoI 19
	AvaI 21	AvaI 19	-
	PstI 32	PstI 30	-
	SmaI 23	SmaI 21	-
	XbaI 20	XbaI 18	-
	XhoI 23	XhoI 21	-

Table 4. Fraction of common sites between chimpanzee-gorilla, chimpanzee-human and gorilla-human clades.

Error	Chimpanzee-Gorilla	Chimpanzee-Human	Gorilla-Human
0	0.0163 (0.9837)	0	0
±1	0.068 (0.932)	0	0
±2	0.042 (0.958)	0	0.043 (0.957)

Percentage of sequence divergence is given in parenthesis.

As it is reported earlier that local point mutations continually generate considerable genetic variation that is capable of altering gene expression (Jonathon and Gregory, 2001) that we can consider as evolution, the error of ±1 between the sites digested by restriction enzymes in different organisms can be taken closer to the exact sites digested by the same restriction enzymes. Using this approach, I have tried to analyze the number of sites shared between chimpanzee, gorilla and human with ±1 error. Extending the same approach to ±2 error, number of sited shared are calculated and sequence divergence is calculated. The percentage of sequence divergence at increased levels of error is tabulated in Table 4.

Conclusion

We have analyzed the phylogeny between three members of the Hominidae family that is, human, gorilla and chimpanzee using parsimony, BIONJ and PHYML methods and calculated the sequence divergence between them using *in silico* restriction digestion. For our analysis, we have taken the genome, 12s and 16s rRNA and a set of 13 proteins coded by the mitochondrial DNA. Phylogeny based upon mitochondrial genome, 12s and 16srRNA supported the chimpanzee-human clade. Mitochondrial genome phylogeny was not found to predict the correct phylogeny by any of the three methods. However, some mitochondrial proteins were also found to be supporting the chimpanzee-gorilla clade. Moreover, not a single protein was found for which the phylogeny predicted by parsimony, BIONJ and PhyML methods were same. PhyML and BIONJ methods were found to predict correct phylogeny often. However, neither mitochondrial genome, rRNA nor any of the mitochondrial proteins was found for which the three methods predicted similar results. In an attempt to analyze the phylogenies more clearly, we calculated the sequence divergence between the genome of these three organisms. The results suggest the human mitochondrial genome to have diverged more from gorilla in comparison to chimpanzee. Even considering the evolutionary process to be influenced more by point mutation, we analyzed the digested sites of these three organisms and achieved the similar results. At ±2 error, human mitochondrial genome was found to have diverged 95.7% from gorilla genome compared to the 95.8% divergence of chimpanzee genome. No similar cut sites were found between human and chimpanzee at 0, ±1 and ±2 errors. This indicate gorilla to be having similarity with both human and chimpanzee at increased levels of error and hence to be the common ancestor. The results from this study might be helpful in further evolutionary studies of these species.

REFERENCES

Atsushi M, Felix R, Isao M, Hasegawa M, Horai S (2009). Molecular phylogeny and evolution of prosimians based on complete sequences of mitochondrial DNAs. Gene, 441: 53–66.

Brown WM, George M, Wilson AC (1979). Rapid evolution of animal mitochondrial dna (primates/restriction endonuclease cleavage maps/gel electrophoresis/dna melting) Proc. Natl. Acad. Sci., 76(4): 1967-1971.

Ferris SD, Wilson AC, Brown WM (1981). Evolutionary tree for apes and humans based on cleavage maps of mitochondrial DNA. Proc. Nat. Acad. Sci., 78: 2432-2436.

Galina G, Veeramachaneni V, Nei M, Makayowski W (2005), Eighty percent of proteins are different between humans and chimpanzees. Gene, 346: 215–219.

Galtier N, Gouy M, Gautier C (1996). SeaView and Phylo_win, two graphic tools for sequence alignment and molecular phylogeny. Comput. Appl. Biosci., 12: 543-548.

Gascuel O (1997). Molecular Biology and Evolution. 14: 685-695.

Guindon S and Gascuel O (2003). A simple, fast, and accurate algorithm to estimate large phylogenies by maximum likelihood. Syst. Biol., 52(5): 696-704.

Jeff Hecht (2003). Chimps are human, gene study implies. New Scientist.

Jonathon RS, Gregory AW (2001). Rapid Evolution of cis-Regulatory Sequences via Local Point Mutations. Mol. Biol. Evol., 18: 1764-1770.

Lockwood CA, Kimbel WH, Lynch JM (2004), Morphometrics and hominoid phylogeny: Support for a chimpanzee–human clade and differentiation among great ape subspecies. PNAS, 101(13): 4356-4360.

Maarek Y and I Shaul (1997). Webcutter: A System for dynamic and tailorable site mapping. Comput. Netw., ISDN Syst., 29: 1269-1279.

Thompson JD, Gibson TJ, Plewniak F, Jeanmougin F, Higgins DG (1997). The ClustalX windows interface: flexible strategies for multiple sequence alignment aided by quality analysis tools. Nucleic Acids Res., 25: 4876-4882.

Xinli S, Yinglong C, Shiping W, (2006). Point Mutations with Positive Selection Were a Major Force during the Evolution of a Receptor-Kinase Resistance Gene Family of Rice. National Key Laboratory of Crop Genetic Improvement, National Center of Plant Gene Research (Wuhan), Huazhong Agricultural University, Wuhan 430070, China. 140(3): 998-1008.

## 7

Nine linked SNPs found in goat *melanophilin* (*mlph*) gene

Xiang-Long Li*, Fu-Jun Feng, Rong-Yan Zhou, Lan-Hui Li, Hui-qin Zheng and Gui-ru Zheng

College of Animal Science and Technology, Hebei Agricultural University, Baoding 071001, China.

Melanophilin (*mlph*) gene was characterized as the candidate gene for dilute coat color in human, mice and dog, but little is known in goat. Nine linked SNPs were found in goat *mlph* gene by sequencing a total of 108 individuals from 5 goat populations. No homozygous mutation of the linked SNPs was detected, so we made a hypothesis that the mutation allele might be or might be linked with a recessive lethal gene. In addition, the nine mutational sites as well as a 205 bp coding region in the sequenced segment were compared with homologous sites or region from other species. Result showed that the overall mean distance (p-distance model) and Std. Err are 0.35 and 0.02 among goat, sheep and other eight mammals for the 205 bp coding region. Phylogenetic analysis showed that the codon used in primates may be more similar to that in bovid rather than in rodent animals.

Key words: Melanophilin, goat, coding SNPs, linkage.

INTRODUCTION

Melanophilin, together with myosin Va and Rab27A in mammalian, was characterized to form a tripartite protein complex, taking responsible for transfering melanosomes from the cell body to the tips of their dendrites by an actin-dependent movement (Matesic et al., 2001). Defects in the transfer process can cause pigment dilution of skin and hair in human diseases (Fukuda et al., 2002; Menasche et al., 2003; Kuroda et al., 2005) and the corresponding coat-color mutant mice (Provance et al., 2002; Fukuda and Kuroda, 2004). Among the three candidate gene (*mlph*, *Rab27a*, and *Myo5a*) for dilute coat color phenotype, mutation in *mlph* gene was responsible for color dilution without any future impair- ment in human Griscelli syndrome 3 (GS3) patients or leaden mice, thus it was considered as the most suitable candidate gene for color dilution (Matesic et al., 2001; Menasche et al., 2003; Philipp et al., 2005).

Genetic effect of dilute coat color associated with *mlph* gene mutation has been reported in mice (Menasche et al., 2003), cats (Ishida et al., 2006), and dogs (Philipp et al., 2005; Philipp et al., 2005; Drogemuller et al., 2007). No paper was published on *mlph* gene for ruminant. In order to extend knowledge of *mlph* gene and provide some useful information for goat breeding, sequence determination and characterization of goat *mlph* gene are being processed. In this paper, we reported 9 linked SNPs in goat *mlph* gene and their variation within and among different species.

MATERIALS AND METHODS

Goat population used and PCR amplification

A total of 108 goat individuals with detailed coat color records from 6 breeds in China were used. The sample size of each population and their distribution were shown in Figure 1 and Table 1.

Genomic DNA from goat blood sample was isolated according to the standard phenol: chloroform extraction method. According to the *mlph* gene sequence of sheep we have got previously (GeneBank accession number: EU218540), the primers we used for PCR amplification were designed as follows: Forward: 5' TGAAAGGGAGTTGAATTGCT 3', and reverse: 5' CACGGTCAAGCGCACTTAC 3'. The PCR product containing exon 8 was 382 bp, which had been submitted to GeneBank (EU195227). PCR amplification was carried out with a total reaction volume of 50 µL containing 150 ng DNA, 400 pmol/L each forward and reverse

---

*Corresponding author. E-mail: lixianglongcn@yahoo.com.

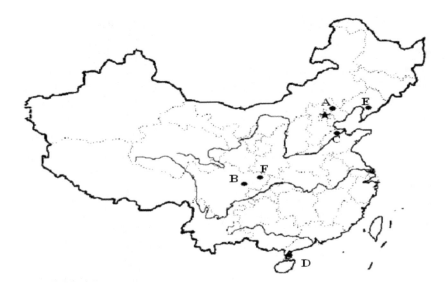

Figure 1. Geographic distribution of six goat populations in China (A: Chengde polled goat; B: Chengdu Ma goat; C: Jining gray goat; D: Leizhou black goat; E: Liaoning cashmere goat; F: Nanjiang brown goat Black strain).

Table 1. Genetype and gene frequency of the linked SNPs in six goat populations.

Goat population	Coat color	Population size	* Individual number of Genetype			Gene frequencies	
			AA(%)	AB(%)	BB(%)	A%	B%
Chengdu Ma goat	Brown (Dilute)	21	21 (100)	0 (0)	0 (0)	100	0
Jining gray goat	**Gray (Dilute)	25	20 (80)	5(20)	0 (0)	90	10
Leizhou black goat	Black	26	16 (61.54)	10 (38.46)	0 (0)	80.77	19.23
Liaoning cashmere goat	White	15	14 (93.33)	1 (6.67)	0 (0)	96.67	3.33
Nanjiang brown goat (Black strain)	Black	21	21 (100)	0 (0)	0 (0)	100	0
In total	-	108	92 (85.19)	16 (14.81)	0 (0)	92.59	7.41

*The percentages in brackets are frequencies comparing to their corresponding population size. ** Not strict, several individuals exhibited mottle or other colors.

primer, 5 μL 10×PCR reaction buffer (Mg^{2+} plus), 200 pmol/μL dNTPs, and 2 U Taq DNA polymerase from TIANGEN BIOTECH Co., Ltd (Beijing, China).

The PCR protocol was as follows: denaturizing at 94°C for 4 min, followed by 35 amplification cycles comprising denaturizing at 94°C for 30 s, annealing at 54°C, and extension at 72°C for 30 s, followed by an extended elongation at 72°C for 10 min. PCR products were detected on 2% agarose gel including 0.5 μg/mL of ethidium bromide, photographed under UV light, and sequenced by Shanghai Sangon Biological Engineering Technology and Service Co., Ltd. (Shanghai, China).

Coding region and SNPs identification

First, we retrieved cattle genome sequence containing *mlph* gene from Mapviewer (NW_001494842.1) and the corresponding mRNA sequence (NM_001081597.1). Then the exons were numbered by aligning genome and mRNA sequences using Spidey program

(http://www.ncbi.nlm.nih.gov/IEB/Research/Ostell/Spidey/). Coding region of goat sequence we determined was concluded by comparing with the catttle protein data (NP_001075066.1), and the SNPs among the 108 individuals were detected by aligning, together with examining the sequencing chromatograms carefully for heterozygote at the SNP sites.

Sequence analysis among species

For comparison and identification of the melanophilin polypeptide product, sequences of other species with a wide zootaxy range were obtained from GenBank (Table 2), together with sheep sequence (EU218540) mentioned above. The coding region identified was aligned with those available for other species, using ClustalW program as implemented in BioEdit (Version 7.0.5.2). Pairwise nucleotide and amino acid sequence divergences were calculated, and the phylogenetic tree among species was reconstructed using the MEGA version 3.1 (Kumar et al., 2004).

Table 2. *MLPH* mRNA and protein sequences of different species from GeneBank.

Species	mRNA Accession No.	Protein Accession No.
Monodelphis domestica	XM_001375200.1	XP_001375237.1
Mus musculus	AF384098.1	NP_443748.2
Rattus norvegicus	NM_001012135.1	AAH81894.1
Homo sapiens	NM_024101.5	AAH01653.1
Pan troglodytes	XM_516180.2	XP_516180.2
Canis familiaris	XM_843654.1	NP_001096689.2
Felis catus	DQ469742.1	NP_001073123.1
Gallus gallus	XM_421876.2	XP_421876.2
Bos taurus	BC133411.1	AAI33412.1
Danio rerio	NM_001079679.1	NP_001073147.1

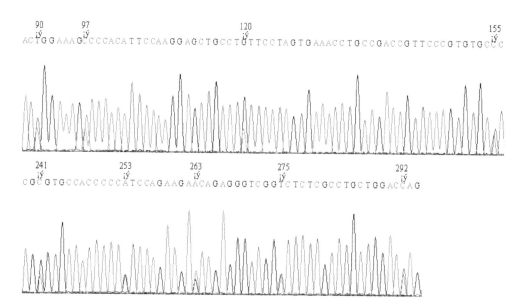

Figure 2. Nine SNPs in heterozygote sequencing chromatograms (Numbers labeled above are base positions of the SNPs in the 382 bp sequence).

RESULTS AND DISCUSSION

Coding region in the sequence determined

The 205 bp coding region was defined by aligning with cattle protein data (AAI33412.1), with the boundaries determined by GT-AG rule. When aligned with the corresponding cattle protein sequence using blastx program, the 205 bp coding region in goat showed high similarity with polypeptide from cattle exon 8 (Identities = 94%, E value = 5e-038), based on which we deduced it to be exon 8 of goat *mlph* gene with 71.22% of GC content.

Completely linked SNPs detected in goat *mlph* gene

Among the 108 determined sequences, nine SNPs in total were detected, 90 (A→T), 97 (C→A), 120 (A→G), 155 (C→T), 241(C→G), 253 (G→A), 263 (G→A), 275 (C→T), and 292 (C→T) respectively, corresponding to the goat *mlph* gene we sent to GeneBank (382bp, EU195227), of which the first four SNPs as stated above were in intron 7 and the rest five were in exon 8.

Among the five SNPs in exon 8, two were synonymous mutation at the position 263 and 275, while three were missense mutation at the position 241(Ala→Gly), 253(Arg→His), and 292(Pro→Leu). An interesting thing was found that only two haplotypes were found, ACACCGGCC represented as A and TAGTGAATT represented as B with frequency of 92.59% and 7.41% respectively (Table 1). Meanwhile, only two genotypes were detected in all individuals, AA and AB as shown in Figure 2, with the frequency of 85.19 and 14.81% respectively. No BB was found. So we deduced that the nine SNPs were completely linked and allele B might be linked with a recessive lethal gene. Given that, mutation in

Table 3. Base information in the five coding SNPs among ruminant available.

Species (haplotype)	Base information of the five SNPs found in goat mlph gene exon 8				
	241	253	263	275	292
Goat (wild type)	C	G	G	C	C
Goat (mutation)	G	A	A	T	T
Sheep	G	G	G	C	T
Cattle	G	G	G	C	C

Table 4. The disparity index test matrix generated from 12 species (1000 reps; seed = 86885).

	1	2	3	4	5	6	7	8	9	10	11	12
1 Goat		0.000	0.000	0.204	0.265	0.020	0.041	0.449	0.306	0.306	0.633	1.388
2 Sheep	1.000		0.000	0.143	0.347	0.082	0.061	0.408	0.224	0.184	0.571	1.224
3 Cattle	1.000	1.000		0.204	0.367	0.000	0.000	0.265	0.245	0.204	0.408	1.102
4 Cat	0.150	0.209	0.126		0.776	0.000	0.000	0.143	0.327	0.000	0.265	0.571
5 Dog	0.141	0.106	0.086	0.008		0.286	0.367	1.224	0.245	0.571	1.490	1.551
6 Opossum	0.417	0.332	1.000	1.000	0.191		0.000	0.388	0.082	0.286	0.000	0.449
7 House mouse	0.407	0.350	1.000	1.000	0.075	1.000		0.143	0.000	0.000	0.102	0.551
8 Norway rat	0.054	0.071	0.121	0.244	0.002	0.150	0.040		0.429	0.000	0.306	0.694
9 Human	0.149	0.194	0.159	0.091	0.166	0.345	1.000	0.054		0.041	0.796	0.918
10 Chimpanzee	0.144	0.244	0.239	1.000	0.040	0.219	1.000	1.000	0.248		0.714	0.837
11 Chicken	0.080	0.091	0.149	0.213	0.003	1.000	0.345	0.174	0.040	0.044		0.000
12 Zebrafish	0.005	0.007	0.007	0.077	0.006	0.093	0.090	0.057	0.030	0.029	1.000	

*The upper triangle are pairwise disparity index, and the lower triangle Probability computed (must be <0.05 for hypothesis rejection at 5% level [gray background]).

mlph gene would cause future impairment at least in goat, and it would be a supplementary to previous study on the relationship between coat color and viability in mammalian (Matesic et al., 2001; Menasche et al., 2003; Philipp et al., 2005). Certainly, the hypothesis of recessive lethal effect of BB needs to be investigated in future.

It was also found that allele B was not found in Chengdu Ma goat and Nanjiang brown goat (Black strain). Nanjiang brown goat was bred with a pedigree of Chengdu Ma goat. So the absence of allele B might be related with the special dilute coat color (tan) of Chengdu Ma goat.

Comparing of the coding region among species

Base information in the five coding SNPs among ruminant were shown in Table 3. Among the five sites, sheep and cattle shared the same base with goat mutant haplotype (at position 241 and 292) whose homozygote was not determined). While at the three sites (position 253, 263 and 275) sheep and cattle shared the same base with goat wild type haplotype. Combined with the synonymous or missense mutation data determined above, base at position 275 may be the most possible site for the hypothesis of the recessive lethal allele.

Generally speaking, high variance of the mlph gene exits among species. Comparing with cattle whole protein sequence, the identities were as follows: cat, 64.1%; dog, 64.0%; human, 59.6%; Norway rat, 53.5%; chimpanzee, 55.0%; house mouse, 54.0%; opossum, 28.2%; chicken, 39.4% and zebra fish, 26.7%. Similarity is much lower than other gene such as kappa-casein gene (Mukesh et al., 2006). For the 205 bp coding region determined, variability was found very high: the overall mean distance (p-distance model) and Std. Err are 0.35 and 0.02 among goat, sheep and the homologous region of eight mammals shown in Table 2. When comparing the sequences among a broader range of taxa (mammal, bird, and fish) the overall mean distance is 0.43 (With Std. Err 0.02). When the values above were recalculated using the deduced protein data, the overall mean distance became much higher: 0.57 (With Std. Err 0.03) among 10 mammals and 0.67 (With Std. Err 0.02) among all the 12 species.

The disparity index test matrix (Table 4) was computed using the UPGMA method (bootstrap value with 1000) based on p-distance of the homologous deduced protein data among the 11 species using Mega 3.1 software with gap/missing data complete deletion parameter. Phylogenetic analysis based on nucleotide sequence of the 12 species revealed grouping of goat close to sheep in one

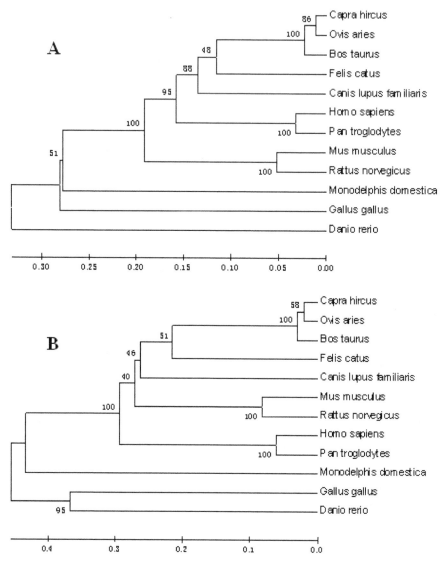

Figure 3. The UPGMA phylogenetic tree based on p-distance of *MLPH* gene (A) exon 8 coding region, and (B) deduced protein sequence data among species.

cluster with cattle forming a separate cluster close to them. However, the primates and rodent formed separate lineages, with rodent at the outer position, and opossum being placed most distantly excluding the non-mammals in the phylogenetic tree (Figure 3 (A)). Based on translated amino acid sequence also, goat, sheep and cattle are grouped close to each other, while primates were placed more distantly than rodent (Figure 3 (B)). The difference between the two phylogenetic tree based on mRNA and protein sequence respectively revealed that the codon used in primates may be nearer with that in bovid animals than in rodent animals.

ACKNOWLEDGEMENT

This work was funded by Natural Science Foundation of Hebei (C2010000775) and development foundation of scientific research of Agricultural University of Hebei.

REFERENCES

Drogemuller CU, Philipp B, Haase AR, Gunzel-Apel TL (2007). "A Noncoding Melanophilin Gene (MLPH) SNP at the Splice Donor of Exon 1 Represents a Candidate Causal Mutation for Coat Color Dilution in Dogs." J. Hered, 98(5): 468-473.

Fukuda M, Kuroda TS (2004). "Missense mutations in the globular tail of myosin-Va in dilute mice partially impair binding of Slac2-a/melanophilin." J. Cell Sci., 117(Pt 4): 583-591.

Fukuda M, Kuroda TS, Mikoshiba K (2002). "Slac2-a/melanophilin, the missing link between Rab27 and myosin Va: implications of a tripartite protein complex for melanosome transport." J. Biol. Chem., 277(14): 12432-12436.

Ishida Y, David E, Eizirik AA, Schaffer BA, Neelam ME, Roelke SS, Hannah S, O'Brien M. Menotti-Raymond (2006). "A homozygous single-base deletion in MLPH causes the dilute coat color phenotype in the domestic cat." Genomics, 88(6): 698-705.

Kumar S, Tamura K, Nei M (2004). "MEGA3: Integrated software for Molecular Evolutionary Genetics Analysis and sequence alignment." Brief Bioinform, 5(2): 150-163.

Kuroda TS, Itoh T, Fukuda M (2005). "Functional analysis of slac2-a/melanophilin as a linker protein between Rab27A and myosin Va in melanosome transport." Methods Enzymol., 403: 419-431.

Matesic LE, Yip R, Reuss AE, Swing DA, O'Sullivan TN, Fletcher CF, Copeland NG, Jenkins NA (2001). "Mutations in Mlph, encoding a member of the Rab effector family, cause the melanosome transport defects observed in leaden mice." Proc. Natl. Acad. Sci. USA, 98(18): 10238-10243.

Menasche G, Ho CH, Sanal O, Feldmann J, Tezcan I, Ersoy F, Houdusse A, Fischer A, de Saint Basile G (2003). "Griscelli syndrome restricted to hypopigmentation results from a melanophilin defect (GS3) or a MYO5A F-exon deletion (GS1)." J. Clin. Invest.. 112(3): 450-456.

Mukesh M, Mishra BP, Kataria RS, Sobti RC, Ahlawat SP (2006). "Sequence analysis of UTR and coding region of kappa-casein gene of Indian riverine buffalo (Bubalus bubalis)." DNA Seq., 17(2): 94-98.

Philipp U, Hamann H, Mecklenburg L, Nishino S, Mignot E, Gunzel-Apel AR, Schmutz SM, Leeb T (2005). "Polymorphisms within the canine MLPH gene are associated with dilute coat color in dogs." BMC Genet., 6: 34.

Philipp U, Quignon P, Scott A, Andre C, Breen M, Leeb T (2005). "Chromosomal assignment of the canine melanophilin gene (MLPH): a candidate gene for coat color dilution in Pinschers." J. Hered, 96(7): 774-776.

Provance DW, James TL, Mercer JA (2002). "Melanophilin, the product of the leaden locus, is required for targeting of myosin-Va to melanosomes."Traffic, 3(2): 124-132.

## 8

UniDPlot: A software to detect weak similarities between two DNA sequences

Marc Girondot[1,2]* and Jean-Yves Sire[3]

[1]Laboratoire d'Écologie, Systématique et Évolution, UMR 8079 Centre National de la Recherche Scientifique, Université Paris Sud et ENGREF, 91405 Orsay cedex 05, France.
[2]Département de Systématique et Evolution, Muséum National d'Histoire Naturelle de Paris, 25 rue Cuvier, 75005 Paris, France.
[3]Université Pierre and Marie Curie-Paris 6, UMR 7138 "Systématique, Adaptation, Evolution", 7 quai St-Bernard, 75005 Paris, France.

Search for DNA sequence similarity is a crucial step in many evolutionary analyses and several bioinformatic tools are available to fulfill this task. Basic Local Alignment Search Tool (BLAST) is the most commonly and highly efficient algorithm used. However, it often fails in identifying sequences showing very weak similarity. An alternative method is to use Dot Plot, but such a graphical method is not suitable for the analysis of large sequences (e.g. hundreds of kilobases) as this is now more often required in the context of genome sequencing programs. As an alternative to the classical Dot Plot method, we designed UniDPlot, which permits to search for weak similarity either between two large sequences (e.g., genome regions, ...) or between one large sequence and a short one (e.g., exons, ...). UniDPlot methodology contracts the output of the Dot Plot similarity matrix along the length of the largest sequence, while defining statistical limits of significance using a bootstrap procedure. To illustrate the efficiency of this method, we used UniDPlot to search for the fate of the gene that encodes the major enamel protein, amelogenin, in chicken. Although we showed that amelogenin was invalidated through a pseudogeneization process, we recovered the entire sequence in the chicken genome. Using UniDPlot, we have identified a pseudogene, which was not detected by classical methods. UniDPlot can be used to search for missing genes, or motifs of various sizes in different genomic contexts.

Key words: DNA sequence similarity, UniDimensional plot (UniDPlot) software, genomes.

INTRODUCTION

Search for similar sequences among genomes or within a target genome is one of the more classical tasks in Bioinformatics. Until now, many tools were developed, and one of the most commonly used algorithms is Basic Local Alignment Search Tool (BLAST) (Altschul et al., 1990). Although BLAST supports many different options, it could fail to detect similarity when two evolutionary distant sequences are used (Miller, 2001). Position-Specific Iterated BLAST (PSI-BLAST) is an alternative to search for weak similarity using amino acid sequences

(Altschul et al., 1997). PSI-BLAST is designed to detect relationships between the query and members of the database, when they are not detectable by standard BLAST searches. The added sensitivity of this program compared to regular BLAST is provided by the use of a profile that is automatically constructed from a multiple alignment of the highest scoring hits in the initial BLAST search. However, PSI-BLAST cannot be run with nucleotide sequences, as for instance in searching pseudogenes or regulatory sequences. Another alternative to regular BLAST is provided by Dot Plot. Originally called diagram (Gibbs and Mcintyre1, 1970), Dot Plot regroups several methods that visually compare two sequences and look for regions of close similarity. A

*Corresponding author. E-mail: marc.girondot@u-psud.fr.

dot plot is a visual representation of the similarities between two sequences. Each axis of a rectangular array represents one of the two sequences to be compared. Whenever one base in one sequence is identical in the other sequence, a dot is drawn at the corresponding position of the array. Thus, when two sequences share similarity over their entire length a diagonal line will extend from one corner of the dot plot to the diagonally opposite corner. If two sequences only share patches of similarity this will be revealed by diagonal stretches.

Maizel and Lenk (1981) popularized Dot Plot and suggested the use of a filter to reduce the noise resulting from matches that occur by chance. As there are combinations of only four different nucleotides, the probability is high that a nucleotide matches another nucleotide in a region of the sequences with no homology. Therefore, the result does not reflect a similarity between the two sequences but the only limited number of bases permitted in DNA sequences. A large variety of filters can be used (Sonnhammer and Durbin, 1995). Maizel and Lenk (Maizel and Lenk, 1981) suggested to place a dot only when there is a significant proportion of successive matching bases. Recent advances in Dot Plot methodology involved parallelization (Mueller et al., 2006) but the visualization of the results is still a bottleneck for using the method. This is particularly well illustrated when a short sequence is to be compared to a large one as, for instance, a genomic fragment. In this case, the result of the Dot Plot will resume into a narrow black line for identical scales in both axes.

Here, we present a new method that we have called UniDimensional Plot (UniDPlot). It is an adaptation of the original Dot Plot method. UniDPlot was designed to compare a short sequence to a large one, while testing the significance of the similarity obtained. In order to illustrate the usefulness of this new method, we used UniDPlot to detect a missing gene in the annotated chicken (*Gallus gallus*) genome (build 2.1, November 30, 2006).

IMPLEMENTATION

DotPlot projection

The classical dot plot algorithm uses a pairwise comparison between two sequences, and the results are presented as a dot-matrix. For a particular position in both sequences, the same base present is shown as a dot and two different bases are shown as a blank. A sliding window is often used to filter the output for better visualisation (Maizel and Lenk, 1981). For UniDPlot method, a projection of the maximum score for each position along the largest sequence against all possible positions of the shortest sequence is plotted. This creates a plot that permits to visualize regions with various values of similarity between the two sequences compared.

Substitution model

Evolutionary divergent sequences could have a known pattern of nucleotide divergence. In the classical Dot Plot algorithm, only 0 - 1

outputs are possible (Gibbs and Mcintyre1, 1970) and gray levels have been further added (Wimmer, 2007). Here, the output can use a matrix in which all base pairs have different weights. Such a matrix can be directly calculated by the software from two aligned sequences. The models implemented are: identical, transition and transversion, and complete matrix obtained by a simple comparison of the two aligned sequences.

Test of significance

The basics of significant test for dot-plot have been given by Gibbs and Mcintyre1 (Gibbs and Mcintyre1, 1970). However, this procedure is applicable only for identical model of substitution without filter. Here, the expected number of maximum matches between the two sequences compared is calculated using a resampling procedure. Briefly, the same number of comparisons are done with two random sequences obtained using the observed frequencies of ATGC for each sequences applying the same substitution model. This permits to define a limit above which such a similarity has never been reached in the same number of trials. During this resampling, the mean and standard deviation of proportion of maximum identities between two sequences are also calculated. This procedure is used rather than an analytical one, due to the complexity of the model of maximum identities proportion based on a sliding window procedure.

Biological background for the test

The ability to form teeth was lost in an ancestor of all modern birds, approximately 80 - 100 million years ago. However, experiments in chicken have revealed that the oral epithelium can respond to inductive signals from mouse mesenchyme, leading to reactivation of the odontogenic pathway (Mitsiadis et al., 2003). Recently, tooth germs similar to crocodile rudimentary teeth were found in a chicken mutant (Harris et al., 2006). These "chicken teeth" did not develop further, but the question remains whether true teeth would have been obtained if the experiments were performed longer. An alternative approach to check whether or not obtaining true hens' teeth in the next future was not utopia was to look for the fate of the dental protein genes, 100 million years after tooth loss. Previous molecular attempts to localise amelogenin gene, the major protein in enamel formation, in chicken DNA were unsuccessful (Girondot and Sire, 1998). Blast searching (BLASTN) for these genes using either full length amniotic sequences or various e-primers defined from conserved regions proved to be unfruitful, even when using low search sensitivity (distant homology).

As an alternative we used gene synteny between mammals and birds to try to locate amelogenin gene in the chicken genome.

In placental mammals, AMEL is located close to the rhoGTPase activating protein 6 gene (ARHGAP6). For instance, in humans AMELX is located at position Xp22.3, between ARHGAP6 and HCCS (holocytochrome C synthetase) gene. MID1 (midline 1) and MSL3L1 (male-specific lethal 3-like 1) mark out this region. AMELX codes in antisense within the 200 kb large intron 1 of ARHGAP6, and its 5' UTR is located at approximately 40 kb far from the 5' region of ARHGAP6 exon 2. In the opossum, AMEL is similarly located, but 58 kb far from ARHGAP6 exon 2.

In chicken, ARHGAP6 (LOC418642), MID1 and MSL3L1 (LOC418641) are found close, one to another on chromosome 1, but compared to their location in humans, chicken MID1 and MSL3L1 are inverted, while HCCS is located on chicken chromosome 8 (LOC424482). In the target region, i.e. between ARHGAP6 and MID1, the Genbank prediction program indicates neither the presence of a putative candidate gene locus nor of a pseudogene.

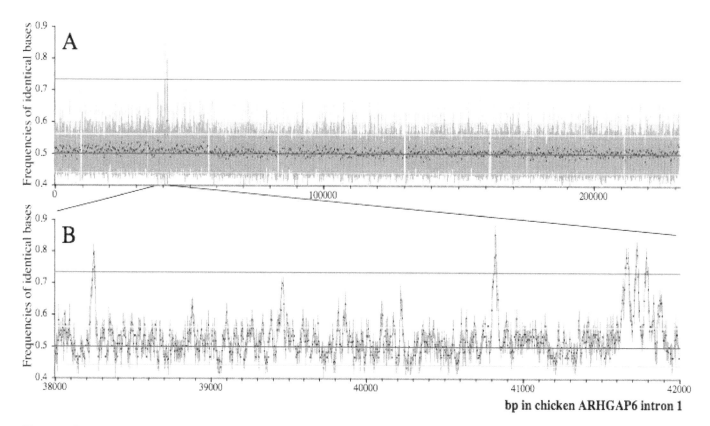

Figure 1. Similarity of crododilian amelogenin cDNA against intron 1 of chicken ARHGAP6 (A) and enlargement of the region with highest similarities (B). The blue line indicates the maximum observed similarity in random resamplings. The green lines represent twice the standard deviation of similarity around the mean value in red. The vertical grey lines indicate the maximum and minimum observed similarity at each corresponding position and each black dot is the similarity average at each position. One pixel summarized 238 bp in (A) and 4 bp in (B). The position 1 for the intron 1 of chicken ARHGAP6 is its first base.

We searched for sequence similarity in the target region with UniDPlot software, using crocodilian AMEL sequence.

RESULTS AND DISCUSSION

The exons of the entire coding sequence of crocodilian AMEL were separated with stretches of 30 X, which is the size of the window that will be used. This permits to ensure that the search will not be confused by artefactual adjacent bases that are normally separated by introns.

When running on entire intron 1 of chicken ARHGAP6 (231,857 bp), UniDPlot revealed several successive hits located approximately 40,000 pb far from ARHGAP6 exon 2 (Figure 1). The similarity was higher than observed for random resamplings of sequences (blue line). When this region was enlarged, three significant peaks were observed (that is above the blue line) and an additional peak was observed in this region, just below the blue line. Such an organisation is compatible with the known structure of the crocodilian AMEL gene that is four coding exons.

In order to confirm this organization, similarity search was performed using crocodilian AMEL exons 2, 3, 5 and

6, separately. Indeed, the first exon is non-coding, exon 4 does not exist in crocodilian AMEL and exon 7 could not be used (3 coding bases only).

The results indicate clearly that the organization of these exons in the chicken genome is similar to the expected one if they belong to AMEL (Figure 2). These sequences were aligned with the crocodilian AMEL (Figure 3). The chicken AMEL gene is a pseudogene, due to an insertion of four bases in the sequence of the first translated exon 2 (signal peptide).

Conclusions

The method proposed here permits to find significant similarity that has been overlooked by automatic procedure used to annotate the *Gallus* genome. The reason is probably due to both the divergence between sequences but also the fact that the bird gene is now a pseudogene and cannot be automatically translated. More generally, this software can be used to search for missing genes in distant organisms and in comparing highly derived sequences. The methodology presented here could have a large range of use, to find missing or

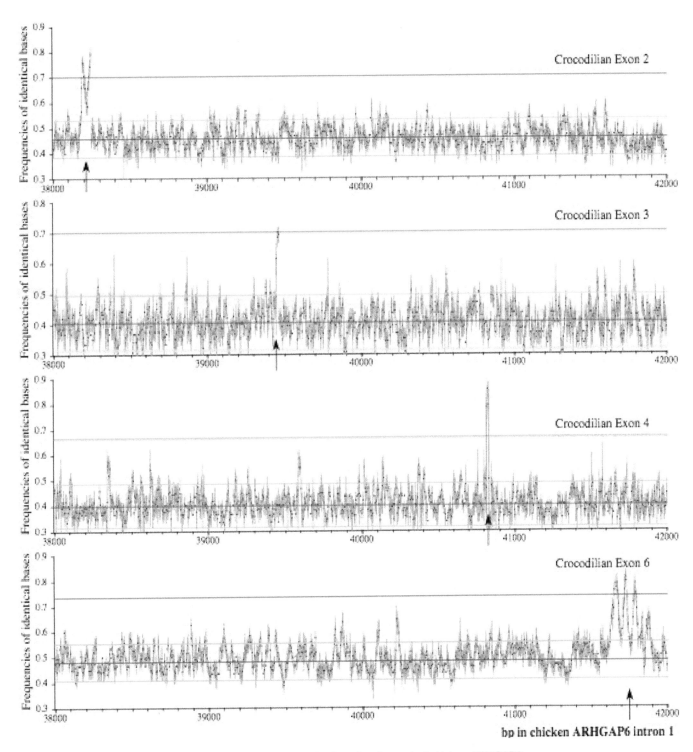

Figure 2. Similarity of the exons of crododilian amelogenin cDNA against intron 1 of chicken ARHGAP6.

duplicated exons or tracks of old insertion of retrovirus for example (Jamain et al., 2002).

UniDPlot can also be used as a combination with various other tools available to visualize alignments (Edwards et al., 2003; Jareborg and Durbin, 2000; Mayor et al., 2000). It proves to be easy to use and permits to get answer in a few minutes, even when using gigabases piece of DNA. At the present stage, no filter for low complexity regions is available and such a region must be removed prior to the analysis to search for similarities or, else, false positive hits could be infrequent. An alternative is to check *a posteriori* for the region in which

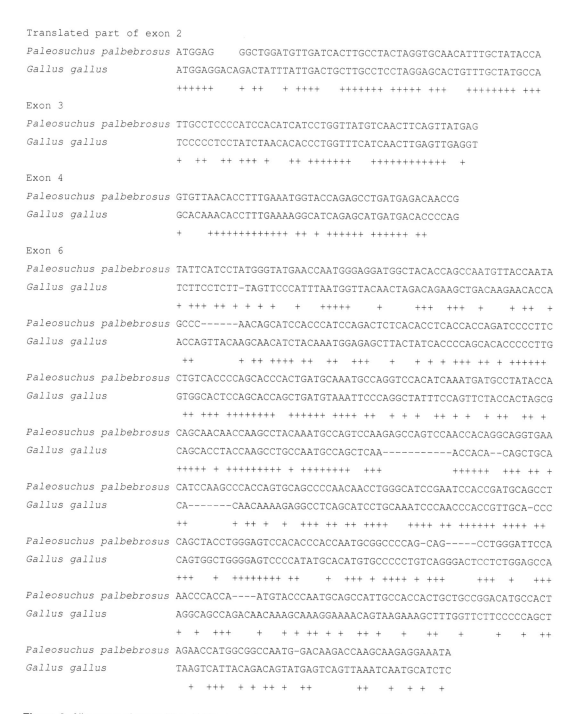

```
Translated part of exon 2

Paleosuchus palbebrosus  ATGGAG    GGCTGGATGTTGATCACTTGCCTACTAGGTGCAACATTTGCTATACCA
Gallus gallus            ATGGAGGACAGACTATTTATTGACTGCTTGCCTCCTAGGAGCACTGTTTGCTATGCCA
                         ++++++   + ++  + ++++  +++++++ +++++ +++  ++++++++ +++
Exon 3

Paleosuchus palbebrosus  TTGCCTCCCCATCCACATCATCCTGGTTATGTCAACTTCAGTTATGAG
Gallus gallus            TCCCCCTCCTATCTAACACACCCTGGTTTCATCAACTTGAGTTGAGGT
                         +  ++  ++ +++ +   ++ +++++++   +++++++++++++  +
Exon 4

Paleosuchus palbebrosus  GTGTTAACACCTTTGAAATGGTACCAGAGCCTGATGAGACAACCG
Gallus gallus            GCACAAACACCTTTGAAAAGGCATCAGAGCATGATGACACCCCAG
                         +  ++++++++++++++ ++ + ++++++ ++++++ ++
Exon 6

Paleosuchus palbebrosus  TATTCATCCTATGGGTATGAACCAATGGGAGGATGGCTACACCAGCCAATGTTACCAATA
Gallus gallus            TCTTCCTCTT-TAGTTCCCATTTAATGGTTACAACTAGACAGAAGCTGACAAGAACACCA
                         + +++ ++ + + + +  +  +++++   +  +++ +++ +  + ++ +

Paleosuchus palbebrosus  GCCC------AACAGCATCCACCCATCCAGACTCTCACACCTCACCACCAGATCCCCTTC
Gallus gallus            ACCAGTTACAAGCAACATCTACAAATGGAGAGCTTACTATCACCCCAGCACACCCCCTTG
                         ++        + ++ ++++ ++  ++  +++   +  + + +++ ++ + ++++++

Paleosuchus palbebrosus  CTGTCACCCCAGCACCCACTGATGCAAATGCCAGGTCCACATCAAATGATGCCTATACCA
Gallus gallus            GTGGCACTCCAGCACCAGCTGATGTAAATTCCCAGGCTATTTCCAGTTCTACCACTAGCG
                         ++ +++ ++++++++ ++++++ ++++ ++ + + + ++ + + + ++  ++ +

Paleosuchus palbebrosus  CAGCAACAACCAAGCCTACAAATGCCAGTCCAAGAGCCAGTCCAACCACAGGCAGGTGAA
Gallus gallus            CAGCACCTACCAAGCCTGCCAATGCCAGCTCAA-----------ACCACA--CAGCTGCA
                         +++++ + +++++++++ + ++++++++  +++         ++++++  +++ ++ +

Paleosuchus palbebrosus  CATCCAAGCCCACCAGTGCAGCCCCAACAACCTGGGCATCCGAATCCACCGATGCAGCCT
Gallus gallus            CA-------CAACAAAGAGGCCTCAGCATCCTGCAAATCCCAACCCACCGTTGCA-CCC
                         ++       + ++ + +  +++ ++ ++ ++++   ++++ ++ ++++++ ++++ ++

Paleosuchus palbebrosus  CAGCTACCTGGGAGTCCACACCCACCAATGCGGCCCCAG-CAG-----CCTGGGATTCCA
Gallus gallus            CAGTGGCTGGGGAGTCCCCATATGCACATGTGCCCCCTGTCAGGGACTCCTCTGGAGCCA
                         +++  +  ++++++++ ++  + +++ + ++++ + +++    +++  +  +++

Paleosuchus palbebrosus  AACCCACCA----ATGTACCCAATGCAGCCATTGCCACCACTGCTGCCGGACATGCCACT
Gallus gallus            AGGCAGCCAGACAACAAAGCAAAGGAAAACAGTAAGAAAGCTTTGGTTCTTCCCCCAGCT
                         +  +  +++    +  + + ++ +  ++ +     +  ++       +     +  ++

Paleosuchus palbebrosus  AGAACCATGGCGGCCAATG-GACAAGACCAAGCAAGAGGAAATA
Gallus gallus            TAAGTCATTACAGACAGTATGAGTCAGTTAAATCAATGCATCTC
                         +  +++ + + ++ +  ++        ++  + + + +
```

Figure 3. Alignment of crocodilian AMEL and orthologous pseugogene AMEL in chicken.

similarities have been detected.

The software is available at the bioinformatics.org web site: http://www.bioinformatics.org/unidplot/wiki/

REFERENCES

Altschul SF, Gish W, Miller W, Myers EW, Lipman. DJ (1990) Basic local alignment search tool. J. Mol. Biol. 215: 403-410.

Altschul SF, Madden TL, Schäffer AA, Zhang J, Zhang Z, Miller W, Lipman DJ (1997) Gapped BLAST and PSI-BLAST: a new generation of protein database search programs. Nucleic Acids Res. 25: 3389-3402.

Edwards YJK, Carver TJ, Vavouri T, Frith M, Bishop MJ, Elgar G (2003) Theatre: a software tool for detailed comparative analysis and visualization of genomic sequence. Nucleic Acids Res. 31: 3510-3517.

Gibbs AJ, Mcintyre1 GA (1970) The Diagram, a method for comparing sequences. Its use with amino acid and nucleotide sequences. Eur. J. Biochem. 16: 1-10.

Girondot M, Sire J-Y (1998) Evolution of the amelogenin gene in toothed and tooth-less vertebrates. Eur. J. Oral Sci. 106 (1): 501-508.

Harris MP, Hasso SM, Ferguson MWJ, Fallon JF (2006). The

development of archosaurian first-generation teeth in a chicken mutant. Current Biology, 16: 371-377.

Jamain S, Girondot M, Leroy P, Clergue M, Quach H, Fellous M, Bourgeron T (2002). Transduction of the human gene AHCP by endogenous retrovirus during primate evolution. Genomics 78: 38-45.

Jareborg N, Durbin R (2000). Alfresco- A workbench for comparative genomic sequence analysis. Genome Res., 10: 1148-1157.

Maizel JV, Lenk RP (1981). Enhanced graphic matrix analysis of nucleic acid and protein sequences. Proc. Natl. Acad. Sci. U. S. A. 78: 7665-7669.

Mayor C, Brudno M, Schwartz JR, Poliakov A, Rubin EM, Frazer KA, Pachter LS, Dubchak I (2000). VISTA : visualizing global DNA sequence alignments of arbitrary length. Bioinformatics, 16: 1046-1047.

Miller W (2001). Comparison of genomic DNA sequences: solved and unsolved problems. Bioinformatics, 17: 391-397.

Mitsiadis TA, Chéraud Y, Sharpe P, Fontaine-Pérus J (2003). Development of teeth in chick embryos after mouse neural crest transplantations. Proc. Natl. Acad. Sci. U. S. A. 100: 6541-6545.

Mueller C, Dalkilic M, Lumsdaine A (2006). High-performance direct pairwise comparison of large genomic sequences IEEE Trans. Parallel Distrib. Syst., 17: 764-772.

Sonnhammer ELL, Durbin R (1995). A dot-matrix program with dynamic threshold control suited for genomic DNA and protein sequence analysis. Gene, 167: 1-10.

## 9

Evaluation of cassava mash dewatering methods

Oladele Peter Kolawole[1,2]*, Leo Ayodeji Sunday Agbetoye[1] and Agboola Simeon Ogunlowo[1]

[1]Federal university of Technology Akure, Nigeria.
[2]International Institute of Tropical Agriculture, Ibadan, Nigeria.

Using different cassava maturity age of 9, 12 and 15 months, evaluation study was carried out on cassava mash dewatering methods. Dewatering tanks with square and cylindrical shapes were made with steel for the experiment. Pressure devices from screw bolts, hydraulic jack press and rope / stick methods were used to squeezed cassava juice from the mash in the tanks. TMS 4(2) 1425 variety of cassava was used. Cylindrical tank containing a 12 months old sample with hydraulic jack gave mash cake with moisture content of the sample at 44% wet basis in the shortest time.

Key words: Dewatering, screw press, hydraulic press, cassava mash.

INTRODUCTION

Cassava is a major source of carbohydrates in human and animal diet; other areas of uses of cassava are being implored. The crop tolerates many cultivation processes, this make its cultivation more popular. The tubers of cassava cannot be stored longer after harvest before decaying, so processing follows immediately after harvesting; this involves peeling, grating, dewatering, cake milling and sieving. The mash can be transformed into two principal products, flour and gari after dewatering. Proper dewatering method to obtain the best product is a requirement, added to this factor is the high cost of fuel needed for drying flour or frying of garri. The engineering improvements required for cassava processing into food depends on the development that can be given to the traditional equipment technology, with the aim of developing low cost with low energy demanding equipment. Traditional processing procedures aimed at reducing cyanide, improving storability, providing convenience and palatability. These starts with dewatering methods adopted. Cassava contains about 70% moisture content, which must be reduced to acceptable level; this process may include fermentation, with the dewatering taking place-using available and suitable methods. Some with stones placed on the sack (Figure 1) or with the use of jacked-wood platforms (Figure 2) to press off the excess liquid from the pulp (Igbeka et al., 1982). The objective of this paper is to evaluate some commonly use-dewatering systems,

showing their merit and demerit under different cassava maturity in order to predict areas requiring engineering improvement. The results obtained can lead to understanding and need for better-developed process handling equipment. This is vital as cassava food is becoming commercialized leading to higher demands for its flour.

Literature review

Dewatering in cassava processing involves applying pressure on the grated pulp to reduce its moisture content. In the dewatering of cassava mash, the particles are constrained while the liquid is free. The pressure applied, varied depth, time, moisture content, volume of material and the particles of material, these are some of the parameters identified by Kolawole et al. (2007). The material moisture content, the mass and the volume were easier to identify.

Diop (1998) reported that the Amerindians developed an ingenious press shaped like a long thin basket-weave tube called ´tipiti´. The operation of the tipiti-involved fillings it with cassava mash, hung on a branch of a tree and stretched from the bottom; the reduced volume at the base reduces the mash volume, water is then squeezed out of the mash. Some other methods involves placing of heavy stone on top of the mash and this was used by Ajibola (1987) when he places heavy stone on cylindrical tank filled with cassava mash to effect dewatering mechanically.

Operation of dewatering is mainly carried out manually

*Corresponding author. E-mail: P.KOLAWOLE@cgiar.org.

Twisting sack to effect
dewatering

Heavy stone
on top of mash
sack

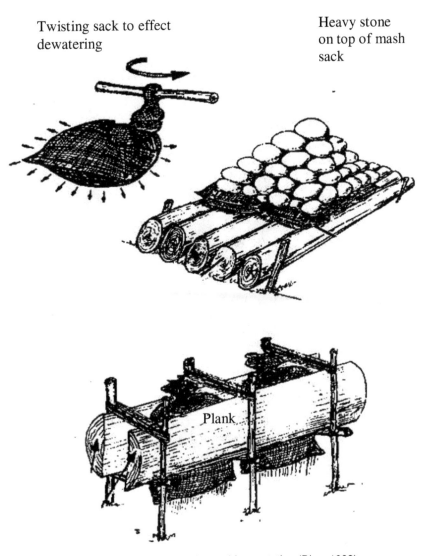

Figure 1. Traditional methods of pressing and fermentation (Diop, 1998).

under rural conditions. So many methods are in use for cassava mash dewatering as; boulders or logs method, use of sticks, parallel board method, tree stumps method, chain or string methods and screw jack (Kolawole and Agbetoye, 2007). Pressing cassava mash have been industrialized with hydraulic presses providing pressures of up to 25 kg/cm^2 (Igbeka et al., 1982) the pressing time can be as short as 15 min with the hydraulic press or as long as 4 days or more when stones are relied upon the only one available to the the local processors in some locality. The main reason for dewatering in cassava mash is same in all crops processing to food; it is a pre-drying alternative (Sinha et al., 2000). Study of centrifugation and direct pressure as means of dewatering was done for cassava starch production by Klanarong et al. (1999). Straub and Bruhn (1978) used a comparison study of centrifugation and direct pressure as dewatering means, while studying the dewatering characteristics of alfalfa

protein concentrate. The result indicated that comparable dewatering could be obtained. Increased acceleration or increased holding time did not give large decreases in final moisture content of the sample.

The improved and available process of cassava mash dewatering could bring about faster rate. They are in the form of a circular press cage holding the fresh pulp or square frame exerting pressure on the sacks. Many types' works by moving a heavy circular or square block, which is lowered or raised by means of, threaded shaft. Some design of press uses hydraulic jack used for cars or lorries to apply pressure to the mash (Igbeka et al., 1982). The frame may consists of two vertical metal posts as shown in Figure 2, all require some amount of human effort to operate them, this in turn compressed the mash to cake. Compression of mash into cakes results in the increasing resistance of cakes. Cassava mash cake is compressible and their specific resistance α change with

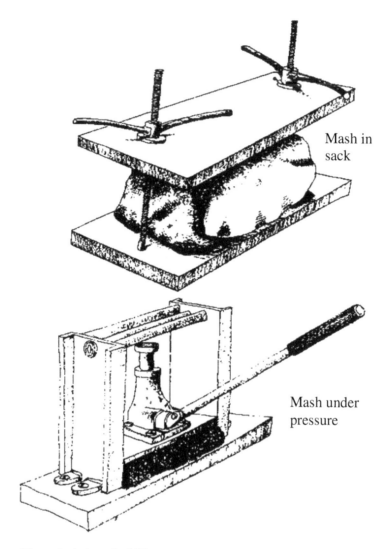

Figure 2. Jack method (Diop, 1998).

the pressure drop across the cake Δp_c as reported by Kolawole (2005).

With constant pressure operations the function:

$$\alpha = f(\Delta p) \tag{1}$$

may be employed directly. Using the equation

$$\Delta p = \Delta p_c + \Delta p_m \tag{2}$$

Where $\Delta P m$ = Pressure drop across the medium; $\Delta P c$ = Pressure drop across the cake; ΔP= Pressure drop. With μ as the viscosity, R as the sack resistance, Q as the flow rate of the juice, A as the pressure operating area, the average mash cake resistance α_{av} and the mash cake **c** concentration playing a role. Then the pressure across the filter medium becomes:

$$\Delta p_m = \frac{\mu R Q}{A} \tag{3}$$

The pressure on cassava mash cake, becomes

$$\Delta p_c = \alpha_{av} \frac{\mu c V Q}{A^2} \tag{4}$$

MATERIALS AND METHODS

Materials

Experimental equipment was designed to obtain the applied pressure, such away that it can be used with the rest of the selected devices. The conception was based on ideas and discussions made during brain storming section with IITA farm engineering staff. An hydraulic system of confining liquid in a tube was the choice in sensing the pressure differences using Pascal's

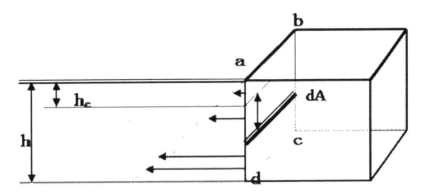

Figure 3. Pressure on the experimental box walls.

Principle, which states that pressure transmitted is undiminished in an enclosed static fluid:

$$P_2 = P_1 + \rho gh \tag{5}$$

Where ρgh is Static fluid pressure P = F/A expressed in N/m² as the force acting normally on a unit area. Equal pressure throughout the area of confinement is characteristics of any pressurised fluid were used as means of obtaining the value of applied pressure, (Sperry and Vickers 1979). Where a fluid exhibits pressure- driven flow, we get:

$$\frac{p_1 - p_2}{\rho g} = \frac{\Delta p}{\rho g} \tag{6}$$

Darcy – Weisbash friction factor F (viscous forces divided by inertial forces). The pressure due to a fluid pressing against a body tends to compresses the body. The ratio of the pressure to the frictional decrease in volume is given as:

$$B = \frac{P}{\Delta V / V} \tag{7}$$

Where B is the Bulk modulus. Mash decreases in volume when they are subjected to external pressure. A minus sign was introduced in the equation to make B positive. The pressure extended by a fluid is equivalent to a compressive stress

The fraction decrease in volume - $\dfrac{\Delta V}{V}$ is compressive strain.

The inverse of the bulk modulus is compressibility K:

$$K = \frac{1}{B} = -\frac{\Delta V / V}{p} \tag{8}$$

The absolute pressure is obtained from gauge pressure by adding atmospheric pressure to it

P = P[gauge] + P[atm.] but Poiseuille's law of flow of liquids through a tube:

$$v = \pi r^4 \, p/8cl \tag{9}$$

Where: l = the length of the tube in cm, r = the radius of the tube in cm, p = the difference in pressure of the two ends of the tube in dynes per cm², c = the coefficient of Viscosity in poises (dyne-seconds per cm²), v = volume in cm³ per second.

Also put into consideration during the design is the bought out components, which was designed for pressure measurement, pressure gauge for measuring pressure above atmospheric. Spring-element pressure gauge was used for this experiment as bought out item. The sealed end connected to a pointer, the deflection shows the pressure of the fluid from the experimental box connected to the nipple of the gauge. Pressure on the walls of the box was considered (Figure 3). Pressure on one side is the same as the pressure on other sides In finding the direction of the resultant force R pressure on one side of the wall abcd ab =bc=cd=ab = 0.3 m.

Area of the wetted surface of abcd = A; Hieght of liquid in the box= h; h_c =distance of centroid of the wall from the free surface.

$$P_{max} = \rho gh + P_o \tag{10}$$

P_{max} is the maximum pressure expected on the samples, Pressure at the centroid the area:

$$P_c = \rho gh_c \tag{11}$$

Then pressure on the constant element dA:

$$P = P_c + \rho hz$$

Where z is the ordinate of Area dA

The total force $R = \int P dA$
$= \int (Pc + Pgz) dA$
$= Pc \int dA + \rho g \int z dA$
$= PcA + 0$
$R = PcA$ or $(h_c \rho g + P_o) \times A$

Pressure on the wall of the copper tube with a diameter D wall thickness t and a minimum tensile strength of 205 N/mm² per unit area at any point on the tube was considered and used for the experiment, the actual tensile stress was not expected to be more than the permissible stress. Expected failure points were near two surfaces of the diametrical cross section.

Each of them has an area:

$$A = tl \tag{12}$$

The tensile stress in these areas are:

$$= pD \, l/2lt, \; = pD/2t \tag{13}$$

Table 1. Design/layout.

Cassava variety	Number of sample	Container shape	Dewatering method
IITA TMS 4(2) 1425	C9 C12 C15	Cylindrical	Rope/stick
	C9 C12 C15	Square	
	C9 C12 C15	Sack	
IITA TMS 4(2) 1425	C9 C12 C15	Cylindrical	Hydraulic
	C9 C12 C15	Square	
	C9 C12 C15	Sack	
IITA TMS 4(2) 1425	C9 C12 C15	Cylindrical	Screw
	C9 C12 C15	Square	
	C9 C12 C15	Sack	

The permissible strength was found grater than the calculated tensile stress. Further, the deflection of the material that host the pressure was calculated by using $wl^4/384EI$ Where w is the force on the longest part, l the length of box E young' modulus and Moment of Inertia. $I = bh^2/12$.

Experimental tool calibration and verification

Objects of different mass were used to exert pressure on the equipment tool; six different gauge types were used. Several weights of objects were tested with the equipment including the weight of workshop staff on top of the platform; these readings were the same for the repeated measurement readings. A measured variable was compared to a reference variable from those earlier measured at pressures of 40, 50, 70 and 80 KN/mm^2 using workshop press. During the calibration process, the measurement system was balanced in such a way that the measured variable deviates as minimally as possible from the true value (reference value), and is within the tolerance range. Measuring device was verified on the basis of what is obtained from hydraulic presses in the workshop and at post harvest unit of IITA. A confirmation of verification-specific, such as verification error limits, was not breached. A verification group within the workshop additionally identifies the measuring device before the commencement of the experiment.

Method

Dewatering was effected using two tanks made of 1 mm galvanized steel plate. The tanks were drilled at the base with 7 mm diameter drill to provide passages for the fluid flowing from the mash. Grated cassava mashes in sacks, in the square and cylindrical containers, were tested with screw bolts, hydraulic jack press and rope / stick methods. The procedure involve each of cassava-grated samples dewatered with the mash carefully and measured at 10 kg into a well-labeled sacks as shown in table one.

The purpose of putting the mash in a sack was to provide filtration at all sides at the same time preventing upward seepage. The sample tanks keep the same standard, since the sacks can be moved out of the containers easily.

For dewatering methods and effect of container shape, each had nine treatments and repeated 5 times this was varied with the age of cassava. The best method was discovered from the most

efficient, the best to meet set moisture content required at a given time for gari production.

Material mass and height measurement

The heights of samples were measured using steel rule before dewatering and after the experiment. Mass of samples was also obtained by weighing the container and sample before and after the experiment.

Applied pressure

The pressure applied was read from the gauge in the experimental equipment. The samples in the dewatering tank placed on the equipment with the pressure applied using a hydraulic jack, screw and rope/sticks methods at different time. The observed pressure reading from the attached pressure gauge was recorded (Table 1).

Time/volume of liquid

The measurement of time was done using a stopwatch. The starting time noted with the volume of expressed liquid. The pressure was kept constraint at the pick, for every 30 s as the liquid gradually drops in flow rate the change in volume is always noted. The cumulative filtrate volume and time presented in data sheet.

Moisture content of samples

The moisture content of the cassava mash samples was noted before and after the experiments. The moisture content of samples was obtained by drying the samples in an oven at $100°C$ until no further change in weight occurred. This took three days of 70 – 72 h in a try-temp hot pack oven and weighing took place daily.

Cassava mash resistance

Mash resistance was noted as internal resistance developed as opposed to applied pressure, only determined with calculation from the data obtained when a constant pressure operation was carried out on the samples.

9 months cassava sample under pressure

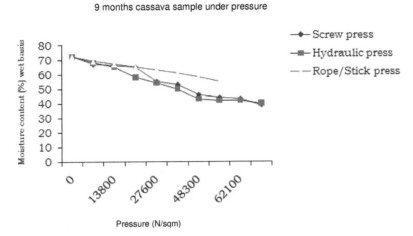

Figure 4. Effect of pressure application on 9 months old graph.

12 months cassava sample under pressure

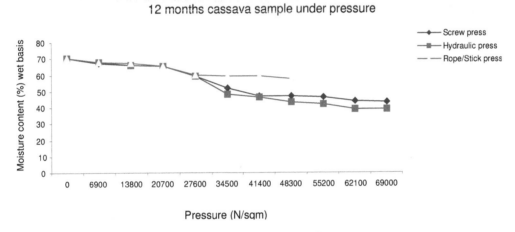

Figure 5. Effect of pressure application on 12 months old graph.

Filtrating surface area

Dewatering tanks made into shapes that the filtration area was calculated with ease, the base area of containers in use when pressure was applied to the mash during the experiment.

RESULT

TMS 4(2) 1425 variety of cassava was available in large quantity for the experiment the chosen variety is of known value of garification as reported by IITA (1987).

Effect of type of container

Grated sample of cassava mash in container was used in testing square and cylindrical container by applying pressure, the statistical analysis using t-test for related measures t=1.8999 df=N-1 at 0.5 level gives 2.262 which is smaller, that proved that cylindrical container performed

better as the moisture content of the sample in cylindrical container meets the set standard of 40 to 45% moisture content wet basis in shortest time.

Effect of applied pressure

Samples tested from screw, hydraulic jack press and rope/stick methods, the result obtained using the cylindrical container with the hydraulic jack press reduce the moisture content of mash to the acceptable level for garri production at a pressure of 69000 N/m^2 while the method of rope/sticks gave the poorest result in the experiment carried out, the required moisture content for garri production process was expected to be 40 to 45% mcwb. Obtained result from the rope/stick and sack method at 20700 N/m^2 was 58.7% mcwb. Advancing beyond this pressure point was difficult. Using hydraulic jack at 48300 N/m^2, 44% moisture content was obtained Figures 4, 5, and 6.

15 months cassava sample under pressure

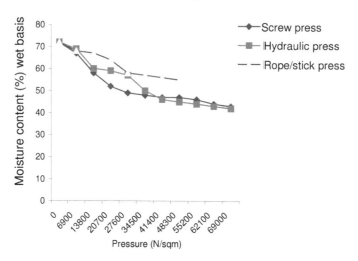

Figure 6. Effect of pressure application on 15 months old graph.

Mash level in container vs moisture content (%)

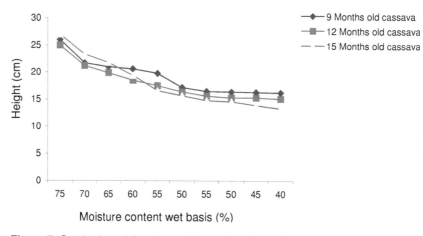

Figure 7. Graph of mash level in container after dewatering.

Effect of cassava age on the dewatering

The volume of filtrate obtained from the samples show that the C9 contains more water than the C12 and C15 at the start of the experiment but C12 had more fluid at the end, this may be due to maturity at peak for the variety while C15 compressed more than the C9 and C15 as shown in Figure 7 this can be due to fibre formation within the cassava.

Conclusion

The results obtained show that not much pressure can be sustained by stick/rope method, as more time will be required. The screw and the hydraulic methods are very efficient. The hydraulic jack method of dewatering shows clear efficiency with the C12 sample as shown in Figures 4, 5 and 6, but no significant differences were noticed between the screw jack method and hydraulic methods when used on C9 and C15 samples. This confirms Igbeka et al. (1982) statement that screw presses and jack presses are used for greater efficiency and speed.

REFERENCES

Ajibola OO (1987). Mechanical Dewatering of Cassava Mash; Transactions of ASAE, 30(2): 539-542.
Diop A (1998). Storage and Processing of Roots and Tubers in Tropics; Food and Agricultural Organisation of UN Agro-Industries and Post-

Harvest Management Service Agro Supports System Division. www.fao.org/docrep/x5415e/5415e00.HTM.

Klanarong S, Sittichoke W, Rungsima C, Sunee C, Kukakoon P, Christopher GO (1999). An Improved Dewatering Performance in Cassava Starch Process by A Pressure Filter, Kasetsart Agricultural and Agro-Industrial Product Improvement, Kasetsart, University Thailand. http://cstru.00go.com/1999/1999_03.htm.

FAO (1994). African Experience in the Improvement of Post-harvest Techniques, Food and Agricultural organization of the United Nations, Agricultural Engineering service (AGSE) Support Systems Division Workshop, ACCRA, Ghana 4th to 8th July, Rome, Italy.www.fao.org/docrep/W1544E/W1544E07.HTM.

Igbeka JC, Jory M Griffon D (1992). Selective Mechanization for Cassava Processing. Agricultural Mechanization in Asia, Africa and Latin America, 23(1): 45-50.

IITA (1987). Elite Cassava Clones Assessed for Gari Quality. IITA Annual Report and Research Highlights. Ibadan, pp. 96-97.

Kolawole OP (2005). Investigation into Cassava Mash Dewatering Parameters Unpublished Master of Engineering Thesis, Agricultural Engineering Dept. Federal University of Technology Akure.

Kolawole OP, Agbetoye LAS, Ogunlowo AS (2007). Cassava Mash Dewatering Parameters. Int. J. Food Eng., 3(1): 4. http://www.bepress.com.

Kolawole OP Agbetoye LAS (2007). Engineering Research to Improve Cassava Processing Technology, Int. J. Food Eng., 3(6): 9. http://www.bepress.com

Sperry V (1979). Mobile Hydraulic Manual, M-2990A, 2nd Edition Sperry Corporation, Troy Michigan 48084, p. 4-20.

Straub RJ, Bruhn HD (1978). Mechanical Dewatering of Alfalfa Concentrate. Transactions of ASAE, 21(3): 414-421.

## 10

Molecular docking of human histamine H1 receptor with chlorpheniramine to alleviate cat allergies

Uma Maheshwari

Department of Bioinformatics, Aloysius Institute of Management and Information Technology, St. Aloysius College (Autonomous), 2nd Cross, Sharada Nagar, Beeri, Kotekar Post, Madoor, Mangalore -575022, Karnataka, India. E-mail: ugdreams@gmail.com.

Cat allergen Fel d 1, secreted by the cat's sebaceous glands and that covers the cat's skin and fur is the major cat allergen responsible for cat allergies in human. It interacts with and cross-links surface IgE antibodies on mast cells and basophils. Once the mast cell-antibody-antigen complex is formed, a complex series of events occurs that eventually leads to cell-degranulation and the release of histamine from the mast cell or basophil. Histamine, acting on H1-receptors, produces pruritis, vasodilatation, hypotension, flushing, headache, tachycardia, and bronchoconstriction and also increases vascular permeability and potentiates pain. Chlorpheniramine is a histamine H1 antagonist of the alkyl amine class. It competes with histamine for the normal H1-receptor sites on effector cells of the gastrointestinal tract, blood vessels and respiratory tract. It binds to the histamine H1 receptor and blocks the action of endogenous histamine there by providing effective, temporary relief of sneezing, watery and itchy eyes, and runny nose due to hay fever and other upper respiratory allergies. Homology modeling of Histamine H1 Receptor is done using SWISSPDBVIEWER – SWISSMODEL. It showed 27 helices, 6 strands and 37 turns. The stereochemistry of the theoretical model of Histamine H1 Receptor is studied by subjecting it into energy minimization in SWISSPDBVIEWER. The model was subjected to structure verification and evaluation using PROCHECK. The Ramachandran plot for the model showed 92.5% residues in most favored regions and hence the model was revealed to have good stereo chemistry. A molecular docking study of modeled structure of Histamine H1 Receptor with the drug chlorpheniramine is done using PatchDock program. Receptor–Drug complex has a complementarity score of 4846, Atomic Contact Energy (ACE) of -139.35. The docking studies which involves the interaction of Histamine H1 Receptor with the drug chlorpheniramine provided valuable insight into the role of chlorpheniramine having anti histamine activity and in alleviating cat allergies produced by the cat allergen namely Fel d 1 protein.

Key words: Fel d 1 protein, cat allergy, histamine H1 receptor, chlorpheniramine, SWISSPDBVIEWER, SWISSMODEL, PROCHECK, PatchDock, homology modeling, molecular docking, receptor-drug complex.

INTRODUCTION

Cat allergen, Fel d 1, is the major cat allergen responsible for cat allergies in human. It is a small, sticky protein secreted by the cat's sebaceous glands and covers the cat's skin and fur which is rubbed off on furniture, carpeting, clothing, etc. Further, the allergen is so light that it easily becomes airborne and contaminates the entire indoor environment. When people allergic to cats come in contact with Fel d 1, they develop a type 1 allergic hypersensitivity reaction which may include the rapid onset of sneezing, runny nose, itchy and swollen eyes, mucus production and difficulties breathing (http://www.felixpets.com). Studies have shown that significant concentrations of cat allergen remain in a home years after a cat has left the house. Cat allergen Fel d 1 has also been identified as one of the three major risk factors for developing childhood allergies, asthma, and other respiratory diseases. The cat allergen Fel d 1 interacts with and cross-links surface IgE antibodies on mast cells and basophils. Once the mast cell-antibody-antigen complex is formed, a complex series of events

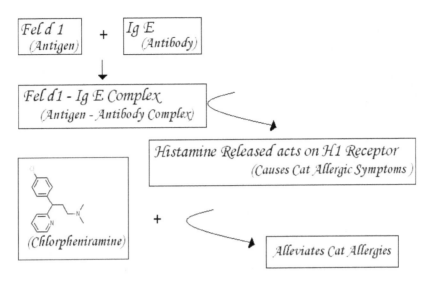

Figure 1. Mechanism of alleviating cat allergies.

occurs that eventually leads to cell-degranulation and the release of histamine (and other chemical mediators) from the mast cell or basophil. Once released, histamine can react with local or widespread tissues through histamine receptors. Histamine, acting on H1-receptors, produces pruritis, vasodilatation, hypotension, flushing, headache, tachycardia, and bronchoconstriction. Histamine also increases vascular permeability and potentiates pain. Chlorpheniramine, is a histamine H1 antagonist of the alkylamine class (http: //redpoll. pharmacy.ualberta.ca/drugbank/index.html). It competes with histamine for the normal H1-receptor sites on effector cells of the gastrointestinal tract, blood vessels and respiratory tract. Chlorpheniramine binds to the histamine H1 receptor and blocks the action of endogenous histamine (Figure 1) there by providing effective, temporary relief of sneezing, watery and itchy eyes, and runny nose due to hay fever and other upper respiratory allergies (http://www.drgreene.com).

This work is an attempt of the three dimensional structure prediction of the Histamine H1 Receptor followed by an *in silico* study of the binding interactions of the drug chlorpheniramine with the histamine H1-receptors which alleviates the cat allergies in humans.

METHODOLOGY

The protein sequence of Histamine H1 receptor with primary accession number P35367 is extracted from the UniProtKB/Swiss-prot (http://www.expasy.org/uniprot) database. The program SWISSPDBVIEWER is employed in the construction of theoretical three dimensional structure of Histamine H1 receptor. SWISS-MODEL, a fully automated protein structure homology-modeling server, accessible via the program DeepView (SWISSPDBVIEWER) is used to model the protein sequence of Histamine H1 receptor with primary accession number P35367 that's extracted from the UniProtKB/Swiss-prot.

The theoretical model generated is subjected to validation using the program PROCHECK for assessing the stereochemistry of the model. The program PROCHECK (Morris et al., 1992) concentrates on the parameters such as bond length, bond angle, main chain and side chain properties, residue-by residue properties, RMS distance from planarity and distorted geometry plots. It assess how normal, or conversely how unusual, the geometry of the residues in a given protein structure is, as compared with stereo chemical parameters derived from well-refined, high-resolution structures (Laskowski et al., 1993).

The model of Histamine H1 receptor is docked with the drug chlorpheniramine using the molecular docking algorithm called PatchDock (Schneidman-Duhovny et al., 2005). This algorithm is inspired by object recognition and image segmentation techniques used in Computer Vision. Docking using this algorithm is compared to assembling a jigsaw puzzle which involves matching two pieces by picking one piece and searching for the complementary one (Schneidman-Duhovny et al., 2003). It concentrates on the patterns that are unique for the puzzle element and look for the matching patterns in the rest of the pieces. It employs a technique in which the surfaces are divided into patches according to the surface shape and these patches correspond to patterns that visually distinguish between puzzle pieces. Once the patches are identified, they can be superimposed using shape matching algorithms which notify that a hybrid of the Geometric Hashing and Pose-Clustering matching techniques are applied to match the patches detected. Concave patches are matched with convex and flat patches with any type of patches. All complexes with unacceptable penetrations of the atoms of the receptor to the atoms of the ligand are discarded. Finally, the remaining candidates are ranked according to a geometric shape complementarity score.

RESULTS AND DISCUSSION

Target sequence of histamine H1 receptor

The protein sequence of Histamine H1 receptor of Homo sapiens (Uniprot/SwissProt ID: P3536) extracted from the UniProtKB/Swiss-prot database (Bairoch et al., 2004) shown below is 487 amino acids in total length, and is of

Figure 2. Structure of template - human B2-adrenergic G protein-coupled receptor.

```
Score = 154 bits (386), Expect = 2e-37

Identities = 121/464 (26%) Positives = 212/464 (46%) Gaps = 45/464 (10%)

Query:   32  VVLSTICLVTVGLNLLVLYAVRSERKLHTVGNLYIVSLSVADLIVGAVVHPHNILYLLHS  91
             VSIL   V  NLV  A       LTVN  I SL  ADL   G  VP      LH
Sbjct:   10  IVHSLIVLAIVFGNVLVITAIAKFERLQTVTNYFITSLACADLVHGLAVVPFGAAHILHK  69

Query:   92  KWSLGRPLCLFWLSHDYVASTASIFSVFILCIDRYRSVQQPLRYLKYRTKTRASATILGA  151
             W  G   CFW SD    TASI      DRY     P  Y    TK  A    IL
Sbjct:   70  HWTFGNFWCEFWTSIDVLCVTASIETLCVIAVDRYFAITSPFKYQSLLTKNKARVIILHV  129

Query:  152  WFLSFLW-VIPI-LGWNHFHQQTSVR--REDKCETDFYDVTWFKVHTAIINFYLPTLLHL  207
             W  SL    PI W    Q      E  C  DF       I  FY P    H
Sbjct:  130  WIVSGLTSFLPIQHHWYRATHQEAINCYABETC-CDFFTNQARYAIASSIVSFYVPLVIHV  188

Query:  208  WFYAKIYKAVRQHCQHRELINRSLPSFSEIKLRPENPKGDAKKPGKESPWEVLKRKPKDA  267
             Y                R L F      G K  K
Sbjct:  189  FVYSRVFQEAK--------RQLMIFEHLRI---DEGLRLKIYKDTEGYY------TI  228

Query:  268  GGGSVL-KSPSQTPKEHKSPVVFSQEDDREVDKLYCFPLDIVHHQARAEGSSRDYVAVNR  326
             G G  L KSPS        K   L    AA  G  R
Sbjct:  229  GIGHLLTKSPSLNRAAKSELDKAIGRNTNGVITKDEAEKLENQDVIRAVRGILRN-AKLKP  287

Query:  327  SHGQLKTDEQGLNTHGASEISEDQHLGDSQSFSRTDSDTTTETAPGKGKLRSGSNTG---  383
             L              E    G   S         EA    KR   T
Sbjct:  288  VYDSLDAVRRAALIMHVFQHGETGVAGFTNSLRHLQQKRWDEARVNLAKSRWYNQTPNRA  347

Query:  384  ----LDYIKFTWKRLRSHSRQYVSGLHMNRERKAAKQLGFIMAAFILCWIPYFIFFMVIA  439
                 TW               KA KLG IH  F LCW P FI   V
Sbjct:  348  KRVITTFRTGTWDAYKFCLKEH---------KRLKTLGIIHGTFTLCWLPFFIUNIVHV  397

Query:  440  FCKNCCNEHLHHFTIWLGYINSTLNPLIYPLCNENFKKTFKRIL  483
             N        W GY NS  NPLIY  F   F  L
Sbjct:  398  IQDNLIRKEVYILLNWIGYVNSGFNPLIY-CRSPDFRIAFQELL  440
```

Figure 3. The sequence alignment between Histamine H1 Receptor and Human B2-Adrenergic G Protein-Coupled Receptor (EXPDB ID: 1rh1a) performed using SWISSMODEL template selection.

molecular weight 55784 Da.

>P35367|HRH1_HUMAN Histamine H1 receptor - Homo sapiens (Human).
MSLPNSSCLLEDKMCEGNKTTMASPQLMPLVVVLSTIC
LVTVGLNLLVLYAVRSERKLHTVGNLYIVSLSVADLIVGA
VVMPMNILYLLMSKWSLGRPLCLFWLSMDYVASTASIF
SVFILCIDRYRSVQQPLRYLKYRTKTRASATILGAWFLS
FLWVIPILGWNHFMQQTSVRREDKCETDFYDVTWFKV
MTAIINFYLPTLLMLWFYAKIYKAVRQHCQHRELINRSLP
SFSEIKLRPENPKGDAKKPGKESPWEVLKRKPKDAGG
GSVLKSPSQTPKEMKSPVVFSQEDDREVDKLYCFPLDI
VHMQAAAEGSSRDYVAVNRSHGQLKTDEQGLNTHGA
SEISEDQMLGDSQSFSRTDSDTTTETAPGKGKLRSGS
NTGLDYIKFTWKRLRSHSRQYVSGLHMNRERKAAKQL
GFIMAAFILCWIPYFIFFMVIAFCKNCCNEHLHMFTIWLG
YINSTLNPLIYPLCNENFKKTFKRILHIRS

Template identification

Selecting appropriate ExPDB template for the protein

sequence of Histamine H1 receptor of Homo sapiens (Uniprot/SwissProt ID: P3536) via the SWISSPDBVIEWER yielded a structure of human B2-adrenergic G protein-coupled receptor (ExPDB ID: 1rh1A, Figure 2) as a template with a length of 442 residues.

Target-template sequence alignment

The most successful techniques for prediction of three dimensional structures of protein rely on aligning the sequence of a protein of to a homolog of known structure. Histamine H1 receptor showed 26% identity, 46% positives, 154 score bits, and 2e-37 e-value with the template human B2-adrenergic G protein-coupled receptor (Figure 3).

Homology modeling of histamine H1 receptor

The lack of 3D structure for Histamine H1 receptor

Figure 4. Homology model of histamine H1 receptor.

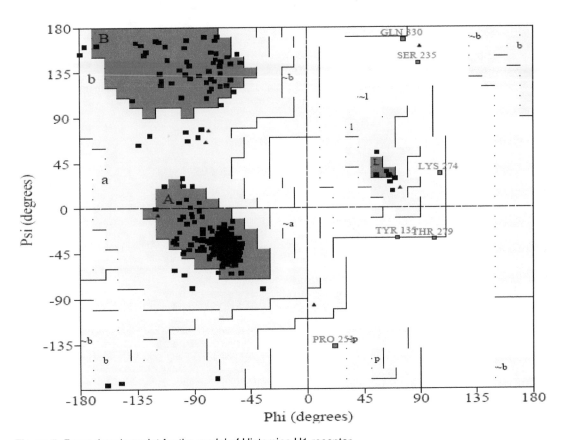

Figure 5. Ramachandran plot for the model of Histamine H1 receptor.

initiated to construct the 3D model for Histamine H1 receptor.

In order to understand the binding characteristics as well as the structural and molecular level properties of the Histamine H1 receptor homology, modeling is carried out based on the structure of human B2-adrenergic G protein-coupled receptor (ExPDB ID: 1rh1A) as the template. The structure of Histamine H1 receptor was modeled using the program SWISSPDBVIEWER - SWISSMODEL (Figure 4).The modeled structure has 27 helices, 6 strands and 37 turns.

Refinement and evaluation of the quality of the model

The stereochemistry of the theoretical model of Histamine H1 Receptor is done by subjecting it into energy minimization in SWISSPDBVIEWER. The model was subjected to structure verification and evaluation using PROCHECK. The Ramachandran plot for the model showed 92.5% residues in most favored regions and other parameters for PROCHECK was in the allowed range (Figure 5). A good quality model would be expected to have over 90% in the most favored regions.

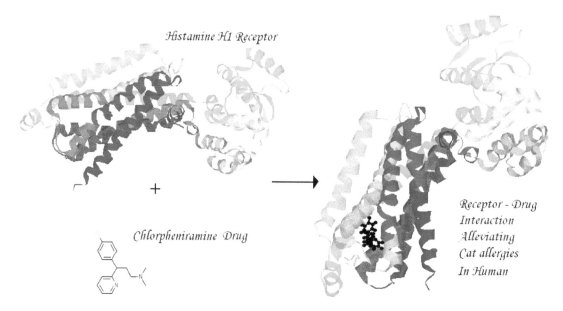

Figure 6. Representation of interaction between Histamine H1 (Receptor) and chlorpheniramine (Drug). Receptor is represented in ribbons format and drug is represented in ball and sticks format. The Docking is performed in Patch Dock software.

The theoretical model is a good quality model since 92.5% of the residues are in most favored region.

Interaction of histamine H1 receptor with chlorpheniramine

The drug chlorpheniramine is downloaded in PDB format from Drug Bank. Downloaded drug is then subjected to molecular docking (Figure 6) with the model of Histamine H1 Receptor using PatchDock program. Receptor–Drug complex has a complementarity score of 4846, Atomic Contact Energy (ACE) of -139.35.

Conclusion

The work involved the homology modeling of Histamine H1 Receptor, and molecular docking studies of modeled structure of Histamine H1 Receptor with the drug chlorpheniramine. The docking studies which involves the interaction of Histamine H1 Receptor with the drug chlorpheniramine provided valuable insight into the role of chlorpheniramine having anti histamine activity and in alleviating cat allergies produced by the cat allergen namely Fel d 1 protein.

REFERENCES

Bairoch A, Boeckmann B, Ferro S, Gasteiger E (2004). Swiss-Prot: Juggling between evolution and stability. Brief. Bioinform., 5: 39-55.

Laskowski RA, MacArthur MW, Moss DS, Thornton JM (1993). PROCHECK: A program to check the stereochemical quality of protein structures. J. Appl. Cryst., 26: 283-291.

Morris AL, MacArthur MW, Hutchinson EG, Thornton JM (1992). Stereochemical quality of protein structure coordinates. Proteins. 12: 345-364.

Schneidman-Duhovny D, Inbar Y, Nussinov R, Wolfson HJ (2005). PatchDock and SymmDock: servers for rigid and symmetric docking. Nucleic Acids Res., Jul 1(33): W363-W367.

Schneidman-Duhovny D, Inbar Y, Polak V, Shatsky M, Halperin I, Benyamini H, Barzilai A, Dror O, Haspel N, Nussinov R, Wolfson HJ (2003). Taking geometry to its edge: Fast unbound rigid (and hinge-bent) docking. Proteins. 52(1): 107-112.

http://redpoll.pharmacy.ualberta.ca/drugbank/index.html.

http://www.drgreene.com/.

http://www.expasy.org/uniprot.

http://www.felixpets.com.

## 11

In silico identification of potential horizontal gene transfer events between archaea and pathogenic bacteria

Hasan Bilal Mirza*, Maryam Anwar and S. Habib Bokhari

Department of Biosciences, COMSATS Institute of Information Technology, Chak Shehzad Campus, Islamabad, Pakistan.

Horizontal gene transfer plays a potent role in the evolution of prokaryotes. A rigorous sequence and phylogenetic analysis was carried out using the robust ClustalW, motifs/domains finding suites and neighbor-joining based ProtDist and BioNJ. This paper reports a few cases of horizontal gene transfer events between archaea and bacteria. Some of these events have been found to be unique to the bacterial pathogenic members and have not been observed in respective non-pathogenic counterparts. Two cases have been shown to exhibit particular importance. The first one is a Cps4I gene that codes for capsule polysaccharide biosynthesis protein in *Streptococcus pneumoniae*. The other gene has been detected in *Streptococcus agalactiae* that codes for N-acetyl neuramic acid synthetase, which is involved in the synthesis of N-acetyl neuramic acid or sialic acid. We believe that these genes, having been retained in the genome through selective advantage, have key functions in the organism's biology and may play a role in pathogenesis.

Key words: Horizontal gene transfer, BLAST, ClustalW, conserved domain, motif, bootstrap value, bit score.

INTRODUCTION

In prokaryotes, the principal mode of genetic flexibility is the natural genetic transformation. However, in order to adapt to new environments, microbes acquire novel genes through horizontal gene transfer (HGT) from the inhabitants of the environment (Doolittle, 1999). It has also been observed that horizontal gene transfer events play a more important role as compared to alterations in gene functions mediated by point mutations, in the adaptation of microbes to new environments (Wiezer et al., 2005). For the same reason, certain microbial species may look similar to each other although there is no ancestor-descendent relationship between them.

Like bacteria, archaea are widely distributed. While they resemble bacteria in their shapes and various cell structures, they differ immensely in the chemical composition of their structures. Extensive analysis on DNA and biochemical features of archaea has revealed many differences in comparison to bacteria including that of ribosomal RNA, cell wall composition, types of lipids used in the cell membrane, and the way DNA is packaged and transcribed (Rossi et al., 2003). Archaea consist of molecular features that are encoded by two different groups of genes. One group is eukaryotic in nature and is called the group of informational genes,

---

*Corresponding author. E-mail: hasan_bilal@comsats.edu.pk.

Abbreviations: HGT, Horizontal gene transfer; **NCBI,** national centre for biotechnology information; **BLAST,** basic local alignment search tool; **MEME,** multiple Em for motif elicitation; **MAST,** motif alignment and search tool; **VFDB,** virulence factor database; **MVirDB,** a microbial database of protein toxins, virulence factors and antibiotic resistance genes; **LLNL,** lawrence livermore national laboratory; **CD-SEARCH,** converved domain search; **ABC-** Transporter, **ATP**-binding cassette transporter; **CPS4I,** gene that codes for capsule polysaccharide biosynthesis protein in Streptococcus pneumonia; **NeuB,** gene that codes for N-acetyl neuramic acid synthetase in Streptococcus agalactiae.

which are involved in transcription, translation and other such processes. The other group of genes is similar to bacterial genes and includes the operational genes that encode housekeeping functions (Garcia-Vallve et al., 2000; Jain et al., 1999).

Recent studies have indicated that horizontal transfer events are greater for operational genes than the informational genes. It has been suggested that the reason for this partiality is the fact that informational genes are associated to large complex systems as compared to operational genes making HGT of informational genes difficult (Jain et al., 1999). Despite extensive genome sequencing and DNA analysis, there are certain features of archaea that are still unknown due to the fact that they are difficult to isolate and culture.

Archaea have been found to be capable of colonizing in the human host as the normal flora. There are anaerobic archaea in the human colon, vagina and oral cavity (Eckburg et al., 2003). However, no virulence genes have been identified in archaea till now. Recent studies have led to the identification of certain characteristics in archaea that are common to known pathogens indicating towards the possibility of a probable role of archaea in causing virulence. Since Griffith, HGT has been thought of as a mode to acquire novel virulence genes in pathogens. Recent sequencing of bacterial and archaeal genomes has shown that inter-domain transfer is common. For instance, a large fraction of *Thermotoga maritima* genes appear to be of archaeal origin (Mongodin et al., 2005). Since archaea are not directly involved in causing a disease but there are similarities between pathogenic bacterial genome and archaeal genome, archaea might be linked to virulence as donors of virulence-promoting genes to pathogenic bacteria through the process of lateral gene transfer (Faguy, 2003).

To explore the issue of horizontal gene transfer between archaea and bacteria and to determine the probable direction of transfer, we have analyzed and compared the genomes of archaea and pathogenic bacteria through the use of web-based computational and statistical tools including specialized softwares such as MEME (Multiple Em for motif elicitation) and MAST (Motif alignment and search tool) for the identification of highly conserved motifs and protein function and Neighbor-Joining packages for phylogenetic analysis. In order to establish if the transfer events between archaea and bacteria also contribute to virulence, we searched and compared the probable candidates of horizontal transfer in pathogenic strains with their non-pathogenic counterparts to examine if they met specific criteria for archaea to bacteria gene transfer or vice versa.

MATERIALS AND METHODS

In order to find the horizontal gene transfer of potential virulence candidate proteins between archaea and pathogenic bacteria, the following scheme was implemented:

Retrieval of pathogenecity-associated sequences

In the first part of this step, updated organism lists of bacterial pathogens, bacterial non-pathogens and archaeal species/strains were obtained from National centre for biotechnology information (NCBI) (http://www.ncbi.nlm.nih.gov/.html). Only those bacterial pathogens were selected for further study whose non-pathogenic counterparts were available at the genus level. About 20 bacterial pathogens were selected in the first part. In the second part of this step, sequences of pathogenecity-associated proteins of the 20 selected bacterial pathogens were retrieved from two major databases: The Virulence Factors Database (VFDB) (Chen et al., 2005) and MvirDB (a microbial database of protein toxins, virulence factors and antibiotic resistance genes) Virulence Database at Lawrence Livermore National Laboratory (LLNL) (Zhou et al., 2007).

Sequence BLASTs

The pathogenecity-associated sequences obtained in the first step were subjected to a series of BLASTs (Altschul et al., 1990) against the genomes and proteomes of bacterial pathogens (excluding pathogens of the same species and genus), bacterial non-pathogens and archaea. From the Blast results, Protein sequences from pathogenic bacteria were selected as probable HGT candidates if they matched the following criteria:

(A) A bit score of at least 105 in BLAST with Archaea and at most 90 in BLAST with Non-Pathogenic counterparts.
(B) At least 2 matches in BLAST with Archaea.
(C) If BLAST with bacterial pathogens resulted in matches with a bit score value greater than that of the best match in archaea, then the candidate protein was selected only if the best matches in bacterial pathogens were from the same species or genus as the candidate. In cases where the number of matches of a specific protein sequence exceeded 15, only first 15 matches were considered.

Multiple sequence alignment

The sequences selected in the second step were subjected to multiple sequence alignment to check for the presence of conserved regions. For this purpose the robust ClustalW tool (Thompson et al., 1994), present at the EBI web server was used.

Identification of conserved motifs and domains

In the first part of this step, each set of similar sequences (HGT candidate, archaeal, bacterial) was given as input to two collaborative web-based softwares MEME and MAST (http://meme.sdsc.edu) to identify highly conserved regions in the sequences. In the second part of this step, the consensus sequences of conserved regions in each set were given as input to CD-Search (Conserved domain search, Marchler et al., 2004) to identify the domains to which the conserved motifs corresponded.

Construction of phylogenetic trees

To ensure optimality of results, the ClustalW alignments of the selected proteins were subjected to refinement using the JALVIEW alignment editor (Clamp et al., 2004). The edited multiple sequence alignments were used to build Distance based Neighbor-Joining Trees using ProtDist and BioNJ packages of Phylip. PhyloDraw (Jeong et al., 2000) was used to display phylogenetic

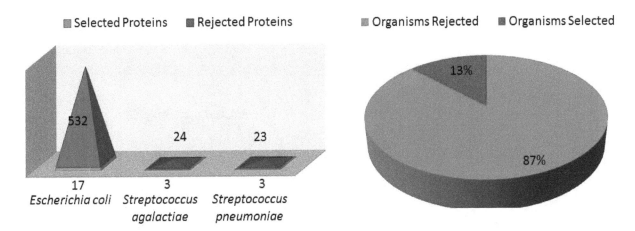

Figure 1. Statistics of the selected and rejected bacteria and their proteins. Of all the bacteria, only 13% were selected for the study as their non-pathogenic counterparts were available at genus level. After BLAST results, proteins from only three bacteria, that is, *Escherichia coli*, *Streptococcus agalactiae* and *Streptococcus pneumonia* fit into selected criteria.

Table 1. Categorical division of the selected proteins. The majority of selected proteins belong to 5 protein classes except for three individual proteins. Here ABC ~ ATP-binding cassette transporter.

Protein groups	Individual proteins
ABC transporters family	DNA methylase
Bacterial capsular proteins	
Transposases and helper proteins	Helicase
Reverse transcriptases	
Restrictions enzymes	Lysyl t-RNA synthetase

trees in graphical form by manipulating the shape of phylogenetic trees and interactively by using several control parameters.

RESULTS AND DISCUSSION

A total of 23 proteins were selected based on the pre-defined criteria. Their division among bacterial pathogens and further categorical divisions are given in Figure 1 and Table 1, respectively.

Few of the HGT candidates in our analysis were directly or indirectly related to virulence. It appears so that the genes acquired by horizontal gene transfer from archaea are more involved in normal biosynthetic functions rather than in pathogenesis of bacteria. Primarily we identified HGT events for genes involved in capsule biosynthesis and DNA regulatory or modification functions. Two events are of particular importance.

The first one is a protein coded by Cps4I gene in *Streptococcus pneumoniae*. *S. pneumoniae* is a human pathogen that causes a variety of diseases including otitis media, pneumonia, sepsis and meningitis (Roche et al., 2000). Cps4I, a capsule polysaccharide biosynthesis protein is also known as UDP-N-acetylglucosamine-2-epimerase. It catalyzes the reversible epimerization of UDP-N-acetylglucosamine (UDP-GlcNAc) at carbon-2, providing bacteria with UDP-N-acetylmannosamine (UDP-ManNAc), which is the activated donor of ManNAc residues. ManNAc is one of the major virulence factors and plays a very important role in several bacterial processes such as formation of the antiphagocytic capsular polysaccharide in pathogens (Campbell et al., 2000). A homologue of UDP-N-acetyl glucosamine in mammals is a bifunctional enzyme involved in the initiation and regulation of biosynthesis of sialic acids that play a role in cell-cell and cell-matrix interactions (Astrid et al., 2004). According to our analysis, Cps4I appears to have been transferred horizontally from archaea. The relationship between Cps4I of *S. pneumoniae* and N-acylneuraminate-9- phosphate synthase of several archaea was clearly depicted in our phylogenetic tree as shown in Figure 2.

MEME and MAST results showed three highly conserved motifs in CPS4I and its archaeal counterparts as shown in Table 2. Based on these results, two main domains WecB (involved in cell envelope biogenesis) and Epimerase_2 (UPD-N-acetylmannosamine kinase activity) were found to be conserved among Cps4I and methanococcal sequences (Table 3).

The HGT candidate Cps4I matched best with the N-acylneuraminate-9- phosphate synthase of *Methanospirillum hungatei JF-1*, which was also its closest neighbor in the archaeal cluster. Though the function of Cps4I is quite clear, the exact function of N-acylneuraminate-9-phosphate synthase in archaea is unknown as yet (Wilson et al., 2005). Based on our phylogenetic analysis, we infer that an HGT event involving capsular proteins has taken place from archaea to bacteria and may have contributed to virulence in bacteria.

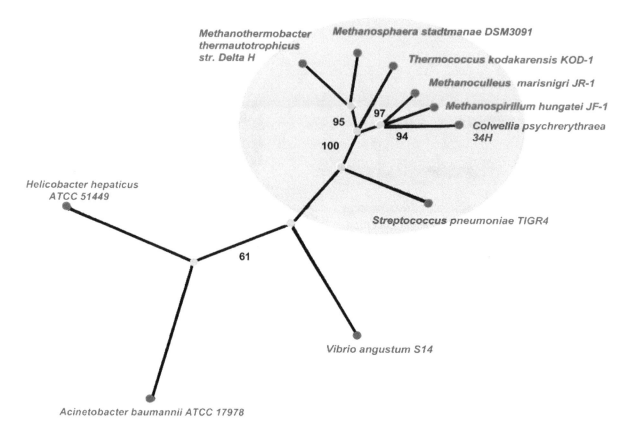

Figure 2. Phylogenetic tree of Cps4I, its archael and bacterial matches. The tree clearly depicts the grouping of *Streptococcus pneumonia* among archaeal sequences.

Table 2. Cps4I motif sequences.

Motif	Width	Consensus sequence
1	50	LIKPLGYLDFLQLLSNAFLVLTDSGGIQEEACTFGVPCVTLRYNTERPET
2	29	QEKPDCVLVQGDTNTVFAGALAAFKLQIP
3	15	GHVEAGLRSYDRYMP

Table 3. Cps4I domains and their functions.

Motifs	Matches with domains	Function of domains
MOTIF 1	WecB	Cell envelope biogenesis
	Epimerase_2	UPD-N-acetylmannosamine kinase activity
MOTIF 2	Epimerase_2	UPD-N-acetylmannosamine kinase activity
MOTIF 3	No significant results	

Our second HGT candidate is a gene for capsular protein and was detected in the pathogen *Streptococcus agalactiae*. *S. agalactiae* is the causative agent of a multitude of infections including sepsis (Maeland et al., 2005), meningitis, bacterimia (Férez et al., 1991) and osteoarticular infections (Gómez et al., 1995). The candidate capsular protein called NeuB (N-acetyl neuramic acid synthetase) is involved in the synthesis of

N-acetyl neuramic acid or sialic acid, which is displayed on the cell surface (Haft et al., 1994). In microbes it is antiphagocytic in nature and therefore weakens immune recognition to enhance pathogenecity (Haft et al., 1994).

MEME and MAST results showed three highly conserved motifs in NeuB and its archaeal counterparts (Table 4). These motifs correspond to a highly conserved and important domain 'NeuB' in the NeuB protein of *S*.

Table 4. NeuB motif sequences.

Motif	Width	Consensus sequence
1	50	VGYSDHTLGIYVPIAAVAMGACVIEKHFTLDRNMPGPDHKASLEPDEFRT
2	32	WKIPSGEITNYPYLRKIGRQQQPVILSTGMAT
3	50	RRSIVAKCDIQKGEIFSEDNLTVKRPGTGISPMYWDQWCGRQARRDYQED

Table 5. NeuB domains and their functions.

Motifs	Matches with domains	Function of domains
MOTIF 1	NeuB	Catalyses the direct formation of Neu5Ac (the most common sialic acid)
MOTIF 2	No significant results	
MOTIF 3	SAF: UxaA/GarD-like hexuronate dehydratases	Present in antifreeze proteins, flagellar FlgA proteins, and CpaB pilus proteins.

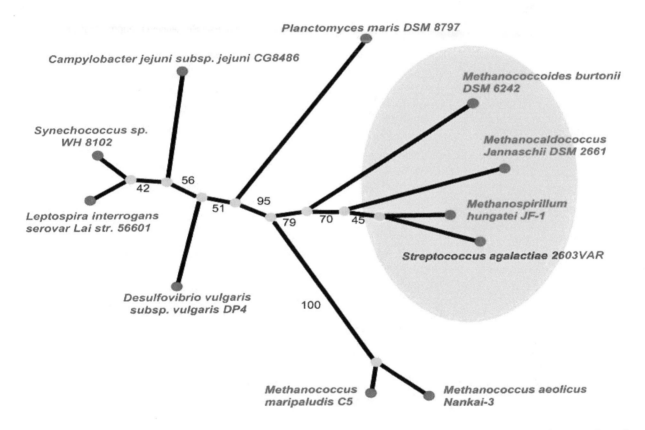

Figure 3. Phylogenetic tree of NeuB, its archael and bacterial matches. The tree clearly depicts the grouping of Streptococcus agalactiae among archaeal sequences.

agalactiae and in N-acylneuraminate-9-phosphate synthases of Methanococci (Table 5).

As the name of the domain 'NeuB' indicates, it is vital to the function of the protein NeuB. The closest match to the NeuB protein of *S. agalactiae* that was determined through phylogenetic analysis is N-acylneuraminate-9-phosphate synthase of *Methanospirillum hungatei JF-1* (Figure 3). As mentioned earlier, N-acylneuraminate-9-

phosphate synthase is categorized as an orphan protein and its function is not well understood in archaea (Wilson et al., 2005). Microarray experiments involving comparison of genomes of *S. agalactiae* and other streptococci revealed differences in the polysaccharides of the capsule as well as in several of the metabolic pathways and transport systems (http://www.innovations-report.com). Such a genetic diversity indicates a probable acquisition of genes horizontally.

Conclusion

The findings suggest that a sequential acquisition of archaeal genes is an important feature in the evolutionary history of bacteria. Our study depicted that the genes acquired by horizontal gene transfer from archaea are more involved in normal biosynthetic functions rather than in pathogenesis of bacteria. Apart from the good cases including capsule biosynthesis proteins, we identified genes involved in DNA regulatory or modify-cation functions. The important aspect of this research is the identification of the role of archaea as a reservoir of a variety of metabolic innovations for bacteria. Such metabolic innovations not only enable the bacteria to adapt to new environment but may also contribute to a better survival in or on the host.

ACKNOWLEDGEMENTS

This work is a part of an undergraduate thesis supported by the department of biosciences, COMSATS Institute of Information Technology. We are grateful to our super-visor, Dr. S. Habib Bokhari for his impetus guidance, to the Chairman of the department of biosciences, Dr. Raheel Qamar for providing us with the facilities to work on this project. We are also thankful to the 'development and maintenance teams' of all the free software tools utilized in this research.

REFERENCES

Altschul SF, Gish W, Miller W, Myers EW, Lipman DJ (1990). Basic local alignment search tool. J. Mol. Biol., 214: 1-8.

Astrid B, Wenke W, Ulrich S, Erich EW, Lothar L, Peter D, Werner R, Rüdiger H, Stephan H (2004). Domain-specific characteristics of the bifunctional key enzyme of sialic acid biosynthesis, UDP-N-acetylglucosamine 2-epimerase/N-acetylmannosamine kinase. Biochem. J., 384: 599-607.

Campbell RE, Mosimann SC, Tanner ME, Strynadka NC (2000). The structure of UDP-N-acetylglucosamine 2-epimerase reveals homology to phosphoglycosyl transferases. Biochemistry, 39(49): 14993-5001.

Chen LH, Yang J, Yu J, Yao ZJ, Sun LL, Shen Y, Jin Q (2005). VFDB: A reference database for bacterial virulence factors. Nucleic Acids Res., 33: 325-328.

Clamp M, Cuff J, Searle SM and Barton GJ (2004). The Jalview Java Alignment Editor. Bioinformatics, 20: 426-427.

Doolittle WF (1999). Phylogenetic classification and the universal tree. Sciences, 284: 2124-2129.

Eckburg PB, Lepp PW, Relman DA (2003). Archaea and their potential role in human disease (Mini Review). Infect. Immun., 71(2): 591-596.

Faguy DM (2003). Lateral Gene Transfer between Archaea and Escherichia coli is a contributor to the emergence of novel infectious disease. BMC Infect. Dis., 3(13): 1471-2334.

Férez A, Fajardo MT, Estellés MA, Moreno R, Esteban A, Martín C, Royo G (1991). Bacteremia caused by Streptococcus agalactiae in adults. Enfermedades Infecciosasy Microbiol. Clin., 9(6): 354-6.

Garcia-Vallve S, Romeu A, Palau J (2000). Horizontal Gene Transfer in Bacterial and Archaeal Complete Genomes. Genome Res., 10(11): 1719-1725

Gómez RN, Ferreiro JL, Willisch A, Muñoz LR, Formigo E, González MG (1995). Osteoarticular infections caused by Streptococcus agalactiae. Enfermedades Infecciosasy Microbiol. Clin., 13(2): 99-103.

Haft RF, Wessels MR (1994) Characterization of CMP-N-acetylneuraminic acid synthetase of group B streptococci. J. Bacteriol., 176(23): 7372-7374.

Jain R, Rivera MC, Lake JA (1999). Horizontal gene transfer among genomes: the complexity hypothesis. Proceedings Nat. Acad. Sci. USA. 96(7): 3801-3806.

Jeong HC, Ho YJ, Hey SK, Hwan G (2000). PhyloDraw: A phylogenetic tree drawing system. Bioinform., 16(11): 1056-1058.

Maeland JA, Bevanger L, Lyng RV (2005) Immunological markers of the R4 protein of Streptococcus agalactiae. Clinical and diagnostic laboratory immunol., 12(11): 1305-10.

Marchler BA, Bryant SH (2004). CD-Search: protein domain annotations on the fly. Nucleic Acids Res., 32: W327-331.

Mongodin EF, Hance IR, DeBoy RT, Gill SR, Daugherty S, Huber R, Fraser CM, Stetter K, Nelson KE (2005). Gene Transfer and Genome Plasticity in Thermotoga maritima, a Model Hyperthermophilic Species. J. Bacteriol., 187(14): 4935-4944.

Roche AM, King SJ, Weiser JN (2007) Live attenuated streptococcus pneumoniae strains induce serotype-independent mucosal and systemic protection in mice. Infect. Immun., 75(5): 2469-75.

Rossi M, Ciaramella M, Cannio R, Pisani FM, Moracci M, Bartolucci S (2003). Extremophiles. J. Bacteriol., 185(13): 3683-3689.

Thompson JD, Higgins DG, Gibson TJ (1994). CLUSTAL W: improving the sensitivity of progressive multiple sequence alignment through sequence weighting, positions-specific gap penalties and weight matrix choice. Nucleic Acids Res., 22: 4673-4680.

Wiezer A, Merkl R (2005). A comparative categorization of gene flux in diverse microbial species. Genomics. 86: 462-475.

Wilson GA, Bertrand N, Patel Y, Hughes JB, Feil EJ, Field D (2005) Orphans as taxonomically restricted and ecologically important genes. Microbiology., 151: 2499-2501.

Zhou CE, Smith J, Lam M, Zemla A, Dyer MD, Slezak T (2007). MvirDB-a microbial database of protein toxins, virulence factors and antibiotic resistance genes for bio-defence applications. Nucleic Acids Res., 35: 391-394.

## 12

Protein ligand interaction analysis an insilico potential drug target identification in diabetes mellitus and nephropathy

Satya vani Guttula[1]*, Allam Appa Rao[2], G. R. Sridhar[3] and M. S. Chakravarthy[4]

[1]Department, Biotechnology, Al-Ameer College of Engineering and IT, Visakhapatam, Andhra Pradesh, India.
[2]Jawaharlal Nehru Technological University, Kakinada, Andhra Pradesh, India.
[3]Endocrine and Diabetes Centre, Visakhapatnam, Andhra Pradesh, India
[4]Department of Marine Living Resources, Andhra University, Andhra Pradesh, India.

Diabetes mellitus is a multisystem disorder leading to hyperglycemia and other metabolic abnormalities leading to complications in many organs of the human body including the kidney. Oxidative stress induced by hyperglycemia can produce dysfunction of pancreatic beta-cells, as well as lead to various other forms of tissue damage in patients with diabetes mellitus. Therefore, it seems reasonable that antioxidants can play a role in the management of diabetic nephropathy. Brain-derived neurotrophic factor (BDNF), which plays a role in human glucose metabolism, has been implicated in the pathogenesis of Alzheimer's disease and depression, which co-exist with type II diabetes. Ras homolog gene is one of the genes associated with Diabetic nephropathy. Three Dimensional structures of the proteins RHOD, BDNF were taken from the PDB databank and the ligands, Astaxanthin, Beta carotene were downloaded from Ligand database. Protein Ligand Docking was done for the target proteins and antioxidant ligands. BDNF and Astaxanthin-Docking Energy range: Emin = -225.39, Emax = -74.12, BDNF and β-carotene- Docking Energy range: Emin = -220.68, Emax = -69.21, RHOD and Astaxanthin Docking Energy range: Emin = -247.72, Emax = -88.39, Rhod and β-carotene Docking Energy range: Emin = -232.07, Emax = -86.55. In docking the lowest minimum energy has the highest affinity. It is concluded that astaxanthin docking score when compared with β-carotene is lowest so, it has the highest affinity with the target proteins. In conclusion, Astaxanthin has powerful antioxidant properties, with the potential to be used in reducing glucose toxicity.

Key words: Diabetes mellitus, antioxidants, docking, Astaxanthin.

INTRODUCTION

In the area of molecular modeling, docking is a method which predicts the preferred orientation of one molecule to a second (Lengauer et al., 1996).

Knowledge of the preferred orientation in turn may be used to predict the strength of association or binding affinity between two molecules using scoring functions. Docking is frequently used to predict the binding orientation of small molecule drug candidates to their protein targets in order to in turn predict the affinity and activity of the small molecule. Hence docking plays an important role in the rational design of drugs. Given the biological and pharmaceutical significance of molecular docking, considerable efforts have been directed toward improving the methods.

Hex is an interactive molecular graphics program for calculating and displaying feasible docking modes of pairs of protein and DNA molecules. Hex calculates protein-ligand docking, assuming the ligand is rigid, and it can superpose pairs of molecules using only knowledge of their 3D shapes. It is still the only docking and superposition program to use spherical polar Fourier correlations to accelerate the calculations, and it is one of the few docking programs which has built-in graphics to view the results (Ritchie et al., 2003).

Oxidative stress is thought to contribute to the development of a wide range of diseases including the pathologies caused by diabetes (Davi et al., 2005). Oxidative stress and oxidative damage to tissues are common end points of chronic diseases, such as atherosclerosis, diabetes, and rheumatoid arthritis. Increased oxidative stress has a primary role in the pathogenesis of diabetic complications and it is a secondary indicator of end-stage tissue damage in diabetes. The increase in glycoxidation and lipoxidation products in plasma and tissue proteins suggests that oxidative stress is increased in diabetes. Elevated levels of oxidizable substrates may also explain the increase in glycoxidation and lipoxidation products in tissue proteins, without the necessity of invoking an increase in oxidative stress.

Diabetes mellitus is characterized by oxidative stress, which in turn determines endothelial dysfunction. Oxidative stress is caused by an imbalance between the production of reactive oxygen and a biological system's ability to readily detoxify the reactive intermediates or easily repair the resulting damage. All forms of life maintain a reducing environment within their cells. This reducing environment is preserved by enzymes that maintain the reduced state through a constant input of metabolic energy. Disturbances in this normal redox state can cause toxic effects through the production of peroxides and free radicals that damage all components of the cell, including proteins, lipids, and DNA.

In chemical terms, oxidative stress is a large rise in the cellular reduction potential, or a large decrease in the reducing capacity of the cellular redox couples, such as glutathione (Schafer et al., 2001). The effects of oxidative stress depend upon the size of these changes, with a cell being able to overcome small perturbations and regain its original state. However, more severe oxidative stress can cause cell death and even moderate oxidation can trigger apoptosis, while more intense stresses may cause necrosis (Lennon et al., 1991).

Early research on the role of antioxidants in biology focused on their use in preventing the oxidation of unsaturated fats, which is the cause of rancidity (German et al., 1999). Antioxidant activity could be measured simply by placing the fat in a closed container with oxygen and measuring the rate of oxygen consumption. However, it was the identification of vitamins A, C, and E as antioxidants that revolutionized the field and led to the realization of the importance of antioxidants in the biochemistry of living organisms (Knight et al., 1998).

Astaxanthin's potent antioxidant activity may be beneficial in cardiovascular, immune, anti-inflammatory, and neurodegenerative diseases. Astaxanthin is a carotenoid that is found in marine animals and vegetables. Several previous studies have demonstrated that AST exhibits a wide variety of biological activities including antioxidant, antitumor, and anti-*Helicobacter pylori* effects (Ohgami et al., 2003).

Astaxanthin has 100-500 times the antioxidant capacity of Vitamin E and 10 times the antioxidant capacity of beta-carotene. Many laboratory studies also indicate astaxanthin is a stronger antioxidant than lutein, lycopene and tocotrienols.

Oxidative stress induced by hyperglycemia possibly causes the dysfunction of pancreatic beta-cells and various forms of tissue damage in patients with diabetes mellitus. Astaxanthin, a carotenoid of marine microalgae, is reported as a strong anti-oxidant inhibiting lipid peroxidation and scavenging reactive oxygen species. Astaxanthin can exert beneficial effects in diabetes, with preservation of beta-cell function. This finding suggests that anti-oxidants may be potentially useful for reducing glucose toxicity (Uchiyama et al., 2002).

β-carotene is an organic compound a terpenoid, a red-orange pigment abundant in plants and fruits. As a carotene with β-rings at both ends, it is the most common form of carotene. It is a precursor (inactive form) of vitamin A being highly conjugated, it is deeply colored, and as a hydrocarbon lacking functional groups, it is very lipophilic (Susan 1998).

The active site of an enzyme contains the catalytic and binding sites. The structure and chemical properties of the active site allow the recognition and binding of the substrate.

Background

Diabetes mellitus is an increasingly common metabolic disorder that affects both large vessels (macrovessels) and small vessels (microvessels) of the body (Sridhar and Rao, 2003). Microvascular involvement of the kidney results in diabetic nephropathy (Satyavani et al., 2010). Both genetic and metabolic causes including oxidative stress are implicated in the pathogenesis of the disease and its complications. Increased levels of oxidative stress indicators occur in individuals with diabetic complications, implying antioxidants can be useful in their prevention and management.

Astaxanthin, a carotenoid of marine microalgae, is reported as a strong anti-oxidant inhibiting lipid peroxidation and scavenging reactive oxygen species. Astaxanthin is a fat-soluble, oxygenated pigment called a xanthophyll and a member of the carotenoid family. It has a unique molecular structure that gives it powerful antioxidant function. It is synthesized by plants and algae, and distributed in marine seafood. Astaxanthin can exert beneficial effects in diabetes, with preservation of beta-cell function.

MATERIALS AND METHODS

Hex calculates protein-ligand docking, assuming the ligand is rigid, and it can superpose pairs of molecules using only knowledge of their 3D shapes. Hex is still the only docking and superpostion

Protein ligand interaction analysis an insilico potential drug target identification in diabetes mellitus and nephropathy

83

Table 1. Docking result energy values in tabular format.

S/No.	Protein	Ligand	Energy range: Emin	Energy range: Emax
1	BDNF	AXT	-225.39	-74.12
2	BDNF	BCR	-220.68	-69.21
3	RHOD	AXT	-247.72	-88.39
4	RHOD	BCR	-232.07	-86.55

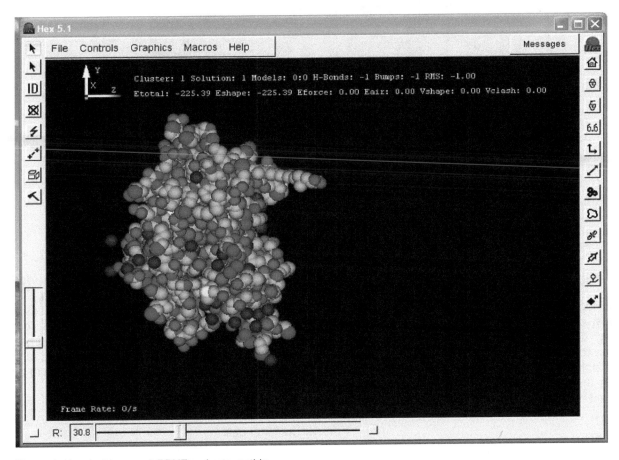

Figure 1. Hex docking result BDNF and astaxanthin.

program to use spherical polar Fourier (SPF) correlations to accelerate the calculations, and its still one of the few docking programs which has built-in graphics to view the results.

Hex can also calculate Protein-Ligand Docking, assuming the ligand is rigid, and it can superpose pairs of molecules using only knowledge of their 3D shapes (Ritchie et al., 2003). It uses Spherical Polar Fourier (SPF) correlations to accelerate the calculations and its one of the few docking programs which has built in graphics to view the result (Ritchie et al., 2000). Hex 5.1 is downloaded on to the system and the molecular Interphase tool is opened.

The PDB (Protein Data Bank) is the single world wide archive of Structural data of Biological macromolecules, established in Brookhaven National Laboratories (BNL) in 1971. It contains Structural information of the macromolecules determined by X-ray crystallographic, NMR methods. The three dimensional structure of the protein BDNF: Brain derieved neurofactor (1BND) and RHOD: Ras homolog gene, memberD (1JIL), are downloaded from the

protein databank website and the Antioxidant ligands Astaxanthin, β-carotene from Ligand Database opened onto the HEX molecular Interface tool. The proteins Brain derieved neurofactor (BDNF) and RHOD: Ras homolog gene member (1JIL), were docked with Astaxanthin and β-carotene. The HEX molecular Interface tool Figure displayed in the results.

RESULTS

Docking result of BDNF and AXT

The Protein- Ligand interaction plays a significant role in structural based drug designing.The proteins were docked with Astaxanthin, B- carotene and the energy values obtained are shown in Table 1, Figures 1 and 2.

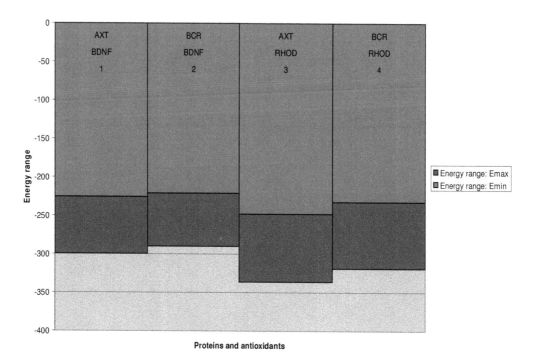

Figure 2. Docking result energy values in graphical format.

Energy range: Emin = -225.39, Emax = -74.12

The docking results are ordered by energy values and the lowest energy docking solution is the seed member for drug design. Lowest energy orientation is the prediction for target (Ritchie, 2002). Using the HEX 5.1 docking software, depending on the energy values I conclude that astaxanthin is the best and the powerful antioxidant to treat Diabetic nephropathy.

DISCUSSION

In this study we have focused on BDNF: Brain-derived neurotrophic factor and RHOD: Ras homolog gene family; proteins from the list of biomarkers of diabetic nephropathy are selected and docked with the antioxidant ligands Astaxanthin and β-carotene. It is observed that the docking energy for Astaxanthin is low when compared with β-carotene. In conclusion, Astaxanthin has powerful antioxidant properties, with the potential to be used in reducing glucose toxicity.

Future works

In future research works, successful re-analysis of the samples to determine appropriate genes, it would be very helpful to assay more individuals with known material backgrounds. All the 46 genes identified as the biomarkers for Diabetic nephropathy are further studied in detail of each protein and checked for any drug molecule or docked with the same antioxidants and results are compared. ADME/T (Absorption, Distribution, Metabolism, Excretion / Toxicity) properties of these compounds can be calculated using the commercial ADME/T tools available thus reducing the time and cost in drug discovery process. These results are studied further in animal models and their response to the drug is monitored.

REFERENCES

Davi G, Falco A, Patrono C (2005). Lipid peroxidation in diabetes mellitus. Antioxidants Redox Sig., 7(1–2): 256–268.

German J (1999). Food processing and lipid oxidation. Adv. Exp. Med. Biol., l459: 23–50.

Knight J (1998). Free radicals: Their history and current status in aging and disease. Ann. Clin. Lab. Sci., 28(6): 331–346.

Lengauer T, Rarey M (1996). Computational methods for biomolecular docking. Curr. Opin. Struct. Biol., 6(3): 402-406.

Lennon SV, Martin SJ, Cotter TG (1991). Dose-dependent induction of apoptosis in human tumour cell lines by widely diverging stimuli. Cell Proliferation, 24(2): 203-214.

Ohgami K, Shiratori K, Kotake S, Nishida T, Mizuki N, Yazawa K, Ohno S (2003). Effects of astaxanthin on lipopolysaccharide-induced inflammation in vitro and in vivo. Invest. Ophthalmol. Visual Sci., 44(6): 2694-2701.

Ritchie DW, Kemp GJL (2000). Protein Docking Using Spherical Polar Fourier Correlations. PROTEINS: Struct. Funct. Genet., 39: 178-194.

Ritchie DW (2003) Evaluation of Protein Docking Predictions Using Hex 3.1 in CAPRI Rounds 1 and 2. PROTEINS: Struct. Funct. Genet., 52(1): 98-106.

SatyaVani G, Allam AR, Sridhar GR, Chakravarthy MS, Kunjum N, Paturi VR (2010). Cluster analysis and phylogenetic relationship in biomarker identification of type 2 diabetes and nephropathy. Int. J. Diabetes Dev. Ctries., 30(1): 52–56. Jan–Mar.

Schafer FQ, Buettner GR (2001). Redox environment of the cell as viewed through the redox state of the glutathione disulfide/glutathione couple. Free Radic. Biol., 30(11): 1191-1212.

Sridhar GR, Rao PV (2003). Prevalence of diabetes among rural Indians. In Das S (ed) Medicine Update (2003). Assoc. Phys. India Mumbai, 13: 370-373.

Susan DVA (1998). Vitamin A in Kirk-Othmer Encyclopedia of Chemical Technology. New York: John Wiley, pp. 99-107.

Uchiyama K, Naito Y, Hasegawa G, Nakamura N, Takahashi J, Yoshikawa T (2002). Astaxanthin protects beta-cells against glucose toxicity in diabetic db/db mice. Redox Rep., 7(5): 290-293.

## 13

Polymorphisms in the transcription factor binding sites of host genes influences evolutionary susceptibility to falciparum malaria

Tabish Qidwai[1], Prabhash K. Pandey[2], Sangram Singh[2] and Farrukh Jamal[2]*

[1]Department of Biochemistry, University of Allahabad, Allahabad, U. P., India.
[2]Department of Biochemistry, Dr. Ram Manohar Lohia Avadh University, Faizabad-224001, U.P., India.

Gene expression at the level of transcription is regulated by a set of transcription factors (TFs) that recognizes *cis* elements. We accessed the human promoters from eukaryotic promoter database. These sequences have been run in P-match tool. MEME software has been used for detection of conserved sequences in the promoter region. All the predicted known TFs and their binding sites along with weight matrices were collected from TRANSFAC database under vertebrate TFs category. P-match tool combines pattern matching and weight matrix approaches thus providing higher accuracy of recognition than each of the methods alone. P-Match is closely interconnected with the TRANSFAC® database. Using results of extensive tests of recognition accuracy, we selected three sets of optimized cut-off values that minimize either false negatives or false positives, or the sum of both errors. In this report, we focus on those polymorphisms of transcription factor binding sites (TFBS) in the regulatory region of host genes and hypothesize that these variation increases the susceptibility/resistance to a particular disease by alteration of gene product in the cell. Therefore, we have concluded that 124 promoter polymorphisms in the 9 genes involved in malaria pathogenesis play important role in susceptibility to falciparum malaria.

Key words: Single-nucleotide polymorphism (SNP), transcription factors, transcription factors binding sites, evolution, infectious diseases.

INTRODUCTION

Although, human cells have the same set of genome but cellular differentiation gives rise to different types of cells and tissues. The formation of different types of tissues from the same genetic material requires coordinated and controlled expression of the genes in the genome. This process involves interplay of a large number of factors involved in gene expression including enhancers, silencers and gene methylation (Frisch et al., 2002; Robertson et al., 2002; Werner, 1999).

Specific nuclear factors called transcription factors binds with selected DNA sequences called transcription factor binding site. The expression of a gene is primarily regulated by transcription factors that interact with regulatory *cis*-elements on DNA sequences. The identification of functional regulatory elements can be done by computer searching using software (s) which can predict TF binding sites using position weight matrices (PWMs) that represent positional base frequencies of collected experimentally determined transcription factor binding sites (TFBS) (Murakami et al., 2004).

Promoter sequences are generally present upstream from the transcription start site but in some cases, it overlaps with first exon of the gene. So promoters are considered as the processors of transcriptional regulation. TF binding site detection is an important tool for the study of transcriptional regulation of gene expression. Zhu et al. (2002) reported the computational modeling of promoter organization as a tool to study the transcriptional regulation. Pipel et al. (2001) used the computational approaches based on DNA array data to study genome wide transcriptional regulation.

*Corresponding author. E-mail: farrukhrmlau@gmail.com, journal.farrukh@gmail.com.

The human genome has more than 2500 genes, which are regulated spatially, temporally and show dramatic diversity (Xueping et al., 2006). All these genes are controlled by less than 2000 transcription factors. Individual genes have binding site for multiple transcription factors. These transcriptional factors bind and work in combination to control the individual genes. This is termed as combinatorial gene regulation, a common process of gene regulation in higher eukaryotes including humans. Xeuping et al. (2006) reported the computational analysis of tissue specific combinatorial gene regulation. They described the interaction of known human TF to their binding sites and predicted the TF pairs that may co-regulate the gene expression. Wasserman and Fickett (1998) employed the concept of a regulatory module (cluster of TFBS) to predict muscle- and liver-specific regulatory regions. In more complex systems, the functional transcription factor binding sites within promoters are organized hierarchically (Klingenhoff et al., 1999, 2002; Krivan and Wasserman, 2001).

In this paper, we used P- match tool for identification of transcription factor binding sites and regulatory analysis of variations in enhancers (RAVEN) tool to predict the polymorphisms in the enhancer region of genes involved in malaria pathogenesis. In addition, the promoters of housekeeping genes (constitutive expression) and regulatory genes have been compared and percent conservation has been calculated to understand their significance during the course of evolution.

METHODOLOGY

Prediction of transcription factor binding sites in human promoters

We accessed the human promoters from eukaryotic promoter database. Promoter sequences are taken from -1000 to +100. These sequences have been run in P-match tool. All the predicted known TFs and their binding sites along with weight matrices were collected from TRANSFAC database (www.gene-regulation.de) under vertebrate TFs category. P-match tool combines pattern matching and weight matrix approaches thus providing higher accuracy of recognition than each of the methods alone. P-Match is closely interconnected with the TRANSFAC® database. In particular, P-match uses the matrix library as well as sets of aligned known TF-binding sites collected in TRANSFAC® and therefore provides the possibility to search for a large variety of different TF binding sites. Using results of extensive tests of recognition accuracy, we selected three sets of optimized cut-off values that minimize either false negatives or false positives, or the sum of both errors. A public version of the P-Match tool is available at http://www.pubmedcentral.nih.gov/redirect3.cgi?&&.

Prediction of conserved motifs in human promoters

MEME software has been used for detection of conserved sequences in the promoter region. We accessed the promoter sequences of different organisms from transcription regulatory element database (TRED) and NCBI (National Center for Biotechnology Information). A set of promoter sequences of different organisms run through MEME software.

Prediction of DNA sequence variation in transcription factor binding sites

We used RAVEN (Regulatory Analysis of Variations in Enhancers) web tool for prediction of SNPs extending in the region -3000 to 500 base pairs, affecting the TFBS (Identification of transcription factor binding sites). RAVEN system is a web tool and is available at http://www.cisreg.ca. According to the keywords entered, search engine gives a list of human gene. By clicking the gene of interest, genome location of gene is displayed by the software. Selection of the genomic regions from -3000 to 500 bp gives results in graphical and in tabulated forms. In the result view, we have option for analysis of SNPs with a particular transcription factor or the entire transcription factor, JASPAR, an open-access database for eukaryotic transcription factor binding profiles.

RESULTS

Table 1 shows TF, their binding site and weight matrices in TRANSFAC database. We have accessed some promoter sequences from NCBI and formed a set of promoters for the same gene in different organisms. These promoter sequences were analyzed through MEME software and results are shown in Table 3. Predicted polymorphisms in transcription factor binding sites are given in Table 2. Table 4 shows comparison of conservation patterns in the promoter region of some genes.

DISCUSSION

The aim of this study was to predict the role of specific sequences involved in the regulation of gene expression of host genes involved in malaria pathogenesis. Interaction of transcription factor to transcription factor binding site mediate the transcriptional response to specific signal transduction pathways, cell type-specific expression and events central to developmental regulation (Stormo, 2000). Several transcription factor binding sites in host genes are present (Table 1). A given promoter module may show a robust stimulus specific response in one tissue but in a second cell type, may not be functional. This can result, for example, from a different complement or concentration of specific transcription factors or from selective signaling events further upstream in an activation pathway. Promoter modules can also exhibit cooperative protein binding and often include one binding element that represents a poor binding site for a specific transcription factor. Through cooperative effects, the stronger binding protein partner can stabilize the binding of the weaker partner, but the loss of either binding site abolishes its function. This highlights an important aspect of transcriptional regulation, namely, that a weak binding site embedded in the correct context can be functionally as important as a

Table 1. Showing TF their binding site and weight matrices in TRANSFAC-DATABASE.

Matrix identifier	Position (strand)	Core match	Matrix match	Sequence (always the (+)- strand is shown)	Factor name
IL-1B (Interleukin-1 beta)					
V$NFKB_Q6	108 (-)	1.000	0.976	ttggaaaGTCCCag	NF-kappaB
V$NFKB_C	109 (-)	1.000	0.997	tggaaaGTCCCa	NF-kappaB
V$CREL_01	110 (-)	1.000	0.990	GGAAAgtccc	c-Rel
V$NFKAPPAB_01	110 (-)	0.986	0.992	ggaaaGTCCC	NF-kappaB
V$HAND1E47_01	792 (-)	1.000	0.961	gtttCCAGAccctgga	Hand1/E47
V$OCT1_Q6	1306 (+)	0.888	0.912	actcatGGAAAtgat	Oct-1
V$AP1_Q4	1706 (+)	1.000	0.990	agTGACTcaag	AP-1
V$CREB_Q2	2055 (-)	1.000	0.983	tgttaCGTCAgg	CREB
V$CREBP1_Q2	2055 (-)	1.000	0.979	tgttaCGTCAgg	CRE-BP1
V$VBP_01	2056 (+)	1.000	0.974	gTTACGtcag	VBP
V$AP1_Q4	2165 (-)	1.000	0.991	gatgAGTCAct	AP-1
V$EVI1_04	2892 (+)	0.842	0.874	agaaaagaaAAGAAa	Evi-1
V$OCT1_Q6	3007 (-)	1.000	0.894	ttaaTTTGCaaagtg	Oct-1
V$COMP1_01	4580 (+)	1.000	0.838	cacaacGATTGtcaggaaaacaat	COMP1
V$OCT1_Q6	4605 (-)	1.000	0.944	cataTTTGCatggtg	Oct-1
IL-1A (Interleukin-1 alpha)					
V$HAND1E47_01	390 (+)	1.000	0.962	cctggtgTCTGGatcc	Hand1/E47
V$NKX25_01	780 (+)	1.000	1.000	tcAAGTG	Nkx2-5
V$SOX9_B1	861 (+)	1.000	0.992	aaggaACAATggca	SOX-9
V$AP1_Q4	929 (-)	1.000	0.982	cttcAGTCAcc	AP-1
V$CREL_01	1097 (-)	1.000	0.982	GGAAAgaccc	c-Rel
V$AP1_Q4	1565 (+)	1.000	0.996	agTGACTcatt	AP-1
V$HNF1_C	1947 (-)	0.829	0.862	ttggggaattaTTTACa	HNF-1
V$HNF1_C	1949 (+)	0.771	0.858	gGGGAAttatttacaac	HNF-1
V$AP1_Q4	2206 (+)	1.000	0.982	agTGACTgaag	AP-1
V$OCT1_Q6	2219 (-)	0.883	0.915	atcaTTAGCattgtc	Oct-1
V$NKX25_01	2771 (+)	1.000	1.000	tcAAGTG	Nkx2-5
IL1R1 (Interleukin-1 receptor-1)					
V$NKX25_01	115 (-)	1.000	1.000	CACTTga	Nkx2-5
V$OCT1_Q6	196 (-)	0.909	0.892	cccaTTTACatgggt	Oct-1
V$AP1_Q4	441 (+)	1.000	0.991	ggTGACTaatc	AP-1
V$FOXD3_01	1225 (-)	1.000	0.966	aaacaAACAAac	FOXD3
V$FOXD3_01	1229 (-)	1.000	0.966	aaacaAACAAac	FOXD3
V$FOXD3_01	1233 (-)	1.000	0.966	aaacaAACAAac	FOXD3
V$FOXD3_01	1237 (-)	1.000	0.966	aaacaAACAAac	FOXD3
V$FOXD3_01	1241 (-)	1.000	0.966	aaacaAACAAac	FOXD3
V$FOXD3_01	1245 (-)	1.000	0.966	aaacaAACAAac	FOXD3
V$FOXD3_01	1249 (-)	1.000	0.966	aaacaAACAAac	FOXD3
V$HNF1_01	1504 (+)	1.000	0.933	ggTTAATatttggga	HNF-1
V$CREL_01	2356 (+)	0.973	0.983	ggggaATTCC	c-Rel
V$COMP1_01	2926 (+)	1.000	0.805	ggatgtGATTGtcacataaagccg	COMP1
V$ELK1_02	2975 (+)	1.000	0.990	gcctcCGGAAgtgg	Elk-1
V$CETS1P54_01	2978 (+)	1.000	0.995	tCCGGAagtg	c-Ets-1(p54)
V$PAX4_01	3465 (-)	0.881	0.835	tcatccccaccCCTCAactct	Pax-4
V$HAND1E47_01	3563 (-)	1.000	0.963	atctCCAGAccccagt	Hand1/E47
V$COMP1_01	4086 (+)	0.856	0.801	tggaagAATTGacttccagaccca	COMP1
V$HAND1E47_01	4097 (-)	1.000	0.970	acttCCAGAcccagga	Hand1/E47

Polymorphisms in the transcription factor binding sites of host genes influences evolutionary susceptibility to falciparum malaria

89

Table 1. Contd.

V$MYOD_01	4271 (+)	1.000	0.971	ggtCAGGTgctg	MyoD
V$CDPCR1_01	5066 (+)	0.929	0.925	aATTGAtggg	CDP CR1
V$COMP1_01	5192 (+)	0.786	0.802	gttattGATGGccattaaaaggcc	COMP1
V$CDPCR1_01	5194 (+)	0.929	0.929	tATTGAtggc	CDP CR1
V$USF_C	5604 (+)	1.000	1.000	cCACGTgc	USF

IL1RN (Interleukin-1 receptor antagonist)

V$COMP1_01	467 (-)	0.914	0.801	agcctccttttgcCAATGttgcaa	COMP1
V$OCT1_Q6	822 (+)	1.000	0.951	gaaaatGCAAAttga	Oct-1
V$PAX4_01	907 (-)	0.979	0.842	tctgccccaagCCTGAggccc	Pax-4
V$PAX6_01	1812 (-)	0.792	0.845	aaatagtcaagCTTAAagaag	Pax-6
V$EVI1_06	1914 (+)	1.000	1.000	ACAAGataa	Evi-1
V$OCT1_06	2144 (+)	0.982	0.971	ctaatTGAGAtgta	Oct-1
V$COMP1_01	2175 (-)	0.842	1.000	gctttttgtatgtCAATCgtacct	COMP1
V$ELK1_01	2542 (+)	0.955	1.000	gtgacaGGAAGtgcag	Elk-1
V$EVI1_04	2594 (+)	0.842	0.862	agttatgagAAGTTa	Evi-1
V$PAX4_01	2749 (+)	0.979	0.857	tggatTCAGGagtcctcagtt	Pax-4
V$GATA3_03	3264 (+)	0.981	0.982	acaGATATta	GATA-3
V$HAND1E47_01	3454 (+)	1.000	0.961	agctgagTCTGGaagc	Hand1/E47
V$IK1_01	4305 (+)	1.000	0.989	acctGGGAAtgcc	Ik-1
V$COMP1_01	4326 (+)	1.000	0.803	tgtgctGATTGacttgtagtccc	COMP1
V$HNF1_C	4444 (+)	0.942	0.852	gGCTAAtacttaaataa	HNF-1
V$ELK1_01	4886 (+)	1.000	0.922	agaacaGGAAGtgaag	Elk-1
V$CREL_01	4954 (+)	1.000	1.000	ggggcTTTCC	c-Rel
V$OCT1_Q6	5109 (+)	1.000	0.891	ccttctGCAAAtgag	Oct-1
V$ELK1_02	5296 (-)	1.000	0.987	atgcTTCCGgtgag	Elk-1
V$HNF4_01	5743 (-)	1.000	0.931	acaaggcCTTTGcccttgc	HNF-4
V$AP1_Q4	6194 (-)	1.000	0.995	cctgAGTCAcc	AP-1
V$VMYB_01	741 (+)	1.000	0.960	attAACGGct	v-Myb
V$HNF1_C	938 (-)	0.771	0.843	ttggccattcaTTCCCc	HNF-1
V$PAX4_01	1038 (-)	1.000	0.847	ggaaggcaaggCATGAaccca	Pax-4
V$ELK1_02	1355 (-)	1.000	0.991	cgacTTCCGgcctc	Elk-1
V$CETS1P54_01	1356 (-)	1.000	0.995	gactTCCGGc	c-Ets-1(p54)
V$HAND1E47_01	1386 (-)	1.000	0.965	agttCCAGAttcctgt	Hand1/E47
V$OCT1_Q6	1472 (-)	0.893	0.922	ttgaTTTTCattcac	Oct-1
V$NKX25_01	1555 (+)	1.000	1.000	tcAAGTG	Nkx2-5
V$FOXJ2_02	1775 (-)	1.000	0.970	caaaatATTATtgg	FOXJ2
V$GRE_C	2666 (+)	0.978	0.951	ggcacaggatGTCCTg	GR
V$VMAF_01	2709 (+)	1.000	0.896	aactGCTGAcgttggagct	v-Maf
V$PAX5_01	2813 (-)	0.988	0.911	tttctcgctatgctgCCCTGccctttgc	BSAP
V$NKX25_01	3229 (-)	1.000	1.000	CACTTga	Nkx2-5
V$PAX4_01	3442 (+)	0.979	0.847	gcaggTCAGGggtgcctgcca	Pax-4
V$PAX6_01	4255 (+)	0.842	0.856	cccctTCATGgttgacttcag	Pax-6
V$NKX25_01	4738 (-)	1.000	1.000	CACTTga	Nkx2-5
V$NKX25_01	5096 (+)	1.000	1.000	tcAAGTG	Nkx2-5
V$HNF1_C	5363 (-)	1.000	0.884	atagcaactcaTTAACa	HNF-1
V$NFY_Q6	5559 (-)	1.000	0.988	gttATTGGtta	NF-Y
V$NKX25_01	6048 (-)	1.000	1.000	CACTTga	Nkx2-5
V$OCT1_Q6	6065 (+)	1.000	0.903	agcagtGCAAAtaat	Oct-1
V$OCT1_Q6	6115 (+)	0.893	0.926	cagaatGAAAAtcag	Oct-1
V$COMP1_01	6826 (-)	1.000	0.823	tatgctttctagaCAATCttagcc	COMP1
V$COMP1_01	7233 (-)	1.000	0.818	tggaactcgtggcCAATCttcctg	COMP1

Table 1. Contd.

V$OCT1_Q6	7977 (+)	0.909	0.906	ggttatGTAAAttcc	Oct-1
V$ELK1_01	8082 (-)	1.000	0.931	gtgggCTTCCtgtgtt	Elk-1
V$HNF1_C	8094 (+)	0.853	0.841	tGTTATttaatgaaccg	HNF-1
V$HNF4_01	8287 (-)	1.000	0.924	atttgtgCTTTGttcttca	HNF-4
V$HNF4_01	9432 (+)	0.915	0.904	cactggcTAAAGatcaaaa	HNF-4
II-3 (Interleukin-5)					
V$PAX4_01	355 (-)	0.979	0.833	tgccactcactCCTGAccctg	Pax-4
V$HAND1E47_01	696 (+)	1.000	0.962	ggctgtgTCTGGctgt	Hand1/E47
V$CREL_01	815 (-)	1.000	0.987	GGAAAaccca	c-Rel
V$HNF4_01	975 (-)	0.883	0.896	ctatgtcCTTTCtcccccca	HNF-4
V$USF_C	1056 (-)	1.000	1.000	gcACGTGg	USF
V$PAX4_01	1348 (+)	0.986	0.881	tgaggTCAAGagtttgagacc	Pax-4
V$PAX4_01	1470 (-)	0.986	0.837	cacaaaaatcgCTTGAaccca	Pax-4
V$SOX9_B1	1764 (-)	1.000	0.995	acccATTGTtccct	SOX-9
V$CREL_01	1808 (+)	1.000	1.000	ggggaTTTCC	c-Rel
V$AP1_Q4	2124 (+)	1.000	0.988	ggTGACTgagc	AP-1
V$CREL_01	2194 (-)	1.000	0.989	GGAAAatccc	c-Rel
V$VMAF_01	2317 (+)	1.000	0.892	cactGCTGAcaaagggacc	v-Maf
V$EVI1_04	2453 (+)	0.842	0.823	taataaaatAAAATa	Evi-1
V$HNF4_01	3152 (-)	1.000	0.923	gcaggtaCTTTGacccgga	HNF-4
V$PAX4_01	3940 (-)	1.000	0.847	gagcaagaaccCATGAgtgcc	Pax-4
V$PAX4_01	4248 (-)	0.788	0.833	ggcccagcacgGGTGAgggcg	Pax-4
V$COMP1_01	4950 (+)	1.000	0.832	gccctgGATTGaggccaacagatg	COMP1
V$AP1_Q4	5562 (+)	1.000	0.987	agTGACTgagg	AP-1
V$ARP1_01	6117 (-)	1.000	0.927	tcggtcCAAGGgctca	ARP-1
V$MYOD_01	7355 (-)	1.000	0.992	caccACCTGtct	MyoD
V$PAX4_01	9156 (-)	0.986	0.846	ctttctcctccCTTGAcctca	Pax-4
IL-5 (Interleukin-5)					
V$PAX4_01	867 (-)	0.986	0.837	caggagaatcgCTTGAaccca	Pax-4
V$OCT1_Q6	1057 (-)	0.883	0.903	ttcaTTAGCataagg	Oct-1
V$HNF1_C	1400 (+)	0.853	0.862	tGTTATttattcaatta	HNF-1
V$FOXD3_01	1764 (+)	1.000	0.992	aaTTGTTtattt	FOXD3
V$HFH1_01	1764 (+)	1.000	0.997	aattGTTTAttt	HFH-1
V$PAX4_01	2013 (+)	0.979	0.877	cgaggTCAGGagtttgagacc	Pax-4
V$CP2_01	2594 (-)	0.961	0.976	CTGGAtagggc	CP2
V$HNF1_C	2897 (+)	0.852	0.904	aGTTAGttatttaacaa	HNF-1
V$CDPCR1_01	2958 (-)	1.000	0.934	gagaTCGATt	CDP CR1
V$HNF1_01	3179 (-)	1.000	0.933	aaacaatcATTAAct	HNF-1
V$HNF3B_01	3209 (+)	1.000	0.966	attatTATTTattta	HNF-3beta
V$FOXD3_01	3211 (+)	0.948	0.955	taTTATTtattt	FOXD3
V$STAF_02	3496 (+)	0.938	0.926	ctgACCCAtcatgcctcgccg	Staf
V$SOX9_B1	3617 (-)	1.000	0.990	tcccATTGTtaaca	SOX-9
V$CEBP_C	3670 (-)	0.985	0.953	ggtacATTACtaaactcc	C/EBP
V$HNF4_01	3944 (+)	0.915	0.891	acagggaTAAAGttccttt	HNF-4
V$EVI1_04	3955 (-)	0.772	0.844	gTTCCTttcttatca	Evi-1
V$HNF1_C	4219 (-)	1.000	0.871	gattaaaatcaTTAACt	HNF-1
V$HNF1_01	4221 (-)	1.000	0.936	ttaaaatcATTAAct	HNF-1
V$FOXJ2_02	4793 (-)	1.000	0.925	tgaaatATTATtca	FOXJ2
V$FOXD3_01	5151 (-)	0.996	0.956	aattaAACATtt	FOXD3
V$FOXD3_01	5365 (+)	1.000	0.960	ttTTGTTtgttt	FOXD3

Table 1. Contd.

V$FOXD3_01	5369 (+)	1.000	0.966	gtTTGTTtgttt	FOXD3
V$FOXD3_01	5373 (+)	1.000	0.966	gtTTGTTtgttt	FOXD3
V$RFX1_01	5587 (+)	1.000	0.989	gtgtcacctgGCAACca	RFX1
V$HNF4_01	6145 (-)	1.000	0.908	aagagcaCTTTGaccaagc	HNF-4
V$NKX25_01	6266 (+)	1.000	1.000	tcAAGTG	Nkx2-5
V$GRE_C	6496 (+)	1.000	0.967	ggtaccatctGTTCTt	GR
V$TAL1ALPHAE47_01	6496 (-)	1.000	0.993	ggtacCATCTgttctt	Tal-1alpha/E47
V$TAL1BETAE47_01	6496 (-)	1.000	0.996	ggtaccATCTGttctt	Tal-1beta/E47
V$PAX4_01	6516 (-)	0.979	0.833	ctcaagacaggCCTGAagtca	Pax-4
V$PAX4_01	6529 (+)	0.979	0.852	tgaagTCAGGcttctaggctg	Pax-4
V$CAAT_01	6929 (+)	1.000	0.989	gagagCCAATca	CCAAT box
V$AP1_Q4	7252 (-)	1.000	0.992	ttttAGTCAct	AP-1
V$FOXD3_01	7422 (-)	0.996	0.986	aaaaaAACATtc	FOXD3
V$OCT1_Q6	7533 (+)	1.000	0.951	agaaatGCAAAtgtg	Oct-1

IRF1 (Interferon regulatory factor-1)

V$PAX4_01	351 (-)	0.986	0.874	tagagtccactCTTGAgcaca	Pax-4
V$VMYB_01	1028 (+)	1.000	0.986	aatAACGGct	v-Myb
V$PAX4_01	1218 (+)	1.000	0.867	ggcggTCATGctttctcccac	Pax-4
V$HNF1_C	1975 (-)	0.942	0.904	gtgggtatttaTTAGCt	HNF-1
V$IK1_01	2297 (-)	1.000	0.983	gggaTTCCCaggt	Ik-1
V$AP1_Q4	2308 (-)	1.000	0.990	gttgAGTCAcc	AP-1
V$STAT_01	3658 (+)	1.000	1.000	TTCCCggaa	STATx
V$VMAF_01	4216 (+)	1.000	0.932	agctGCTGAcccggctgca	v-Maf
V$PAX4_01	5269 (+)	0.986	0.837	tgcctTCAAGcttttggatgc	Pax-4
V$CEBP_C	5304 (+)	1.000	0.984	tgtgttctGCAATtcaca	C/EBP
V$PAX4_01	0 (+)	0.979	0.866	tgaggTCAGGagttggagaac	Pax-4
V$PAX4_01	6878 (+)	1.000	0.848	aaggtTCATGcgttcctgttc	Pax-4
V$OCT1_Q6	7691 (+)	0.909	0.939	gtaaatGTAAAtgac	Oct-1
V$OCT1_Q6	7801 (+)	0.888	0.927	aaaaatGGAAAtaac	Oct-1
V$EVI1_04	8365 (-)	0.772	0.832	tTTCCTctcctagct	Evi-1
V$CREL_01	9302 (+)	1.000	0.988	tgggaTTTCC	c-Rel

NOS2A (Inducible form of nitric oxide synthase)

V$PAX6_01	398 (-)	0.925	0.878	actcactcattCGTCAatggt	Pax-6
V$CDPCR1_01	727 (-)	0.929	0.929	gccaTCAATt	CDP CR1
V$USF_Q6	817 (-)	1.000	0.974	gccaCGTGAa	USF
V$BRN2_01	901 (+)	1.000	0.996	aacatccAAAATaagc	Brn-2
V$USF_Q6	1115 (-)	1.000	0.993	ggcaCGTGAc	USF
V$ELK1_02	1574 (-)	1.000	0.982	ttccTTCCGgcatg	Elk-1
V$HNF4_01	1819 (-)	0.915	0.902	ctttgccCTTTAaacagtt	HNF-4
V$MYOD_01	2256 (+)	1.000	0.971	gggCAGGTgctg	MyoD
V$VMYB_01	2438 (-)	1.000	0.995	tgCCGTTatt	v-Myb
V$HAND1E47_01and1/E47	2533 (-)	1.000	0.974	agagCCAGAccccacc	
V$EVI1_04	3021 (+)	1.000	0.875	ggtaaagaaAAGATa	Evi-1
V$NKX25_01	3269 (+)	1.000	1.000	tcAAGTG	Nkx2-5
V$E47_01	3468 (+)	1.000	0.995	actgCAGGTgttcac	E47
V$COMP1_01	4638 (+)	0.786	0.801	ggggagGCTTGacaagaaacgagg	COMP1
V$CP2_01	4696 (+)	0.974	0.972	gcaccaGCCAG	CP2
V$NKX25_01	4916 (-)	1.000	1.000	CACTTga	Nkx2-5
V$USF_Q6	5047 (-)	1.000	0.997	gacaCGTGAc	USF
V$USF_Q6	5047 (+)	0.973	0.976	gACACGtgac	USF

Table 1. Contd.

V$CREL_01	5644 (-)	1.000	0.987	GGAAAgccca	c-Rel
V$MYOD_01	5724 (-)	1.000	0.971	caccACCTGact	MyoD
V$EVI1_04	6481 (+)	0.930	0.838	ggttaagagAGGATt	Evi-1
V$OCT1_02	6521 (-)	0.992	0.989	attgtGAATAttcta	Oct-1
V$EVI1_04	7145 (+)	1.000	0.835	caagatgagAAGATa	Evi-1
V$EVI1_04	7329 (-)	0.772	0.844	tTTCCTttcctttct	Evi-1
V$EVI1_04	7334 (-)	0.772	0.849	tTTCCTttcttttcc	Evi-1
V$EVI1_04	7339 (-)	0.842	0.869	tTTCTTttcctttcc	Evi-1
V$EVI1_04	7344 (-)	0.772	0.844	tTTCCTttcctttcc	Evi-1
V$EVI1_04	7349 (-)	0.772	0.844	tTTCCTttcctttcc	Evi-1
V$EVI1_04	7354 (-)	0.772	0.844	tTTCCTttcctttcc	Evi-1
V$EVI1_04	7359 (-)	0.772	0.844	tTTCCTttcctttcc	Evi-1
V$EVI1_04	7364 (-)	0.772	0.844	tTTCCTttcctttcc	Evi-1
V$EVI1_04	7369 (-)	0.772	0.844	tTTCCTttcctttcc	Evi-1
V$EVI1_04	7374 (-)	0.772	0.844	tTTCCTttcctttcc	Evi-1
V$EVI1_04	7379 (-)	0.772	0.844	tTTCCTttcctttcc	Evi-1
V$EVI1_04	7384 (-)	0.772	0.844	tTTCCTttcctttcc	Evi-1
V$EVI1_04	7389 (-)	0.772	0.844	tTTCCTttcctttcc	Evi-1
V$EVI1_04	7394 (-)	0.772	0.844	tTTCCTttcctttcc	Evi-1
V$HAND1E47_01	7489 (-)	1.000	0.967	actcCCAGActcaatt	Hand1/E47
V$PAX4_01	7956 (+)	0.986	0.845	tgtccTCAAGcctggtgcttg	Pax-4
V$YY1_02	8502 (+)	1.000	0.959	gcccgGCCATcttgtcactt	YY1
V$PAX6_01	8595 (-)	0.818	0.825	ttgagctgaagCCTGAaggga	Pax-6
V$PAX4_01	8831 (+)	0.986	0.863	tgagaTCAAGggtgactttt	Pax-4
V$NKX25_01	9026 (-)	1.000	1.000	CACTTga	Nkx2-5
V$OCT1_Q6	9320 (-)	0.888	0.908	atcaTTTCCattata	Oct-1
V$NKX25_01	9467 (+)	1.000	1.000	tcAAGTG	Nkx2-5

TGF-beta (Transforming growth factor beat-1)

V$PAX4_01	31 (+)	0.879	0.833	tggcgTGACGcggaaggcggg	Pax-4
V$CREL_01	91 (+)	1.000	1.000	ggggcTTTCC	c-Rel
V$PAX4_01	185 (+)	1.000	0.861	ggcttTCATGggttggcaatt	Pax-4
V$OCT1_Q6	545 (-)	0.888	0.914	ctcaTTTCCatcagt	Oct-1
V$HNF1_01	1010 (-)	1.000	0.939	atttaaatATTAAct	HNF-1
V$HNF4_01	1040 (-)	1.000	0.931	tggagacCTTTGgactcga	HNF-4
V$PAX4_01	1272 (+)	1.000	0.869	agttgTCATGagtactaaacg	Pax-4
V$PAX4_01	1462 (-)	0.979	0.831	atgtcttcaggCCTGAgtcct	Pax-4
V$PAX4_01	1463 (+)	0.979	0.844	tgtctTCAGGcctgagtccta	Pax-4
V$PAX4_01	1879 (+)	0.986	0.837	tgggtTCAAGcgattctccta	Pax-4
V$PAX4_01	2171 (+)	0.986	0.837	tgggtTCAAGcgattctccta	Pax-4
V$PAX4_01	3141 (+)	0.979	0.877	tgaggTCAGGagtttgagacc	Pax-4
V$PAX4_01	3266 (-)	0.986	0.837	caggagaatcgCTTGAaccca	Pax-4
V$EVI1_04	3372 (+)	0.842	0.829	aaataaaatAAAATa	Evi-1
V$FOXJ2_01	3382 (+)	1.000	0.994	aaataaatAAACAgataa	FOXJ2
V$AP1_Q4	3418 (+)	1.000	0.993	ggTGACTcacc	AP-1
V$NKX25_01	3469 (-)	1.000	1.000	CACTTga	Nkx2-5
V$EVI1_04	3752 (+)	0.907	0.825	tgaaaagaaATGATg	Evi-1
V$NKX25_01	3823 (-)	1.000	1.000	CACTTga	Nkx2-5
V$HNF4_01	3906 (+)	1.000	0.922	gccagtgCAAAGgccctga	HNF-4
V$USF_Q6	4019 (-)	0.987	0.972	gccaCGTGGg	USF
V$NKX25_01	4261 (+)	1.000	1.000	tcAAGTG	Nkx2-5
V$GATA1_02	4347 (+)	1.000	0.992	gtagAGATAgggtt	GATA-1

Table 1. Contd.

V$PAX4_01	4514 (-)	0.979	0.887	ggtctcgaaccCCTGAcctca	Pax-4
V$NKX25_01	4532 (+)	1.000	1.000	tcAAGTG	Nkx2-5
V$PAX4_01	4650 (-)	0.979	0.877	ggtctcaaactCCTGAcctca	Pax-4
V$AP1_Q4	4715 (-)	1.000	0.992	cgtgAGTCAct	AP-1
V$PAX6_01	5347 (+)	0.842	0.823	cccatTCATGgattaatgggt	Pax-6
V$PAX4_01	5877 (+)	0.979	0.888	tcctgTCAGGcgtgcgggagg	Pax-4
V$GATA1_02	5918 (+)	1.000	0.991	ccgcAGATAggggga	GATA-1
V$LMO2COM_02	5921 (+)	1.000	1.000	cAGATAggg	Lmo2
V$ARNT_01	7155 (-)	1.000	0.991	acagcCACGTgccacc	Arnt
V$USF_Q6	7158 (+)	0.987	0.983	gCCACGtgcc	USF
V$USF_C	7159 (+)	1.000	1.000	cCACGTgc	USF
V$PAX4_01	7237 (-)	0.979	0.878	ggtctcgaactCCTGAcctca	Pax-4
V$HNF4_01	8601 (-)	0.915	0.897	ggttggaCTTTAtactgag	HNF-4
V$GATA1_06	8699 (+)	1.000	1.000	ataGATAAga	GATA-1
V$USF_Q6	8987 (+)	0.987	0.972	cCCACGtggc	USF
V$PAX4_01	9251 (+)	0.986	0.839	agtggTCAAGagcacagactc	Pax-4
V$LMO2COM_02	9357 (-)	1.000	1.000	cccTATCTg	Lmo2
V$CP2_01	9909 (-)	1.000	0.988	CTGGGtggggc	CP2
(IFNAR1) Interferon –alpha receptor-1					
V$EVI1_04	16 (+)	0.842	0.845	agatatggcAAAATa	Evi-1
V$HNF1_C	20 (-)	1.000	0.841	atggcaaaataTTAACg	HNF-1
V$XFD2_01	693 (-)	1.000	1.000	tcaatgTTTATaat	XFD-2
V$FOXJ2_02	935 (-)	1.000	0.940	ataagtATTATttt	FOXJ2
V$PAX6_01	1066 (-)	0.960	0.817	aatcgatgaatCGTAAagtga	Pax-6
V$COMP1_01	1120 (+)	1.000	0.829	tggataGATTGcctaaaaatcatt	COMP1
V$AP1_Q4	1227 (+)	1.000	0.992	ggTGACTcacg	AP-1
V$CREL_01	1320 (-)	1.000	0.988	GGAAAtccca	c-Rel
V$PAX4_01	1405 (-)	0.986	0.837	caggagaatcgCTTGAacccg	Pax-4
V$OCT1_02	2367 (+)	0.992	0.989	tggaaTATTCacgta	Oct-1
V$HLF_01	4248 (-)	0.939	0.938	attatGTAAT	HLF
V$HNF1_C	4258 (+)	0.942	0.861	tGCTAAttaattgcttg	HNF-1

strong binding site. Additional transcription elements working in concert with modules appear to fine-tune promoter regulation (Malin et al., 2008; Wasserman and Fickett, 1998). Promoters that are constitutively expressed often referred to as housekeeping genes have upstream sequence elements that are recognized by ubiquitous activators. Promoters that are expressed only in certain times or place have sequence elements that require activators that are available only at those times or places.

Different types of variations in the genome alter this interaction of TF to TFBS, thereby effecting the gene expression. Two alterations interfere with gene regulation viz., epigenetic changes and DNA sequence variations and may thus be responsible for the final outcome of disease (Jones and Stephen, 2002). The presence of polymorphisms in coding region affects the activity of protein, while in regulatory region affect the expression levels of genes and thus play important roles in the pathogenesis of many complex diseases. Nucleotide variations in the TFBS may alter the DNA cis-elements and protein (TF) interaction and expression of the gene. Promoter polymorphisms affects the level of gene product thus susceptibility to disease (Teeranaipong et al., 2008; Sinha, et al., 2008). A study from Japan reported association of the -1031 (rs1799964), -863A (1800630) and -857 polymorphisms with increased reporter gene expression and increased concanavalin A-stimulated TNF production from peripheral blood mononuclear cells (Higuchi et al., 1998). Predicted124 SNPs in TFBS of host genes involved in malaria pathogenesis might alters the level of gene product by influencing the binding of transcription factor to transcription factor binding site (Table 2).

Falciparum malaria and selection

In response to disease pressure, genome selects those variations/ polymorphisms (SNP) that are beneficial, providing resistance against the disease. The best

Table 2. Single nucleotide polymorphism lies in transcription factor binding sites of genes involved in malaria pathogenesis. Predicted polymorphisms in conserved regions are more likely to influence the regulation of gene.

SNP ID	Position	TF	Std	Start	End	Allele 1	Score 1 (%)	Allele 2	Score 2 (%)	Diff	Con?
IL-1 (Interleukin-1)											
rs6542093	113244767	E74A	-	113244762	113244768	CTGGCAG	2.967 (69.2)	CCGGCAG	6.627 (83.7)	-3.66	No
rs6542093	113244767	NRF-2	-	113244760	113244769	ACTGGCGAGGC	5.006 (71.7)	ACCGGCGAGGC	8.338 (82.4)	-3.332	No
rs6542093	113244767	SOX17	+	113244764	113244772	GCCAGTGTC	6.273 (82.6)	GCCGGTGTC	1.778 (68.1)	4.495	No
rs6542093	113244767	Snail	+	113244765	113244770	CCAGTG	2.989 (72.3)	CCGGTG	6.063 (83.3)	-3.074	No
rs6542094	113244856	E74A	+	113244855	113244861	AAGGAAG	7.540 (87.3)	AGGGAAG	4.991 (77.2)	2.549	No
rs10169524	113245103	Broad-complex_1	+	113245101	113245114	ATAAAAAGAAAAAT	9.120 (83.2)	ATGAAAAGAAAAAT	7.404 (78.7)	1.716	No
rs10169524	113245103	Broad-complex_4	+	113245102	113245112	TAAAAAGAAAA	7.405 (82.1)	TGAAAAGAAAA	4.492 (72.8)	2.913	No
rs10169524	113245103	HMG-IY	+	113245099	113245114	TGATAAAAAGAAAAAT	10.306 (86.3)	TGATGAAAAGAAAAAAT	8.706 (82.7)	1.6	No
rs10169524	113245103	Hunchback	+	113245099	113245108	TGATAAAAAG	7.917 (84.9)	TGATGAAAAG	4.109 (73.2)	3.808	No
rs10169524	113245103	Hunchback	+	113245103	113245112	AAAAAGAAAA	5.356 (77.0)	GAAAAGAAAA	7.525 (83.7)	-2.169	No
rs10169524	113245103	SQUA	+	113245099	113245112	TGATAAAAAGAAAA	8.817 (83.8)	TGATGAAAAGAAAA	4.664 (75.2)	4.153	No
rs10169524	113245103	SQUA	+	113245101	113245114	ATAAAAAGAAAAAT	8.112 (82.3)	ATGAAAAGAAAAAT	5.872 (77.7)	2.24	No
rs10169524	113245103	TBP	+	113245099	113245113	TGATAAAAAGAAAAAA	6.008 (80.7)	TGATGAAAAGAAAAAA	0.832 (70.4)	5.176	No
rs6542095	113245414	CF2-II	+	113245414	113245423	CTATAGataa	7.044 (82.3)	ttatCTATAA	5.512 (78.5)	1.532	No
rs6542095	113245414	MEF2	-	113245414	113245423	ttatCTATAG	9.782 (84.9)	ttatCTATAA	7.067 (79.2)	2.715	No
rs10539616	113245450	AGL3	-	113245441	113245450	Catataataa	1.274 (69.6)	CAATATatat	7.050 (83.1)	-5.776	No
rs10539616	113245450	Broad-complex_1	+	113245444	113245457	ttatatGTCATATA	4.079 (69.9)	GTATATGACAATAT	9.219 (83.5)	-5.14	No
rs10539616	113245450	Broad-complex_1	-	113245445	113245458	GTATATGACatata	7.666 (79.4)	GTATATGACAATAT	9.219 (83.5)	-1.553	No
rs10539616	113245450	CF2-II	+	113245444	113245453	ttatatGTCA	6.180 (80.1)	ATATatataa	12.441 (95.6)	-6.261	No
rs10539616	113245450	CF2-II	-	113245444	113245453	TGACatataa	2.537 (71.1)	ATATatataa	12.441 (95.6)	-9.904	No
rs10539616	113245450	CF2-II	-	113245449	113245458	GTATATGACa	5.446 (78.3)	ATATatataa	12.441 (95.6)	-6.995	No
rs10539616	113245450	E4BP4	-	113245441	113245451	ACataataa	3.464 (70.2)	ATataataa	7.675 (80.9)	-4.211	No
rs10539616	113245450	E4BP4	+	113245444	113245454	ttatatGTCAT	3.725 (70.8)	ATataataa	7.675 (80.9)	-3.95	No
rs10539616	113245450	E4BP4	-	113245446	113245456	ATATGACatat	2.652 (68.1)	ATataataa	7.675 (80.9)	-5.023	No
rs10539616	113245450	E4BP4	-	113245448	113245458	GTATATGACat	3.725 (70.8)	ATataataa	7.675 (80.9)	-3.95	No
rs10539616	113245450	HFH-3	+	113245442	113245453	tattatatATAT	2.046 (68.5)	tattatatATAT	6.838 (80.1)	-4.792	No
rs10539616	113245450	RORalfa-1	+	113245444	113245453	ttatatGTCA	7.555 (81.2)	tATATTGTCA	2.536 (67.3)	5.019	No
rs10539616	113245450	SOX17	+	113245444	113245452	ttatatGTC	1.308 (66.6)	tATATTGTC	10.360 (95.8)	-9.052	No
rs10539616	113245450	SQUA	-	113245440	113245453	TGACatataataat	4.217 (74.3)	ATATatataataat	10.072 (86.3)	-5.855	No
rs10539616	113245450	SQUA	+	113245441	113245454	ttattatatGTCAT	2.525 (70.8)	ATATatataataat	10.072 (86.3)	-7.547	No
rs10539616	113245450	bZIP910	-	113245448	113245454	ATGACat	7.070 (85.2)	ATGACAA	2.446 (70.4)	4.624	No
rs10539616	113245450	TBP	-	113245437	113245451	ACatataatattta	2.619 (73.9)	ATATatataatt	6.078 (80.8)	-3.459	No
rs10539616	113245450	TBP	-	113245444	113245458	GTATATGACatataa	2.177 (73.1)	ATATatataatt	6.078 (80.8)	-3.901	No
rs11677416	113245471	AGL3	+	113245471	113245480	CTTTTAAAAG	6.120 (80.9)	TTTTTAAAAG	1.686 (70.6)	4.434	No
rs11677416	113245471	AGL3	-	113245471	113245480	CTTTTAAAAG	6.120 (80.9)	TTTTTAAAAG	1.686 (70.6)	4.434	No
rs11677416	113245471	Athb-1	+	113245465	113245472	CATTCACT	2.314 (66.9)	CATTCATT	6.650 (80.6)	-4.336	No
rs11677416	113245471	Broad-complex_4	-	113245467	113245477	TTAAAAGTGAA	5.421 (75.8)	TTAAAAATGAA	7.220 (81.5)	-1.799	No
rs11677416	113245471	COUP-TF	-	113245470	113245483	TGACTTTTAAAAGT	6.613 (75.5)	TGACTTTTAAAAAT	8.727 (80.1)	-2.114	No

Table 2. Contd.

rs1167416	113245471	Sox-5	-	113245470	113245476	TAAAAGT	2.350 (68.1)	TAAAAAT	6.624 (84.1)	-4.274	No
rs3783560	113246025	Broad-complex_1	-	113246016	113246029	ttaaTataaaaata	8.628 (81.9)	ttaaCataaaata	5.458 (73.5)	3.17	No
rs3783560	113246025	Broad-complex_4	-	113246016	113246026	aTataaaaata	6.868 (80.4)	aCataaaaata	4.775 (73.7)	2.093	No
rs3783560	113246025	Broad-complex_4	-	113246018	113246028	taaTataaaa	7.571 (82.7)	taaCataaaa	4.375 (72.4)	3.196	No
rs3783560	113246025	HFH-3	-	113246023	113246034	atatattaaTat	7.252 (81.1)	atatattaaCat	3.063 (71.0)	4.189	No
rs3783560	113246025	Hunchback	-	113246017	113246026	aTataaaat	6.162 (79.5)	aCataaaat	9.332 (89.2)	-3.17	No
rs3783560	113246025	SQUA	-	113246017	113246030	attaaTataaaat	8.084 (82.2)	attttatGttaat	4.918 (75.7)	3.166	No
rs3783560	113246025	SQUA	-	113246019	113246032	atattaaTataaa	8.086 (82.2)	atattaaCataaa	4.056 (73.9)	4.03	No
rs3783560	113246025	TBP	-	113246012	113246026	aTataaaataattc	9.213 (87.0)	aCataaaataattc	6.589 (81.8)	2.624	No
rs1040193	113246330	Broad-complex_4	-	113246325	113246335	aaggaGaaaaa	3.679 (70.2)	aaggaAaaaaa	7.111 (81.2)	-3.432	Yes
rs1040193	113246330	E74A	-	113246329	113246335	aaggaGa	2.540 (67.5)	aaggaAa	6.669 (83.8)	-4.129	Yes
rs1040193	113246330	HMG-IY	-	113246321	113246336	gaaggaGaaaaagagc	6.036 (76.6)	gaaggaAaaaaagagc	8.059 (81.2)	-2.023	Yes
rs1040193	113246330	HMG-IY	-	113246325	113246340	agtggaggaGaaaaa	5.536 (75.4)	agtggaggaAaaaaa	7.743 (80.5)	-2.207	No
rs1040193	113246330	Hunchback	-	113246325	113246334	aggaGaaaaa	3.413 (71.0)	aggaAaaaaa	7.221 (82.7)	-3.808	Yes
rs1040193	113246330	Hunchback	-	113246326	113246335	aggaGaaaa	3.034 (69.8)	aggaAaaaa	7.121 (82.4)	-4.087	Yes
rs1040193	113246330	Hunchback	-	113246327	113246336	gaggaGaaa	2.396 (67.9)	gaggaAaaa	6.484 (80.5)	-4.088	Yes
rs1516789	113247255	E74A	-	113247254	113247260	cgggaGg	2.967 (69.2)	cgggaAg	7.095 (85.5)	-4.128	No
rs3783555	113247324	Broad-complex_4	+	113247320	113247330	tacaAaaaaaa	7.111 (81.2)	tacaGaaaaaa	5.312 (75.4)	1.799	No
rs3783555	113247324	HFH-2	-	113247321	113247332	attttttTtgt	7.084 (81.1)	attttttCtgt	4.083 (75.1)	3.001	No
rs3783555	113247324	HFH-2	-	113247323	113247334	tcattttttT	7.353 (81.6)	tcattttttCt	3.864 (74.7)	3.489	No
rs3783555	113247324	Hunchback	+	113247319	113247328	ctacaAaaaa	7.899 (84.8)	ctacaGaaaa	3.811 (72.2)	4.088	No
rs3783555	113247324	Hunchback	+	113247320	113247329	tacaAaaaa	8.706 (87.3)	tacaGaaaa	4.899 (75.6)	3.807	No
rs3783555	113247324	SQUA	+	113247319	113247332	ctacaAaaaaaaat	8.043 (82.2)	ctacaGaaaaaat	4.297 (74.4)	3.746	No
rs3783555	113247324	SQUA	+	113247324	113247337	Aaaaaaatgaaaa	7.022 (80.1)	Gaaaaaatgaaaa	4.638 (75.1)	2.384	No
rs3783555	113247324	TBP	+	113247319	113247333	ctacaAaaaaaaatg	6.787 (82.2)	ctacaGaaaaaatg	0.997 (70.7)	5.79	No
rs1516790	113247522	HLF	+	113247511	113247522	GTATGTGTAATA	3.001 (70.3)	CATTACACATAC	7.247 (81.4)	-4.246	No
rs1516790	113247522	TEF-1	-	113247513	113247524	CATATTACACAT	5.448 (72.9)	CACATTACACAT	9.341 (82.8)	-3.893	No
rs3783592	113247718	Athb-1	+	113247715	113247722	ACATTATT	7.756 (84.1)	AAACTATG	3.770 (71.5)	3.986	No
rs3783592	113247718	HFH-1	+	113247716	113247726	CATTATTCATT	6.517 (76.9)	CATAGTTTATT	12.868 (93.2)	-6.351	No
rs3783592	113247718	HFH-2	-	113247712	113247723	GAATAATGTGTC	2.298 (71.5)	CATAGTTTATTC	7.928 (82.8)	-5.63	No
rs3783592	113247718	HFH-2	+	113247716	113247727	CATTATTCATTG	3.259 (73.5)	CATAGTTTATTC	7.928 (82.8)	-4.669	No
rs3783592	113247718	Sox-5	+	113247713	113247719	ACACATT	2.413 (68.4)	AAACTAT	6.563 (83.8)	-4.15	No
rs3783592	113247718	Staf	+	113247709	113247728	TCTGACACATTATTCATTGC	10.260 (80.0)	TCTGACACATAGTTATTCA	4.843 (70.8)	5.417	No
rs3783591	113247745	AGL3	+	113247736	113247745	CTAAATAAA	4.306 (76.7)	CTAAATAAAG	9.505 (88.8)	-5.199	No
rs3783591	113247745	AGL3	-	113247736	113247745	TTTTATTTAG	3.948 (75.9)	CTAAATAAAG	9.505 (88.8)	-5.557	No
rs3783591	113247745	HFH-3	-	113247734	113247745	TTTTATTTAGTT	11.465 (91.3)	CTTTATTTAGTT	9.214 (85.8)	2.251	No
rs3783591	113247745	HNF-3beta	-	113247734	113247745	TTTTATTTAGTT	6.836 (79.9)	CTTTATTTAGTT	8.820 (85.0)	-1.984	No
rs3783591	113247745	MEF2	+	113247736	113247745	CTAAATAAA	4.372 (73.6)	CTTTATTTAG	9.128 (83.5)	-4.756	No
rs3783591	113247745	MEF2	-	113247736	113247745	TTTTATTTAG	6.584 (78.2)	CTTTATTTAG	9.128 (83.5)	-2.544	No
rs3783553	113247947	Chop-cEBP	-	113247938	113247949	AATTGAAACAAG	3.701 (71.3)	TCATTCAATTCC	7.325 (80.4)	-3.624	Yes
rs3783553	113247947	Chop-cEBP	-	113247944	113247955	AGGTGGAATTGA	3.109 (69.9)	TCATTCAATTCC	7.325 (80.4)	-4.216	Yes

Table 2. Contd.

rs16347	113247951	Chop-cEBP	-	113247944	113247955	AGGTGGAATTGA	TCATTCAATTCC	3.109 (69.9)	7.325 (80.4)	-4.216	Yes
rs3783553	113247947	Irf-1	-	113247940	113247951	GGAATTGAAACA	GGAATTGAATGA	8.779 (81.1)	3.552 (69.4)	5.227	Yes
rs16347	113247951	Irf-1	-	113247940	113247951	GGAATTGAAACA	GGAATTGAATGA	8.779 (81.1)	3.552 (69.4)	5.227	Yes
rs3783553	113247947	Chop-cEBP	+	113247944	113247955	AATTGAAACAAG	TCATTCAATTCC	3.701 (71.3)	7.325 (80.4)	-3.624	Yes
rs16347	113247951	Chop-cEBP	+	113247944	113247955	AATTGAAACAAG	TCATTCAATTCC	3.701 (71.3)	7.325 (80.4)	-3.624	Yes
rs16347	113247951	Hunchback	+	113247949	113247958	AAACAAGAAT	GAAACAAGAA	3.712 (71.9)	6.484 (80.5)	-2.772	No
rs3783590	113247956	Hunchback	+	113247949	113247958	AAACAAGAAT	GAAACAAGAA	3.712 (71.9)	6.484 (80.5)	-2.772	No
rs3783553	113247947	Irf-1	+	113247942	113247953	GGAATTGAAACA	GGAATTGAATGA	8.779 (81.1)	3.552 (69.4)	5.227	Yes
rs16347	113247951	Irf-1	+	113247942	113247953	GGAATTGAAACA	GGAATTGAATGA	8.779 (81.1)	3.552 (69.4)	5.227	Yes
rs3783553	113247947	Sox-5	-	113247945	113247951	TTTCAAT	AAACAAG	3.288 (71.6)	6.563 (83.8)	-3.275	Yes
rs16347	113247951	Sox-5	-	113247945	113247951	TTTCAAT	AAACAAG	3.288 (71.6)	6.563 (83.8)	-3.275	Yes
rs3783590	113247956	HFH-2	+	113247952	113247963	GCATACTTGTTT	GCATTCTTGTTT	7.259 (81.4)	4.922 (76.8)	2.337	No
rs3783590	113247956	HFH-3	+	113247952	113247963	GCATACTTGTTT	GCATTCTTGTTT	9.604 (86.8)	6.234 (78.6)	3.37	No
rs3783590	113247956	HNF-3beta	+	113247952	113247963	GCATACTTGTTT	GCATTCTTGTTT	8.731 (84.8)	5.186 (75.7)	3.545	No
rs3783590	113247956	Hunchback	-	113247955	113247964	GAAACAAGTA	GAAACAAGAA	2.484 (68.1)	6.484 (80.5)	-4	No
rs3783590	113247956	Sox-5	-	113247954	113247960	CAAGTAT	CAAGAAT	1.465 (64.8)	5.801 (81.0)	-4.336	No
rs16347	113247951	c-REL	+	113247949	113247958	TGGGCATACT	TGGGCATTCT	4.576 (74.3)	6.979 (81.7)	-2.403	No
rs3783590	113247956	c-REL	+	113247949	113247958	TGGGCATACT	TGGGCATTCT	4.576 (74.3)	6.979 (81.7)	-2.403	No
rs3783589	113248186	Brachyury	+	113248184	113248194	CTAAGTGTGAC	CTGAGTGTGAC	11.785 (85.5)	7.068 (75.8)	4.717	No

IL-1R (Interleukin-1 receptor)

rs6758647	102215391	CFI-USP	+	102215387	102215396	GGGGACAGGG	GGGGTCAGGG	8.380 (81.3)	13.061 (93.4)	-4.681	No
rs4141633	102215556	FREAC-4	-	102215555	102215562	GTAAGCGG	GTAAGCAG	3.949 (71.2)	8.188 (85.5)	-4.239	No
rs4141632	102215657	E4BP4	-	102215653	102215663	TTACGGGAGCC	TTACGGAAGCC	3.155 (69.4)	7.490 (80.5)	-4.335	No
rs4141632	102215657	E4BP4	+	102215656	102215666	TCCGTAAGGT	TTCCGTAAGGT	4.597 (73.1)	8.808 (83.8)	-4.211	No
rs4141632	102215657	E74A	-	102215655	102215661	ACGGGAG	ACGGAAG	4.523 (75.4)	8.651 (91.7)	-4.128	No
rs4141632	102215657	c-REL	+	102215650	102215659	GGAGGCTCCC	GGAGGCTTCC	2.778 (68.8)	6.737 (80.9)	-3.959	No
rs4141632	102215657	c-REL	-	102215650	102215659	GGGAGCCTCC	GGAGGCTTCC	4.938 (75.4)	6.737 (80.9)	-1.799	No
rs4141631	102215734	bZIP910	+	102215728	102215734	CTGACTC	CTGACTT	2.446 (70.4)	7.070 (85.2)	-4.624	No
rs4141631	102215734	c-FOS	+	102215728	102215735	CTGACTCT	CTGACTTT	5.981 (80.9)	2.288 (68.6)	3.693	No
rs4141631	102215734	c-FOS	-	102215729	102215736	GAGAGTCA	GAAAGTCA	7.560 (86.1)	3.429 (72.4)	4.131	No
rs6708048	102216173	HMG-IY	+	102216169	102216184	ACAGAAATGGCATCAC	ACAGTAATGGCATCAC	9.430 (84.3)	5.757 (75.9)	3.673	No
rs6708048	102216173	SOX17	-	102216168	102216176	ATTTCTGTG	ATTACTGTG	2.332 (69.9)	6.046 (81.9)	-3.714	No
rs6708048	102216173	SQUA	+	102216169	102216182	ACAGAAATGGCATC	ACAGTAATGGCATC	9.353 (84.9)	7.811 (81.7)	1.542	No
rs6708048	102216173	ATHB5	-	102216170	102216178	CCATTTCTG	CCATTACTG	3.684 (71.4)	8.346 (83.1)	-4.662	No
rs2871448	102216405	AGL3	+	102216403	102216412	CTCTTAATGC	GCATTAAAAG	2.497 (72.5)	5.769 (80.1)	-3.272	No
rs2871448	102216405	Athb-1	+	102216398	102216405	GAATTCTC	GAATTCTT	2.753 (68.3)	7.031 (81.8)	-4.278	No
rs2871448	102216405	Hunchback	-	102216403	102216412	GCATTAAGAG	GCATTAAAAG	6.542 (80.6)	8.864 (87.8)	-2.322	No
rs2871448	102216405	NF-kappaB	-	102216396	102216405	GAGAATTCCT	AGGAATTCTT	6.814 (80.1)	2.968 (70.7)	3.846	No
rs2871448	102216405	SQUA	-	102216399	102216412	GCATTAAGAGAATT	GCATTAAAAGAATT	6.588 (79.2)	8.571 (83.2)	-1.983	No
rs2871448	102216405	Sox-5	-	102216400	102216406	AGAGAAT	AAAGAAT	3.288 (71.6)	6.624 (84.1)	-3.336	No

Table 2. Contd.

rs ID	Position	TF	Strand	Sequence	Score (%)	Position	Position	Sequence	Score (%)	Δ	Sig.
rs2871448	102216405	TBP	-	GCATTAAGAGAGAATTC	3.815 (76.3)	102216398	102216412	GCATTAAAAGAATTC	6.029 (80.7)	-2.214	No
rs956730	102216634	HMG-IY	-	TTAGAAACTCAAGAAT	8.383 (81.9)	102216620	102216635	TCAGAAACTCAAGAAT	5.984 (76.4)	2.399	No
rs2234650	102216845	Chop-cEBP	-	GTCTGCAGCTCC	3.949 (71.9)	102216841	102216852	GTCTGCAACTCC	7.824 (81.6)	-3.875	No
rs2234650	102216845	Myf	+	AGGGAGCTGCAG	11.907 (90.6)	102216839	102216850	AGGGAGTTGCAG	7.907 (81.5)	4	No
rs2234650	102216845	Thing1-E47	-	AGTCTGCAGC	4.827 (76.6)	102216844	102216853	AGTCTGCAAC	6.824 (82.5)	-1.997	No
rs2234650	102216845	Spz1	+	GGAGCTGCAGA	4.042 (72.2)	102216841	102216851	GGAGTTGCAGA	7.691 (81.7)	-3.649	No
rs2234652	102217009	Broad-complex_4	-	TTTTAGActta	3.555 (69.8)	102217004	102217014	TTTTAAActta	6.987 (80.8)	-3.432	No
rs2234652	102217009	COUP-TF	-	TAGAActtaaaaccc	6.515 (75.3)	102216998	102217011	TAAActtaaaaccc	9.278 (81.2)	-2.763	No
rs2234652	102217009	Hunchback	-	GActtaaaac	7.180 (82.6)	102217000	102217009	AActtaaaac	5.010 (75.9)	2.17	No
rs2234652	102217009	Hunchback	+	gTCTAAAAAT	7.010 (82.1)	102217007	102217016	gTTTAAAAAT	5.010 (75.9)	2	No
rs10168222	102217186	Broad-complex_1	-	tttTaaaaaaatg	6.580 (76.5)	102217176	102217189	tttAaaaaaaatg	8.727 (82.2)	-2.147	No
rs10168222	102217186	Broad-complex_4	-	tttTaaaaaaa	6.291 (78.6)	102217178	102217188	ttAaaaaaaaa	8.384 (85.3)	-2.093	No
rs10168222	102217186	Broad-complex_4	-	tttTaaaaaaa	8.091 (84.3)	102217179	102217189	tttAaaaaaaa	6.291 (78.6)	1.8	No
rs10168222	102217186	Broad-complex_4	-	ttttTaaaaaa	4.894 (74.1)	102217180	102217190	ttttAaaaaa	8.091 (84.3)	-3.197	No
rs10168222	102217186	Broad-complex_4	+	ttttTaaaaac	6.927 (80.6)	102217182	102217192	ttttTaaaaac	3.731 (70.4)	3.196	No
rs10168222	102217186	HFH-2	+	tcattttttA	2.932 (72.8)	102217175	102217186	tcatttttttT	7.353 (81.6)	-4.421	No
rs10168222	102217186	Hunchback	+	tTaaaaaaaa	7.221 (82.7)	102217178	102217187	tAaaaaaaaa	10.028 (91.4)	-2.807	No
rs10168222	102217186	Hunchback	-	ttTaaaaaaa	3.899 (72.5)	102217179	102217188	ttAaaaaaa	7.221 (82.7)	-3.322	No
rs10168222	102217186	TBP	-	tttTaaaaaaaatga	5.858 (80.4)	102217175	102217189	tttAaaaaaaatga	0.280 (69.3)	5.578	No
rs10168222	102217186	TBP	+	ttttTaaaaaaatg	2.871 (74.4)	102217176	102217190	ttttAaaaaaatg	6.232 (81.1)	-3.361	No
rs10168222	102217186	TBP	+	ttttTaaaaactgtt	6.090 (80.8)	102217182	102217196	ttttTaaaaactgtt	2.729 (74.2)	3.361	No
rs1800919	102217811	E74A	+	ccggagA	5.756 (80.2)	102217805	102217811	ccggagC	4.185 (74.0)	1.571	No
IL-1RN (Interleukin-1 receptor antagonist)											
rs315920	113589249	NRF-2	-	AATGGAGGAG	5.186 (72.3)	113589246	113589255	AATGGAAGAG	8.720 (83.6)	-3.534	No
rs4251954	113589830	AML-1	-	catGtggtt	9.467 (91.1)	113589825	113589833	catAtggtt	4.823 (77.9)	4.644	No
rs4251954	113589830	ARNT	+	caCatg	6.112 (83.1)	113589828	113589833	caTatg	1.872 (66.2)	4.24	No
rs4251954	113589830	ARNT	-	catGtg	6.112 (83.1)	113589828	113589833	caTatg	1.872 (66.2)	4.24	No
rs4251954	113589830	Max	+	aaccaCatgc	9.213 (88.2)	113589825	113589834	aaccaTatgc	5.084 (75.6)	4.129	No
rs4251954	113589830	Myc-Max	-	tggcatGtggt	9.949 (85.0)	113589826	113589836	tggcatAtggt	6.648 (76.7)	3.301	No
rs4251954	113589830	Snail	-	catGtg	6.136 (83.5)	113589828	113589833	caTatg	2.669 (71.1)	3.467	No
rs4251954	113589830	Sox-5	+	caaccaC	1.405 (64.6)	113589824	113589830	caaccaT	5.740 (80.8)	-4.335	No
rs4251954	113589830	Tal1beta-E47S	+	caaccaCatgcc	5.355 (76.1)	113589824	113589835	caaccaTatgcc	9.018 (84.1)	-3.663	No
rs4251954	113589830	USF	-	catGtgg	8.367 (89.2)	113589827	113589833	catAtgg	4.687 (76.6)	3.68	No
rs4251954	113589830	n-MYC	+	caCatg	7.418 (88.4)	113589828	113589833	caTatg	3.703 (74.5)	3.715	No
rs4251954	113589830	n-MYC	-	catGtg	6.819 (86.2)	113589828	113589833	caTatg	3.703 (74.5)	3.116	No
rs4251955	113590102	HFH-2	-	AAATGTCAATTT	7.780 (88.4)	113590100	113590111	AAATGTCAACTT	5.745 (78.4)	2.035	No
rs4251955	113590102	SQUA	+	ACAAATTGACATT	7.437 (80.9)	113590097	113590110	ACAAAGTTGACATT	3.691 (73.2)	3.746	No
rs4251956	113590240	E74A	+	GCGGAAG	8.651 (91.7)	113590239	113590245	GTGGAAG	4.991 (77.2)	3.66	No
rs4251956	113590240	NRF-2	+	GGCGGAAGAG	10.283 (88.6)	113590238	113590247	GGTGGAAGAG	6.951 (77.9)	3.332	No
rs4251956	113590240	Snail	+	AAGGCG	1.346 (66.4)	113590236	113590241	AAGGTG	6.063 (83.3)	-4.717	No

Table 2. Contd.

rs4251958	113590307	RREB-1	-	113590298	113590317	CCCCCCACCGCGCGCCCGC	12.018 (80.6)	CCCCCCACCCCCGCCCCGC	15.257 (85.6)	-3.239	No
rs4251958	113590307	RREB-1	-	113590301	113590320	AAGCCCCCACCCGCCCCGCCCC	10.062 (77.6)	AAGCCCCCACCCCCGCCCCGCCCC	11.963 (80.5)	-1.901	No
rs4251958	113590307	Snail	+	113590307	113590312	CGGGTG	6.063 (83.3)	GGGGTG	2.088 (69.1)	3.975	No
rs4251959	113590353	AGL3	+	113590351	113590360	CCAATTCAGG	5.912 (80.4)	CCCATTCAGG	2.256 (71.9)	3.656	No
rs4251959	113590353	AGL3	-	113590351	113590360	CCTGAATTGG	6.094 (80.9)	CCCATTCAGG	2.256 (71.9)	3.838	No
rs4251959	113590353	AML-1	-	113590347	113590355	ATTGGGGTG	5.689 (80.4)	ATGGGGTG	1.203 (67.6)	4.486	No
rs4251959	113590353	RREB-1	+	113590339	113590358	GCCCTCCCACCCCAATTCA	9.994 (77.5)	GCCCTCCCACCCCCATTCA	11.791 (80.2)	-1.797	No
rs4251960	113590408	Thing1-E47	+	113590400	113590409	GGTCTGCAAG	7.910 (85.7)	GGTCTGCAGG	5.913 (79.8)	1.997	No
rs4251960	113590408	Spz1	+	113590407	113590417	AAGGTTAGAGG	6.932 (79.8)	AGGGTTAGAGG	10.442 (88.9)	-3.51	No
rs4251961	113590698	SAP-1	-	113590695	113590703	ACCTGGTGC	3.301 (68.6)	ACCTGATGC	7.540 (80.5)	-4.239	No
rs4251961	113590698	Snail	-	113590696	113590701	CTGGTG	6.770 (85.8)	CTGATG	3.303 (73.4)	3.467	No
rs4251962	113590873	FREAC-4	-	113590869	113590876	GCAGACAA	3.862 (70.9)	GCAAACAA	8.102 (85.2)	-4.24	No
rs4251962	113590873	HFH-2	+	113590867	113590878	AGTTGTCTGCTC	2.857 (72.7)	AGTTGTTTGCTC	7.656 (82.2)	-4.799	No
rs4251962	113590873	HNF-3beta	+	113590867	113590878	AGTTGTCTGCTC	6.227 (78.4)	AGTTGTTTGCTC	9.295 (86.2)	-3.068	No
rs4251962	113590873	Hunchback	-	113590869	113590878	GAGCAGACAA	2.297 (67.6)	GAGCAAACAA	6.384 (80.2)	-4.087	No
rs4251962	113590873	Sox-5	-	113590868	113590874	AGACAAC	3.227 (71.4)	AAACAAC	6.563 (83.8)	-3.336	No
rs4251963	113590924	HMG-IY	+	113590922	113590937	CTACCAACGGCAAAA	9.067 (83.5)	CTCCCAACGGCAAAAA	6.707 (78.1)	2.36	No
rs4251964	113590925	HMG-IY	+	113590922	113590937	CTACCAACGGCAAAA	9.067 (83.5)	CTCCCAACGGCAAAAA	6.707 (78.1)	2.36	No
rs4251965	113590926	HMG-IY	+	113590922	113590937	CTACCAACGGCAAAA	9.067 (83.5)	CTCCCAACGGCAAAAA	6.707 (78.1)	2.36	No
rs4251966	113591023	AGL3	+	113591023	113591032	CCAGGTATAG	6.967 (82.9)	TCAGGTATAG	2.533 (72.6)	4.434	No
rs4251966	113591023	CFI-USP	+	113591019	113591028	GAGGCCAGGT	3.277 (68.1)	GAGGTCAGGT	7.958 (80.2)	-4.681	No
rs4251966	113591023	COUP-TF	-	113591012	113591025	TGGCCTCTGCCGTG	8.503 (79.6)	TGACCTCTGCCGTG	11.265 (85.5)	-2.762	No
rs4251966	113591023	RORalfa-1	+	113591016	113591025	GCAGAGGCCA	2.958 (68.5)	GCAGAGGTCA	7.350 (80.6)	-4.392	No
rs4251966	113591023	Thing1-E47	+	113591021	113591030	GGCCAGGTAT	4.087 (74.4)	GGTCAGGTAT	7.008 (83.0)	-2.921	No
rs4251966	113591023	bZIP910	-	113591020	113591026	CTGGCCT	2.446 (70.4)	CTGACCT	7.070 (85.2)	-4.624	No
rs4251967	113591199	NF-kappaB	+	113591198	113591207	aCggcttccc	4.172 (73.7)	aGggcttccc	8.853 (85.0)	-4.681	No
rs11677397	113591312	Broad-complex_1	-	113591306	113591319	caagttaGcaaata	6.524 (76.4)	caagttaAcaaata	8.671 (82.0)	-2.147	No
rs11677397	113591312	Broad-complex_4	-	113591308	113591318	aagttaGcaaa	6.476 (79.2)	aagttaAcaaa	8.275 (84.9)	-1.799	No
rs11677397	113591312	FREAC-4	-	113591309	113591316	gttaGcaa	4.998 (74.7)	gttaAcaa	8.172 (85.4)	-3.174	No
rs11677397	113591312	HFH-2	+	113591303	113591314	ttttatttgCta	6.016 (79.0)	ttttatttgTta	8.051 (83.0)	-2.035	No
rs11677397	113591312	HFH-2	+	113591307	113591318	atttgCtaactt	4.674 (76.3)	atttgTtaactt	9.503 (85.9)	-4.829	No
rs11677397	113591312	HFH-3	+	113591303	113591314	ttttatttgCta	6.055 (78.2)	ttttatttgCta	10.244 (88.3)	-4.189	No
rs11677397	113591312	HMG-IY	-	113591299	113591314	taGcaaataaataac	9.882 (85.4)	taAcaaataaataac	12.242 (90.8)	-2.36	No
rs11677397	113591312	HMG-IY	-	113591307	113591322	aaacaagttaGcaaat	5.794 (76.0)	aaacaagttaAcaaat	8.001 (81.1)	-2.207	No
rs11677397	113591312	HNF-1	-	113591304	113591317	agttaGcaaataaa	6.631 (74.7)	agttaAcaaataaa	9.629 (80.8)	-2.998	No
rs11677397	113591312	HNF-3beta	+	113591307	113591318	atttgCtaactt	4.523 (74.0)	atttgTtaactt	7.591 (81.9)	-3.068	No
rs11677397	113591312	Hunchback	-	113591303	113591312	Gcaaataaaa	7.888 (84.8)	Acaaataaaa	5.718 (78.1)	2.17	No
rs11677397	113591312	SQUA	-	113591299	113591312	Gcaaataaaataac	7.405 (80.8)	Acaaataaaataac	9.789 (85.8)	-2.384	No
rs11677397	113591312	Sox-5	-	113591308	113591314	taGcaaa	3.164 (71.2)	taAcaaa	6.563 (83.8)	-3.399	No
rs4251968	113591448	TEF-1	+	113591441	113591452	CACATGCATGAG	6.924 (76.7)	CACATGCCTGAG	10.701 (86.3)	-3.777	No
rs4251968	113591448	TEF-1	-	113591441	113591452	CTCATGCATGTG	3.846 (68.8)	CACATGCCTGAG	10.701 (86.3)	-6.855	No

Table 2. Contd.

rs2234678	113591796	AML-1	113591798	-	TCTGAGGTC	7.747 (86.2)	TCCGAGGTC	4.461 (76.9)	3.286	No
rs2234678	113591796	Dorsal_2	113591805	-	GAGGTCTTCT	5.445 (74.2)	GAGGTCTTCC	8.989 (84.5)	-3.544	No
rs2234678	113591796	E74A	113591800	+	TCAGAAG	3.945 (73.1)	TCGGAAG	8.074 (89.4)	-4.129	No
rs2234678	113591796	NRF-2	113591802	+	CTCAGAGAC	4.612 (70.4)	CTCGGAAGAC	8.146 (81.8)	-3.534	No
rs2234678	113591796	bZIP910	113591797	-	CTGAGGT	7.070 (85.2)	CCGAGGT	2.446 (70.4)	4.624	No
rs4251970	113592004	SU_h	113592017	+	CCATGGGAGACCATGC	5.737 (71.1)	CCGTGGGAGACCATGC	9.508 (80.1)	-3.771	No
rs4252038	113592123	Dorsal_1	113592133	+	GAGTCATTTCC	4.151 (71.4)	GGGTCATTTCC	7.990 (81.0)	-3.839	No
rs4252038	113592123	RORalfa-1	113592118	+	GTGAGAGTCA	4.232 (72.0)	GTGAGGGTCA	8.624 (84.1)	-4.392	No
rs4252038	113592123	c-FOS	113592120	+	GAGAGTCA	7.560 (86.1)	GAGGGTCA	3.429 (72.4)	4.131	No
rs4252038	113592123	c-FOS	113592121	-	ATGACTCT	6.960 (84.1)	ATGACCCT	3.846 (73.8)	3.114	No

CR1 (Complement receptor-1)

rs11807805	204054992	AGL3	204054995	+	cgatatCtgg	4.995 (78.3)	ccaCatatcg	7.404 (83.9)	-2.409	No
rs11807805	204054992	AML-1	204054997	+	tatCtgggc	1.600 (68.8)	tatGtgggc	6.245 (81.9)	-4.645	No
rs11807805	204054992	SU_h	204055005	-	atCtgggcaaagagca	5.679 (71.0)	atGtgggcaaagagca	9.449 (80.0)	-3.77	No
rs9429780	204055585	AML-1	204055591	+	tttgctGtc	6.955 (83.9)	tttgctCtc	2.273 (70.7)	4.682	No
rs9429781	204055617	E74A	204055620	+	cagGaat	7.203 (86.0)	cagTaat	3.074 (69.6)	4.129	No
rs9429781	204055617	HFH-2	204055628	+	Gaatgttgtttt	14.310 (95.5)	Taatgttgtttt	12.640 (92.2)	1.67	No
rs9429781	204055617	TEF-1	204055623	-	aacattCctggt	11.517 (88.4)	aacattActggt	7.624 (78.5)	3.893	No
rs9429941	204055698	Broad-complex_4	204055692	+	ttataaAgaca	6.987 (80.8)	ttataaTgaca	3.791 (70.6)	3.196	No
rs9429941	204055698	TBP	204055685	-	cTttataatcaccat	6.337 (81.3)	cAttataatcaccat	2.430 (73.6)	3.907	No
rs9429941	204055698	TBP	204055692	+	ttataaAgacagagt	8.906 (86.4)	ttataaTgacagagt	3.845 (76.4)	5.061	No
rs12078329	204055892	Athb-1	204055893	+	aaatcaCt	4.960 (75.3)	aaatcaTt	9.297 (88.9)	-4.337	No
rs12078329	204055892	Athb-1	204055894	+	caAtgatt	4.328 (73.3)	caAtgatt	8.720 (87.1)	-4.392	No
rs12078329	204055892	SOX17	204055896	+	atcaCtgag	2.498 (70.4)	atcaTtgag	6.212 (82.4)	-3.714	No
rs12078329	204055892	SOX17	204055896	+	ctcaGtgat	0.946 (65.4)	atcaTtgag	6.212 (82.4)	-5.266	No
rs12078329	204055892	ATHB5	204055894	+	aaatcaCtg	2.881 (69.3)	caAtgattt	10.084 (87.4)	-7.203	No
rs12078329	204055892	ATHB5	204055894	+	caAtgattt	5.421 (75.7)	caAtgattt	10.084 (87.4)	-4.663	No
rs11117911	204056380	E74A	204056383	+	GAGAAAG	3.411 (71.0)	GAGGAAG	7.540 (87.3)	-4.129	No
rs11117913	204056630	AGL3	204056634	+	CCATACTTCT	2.315 (72.1)	CCATATTTCT	5.786 (80.1)	-3.471	No
rs11117913	204056630	Broad-complex_4	204056639	-	AAATAAGAAGT	4.024 (71.3)	AAATAAGAAAT	7.220 (81.5)	-3.196	No
rs11117913	204056630	SQUA	204056642	-	CTGAAATAAGAAGT	7.450 (80.9)	CTGAAATAAGAAAT	9.806 (85.8)	-2.356	No
rs7525160	204056809	Dorsal_1	204056819	-	GGGTTTTCTGT	6.163 (76.4)	GGGTTTTCTCT	8.543 (82.4)	-2.38	No
rs7525160	204056809	Hunchback	204056817	+	ACAGAAAAAC	6.747 (81.3)	AGAGAAAAAC	5.162 (76.4)	1.585	No
rs7525160	204056809	MEF2	204056809	+	TTATTTTAAC	5.099 (75.1)	TTATTTTAAG	9.868 (85.0)	-4.769	No
rs12069288	204056859	COUP-TF	204056866	-	TGTCCTTTGACAT	8.844 (80.3)	TGTCCTTCTGACAT	5.005 (72.1)	3.839	No
rs12069288	204056859	Thing1-E47	204056862	-	CTTTTGACAT	2.949 (71.0)	CTTCTGACAT	6.593 (81.8)	-3.644	No
rs12069288	204056859	bZIP910	204056859	-	TTGACAT	3.592 (74.1)	CTGACAT	7.070 (85.2)	-3.478	No
rs9429942	204057025	CF2-II	204057027	+	acatatgCat	6.294 (80.4)	atAcatatgt	9.387 (88.1)	-3.093	No
rs9429942	204057025	CF2-II	204057027	-	atGcatatgt	5.775 (79.1)	atAcatatgt	9.387 (88.1)	-3.612	No
rs9429942	204057025	CF2-II	204057029	+	atatgCatac	4.797 (76.7)	gtatAcatat	10.344 (90.4)	-5.547	No

Table 2. Contd.

rs9929942	204057025	204057020	204057029	-	CF2-II	gtatGcatat	gtatAcatat	5.179 (77.6)	10.344 (90.4)	-5.165	No
rs9929942	204057025	204057022	204057031	+	CF2-II	atgCatacat	atgTatacat	4.443 (75.8)	7.067 (82.3)	-2.624	No
rs9929942	204057025	204057024	204057033	+	CF2-II	gCatacatgt	gTatacatgt	4.824 (76.8)	9.031 (87.2)	-4.207	No
rs9929942	204057025	204057024	204057033	-	CF2-II	acatgtatGc	gTatacatgt	2.889 (72.0)	9.031 (87.2)	-6.142	No
rs9929942	204057025	204057022	204057029	-	FREAC-4	gtatGcat	gtatAcat	5.095 (75.1)	8.269 (85.7)	-3.174	No
rs9929942	204057025	204057024	204057031	+	FREAC-4	gCatacat	gTatacat	4.030 (71.5)	8.269 (85.7)	-4.239	No
rs9929942	204057025	204057014	204057025	-	HLF	Gcatatgtaaca	tgttacatagT	3.516 (71.7)	7.823 (82.9)	-4.307	No
rs9929942	204057025	204057024	204057038	+	TBP	gCatacatgtgcgac	gTatacatgtgcgac	3.296 (75.3)	5.920 (80.5)	-2.624	No
rs2296878	204058097	204058095	204058103	+	AML-1	GTCGTGGTG	GTTGTGGTG	3.694 (74.7)	6.980 (84.0)	-3.286	No
rs4097396	204058347	204058345	204058350	+	ARNT	CACGTG	CAGGTG	10.351 (100.0)	6.112 (83.1)	4.239	No
rs4097396	204058347	204058345	204058350	-	ARNT	CACGTG	CAGGTG	10.351 (100.0)	6.112 (83.1)	4.239	No
rs4097396	204058347	204058342	204058351	+	Max	TCCCACGTGC	TCCCAGGTGC	9.232 (88.2)	5.103 (75.6)	4.129	No
rs4097396	204058347	204058334	204058349	-	SU_h	ACGTGGGAACTCCACG	ACCTGGGAACTCCACG	10.820 (83.3)	7.049 (74.3)	3.771	No
rs4097396	204058347	204058345	204058350	+	Snail	CACGTG	CAGGTG	6.136 (83.5)	10.744 (100.0)	-4.608	No
rs4097396	204058347	204058345	204058350	-	Snail	CACGTG	CAGGTG	6.136 (83.5)	10.744 (100.0)	-4.608	No
rs4097396	204058347	204058344	204058350	-	USF	CACGTGG	CACCTGG	11.491 (100.0)	7.020 (84.6)	4.471	No
rs4097396	204058347	204058345	204058351	+	USF	CACGTGC	CAGGTGC	9.302 (92.5)	4.879 (77.2)	4.423	No
rs4097396	204058347	204058345	204058350	+	n-MYC	CACGTG	CACCTG	10.533 (100.0)	6.914 (86.5)	3.619	No
rs4097396	204058347	204058345	204058350	-	n-MYC	CACGTG	CACCTG	10.533 (100.0)	6.914 (86.5)	3.619	No
TNF-α (Tumor necrosis factor-alpha)											
rs5875327	31648480	31648476	31648485	-	NRF-2	aGagaaagag	aCagaaagag	6.514 (76.5)	8.283 (82.2)	-1.769	Yes
rs4647194	31648484	31648476	31648485	-	NRF-2	aGagaaagag	aCagaaagag	6.514 (76.5)	8.283 (82.2)	-1.769	Yes
rs2857713	31648535	31648528	31648537	-	Thing1-E47	TGTGTGGCAC	TGCGTGGCAC	6.189 (80.6)	3.268 (72.0)	2.921	No
rs1041981	31648763	31648762	31648770	-	AML-1	TTTGAGGTT	TTTGAGGGT	9.354 (90.7)	5.508 (79.8)	3.846	No
rs4647195	31648936	31648928	31648939	+	Chop-cEBP	CCCTGCCACCCC	CCCTGCCATCCC	5.236 (75.2)	7.428 (80.6)	-2.192	No
rs4647195	31648936	31648926	31648945	+	RREB-1	CCCCCTGCCACCCCCCAGGA	CCCCCTGCCATCCCCCAGGA	12.495 (81.3)	9.256 (76.3)	3.239	No
rs4647195	31648936	31648929	31648939	-	Spz1	GGGGTGGCAGG	GGGATGGCAGG	7.123 (80.2)	3.347 (70.4)	3.776	No
rs3093544	31649758	31649750	31649760	+	Spz1	AGAGGAAGAGC	AGAGGAAGGGC	8.473 (83.8)	6.550 (78.8)	1.923	No
rs4645834	31649818	31649815	31649825	+	Broad-complex_4	AAGGCaaaaa	AAGTCaaaaa	3.915 (71.0)	7.111 (81.2)	-3.196	Yes
rs4645834	31649818	31649810	31649825	+	HMG-IY	TTATGAAGGCaaaaaa	TTATGAAGTCaaaaaa	7.959 (81.0)	5.752 (75.9)	2.207	Yes
rs4645834	31649818	31649815	31649824	+	Hunchback	AAGGCaaaaa	AAGTCaaaaa	4.314 (73.8)	6.484 (80.5)	-2.17	Yes
rs4645834	31649818	31649816	31649825	+	Hunchback	AGGCaaaaa	AGTCaaaaa	6.899 (81.7)	4.577 (74.6)	2.322	Yes
rs4645834	31649818	31649817	31649826	+	Hunchback	GGCaaaaa	GTCaaaaa	9.069 (88.4)	7.484 (83.5)	1.585	Yes
rs4645834	31649818	31649818	31649827	+	Hunchback	GCaaaaaat	TCaaaaaat	10.654 (93.3)	9.069 (88.4)	1.585	Yes
rs3093547	31649827	31649818	31649827	+	Hunchback	GCaaaaaat	TCaaaaaat	10.654 (93.3)	9.069 (88.4)	1.585	Yes
rs4645834	31649818	31649812	31649818	+	bZIP910	ATGAAGG	ATGAAGT	2.446 (70.4)	7.070 (85.2)	-4.624	Yes
rs3093547	31649827	31649822	31649829	-	Athb-1	taTtttt	taAtttt	2.890 (68.7)	7.282 (82.6)	-4.392	Yes
rs3093547	31649827	31649826	31649833	-	Athb-1	aatttaTt	aatttaAt	6.670 (80.7)	3.182 (69.7)	3.488	Yes
rs3093547	31649827	31649820	31649833	+	Broad-complex_1	aaaaaaaAtaatt	aaaaaaAtaaatt	8.373 (81.2)	6.226 (75.6)	2.147	Yes
rs3093547	31649827	31649821	31649831	+	Broad-complex_4	aaaaaaAtaaa	aaaaaaTtaa	7.688 (83.0)	4.492 (72.8)	3.196	Yes

Table 2. Contd.

rs3093547	31649827	Broad-complex_4	+	31649825	31649835	aaAtaaattat	aaTaaattat	8.552 (85.8)	6.459 (79.1)	2.093	Yes
rs3093547	31649827	HFH-1	-	31649826	31649836	aataatttaTt	aataatttaAt	8.701 (82.5)	4.972 (72.9)	3.729	Yes
rs3093547	31649827	HFH-2	-	31649820	31649831	tttaTtttttt	tttaAtttttt	5.397 (77.7)	7.734 (82.4)	-2.337	Yes
rs3093547	31649827	HFH-2	-	31649821	31649832	atttaTttttt	atttaAttttt	12.289 (91.5)	7.460 (81.8)	4.829	Yes
rs3093547	31649827	HFH-2	+	31649825	31649836	aaAtaaattatt	aataaattaAtt	2.154 (71.3)	7.189 (81.3)	-5.035	Yes
rs3093547	31649827	HFH-2	-	31649825	31649836	aataatttaTt	aataatttaAtt	9.400 (85.7)	7.189 (81.3)	2.211	Yes
rs3093547	31649827	HFH-3	-	31649821	31649832	atttaTttttt	atttaTttttt	8.881 (85.0)	4.340 (74.1)	4.541	Yes
rs3093547	31649827	HFH-3	-	31649825	31649836	aataatttaTt	aataatttaAtt	7.260 (81.1)	3.071 (71.0)	4.189	Yes
rs3093547	31649827	HNF-3beta	-	31649821	31649832	atttaTttttt	atttaTttttt	8.477 (84.1)	4.430 (73.8)	4.047	Yes
rs3093547	31649827	HNF-3beta	-	31649825	31649836	aataatttaTt	aataatttaAtt	9.702 (87.3)	6.571 (79.2)	3.131	Yes
rs3093547	31649827	Hunchback	+	31649819	31649828	CaaaaaaaAt	CaaaaaaaAt	9.706 (90.4)	5.706 (78.1)	4	Yes
rs3093547	31649827	Sox-5	+	31649821	31649827	aaaaaA	aaaaaT	2.289 (67.9)	6.624 (84.1)	-4.335	Yes
rs3093547	31649827	Sox-5	+	31649822	31649828	aaaaaAt	aaaaaTt	6.624 (84.1)	2.350 (68.1)	4.274	Yes
rs4248157	31650122	NF-kappaB	+	31650113	31650122	GAGAACTTCC	GAGAACTTCT	6.878 (80.2)	3.472 (72.0)	3.406	No
rs4248157	31650122	NF-kappaB	-	31650114	31650123	GGGAAGTTCT	GAGAAGTTCT	8.991 (85.3)	4.309 (74.0)	4.682	No
rs9282875	31650245	Thing1-E47	-	31650244	31650253	AGTCTGGCGG	AGTCTGGCAG	7.996 (85.9)	9.992 (91.8)	-1.996	Yes
rs4647198	31650314	COUP-TF	+	31650309	31650322	TGACCCCCGCCCCT	TGACCCCCACCCCT	9.975 (82.7)	7.938 (78.4)	2.037	No
rs4647198	31650314	RORalfa-1	+	31650313	31650322	GCGGGGGTCA	GTGGGGGTCA	4.801 (73.6)	7.654 (81.5)	-2.853	No
rs2507961	31650433	TBP	-	31650424	31650438	CTATGAAAGTCGAGT	CTATGAAAGTCGAGT	1.619 (72.0)	7.410 (83.5)	-5.791	No
rs1800630	31650455	NF-kappaB	+	31650446	31650455	GGGACCCCCA	GGGGGGTCCC	3.021 (70.9)	8.366 (83.8)	-5.345	No
rs1800630	31650455	NF-kappaB	-	31650446	31650455	TGGGGGTCCC	GGGGGGTCCC	3.685 (72.5)	8.366 (83.8)	-4.681	No
rs1800630	31650455	p50	+	31650445	31650455	GGGGACCCCCA	GGGGGGTCCCC	9.183 (82.2)	13.895 (93.4)	-4.712	No
rs1800630	31650455	p50	-	31650445	31650456	TGGGGGTCCCC	GGGGGGTCCCC	9.727 (83.5)	13.895 (93.4)	-4.168	No
rs1800630	31650455	p50	-	31650446	31650456	GTGGGGGTCCC	GGGGGGGGTCCC	6.535 (75.9)	10.702 (85.8)	-4.167	No
rs4645836	31650456	p50	+	31650446	31650456	GTGGGGGTCCC	GGGGGGGGTCCC	6.535 (75.9)	10.702 (85.8)	-4.167	No
rs1800630	31650455	p50	+	31650446	31650456	GGGACCCCCCA	GGGGGGGGTCCC	4.155 (70.2)	10.702 (85.8)	-6.547	No
rs4645836	31650456	p50	-	31650446	31650456	GGGACCCCCCA	GGGGGGGGTCCC	4.155 (70.2)	10.702 (85.8)	-6.547	No
rs1800630	31650455	p50	-	31650446	31650456	TGGGGGGTCCC	GGGGGGGTCCC	6.535 (75.9)	10.702 (85.8)	-4.167	No
rs4645836	31650456	p50	-	31650446	31650456	TGGGGGGTCCC	GGGGGGGTCCC	6.535 (75.9)	10.702 (85.8)	-4.167	No
rs4248158	31650512	E74A	-	31650511	31650517	CTGGAGG	CTGGAAG	2.967 (69.2)	7.095 (85.5)	-4.128	No
rs4248158	31650512	Thing1-E47	-	31650511	31650520	TACCTGGAGG	TACCTGGAAG	4.622 (76.0)	6.618 (81.9)	-1.996	No
rs4987086	31650536	bZIP910	+	31650531	31650537	GGGACAT	GGGACGT	1.099 (66.1)	5.723 (80.9)	-4.624	No
rs4248159	31650559	SOX17	+	31650555	31650563	CACAATGGG	CCCAGTGTG	2.910 (71.7)	6.074 (82.0)	-3.164	No
rs4248159	31650559	SOX17	-	31650555	31650563	CCCATTGTG	CCCAGTGTG	10.569 (96.5)	6.074 (82.0)	4.495	No
rs4248159	31650559	Sox-5	+	31650554	31650560	ACACAAT	ACACACT	6.687 (84.3)	3.288 (71.6)	3.399	No
rs2857712	31650632	HFH-2	+	31650623	31650634	TAATGCTGGGTT	TAATGCTGGTTT	4.158 (75.3)	8.539 (84.0)	-4.381	Yes
rs2736196	31650634	HFH-2	+	31650623	31650634	TAATGCTGGGTT	TAATGCTGGTTT	4.158 (75.3)	8.539 (84.0)	-4.381	Yes
rs2857712	31650632	HNF-3beta	+	31650623	31650634	TAATGCTGGGTT	TAATGCTGGTTT	4.638 (74.3)	7.769 (82.3)	-3.131	Yes
rs2736196	31650634	HNF-3beta	+	31650623	31650634	TAATGCTGGGTT	TAATGCTGGTTT	4.638 (74.3)	7.769 (82.3)	-3.131	Yes
rs2857712	31650632	Irf-1	-	31650630	31650641	AAGACTGAACCC	AAGACTGAAACC	6.671 (76.4)	10.910 (85.8)	-4.239	No
rs2736196	31650634	Irf-1	-	31650630	31650641	AAGACTGAACCC	AAGACTGAAACC	6.671 (76.4)	10.910 (85.8)	-4.239	No

Table 2. Contd.

rs2857712	31650632	Athb-1	-	31650628	31650635	CCAGCATT	CAAGCATT	3.344 (70.2)	6.650 (80.6)	-3.306	Yes
rs2736196	31650634	Athb-1	-	31650628	31650635	CCAGCATT	CAAGCATT	3.344 (70.2)	6.650 (80.6)	-3.306	Yes
rs2857712	31650632	HFH-2	+	31650627	31650638	TAATGCTGGTTT	TAATGCTTGTTT	8.539 (84.0)	10.064 (87.0)	-1.525	No
rs2736196	31650634	HFH-2	+	31650627	31650638	TAATGCTGGTTT	TAATGCTTGTTT	8.539 (84.0)	10.064 (87.0)	-1.525	No
rs2857712	31650632	HFH-3	+	31650627	31650638	TAATGCTGGTTT	TAATGCTTGTTT	4.259 (73.9)	8.800 (84.8)	-4.541	No
rs2736196	31650634	HFH-3	+	31650627	31650638	TAATGCTGGTTT	TAATGCTTGTTT	4.259 (73.9)	8.800 (84.8)	-4.541	No
rs2736196	31650634	Irf-1	-	31650634	31650645	AAGACTGAAACC	AAGACTGAAACA	10.910 (85.8)	8.174 (79.7)	2.736	No
rs2857712	31650632	Sox-5	-	31650632	31650638	AAACCAG	AAACAAG	2.228 (67.7)	6.563 (83.8)	-4.335	No
rs2736196	31650634	Sox-5	-	31650632	31650638	AAACCAG	AAACAAG	2.228 (67.7)	6.563 (83.8)	-4.335	No
rs2736195	31650670	NF-kappaB	-	31650661	31650670	GGGCCTGCCC	AGGCCTGCCC	7.010 (80.5)	2.329 (69.2)	4.681	Yes
rs4248160	31650672	Snail	-	31650671	31650676	CAGGTC	CAGGCC	6.099 (83.4)	1.382 (66.5)	4.717	Yes
rs1800195	31650743	Spz1	-	31650740	31650750	GGGGTAGTAGG	GGGGTAGCAGG	6.969 (79.8)	10.479 (89.0)	-3.51	No
rs4248161	31650746	Spz1	-	31650740	31650750	GGGGTAGTAGG	GGGGTAGCAGG	6.969 (79.8)	10.479 (89.0)	-3.51	No
rs4248162	31650748	Spz1	-	31650740	31650750	GGGGTAGTAGG	GGGGTAGCAGG	6.969 (79.8)	10.479 (89.0)	-3.51	No
rs2857711	31650750	Spz1	-	31650740	31650750	GGGGTAGTAGG	GGGGTAGCAGG	6.969 (79.8)	10.479 (89.0)	-3.51	No
rs1800195	31650743	Spz1	-	31650740	31650750	GGGGTAGCAGG	GGGGGAGCAGG	10.479 (89.0)	7.938 (82.4)	2.541	No
rs4248161	31650746	Spz1	-	31650740	31650750	GGGGTAGCAGG	GGGGGAGCAGG	10.479 (89.0)	7.938 (82.4)	2.541	No
rs4248162	31650748	Spz1	-	31650740	31650750	GGGGTAGCAGG	GGGGGAGCAGG	10.479 (89.0)	7.938 (82.4)	2.541	No
rs2857711	31650750	Spz1	-	31650740	31650750	GGGGTAGCAGG	GGGGGAGCAGG	10.479 (89.0)	7.938 (82.4)	2.541	No
rs1800195	31650743	Spz1	-	31650740	31650750	GGTGTAGCAGG	GGGGTAGCAGG	6.830 (79.5)	10.479 (89.0)	-3.649	No
rs4248161	31650746	Spz1	-	31650740	31650750	GGTGTAGCAGG	GGGGTAGCAGG	6.830 (79.5)	10.479 (89.0)	-3.649	No
rs4248162	31650748	Spz1	-	31650740	31650750	GGTGTAGCAGG	GGGGTAGCAGG	6.830 (79.5)	10.479 (89.0)	-3.649	No
rs2857711	31650750	Spz1	+	31650750	31650760	CGGGTAGCAGG	GGGGTAGCAGG	8.321 (83.4)	10.479 (89.0)	-2.158	No
rs3093548	31650799	Hen-1	+	31650790	31650801	CCCCAGCTCCTT	CCCCAGCTCTTT	8.205 (80.7)	5.896 (75.7)	2.309	No
rs3093548	31650799	Myf	+	31650790	31650801	CCCCAGCTCCTT	AAAGAGCTGGGG	2.679 (69.6)	7.632 (80.8)	-4.953	No
rs4248163	31650807	E74A	-	31650802	31650808	CGGGGAG	CCGGGAG	2.967 (69.2)	6.627 (83.7)	-3.66	No
rs4248163	31650807	E74A	+	31650805	31650811	CCCGCAG	CCGGCAG	2.498 (67.4)	6.627 (83.7)	-4.129	No
rs4248164	31651327	Hen-1	+	31651320	31651331	CAGCAGACGCTC	CAGCAGATGCTC	5.499 (74.9)	9.745 (84.0)	-4.246	Yes
rs4248164	31651327	Hen-1	-	31651320	31651331	GAGCGTCTGCTG	GAGCATCTGCTG	4.037 (71.7)	9.745 (84.0)	-5.708	Yes
rs4248164	31651327	Myf	+	31651317	31651328	AGCCAGCAGACG	AGCCAGCAGATG	6.113 (77.4)	9.573 (85.2)	-3.46	Yes
rs4248164	31651327	Myf	+	31651320	31651331	CAGCAGACGCTC	GAGCATCTGCTG	4.504 (73.7)	10.559 (87.5)	-6.055	Yes
rs4248164	31651327	Myf	-	31651320	31651331	GAGCGTCTGCTG	GAGCATCTGCTG	6.471 (78.2)	10.559 (87.5)	-4.088	Yes
rs4248164	31651327	Myf	-	31651323	31651334	AGGGAGCGTCTG	AGGGAGCATCTG	5.012 (74.9)	7.819 (81.3)	-2.807	Yes
rs4248164	31651327	Snail	+	31651323	31651328	CAGACG	CAGATG	2.561 (70.8)	7.278 (87.6)	-4.717	Yes
rs4248164	31651327	Tal1beta-E47S	-	31651321	31651332	GGAGCGTCTGCT	GGAGCATCTGCT	4.566 (74.4)	9.349 (84.9)	-4.783	Yes
rs4645838	31651391	Dorsal_1	-	31651389	31651400	GTTGTTTTCAGG	GGTTGTTTTCAG	3.911 (70.8)	7.863 (80.7)	-3.952	No
rs4645838	31651391	E74A	+	31651390	31651396	CTGAAAA	CCTGAAA	2.096 (65.8)	5.756 (80.2)	-3.66	No
rs2515924	31651470	CREB	+	31651463	31651474	GAGGGTGAAGCC	GAGGGTGGAGCC	7.769 (83.5)	3.681 (72.5)	4.088	No
rs2228088	31651584	Myf	-	31651578	31651589	AAGCACCGCCTG	AAGCAACGCCTG	5.012 (74.9)	8.012 (81.7)	-3	Yes
rs3179060	31651651	COUP-TF	+	31651649	31651662	TGAACTTTGGAGTG	TGCACTTTGGAGTG	13.003 (89.2)	9.164 (81.0)	3.839	Yes

Table 2. Contd.

rs ID		TF					GGGGAAATGGAGACAC		GGGGAAATGGAGACGC			
rs3093661	31651737	HMG-IY	31651804	+	31651723	31651738	GGGGAAATGGAGACAC	10.540 (86.9)	GGGGAAATGGAGACGC	8.939 (83.2)	1.601	No
rs4645839	31651804	ARNT	31651808	+	31651803	31651808	aAcgtg	8.609 (93.0)	aTcgtg	4.440 (76.4)	4.169	No
rs1800610	31651806	ARNT	31651808	+	31651803	31651808	aAcgtg	8.609 (93.0)	aTcgtg	4.440 (76.4)	4.169	No
rs4645839	31651804	ARNT	31651808	-	31651803	31651808	cacgTt	6.112 (83.1)	aTcgtg	4.440 (76.4)	1.672	No
rs1800610	31651806	ARNT	31651808	-	31651803	31651808	cacgTt	6.112 (83.1)	aTcgtg	4.440 (76.4)	1.672	No
rs4645839	31651804	HFH-2	31651809	-	31651798	31651809	ccacgTtttttt	7.249 (81.4)	ccacgAtttttt	2.421 (71.8)	4.828	No
rs1800610	31651806	HFH-2	31651809	-	31651798	31651809	ccacgTtttttt	7.249 (81.4)	ccacgAtttttt	2.421 (71.8)	4.828	No
rs4645839	31651804	Hunchback	31651805	+	31651796	31651805	agaaaaaaAc	6.484 (80.5)	agaaaaaaTc	2.484 (68.1)	4	No
rs4645839	31651804	Hunchback	31651806	+	31651797	31651806	gaaaaaaAcg	6.876 (81.7)	gaaaaaaTcg	2.969 (69.6)	3.907	No
rs1800610	31651806	Hunchback	31651806	+	31651797	31651806	gaaaaaaAcg	6.876 (81.7)	gaaaaaaTcg	2.969 (69.6)	3.907	No
rs4645839	31651804	Max	31651809	+	31651800	31651809	aaaaAcgtgg	8.321 (85.4)	aaaaTcgtgg	4.274 (73.1)	4.047	No
rs1800610	31651806	Max	31651809	+	31651800	31651809	aaaaAcgtgg	8.321 (85.4)	aaaaTcgtgg	4.274 (73.1)	4.047	No
rs4645839	31651804	Myc-Max	31651810	+	31651800	31651810	aaaaAcgtgga	8.801 (82.1)	aaaaTcgtgga	4.528 (71.3)	4.273	No
rs1800610	31651806	Myc-Max	31651810	+	31651800	31651810	aaaaAcgtgga	8.801 (82.1)	aaaaTcgtgga	4.528 (71.3)	4.273	No
rs4645839	31651804	Sox-5	31651804	+	31651798	31651804	aaaaaaA	2.289 (67.9)	aaaaaaT	6.624 (84.1)	-4.335	No
rs4645839	31651804	USF	31651808	-	31651802	31651808	cacgTtt	5.702 (80.1)	cacgAtt	1.280 (64.9)	4.422	No
rs1800610	31651806	USF	31651808	-	31651802	31651808	cacgTtt	5.702 (80.1)	cacgAtt	1.280 (64.9)	4.422	No
rs4645839	31651804	USF	31651809	+	31651803	31651809	aAcgtgg	6.973 (84.5)	aTcgtgg	2.455 (68.9)	4.518	No
rs1800610	31651806	USF	31651809	+	31651803	31651809	aAcgtgg	6.973 (84.5)	aTcgtgg	2.455 (68.9)	4.518	No
rs4645839	31651804	n-MYC	31651808	+	31651803	31651808	aAcgtg	5.992 (83.1)	aTcgtg	2.829 (71.3)	3.163	No
rs1800610	31651806	n-MYC	31651808	+	31651803	31651808	aAcgtg	5.992 (83.1)	aTcgtg	2.829 (71.3)	3.163	No
rs4645839	31651804	n-MYC	31651808	-	31651803	31651808	cacgTt	5.992 (83.1)	aTcgtg	2.829 (71.3)	3.163	No
rs1800610	31651806	n-MYC	31651808	-	31651803	31651808	cacgTt	5.992 (83.1)	aTcgtg	2.829 (71.3)	3.163	No
rs4645839	31651804	ARNT	31651809	+	31651804	31651809	caCgtt	6.112 (83.1)	aacAtg	4.370 (76.1)	1.742	No
rs1800610	31651806	ARNT	31651809	+	31651804	31651809	caCgtt	6.112 (83.1)	aacAtg	4.370 (76.1)	1.742	No
rs4645839	31651804	ARNT	31651809	-	31651804	31651809	aacGtg	8.609 (93.0)	aacAtg	4.370 (76.1)	4.239	No
rs1800610	31651806	ARNT	31651809	-	31651804	31651809	aacGtg	8.609 (93.0)	aacAtg	4.370 (76.1)	4.239	No
rs4645839	31651804	HFH-2	31651814	+	31651803	31651814	ccaCgtttttt	7.249 (81.4)	ccaTgtttttt	10.185 (87.3)	-2.936	No
rs1800610	31651806	HFH-2	31651814	+	31651803	31651814	ccaCgtttttt	7.249 (81.4)	ccaTgtttttt	10.185 (87.3)	-2.936	No
rs4645839	31651804	HFH-3	31651814	+	31651803	31651814	ccaCgtttttt	3.705 (72.5)	ccaTgtttttt	8.246 (83.5)	-4.541	No
rs1800610	31651806	HFH-3	31651814	+	31651803	31651814	ccaCgtttttt	3.705 (72.5)	ccaTgtttttt	8.246 (83.5)	-4.541	No
rs1800610	31651806	HMG-IY	31651820	-	31651805	31651820	ggagagaaaaaacGt	7.221 (79.3)	ggagagaaaaaacAt	8.822 (82.9)	-1.601	No
rs4645839	31651804	HNF-3beta	31651814	+	31651803	31651814	ccaCgtttttt	5.819 (77.3)	ccaTgtttttt	8.887 (85.2)	-3.068	No
rs1800610	31651806	HNF-3beta	31651814	+	31651803	31651814	ccaCgtttttt	5.819 (77.3)	ccaTgtttttt	8.887 (85.2)	-3.068	No
rs1800610	31651806	Hunchback	31651815	-	31651806	31651815	gaaaaaaacG	6.876 (81.7)	gaaaaaaacA	8.613 (87.0)	-1.737	No
rs4645839	31651804	Max	31651812	-	31651803	31651812	aaaaacGtgg	8.321 (85.4)	aaaaacAtgg	5.253 (76.1)	3.068	No
rs1800610	31651806	Max	31651812	-	31651803	31651812	aaaaacGtgg	8.321 (85.4)	aaaaacAtgg	5.253 (76.1)	3.068	No
rs4645839	31651804	Myc-Max	31651812	-	31651802	31651812	aaaaacGtgga	8.801 (82.1)	aaaaacAtgga	5.500 (73.8)	3.301	No
rs1800610	31651806	Myc-Max	31651812	-	31651802	31651812	aaaaacGtgga	8.801 (82.1)	aaaaacAtgga	5.500 (73.8)	3.301	No
rs4645839	31651804	USF	31651809	-	31651803	31651809	aacGtgg	6.973 (84.5)	aacAtgg	3.293 (71.8)	3.68	No
rs1800610	31651806	USF	31651809	-	31651803	31651809	aacGtgg	6.973 (84.5)	aacAtgg	3.293 (71.8)	3.68	No

Table 2. Contd.

rs4645839	31651804	31651804	+	USF	caCgtt	5.702 (80.1)	31651810	caTgtt	2.579 (69.3)	3.123	No
rs1800610	31651806	31651804	+	USF	caCgtt	5.702 (80.1)	31651810	caTgtt	2.579 (69.3)	3.123	No
rs4645839	31651804	31651804	+	n-MYC	caCgtt	5.992 (83.1)	31651809	caCgtt	2.877 (71.5)	3.115	No
rs1800610	31651806	31651804	+	n-MYC	caCgtt	5.992 (83.1)	31651809	caCgtt	2.877 (71.5)	3.115	No
rs4645839	31651804	31651804	-	n-MYC	aacGtg	5.992 (83.1)	31651809	aacAtg	2.877 (71.5)	3.115	No
rs1800610	31651806	31651804	-	n-MYC	aacGtg	5.992 (83.1)	31651809	aacAtg	2.877 (71.5)	3.115	No
IFR-1 (Interferon regulatory factor-1)											
rs960757	131854209	131854207	+	E2F	CTCCGCGC	4.558 (72.3)	131854214	CTCCGCGC	8.329 (85.3)	-3.771	No
rs10900809	131854221	131854217	+	ARNT	CACTCG	1.872 (66.2)	131854222	CACTTG	6.112 (83.1)	-4.24	No
rs10900809	131854221	131854217	-	ARNT	CGAGTG	2.864 (70.1)	131854222	CACTTG	6.112 (83.1)	-3.248	No
rs10900809	131854221	131854217	-	Snail	CGAGTG	2.989 (72.3)	131854222	CAAGTG	7.670 (89.0)	-4.681	No
rs10900809	131854221	131854216	-	USF	CGAGTGG	2.550 (69.2)	131854222	CAAGTGG	7.068 (84.8)	-4.518	No
rs10900809	131854221	131854217	+	USF	CACTCGG	3.388 (72.1)	131854223	CACTTGG	7.020 (84.6)	-3.632	No
rs10900809	131854221	131854217	+	n-MYC	CACTCG	3.390 (73.4)	131854222	CACTTG	6.133 (83.6)	-2.743	No
rs10900809	131854221	131854217	-	n-MYC	CGAGTG	1.589 (66.7)	131854222	CACTTG	6.133 (83.6)	-4.544	No
rs2549009	131854664	131854658	+	CFI-USP	GGGGCCAGGG	8.380 (81.3)	131854667	GGGGCCGGGG	5.371 (73.5)	3.009	No
rs2549009	131854664	131854663	+	Snail	CAGGGG	6.028 (83.1)	131854668	CAGGGG	1.346 (66.4)	4.682	No
rs2549008	131854752	131854744	-	c-REL	GGGGTATATC	6.482 (80.1)	131854753	GAGGTATATC	2.523 (68.0)	3.959	No
rs2549007	131854774	131854773	+	ARNT	CACCTG	6.112 (83.1)	131854778	CGCCTG	2.864 (70.1)	3.248	No
rs2549007	131854774	131854773	+	ARNT	CAGGTG	6.112 (83.1)	131854778	CGCCTG	2.864 (70.1)	3.248	No
rs2549007	131854774	131854770	+	Hen-1	CCTCACCTGCGT	10.729 (86.1)	131854781	CCTCGCCTGCGT	5.803 (75.5)	4.926	No
rs2706384	131854779	131854770	+	Hen-1	CCTCACCTGCGT	10.729 (86.1)	131854781	CCTCGCCTGCGT	5.803 (75.5)	4.926	No
rs2549007	131854774	131854770	-	Hen-1	ACGCAGGTGAGG	9.731 (84.0)	131854781	CCTCGCCTGCGT	5.803 (75.5)	3.928	No
rs2706384	131854779	131854770	-	Hen-1	ACGCAGGTGAGG	9.731 (84.0)	131854781	CCTCGCCTGCGT	5.803 (75.5)	3.928	No
rs2549007	131854774	131854773	+	Snail	CACCTG	1.490 (66.9)	131854778	CAGGCG	6.028 (83.1)	-4.538	No
rs2549007	131854774	131854773	-	Snail	CAGGTG	10.744 (100.0)	131854778	CAGGCG	6.028 (83.1)	4.716	No
rs2549007	131854774	131854772	-	USF	CAGGTGA	6.501 (82.8)	131854778	CAGGCGA	2.869 (70.3)	3.632	No
rs2549007	131854774	131854773	+	n-MYC	CACCTG	6.914 (86.5)	131854778	CAGGCG	3.295 (73.0)	3.619	No
rs2549007	131854774	131854773	-	n-MYC	CAGGTG	6.038 (83.2)	131854778	CAGGCG	3.295 (73.0)	2.743	No
rs2706384	131854779	131854777	+	NF-kappaB	GGGGATCGCC	7.158 (80.9)	131854786	GGCGATCACC	3.714 (72.6)	3.444	No
rs2706384	131854779	131854775	+	Snail	GAGGGG	2.053 (68.9)	131854780	GAGGTG	6.770 (85.8)	-4.717	No
rs2549007	131854774	131854773	+	bZIP910	GTGAGGG	1.099 (66.1)	131854779	GTGAGGT	5.723 (80.9)	-4.624	No
rs2706384	131854779	131854773	+	bZIP910	GTGAGGG	1.099 (66.1)	131854779	GTGAGGT	5.723 (80.9)	-4.624	No
rs2706384	131854779	131854779	-	c-REL	CGGGCGATCC	6.649 (80.6)	131854788	CGGGCGATCA	3.581 (71.2)	3.068	No
rs2706384	131854779	131854776	-	p50	GGCGATCCCCT	8.523 (80.7)	131854786	GGCGATCACCT	4.794 (71.8)	3.729	No
rs2706384	131854779	131854777	+	p50	GGGGATCGCCC	11.924 (88.8)	131854787	GGTGATCGCCC	7.756 (78.8)	4.168	No
rs2706384	131854779	131854777	-	p50	GGGGATCGCCC	10.873 (86.2)	131854787	GGTGATCGCCC	7.756 (78.8)	3.117	No
rs2706384	131854779	131854776	+	Spz1	AGGGGATCGCC	7.357 (80.9)	131854786	AGGTGATCGCC	4.688 (73.9)	2.669	No
rs2549006	131854955	131854955	+	Thing1-E47	TTTCTGCCTC	5.811 (79.5)	131854964	TTTCTGCCTT	7.509 (84.5)	-1.698	No
rs2549005	131855090	131855088	+	Athb-1	ctAttatt	10.419 (92.5)	131855095	ctGttatt	6.027 (78.6)	4.392	No

Table 2. Contd.

rs2549005	131855090	SQUA	-	131855084	131855097	aaaataaTagtagc	7.040 (80.1)	aaaataaCagtagc	3.010 (71.8)	4.03	No
rs2549005	131855090	Sox-5	-	131855087	131855093	taaTagt	3.225 (71.4)	taaCagt	6.624 (84.1)	-3.399	No
rs2549005	131855090	Sox-5	-	131855090	131855096	aaataaT	7.499 (87.3)	aaataaC	3.164 (71.2)	4.335	No
rs3840527	131855552	Dorsal_2	+	131855547	131855556	GGGGCTTACC	9.321 (85.5)	GGGGCCTTAC	7.217 (79.3)	2.104	No
rs3840527	131855552	NF-kappaB	+	131855547	131855556	GGGGCTTACC	11.146 (90.5)	GGGGCCTTACC	7.908 (82.7)	3.238	No
rs3840527	131855552	NF-kappaB	-	131855547	131855556	GGTAAGCCCC	4.319 (74.0)	GGGGCCTTACC	7.908 (82.7)	-3.589	No
rs3840527	131855552	c-REL	+	131855546	131855555	AGGGGCTTAC	2.628 (68.3)	GGGGCCTTACC	8.033 (84.9)	-5.405	No
rs3840527	131855552	c-REL	+	131855547	131855556	GGGGCTTACC	10.338 (92.0)	GGGGCCTTACC	8.033 (84.9)	2.305	No
rs3840527	131855552	c-REL	-	131855548	131855557	TGGTAAGCCC	1.515 (64.9)	GGGGCCTTACC	8.033 (84.9)	-6.518	No
rs3840527	131855552	p65	+	131855547	131855556	GGGGCTTACC	9.235 (84.2)	GGGGCCTTACC	6.309 (76.6)	2.926	No
rs2549004	131855724	CFI-USP	+	131855723	131855732	GGGGTGAAGG	5.096 (72.8)	GGGGTGAAGG	9.703 (84.7)	-4.607	Yes
rs12657668	131856363	AGL3	+	131856361	131856370	CCATATATGC	9.097 (87.8)	CCGTATATGC	5.199 (78.8)	3.898	No
rs12657668	131856363	AGL3	-	131856361	131856370	GCATATATGG	8.347 (86.1)	CCGTATATGC	5.199 (78.8)	3.148	No
rs12657668	131856363	CF2-II	-	131856359	131856368	ATATATGGGT	7.393 (83.1)	ATATACGGGT	3.781 (74.2)	3.612	No
rs12657668	131856363	CF2-II	+	131856361	131856370	CCATATATGC	7.217 (82.7)	GCATATACGG	5.186 (77.7)	2.031	No
rs12657668	131856363	CF2-II	-	131856361	131856370	GCATATATGG	7.830 (84.2)	GCATATACGG	5.186 (77.7)	2.644	No
rs12657668	131856363	CF2-II	-	131856363	131856372	ATGCATAT	7.088 (82.4)	GTATATGCAT	11.134 (92.4)	-4.046	No
rs12657668	131856363	SQUA	+	131856351	131856364	ATAAATATACCCAT	7.676 (81.4)	ATAAATATACCCGT	5.320 (76.5)	2.356	No
rs12657668	131856363	SQUA	+	131856361	131856374	CCATATGCATAT	7.962 (82.0)	CCGTATGCATAT	5.722 (77.4)	2.24	No
rs12657668	131856363	SRF	+	131856359	131856370	ACCCATATGC	12.487 (86.0)	ACCCGTATATGC	8.174 (78.0)	4.313	No
rs12657668	131856363	TBP	-	131856356	131856370	GCATATATGGGTATA	7.456 (83.5)	GCATATACGGGTATA	3.273 (75.2)	4.183	No
rs12657668	131856363	TBP	+	131856361	131856375	CCATATGCATATG	7.470 (83.6)	CCGTATGCATATG	1.784 (72.3)	5.686	No
rs2549003	131857196	E74A	-	131857194	131857200	TAGGGAA	1.962 (65.2)	TAGGAAA	6.091 (81.6)	-4.129	Yes
rs2549003	131857196	Irf-2	-	131857180	131857197	GGAAGATGAAACTAAAGG	12.031 (81.5)	GAAAGATGAAACTAAAGG	10.108 (78.1)	1.923	Yes
rs2549003	131857196	Staf	+	131857190	131857209	CATCTTCCCTACTGCCAAGG	12.148 (83.3)	CATCTTCCTACTGCCAAGG	8.377 (76.8)	3.771	No

TGF-β-1 (Transforming growth factor-beta-1)

rs11466316	46551176	E74A	-	46551175	46551181	CGGGAGG	2.967 (69.2)	CGGGAAG	7.095 (85.5)	-4.128	Yes
rs11551226	46551242	CFI-USP	+	46551237	46551246	GGGGGCAGGG	8.380 (81.3)	GGGGGTAGGG	4.495 (71.2)	3.885	No
rs1799753	46551551	NF-kappaB	-	46551551	46551560	ggggtgccc	6.444 (79.2)	ggggaCccc	8.508 (84.2)	-2.064	Yes
rs1800999	46551557	NF-kappaB	-	46551552	46551560	ggggtgccc	6.444 (79.2)	ggggaCccc	8.508 (84.2)	-2.064	Yes
rs1800999	46551557	NF-kappaB	+	46551553	46551561	gggcacccc	4.019 (73.3)	ggggaCccc	8.508 (84.2)	-4.489	Yes
rs1800999	46551557	NF-kappaB	+	46551553	46551562	ggcacccc	2.983 (70.8)	ggggaCccc	8.508 (84.2)	-5.525	Yes
rs1800999	46551557	NF-kappaB	-	46551553	46551562	gggggtgc	4.777 (75.1)	ggggaCccc	8.508 (84.2)	-3.731	Yes
rs1799753	46551551	p50	+	46551550	46551560	cgggcacccc	4.691 (71.5)	ggggGtgcccc	13.895 (93.4)	-9.204	Yes
rs1800999	46551557	p50	+	46551550	46551560	cgggcacccc	4.691 (71.5)	ggggGtgcccc	13.895 (93.4)	-9.204	Yes
rs1799753	46551551	p50	-	46551550	46551560	gggtgcccg	7.205 (77.5)	ggggGtgcccc	13.895 (93.4)	-6.69	Yes
rs1800999	46551557	p50	-	46551550	46551560	gggtgcccg	7.205 (77.5)	ggggGtgcccc	13.895 (93.4)	-6.69	Yes
rs1799753	46551551	p50	+	46551551	46551561	ggggcacccc	12.111 (89.2)	ggggGtgcccc	13.895 (93.4)	-1.784	Yes
rs1800999	46551557	p50	+	46551551	46551561	ggggcacccc	12.111 (89.2)	ggggGtgcccc	13.895 (93.4)	-1.784	Yes
rs1800999	46551557	p50	+	46551552	46551562	gggcacccc	8.138 (79.7)	ggggGtgcccc	13.895 (93.4)	-5.757	Yes

Table 2. Contd.

rs ID	Pos 1	Pos 2	Strand	TF	Seq 1	Score 1	Seq 2	Score 2	Value	Disease
rs1800999	46551557	46551552	-	p50	gggggtgtcccc	10.166 (84.6)	ggggGtgcccc	13.895 (93.4)	-3.729	Yes
rs12985978	46551621	46551617	+	E74A	GCGGAAG	8.651 (91.7)	GCGGAAG	4.523 (75.4)	4.128	Yes
rs12977601	46551622	46551617	+	E74A	GCGGAAG	8.651 (91.7)	GCGGAAG	4.523 (75.4)	4.128	Yes
rs12985978	46551621	46551618	+	Myf	CGGAAGGAGGTG	7.425 (80.4)	CGGAAGGAGGTG	3.337 (71.0)	4.088	Yes
rs12977601	46551622	46551618	+	Myf	CGGAAGGAGGTG	7.425 (80.4)	CGGAAGGAGGTG	3.337 (71.0)	4.088	Yes
rs12985978	46551621	46551618	-	TEF-1	CACCTCCTTCCG	5.595 (73.3)	CACCTCCTTCCG	8.264 (80.1)	-2.669	Yes
rs12977601	46551622	46551618	-	TEF-1	CACCTCCTTCCG	5.595 (73.3)	CACCTCCTTCCG	8.264 (80.1)	-2.669	Yes
rs11466314	46552076	46552070	-	Thing1-E47	GGTTTGTCAA	4.192 (74.7)	GGTCTGTCAA	7.836 (85.4)	-3.644	No
rs1800469	46552136	46552135	-	E74A	CCTGAGG	2.498 (67.4)	CCTGAAG	6.627 (83.7)	-4.129	No
rs1800468	46552427	46552424	-	CREB	GGTGGTGATGTT	7.935 (83.9)	GGTGGTGACGTT	12.023 (94.9)	-4.088	No
rs1800468	46552427	46552425	-	bZIP910	GTGATGT	5.723 (80.9)	GTGACGT	10.348 (95.7)	-4.625	No
rs1054797	46552599	46552596	+	ARNT	CACAGG	1.872 (66.2)	CCCGTG	6.182 (83.4)	-4.31	Yes
rs1054797	46552599	46552596	-	ARNT	CCTGTG	1.942 (66.4)	CCCGTG	6.182 (83.4)	-4.24	Yes
rs1054797	46552599	46552595	-	Max	AAGCCTGTGC	3.101 (69.5)	AAGCCCGTGC	7.230 (82.1)	-4.129	Yes
rs1054797	46552599	46552598	+	c-REL	CAGGCTTTCG	4.153 (73.0)	CGGGCTTTCG	8.112 (85.1)	-3.959	Yes
rs1054797	46552599	46552596	+	n-MYC	CACAGG	3.017 (72.0)	CACGGG	6.133 (83.6)	-3.116	Yes
rs1054797	46552599	46552596	-	n-MYC	CCTGTG	2.370 (69.6)	CACGGG	6.133 (83.6)	-3.763	Yes
rs1054797	46552599	46552598	+	p65	CAGGCTTTCG	3.732 (69.8)	CGGGCTTTCG	7.822 (80.5)	-4.09	Yes
rs1800820	46552615	46552605	+	Myf	GGGCAGTTGGAG	8.255 (82.2)	CGCCAACTGCCC	5.986 (77.1)	2.269	Yes
rs2317130	46553514	46553519	+	Snail	Cagatg	7.278 (87.6)	Tagatg	2.596 (70.9)	4.682	Yes
rs2317130	46553514	46553521	+	Tal1beta-E47S	agatCagatggt	9.456 (85.1)	agatTagatggt	4.704 (74.7)	4.752	Yes
rs2317130	46553514	46553523	-	Tal1beta-E47S	ccaccatctGat	11.614 (89.8)	ccaccatctAat	6.863 (79.4)	4.751	Yes
rs11466311	46553588	46553579	-	CFI-USP	Gggatcaagg	8.906 (82.6)	Aggatcaagg	4.262 (70.6)	4.644	No
rs11466310	46553698	46553692	+	AML-1	cttgctAtt	1.650 (68.9)	cttgctGtt	6.332 (82.2)	-4.682	No
rs11466310	46553698	46553706	+	Androgen	cttggcacttgctAttccctct	7.046 (75.2)	cttggcacttgctGttccctct	11.411 (82.2)	-4.365	No
rs11466310	46553698	46553701	-	Myf	gaaTagcaagtg	3.352 (71.1)	gaaCagcaagtg	7.352 (80.2)	-4	No
rs11466310	46553698	46553699	-	NRF-2	aTagcaagtg	4.725 (70.8)	aCagcaagtg	7.823 (80.7)	-3.098	No
rs11466310	46553698	46553705	-	Spz1	gagggaaTagc	3.807 (71.6)	gagggaaCagc	7.317 (80.8)	-3.51	No
rs11666933	46554093	46554089	+	CF2-II	ggatAtattt	6.213 (80.2)	aaataCatcc	1.968 (69.7)	4.245	No
rs13345981	46554303	46554295	+	Chop-cEBP	aagtgaaaCctc	7.396 (80.5)	aagtgaaaTctc	9.588 (86.0)	-2.192	No
rs13345981	46554303	46554293	+	Irf-1	aaaagtgaaaCc	16.637 (98.6)	aaaagtgaaaTc	12.978 (90.4)	3.659	No
rs13345981	46554303	46554292	+	Irf-2	taaaagtgaaaCctcagc	12.732 (82.8)	taaaagtgaaaTctcagc	9.745 (77.5)	2.987	No
rs13345981	46554303	46554302	-	bZIP910	ctgagGt	7.070 (85.2)	ctgagAt	2.446 (70.4)	4.624	No

MBL-2 (Mannose binding lectin-2)

rs ID	Pos 1	Pos 2	Strand	TF	Seq 1	Score 1	Seq 2	Score 2	Value	Disease
rs3737613	11041105	11041106	+	bZIP910	CTGATCT	2.446 (70.4)	CTGATGT	7.070 (85.2)	-4.624	No
rs12751228	11042418	11042425	-	AML-1	tttgaggTg	6.411 (82.4)	tttgaggGg	2.565 (71.5)	3.846	No
rs12751228	11042418	11042427	+	Hunchback	Acctcaaaaa	6.524 (80.6)	Ccctcaaaa	8.109 (85.5)	-1.585	No
rs12751228	11042410	11042419	+	NF-kappaB	gagactccAc	3.068 (71.0)	gGggagtctc	7.535 (81.8)	-4.467	No
rs12751228	11042410	11042419	-	NF-kappaB	gTggagtctc	2.854 (70.5)	gGggagtctc	7.535 (81.8)	-4.681	No
rs12751228	11042417	11042422	-	Snail	gaggTg	6.770 (85.8)	gaggGg	2.053 (68.9)	4.717	No

Table 2. Contd.

rs12751228	11042418	11042409	p50	-	gTggagtctca	4.405 (70.8)	gGggagtctca	8.573 (80.8)	-4.168	No
rs12737148	11043642	11043641	NF-kappaB	+	gCgagactcc	2.326 (69.2)	gGgagactcc	7.007 (80.5)	-4.681	No
rs12737148	11043642	11043641	c-REL	+	gCgagactcc	3.527 (71.1)	gGgagactcc	6.508 (80.2)	-2.981	No
rs12737148	11043642	11043642	c-REL	-	tgagtctcG	2.489 (67.9)	tgagtctcC	6.535 (80.3)	-4.046	No
rs12737148	11043642	11043642	p65	-	tgagtctcG	4.236 (71.1)	tgagtctcC	8.403 (82.0)	-4.167	No
rs12757026	11043657	11043653	Broad-complex_1	+	ctcaAaaaaaaaa	9.103 (83.1)	ctcaCaaaaaaaa	6.781 (77.0)	2.322	No
rs12757026	11043657	11043654	Broad-complex_1	+	tcaAaaaaaaaaa	8.220 (80.8)	tcaCaaaaaaaaa	4.851 (71.9)	3.369	No
rs12757026	11043657	11043655	Broad-complex_4	+	caAaaaaaaaa	7.688 (83.0)	caCaaaaaaaa	5.595 (76.3)	2.093	No
rs12757026	11043657	11043656	Broad-complex_4	+	aAaaaaaaaa	7.688 (83.0)	aCaaaaaaaa	4.775 (73.7)	2.913	No
rs12757026	11043657	11043656	HFH-2	-	ttttttttTt	9.407 (85.7)	ttttttttGt	6.539 (80.0)	2.868	No
rs12757026	11043657	11043657	HFH-2	-	ttttttttT	9.407 (85.7)	ttttttttG	4.986 (76.9)	4.421	No
rs12757026	11043657	11043653	HMG-IY	+	ctcaAaaaaaaaa	8.479 (82.2)	ctcaCaaaaaaaaa	4.806 (73.7)	3.673	No
rs12757026	11043657	11043655	HMG-IY	+	caAaaaaaaaaa	11.524 (89.1)	caCaaaaaaaaaa	9.164 (83.7)	2.36	No
rs12757026	11043657	11043656	HMG-IY	+	aAaaaaaaaaaaa	10.932 (87.8)	aCaaaaaaaaaaaa	7.847 (80.7)	3.085	No
rs12757026	11043657	11043652	Hunchback	+	tctcaAaaa	6.747 (81.3)	tctcaCaaa	2.659 (68.7)	4.088	No
rs12757026	11043657	11043653	Hunchback	+	ctcaAaaaa	6.899 (81.7)	ctcaCaaaa	4.091 (73.1)	2.808	No
rs12757026	11043657	11043657	Hunchback	+	Aaaaaaaaa	9.443 (89.6)	Caaaaaaaa	11.028 (94.5)	-1.585	No
rs12757026	11043657	11043655	SOX17	-	tttttTtg	1.814 (68.2)	tttttGtg	6.355 (82.9)	-4.541	No
rs12757026	11043657	11043654	SQUA	+	tcaAaaaaaaaa	9.768 (85.7)	tcaCaaaaaaaaa	7.402 (80.8)	2.366	No
rs12757026	11043657	11043655	SQUA	+	caAaaaaaaaaa	7.192 (80.4)	caCaaaaaaaaaa	2.981 (71.7)	4.211	No
rs12757026	11043657	11043656	SQUA	+	aAaaaaaaaaaa	6.879 (79.8)	aCaaaaaaaaaaa	10.972 (88.2)	-4.093	No
rs12402525	11044252	11044245	CFI-USP	-	ggGttcacgc	10.323 (86.3)	ggCttcacgc	5.642 (74.2)	4.681	No
rs12402525	11044252	11044244	CREB	-	cggGttcacgcc	7.593 (83.0)	cggCttcacgcc	6.008 (78.7)	1.585	No
rs11577987	11044286	11044282	ARNT	+	ctcgCg	1.942 (66.4)	ctcgTg	6.182 (83.4)	-4.24	No
rs11577987	11044286	11044282	ARNT	-	cGcgag	2.864 (70.1)	ctcgTg	6.182 (83.4)	-3.318	No
rs11577987	11044286	11044282	n-MYC	+	ctcgCg	4.627 (78.0)	ctcgTg	7.369 (88.2)	-2.742	No
rs11577987	11044286	11044282	n-MYC	-	cGcgag	1.684 (67.0)	ctcgTg	7.369 (88.2)	-5.685	No
rs754311	11044480	11044477	Snail	+	cagCtt	2.632 (71.0)	cagGtt	7.278 (87.6)	-4.646	No
rs754311	11044480	11044477	Snail	-	aaGctg	1.417 (66.7)	cagGtt	7.278 (87.6)	-5.861	No

example of this is the selection of sickle cell anemia, thalassemia, and glucose-6-phosphate dehydrogenase deficiency against the pressure of malaria. Falciparum malaria is an example of evolutionary selection. Certain traits are positively selected in malaria endemic region causing aminoacid change, modified protein in such a way as it provide resistance against malaria. Several host genes selects non-synonymous amino acid changes. What happens in regulatory region? It will be clear from this example. Sickle-cell trait, non-synonymous amino acid changes (HbAS) protects against severe outcomes of malaria, and it is highly prevalent in East African populations who live in malaria endemic areas (Aidoo et al., 2002). iNOS, −1173 C→T polymorphism is as prevalent as the sickle-cell trait in the two East African populations studied (Figure 1). The −1173 C→T polymorphism is significantly associated with protection from both cerebral malaria and severe malarial anemia, and with increased NO production *in vivo*. The C to T change predicts the creation of a new sequence recognition site for the GATA-1 or GATA-2 transcription factors and is responsible for, an increased degree of transcription from the -1173 C→T promoters (Heinemeyer et al., 1998). Some investigators

Table 3. Conservation pattern in the promoter region of genes involved in malaria pathogenesis and their comparison with other genes.

Gene	Motif-1	Motif-2	Motif-3
G6PD			
Cdk-7			
Ldha			
GSTP1			
iNOS			
iNOS			

CDK7- *H. sapiens, P. troglodytes, C. lupus, B. taurus, M. musculus, R. norvegicus, D. rerio, D. melanogaster and C.elegans. LDHA, GSTP1,* **iNOSb-** *Human, rat, mouse.* **iNOSc-** *H. sapiens, P. troglodytes, C. lupus, B. taurus, M. musculus, R. norvegicus, D. rerio) with different length of sequences.* **G6PD-** *H. sapiens, C. lupus G6PD, B. taurus G6PD, M. musculus G6pdx, R. norvegicus G6pdx, D. rerio LOC100148915, D. rerio wu:fj78b06, D. melanogaster Zw gene, C. elegans G6PD, S. pombe zwf1.*

have reported significant protection by the -954 G→C or CCTTT long repeat polymorphisms genes from *NOS2* promoters with deletions in the proximal portion of the *NOS2* promoter. In the light of these facts and our finding in the supplementary data Table 2, our hypothesis is that in the regulatory region, those variations are selected, which alters the expression of genes in such a way as to reduce the infection of parasite.

High level of iNOS is beneficial against the infection of *Plasmodium falciparum*, as it reduces the TNF-alpha toxicity and expression of PECAM1, ICAM1 (adhesion molecules). Changes in their structure or levels in individuals can influence the outcome of infection. Interestingly, a SNP of the *PECAM1* gene (rs668, exon 3, C/G) with low minor allele frequency in populations of the endemic region compared to the non-endemic

region exhibited differential association with disease in these regions; the G allele was a risk factor for malaria in the endemic region, but exhibited significant association with protection from disease in the non-endemic region (Sinha et al., 2008, 2009). So variations occur according to disease prevalence and selected if it play beneficial role against the disease.

In mammalian genome, methylation of cytosine

Table 4. Comparison of percentage conservation in the promoters of different genes in different organisms. Polymorphisms in conserved region are more likely to influence the regulation of gene.

Gene	% Conservation		
	Logo1	Logo2	Logo3
LDHA (Human, rat, mouse)	87.23	81.63	65.21
HSPCB*	38	32	30
GSTP1 (Human, rat, mouse)	85	58.62	69.23
iNOS**	72	62	17.64

*H .sapiens, P. troglodytes, C .lupus, B. taurus, M. musculus, R. norvegicus, D. rerio, D. melanogaster and C. elegans. ** H. sapiens, P. troglodytes, C .lupus, B .taurus, M. musculus, R. norvegicus and D. rerio.

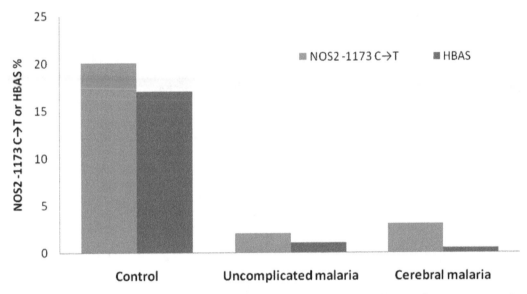

Figure 1. NOS2 −1173 C→T genotype or sickle cell trait (HBAS) relative to disease category in Tanzanian children. Source: Maurine et al. (2002), Lancet [13].

in CpG dinucleotide play role in outcome of disease. Half of the genes in mammalian genome in the proximal promoter regions (0.5 to 4 kb) have CpG Islands. In normal cells, these are unmethylated whereas DNA methylation in the promoter of certain genes is associated with transcriptional silencing. Methylation affects gene expression directly by interfering with transcription factor binding and/or indirectly by recruiting histone deacetylases through methyl-DNA binding proteins (Wei-Guo et al., 2003). The reports indicate that hypermethylation may interfere with Sp1/Sp3 binding. Methylation outside the consensus of Sp1 element induces a significant decrease in Sp1/Sp3 binding.

Polymorphisms in transcription factor binding sites play role in expression divergence, fitness and evolution

In case of HIV, there is evidence of positive selection in early HIV-1 infection which appears to be driven in many cases by escape from early cytotoxic T lymphocyte (CTL) responses via mutations in the APOBEC sequence, suggesting a role for APOBEC in determining the pathway of immune escape (Wood et al., 2009). The study holds significance in understanding the regulation of gene expression at the level of TF and TF binding sites using the aforesaid tools. Further, the variations in the DNA region alter the interaction thereby modulating the host parasite interaction or the genetic disorders. Wittkopp (2010) reported that, natural selection has played some role in expression divergence, but the relative frequency of adaptive and neutral changes remains unclear. Bradley et al. (2010) observed differences in transcription factor binding between species that were similar in regions of the genome thought to act as functional cis-regulatory elements and those thought to have no such activity. The majority of changes in transcription factor binding may have little to no effect on gene expression. All changes in transcription factor binding are neutral. They also reported that changes in transcription factor binding alter gene expression and may have contributed to adaptive evolution (Sequence variation to transcription factor binding, transcription factor binding to gene expression, gene expression to phenotypic variation, and phenotypic variation to fitness in the wild).

Interactions of TF to TFBS are mediated by the DNA binding domain of the transcription factor and the nucleotides within the cis-regulatory DNA to which it binds. Most cis-regulatory sequences are bound by more than one type of transcription factor, and most transcription factors bind to the cis-regulatory sequences from several genes. The recruitment of different combinations of transcription factors to different genes allows expression of each gene to be regulated independently. Mutations that alter the activity or availability of transcription factors, as well as mutations that alter the cis-regulatory sequences to which they bind, can change gene expression. Both types of changes contribute to evolution; however, studies from a variety of organisms suggest that mutations affecting cis-regulatory activity are the predominant source of expression divergence between species (Tirosh et al., 2009, Wittkopp et al., 2008, Wilson et al., 2008, Graze et al., 2009). Changes in gene expression often alter phenotypes; mutations that affect gene expression can affect fitness and contribute to adaptive evolution. Bradley et al. (2010) consistently detected binding of the same transcription factors to regions of DNA in D. melanogaster and D. yakuba that have a common evolutionary origin; however, the relative affinity of these binding sites often differed between species. This suggests that evolutionary changes in the DNA sequence of cis-regulatory regions have occurred that alter the strength of the interaction between transcription factors and their binding sites without eliminating binding.

We have checked the conservation pattern in the promoter region and found that most of the region in the promoter is conserved. It is also suggestive of the fact that if a polymorphism or any variation in the DNA sequence occurs in the conserved region then it effects the interaction of TF with TFBS largely. Table 4 shows comparison of conservation patterns in the promoter region of some genes viz., G6PD, CDK7, LDHA, GSTP1 and iNOS. Understanding the conservation and change of regulatory sequences is critical to our knowledge of the unity as well as diversity of animal development and phenotypes. It can be deciphered from this data that as the number of organisms increases, the percent conservation decreases although certain position in the sequence remains constant throughout. These conserved sequences are thought to be the essential sites that are controlling the regulatory activity for the normal expression of the gene. Genome tries to preserve these conserved sequences irrespective of whether the gene is a housekeeping gene or a highly regulatory gene. Kim et al. (2009) reported that the evolution of sequences

involved in the regulation of body patterning in Drosophila embryo. The mutations of nucleotides within a binding site are constrained by evolutionary forces to preserve the site's binding affinity to the cognate transcription factor. Functional binding sites are frequently destroyed during evolution and the rate of loss across evolutionary spans is roughly constant.

In this report, we focus those polymorphisms of TFBS in the regulatory region of host genes and hypothesize that these variation increases the susceptibility/resistance to a particular disease by alteration of gene product in the cell. Therefore, we have concluded that 124 promoter polymorphisms in the 9 genes involved in malaria pathogenesis play important role in susceptibility to falciparum malaria. The individual SNP has no contribution in risk of disease but SNP-SNP interaction is associated with risk of disease. SNP-SNP interaction analysis of the predicted SNPs will be important in case/control study. This is the first report in which an attempt has been made to associate SNP, variations in promoter sequences in relation with gene deregulation and susceptibility/resistance to various genetic and infectious diseases. A given transcription factor can have different effects on different promoters and multiple transcription factor affects the activity of a single gene. The regulatory sequence of DNA (cis elements) tries to preserve itself. A large number of diseases have been reported in which, variations in regulatory region is responsible for outcome of disease. Polymorphisms and methyl group resulting from methylation of promoter, affects the interaction of TF to TFBS in the studied gene (involved in malaria pathogenesis). DNA sequence variation in the regulatory region and aberrant promoter hypermethylation interfere with regulation of gene expression at transcription level, altering the level of gene product and thus responsible for susceptibility/ resistance to genetic and infectious disease. Further studies are required to validate the predicted SNPs in Indian and other populations. Haplotype and individual SNP analysis does not give the clear picture of case-control study. Therefore, SNP-SNP interaction (gene-gene interaction) and SNP-environment interactions (gene environment interaction) are required for the analysis.

ACKNOWLEDGMENTS

The authors express their gratitude to Ministry of Science and Technology, Government of India and University Grants Commission, New Delhi for providing financial support to the department of Biochemistry, Dr. R.M.L. Avadh University, Faizabad, U. P., India, under the DST-FIST and UGC-SAP schemes, for developing infrastructure to carry out work on such aspects.

REFERENCES

Aidoo M, Terlouw DJ, Kolczak MS, McElroy PD, Kuile FO, Kariuki S,

Nahlen BL, Lal AA, Udhayakumar V (2002). Protective effects of the sickle cell gene against malaria morbidity and mortality. Lancet, 359: 1311–1312.

Bradley RK, Li XY, Trapnell C, Davidson S, Pachter L, Chu HC, Tonkin LA, Biggin MD, Eisen MB (2010). Binding site turnover produces pervasive quantitative changes in transcription factor binding between closely related Drosophila species. PLoS Biol., 8: e1000343.doi:10.1371/journal.pbio.1000343.

Frisch M, Frech K, Klingenhoff A, Cartharius K, Liebich I, Werner T (2002). In silico prediction of scaffold/matrix attachment regions in large genomic sequences. Genome Res., 12: 349–354.

Graze RM, McIntyre LM, Main BJ, Wayne ML, Nuzhdin SV (2009). Regulatory Divergence in Drosophila melanogaster and D. simulans, a Genome-wide Analysis of Allele-specific Expression. Genetics, 183: 547–551.

Heinemeyer T, Wingender E, Reuter I, Hermjakob H, Kel AE, Kel OV, Ignatieva EV, Ananko EA, Podkolodnaya OA, Kolpakov FA, Podkolodny NL, Kolchanov NA (1998). Databases on transcriptional regulation: TRANSFAC, TRRD and COMPEL. Nucleic Acids Res., 26: 362–367.

Higuichi T, Seki N, Kamizono S, Yamada A, Kimura A, Kato H, Itoh K (1998). Polymorphism of the 5′-flanking region of the human tumor necrosis factor TNF-A gene in Japanese. Tissue Antigen, 51: 605-612.

Hobbs MR, Udhayakumar V, Levesque MC, Booth J, Roberts JM, Tkachuk AN (2002). A new NOS2 promoter polymorphism associated with increased nitric oxide production and protection from severe malaria in Tanzanian and Kenyan children. Lancet, 360: 1468–1475.

Jones PA, Stephen BB (2002). The fundamental role of epigenetic events in cancer. Nat. Genet., 3: 415-428.

Kim J, Xin H, Sinha S (2009). Evolution of Regulatory Sequences in 12 Drosophila species PLoS Genet., 5(1): e1000330. doi:10.1371/journal.pgen.1000330.

Klingenhoff A, Frech K, Quandt K, Werner T (1999). Functional promoter modules can be detected by formal models independent of overall nucleotide sequence similarity. Bioinformatics, 15: 180–186.

Klingenhoff A, Frech K, Werner T (2002). Regulatory modules shared within gene classes as well as across gene classes can be detected by the same in silico approach. In Silico Biol., 2: S17–S26.

Krivan W, Wasserman WW (2001). A predictive model for regulatory sequences directing liver-specific transcription. Genome Res., 11: 1559–1566.

Murakami K, Kojima T, Sakaki Y (2004). Assessment of clusters of transcription factor binding sites in relationship to human promoter, CpG islands and gene expression. BMC Genom., 5: 16.

Phairote T, Ohashi J, Patarapotikul J, Kimura R, Nuchnoi P (2008). A Functional single nucleotide polymorphism in the CR1 promoter region contributes to protection against cerebral malaria. J. Infect. Dis., 198: 1880–1891.

Pilpel Y, Sudarsanam P, Church GM (2001). Identifying regulatory networks by combinatorial analysis of promoter elements. Nat. Genet., 29: 153–159.

Robertson KD (2002). DNA methylation and chromatin — Unraveling the tangled web. Oncogene, 21: 5361–5369.

Sinha S, Jha GN, Anand P, Qidwai T, Pati SS, Mishra SK, Tyagi PK, Sharma SK., IGVC, Venkatesh V, Habib S (2009). CR1 levels and gene polymorphisms exhibit differential association with falciparum malaria in regions of varying disease endemicity. Hum. Immunol., 70: 244-250.

Sinha S, Mishra SK, Sharma S, Patibandla PK, Mallick PK, Sharma SK, Mohanty S, Pati SS, Mishra SK, Ramteke BK, Bhatt RM, Joshi H, Dash AP, Ahuja RC, Awasthi S, IGVC, Venkatesh V, Habib S (2008). Polymorphisms of TNF-enhancer and gene for FcγRIIa correlate with the severity falciparum malaria in the ethnically diverse Indian population. Malaria J., 7: 12.

Stormo GD (2000). DNA binding sites: Representation and discovery. Bioinformatics, 16: 16–23.

Tirosh I, Reikhav S, Levy AA, Barkai N (2009). A yeast hybrid provides insight into the evolution of gene expression regulation. Science, 324: 659–662.

Wasserman WW, Fickett JW (1998). Identification of regulatory regions which confer muscle-specific gene expression. J. Mol. Biol., 278: 167–181.

Wei-Guo Z, Srinivasan K, Dai Z, Duan W, Druhan LJ, Haiming D, Lisa Y, Villalona-Calero MA, Christoph P, Gregory A (2003). Otterson. Methylation of adjacent CpG Sites affects Sp1/Sp3 binding and activity in the $p21^{Cip1}$ promoter. Mol. Cell. Biol., 27: 4056-4065.

Werner T (1999). Models for prediction and recognition of eukaryotic promoters. Mammalian Genom., 10: 168–175.

Wilson MD, Barbosa-Morais NL, Schmidt D, Conboy CM, Vanes L, Tybulewicz VLJ, Fisher EMC, Tavaré S, Odom DT (2008). Species-specific transcription in mice carrying human chromosome 21. Science, 322: 434–438.

Wittkopp PJ (2010). Variable Transcription Factor Binding: A Mechanism of Evolutionary Change. PLoS Biol., 8(3): e1000342. doi:10.1371/journal.pbio. 1000342.

Wood N, Bhattacharya T, Keele BF, Giorgi E, Liu M, Gaschen B, Daniels M, Ferrari G, Haynes BF, McMichael A, Shaw GM, Hahn BH, Korber B, Seoighe C (2009). HIV Evolution in Early Infection: Selection Pressures, Patterns of Insertion and Deletion, and the impact of APOBEC. PLoS Pathog., 5(5): e1000414. doi:10.1371/journal.ppat.

Xueping Yu, Jimmy L, Zack DJ, Qian J (2006). Computational analysis of tissue-specific combinatorial gene regulation: Predicting interaction between transcription factors in human tissues. Nucleic Acids Res., 34: 4925–4936.

Zhu Z, Pilpel Y, Church GM (2002). Computational identification of transcription factor binding sites via a transcription-factor-centric clustering (TFCC) algorithm. J. Mol. Biol., 318: 71–81.

## 14

Molecular docking studies on oxidosqualene cyclase with 4-piperidinopyridine and 4-piperidinopyrimidine as its inhibitors

G. Jhansi Rani*, M. Vinoth and P. Anitha

Department of Biochemistry and Bioinformatics, Hindustan College of Arts and Science, Chennai, India.

Oxidosqualene cyclase (OSC) or Lanostrol Synthase is one of the major enzyme in cholesterol biosynthesis. OSC is involved in conversion of squalene to lanosterol. Increased level of cholesterol in blood leads to hypercholesterolemia and major risk factor for cardiovascular diseases. Statin drug molecule is developed to inhibit HMGCoA, which is the first enzyme of cholesterol biosynthesis showed major side effects. Insilico predictions based on the crystal structure of OSC are performed. Active molecular docking studies using GOLD software reveals 4-piperidinopyridine and 4-piperidinopyrimidine (piperidino derivatives) are potent inhibitors of OSC and satisfy ADME properties. The PASS (Prediction of Activity Spectra for Substances) prediction results show the inhibiting activity of OSC enzyme.

Key words: Oxidosqualene cyclase (OSC), piperidino derivatives, molecular docking, toxicity testing, prediction of activity spectra for substances (PASS).

INTRODUCTION

Hypercholesterolemia is a condition characterized by very high levels of cholesterol in blood, have a high risk of developing heart disease and also cause angina, tendon xanthomas, xanthalasmata, achilles tendons (Genetic Home, 2007). A large scale trials therapy demonstrated that cholesterol level lowered by 3-hydroxy 3-methyl coenzyme A (HMGCoA) reductase inhibitors (Gavin, 2000). Statins, a class of hypercholesterolemia agents are well established agents for lowering plasma cholesterol levels and have wide spread agent for lowering plasma cholesterol levels, have wide spread therapeutic used in the treatment of cardiovascular disease that led to search for other novel inhibitors of cholesterol biosynthesis pathway (David, 1987; John et al., 2006)

Oxidosqualene cyclase (OSC) is involved in conversion of squalene to lanosterol in cholesterol biosynthesis pathway, identifying drug-drug interactions involving OSC is vital for improving therapy of hypercholesterolemia, thus would lead to the development of more effective less toxic drug regimes (Jean-Didier, 2005; Michael et al. 1996).

Insilico models have potential use in the discovery and optimization of novel molecules, with affinity to the target, clarification of absorption, distribution, metabolism, excretion and toxicity properties as well as physiochemical characterization (Ekins et al., 2007).

Docking is an important in the study of protein ligand interaction properties such as binding energy, geometry complementarity, electron distribution, hydrogen bond donor acceptor, hydrophobicity and polarizability thus molecular docking contribute a major role in the drug discovery in the identification of innovative small molecular scaffold, exhibiting the important properties with selectivity for the target together with reasonable ADME profile, lead and or drug likeness (Krvoat et al., 2005)

GOLD, the first algorithm to be evaluated on a large data set of complex posses, an empirical free energy scoring function that estimates the free energy of binding permitting inhibition constant for protein ligand complex. It is a package of program for structure visualization and manipulation for docking, the post processing and visualization of the results (Jones, 1997).

MATERIALS AND METHODS

Preparation of protein molecule

The experimental structure of human oxidosqualene cyclase (OSC) (PDB ID: 1GSZ) as shown in Figure 2 was retrieved from the RCSB protein data bank as a PDB file. The protein molecules were prepared mainly by using the software Swiss PDB viewer. Active site residues within a range of 4.0 A^0 were selected and saved in PDB format. Later, the active site residues were minimized in Argus Lab (4.0.1) after adding hydrogen bonds (Akifumi, 2009).

Preparation of ligand

The ligand compounds 4- piperidino pyridine and 4- piperidino pyrimidine were drawn using ACD/ Chemsketch (12.0) (Alex, 2009) and saved in mol 2 format. The saved ligand compounds were later imported and minimized in Argus Lab after adding hydrogen bonds. The molecules thus obtained were saved in PDB format.

Argus Lab

Argus Lab is an electronic structure program that is based on the quantum mechanics; it predicts the potential energies, molecular structures, geometry optimization of structure, vibration frequencies of co-ordinates of atoms, bond length, bond angle and reaction pathway (Cheng, 2003).

The energy (E) of the molecule is calculated as E= E stretching + E bending + E torsion + E vander Waals + E electrostatic + E hydrogen bond +cross term. These terms are of importance for the accurate calculation of geometric properties of molecules. The set of energy functions and the corresponding parameters are called a force field (Afshan, 2009).

Genetic algorithm

Genetic algorithm (GA) is a computer program that mimics the process of evolution by manipulating a collection of data structures called chromosomes. It is also stochastic optimization methods and provides a powerful means to perform directed random searches in drug designing (Shahper, 2008). It study properties of QSAR, utilizes the novel representation of the docking process, each chromosome encodes an internal conformation and protein active site and includes a mapping from hydrogen-bonding sites in the ligand and protein (Seiburg, 1990; Rajasekhar et al., 2010). On decoding a chromosome, fitness is evaluated by PLS (partial least squares) cross validation to position the ligand within the active site of the protein, in such a way that as many of the hydrogen bonds suggested by the mapping are formed (Kimura et al., 1998). Docking of flexible ligands to macromolecules is paramount in structure based drug design, few programs that work with GA also enable automated docking; another application of GA is the automated generation of small organic molecules using lipophilicity, electronic properties and shape related properties for calculation of the scoring function (Nissink et al., 2002).

Docking using GOLD

Genetic algorithm was implemented in GOLD v 3.2 that was applied to calculate the possible conformations of the drug that binds to the protein (Selvaraj, 2008). The genetic algorithm parameters used are population size-100, number of islands-5, niche size-2, selection pressure-1.1, migrate-2, number of operators-100,000, mutate-95, cross over-95. During docking process, a maximum of 10 different conformations was considered for the drug. The conformer with highest binding score was used for further analysis (Girija et al., 2010)

ADME/ toxicity testing

\ADME (absorption, distribution, metabolism, and excretion) determines drug like activity of the ligand molecules based on Lipinski rule of 5 (Konstantin, 2005). Increasing clinical failures of new drugs call for a more effective use of ADME/TOX technologies, becoming more advanced and reliable in terms of accuracy and predictiveness, an increase in their usage is expected during the initial development and screening phase of innovative drugs. New computational methods including consensus modeling show promise for increase in the accuracy of Insilco ADME-TOX prediction used for virtual screening in lead optimization (Gregory, 2004).

PASS prediction

The prediction of activity spectra for substances predicts the biological activity spectrum (BAS) (Sohelia et al., 2001) of a compound represents the complex of pharmacological and physiological effects and biochemical mechanisms of actions, specific toxicity (mutagenecity, carcinogenecity, teratogenecity and embryotoxicity) for a compound on the basis of its structural formula (Poroikov, 2000).

Figure 1 show the structure of piperidinoderivatives of 4-piperidinopyridine and 4-piperidinopyrimidine.

RESULTS AND DISCUSSION

In assessment using GOLD 3.2, OSC showed better affinity with piperidino derivatives. Our receptor retrieved from protein data bank (PDB ID: 1GSZ) is a complex structure of OSC with anticholesteremic drug (drug Id RO-4A-8071). Target protein has four identical chains A, B, C, D with similar active sites, Hence B chain has chosen for analysis. The possible active site was identified using Swiss PDB viewer, It is found 12 active site amino acid residues as TRP 169, ALA 170, ILE 261, PRO 263, TRP 312, PHE 365, ASP 374, ASP 376, ASP 377, TYR 420, PHE 437, TRP 489 by the removal of complexed anticholesteremic drug. Therefore it is chosen as a most biologically favorable site for docking. The conformational stability structure of OSC and piperidino derivatives were obtained by energy minimization using Universal Force Field performed in Argus Lab software.

Docking of piperidino derivatives to OSC

Docking of piperidino derivatives with OSC was performed using GOLD. The algorithm exhaustively searches the entire rotational and translational space of the ligand with respect to the receptors. The various solutions evaluated by a score, which is equivalent to the absolute value of the total energy of the ligand in the protein environment. The best docking solutions GOLD

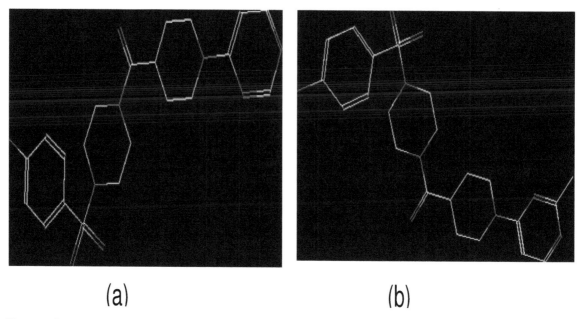

(a)   **(b)**

Figure 1. Structure of piperidinoderivatives (a) 4-piperidinopyridine and (b) 4-piperidinopyrimidine.

Table 1. GOLD scores and interactions of anticholesteremic drug and piperidino derivatives.

S/N	Compound	Interaction (D-H...A)	Hydrogen bond distance between donor and acceptor (Å)	GOLD score
1	Anticholesteremic (Co-crystal ligand)	TYR420 (NH...N)	2.606	52.04
2	4-piperidino pyridine	(TYR 420) N-H...O, (TRP312) N-H...N	2.471 2.490	62.21
3	4-piperidino pyrimidine	ASP376 (NH...O)	2.296	64.7

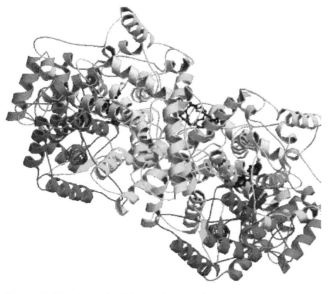

Figure 2. Structure of oxidosqualene cyclase.

score for each compound was considered.

It was noted that GOLD scores of 4-piperidinopyridine and 4-piperidinopyrimidine was 64.7 and 62.21, respectively, which is greater than anticholesteremic drug score value 52.04 as shown in Table 1, Figures 3 and 4.

The drug like activity of the ligand molecules are characterized using ADME properties. Anticholesteremic drug and piperidino derivatives satisfy Lipinski rule of 5 and ADME properties results are shown in Table 2.

The biological activity of piperidino derivatives were predicted using PASS by analyzing the parameters of probabilities of presence (pa) and probabilities of absence (pi). Activities of the molecules are shown in Tables 3 and 4.

Conclusion

OSC is the most recent potent drug target for hypercholesterolemia; the active site residues of OSC

Table 2. Shows ADME properties of piperidino derivatives and anticholesteremic drugs.

S/N	Lig	M.W Min: 200 Max: 600	DRS Min: 0 Max: 6	ARS Min: 0 Max: 12	FB Min: 0 Max: 15	RB Min: 0 Max: 50	#R Min: 0 Max: 7	RL Min: 0 Max: 12	C Min: 5	nC Min: 2	C/nC Min: 0.1 Max: 1.0	#Chr Min: 0 Max: 2	Chr Min: 2 Max: 2	Logp Min: 2 Max: 6	PSA Min: 0 Max: 150
1	4-piperidino pyridine	494.2	0	8	5	27	4	6	21	10	0.500	0	0	1.92	95.09
2	4-piperidino pyrimidine	508.2	0	8	5	27	4	6	21	10	0.470	0	0	2.24	95.09
3	Anticholesteremic drug	380.3	2	6	4	25	4	7	21	7	0.333	0	0	2.84	78.35

Lig- ligand, M.W- molecular weight, DRS- donors, ARS- acceptors, FB- flexible bonds, RB- rigid bonds, R- ring number, RL- ring length, C- carbons, nC- non carbons, C/nC- ratio non carbons/carbons. #Chr- number of charges, Chr- total charge, Log p- log p (octanol/water), PSA- polar surface area.

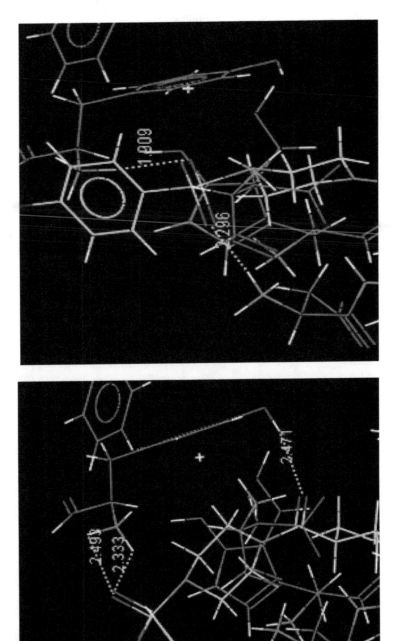

4-piperidino pyridine   4-piperidino pyrimidine

Figure 3. Shows the docking results of piperidino derivatives with OSC.

Table 3. Activity for 4-piperidino pyridine.

		Activity prediction
		2.3-Oxidosqualene-lanosterol cyclase inhibitor
		Possible activities at Pa > 30%
Pa	**Pi**	**Activity**
0.807	0.013	Neuropeptide agonist
0.632	0.007	Polarisation stimulant
0.670	0.046	Nootropic
0.564	0.025	Cognition disorders treatment
0.523	0.048	**Vasodilator. cerebral**
0.456	0.001	**2.3-Oxidosqualene-lanosterol cyclase inhibitor**
0.442	0.016	Antiobesity
0.434	0.034	Atherosclerosis treatment
0.461	0.061	Alpha-7 nicotinic receptor agonist

Table 4. Activity for 4-piperidino pyrimidine.

		Activity prediction
		2.3-Oxidosqualene-lanosterol cyclase inhibitor
		Possible activities at Pa > 30%
Pa	**Pi**	**Activity**
0.877	0.004	Neuropeptide agonist
0.637	0.007	Polarisation stimulant
0.593	0.001	**2.3-Oxidosqualene-lanosterol cyclase inhibitor**
0.570	0.024	Cognition disorders treatment
0.600	0.075	Nootropic
0.533	0.008	Antiobesity
0.472	0.057	Alpha7 nicotinic receptor agonist
0.877	0.004	Neuropeptide agonist

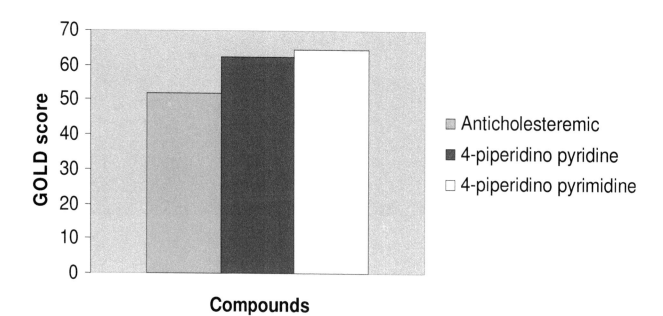

Figure 4. Comparisons of GOLD scores.

were predicted using Swiss PDB viewer. The refined models of OSC and piperidino derivatives were obtained after energy minimization using the Argus Lab software. The stable model of OSC was further used for virtual docking of piperidino derivatives. It is well known that hydrogen bonding plays an important role in the structure and function of biological molecules, especially for inhibition in a complex. Piperidino derivatives play a vital role in holding the molecule at a place at the active site of OSC by hydrogen bonds. Applying Lipinski's rule of 5 to piperidino derivatives to evaluate drug likeness (absorption, distribution, metabolism and excretion), there was no violation of the rule determining drugs pharmacological activity in the body. PASS prediction reveals that 4-piperidino pyridine and 4- piperidino pyrimidine are potential inhibitor for OSC as target for hypercholesterolemia forming a hydrogen bonding and with non-bonded interaction to act as a drug candidate yet pharmacological study will confirm it to be promising in future.

REFERENCES

Afshan N, Khalida B, Farhat B, Najaf AG, Naheed A (2009). Confirmational analysis (geometry optimization) of nucleosidic antitumor antibiotic showdomycin by Argus Lab software. Pak. J. Pharm. Sci., 22(1): 78-82.

Akifumi O, Ohgi T (2009). Validation of Argus Lab efficiencies for binding free energy calculations. Chem. Bioinforma. J., 9: 52-61.

Alex MJ (2009). Docking studies on anticancer drugs for breast cancer using Hex. Proceedings of the International Multi conference of Engineers and Computer Scientists, 1.

Girija CR, Prasantha K, Chtan SP, Noor SB, Akheel AS (2010). Molecular docking studies of curcumin derivatives with multiple protein targets for procarcinogen activating enzyme inhibition. J. Proteomics Bioinforma., 3(6): 200-203.

Cheng A, Merz KM (2003). Prediction of aqueous solubility of a divers set of compounds using quantitative structure- property relationships J. Med. Chem., 46: 3572-3580.

David K (1987). Inhibition of cholesterol biosynthsis. J. Nutr., 117: 1330-1334.

Krovat EM, Steindl T, Lange T (2005). Recent advance in docking and scoring. Curr. Computer-aided Drug Des., 1: 93-102.

Gavin JB, Paul MR (2000). Are statin anti-inflammatory? Curr. Control Trials Cardiovasc. Med., 1: 161-165.

Gregory MB (2004). In silico ADME-TOX prediction: The more, the merrier. Current Drug Discovery.

Hypercholesterolemia, Genetics Home Reference (2007).

Jean-Didier M, Jinglei Y, Simon B, Louri K, Elain MR, Wolf CR, Gordon CKR, Mark JIP Michael JS (2006). In silico and in vitro screening for inhibition of cytochrome p450 CYP3A4 by comedications commonly used by patients with cancer. Drug Metab. Disposition, 34: 534-538.

John G, Lawrence S, Scott SL (2006). Statin therapy and autoimmune disease: From protein prenylation to immunomodulation. Nat. Med., 6: 358-370.

Jones G, Willett P, Glen RC, Leach AR, Taylor R (1997). Development and validation of a genetic algorithm for flexible docking. J. Mol. Biol., 267: 727-748.

Kimura T, Kiyoshi H, Kimito F (1998). GA strategy for variable selection in QSAR studies. Application of GA based region selection to a 3D-QSAR study of acetylcholinesterase inhibitors. J. Chemoinforma. Comp. Sci., 39: 112-120.

Konstantin VB, Yan AI, Nikolay PS, Andrey AI Sean E (2005). Comprehensive computational assessment of ADME properties using mapping techniques. Curr. Drug Discov. Technol., 2: 99-113.

Michael M, Muller P, Maier R, Eisel B (1996). Effects of novel 2,3 oxidosqualene cyclase inhibitor on the regulation of cholesterol biosynthesis in Hep G2 cells. J. Lipid Res., 37: 148-159.

Nissink JW Murray C, Hartshorn M, Verdonk ML, Cole JC, Taylor R (2002). A new test set for validating predictions of protein-ligand interaction. Proteins, 49: 457-471.

Rajasekhar C, Anuradha CM, Chaitanya M, Babujan B, Yogiprasad P, Chitta SK (2010). Structural characterization of pf serine hydroxymethyl transferase: A novel target for malaria. J. Bioinforma. Seq. Anal., 2: 13-24.

Ekins S, Mestres J, Testa B (2007). In silico pharmacology for drug discovery: Applications to targets and beyond. Brit. J. Pharm., 152(1): 21-37.

Selvaraj M, Malik BK (2008). Modeling of human CCR5 as target for HIV-I and virtual screening with therapeutic compounds. Bioinformation, 3(2): 89-94.

Shahper NK, Asad UK (2008). Computational simulation of Mitoxantrone binding with Human Serum Albumin. J. Proteomics Bioinforma., 1: 17-20.

Sieburg HB (1990). Physiological studies in silico studies in the scinces of complexity, 12: 321-342.

Soheila A, Gerhard B, Bertram C, Michael K, Dmitri F, Vladimir P (2001). Discriminating between drugs and non drugs by prediction of activity spectra for substances (PASS). J. Med. Chem., 44: 2432-2437.

Poroikov VV, Filimonov DA, Yu VB, Lagunin AA, Kos A (2000). Robustness of biological activity spectra predicting by computer program PASS for noncongeneric sets of chemical compounds. J. Chem. Inf. Comput. Sci., 40(6): 1349-1355.

## 15

Modern drug discovery process: An *in silico* approach

V. Srinivasa Rao and K. Srinivas*

Department of Computer Science and Engineering, V.R Siddhartha Engineering College, Kanuru, Vijayawada-520 007, India.

Drug discovery process is a critical issue in the pharmaceutical industry since it is a very cost-effective and time consuming process to produce new drug potentials and enlarge the scope of diseases incurred. Drug target identification, being the first phase in drug discovery is becoming an overly time consuming process. In many cases, such produces inefficient results due to failure of conventional approaches like *in vivo* and *in vitro* to investigate large scale data. Sophisticated *in silico* approaches has given a tremendous opportunity to pharmaceutical companies to identify new potential drug targets which in turn affect the success and time of performing clinical trials for discovering new drug targets. The main goal of this work is to review *in silico* methods for drug discovery process with emphasis on identifying drug targets, where there are genes or proteins associated with specific diseases. This review provides a succinct overview of several recent approaches that employ bioinformatics for the systematic characterization of the targets of bioactive compounds.

Key words: *In silico*, infectious vector, drug, pharmaceutical industry.

INTRODUCTION

In silico is an expression used to mean "performed on computer or via computer simulation (http://en.wikipedia.org/wiki/Binding_site). *In silico* drug designing is a form of computer-based modeling whose technologies are applied in drug discovery processes. Unlike the historical method of drug discovery, by trial-and-error testing of chemical substances on animals, and matching the apparent effects to treatments, *in silico* drug design begins with a knowledge of specific chemical responses in the body or target organism and tailoring combinations of these to fit a treatment profile (http://www.scfbio-iitd.res.in/tutorial/drugdiscovery.htm). A drug is a substance used in the diagnosis, treatment, or prevention of a disease or as a component of a medication. The drug discovery process is aimed at discovering molecules that can be very rapidly developed into effective treatments to fulfill unmet medical needs for both endogenous diseases, that arise from in-born sequence errors in germ cells or spontaneous (or age-related) mutations in somatic cells and exogenous diseases, that arise from an infectious vector (virus,

bacterium or parasite) that has its origins outside (Yongliang et al., 2009). In most basic sense, drug design involves design of small molecules that are complementary in shape and charge to the bimolecular target to which they interact and therefore will bind to it. The identification of potential drug target is valuable and significant in the research and development of drug molecules at early stage, safety evaluation and old drugs with new use. Due to the limitation of throughput, accuracy and cost, experimental techniques cannot be applied widely, therefore, the development of *in silico* target identification algorithms, as a strategy with the advantage of fast speed and low cost, has been receiving more and more attention worldwide. It has been of great importance to develop fast and accurate target identification and prediction method for the discovery of targeted drugs, construction of drug-target interaction network as well as the analysis of small molecule regulating network (Markus et al., 2007). Computational tools offer the advantage of delivering new drug candidates more quickly and at a lower cost. Major roles of computation in drug discovery are: 1) Virtual screening and de novo design, 2) *in silico* ADME/T prediction and 3) advanced methods for determining protein-ligand binding and structured based drug design.

*Corresponding author. E-mail: kudipudi72@gmail.com.

The process of finding a drug molecule that attaches itself to the target protein in the body has now moved from the lab to the computer. When a protein target has been identified, it needs to be screened against a large database of known molecules, a method called virtual high-throughput screening (http://www.minglebox.com/blog/l7530/post/in_silico_drug_design). If a molecule fits the target protein, it can be further tested. Knowledge from molecular modeling, molecular biology and combinatorial chemistry is coded into software programs that help predict how the protein target and the drug molecule will come together. The techniques used today, which are continually being improved, do an approximate match to come up with possible hits or pairings. It would be impossible to test millions of molecules in a lab against a given target, but the computerized screening process helps in choosing a small set of molecules that can then be tested in a wet lab (http://www.kauhort.in/Download/SBDD.pdf). This review provides a succinct overview of several recent approaches that employ bioinformatics for the systematic characterization of the targets of bioactive compounds.

TYPES OF DRUG DESIGN

There are two types of drug design; one is "rational drug design" and the other is "structure based drug design".

Rational drug design (RDD)

Rational drug design is a process used in the biopharmaceutical industry to discover and develop new drug compounds. RDD uses a variety of computational methods to identify novel compounds, design compounds for selectivity, efficacy and safety, and develop compounds into clinical trial candidates. These methods fall into several natural categories such as, structure-based drug design, ligand-based drug design, de novo design and homology modeling, depending on how much information is available about drug targets and potential drug compounds.

Structure based drug design (SBDD)

Structure-based drug design is one of the first techniques to be used in drug design. Drug targets are typically key molecules involved in a specific metabolic or cell signaling pathway that is known, or believed, to be related to a particular disease state. Drug targets are most often proteins and enzymes in these pathways. Drug compounds are designed to inhibit, restore or otherwise modify the structure and behavior of disease-related proteins and enzymes. SBDD uses the known 3D geometrical shape or structure of proteins to assist in the development of new drug compounds. The 3D structure of protein targets is most often derived from x-ray crystallography or nuclear magnetic resonance (NMR) techniques. X-ray and NMR methods can resolve the structure of proteins to a resolution of a few angstroms (about 500,000 times smaller than the diameter of a human hair) (Suresh et al., 2006). At this level of resolution, researchers can precisely examine the interactions between atoms in protein targets and atoms in potential drug compounds that bind to the proteins. This ability to work at high resolution with both proteins and drug compounds makes SBDD one of the most powerful methods in drug design. Structure- based design refers specifically to finding and complementing the 3D structure (binding and/or active site) of a target molecule such as a receptor protein. Chemists may be guided to subsets of compounds with desired features to complement 3-dimensional shape of the site. From the geometry and functional features of the binding site, complementary structures of a compound (ligand) are so designed as to have high binding affinity with the target molecule. It is a powerful technique to design a corresponding ligand specifically interacting with the target, particularly for the development of a novel therapeutic through stimulation or inhibition of the receptor protein.

MODERN DRUG DISCOVERY PIPELINE

Drug discovery process operates on a target-based approach, in which the organism is seen as a series of genes and pathways and the goal is to develop drugs that affect only one gene or molecular mechanism (that is, the target) in order to selectively treat the deficit causing the disease without producing side effects (api.ning.com/files/.../DrugDiscoveryNewDrugDevelopmentProcess.ppt). Computers can be used to simulate a chemical compound and design chemical structures that might work against it. Enzymes attach to the correct site on a cell's membrane, which causes the disease. A computer can show scientists what the receptor site looks like and how one might tailor a compound to block an enzyme from attaching there (http://www.microcal.com/drug-discovery-development/small-molecule/target-identification.asp.).

Figure 1 shows the stages of modern drug discovery process pipeline to find out the new drugs. Modern drug discovery process pipeline consists of seven important steps: target identification, target validation, hit and lead identification, lead optimization, pre clinical testing, chemical testing and new drug application (NDA) and food and drug administration (FDA) approval.

Target identification

Target-based drug discovery begins with the identification of the function of a potential therapeutic drug target and understanding its role in the disease process

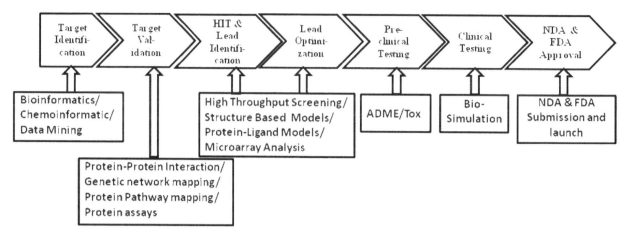

Figure 1. Modern drug discovery process pipeline.

(http://en.wikipedia.org/wiki/Drug_design). A target is generally a single molecule, such as a gene or protein, which is involved in a particular disease. A drug target is a key molecule involved in a particular metabolic or signaling pathway that is specific to a disease condition or pathology, or to the infectivity or survival of a microbial pathogen. Some approaches attempt to inhibit the functioning of the pathway in the diseased state by causing a key molecule to stop functioning. Drugs may be designed that bind to the active region and inhibit this key molecule. Another approach may be to enhance the normal pathway by promoting specific molecules in the normal pathways that may have been affected in the diseased state (Taylor and Francis, 2006). The exact target and the specific patient population are identified with the help of bioinformatics, chemoinformatics and/or data maiming approaches such as, homology based, ligand base, structures base, high throughput screening (HTS), text mining, microarray technologies, pattern matching etc.

Target validation

After a drug target has been identified, a rigorous evaluation needs to occur to demonstrate that modulation of the target will have the desired therapeutic effect. In the drug-discovery process, the major bottleneck is target validation. If this process can be accelerated with computational tools, the target validation step will speed up significantly. The target-validation process includes determining if the modulation of a target's function will yield a desired clinical outcome, specifically the improvement or elimination or a phenotype. *In silico* characterization can be carried by using approaches such as genetic-network mapping, protein-pathway mapping, protein–protein interactions, disease-locus mapping, and subcellular localization predictions. Initial selection of a target may be based on the preliminary

results found between cellular location and disease/health condition, protein expression, potential binding sites, cross-organism confirmation, or pathways involved in a disease/health condition (Bleicher et al., 2003).

HIT and lead identification

For many targets in drug discovery, the identification of a small molecule 'hit' as a starting point for the hit-to lead process. The identification of small molecule modulators of protein function and the process of transforming these into high-content lead series are key activities in modern drug discovery (Robert AG 2006). The "hit-to-lead" phase is usually the follow up of high-throughput screening (HTS). Hits can be identified by one or more of several technology-based approaches like high-throughput biochemical and cellular assays, assay of natural products, structure-based design, peptides and peptidomimetics, chemogenomics and virtual HTS, and literature- and patent-based innovations (Suresh et al., 2006). To develop efficient drug discovery practices, it is useful to consider the various strategies that have been reported for hit and lead identification; assay development, where the target is converted to an HTS assay system.

Lead optimization

Lead optimization is the complex, no-linear process of refining the chemical structure of a confirmed hit to improve its drug characteristics with the goal of producing drug candidate. Lead structures are optimized for target affinity and selectivity. Docking techniques are currently applied to aid on structure-based absorption, distribution, metabolism and excretion (ADME). Drug candidates discovered using this approach needs to be validated on a disease-specific animal model to provide experimental proof of concept. This radical shift in the drug discovery process from physiology-based approach to target-based approach offers high screening capacity and supports to formulate simple, clear requirements to candidate drugs, which allows implementation of rational drug design (Klaus et al., 2001)·

Pre-clinical testing

Preclinical studies and testing strategies with and without the use of animal testing methods have the purpose of limiting risks whenever a new active substance is to be used as a medicinal product in humans. They should be designed in such a way as to achieve as early, risk-free, unproblematic, and economic a transition as possible from preclinical to clinical trials in medicinal products development (Glossary of Clinical Trial Terms, NIH Clinicaltrials.gov).Scientists carry out *in vitro* and *in vivo* tests. *In vitro* tests are experiments conducted in the lab, usually carried out in test tubes and beakers ("*vitro*" is "glass" in Latin) and in vivo studies are those in living cell cultures and animal models ("*vivo*" is "life" in Latin). Preclinical testing involves: pharmacology, toxicology, preformulation, formulation analytical and pharmacokinetics.

Clinical testing

A clinical trial (also clinical research) is a research study in human volunteers to answer specific health questions. Carefully conducted clinical trials are the fastest and safest way to find treatments that work in people and ways to improve health. During the clinical trial, the investigators: recruit patients with the predetermined characteristics, administer the treatment(s), and collect data on the patients' health for a defined time period. The U.S. National Institutes of Health (NIH) organizes trials into five (5) different types: prevention trials, screening trials, diagnostic trials, treatment trials, quality of life trials and compassionate use trials or expanded access (Glossary of Clinical Trial Terms, NIH Clinicaltrials.gov).

NDA and FDA approval

The new drug application (NDA) is the vehicle in the United States through which drug sponsors formally propose that the food and drug administration (FDA) approve a new pharmaceutical for sale and marketing. The goals of the NDA are to provide enough information to permit FDA reviewers. The NDA includes all of the information from the previous years of work, as well as the proposals for manufacturing and labeling of the new medicine. FDA experts review all the information included in the NDA to determine if it demonstrates that the medicine is safe and effective enough to be approved.

SIGNIFICANCE OF *IN-SILICO* DRUG DISCOVERY PROCESS

As structures of more and more protein targets become available through crystallography, NMR and bioinformatics methods, there is an increasing demand for computational tools that can identify and analyze active sites and suggest potential drug molecules that can bind to these sites specifically. Time and cost required for designing a new drug are immense and at an unacceptable level. According to some estimates it costs about $880 million and 14 years of research to develop a new drug before it is introduced in the market. Intervention of computers at some plausible steps is imperative to bring down the cost and time required in the drug discovery process.

BIOINFORMATICS IN COMPUTER-AIDED DRUG DESIGN

Bioinformatics is the interdisciplinary subject to solve the biological problems in the life science using computational approach. Computer-aided drug design (CADD) is a specialized discipline that uses computational methods to simulate drug-receptor interactions. CADD methods are dependent on bioinformatics tools, applications and biological databases. There are several key areas in bioinformatics regarding CADD research.

Homology modeling

Homology modeling, also known as comparative modeling of protein refers to constructing an atomic-resolution model of the "target" protein from its amino acid sequence and an experimental three-dimensional structure of a related homologous protein (the "template"). Most drug targets are proteins, so it is important to know their 3-D structure. It is estimated that the human body has 500,000 to 1 million proteins. Homology modeling relies on the identification of one or more known protein structures likely to resemble the structure of the query sequence, and on the production of an alignment that maps residues in the query sequence to residues in the template sequence. It has been shown that protein structures are more conserved than protein sequences amongst homologues, but sequences falling below a 20% sequence identity can have very different structure (http://en.wikipedia.org/wiki/Homology_modeling). Modeller is a well-known tool in homology modeling, and the Swiss-Model Repository is a database of protein structures created with homology modeling (Richard, 2005).

Interaction networks

Docking is a method used to identify the fit between a receptor and a potential ligand. Docking actually consists of two distinct parts, the "docking" part, which is the search scheme to identify suitable conformations or poses, and "scoring", which is a measure of the affinity of various poses (http://mndoci.com/2007/02/10/evaluating-protein-ligand-interactions/). Interaction network is a network of nodes that are connected by features. If the feature is a physical and molecular, the interaction network is molecular interactions usually found in cells (http://en.wikipedia.org/wiki/Interaction_network). Protein-ligand docking is a molecular modelling technique. The goal of protein-ligand docking is to predict the position and orientation of a ligand (a small molecule) when it is bound to a protein receptor or enzyme. Docking techniques are employed in the virtual screening of large databases of available chemicals in order to select likely drug candidates (http://en.wikipedia.org/wiki/Protein-ligand_docking). The following are the protein-ligand docking software's:

i)   Gold (http://www.ccdc.cam.ac.uk/products/life_sciences/gold).
ii) AutoDock (http://autodock.scripps.edu/).
iii) Dock (http://dock.compbio.ucsf.edu/).
iv) ZDock (http://zlab.bu.edu/zdock/).
v) Docking server: http://www.dockingserver.com/web.

Microarray analysis

Microarray analysis, known as DNA technology is a new technology now promises to advance biotechnology further. Microarrays are simply ordered sets of DNA molecules of known sequence. Usually rectangular, they can consist of a few hundred to hundreds of thousands of sets. Each individual feature goes on the array at precisely defined location on the substrate. The identity of the DNA molecule fixed to each feature never changes. Scientists use that fact in calculating their experimental results. Microarray analysis permits scientists to detect thousands of genes in a small sample simultaneously and to analyze the expression of those genes. As a result, it promises to enable biotechnology and pharmaceutical companies to identify drug targets. Since it can also help identify individuals with similar biological patterns, microarray analysis can assist drug companies in choosing the most appropriate candidates for participating in clinical trials of new drugs. In the future, this emerging technology has the potential to help medical professionals select the most effective drugs, or

those with the fewest side effects, for individual patients. It has potential applications in several fields, such as tissue microarrays for cancer and other diseases, normal tissues and cells during development, and studies of transgenic animals.Microarray technology has the potential to be used to develop new drugs. "It's clearly been demonstrated that the technology can identify genes that have been upregulated or downregulated," says Jeffrey Williams, CEO of Genomic Solutions, based in Ann Arbor, Michigan (http://www.sciencemag.org/site/products/micro.xhtml). DruTiMine (drug target integrative miner), which is an IBM research project conducted at IBM Centre of Advanced Studies in Cairo (Cairo-CAS) is to identify drug targets for a specific disease: genes, proteins, and chemical compounds by utilizing text mining, association rule mining, and machine learning techniques (Hisham KH (2003).

Virtual high-throughput screening (vHTS)

Pharmaceutical companies are always searching for new leads to develop into drug compounds. One search method is virtual high-throughput screening (vHTS). In vHTS, protein targets are screened against databases of small-molecule compounds to see which molecules bind strongly to the target. If there is a "hit" with a particular compound, it can be extracted from the database for further testing. With today's computational resources, several million compounds can be screened in a few days on sufficiently large clustered computers. Pursuing a handful of promising leads for further development can save researchers considerable time and expense. ZINC is a good example of a vHTS compound library (Satyajit et al., 2010).

Drug lead optimization

When a promising lead candidate has been found in a drug discovery program, the next step is to optimize the structure and properties of the potential drug. This usually involves a series of modifications to the primary structure and secondary structure of the compound. This process can be enhanced using software tools that explore related compounds (bioisosteres) to the lead candidate. OpenEye's WABE is one such tool. Lead optimization tools such as WABE offer a rational approach to drug design that can reduce the time and expense of searching for related compounds (Satyajit et al., 2010).

Drug bioavailability and bioactivity

Most drug candidates fail in Phase III clinical trials after many years of research and millions of dollars have been spent on them. And most fail because of toxicity or problems with metabolism. The key characteristics for drugs are: absorption, distribution, metabolism, excretion, toxicity (ADMET) and efficacy—in other words bioavailability and bioactivity. Although these properties are usually measured in the lab, they can also be predicted in advance with bioinformatics such as C2-ADME, TOPKAT, CLOGP, DrugMatrix, AbSolv, Bioprint, GastroPlus etc.

CONCLUSION

The drug discovery and development process is a long and expensive one. It stars from target identification, after that, validates the targets and identifies the drug candidates. Before any newly discovered drug is placed on the market, it must undergo extreme preclinical and clinical tests and get the FDA approval. Due to the limitation of throughput, accuracy and cost, experimental techniques cannot be applied widely, therefore, in recent times the drug discovery process has shifted to *in silico* approaches such as homology modeling, protein-ligand interactions, microarrary analysis, vHTS etc. *In silico* approach has been of great importance to develop fast and accurate target identification and prediction method for the discovery.

REFERENCES

api.ning.com/files/.../DrugDiscoveryNewDrugDevelopmentProcess.ppt.

Richard C (2005). Bioinformatics in Computer-Aided Drug Design, May 10.

Bleicher KH, Bohm HJ, Muller K, Alanine AI (2003). "Hit and lead generation: Beyond high-throughput screening." Nat. Rev. Drug Discov., 2(5): 369-378. May.

Suresh KP, Siddharth M, Rao V, Vadlamudi SV (2006). Current approaches in drug discovery. Pharma Times - Vol 38 - No. 8 - August.

Hisham E, Taysir HA, Soliman IE (2006). "Mining Drug Targets: The Challenges and a Proposed Framework." Proc. 11th IEEE Symp. Comput. Commun. (ISCC'06).

http://en.wikipedia.org/wiki/Binding_site

http://en.wikipedia.org/wiki/Drug_design

http://en.wikipedia.org/wiki/Homology_modeling

http://en.wikipedia.org/wiki/Interaction_network

http://en.wikipedia.org/wiki/Protein-ligand_docking.

http://english.simm.cas.cn/rp/201007/t20100701_55978.html

http://mndoci.com/2007/02/10/evaluating-protein-ligand-interactions/

http://www.kauhort.in/Download/SBDD.pdf

http://www.microcal.com/drug-discovery-development/small-molecule/target-identification.asp.

http://www.minglebox.com/blog/l7530/post/in_silico_drug_design

http://www.scfbio-iitd.res.in/tutorial/drugdiscovery.htm

http://www.sciencemag.org/site/products/micro.xhtml

Klaus ODVM, Peter GU, Nzel DVM, Rolf BMD (2001). "Preclinical Testing Strategies." Drug Inf. J. 35: 321–336.

Markus HJ Seifert JK, Bernd K (2007). "Virtual high-throughput screening of molecular databases." Curr. Opin. Drug Discov. Dev., 10(3): 298-307. May

Robert AG (2006). "Hit and lead identification: Integrated technology-based., 3 (4)

Satyajit D, Sovan S, Kapil S (2010). Computer Aided Drug Design- A New Approach in Drug Design and Discovery. Int. J. Pharm. Sci. Rev. Res., 4(3). September – October.

Suresh KP, Siddharth M, Rao V, Vadlamudi SV (2006). "Current approaches in drug discovery." Pharma Times, 38(8). August.

Yongliang Y, Adelstein SJ, Amin IK (2009). Target discovery from data mining approaches. 20 January.

Taylor, Francis (2006). *"In silico* Technologies in Drug Target Identification and Validation." Taylor and Francis Group, LLC.

Xiaofeng L, Sisheng O, Biao Y, Yabo L, Kai H, Jiayu G, Siyuan Z, Zhihua L, Honglin L, Hualiang J (2010). "PharmMapper server: A web server for potential drug target identification using pharmacophore mapping approach." Nucleic Acids Res., 38: W609-W614.

## 16

Choke point analysis of the metabolic pathways of *Acinetobacter baylyi*: A genomics approach to assess potential drug targets

Shailza Singh*, Priyanka Joshi and Balu Ananda Chopade

Institute of Bioinformatics and Biotechnology, University of Pune, Pune-411007, India.

Numerous species of the genus *Acinetobacter* have been known to cause various nosocomial infections. An insight into the pathogenesis of *Acinetobacter baylyi* reveals that it is a potent organism in causing nosocomial infections. In this study, choke point analysis of the entire metabolic network of *A. baylyi* is performed to assess potential drug targets. Potential drug targets are proposed based on the analysis of the top 8 choke points in the bacterial network. A comparative study between the reported top 8 bacterial choke points and the human metabolic network was performed. Further biological inferences were made on results obtained by performing a homology search against the human genome. The study was successful in listing out of the potential drug targets from these pathways which may be useful for the discovery of broad-spectrum drugs.

Key words: Choke points, *Acinetobacter baylyi*, human genome, drug discovery, metabolic pathway, opportunistic pathogen.

INTRODUCTION

Acinetobacter spp. plays a significant role in the colonization and infection of immunocompromised patients. They have been implicated in a variety of nosocomial infections, including bacteremia, urinary tract infection and secondary meningitis, but their predominant role is as agents of nosocomial pneumonia, particularly ventilator-associated pneumonia in patients confined to hospital intensive care units (Bergogne-Bérézin and Towner, 1996). Such infections are often difficult to be treated by the clinician as these strains have developed resistance to the classical antibiotics used. This calls for an urgent need for identification of novel drug targets to effectively combat nosocomial infections. Infact, these bacteria have a significant capacity for long term survival in the hospital environment, with corresponding enhanced opportunities for transmission between patients, either via human reservoirs or via inanimate materials. In this study, *Acinetobacter baylyi* (also called *Acinetobacter* sp. ADP1), an opportunistic pathogen (Chen et

al., 2008), is used as a model organism for the identification of novel drug targets for effective treatment of nosocomial infections.

A. baylyi is highly competent for natural transformation (Young et al., 2005). Due to this ability, ADP1 can effectively express a wide variety of foreign genes including antibiotic resistance cassettes, essential metabolic genes, negatively selectable catabolic genes and even intact operons from highly divergent bacteria (Metzgar et al., 2004). This makes it an opportunistic pathogen which is capable of causing secondary infections in association with other gram negative bacilli. Moreover, *Pseudomonas aeruginosa* is phylogenetically the closest organism to ADP1 (Jacobs et al., 2003) and shares 1655 orthologous genes with it (V de Berardinis et al., 2008). One thousand one hundred and seventy seven orthologous genes are shared between *E. coli* and ADP1 (V de Berardinis et al., 2008). Due to a considerable degree of homology between the genes of ADP1 and these pathogenic gram-negative bacilli, it is a potent causal organism of secondary infections in association with them. Also, its high competence for natural transformation (Barbe et al., 2004) may favour uptake of DNA from pathogenic strains in the hospital environment. An

---

*Corresponding author. E-mail: shailza_iitd@yahoo.com.

Table 1. The reaction and its EC number are given. The In Human column denotes whether or not the enzymatic activity has a similar enzyme in human as determined by BLAST alignment with an expectation of less than 0.0001.

Target enzyme	EC number	References	Chokepoint	In human
Lipoyl synthase	2.8.1.8	Kok et al., 1995	Yes	Yes
DNA directed RNA polymerase	2.7.7.6	V de Berardinis et al., 2008	Yes	Yes
UDP-N-acetylmuramate:L-alanyl-gamma-D-glutamyl-meso-diaminopimelate ligase (murein peptide ligase)	6.3.2.-	Chakravorty et al., 2007	Yes	No
ssDNA exonuclease, 5'→3' specific, Mg Dependent	3.1.-.-	Kickstein et al., 2007	Yes	No
UDP-N-acetylmuramate-alanine ligase	6.3.2.8	V de Berardinis et al., 2008	Yes	No
Tryptophan synthase	4.2.1.20	Cohn and Crawford, 1976	Yes	No
Phosphopantetheinyl transferase	2.7.8.-	V de Berardinis et al., 2008	Yes	No
GTP cyclohydrolase I	3.5.4.16	El Yacoubi Basma, 2006	Yes	Yes

insight into its pathogenesis has revealed that it also cause nosocomial infections particularly bacteremia in immunocompromised patients (Chen et al., 2008). As certain genes are present in *A. baylyi*, which show resistance to traditional antibiotics (Gomez et al., 2006), there is an urgent need for the identification of novel drug targets.

Understanding the cellular mechanisms and interactions between cellular components is instrumental to the development of new effective drugs and vaccines. Metabolic pathway analysis is increasingly becoming important for assessing inherent properties in biochemical reaction networks. Choke point strategy enables to classify reactions that either uniquely consume a specific substrate or produce a specific product (Yeh et al., 2004). Such reactions, called choke point reactions, are believed to be essential to the pathogen's survival and are therefore potential drug targets. This study identifies such choke points in the metabolic network of *A. baylyi* as potential drug targets.

MATERIALS AND METHODS

Sequence Retrieval and pathway analysis

KEGG (Kyoto Encyclopedia of Genes and Genomes (Kanehisa et al., 2002) pathway database was used as a source of metabolic pathway information. KEGG provides with a typical metabolic network consisting of reactions, metabolites and enzymes. Metabolic pathway identification numbers of the host *Homo sapiens* and the pathogen *A. baylyi* were extracted from the KEGG database. A network based comparative study of the choke points was performed between *A. baylyi* and *Homo sapiens*. BLASTp (Altschul et al., 1997) package was used to infer homology between the sequences. Further, gene ontologies archived in different databases viz. UniProt, Microbial Genome Database and Genoscope were used to predict functions of the enzymes coded by these genes.

Choke point analyses

Here the choke point analyses method of Yeh et al. (2004) has been adopted.

Chokepoint analyses are particularly straightforward to perform with a computational representation of metabolism and there are

certain reactions that are excluded from the chokepoint analysis, namely proteolytic reactions (as the specificity of these reactions is not captured), reactions that do not have clearly defined substrates (e.g., protein disulfide isomerase), and reactions with important side effects (many ATPases). Although these enzymes could be good drug targets, the rationale of the method is not expected to apply in these cases.

If an enzyme catalyzes at least one chokepoint reaction, it is classified as a potential drug target. All the potential metabolic drug targets are listed in Table 1.

To assess the usefulness of identifying chokepoint enzymes for proposing drug targets, chokepoints and non-chokepoints against proposed drug targets from the literature is compared. A complete literature search for proposed *Acinetobacter* drug targets is attempted that were metabolic enzymes and met the criteria outlined above. Of the 12 proposed targets with biological evidence, 8 are chokepoints in Table 1. Due to the high percentage of enzymes identified as choke points, one additional criteria observed in addition to being a choke point enzyme for identifying potential metabolic drug targets is that an enzyme not having an isozyme would make it more likely to be a good drug target. This is because one enzyme would be easier to inhibit than a family of enzymes. NADH Dehydrogenase I in *Acinetobacter* has two isozymes and according to the criteria outlined above, it has not been included in the list of potential drug targets identified in Table 1.

There are further aspects on which the list of potential drug targets can be narrowed down. The drug should adversely affect the parasite but not the human host; therefore, if the drug target has a homologous enzyme in human, it should not be essential or have differential inhibition in human (perhaps due to different protein structure or different regulation). Potential drug targets should be expressed in the human stages of the pathogen.

RESULTS

Potential drug targets are proposed based on the analysis of the top 8 choke points in the bacterial network. A comparative study between the reported top 8 bacterial choke points and the human metabolic network was performed. Further biological inferences were made on results obtained by performing a homology search against the human genome. The study was successful in listing out the potential drug targets from these pathways, which may be useful for the discovery of broad-spectrum drugs.

A total of 8 choke point enzymes have been identified

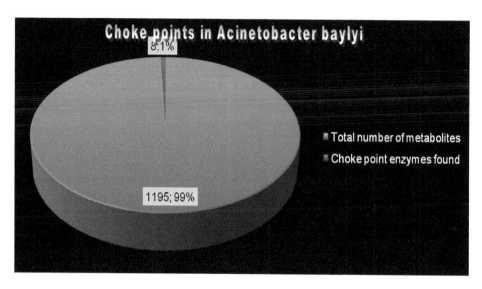

Figure 1. Choke point enzymes in the metabolome of *Acinetobacter baylyi.*

from the metabolome of *A. baylyi,* which comprise 1% of the metabolome of the pathogen (Figure 1). Strategy applied has been explained in Materials and Methods. Of the 8 choke points 3 choke points have homologs in human and may interfere in drug-pathogen enzyme interaction causing some side effects. Therefore 62.5% of the reported targets are choke point enzymes having no human homologs. The 8 choke points are given in Table 1.

DISCUSSION

Drug target identification based on 'omics' networks (di Bernardo et al., 2005; Giaever et al., 2004; Yeh et al., 2004) is a very promising approach that has recently become possible. The concept of choke points (Dawson and Elliot, 1980) in a given network contributes effectively in the identification of drug targets.

Often drugs are identified by a unique pathogen specific metabolic activity approach, as in the case of reverse transcriptase in HIV (Imamichi, 2004). However, the screening of the entire pathogen network to find choke point based potential drug targets followed by a study with the human metabolic network provides additional results. Further, some enzymes for e.g. Lipoyl synthase, show a significant similarity at e-inclusion threshold value of 0.0001, thus have a human homologue. Such enzymes may still be used as drug targets because the e-inclusion value has been set so as to detect closely related homologues. No homologue in such a case may lead to an inference that it is not a drug target as the two protein sequences are divergent due to evolutionary lineage. In such cases the target may be effective without causing any side effects to the host. However, experimental validation of these drug targets may remove any ambiguity. The targets obtained in this

study are obtained by reliable computational approaches and have a sound grounding for future analysis. Annotations provided in *Acineto*Cyc (Genoscope), KEGG Metabolic Pathways and UniProt (Expasy proteomics server) are analyzed to investigate further on the predictability of the enzymes as potential drug targets. Figure 2 depicts the loci of the Open Reading Frames of the genes encoding the choke point enzymes. Such a representation highlights the pathways in which these enzymes are involved and their essentiality.

All the 8 choke point enzymes identified in the study are essential for the pathogen's survival. GTP cyclohydrolase-I is the first enzyme of the Tetrahydrofolate pathway (THF) and serve as a cofactor during the synthesis of purines, glycine, serine and also the initiator formyl methionyl t-RNA (El Yacoubi et al., 2006). The presence of homologous enzymes in both human and bacteria has precluded the development of GTP-cyclohydrolase-I as a viable target. Murein peptide ligase (Mpl) acts in response to DNA damage. Moreover an Mpl deficient mutant is susceptible to β-lactamases. Since *E. coli* mutants do not show susceptibility to β-lactamases so Mpl is a potential target for species-specific antibacterial compounds. Tryptophan synthase is responsible for the synthesis of L-tryptophan from indole and L-serine. It is thus essential for amino acid biosynthesis. DNA dependent RNA polymerase catalyzes the transcription of DNA into RNA using four ribonucleotides as substrates. UDP-N-acetylmuramate-alanine ligase is essential for cell wall formation and peptidoglycan biosynthesis. *recJ* encoded ssDNA exonuclease is essential for genetic transformation and it has been shown that its deletion is lethal (Kickstein et al., 2007) Lipoate synthase is essential for the biosynthesis of cofactors, prosthetic groups, and carriers. Phosphopantethenyl transferase is essential for siderophore synthesis. The iron acquisition systems of many pathogenic and saprophytic bacteria

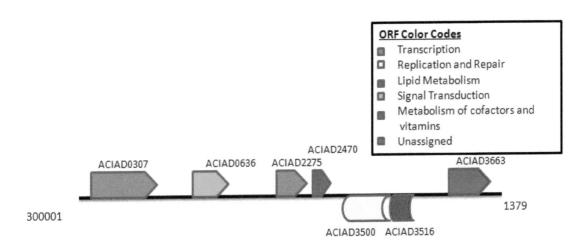

Figure 2. Diagrammatical representation of the chokepoint enzymes coding genes on the genome map of *A. baylyi*. Open Reading Frame (ORF) colour codes depict the various metabolic pathways in which these chokepoint enzymes are involved.

rely on the production of small molecules called sidero-phores. Siderophores allow the pathogen to thrive in the human microenvironment by the uptake of free iron. By identifying choke point reactions, enzymes essential for the pathogen's survival have been identified. The identification of choke point enzymes has led to the enrichment of drug targets as compared to the non choke point enzymes.

Conclusion

The genome sequence has allowed to fill in much of the metabolism of *A. baylyi*, revealing that many pathways normally present in eukaryotes are absent from this organism. It is also possible that some 'missing' pathways are actually present, but they may not be identifiable. In addition, by identifying choke point reactions, it has been tried to identify enzymes that are essential to the parasite's survival. There is an enrichment of drug targets in chokepoints as compared with non-chokepoints. This leads to the conclusion that the classification of an enzyme as a chokepoint has some bearing on whether or not it would make a good drug target. The choke point analysis is limited, because the capabilities of the parasite to transport an accumulating metabolite out of the cell or a limiting metabolite into the cell have not been considered. One reason that chokepoints may not be essential could be that they create unique intermediates to an essential product that are not essential themselves because of another pathway to the essential product. Finally, there could be chokepoint reactions that are not essential due to other pathways that achieve the same metabolic goal within the organism, such that blocking the reaction has no deleterious effects on the parasite. The provisional targets which have been cited here needs to be examined further, both computationally and experimentally for these additional features.

REFERENCES

Altshcul SF, Madden T, Schaffer AA, Zhang J, Zhang Z, Miller W, Lipman DJ (1997). Gapped BLAST and PSI-BLAST: a new generation of protein database search programs. Nucleic Acids Res. 25: 3389-3402

Barbe V, Vallenet D, Fonknechten N, Kreimeyer A, Oztas S, Labarre L, Cruveiller S, Robert C, Duprat S, Wincker P, Ornston LN, Weissenbach J, Marlière P, Cohen GN, Médigue C (2004). Unique features revealed by the genome sequence of *Acinetobacter sp. ADP1*, a versatile and naturally transformation competent bacterium. Nucleic Acids Res. 32: 5766 – 5779

Bergogne-Bérézin E, Towner KJ (1996). *Acinetobacter spp.* as Nosocomial Pathogens: Microbiol.Clin.and Epidemiol. Features. Clin. Microbiol. Rev. 9:148-165

Chakravorty A, Klovstad M, Peterson G, Lindeman RE, Leslie A, Gregg-Jolly(2007). Sensitivity of *Acinetobacter baylyi* mpl mutant to DNA damage. App. and Environ. Biol. 74: 1273-1275

Chen TL, Siu LK, Lee YT, Chen CP, Huang LY, Roy CCW, Cho WL, Fung CP (2008). New insights of *Acinetobacter baylyi* as a pathogen for opportunistic infections. J.Clin. Biol. 46:9

Cohn W, Crawford IP (1976). Regulation of enzyme synthesis in the tryptophan pathway of Acinetobacter calcoaceticus. J Bacteriol. 127:367-379

Dawson SV, Elliot EA (1980). Use of the choke point in the prediction of flow limitation in elastic tubes. Fed. Proc. 39:2765-2770

de Berardinis V, Vallenet D, Castelli V, Besnard M, Pinet A, Cruaud C, Samair S, Lechaplais C, Gyapay G, Richez C, Durot M, Kreimeyer A, Fèvre FL, Schächter V, Pezo V, Döring V, Scarpelli C, Médigue C, Cohen GN, Marlière P, Salanoubat M, Weissenbach J (2008). A complete collection of single-gene deletion mutants of *Acinetobacter baylyi* ADP1. Mol. Syst. Biol. 4:174-4292

Kanehisa M, Goto S, Kawashima S, Nakaya A (2002). The KEGG databases at GenomeNET. Nucleic Acids Res. 30:42-4

di Bernardo D et al. (2005). Chemogenomic profiling on a genome wide scale using reverse-engineered gene networks. Nat. Biotechnol. 23: 377-383

El Yacoubi B, Bonnett S, Anderson JN, Swairjo MA, Iwata-Reuyl (2006).Discovery of a new prokaryotic type I GTP cyclohydrolase family. V. J. Biol. Chem. 14:76-83

Giaever G, Flaherty P, Kumm J, Proctor M, Nislow C, Jaramillo DF, Chu AM, Jordan MI, Arkin AP, Davis RW (2004) Chemogenomic profiling: identifying the functional interactions of small molecules in yeast. Proc. Natl. Acad. Sci. USA. 99:7821-7826

Gomez MJ, Neyfakh AA. (2006). Genes involved in intrinsic antibiotic resistance of *Acinetobacter baylyi* ADP1. Antimicrob. Agents Chemother. 50: 3562-3567

Imamichi T (2004). Action of anti-HIV drugs and resistance: reverse transcriptase inhibitors and protease inhibitors. Curr. Pharm. Des. 10:4039-4053

Jacobs MA, Altwood A, Thaipisuttikul I, Spencer D et al (2003). Comprehensive transposon mutant library of *Pseudomonas aeruginosa.* Proc. Natl. Acad. Sci. USA. 100:14339-14344

Kickstein E, Klaus H, Wilfried W (2007). Deletions of *recBCD* or *recD* influence genetic transformation differently and are lethal together with a *recJ*. deletion. Microbiol. 153: 2259- 2270

Kok RG, Young DM, Ornston LN (1999). Phenotypic Expression of PCR-Generated Random Mutations in a *Pseudomonas putida* Gene after Its Introduction into an *Acinetobacter* Chromosome by Natural Transformation. Appl. Environ. Microbiol. 65: 1675-1680.

Yeh I, Hanekamp T, Tsoka S, Karp PD, Altman RB (2004). Computational analysis of *Plasmodium falciparum* metabolism: Organizing genomic information to facilitate drug discovery. Genome Res. 14:917-924

Young DM, Parke D, Ornston LN (2005). Opportunities for genetic investigation afforded by *Acinetobacter baylyi*, a nutritionally versatile bacterial species that is highly competent for natural transformation. Annu. Rev. Microbiol. 59:519-551

## 17

Effect of physical activity on plasma metabonomics variation using ^{1}H NMR, anthropometric and modeling methods

Mohammad Arjmand[1], Fatemeh Darvizeh[2], Ziba Akbari[1], Reyhaneh Mohabati[1] and Zahra Zamani[1]*

[1]Department of Biochemistry, Pasteur Institute of Iran, Pasteur Ave, Tehran 13164, Iran.
[2]Department of Chemistry, Sharif University of Technology, Tehran 11155-9516, Iran.

The metabolic changes in serum during a sport program were explored using a metabonomic approach, based on proton nuclear magnetic resonance (^{1}H-NMR) spectroscopy and anthropometry. The aim of this study was to classify two groups of female university students with body mass index over 25 kg/m^2, using multiple measured descriptors. The first group (n=16) underwent a complex and well programmed 18-week physical training courses, and the second group (n=8), which was our control group, did not participate in any training course. Our descriptors consist of anthropometric descriptors (including height, weight, circumferences of arm, waist, hip and thigh, lean body mass and fat mass percentiles). Serum levels of growth hormone, insulin, and insulin like growth factor-1 were measured. ^{1}H-NMR spectra was obtained using a 500-MHz Bruker spectrometer and was calculated for certain chemical shift integrals using Chenomx software for all the individuals in both groups. These descriptors were measured both before and after the training program for the experimental group. In order to make a linear model between growth hormone (GH) and ^{1}H-NMR matrix as a set of variables, initially by multiple linear regression (MLR) stepwise as the variable selection method, the most important descriptors were selected by MLR modeling approaches. The results obtained for R^2 training and test show an agreement between experimental and theoretical GH values. By applying counter-propagation Artificial Neural Networks (CP-ANN) classification methods, we significantly separated our 1st group from the other one.

Key words: Physical activity, blood serum, nuclear magnetic resonance, multiple linear regressions, artificial neural network.

INTRODUCTION

Studying human metabolite variations caused by external factors like diet, drugs and physical activity is a subdivision of metabonomic, which is defined as the quantitative measurement of the dynamic multiparametric metabolic response of living systems to pathophysiological stimuli or genetic modification (Gavaghan et al., 2000). The proton nuclear magnetic resonance (^{1}H-NMR) spectroscopy of biofluids (urine, serum/plasma) and tissue generates comprehensive biochemical profiles of low molecular weight endogenous metabolites (Solanky et al., 2003). Nuclear magnetic resonance (NMR) spectroscopy has also emerged as a key tool for understanding metabolic processes in living systems (Brown et al., 1977).

The range of spectroscopic techniques that are used in metabonomics are often so-called 'hyphenated' mode (e.g. liquid chromatography/ nuclear magnetic resonance/ mass spectrometry (LC–NMR–MS). A detailed inspection of NMR spectra and integration of individual peaks can give valuable information on dominant biochemical changes, in this way Pattern recognition method can be used to map the NMR spectra into a lower dimensional

---

*Corresponding author. E-mail: zzahrazamani@yahoo.com.

Table 1. Walking distances.

Week	1	2	3	4	5	6
Average distance of running-walking (m)	2198.7	2858.3	3430	3944.5	4338.9	4555.9

space (implied by the number of points in the digital representation of the NMR spectrum) such that any clustering of the samples that is based on similarities of biochemical profiles can be easily determined (Nicholson et al., 1995; Coen et al., 2005).

Obesity is the heavy accumulation of fat in a body to such a degree that it rapidly increases the risk of diseases such as diabetes and heart disease. The fat may be equally distributed around the body or concentrated on the stomach or the hips and thigh (Fujioka et al., 1991). Urinary creatinine, lactate, pyruvate, alanine, β-hydroxybutyrate, acetate and hypoxanthine profiles shows a change after acute and chronic physical exercise by ^{1}HNMR base metabolomics approaches (Enea et al., 2010). In the present investigation, we used anthropometric variables along with growth hormone (GH), insulin-like growth factor-1 (IGF-1), serum insulin level along with ^{1}HNMR profiles to distinguish a control group of 8 obese girls with body mass index (BMI) > 25 from a group of 16 obese girls who undergone combined aerobic and anaerobic physical exercises for 18 weeks. The aim was to classify two groups of obese students with body-mass index over 25 kg/m², using multiple measured descriptors and find out the key metabolite changes in the experimental group.

MATERIALS AND METHODS

Samples collection and preparation

A group of obese female students from Shariff University with BMI>25 were taken for this study. They have been instructed to use controlled and the same regiment of diet. These were divided into two groups: The first group (n = 16) underwent a complex and well programmed 18-week physical training courses. The test group (average age 18.9 ± 1.3 years, height 159 ± 0.04 cm, weight 73.46 ± 7.75 kg) did a 90-min program consisting of running-walking with 60-70% intensity of a maximum heart beat (made in Finland and with distance Polar; CE0537, F1) and with increasing distance in every week (Table 1), light strength building exercise (using body weight and small weights) and also aerobic exercise consisting of sit up, Swedish push up and etc. 3 times a week, each session lasting 90 min for 6 weeks. The 2nd group (n = 8) was taken as our control group; they did not participate in any physical training program. Our description consisted of the anthropometric descriptors (including height, weight, circumferences of arm, waist, hip and thigh, lean body mass and fat mass percentiles). This study was approved by Department's Ethical Committee.

Fasting blood serum was collected from these groups on the 6th week at 8 o' clock in the morning and stored at -20°C until assayed. Serum total IGF-1 (Biosource, Belgium), insulin (DRG, Germany) and human growth hormone (Radim, Italy) were assayed by

enzyme-linked immunosorbent assay (ELISA) methods. Intra assay and inter-assay coefficient of variation were 6.6 and 13.3% for IGF-1, 2.2 and 4.4% for insulin, and 4.2 and 5.3% for human growth hormone, respectively.

^{1}HNMR spectroscopy

Prior to NMR analysis, serum samples (60 μL) were diluted with 600 μL of 52% Deuterium oxide (D_2O, 99.9 at. % D, Aldrich Chemicals Company, South Africa) and placed in 5 mm high quality NMR tubes (Sigma Aldrich., RSA). Conventional ^{1}H-NMR spectra of each serum sample was measured at 500 MHz on a Bruker Avance with Carr–Purcell–Meiboom–Gill (CPMG) protocol at Shariff University as described by Lin et al. (2007).

Data reduction of NMR data

Each ^{1}H-NMR spectrum was corrected for phase and baseline distortion using Chenomx NMR suite (version 6.0) and the 0.0 - 10.0 parts per million (ppm) spectral region was reduced to 250 integral segments of equal width of 0.04. This optimal width of segmented regions is based on previous studies, which found the regions of 0.04 ppm accommodated any small pH-related shifts in signals and variation in shimming quality (Coen et al., 2005).

Statistical analysis

At preprocessing step to NMR spectroscopy analysis, orthogonal signal correction (OSC) which removed orthogonal variations to the class of interest was done (Gavaghan, et al., 2002). In the OSC, identification of sample classes will be assigned by a vector, Y. Calculation of the first principal component or score vector t, is the first step in OSC method, which describes the maximum separation based on classes. Concerning this corrected vector, the loading vector, p* is measured. The product of the orthogonal score and loading vectors is removed from the data of a spectrum. The residual matrix represents the filtered spectral data and was then used for calculation of multiple linear regression (MLR) and CP-ANNs. Stepwise-MLR was used to select the best descriptors among 250. Then the selected variables were used in order to make a linear model.

Multiple linear regression (MLR) techniques based on least-squares procedures are very often used for estimating the coefficients involved in the model equation (Porter et al., 1981). Artificial Neural networks (ANNs) can solve both supervised and unsupervised problems, such as clustering and modeling of qualitative responses (classification). Among ANN learning strategies, Kohonen Maps (Figure 1) and ANNs are two of the most popular approaches that were applied to our data. Kohonen Maps are self-organizing systems applied to the unsupervised problems (cluster analysis and data structure analysis). CP-ANNs (Figure 2) are very similar to the Kohonen Maps and are essentially based on the Kohonen approach, but combines characteristics from both supervised and unsupervised learning, that is CP-ANNs can be used to build both regression and classification models (Ballabio et al., 2007).

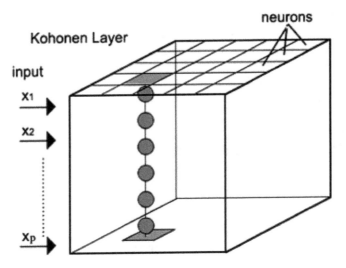

Figure 1. Structure of a Kohonen layer.

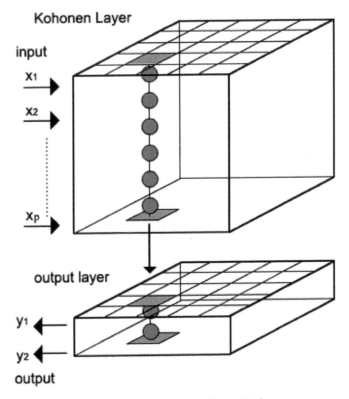

Figure 2. Structure of a counter-propagation network.

RESULTS AND DISCUSSION

To find out the important variables affecting the GH serum levels of two groups (from all 48 samples, 32 and 16 of them related to pre-activity and post-activity tests respectively), we performed stepwise multiple linear regression (MLR) and genetic algorithm –partial least square (GA-PLS) on the data matrix (X) after the application of orthogonal signal correction (OSC). Results indicated that both methods provided same frequency ranges for the participant and non-participant groups as significant descriptors. IGF-1, Insulin serum levels and anthropometric data could not lead us to an acceptable classification or calibration model. For the physical activity participant group, the integral values of low density lipoprotein (LDL), very low density lipoprotein

Table 2. Specifications of the selected MLR Descriptors.

Parameter	Descriptors	NMR Range	Coefficients	Mean	Mean effect [a]
Physical activity experimental groups	Cholesterol/LDL /VLDL	0.84 -0.88	35.90	0.0056	0.20
	Glycerol /Choline (lipid)	3.64 -3.68	100.53	0.0035	0.35
Control Group	Tyrosine	6.44-6.48	182.32	0.0051	0.09
	β-glucose	5.04 -5.08	257.20	0.0024	0.62
	Glutamine /Leucine /Citrulline /α -glucose	3.68 -3.72	205.44	0.0026	0.53

[a]Mean effect of a descriptor is the product of its mean and regression coefficient in the MLR model.

Table 3. The results for MLR model.

Data	Training set			Test Set		
	RMSE	R^2	F-test	RMSE	R^2	F-test
Physical activity experimental group	0.032	0.998	6313.52	0.065	0.989	481.03
Control Group	0.24	0.995	1397.03	0.23	0.950	81.06

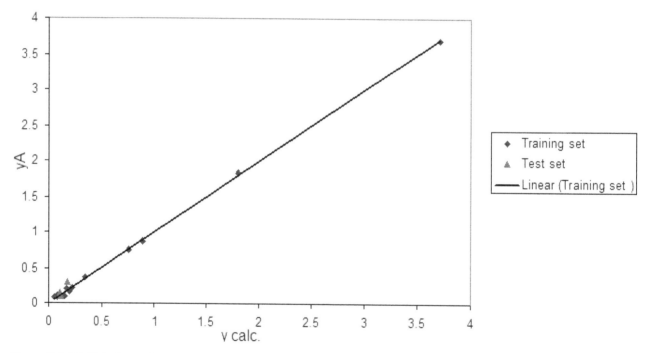

Figure 3. MLR Plot of experimental vs. the calculated values of GH (yA/ycalc.) for the training and test sets in physical activity experimental group 1.

(VLDL) and choline (Lipid) were obtained as the most important descriptors and for control group also, 3 sets of important descriptors in a specific chemical shift range of NMR were measured (Table 2). All these variables were used in the next section to classify the two obese girl groups.

Table 2 shows the most important descriptors with their properties calculated with MLR- stepwise. For the next step (modeling), the GH based on the best descriptors for both two groups is the main goal. The regression results for the selected MLR model are presented in Table 3. The R^2 for training set were shown to be 0.998 and 0.989, respectively. For test set, experimental and control groups were 0.995 and 0.950, accordingly. Figures 3 and 4 show the correlation between the MLR calculated and the experimental values of the GH included in the training and test sets for the physical activity of the experimental and control group, respectively. The results indicate a

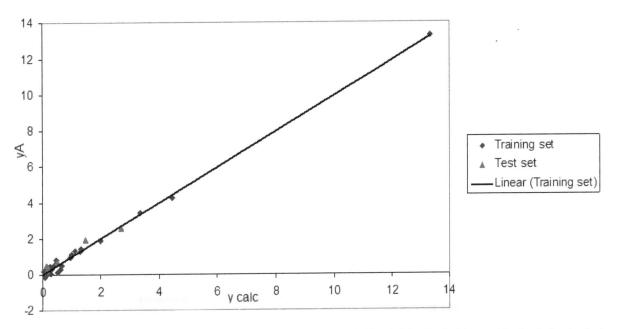

Figure 4. MLR Plot of experimental vs the calculated values of GH (yA/ycalc.) for the training and test sets in physical activity experimental group 2.

Table 4. Results of analysis: error rate(ER) and non -error rate (NER) for model and cross validation.

Data	NER	ER
Model	0.94	0.06
C.V	0.86	0.14

reasonable agreement between these values. After applying Counter Propagation Artificial Neural Network (CPANN) on the selected variables, two groups of physical activity program participants and non-participants were not effectively classified. Applying OSC, with GH serum levels of two groups as dependent "Y" matrix, led to an acceptable classification model.

Samples from obese girls, which gave the most important descriptors, were calculated with MLR-stepwise method. The samples belong to two different groups and consequently, the final aim of the classification model was the determination of influence of physical exercise on obsesses girls. Kohonen maps, which deal with unsupervised issues, are not directly treated here since they are implicitly calculated as the Kohonen layer of CP-ANNs. To find the optimal CP-ANNs settings, several networks are usually evaluated by changing the number of neurons and training epochs. Settings are then selected based on the optimization of a classification parameter, such as non-error rate, present cross- validated samples. Settings were chosen based on personal experience by selecting a reasonable number of epochs (200) and a number of neurons relatively selected

close to the number of samples (49, constituting a squared map with 7 neurons on each side). Data were auto-scaled.

In Table 4 part of the classification indices calculated (error rate, non- error rate) is shown, also the classification performances refer to the cross-validation result. It is important to have an insight into the model by interpreting samples and variables relationships. This can be done by analyzing the Kohonen top map, the neurons constituting the network. In the top map, samples can be projected in order to evaluate the data structure, the presence of cluster or outliers; while variable importance can be analyzed by coloring the neurons based on the neuron weights that are comprised between 0 and 1(Ballabio et al., 2009). The Kohonen top map (Figure 5) represents the space defined by the neurons where the samples are placed. Samples are visualized by randomly scattering their positions within the squares; Different samples are placed far apart, while similar samples occupy the same neuron. Thus visual investigation of the data structure by analyzing the sample positions and their relationships are allowed. The neurons can be colored based on the weight values. Therefore, it is possible to

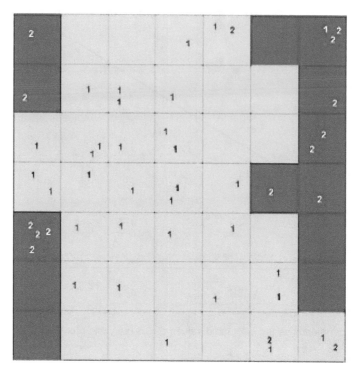

Figure 5. Top map of the classification of samples by Kohonen artificial neural network. 1 is assigned as control and 2 is experimental samples.

interpret the sample relationships as well as the variable influence.

An alternative consists of performing principal component analysis (PCA) on the Kohonen weights, in order to investigate the relationships between variables and samples in a global way and not one variable at a time (Scampicchio et al., 2008). PCA is a well-known pattern-recognition technique, which projects the data in a reduced hyperspace, defined by the first significant principal components (Wold et al., 1987). The weights of the Kohonen layer can be arranged as a data matrix with N2 rows and J columns, where N is the number of neurons on each side of the map and J the number of variables. Therefore, each element wrj of the matrix W represents the weight of the j-th variable in the r-th neuron. By applying PCA on the W matrix, a loading matrix (with dimension J×F, where F is the number of significant principal components) and a score matrix (N2×F) is obtained. By comparing the corresponding loading and score plots, the relationships between variables and neurons can be evaluated. Each neuron can be assigned to a class (when dealing with CP-ANNs) and the relationships between variables and classes can also be investigated (Ballabio et al., 2007). For this reason, a GUI for calculating PCA on the Kohonen weights is provided (Figure 6).

In Figures 4 to 6 the score and loading plots of the first two components (explaining 96.12% of the total information) are shown. In the score plot, each point represents a neuron of the previous CP-ANN model. From each neuron, it is easy to see that neurons assigned to class 1 (Control group) are all clustered and placed at the right side of the score plot. Then, comparing score and loading plots, one can evaluate how all the variables characterize this specific class. Variables 3, 4 and 5 are placed at the right of the loading plot and thus is directly correlated with class 1. On the contrary, variables 1 and 2 have the largest negative loadings in the first component and thus samples of class 2 will be characterized by the values of these variables.

Conclusion

Metabolite profile was significantly altered after 18-week training program. The same method of classification can be used to evaluate several physical activity courses to ascertain their similarities and differences, and therefore, design an optimal physical activity course considering the NMR profile and GH level alterations. Furthermore, we were able to effectively predict GH serum levels by our linear models. So it is applicable to use NMR descriptors for quantitatively predicting the serum level alterations of GH and probably other hormones during physical activity. Since the 0.84 - 0.88 ppm chemical shift is attributable to mainly low density lipoprotein (LDL) and very low density lipoprotein (VLDL), the linear model can also support the hypothesis that increasing LDL and VLDL amounts lead

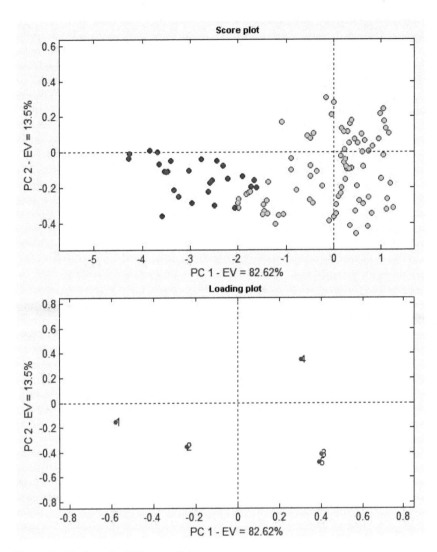

Figure 6. Interface for PCA on weights.

to increase in GH hormone, and the elevated GH hormone by increasing lipoprotein lipase activity, will decrease LDL and VLDL levels.

REFERENCES

Ballabio D, Kokkinofta R, Todeschini R, Theocharis CR (2007). Characterization of the traditional Cypriot spirit Zivania by means of Counter-propagation Artificial Neural Networks. IT. J. Chemometr. Intell. Lab. Syst. 87:52-58.

Ballabio D, Consonni V, Todeschini R (2009). The Kohonen and CP-ANN toolbox: A collection of MATLAB modules for Self Organizing Maps and Counter-propagation Artificial Neural Networks .IT. J. Chemometr. Intell. Lab. Syst. 98:115-122.

Brown FF, CampbellID, Kuchel PW, Rabenstein DC (1977). Human erythrocyte metabolism studies by 1H spin echo NMR.EN. J. FEBS Lett. 82:12-16.

Coen M, O'Sullivan M, Bubb WA, KuchelPW,Sorrell T (2005). Proton nuclear magnetic resonance-based metabonomics for rapid diagnosis of meningitis and ventriculitis. AU. J. Clin. Infect. Dis. 41:1582-1590.

Enea C, Seguin F, Petitpas-Mulliez J, Boildieu N, Boisseau N, Delpech N, Diaz V, Eugene M, Dugue B (2010). (1)H NMR-based metabolomics approach for exploring urinary metabolome modifications after acute and chronic physical exercise. FR. J. Anal. Bioanal. Chem. 396:1167-1176.

Fujioka S, Matsuzawa Y, Tokunaga K, Kawamoto T, Kobatake T, Keno Y, Kotani K, Yoshida S, Tarui S (1991). Improvement of glucose and lipid metabolism associated with selective reduction of intra-abdominal visceral fat in premenopausal women with visceral fat obesity. JA. J. Int. J. Obes.15:853-859.

Gavaghan CL, Holmes E, Lenz E, Wilson ID, Nicholson JK (2000). An NMR-based metabonomic approach to investigate the biochemical consequences of genetic strain differences application to the C57BL10 and Alpk:ApfCD mouse. UK. J. FEBS Lett. 484:169-174.

Gavaghan CL, Wilson ID, Nicholson JK (2002).Physiological variation in metabolic phenotyping and functional genomic studies: use of orthogonal signal correction and PLS-DA. LDN. J. FEBS Lett. 530:191-196.

Lin CY, Wu H, Tjeerdema RS, Viant MR (2007). Evaluation of metabolite extraction strategies from tissue samples using NMR metabolomics.USA. J. Metabol. 3:55-67.

Nicholson JK, Foxall PJ, Spraul M, Farrant RD, Lindon JC (1995).750 MHz 1H and 1H-13C NMR spectroscopy of human blood plasma.LDN. J. Anal. Chem. 67(5):793-811.

Porter AL, Connolly T, Heikes RG, Park CY (1981). Misleading indicators: The limitations of multiple linear regression in formulation of policy recommendations. U.S.A. J. Policy Sci.13:397-418.

Scampicchio M, Ballabio D , Arecchi A , Cosio SM , Mannino S (2008). Amperometric electronic tongue for food analysis.IT. J. Microchim. Acta.163:11-21.

Solanky KS, Bailey NJ, Beckwith-Hall BM, Davies A, Bingham S, Holmes E, Nicholson JK, Cassidy A (2003). Application of biofluid 1H nuclear magnetic resonance-based metabonomic techniques for the analysis of the biochemical effects of dietary isoflavones on human plasma profile. LDN. J. Anal. Biochem. 323:197-204.

Wold S, Esbensen K, Geladi P (1987). Principal component analysis. SW. J. Chemometr. Intell. Lab. Syst. 2:37-52.

## 18

In silico analysis of amino acid sequences in relation to specificity and physiochemical properties of some aliphatic amidases and kynurenine formamidases

Naresh Kumar[1]* and T. C. Bhalla[2]

Department of Biotechnology, Himachal Pradesh University (HPU), Summer Hill, Shimla, Himachal Pradesh-171005, India.

Computational analysis of amino acid sequences of aliphatic amidases and kynurenine formamidases for some of their physiochemical properties and their substrate specificity has been done. Multiple sequence alignment of 18 amino acid sequences shows a clear difference between the two classes of aminohydrolases. Statistical analysis indicated a clear distinction between aliphatic amidases and kynurenine formamidases. The kynurenine formamidases and aliphatic amidases mainly differ in the total number of amino acid and composition of amino acid. Catalytic triad was found to be conserved and difference in amino acids makes them substrate specific. The results of the present work will be quite useful in prediction and selection of kynurenine formamidases/aliphatic amidases either from reported amidases or from the large number of sequenced microbial genome.

Key words: Aliphatic amidases, kynurenine formamidases, amino acids, substrate specificity, multiple alignments.

INTRODUCTION

A variety of cyclic amide-metabolizing systems occur in nature and play important roles in various metabolisms such as pyrimidine and purine; amino acid and antibiotic (Soong et al., 2000).The enzyme physiologically functions in the second step of cyclic imide degradation, that is, the hydrolysis of monoamidated dicarboxylates (half-amides) to dicarboxylates and ammonia. Amidases (EC 3.5.1 and 3.5.2) a subclass of acylamide amidohydrolases are mainly involved in nitrogen exchange of pro and eukaryotes utilizing nitriles. Reaction catalyzed by these complex enzyme, are of primary interest for large scale production of acrylamide and acrylic acid in industry (Novo et al., 2002). The importance of amidases in biotechnology is growing rapidly, because of their potential applications that are span through chemical and pharmaceutical industries as well as in bioremediation (Jorge et al., 2007). Microbial Amidases are a class of enzymes that have potential

value for the development of commercial bioprocesses (Wu et al., 1998). They are used in detoxification of industrial effluents containing toxic amides such as acrylamide and formamide.

Additionally, immobilized amidase can be used efficiently for production of acrylic acid from acrylamide, thus converting a toxic ambient contaminant into widely used industrial raw material (Nawaz et al., 1996; Nagasawa et al., 1989a; Madhavan et al., 2005). Most of the currently known amidases have been found and described in bacteria. Many genera are concerned: *Rhodococcus, Corynebacterium, Mycobacterium, Pseudomonas, Bacillus, Micrococcus, Brevibacterium, Nocardia, Streptomyces, Blastobacter, Arthrobacter, Alcaligenes, Helicobacter, Lactobacillus,* and *Methylophilus.* Amidases (EC 3.5.1.4) are ubiquitous enzymes in the living world and can be divided into two types. They include aliphatic amidases (hydrolyzing short and mid chain aliphatic amides) and broad range amidases (hydrolyzing various substrates, some arylamides, a-aminoamides, a-hydroxyamides and kynurenine formamidases). Amidases can be assigned to

*Corresponding author. E-mail: nareshkumariitr@gmail.com.

Table 1a. Name of microorganism with there SwissProt accession number for aliphatic amidases.

S/N	Abbreviation	Accession No.	Source	No. of amino acids
1	AMIE_RHOER	Q01360	*Rhodococcus erythropolis*	345
2	AMIE_HELPY	O25067	*Helicobacter pylori*	339
3	AMIE_PSEAE	P11436	*Pseudomonas aeruginosa*	346
4	AMIE_BACSP	Q9L543	*Bacillus sp.*	348
5	AMIE_MARAV	A1U7G1	*Marinobacter aquaelei VT8*	348
6	AMIE_BURCH	A0B137	*Burkholderia cenocepacia I2424*	341
7	AMIE_ALCBS	Q0VN20	*Alcanivorax borkumensis SK2*	348
8	AMIE_NOCFA	Q5Z1VO	*Nocardia farcinia*	345
9	AMIE_DELAS	A9C011	*Delpha acidovorans SPH-1*	345

phylogenetically unrelated families on the basis of amino acid sequence. One family comprises the kynurenine formamidases group (3.5.1.9), and other may be termed as aliphatic amidase on the basis of substrate specificity (Fournand and Arnaud, 2001). Amidases turned out to be efficient tools for the synthesis of various compounds. Many microbial amidases have been purified and characterized.

To this end, these can be divided into two types based on their catalytic activity functions. Bacterial aliphatic amidases are the most extensively characterized, particularly as a consequence of their potential in the large-scale production of acrylic as well as other acidic products in industry (Hughes et al., 1998). Amidases exhibit a wide range of substrate specificities and some exhibit stereoselectivity (Mayaux et al., 1990; Mayaux et al., 1991; Hashimoto et al., 1991; Hirrlinger et al., 1996) a property that can be exploited to allow the production of enantiopure acids that would be difficult to produce by other methods. Microbial amidases with altered substrate specificity have attracted growing interest in the last decade because they can be used in detoxification of industrial effluents containing toxic amides such as acrylamide and formamide. Additionally, immobilized amidase can be used efficiently for production of acrylic acid from acrylamide, thus converting a toxic ambient contaminant into widely used industrial raw material (Jorge et al., 2007).

A number of physiochemical properties e.g. number of amino acid residues, molecular mass, theoretical pI, amino acid composition, negatively charged residues (Asp+Glu), positively charged residues (Arg+Lys), atomic composition, total number of atoms, extinction coefficients (M^{-1} cm^{-1}) at 280 nm, instability index/ aliphatic index, grand average hydropathicity (GRAVY), etc. of enzymes immensely influence their applications and need to be carefully studied. These properties can be either determined experimentally or deduced from the *in silico* analysis of amino acid sequences of enzymes available in the databases. Amidases are still not sufficiently investigated and their classification is not definitely formulated. The classification based on

substrate specificity (Fournand and Arnaud, 2001) occasionally integrates enzymes with different structural organization, mechanism, and catalytic properties.

In spite of significant progress in expanding our knowledge of amidases, the spatial organization of these proteins remains unknown and systematic comparative analysis of formamidases and aliphatic amidases is far from complete. The novel approach taken in this paper is to study general physiochemical properties that are true for the sequences analysis and these properties of the sequence can then be used to predict there substrate specificity.

MATERIALS AND METHODS

Data collection and analysis

Information about the affinity (kynurenine formamidases /aliphaticity) of formamidases and aliphatic amidases of some microorganisms was obtained from the SwissProt data (Table 1a and b). Amino acid sequences for both from 18 microorganisms having experimentally proved substrate specificity as well as complete nucleotide sequences and these sequences are not fragmented, pseudo, putative or hypothetical. The amino acid sequences for formamidases and aliphatic amidases were downloaded from the ExPASy proteomic server. Physiochemical data were generated from the Swiss Prot and Expert Protein Analysis System (ExPASy) that is the proteomic server of Swiss Institute of Bioinformatics (SIB). FASTA format of sequences were used for analysis. Blastp (Protein BLAST) was performed to study the homology among the various amidase sequences and 18 sequences belonging to same E.C. number (E.C.3.5.1.4) of microbial amidases were selected (Table 1a and b). All the selected microorganism organisms have complete nucleotide sequences for its amidase gene as well as experimentally proved substrate specificity. Clustal W was used for multiple sequence alignment.

Various tools in the Proteomic server {ProtParam, Protein calculator, Compute pI/Mw, ProtScale (14)} were applied to calculate/deduce different physiochemical properties of amidases from the protein sequences. The molecular weights (Kda) of kynurenine formamidases and aliphatic amidases were calculated by the addition of average isotopic masses of amino acid in the protein and deducting the average isotopic mass of one water molecule. The pI of amidases was calculated using pK values of amino acid (Bjellqvist et al., 1993). The atomic composition of amidases was derived using the ProtParam tool, available at

Table 1b. Name of microorganism with there SwissProt accession number for Kynurenine formamidases.

S/N	Abbreviation	Accession No.	Source	No. of amino acids
1	KYNB_BURA4	B1YVH0	*Burkholderia ambifaria Str. C40-6*	213
2	KYNB_CUPTR	B3R5Q1	*Cupriavidus taiwanensis (Str. R1 / LMG 19424)*	216
3	KYNB_ERYLH	Q2N5X0	*Erythrobacter litoralis (Str. HTCC2594)*	216
4	KYNB_PSEFL	Q84HF4	*Pseudomonas fluorescens*	218
5	KYNB_RALME	P0C8P4	*Ralstonia metallidurans ATCC 43123*	218
6	KYNB_DEIGD	Q1IY56	*Deinococcus geothermalis (Str. DSM 11300)*	213
7	KYNB_ACIAC	A1TLB1	*Acidovorax avenae Subsp. Citruli (Str. AAC00-1)*	216
8	KYNB_BORPE	Q7VYS5	*Bordetella pertussis*	209
9	KYNB_MARMM	Q0APM5	*Maricaulis maris (strain MCS10)*	209

ExPASy. The extinction coefficient of various amidases was calculated using the following equation (Stanley et al., 1989):

$$E(Prot) = Numb(Tyr)*Ext(Tyr) + Numb(Trp)*Ext(Trp) + Numb(Cystine)*Ext(Cystine)$$

The values of aliphatic index of various amidase sequences were obtained using Prot Param (ExPASy) tool (Kyte and Doolittle, 1982). The instability index and grand average of hydropathicity (GRAVY) were estimated following the method of Guruprasad et al. (1990), and Kyte and Doolittle (1982) respectively.

Statistical analysis

An analysis of variance (ANOVA) was conducted on various physiochemical parameter variables for each study with the statistical packages 'Asistat version-7.4 beta 2008'. F-tests were used to determine the statistical significance. When significant effects were detected, a Tukey test was applied for all pairwise comparisons of mean responses.

RESULTS

In the present study, attempts to find differences between the physiochemical properties of eighteen (18) amino acid sequences of aliphatic amidases (9) and kynurenine formamidases (9) has been done (Table 2a and b). The total number of amino acid residues in these amidases differed substantially as kynurenine formamidases have lesser number of amino acid residues ranging between 209 to 218 amino acid as whereas aliphatic amidases ranging between 339 to 348. The molecular weight of kynurenine formamidases ranges between 22546.4 to 24015.0 and that of aliphatic amidases ranges between 37712.9 to 38596.9. Theoretical pI varied between 4.61 to 6.07 in case of kynurenine formamidases and it was found to be 4.94 to 6.20 for aliphatic amidases. It was further found that the average pI value of aliphatic amidases were insignificantly higher than that of kynurenine formamidases (Table 2a). Negative charge residues (Asp and Glu) were found to be substantially higher in aliphatic amidases that is 45.33 in aliphatic amidases and 26.77 in kynurenine formamidases.

Significant difference was found between kynurenine formamidases (16.15) and aliphatic amidases (34.00) for positively charged amino acid residues also. Instability indices of these two groups of amidases indicated that aliphatic amidases (33.98) were more stable as compared to kynurenine formamidases (45.53) (Table 2a).

The aliphatic index values were found to be higher (1.31 fold) in kynurenine formamidases and values for grand average hydropathicity (GRAVY) was substantially higher (5.61 fold) for aliphatic amidases than that of kynurenine formamidases. Results of amino acid analysis of two types of amidases are shown in Table 2a and b. These enzymes contained all the common amino acids. The comparison of the amino acid composition of the kynurenine formamidases and aliphatic amidases has shown that alanine (Ala), one of the simplest amino acid is found to be the predominant residue in kynurenine formamidases and glycine (Gly) in aliphatic amidases. The amino acid cysteine (Cys) is considered to be an important parameter in the calculation of extinction co-efficient of proteins and its content was 1.61 fold higher in aliphatic amidases as compared to kynurenine formamidases. The amino acid Ser, Thr, Trp and Val are (1.10, 1.11, 1.28 and 1.04) non-significantly higher in kynurenine formamidases while the amino acid, Ala, Arg, Asp, His, Leu and Pro are (1.39, 1.38, 1.43, 1.78, 2.20 and 2.12) significantly higher in kynurenine formamidases. The amino acid Asn, Glu, Gly, Ile, Lys, Met, Phe and Tyr are (4.5, 1.73, 1.43, 1.19, 3.56, 2.58, 2.03 and 2.70) significantly higher in aliphatic amidases while only Gln (1.19x) is found to be non-significantly higher in aliphatic amidases.

The multiple sequence alignment of aliphatic amidases and kynurenine formamidases showed some unique differences for the position specific presence of some amino acids. The position specific (conserved) amino acid in these amidases comprised of active site domain and the N-terminal regions. However, no differences were observed in the conserved amino acid in the C-terminal regions of the enzymes compared in the present study. The present work has contributed to conclude that

Table 2a. Comparative analysis of physiochemical properties of aliphatic amidases and kynurenine formamidases.

Parameter	SS[1]	1	2	3	4	5	6	7	8	9	Avg.	(P < 0.01)
Number of amino acids	AA[2]	345	339	346	348	348	348	345	346	345	345.55	7871.12**
	KF[3]	213	216	216	218	218	213	216	209	209	214.22	
Molecular weight	AA	38200.1	37712.9	384947	38596.9	38460.5	38359.4	38183	38441.7	38564.7	38334.88	6704.56**
	KF	22699	23164.4	24015	23629.1	23382.7	22784.8	23229.6	22776	22546.4	23136.33	
Theoretical pI	AA	4.94	6.20	5.31	5.38	5.06	4.96	4.98	5.65	5.69	5.35	0.01 ns
	KF	5.24	5.57	4.61	6.07	5.73	5.11	5.37	5.47	4.80	5.33	
Negatively charged residues (Asp+Glu)	AA	48	41	45	45	47	47	48	43	44	45.33	100.14**
	KF	26	22	38	22	24	29	25	25	30	26.77	
Positively charged residues (Arg+Lys)	AA	32	38	35	36	33	31	31	35	35	34.00	312.01**
	KF	17	14	20	16	15	18	17	16	16	16.55	
Extinction coefficients ($M^{-1}cm^{-1}$) at 280 nm	AA	60320	58955	58830	57340	57465	57465	60320	64790	54945	58936.67	90.59**
	KF	28210	28210	48595	24200	28210	21200	29575	39085	33710	32221.67	
Instability index	AA	30.15	40.47	35.61	30.20	28.78	32.92	31.57	38.05	38.09	33.98	21.16**
	KF	46.28	47.36	50.54	40.54	51.15	42.18	50.03	49.57	32.14	45.53	
Aliphatic index	AA	74.96	77.35	74.74	74.57	68.13	68.16	76.90	73.58	69.54	73.10	70.87**
	KF	99.39	100.83	80.06	102.06	96.79	94.88	101.67	102.78	89.28	96.41	
Grand average of hydropathicity (GRAVY)	AA	-0.319	-0.347	-0.330	-0.324	-0.360	-0.333	-0.279	-0.348	-0.397	-0.337	45.16**
	KF	0.081	-0.001	-0.302	0.002	-0.052	-0.168	0.040	-0.013	-0.128	-0.060	

[1]-Substarte specificity; [2]-Aliphatic amidase; [3]-Kynurenine formamidases. (1) *Rhodococcus erythropolis* Q01360 (2). *Helicobacter pylori* O25067 (3). *Pseudomonas aeruginosa* P11436 (4). *Bacillus sp.* Q9L543 (5). *Marinobacter aquaelei* VT8 A1V7G1 (6) *Burkholderia cenocepacia* HI2424 A0B137 (7). *Alcanivorax borkumensis* SK2 Q0VN20 (8). *Nocardia farcinia* Q5Z1VO (9). *Delpha acidovorans* SPH-1 A9C011. ** Significant at a level of 1% of probability (P < 0.01); * Significant at a level of 5% of probability (0.01 =< P < 0.05); ns: Non-significant (P >= 0.05).

there is a clear difference between kynurenine formamidases and aliphatic amidases in terms of position specific presence of certain amino acid. Amino acid Proline (Pro) at 50 and Glycine (Gly) at positions 247, 252 and 291 is conserved aliphatic and kynurenine formamidases, respectively. Amino acid residues at position 59, 60, 87, 91, 97, 100, 117, 119, 184, 244, 254, 259, 263, 281, 304, 308 and 320 in aliphatic amidases are invariable Glu, Tyr, Phe, Cys, Trp, Phe, Asn, Leu, Glu, Gly, Gln, Ser, Ile, His, Phe, Trp and Glu respectively, while these positions are occupied by Gly, Asp, Ser, Gly, Pro, Tyr, Gly, Cys, Arg, Ala, Asp, Asp, Ser, Glu, Leu, Pro and Arg respectively in kynurenine formamidases.

Table 2b. Comparison between amino acids presents in aliphatic amidases and kynurenine formamidases.

Amino acid composition	SS[1]	Micro-organism*** 1 2 3 4 5 6 7 8 9									Avg.	(P<0.01)
Ala (A)	AA[2]	9.6	7.4	9.2	8.3	8.9	9.5	9.3	8.7	7.2	8.86	24.62**
	KF[3]	12.7	14.4	7.9	11	14.2	11.3	13	12.9	13.9	12.36	
Arg (R)	AA	4.6	3.5	5.8	3.7	4.0	4.0	5.2	4.3	5.2	4.47	27.02**
	KF	6.6	6.0	6.5	5.0	6.0	7.0	6.9	6.2	5.7	6.21	
Asn (N)	AA	4.1	4.4	4.0	4.6	4.9	4.3	2.3	4.6	4.9	4.23	109.34**
	KF	0.5	1.4	0.5	0.9	0.5	1.9	0.9	1.4	0.5	0.94	
Asp (D)	AA	7.0	5.6	4.9	4.6	6.6	6.3	7.2	5.2	5.2	5.84	15.50**
	KF	8.5	8.8	10.2	6.9	7.3	6.1	8.3	7.7	11.5	8.36	
Cys (C)	AA	2.3	3.2	2.6	2.3	2.9	2.9	2.6	2.3	2.9	2.66	39.95**
	KF	1.9	1.9	0.9	1.8	1.8	1.9	1.4	1.4	1.9	1.65	
Gln (Q)	AA	3.5	4.7	4.0	3.2	3.2	3.4	4.1	2.6	2.6	3.47	1.38[ns]
	KF	0.9	5.1	2.3	4.1	3.7	1.4	2.8	2.9	2.9	2.90	
Glu (E)	AA	7.0	6.5	8.1	7.8	6.9	7.2	6.7	7.2	7.5	7.21	19.10**
	KF	3.8	1.4	7.4	3.2	3.7	7.5	3.2	4.3	2.9	4.15	
Gly (G)	AA	9.6	9.4	9.8	9.8	9.8	9.8	9.6	9.5	9.9	9.68	59.72**
	KF	6.6	5.6	8.3	6.0	6.4	8.9	6.5	5.7	6.7	6.74	
His (H)	A	2.3	2.1	2.0	2.3	2.3	2.3	2.9	2.6	3.2	2.44	28.08**
	KF	3.8	4.6	3.2	6.0	6.0	3.8	3.7	3.8	4.3	4.35	
Ile (I)	AA	7.0	6.2	6.1	7.8	5.7	5.7	5.2	6.4	6.4	6.27	6.99**
	KF	4.7	5.1	5.1	6.4	6.0	3.8	5.6	6.2	4.3	5.24	
Leu (L)	AA	4.6	5.6	5.8	4.3	4.3	4.6	6.1	4.9	4.6	4.99	211.78**
	KF	9.9	11.6	10.6	11.5	10.1	13.1	10.6	11.5	10.0	10.98	
Lys (K)	AA	4.6	7.7	4.3	6.6	5.5	4.9	3.8	5.8	4.9	5.34	66.41**
	KF	1.4	0.5	2.8	2.3	0.9	1.4	0.9	1.4	1.9	1.50	
Met (M)	AA	3.8	2.1	4.3	3.7	4.9	5.5	3.2	4.3	4.6	4.04	34.20**
	KF	1.9	0.9	3.2	1.4	1.4	0.5	1.9	1.0	1.9	1.56	
Phe (F)	A	2.6	3.2	2.6	3.2	2.9	2.6	2.6	2.0	2.9	2.73	59.80**
	KF	0.9	1.4	1.9	1.4	0.9	1.4	0.9	1.4	1.9	1.34	
Pro (P)	AA	4.0	5.0	4.6	4.3	4.3	4.6	4.6	5.2	5.2	4.64	58.84**
	KF	11.3	12.5	6.0	9.2	11.9	9.9	10.2	9.6	8.1	9.85	
Ser (S)	AA	4.1	4.4	4.6	4.0	4.3	4.9	4.6	5.2	4.6	4.52	1.16[ns]
	KF	5.2	3.7	7.4	6.0	3.7	3.8	4.6	5.7	4.8	4.98	
Thr (T)	AA	5.2	3.8	3.8	6.0	5.5	4.9	4.9	4.0	4.6	4.74	1.40[ns]
	KF	5.6	4.2	4.2	6.0	5.0	7.5	5.6	3.8	5.7	5.28	

Table 2b. Contd.

Trp (W)	AA	1.7	1.8	1.7	1.7	1.7	1.7	1.7	1.7	1.4	1.67	3.44[ns]
	KF	1.9	1.9	3.7	1.4	1.8	1.4	1.9	2.9	2.4	2.14	
Tyr (Y)	AA	5.2	5.0	4.9	4.6	4.6	4.6	5.2	6.1	5.2	5.04	277.27**
	KF	1.9	1.9	1.4	2.3	1.8	1.4	2.3	1.9	1.9	1.86	
Val (V)	AA	7.0	8.3	6.6	6.6	6.9	6.3	8.1	7.2	6.7	7.07	0.62[ns]
	KF	10.3	7.4	6.5	7.3	6.9	6.1	8.8	7.2	6.7	7.40	

[1]Substarte specificity; [2]Aliphatic amidase; [3] Kynurenine formamidases. (1) *Burkholderia ambifaria* Str. MC40-6 B1YVH0 (2). *Cupriavidus taiwanensis* (Str. R1 / LMG 19424) B3R5Q1 (3). *Erythrobacter litoralis* (Str. HTCC2594) Q2N5X0 (4). *Pseudomonas fluorescens* Q84HF4 (5). *Ralstonia metallidurans* ATCC 43123 P0C8P4 (6). *Deinococcus geothermalis* (Str. DSM 11300) Q1IY56 (7). *Acidovorax avenae Subsp. Citruli* (Str. AAC00-1) A1TLB1 (8). *Bordetella pertussis* Q7VYS5 (9). *Maricaulis maris* (strain MCS10) Q0APM5. ** Significant at a level of 1% of probability (P < 0.01); * Significant at a level of 5% of probability (0.01 =< P < 0.05); ns: Non-significant (P >= 0.05).

The other conserved amino acid residues in both aliphatic amidases included Ala -16, 39, 76, 90, 179, 208, 216, 218, 220, 256 and 298; Gln- 130, 190, 199, 200, 271 and 273; Pro-23, 50, 80, 115, 140, 146, 156, 172, 195, 301 and 338; Glu-71, 83, 105, 108, 127, 142, 173, 245 and 249 ; Tyr- 20, 67, 116, 151, 171, 194, 214, 227, 229, 255 and 305; Arg-2, 24, 133, 176, 188, 264 and 282 ; Lys- 113, 157, 166, 197, 205 and 278, ; Gly- 4, 14, 44, 48, 51, 64, 81, 98, 104, 126, 147, 155, 158, 169, 182, 191, 222, 225, 231, 237, 240, 286, 293, 296 and 328 ; Cys-166, 178, 189 and 332; Trp-144 and 175; Val-13, 17, 18, 31, 129, 152, 187, 215 and 226; Thr-75, 84, 103, 118 and 242; Asp- 5, 11, 53, 167, 168, 177, 224, 239, 265 and 311; His- 26, 107 and 232 (Figure 1). The conserved amino acid residues present in kynurenine formamidases comprised His- 90, 94, 99 and 269; Tyr- 302; Asp-40, 95 and 315; Asp- 40, 95 and 315 (Figure 1).

DISCUSSION

The present article aims to differentiate two groups of amidases that is kynurenine formamidases and aliphatic amidase on the basis of their amino acid sequences and physiochemical properties. The sequence redundancy was removed by 40, 60, 80 and 100% by the use of CD-HIT software. The selected sequences in each group that is aliphatic amidases and kynurenine formamidases were 100% homologous and more than 40% identical with respect to model sequence of each group that is aliphatic amidase amino acid sequence of *Marinobacter aquaelei* VT8 (A1U7G1,UniProtKB/Swiss-Prot) were selected. Variation in total number of amino acid residues between aliphatic amidases and kynurenine formamidases result shows that total number of amino acid and molecular weight might be playing some role in providing the substrate specificity to these two groups of amidases. No significant difference for pI values was found between the two groups of amidases. This indicates that pI value is

not responsible with the substrate specificity of the amidase enzymes considered in the present study.

As 20 amino acids differ in their chemical composition and physiochemical properties, also proteins differ widely in physiochemical properties as well as in substrate specificity (O'Reilly and Turner, 2003; Yeom et al., 2008). The results of this work have confirmed that amino acid number and their percentage composition in amidases significantly affect the substrate specificity. Ala is the predominant amino acid in the kynurenine formamidases and Gly in the aliphatic amidases has confirmed there presence in amino acid sequences of compared amidases in the present investigation. An important amino acid that is found to play a significant role in amidases is Cys (Kobayashi et al., 1993) that generally provides stability to proteins due to the formation of disulphide bonds. The results in the present work also indicate that aliphatic amidases are more stable as is shown by the instability index values (Table 2a) of various amidases considered in present work. This finding is further supported by the fact that aliphatic amidases have higher percentage of Cys content as compared to kynurenine formamidases.

Conclusion

A number of physiochemical properties of aliphatic amidases and kynurenine formamidases have been derived from amino acid sequences of some amidases. The kynurenine formamidases and aliphatic amidase mainly differs in the total number of amino acid, molecular weights and composition of amino acid. This study has clearly found differences between these two types of amidases in conserved amino acid residues at several positions. The results of the present work will be quite useful in prediction and selection of kynurenine formamidases / aliphatic amidases from hitherto reported amidases or from the large number of sequenced

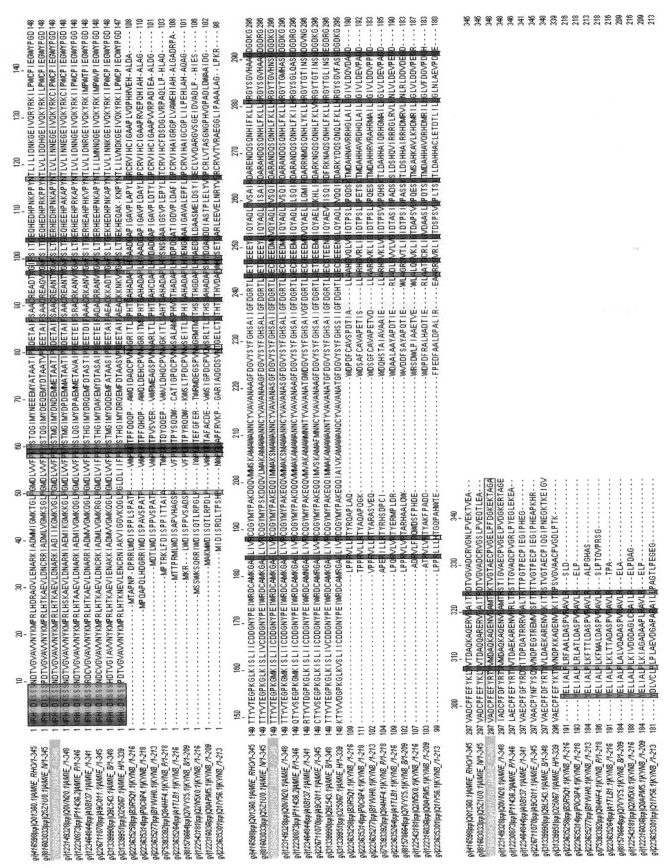

Figure 1. Alignment of the amino acid sequences of aliphatic amidases and kynurenine formamidases. #Reference sequence A1U7G1 (*Marinobacter aquaelei* VT8).

microbial genomes.

REFERENCES

Bjellqvist B, Hughes GJ, Pasquali C, Paquet N, Ravier F, Sanchez JC, Frutiger S, Hochstrasser D (1993). The focusing positions of polypeptides in immobilized pH gradients can be predicted from their amino acid sequences. Electrophoresis, 14: 1023-1031.

Fournand D, Arnaud A (2001). Aliphatic and enantioselective amidases: from hydrolysis to acyl transfer activity. J. Appl. Microbiol., 91: 381-393.

Guruprasad K, Reddy BVB, Pandit MW (1990). Correlation between stability of a protein and its dipeptide composition: a novel approach for predicting in vivo stability of a protein from its primary sequence. Protein Eng., 4: 155-161.

Hashimoto Y, Nishiyama M, Ikehata O, Horinouchi S, Beppu T (1991). Cloning and characterization of an amidase gene from *Rhodococcus* species N-774 and its expression in *Escherichia coli*. Biochim. Biophys. Acta, 1088: 225-233.

Hirrlinger B, Stolz A, Knackmuss HJ (1996). Purification and properties of an amidase from *Rhodococcus erythropolis* MP50 which enantioselectively hydrolyzes 2- arylpropionamides. J. Bacteriol., 178: 3501-3507.

Hughes J, Armitage YC, Symes KC (1998). Application of whole cell rhodococcal biocatalysts in acrylic polymer manufacture. Antonie Van Leeuwenhoek, 74: 107-118.

Jorge A, Amin K, Maria A, Carrondo, Carlos F (2007). Structure of Amidase from *Pseudomonas aeruginosa* showing a Trapped Acyl Transfer Reaction Intermediate State. J. Biol. Chem., 282(27): 19598-19605.

Kobayashi M, Komeda H, Nagasawa T, Nishiyama M, Horinouchi S, Beepu T, Yameda H, Shimizu S (1993). Amidases coupled with low molecular mass nitrile hydratase from *Rhodococcus rhodochrous* J1 Eur. J. Biochem., 217: 327- 336.

Kyte J, Doolittle RF (1982). A simple method for displaying the hydropathic character of a protein. J. Mol. Biol., 157: 105-132.

Madhavan NK, Roopesh K, Chacko S, Pandey A (2005). Competitive study of amidase production by free and immobilized *Escherichia coli* cells. Appl. Biochem. Biotechnol., 120:97-108.

Mayaux JF, Cerbelaud E, Soubrier F, Yeh P, Blanche F, Petre D (1991). Purification, cloning, and primary structure of a new enantiomer-selective amidase from a *Rhodococcus* strain: structural evidence for a conserved genetic coupling with nitrile hydratase. J. Bacteriol., 173: 6694-6704.

Mayaux JF, Cerebelaud E, Soubrier F, Faucher D, Petre D (1990). Purification, cloning, and primary structure of an enantiomer-selective amidase from *Brevibacterium* sp. strain R312: structural evidence for genetic coupling with nitrile hydratase. J. Bacteriol., 172: 6764-6773.

Nagasawa T, Ryuno K, Yamada H (1989a). Superiority of Pseudomonas chlororaphls B23 nitrile hydratase as a catalyst for the enzymatic production of acrylamide. Experientia, 45: 1066-1070.

Nawaz MS, Khan AA, Bhattacharya D, Silton PH, Cerniglia CE (1996). Physical, biochemical and immunological characterization of a thermostable amidase from *Klebsiella pnumoniae* NCTR1. J. Biotechnol., 178: 2397-2401.

Novo C, Fournand S, Tata R, Clemente A, Brown PR (2002). Support for a three-dimensional structure predicting a Cys-Glu-Lys catalytic triad for *Pseudomonas aeruginosa* amidase comes from site-directed mutagenesis and mutations altering substrate specificity. Biochem. J., 365: 731-738.

O'Reilly C, Turner PD (2003). The nitrilase family of CN hydrolyzing enzymes – A comparative study. J. Appl. Microbiol., 95: 1161-1174.

Soong CL, Ogawa J, Shimizu S (2000). A Novel Amidase (Half-Amidase) For Half-Amide Hydrolysis involved in the Bacterial Metabolism of Cyclic Amides. Appl. Environ. Microbiol., 66: 1947-1952.

Stanley C, Gill, Peter H, Von-Hippel (1989). Calculation of protein extinction coefficients from amino acid sequence data. Analytical Biochemistry, 1 November, 182(2): 319-326.

Wu S, Fallon RD, Payne MS (1998). Cloning and nucleotide sequence of amidase gene from *Pseudomonas putida*. DNA Cell Biol., 17(10): 915-920.

Yeom SJ, Kim HJ, Lee JK, Kim DE, Oh DK (2008). An amino acid at position 142 in nitrilase from *Rhodococcus rhodochrous* ATCC 33278 determines the substrate specificity for aliphatic and aromatic nitrile. Biochem. J., 415: 401- 407.

## 19

Generation of a 3D model for human cereblon using comparative modelling

Samina Bilal*, Shumaila Barkat Ali, Sahar Fazal and Asif Mir

Department of Computer Sciences and Bioinformatics, Mohammad Ali Jinnah University Islamabad Sihala Road, Pakistan.

Three-dimensional (3D) protein structures provide helpful insights into the molecular association of a gene, its purpose also allow efficient drug designing experiments, such as the structure-based design of specific inhibitors. Recently, it has been shown that protein (cereblon) is involved in various tissues and brain and is revealed to be related with mental retardation. After this first report of cereblon (CRBN) involvement, it was necessary to further study this protein. Therefore a 3D structure of cereblon was developed using comparative modeling approach. By comparing the templates-target sequence, a model was created using MODELLER, a program for homology modeling. The accuracy of the predicted structure was checked using Ramachandran plot which showed that the residue falling in the favoured region was 88.4%. The predicted cereblon model can be used to understand the pathogenesis of mutations in cereblon that causes adenosine-5'-triphosphate (ATP)-dependent degradation of proteins in memory and learning.

Key words: CRBN, 3D structure, 1M4Y, MODELLER, comparative homology modeling.

INTRODUCTION

Mental retardation (MR) is the most common developmental disability and ranks first among the chronic conditions which are causing major activity limitations. A genetic or inherited metabolic etiology was implicated in two-thirds of mental retardation cases (Xin et al., 2008; Curry et al., 1997) and a recessive mode of transmission accounts for nearly one-fourth of these cases (Wright et al., 1959). Several of these cases affected basic cellular mechanisms such as cell signaling pathways (Matsuura et al., 1997; Albrecht et al., 1997; Costa et al., 2002; Xing et al., 1996) regulation of gene expression (Galdzicki et al., 2001; Shahbazian et al., 2002; Petrij et al., 1995; Wang et al., 1994; Darnell et al., 2001) and alterations in hippocampal dendrite morphology (Yang et al., 2004). There are three different types of non syndromic intellectual disability, one is X-linked (NS-XLMR), second is autosomal dominant (NS-ADID) and third one is autosomal recessive (NS-ARID)

(Chelly et al., 2006). There are 6 genes accountable for NS-ARID these are TUSC3, TRAPPC9, PRSS12, CRBN, GRIK2 and CC2DIA. All of these six genes play a crucial role in the involvement of many biochemical pathways (Najmabadi et al., 2007). Higgins and colleagues found that the homozygous C > T nonsense mutation at nucleotide position 1,274 of a novel complementary deoxyribonucleic acid (cDNA) (1,274C > T) is involved in autosomal recessive nonsyndromic- mental retardation (ARNSMR) in a large kindred.

The gene was named CRBN (cereblon, NM_016302) based on its putative role in cerebral development and the presence of its large, highly conserved Lon domain. The nonsense mutation causing a premature stop codon in CRBN interrupts an N-myristoylation site and eliminates a casein kinase II phosphorylation site at the C terminus (Xin et al., 2008). CRBN are specifically involved in neural development and calcium signaling in the cerebral cortex and hippocampus. Although little is known about the function of human CRBN, its relationship to mild cognitive deficits suggests that it is involved in the basic processes of human memory and learning (Higgins et al., 2008). ARNSMR which is

*Corresponding author. E-mail: shumaila.ali86@gmail.com.

Table 1. Percentage similarity between target and template sequence.

Model number	Tool used	Template	Similarity (%)	No. of residues modeled
1	Modeller	1M4Y	56	442
2		2Q9U	29	442
3	3Djigsaw	------	------	105
4	CPH models	1M4Y	56	237
5	ESyPred3D	2ANE	8.4	107

associated with IQs ranging from 50 to 70 was widely studied (Xin et al., 2008). The predicted protein of CRBN, LON protease might belong to a family of ATP-dependent protease which is highly conserved across species (Lu et al., 2003).

Energy-dependent proteolysis plays a key role in prokaryotic and eukaryotic cells by regulating the availability of certain short-lived regulatory proteins, ensuring the proper stoichiometry of multiprotein complexes, and ridding the cell of abnormal and damaged proteins (Wang et al., 1993). Some ATP-dependent Lon proteases were reported to be associated with mental retardation. Comparative modeling is a useful technique in bioinformatics because this process constructs three dimensional models that are related to known protein structure (template) (Sali and Blundell, 1993; Marti-Renom et al., 2000). Thus this approach is relevant to structural based functional annotation. As a result, it enhances impact of structure and function on biology and medicine. By using bioinformatics tools, three dimensional structure of CRBN was constructed in the present study through comparative homology modeling approach.

MATERIALS AND METHODS

Comparative modeling consists of the following steps.

1. Search for related protein structures, selection of one or more templates.
2. Target-template alignment.
3. Model building and model evaluation. If model is not satisfactory, some or all of the steps can be repeated.

The amino acid sequence of cereblon was obtained from sequence database at National Center for Biotechnology Information (NCBI). It contains 442 amino acids. It was ensured that the three-dimensional structure of the protein was not available in Protein Data Bank therefore the present work of predicting the 3D modeling of the cereblon was performed. Template protein was searched by BLASTP, scanning the non redundant protein sequence database at NCBI with e-value cut off lesser than threshold, and retaining up to two templates with significant e-value. This searching provides us two templates. We used templates 1M4Y and 2Q9U high resolution X-ray diffraction in cereblon. Web based tools 3Djigsaw CPH models (Lund et al., 2002), ESyPred3D (Lambert et al., 2002) obtained templates automatically without any user intervention. 3Djigsaw looks for homologue templates in sequence database (PFAM+PDB+nr).

CPH models sought templates by iteratively aligning the target sequence to non redundant protein sequence database and searching the template pdb in protein structure database. ESyPred3D uses PSI-Blast at NCBI. All the templates are listed in Table 1. The target and template sequences were then aligned using the align2d command of MODELLER [http://www.salilab.org/modeller/8v1/] which uses global dynamic programming, with linear gap penalty function for aligning the two profiles. MODELLER takes target-template alignment file as input and without user intervention it generates 3D model. Initial step of model building is, identification of spatial restraints for example, distances and dihedral angles lying on the target sequence by aligning with template sequence. Interaction of many features of protein structure is analyzed statistically and used to derive spatial restraints on the target sequence. ESyPred3D use neural network method for increasing the alignment performance between the query and template sequence. CPH model uses profile-profile alignment between target and template.

Alignment between target and template that is, 1M4Y is shown in Figure 1 obtained through ClustalW web based tool. A three dimensional structure was developed from sequence alignment between CRBN and template protein using MODELLER8v1. It constructs model by satisfaction of spatial restraints. Distance and dihedral angle restraints on target sequence were derived from alignment with template structure. Stereochemical restraints such as bond angles and bond lengths were extracted from CHARM22 molecular mechanics force field. Statistical correlation of dihedral angles and non-bonded interatomic distance were extracted from database of family alignments that includes proteins with known three dimensional structures. CHARMM energy function and these spatial restraints were combined to obtain objective function. Final model was obtained by optimization of objective function using conjugate gradients and molecular dynamics with simulated annealing. 3Djigsaw, CPH models, ESyPred3D automatically build model by using their own set of modelling algorithms. CPH model uses segmod program from the GeneMine package.

It further refines the model using encad program from the GeneMine package. The constructed models were subjected to energy minimization by steepest descent, using GROMOS96 force field, implementation of Swiss-pdb Viewer Accuracy of the predicted model determines information that can be deduced from it; therefore all the models were subjected through a series of tests. Stereochemical properties were evaluated through procheck (Laskowski et al., 1993). Backbone conformation was evaluated by investigating PSi/Phi Ramachandran plot using Procheck and RAMPAGE (Sali, 1998). Packing quality and RMS of model was evaluated using Whatif packing quality control and protein analysis (Hooft et al., 1993).

RESULTS

Three dimensional structures are primarily important for providing valuable insight into molecular functions of

```
CRBN   MAGEGDQQDAAHNMGNHLPLLPAESEEEDEMEVEDQDSKEAKKPNIINFDTSLPTSHIYL 60
1M4Y   TTILVVRRNGQTVMGGDGQVTFGSTVLKGNARKVRKLGEGKVLAGFAGSVADAMTLFDRF 60
       :    :::.  **..  :  ..: :.: . : .:   ..: .: *. :

CRBN   GADMEEFHG----RTLHDDDSCQVIPVLPQVMMILIPGQTLPLQLFHPQEVSMVRN---- 112
1M4Y   EAKLREWGGNLTKAAVELAKDWRTDRVLRRLEALLLVADKENIFIISGNGEVIQPDDDAA 120
       *.:.*: *    ::.  .. .: ** :: :*:.:. ::: : :

CRBN   LIQKDRTFAVLAYSNVQE---------REAQFGITAEIYAYREEQDFGIEIVKVKAIGRQ 163
1M4Y   AIGSGGPYALAAAKALLRNTDLSAREIVEKAMTIAGEICIYTNQNIVIEEVTTILVVRRN 180
       *  .. .:*: * . :.      * :  :.** * ::: .  *:..: .: *:

CRBN   RFKVLELRTQSDG------IQQAKVQILPECVLPSTMSAVQLESLNKCQIFPSKP----- 212
1M4Y   GQTVMGGDGQVTFGSTVLKGNARKVRKLGEGKVLAGFAGSVADAMTLFDRFEAKLREWGG 240
       .*:   *        :  **: * *  : : ::.   :::.  : * :*

CRBN   --VSREDQCSYKWWQKYQKRKFHCANLTSWPRWLYSLY----------DAETLMDRIKKQ 260
1M4Y   NLTKAAVELAKDWRTDRVLRRLEALLLVADKENIFIISGNGEVIQPDDDAAIGSGGPYA 300
       ..  :  : :.*  .  *::.. *.:  .:: :    ** ::.

CRBN   LREWDENLKDDSLPS-NPIDFSYRVAACLPIDDVLRIQLLKIGSAIQRLRCELDIMN--- 316
1M4Y   LAAAKALLRNTDLSAREIVEKAMTIAGEICIYTNQNIVIEEVTTILVVRRNGQTVMGGDG 360
       *   . *:: .*.: : :: : *   :*. .*  : :: : :   *   :*.

CRBN   ---KCTSLCCKQCQETEITTKNEIFS---------LSLCGPMAAYVNPHG--YVHETLTV 362
1M4Y   QVTFGSTVLKGNARKVRKLGEGKVLAGFAGSVADAMTLFDRFEAKLREWGGNLTKAAVEL 420
       :::  :.::..   :.:::::        ::*.  : * :.  *   .: ::

CRBN   YKACNLNLIGR--------PSTEHSWFPGYAWTVAQCKICASHIG----WKFTATKKDMS 410
1M4Y   AKDWRTDRVLRRLEALLLVADKENIFIISGNGEVIQPDDDAAAIGSGGPYALAAAKALLR 480
       *   .: : *     ...*: ::.  * * .  *: **     : ::*:* :

CRBN   PQKFWGLTRSALLPTIPDTEDEISPDKVILCL- 442
1M4Y   NTDLSAREIVEKAMTIAGEICIYTNQNIVIEEV 513
       .: .        **..    : :::::
```

Figure 1. Alignment between CRBN and 1M4Y obtained through clustalW.

Table 2. Ramachandran plot values obtained through PROCHECK.

Model number	Ramachandran plot values			
	Core (%)	Allowed (%)	Generously (%)	Disallowed (%)
1	81.7	13.3	2.8	2.3
2	87.9	8.8	2.0	1.3
3	80.0	15.6	3.3	1.1
4	67.8	22.7	6.2	3.3
5	87.5	10.4	2.1	0.0

proteins. It plays a major role in site-directed mutagenesis, in studying disease related mutations and in drug designing process. Protein sequence of CRBN was obtained through NCBI, sequence database. Templates, high resolution X-ray diffraction 1M4Y and 2Q9U were obtained using blastp at NCBI. Secondary structure of predicted cereblon consists of 166 hydrogen bonds, 6 Helices, 11 strands and 58 Turns. Webs based tools obtained templates automatically and are shown in Table 1. Comparative modeling builds a three dimensional structure of the target protein based on sequence identity to known protein structures (Sali, 1998; Vitkup et al., 2001). Therefore, sequence identity is good determinant for the quality of the model. In general, sequence of at least one related structure must have more than 30%

identity (Roberto and Andrej, 2000). Sequence similarity between target and template sequences has been shown in Table 1. Among the different alignments, the more related alignment is of models obtained through MODELLER and CPH models.

The template most used tools is 1M4Y. MODELLER and web-based tools were used for building the model and global energy minimization. After model building, the structures were validated through energy minimization. Refined models were checked through PROCHECK and RAMPAGE.

Values for the Ramachandran plot obtained through Procheck are shown in Table 2. The plot is subdivided in core, allowed, generously allowed and disallowed regions. The models obtained through MODELLER and

Table 3. Ramachandran plot values obtained through RAMPAGE.

Model number	Ramachandran plot values		
	No of residues in favoured region (%)	No of residues in allowed region (%)	No of residues in outlier region (%)
1	88.4	6.8	4.8
2	93.2	4.5	2.3
3	90.0	7.0	3.0
4	81.3	11.7	7.0
5	95.3	2.8	1.9

Table 4. Ramachandran plot values obtained through Whatif server.

Model number	Z-Score
1	-1.094
2	-0.549
3	-3.600
4	-5.612
5	-0.754

for models obtained through MODELLER and Esypred were significant, as denser number of residues in favored region (>90%) is the measure of good quality of a model (Morris et al., 1992), but Esypred3D created the model for 107 residues while MODELLER created the model for all 442 residues.

Values for Ramachandran plot obtained through Whatif Server are shown in Table 4. The score expressing how well the backbone conformations of all residues are corresponding to the known allowed areas in the Ramachandran plot is within expected ranges for well-refined structures. These results demonstrate that prediction of the best possible target would be a difficult task because the target performing well in one case was not found good in other cases. Esypred3D model tends to have better stereochemistry, whereas it does not hold good sequence similarity and is modeled for 107 residues only. For all the targets described herein, the structure obtained through MODELLER, using 1M4Y template, was found to be satisfactory based on the above results. This model is shown in Figure 2. Ramachandran plot analysis through procheck showed that 81.7% residues are within the core region (Figure 3). RMS and packing quality was evaluated through Whatif and found satisfactory for this model.

DISCUSSION

The identification of human monogenic disorders that solely affect cognition provides rare opportunities to study the mechanisms of human memory and learning. Studies have shown that CRBN, results in a phenotype characterized by mild mental retardation without the presence of dysmorphic features or physical anomalies (Higgins et al., 2004; 2000). The CRBN protein contains an N-terminal domain of the ATP-dependent Lon protease, a regulator of G-protein- signaling-like domain, a leucine zipper motif, and four putative protein kinase C phosphorylation sites (Jo et al., 2005). CRBN is highly expressed in the hippocampus and cerebral cortex. CRBN is also involved in regulating the surface expression and electrical properties of BKCa channels (Darnell et al., 2001). Mutations in CRBN cause

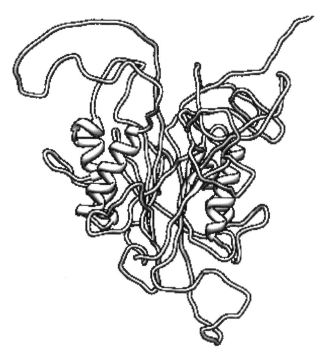

Figure 2. 3D Structure of human CRBN in raswin 2.7.5.

Esypred3D showed better Ramachandran plot values, as core region (>80%) accounts for better structure (Morris et al., 1992). Rampage assessment is shown in Table 3. Rampage derives Phi/Psi plots for Gly, Pro, Pre-Pro and other residues. The plot was divided into three regions that is, favored, allowed, and outlier regions. The result

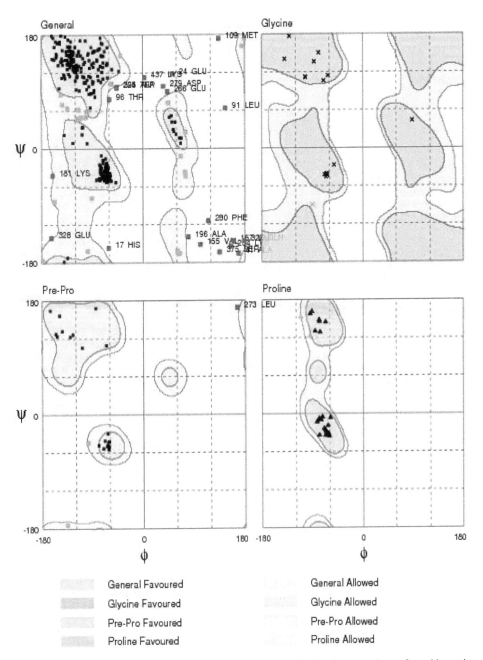

Figure 3. RAMPAGE values for best predicted model showing number of residues in favoured, allowed and outlier region.

mental retardation. This three dimensional structure of CRBN is useful for studying these disease-related mutations. Further analysis of this structure will help in finding binding clefts, for finding novel drug leads.

REFERENCES

Albrecht U, Sutcliffe JS, Cattanach BM (1997). Imprinted expression of the murine Angelman syndrome gene, Ube3a, in hippocampal and Purkinje neurons. Nat. Genet. 17:75-78 biologie/urbm/bioinfo/esypred/)

Costa RM, Federov NB, Kogan JH (2002). Mechanism for the learning deficits in a mouse model of neurofibromatosis type 1. Nature 415:526-530

Curry CJ, Stevenson RE, Aughton D (1997). Evaluation of mental retardation: recommendations of a Consensus Conference: American College of Medical Genetics. Am. J. Med. Genet. 72:468-477.

Darnell JC, Jensen KB, Jin P (2001). Fragile X mental retardation protein targets G quartet mRNAs important for neuronal function. Cell 107:489-499

Galdzicki Z, Siarey R, Pearce R (2001). On the cause of mental retardation in Down syndrome: extrapolation from full and segmental trisomy 16 mouse models. Brain Res. Rev. 35:115-145.

Higgins JJ, Pucilowska J, Lombardi RQ, Rooney JP (2004). A mutation in a novel ATP-dependent Lon protease gene in a kindred with mild mental retardation. Neurology 63:1927-1931.

Higgins JJ, J Hao, BE Kososky (2008). Dysregulation of large conductance Ca^{2+}-activated K^{+} channel expression in nonsyndromal mental retardation due to a cerebelon p.R419X mutation. Neurogenetics. 9:219-223.

Higgins JJ, Rosen DR, Loveless JM, Clyman JC, Grau MJ (2000). A gene for nonsyndromic mental retardation maps to chromosome 3p25-pter. Neurology 55:335-340.

Hooft RWW, Vriend G, Sander C, Abola EE (1993). Errors in protein structures. Nature 381: 272-272. (Server: http://swift.cmbi.kun.nl/WIWWWI/)

Jo S, Lee KH, Song S, Jung YK, Park CS (2005). Identification and functional characterization of cereblon as a binding protein for large-conductance calcium-activated potassium channel in rat brain. J. Neurochem. 94:1212–1224

Lambert C, Leonard N, De Bolle X, Depiereux E (2002). ESyPred3D: Prediction of proteins 3D structures. Bioinformatics 18(9):1250-1256. (Server:http://www.fundp.ac.be/sciences)

Laskowski RA, MacArthur MW, Moss DS, Thornton JM (1993). PROCHECK: a program to check the stereochemical quality of protein structures. J. Appl. Cryst., 26: 283-291. (Server: http://www.csb.yale.edu/userguides/datamanip/prochec k/)

Lu B, Liu T, Crosby JA (2003). The ATP-dependent Lon protease of *Mus musculus* is a DNA-binding protein that is functionally conserved between yeast and mammals. Gene 306:45-55.

Lund O, Nielsen M, Lundegaard C, Worning P (2002). X3M a Computer Program to Extract 3D Models. CASP5 conference A102. (Server:http://www.cbs.dtu.dk/services/CPHmodels/output.php)

Marti-Renom MA, Stuart AC, Fiser A, Sanchez R, Melo F, Sali A (2000). Comparative protein structure modeling of genes and genomes. Annu. Rev. Biophys. Biomol. Struct. 29:291-325.

Matsuura T, Sutcliffe JS, Fang P (1997). *De novo* truncating mutations in E6-AP ubiquitin-protein ligase gene (UBE3A) in Angelman syndrome. Nat. Genet. 15:74-77.

Morris AL, MacArthur MW, Hutchinson EG, Thornton JM (1992). Stereochemical quality of protein structure coordinates. Proteins 12:345-364.

Petrij F, Giles RH, Dauwerse HG (1995). Rubinstein–Taybi syndrome caused by mutations in the transcriptional co-activator CBP. Nature 376:348–351

Roberto S, Andrej S (2000). Comparative protein structure modeling: Introduction and practical examples with MODELLER. In: Protein Structure Prediction: Methods and Protocols. Ed: Webster, D. M., 97-129. Humana Press.

Sali A (1998). 100,000 protein structures for the biologist. Nat. Struct. Biol. 5:1029-1032.

Sali A, Blundell TL (1993). Comparative protein modelling by satisfaction of spatial restraints. J. Mol. Biol. 234:779-815.

Shahbazian M, Young J, Yuva-Paylor L (2002). Mice with truncated MeCP2 recapitulate many Rett syndrome features and display hyperacetylation of histone H3. Neuron 35:243-254.

Vitkup D, Melamud E, Moult J, Sander C (2001). Completeness in structural genomics. Nat. Struct. Biol. 8(6):559-566.

Wang N, Gottesman S, Willingham MC (1993). A human mitochondrial ATPdependent protease that is highly homologous to bacterial Lon protease. Proc. Natl. Acad. Sci. USA 90:11247-11251.

Wang YH, Amirhaeri S, Kang S (1994). Preferential nucleosome assembly at DNA triplet repeats from the myotonic dystrophy gene. Science 265:669-671.

Wright SW, Tarjan G, Eyer L (1959). Investigation of families with two or more mentally defective siblings; clinical observations. Am. J. Dis. Child 97:445-463

Xin W, Xiaohua N, Peilin C (2008). Primary function analysis of human mental retardation related gene CRBN. Mol. Biol. Rep. 35:251-256.

Xing J, Ginty DD, Greenberg ME (1996). Coupling of the RASMAPK pathway to gene activation by RSK2, a growth factor regulated CREB kinase. Science 273:959-963

Yang EJ, Yoon JH, Min do S (2004). LIM kinase 1 activates cAMP-responsive element-binding protein during the neuronal differentiation of immortalized hippocampal progenitor cells. J. Biol. Chem. 279:8903–8910.

## 20

Measurement of urinary calcium/creatinine and sodium/potassium excretion in healthy children aged 1-7 years in Imam Ali Hospital, Andimeshk in 2008

Morad Rostami[1]*, Mohammad Aberomand[1], Alireza Khirollah[1] and Masoomeh Jorfi[2]

[1]Biochemistry Department, Faculty of Medicine, Ahvaz Jundishapur University of Medical Sciences, Iran.
[2]Microbiology Department, Faculty of Medicine, Ahvaz Jundishapur University of Medical Sciences, Iran.

Due to the difficulty in obtaining a 24 h urine collection in children, a random sample of urine is often used to calculate the urine calcium to creatinine ratio. Also, urinary calcium excretion might be influenced by genetic, geographic area, etc. we decided to evaluate the urinary calcium, creatinine, sodium and potassium excretion in healthy children with 1-7 years and determine age-related reference values for urine calcium to creatinine and sodium to potassium ratio in Andimeshk City in Khozestan Province of Iran. From 1155 healthy children (528 boys and 627 girls) with ages between 1-7 years, that referred to check-up to Imam Ali Hospital in Andimeshk, between January and December 2008, urine sample was collected and calcium, creatinine, sodium and potassium were measured. From 1155 healthy children, 528 (45.7%) were boys and 627 (54.3%) were girls. Mean ± SD ratio of urine calcium to creatinine in all children was 0.165 ± 0.115. This ratio was 0.168 ± 0.114 and 0.163 ± 0.093 for boys and girls, respectively, but not significant (p=0.37). Also, the mean ± SD ratio of urine sodium to potassium in all children was 1.981 ± 1.322. This ratio was 1.982 ± 0.912 and 1.980 ± 1.108 for boys and girls, respectively, it was higher in boys than girls, but not significant (p=0.28). Because of warm climate in Khuzestan Province in Iran and relatively, high quantities of solutes in children's urine of this region, suggested that more investigation is done and prevalence of kidney's stone will particularize.

Key words: Hypercalciuria, calcium, creatinine, sodium, potassium.

INTRODUCTION

Idiopathic hypercalciuria has been increasingly recognized as a cause of urinary tract complication in pediatrics (Langman and Moore, 1984). Clinical manifestations of hypercalciuria in children are gross or microscopic hematuria, renal calculi, dysuria, enuresis, osteopenia/rickets, abdominal pain, sterile pyuria, renal colic, urinary frequency/urgency, short stature and polyuria, while most children with idiopathic hypercalciuria are asymptomatic (Langman and Moore,

1984; So et al., 2001). Hypercalciuria is defined as urinary calcium excretion more than 4 mg/kg/day (Langman and Moore, 1984). Urinary solute to creatinine ratio is a useful and reliable factor for determining hypercalciuria and also is a non-invasive and relative cheap method and other hand, for every age-group, different urine calcium to creatinine ratio was reported (Ginsbery et al., 1993). Also, urinary calcium excretion might be influenced by genetic, geographic area, sun or light exposure, climate, ethnicity, drinking water and nutrition (Honarpisheh et al., 2009).

Due to the difficulty in obtaining a 24 h urine collection in children, a random sample of urine is often used to calculate the urine calcium to creatinine ratio and this

*Corresponding author. E-mail: morad_r56@yahoo.com.

Table 1. Urinary Calcium/Creatinine and Sodium/Potassium excretion ratios among 1-7 years old healthy children's in Andimeshk city, Iran.

Age groups	Sex†	N	Mean ± SD*				p-value
			Calcium/Creatinine	95th percentile	Sodium/Potassium	95th percentile	
1-2	M	65	0.181±0.110	0.41	2.015±1.020	4.21	0.46
	F	53	0.175±0.090	0.39	1.997±1.005	3.83	
2-3	M	90	0.176±0.098	0.43	2.033±0.895	5.42	0.47
	F	103	0.173±0.068	0.41	2.010±1.010	4.65	
3-4	M	98	0.172±0.095	0.39	1.885±1.025	4.13	0.35
	F	88	0.155±0.082	0.35	1.998±0.980	4.58	
4-5	M	87	0.161±0.085	0.37	2.000±1.022	4.46	0.48
	F	114	0.163±0.072	0.39	1.887±0.995	4.12	
5-6	M	103	0.165±0.087	0.36	2.003±1.005	5.28	0.42
	F	117	0.158±0.064	0.31	1.978±0.884	4.73	
6-7	M	121	0.150±0.090	0.32	1.955±0.990	4.37	0.10
	F	116	0.152±0.096	0.37	2.010±1.032	5.69	

*Standard deviation, †M: Male; F: Female.

ratio is routinely used in clinical practice to screen for hypercalciuria as it is found to have a good correlation with the 24 h calcium excretion (So et al., 2001). Traditionally, if a urine calcium to creatinine ratio is greater than 0.21, considered abnormal and suggestive of hypercalciuria in children (Pak et al., 1975). Also, some of the researches showed a direct association between urinary sodium/potassium ratio with urinary calcium/creatinine ratio in hypercalciuric patients (Osorio and Alon, 1997) and increased risk of urolithiasis (Cirllo et al., 1996).

Due to our search in internet, no study has been done in children of 1 to 7 years in the world, and also, no study has been done on this subject in Khozestan province up to now. Therefore, we decided to evaluate the urinary calcium, creatinine, sodium and potassium excretion in healthy children with 1 to 7 years and determine age related reference values for urine calcium to creatinine ratio in Andimeshk city in Khozestan province of Iran.

MATERIALS AND METHODS

This is a descriptive study conducted in Andimeshk city in the north of Khozestan province. Khozestan province is located at the south-western of Iran with very hot and humid climate in the most months of the year. In this study, from 1155 healthy children (528 boys and 627 girls) with ages between 1 to 7 years, that referred to check-up to Imam Ali hospital in Andimeshk, between January and December 2008, urine sample is collected. All of the children had normal examination and growth and not eating habits, physical activities, any history of kidney or urinary tract diseases. This finding is

obtained according to physical examination by hospital's physician and questionnaire that are filled by their parents. The consent form was obtained from all participants. Random urine samples were obtained from each subject, collected in a coded plastic sealed container and sent to biochemistry department of laboratory immediately. Calcium and creatinine of urine samples, were measured by BS-300 Mindry Autoanalyzer and sodium and potassium were measured by Convergys ISE Analyzer (Flameless flame photometer), immediately.

RESULTS

From 1155 healthy children, 528 (45.7%) were boys and 627 (54.3%) were girls. The number of each groups are listed in Table 1. Mean ± SD ratio of urine calcium to creatinine in all children was 0.165±0.115. The mean ± SD of urine calcium to creatinine ratio for boys and girls was 0.168±0.114 and 0.163±0.093, respectively. The urine calcium to creatinine ratio is higher in boys than girls, but not significant (p=0.37). Also, the mean ± SD ratio of urine sodium to potassium in all children was 1.981±1.322. The mean ± SD of urine sodium to potassium ratio for boys and girls was 1.982±0.912 and 1.980±1.108, respectively. The urine sodium to potassium ratio is higher in boys than girls, but not significant (p=0.28).

Conclusions

According to our study, the mean±SD urinary calcium to creatinine and sodium to potassium ratio in 1 to 7 healthy children in Andimeshk City were 0.165 ± 0.115 and

1.981±1.322, respectively. In our study, the urinary calcium to creatinine and sodium to potassium ratio are higher in boys than girls, but this differences not significant.

In the study of Nikibakhsh et al. (2008), the mean calcium to creatinine ratio in primary school children in Urmia (the city in the north-west of Iran), was 0.11. In their study, have not find any differences between males and females that compatible with our study. Esbjorner and Jones (1995) reported normal urine calcium to creatinine ratio as high as 0.44 in 2 to 18 years healthy Swedish children. Ceran et al. (2003) reported urine calcium to creatinine ratio equal to 0.1 in Turkish children that lower than our results. Safarinejad (2003) reported extremely low calcium to creatinine ratio as low as 0.04 in an Iranian healthy children population.

Ceran et al. (2003) reported that children under 7 months have 3 fold higher urine calcium to creatinine ratio compared to ones above 7 years. Also, So et al. (2001) reported that urine calcium to creatinine ratio is decreased by aging.

Sargent et al. (1993) suggested that high levels of urine calcium to creatinine ratio in infants may be secondary to low creatinine excretion per unit body mass. Cirllo et al. (1996) showed an association between high urinary sodium to potassium ratio and increased risk of urolithiasis. A direct correlation between urine calcium to creatinine ratio and urine sodium to potassium ratio in hypercalciuric patients has been shown by Osorio and Alon (1997). They suggested that increased potassium intake in hypercalciuric children has beneficial effect on urine calcium to creatinine ratio and patient's symptoms. S factors such as dietary habits, warm climate, etc. are involved in kidney stone formation (Curhan et al., 1997). Because of high quantities of solutes in children's urine of this region and warm climate in Khuzestan province in Iran, the risk of renal stone formation are high and therefore, it is suggested that more investigation in other Khuzestan cities will be done and also, the prevalence of kidney's stone in this children will particularize.

ACKNOWLEDGEMENT

This study was supported by Ahvaz Jundishapur University of Medical Sciences, grant No. 88.S.51. We thank Imam Ali laboratory personals for their expert laboratory assistance.

REFERENCES

Ceran O, Akin M, Akturk Z et al., (Provide Complete Name) (2003). Normal calcium/creatinine ratios in Turkish children. Indian Pediatr. 40(9):884-887.

Cirllo M, Laurenzi M, Panarelli W et al., (Provide Complete Name) (1996). Urinary sodium to potassium ratio and urinary stone disease. Kidney Int. 46(4):1133-1139.

Curhan GC, Willett WC, Rimm EB et al., (Provide Complete Name) (1997). Family history and risk of kidney stones. J. Am. Soc. Nephrol. 8:1568-1573.

Esbjorner E, Jones IL (1995). Urinary calcium excretion in Swedish children. Acta Pediatr. 84(2):156-159.

Ginsbery JM, Chang BS, Matarese RA et al., (Provide Complete Name) (1993). Use of single voided urine samples to estimate proteinuria. Engl. J. Med. 309:1543-1546.

Honarpisheh A, Hooman N, Taghavi A (2009). Urinary calcium excretion in healthy children living in Kashan/Iran. Iran J. Pediatr. 19:154-158.

Langman CB, Moore ES (1984). Hypercalciuria in clinical pediatrics. Clin. Pediatr. 23(3):135-137.

Nikibakhsh A, Seyedzadeh A, Mahmoodzadeh H et al., (Provide Complete Name) (2008). Normal values for random urinary calcium to creatinine ratio in Iranian children. Iran J. Pediatr. 18:263-266.

Osorio AV, Alon US (1997). The relationship between urinary calcium, sodium and potassium excretion and the role of potassium in treating idiopathic hypercalciuria. Pediatrics 100(4):675-681.

Pak CY, Kaplan R, Bone H et al., (Provide Complete Name) (1975). A simple test for the diagnosis of absorptive and renal hypercalciurias. N. Engl. J. Med. 292:497-500.

Safarinejad MR (2003). Urinary mineral excretion in healthy Iranian children. Pediatr. Nephrol. 18(2):140-144.

Sargent JD, Stukel TA, Kresel J (1993). Normal values random urinary calcium to creatinine ratios in infancy. J. Pediatr. 123:393-397.

So NP, Osorio AV, Simon SD, Alan US (2001). Normal Urinary calcium/creatinine ratio in African–American and Caucasian children. Pediatr. Nephrol. 16(2):133-139.

## 21

Evaluation of the risk of drug addiction with the help of fuzzy sets

Manoranjan Kumar Singh[1], L. Rakesh[2*] and Aniket Ranjan[3]

[1]Department of Mathematics, Magadh University, Bodhagaya, Gaya, Bihar, India-823001.
[2]Magadh University, Bodhgaya, Gaya, India-823001.
[3]Department of Computer-Science, SCT Institute of Technology, Bangalore, India-560075.

The primary focus of this paper is to present a general view of the current applications of fuzzy logic in medical analogy of consumption of drugs. The paper also deals with the origin, structure and composition of fuzzy sets. The authors particularly review the medical literature using fuzzy logic. Fuzzy set theory can be considered as a suitable formalism to deal with the imprecision intrinsic to many real world problems. Fuzzy set theory provides an appropriate framework for the representation of vague medical concepts and imprecise modes of reasoning. The authors present two concrete illustrations to investigate the impact of the risk related to drug addictions, like smoking and alcohol drinking and thereby highlighting the social problem related to health.

Key words: Estimation, classical set, validation, diagnostic test.

INTRODUCTION

Logic studies the notions of consequence; it deals with propositions, set of propositions and the relation of consequence among them. Formal logic represents this by means of well-defined logical calculi. Logical calculus has two notions of consequence; they are syntactical, based on a notion of proof and semantically which are based on notions of truth. Fuzzy propositions use linguistic variables such as age; with values- young, very old and old. The truth of a fuzzy proposition is a matter of degree. Aristotle in his, laws of thought and law of the excluded middle described every proposition must either be True or False. Plato laid the foundation, for what would become fuzzy logic, indicating that there was a third region beyond True and False. Lukasiewicz, who first proposed a systematic alternative to the bi-valued logic of Aristotle described the 3-valued logic; where the third value is possible. He showed that, it is possible to derive infinite-valued logic. In 1965, Lotfi Zadeh published his seminal work on "Fuzzy Sets" describing the mathematics of fuzzy set theory.

In 1973, Lotfi Zadeh proposed his theory of fuzzy logic where the membership function operates over the range of real numbers [0, 1]. New operations for the calculus of logic were proposed, and shown to be in principle at least a generalization of classic logic. Lotfi Zadeh is regarded as the father of fuzzy theory. He was born in Iran and graduated from the University of Tehran. In the United States, he received his doctoral degree at Columbia University. He worked at Princeton University and then became a professor at the University of California in 1959. He was brilliant researcher in control theory and system theory before he proposed a theory whose objects, that is, fuzzy sets are sets with boundaries that are not precise. The membership in a fuzzy set is not a matter of affirmation or denial, but rather a matter of a degree. The word fuzzy means indistinct, imprecise, obscure, blurred, vague, ambiguous etc. Hence, one may be tempted to interpret fuzzy set as a vague set or ambiguous set but this would be a wrong interpretation. In fact, 'fuzzy set' is a well defined concept in mathematics. The driving force behind this change is the realization that classical set theory is in adequate for dealing with imprecision, uncertainty and the complexity of the real world. This motivates the evolution of fuzzy set theory. The example

*Corresponding author. E-mail: rakeshsct@yahoo.co.in.

theory. The example of age with different values; young, very old, old, containing adjective, verb and adverb may not form sets in the usual mathematical sense, the fact remains that such imprecisely defined classes play an important role in human thinking, particularly in the domain of pattern recognition, digital communication and Information technology. Zadeh describes fuzzy logic as formalization of approximate reasoning.

Although, "fuzzy logic" may seem to imply imprecision, it's based on a reliable and rigorous discipline. Fuzzy logic lets us accurately describe control systems in words instead of complicated math. Fuzzy logic, based on fuzzy set theory, allows us to express the operational and control laws of a system linguistically in words. Although, such an approach might seem inadequate, it can actually be superior to and much easier than a more mathematical approach. The main strength of fuzzy set theory, a generalization of classical set theory, that excels in dealing with imprecision. In classical set theory, an item is either a part of a set or not. There is no in-between, there are no partial members. Fuzzy set theory recognizes that very few crisp sets actually exists Herrera et al., 2004. There is a paradigm shift from crisp set to fuzzy set. The paradigm shift is necessitated by "the need to bridge the gap between mathematical models (biology, medicine, social science) and experience". This paradigm allows expressing observation and measurement uncertainties, managing complexity and capturing human common-sense reasoning and decision making.

NON FUZZY (CLASSICAL) SETS TO FUZZY SETS

One of the important tools in modern mathematics is the theory of sets. Every branch of mathematics can be considered as a study of sets of objects of one kind or another. For instance geometry is the study of set of points. Algebra is concerned with the set of numbers and operations on those sets Singh, 1986. Analysis mainly deals with set of function. The study of sets and their use in the foundation of mathematics began in the latter part of the nineteenth century by German mathematician George Cantor (1845 - 1918). According to Cantor, "A set is a collection into a whole of definite and distinct objects of the intuition or thought and the objects are called 'elements' of the set ". About the turn of the twentieth century paradoxes of various kinds namely Russell's paradox (1901); Cantor's paradox (1932); Burali-Forti's Paradox (1897), were discovered which directly or indirectly originated from the notion of the set and which shook the foundations of mathematics in general and set theory in particular. Frege indeed admitted that Russell's paradox undermines the foundations of his life work to construct arithmetic on the basis of the set theory. There are three principal philosophies of mathematics each of which has a sizable group of adherents. These are logistic school, of which Frege, Russell and White - Head are the main expositors, the intuitionist school was led by the Dutch mathematician L.E.J. Brouwer and Heyting and the formalist school developed principally by David Hilbert. These schools of mathematics were greatly influenced by the appearance of paradoxes. The mathematicians of these schools approached the problem posed by the paradoxes according to the philosophy of mathematics they held. The basic assumption that has been made in any axiomatic set theory as well as in Cantor's intuitive set theory is that given to any set A and any object x of the universe of discourse X, it can be decided whether $x \in A$ holds or not. Hence, corresponding to any subset A of X, they can construct a unique real valued function $f_A(x)$, called characteristic function defined over the universe of discourse X such that:

$f_A : X \rightarrow [0, 1]$ such that

$f_A(x) = 1$ if $x \in$ A is true

$= 0$ if $x \in A$ if false

However, in real physical world, the above assumption ($x \in A$ or $x \in$ A) may not be true. In order to exemplify, let us consider the "Class of new cars", "Class of short men", "Class of new, high buildings", "Class of all real numbers which are much greater than 1", "Class of expensive bike", "Class of highly contagious diseases", "Class of beautiful flowers", "Class of the boy who resembles his father", the class of real number "approximately equal to 3", "Class of sunny days", We observe that due to the presence of the terms 'new', 'short', 'high', 'much', 'expensive', 'highly', 'beautiful', 'sunny', 'approximately', in the formation of above classes some kind of imprecision or ambiguity or vagueness arises in deciding whether an individual element in the context is an element of the class or not. Indeed, classes of such types do not constitute a set in usual mathematical sense Wilder, 2006. Sets of this type that is very often involve some adjectives, verbs and adverbs or some combination thereof which are not sharply defined in their descriptions. Numerous other examples may be found in every branch of science as well as in writings and daily conversations. In fact, most of the classes of objects encountered in the real physical world are this 'fuzzy' not sharply defined type. They do not have precisely defined criteria of membership. In such classes, an object need not necessarily either belong to or not belong to a class; there may be intermediate grades of membership. In other words, they can say the transition from member to non- member appears gradual rather than abrupt. Thus, the fuzzy set introduces vagueness with the aim of reducing complexity by eliminating the sharp boundary and dividing members of the class from non- members.

A fuzzy set can be defined mathematically by assigning each individual in the universe of discourse value representing its grade of membership in the fuzzy set. This grade corresponds to the degree to which individual is "similar" or "compatible" with the concept represented by the fuzzy set Kosko, 1993. Thus, individuals may belong in the fuzzy set to a greater or lesser degree as indicated by a larger or smaller membership grade. These membership grades are very often represented by real-number values ranging in the closed interval between 0 and 1. This concept of a fuzzy set, which is a "class" with a continuum of grades of membership or they can say that a fuzzy set on a set X is sorted of generalized "Characteristic function" on X, whose degree of membership may be more than "yes" or "no". Thus, a fuzzy set representing the concept of sunny days might assign a degree of membership 1 to a cloud of 0%, 0.8 to a cloud cover of 20%, 0.4 to a cloud cover of 30% and 0 to a cloud cover of 75%. These grades signify the degree to which each percentage of cloud cover approximates the subjective concept of sunny days and the set itself models the semantic flexibility inherent in such a common linguistic term. Because full membership and full non-membership in the fuzzy set can still be indicated by the values of 1 and 0, they can consider the "crisp" set to be restricted in case of the more general fuzzy set for which only these two grades of membership are allowed. The notion of fuzzy sets can be represented; Let X denotes a universal set which is also refereed as a field of reference or universe of discourse. Then, the membership function f_A by which a fuzzy set A is usually defined has the form;

$f_A : X \rightarrow [0, 1]$ where $[0, 1]$

denotes the interval of real numbers from 0 - 1, inclusive. The value of f_A at x, $f_A(x)$ is 1 or 0 according as x belongs or does not belong to A. When A is a fuzzy set, then the nearer the value of $f_A(x)$ to 0, the more tenuous is the membership of x in A, with the "degree of belonging" increasing with increase in $f_A(x)$.

MEDICAL LITERATURE

Sources of uncertainty

The complexity of medical practice makes traditional quantitative approaches of analysis inappropriate. In medicine, the lack of information and its imprecision, and many times, contradictory nature are common facts Nieto, 2004. The sources of uncertainty can be classified as follows.

Information about the patient

Medical history of the patient, which is usually, supplied by the patient and/or his/her family. This is usually highly subjective and imprecise.

Physical examination

The physician usually obtains objective data, but in some cases the boundary between normal and pathological status is not sharp.

RESULTS

Results of laboratory and other diagnostic tests are also subject to some mistakes and even to improper behaviour of the patient prior to the examination.

Symptoms

The patient may include simulated, exaggerated, understated symptoms, or may even fail to mention some of them.

Classification

The authors stress the paradox of the growing number of mental disorders versus the absence of a natural classification. The classification in critical (that is, borderline) cases is difficult, particularly when a categorical system of diagnosis is considered.

Fuzzy logic and medicine

Fuzzy logic plays an important role in medicine. Some examples showing that fuzzy logic crosses many disease groups are the following:

(i) Fuzzy information granulation of medical images. Blood vessel extraction from 3-D MRA images.

(ii) Awareness monitoring and decision-making for general anaesthesia.
Acquisition of fuzzy association rules from medical data.
(iii) Fuzzy logic in a decision support system in the domain of Coronary heart disease risk assessment.
(iv) A model-based temporal abductive diagnosis model for an intensive coronary care unit.
(v) A Fuzzy Model for Pattern Recognition in the Evolution of Patients
(vi) To predict the response to treatment with citalopram in alcohol dependence.
(vii) To analyze diabetic neuropathy and to detect early diabetic retinopathy.
(viii) To calculate volumes of brain tissue from magnetic resonance imaging (MRI)], and to analyze functional MRI data.
(ix) To assist the diagnosis of central nervous systems tumors (astrocytic tumors).
(x) To discriminate benign skin lesions from malignant melanomas
(xi) To improve decision-making in radiation therapy and to visualize nerve fibers in the human brain.
(xii) To represent quantitative estimates of drug use.

Many other areas of application, to mention a few, are to study fuzzy epidemics, to make decisions in nursing, to overcome electro acupuncture accommodation. The diagnosis of disease involves several levels of uncertainty and imprecision and it is inherent to medicine. A single disease may manifest itself quite differently, depending on the patient, and with different intensities. A single symptom may correspond to different diseases Papageorgious et al., 2003. On the other hand, several diseases present in a patient may interact and interfere with the usual description of any of the diseases. The best and most precise description of disease entities uses linguistic terms that are also imprecise and vague. Moreover, the classical concepts of health and disease are mutually exclusive and opposite. However, some recent approaches consider both concepts as complementary processes in the same continuum. According to the definition issued by the World Health Organization (WHO), "health is a state of complete physical, mental and social well-being and not merely the absence of disease or infirmity". The loss of health can be seen in its three forms, disease, illness and sickness.

To deal with imprecision and uncertainty, the authors have at the disposal fuzzy logic. Fuzzy logic introduces partial truth values, between true and false. According to Aristotelian logic, for a given proposition or state, they only have two logical values, true-false, black-white, 1 - 0. In real life, things are not either black or white, but most of the times are grey. Thus, in many practical situations, it is convenient to consider intermediate logical values. Let us show this with a very simple medical example. Consider the statement "you are healthy". Is it true if you have only a broken nail? Is it false if you have a terminal

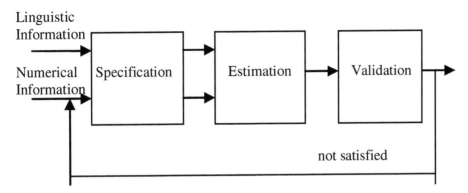

Figure 1. A system identification.

cancer? Everybody is healthy to some degree h and ill to some degree i Szczepaniak et al., 2005. If you are totally healthy, then of course h = 1, i = 0. Usually, everybody has some minor health problems and h < 1, but h + i = 1. In the other extreme situation, h = 0, and i = 1, so that, you are not healthy at all (you are dead). In the case, you have only a broken nail, they may write h = 0.999, i = 0.001; if you have a painful gastric ulcer, i = 0.6, h = 0.4, but in the case you have a terminal cancer, probably i = 0.95, h = 0.05. Uncertainty is now considered essential to science and fuzzy logic is a way to model and deal with it using natural language. The authors can say that, fuzzy logic is a qualitative computational approach. Since uncertainty is inherent in fields such as medicine and fuzzy logic takes into account such uncertainty, fuzzy set theory can be considered as a suitable formalism to deal with the imprecision intrinsic to many biomedical and bioinformatics problems. Fuzzy logic is a method to render precise what is imprecise in the world of medicine.

FUZZY SYSTEM IDENTIFICATION

The concept of a mathematical model is fundamental to system analysis and design which require the representation of systems phenomenon as a functional dependence between interacting input and output variables. Mathematical models are essential for prediction and control purposes Rosen (1982). Conventionally, a mathematical model for a system is constructed by analysing input-output measurements from the system. These numerical measurements are important because they represent the behaviour of the system in a quantitative fashion. Very often, there exists another important information source for many engineering systems, knowledge from human experts. This knowledge known as linguistic information, provides qualitative instructions and descriptions about the system and is especially useful when the input and output measurements are difficult to obtain. Fuzzy models are capable of doing this kind of information naturally and conveniently, while

conventional mathematical models usually fail to do so. Moreover, it is interesting to note that fuzzy models have the same ability to process numerical information as conventional models, if such information is available. Being able to deal with linguistic information and numerical information is one of the important properties of fuzzy models. The second important property of fuzzy models is their ability to handle non linearity. It is well known fact that most engineering systems are non linear to some extent. Interpretability is another salient feature of fuzzy models. A fuzzy model has a transparent model structure. Each rule in the model acts like a "local model" in the sense that it only covers a local region of the input-output space, and its contribution to the whole output of the model is easily understood. Fuzzy system identification consists of three basic sub problems, specification, estimation and validation. This is depicted in the Figure 1.

Specification involves finding the important input variables from all possible input variables, specifying membership functions, partitioning the input space, and determining the number of fuzzy rules comprising the underlying model. Parameter estimation involves the determination of unknown parameters in the model using some optimization method based on both linguistic information obtained from human experts and numerical data obtained from the actual system to be modelled. Specification and estimation are interwoven, and neither of them can be independently identified without resort to other. Validation involves testing the model based on some performance criterion. If the model cannot pass the test, w must modify the model, the model structure and re-estimate the model parameter. It may be necessary to repeat this process many times before a satisfactory model is found. The specification of a fuzzy model involves selection of input variables. The different techniques for selecting input variables are forward selection, backward selection, and best subset procedure. The choice of membership functions affect how well a fuzzy model behaves. Empirical evaluation of different membership functions can be useful in guiding the choice of membership functions. Fuzzy models are constructed

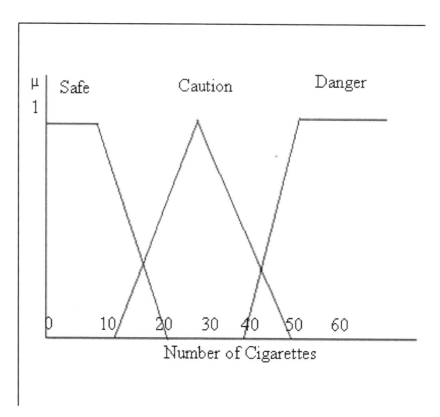

Figure 2. Membership functions of risk of smoking.

using triangular, bell shaped and Gaussian membership function. Triangular membership function is inferior to bell shaped and Gaussian membership function. These membership functions are compared with other membership functions especially, with the sin function sin(x) /x, based on how closely the resultant fuzzy models approximate the real systems. More extensive empirical investigation is needed in this area. Parameter estimation problems, in general, involve the optimization of antecedent membership parameters and the consequent parameters. In evaluating fuzzy models cross validation, residual analysis, and information-theoretic criteria are employed.

SUMMARY OF FINDINGS

Estimation of the risk of smoking

We know that fuzzy control work on fuzzy inference. The idea of fuzzy inference is applied to fuzzy expert system. It is now being used not only in engineering but in several fields of social sciences. In this light we will show the example based on consistencies of fuzzy sets. Let us consider the following situation of smoking which is one of the vital causes behind heart attack, cancer etc. among human beings:

(i) A doctor thinks that smoking less than 10 cigarettes a day is not harmful for health (safe),
(ii) He presumes that smoking more than 50 smokes a day is definitely (absolutely) harmful (dangerous).

The doctor believes that smoking 20 - 30 smokes per day are potentially harmful (suspicious). The doctor understanding about smoking can be illustrated with the help of fuzzy sets as shown in the Figure 2. On the horizontal axis they is, on the x-axis, we express the number of smokes a day, and the membership function that expresses the risk of smoking has been indicated on the vertical axis i.e. on y axis between the real number 0 and 1. Let us suppose that Ajay's satisfaction of smoking is given by the fuzzy set A. That is he is satisfied if he has about 10 - 20 smokes a day. Also, they have Binod's fuzzy set B, which means Binod's requires about 40 - 50 smokes a day. The doctor's diagnosis (understanding) about smoking is given by the points of agreement of each of the fuzzy sets, safe, caution and danger. We know that the points of agreements are given by the highest value at the intersection of two fuzzy sets. The intersection of two fuzzy sets A and B is defined as,

$$(A \cap B)(X) = \min \{ A(X), B(X) \},$$

for all $x \in X$, where X is the universal set, A(X) and B(X) are the membership functions. They may infer that Ajay has the safety degree of 0.9, the degree being Caution of

0.9, and the danger degree of 0.0. Also, the authors have Arun Fuzzy set we infer that Arun's danger degree is 0.85 and his safety degree is almost zero. Here we note that the membership function is used to give the diagnosis that can be provided by the statistics or by the doctor's subjectivity. This example shows a way to give a subjective diagnosis, which might be too simple for real use. If the patient is required to be classified, we can take the label whose value is the highest. Here, they also observe that in this example, the horizontal axis gives continuous numbers.

Estimation of the risk of alcohol drinking

Alcohol drinking and Cigarette smoking during adolescence have been shown to be associated with a greater possibility of concurrent and future substance-related disorders. In order to report patterns of drug use and to describe factors associated with substance use in adolescents, a cross-sectional survey was carried out in a representative population sample of 3000 adolescents, aged 12 - 17 years, from Bangalore, silicon city of India to Bombay, a metro and commercial capital of India. The original survey covered the use of alcohol, tobacco, illicit drugs, and other psychoactive substances. For tobacco smoking and alcohol drinking, each subject of the population sample can be assigned a fuzzy degree of addiction (or risk use). With respect to the other fuzzy variable, if you drink no alcohol, the degree of this variable is 0. If you drink more than 75 cc of alcohol per day, the degree of alcoholism is 1. For 25 cc/d, the degree could be 0.4 and for 50 cc/d, 0.8. Suppose you correspond to the fuzzy set $\lambda = (1, 1)$, have recently had some health problems, and your physician has advised you to reduce your consumption of cigarettes and alcohol by half. The ideal situation for your health is, of course, the point $\mu = (0, 0)$, but it is possibly difficult to achieve. Since uncertainty is inherent in fields such as medicine, fuzzy logic takes into account such uncertainty to render precise, overcome imprecise in the world of medicine.

Conclusions

In this interesting paper the author presents a summary of the basic concepts and techniques underlying the application of fuzzy set theory to solve practical problems related to health. The study finds a number of examples relating to its use as a computational system for dealing with uncertainty and imprecision in the context of evaluation of risk associated with smoking and drinking habits. Health is a vital indicator of human development that will enable every individual to lead a social and economically productive life. Through the process of fuzzification, the authors gain greater generality and enhanced ability to model real world problems and higher expressive power to some extent for respective areas of non fuzzy mathematics.

REFERENCES

Herrera F, Hoffmann F, Magdalena L, Cordon O, Gomide F (2004). Fuzzy Sets and Systems, Int. J. Intelligent Systems, 141(1): 5-31.

Kosko B (1993). Fuzzy Thinking: The New Science of Fuzzy Logic, Hyperion Press, New York. pp. 40-47.

Nieto JJ, Torres A (2005). Midpoints for Fuzzy sets and their application in medicine. Artificial Intelligence in Medicine. 152(1):5–16. 59. Papageorgiou EI, Stylios CD, Groumpos PP (2003). IEEE Transactions on Biomed. Eng., 50(12): 1326–1339.

Rosen Field A (1982). How many are a few, Fuzzy sets, Fuzzy numbers and Fuzzy mathematics, 5th edition, Pearson, pp. 77-80.

Singh MK (1986). Ph.D Thesis Entitled "A study on the Axiomatic foundations of set theory", pp. 95-99.

Szczepaniak, Lisoba, Kacprzyk (2005).Fuzzy Systems in Medicine, 3rd Edition, Germany. pp. 10-15.

Wilder RL (2006). Introduction to foundations of mathematics, International edition Japan. pp. 5-12.

## 22

Competitiveness of Ljubljana city

Art Kovačič

Institute for Economic Research, Kardeljeva pl. Ljubljana, Slovenia. E-mail: kovacica@ier.si.

Ljubljana can be observed through different perspectives. Urban development is often written on the basis of economic level, social development, benchmarking results with similar economies, on the basis of past experiences. By urbanistic way of life we cover the main Slovenian areas in polycentric net, that is well organised in EU space. City is forced to lead a vital, beautiful and clean environment that supports economic and social progress and quality of life. According on the Central Europe programme we can realise the new competitiveness strategy. Competitiveness is now more regional oriented and cover the needs of economy and citizens on specific area. We would like to increase the competitiveness level by providing equal opportunities for larger set of regions and border regions. The research can be understood as a sum of economic and social success of all regions in the area. The concept of local economy and the connections among city and surrounds as investment bases, industrial capacities can increase the investment potential. Well conditions for business development in Central Slovenia are can supported the city competitiveness. In article I will show the business importance of the city and also the business circumstances in Ljubljana's area. Creating a better circumstance for competitive growth in more ubranistic Europe, with high share of elderly citizens, and with important cultural heritage can be explained with next instruments. The modern concept of city development (case Ljubljana) will be analysed through different perspectives. European perspectives give a more modern view on city development. City development can be seen as a balance of different interests among investors, households, citizens, tourists and government. SMEs companies usually take more modern concept of planning development. But urban development has to involve the competitiveness research. So, by increasing the competitive level we improve the position of enterprises in the city.

Key words: Productivity and competitiveness, benchmarking, development strategy, national development, JEL classification: 011, 024, 038, 057: UDC: 339, 9.

INTRODUCTION

City competitiveness can be seen as creation of well circumstances from citizens and for business sector. If we don't provide well conditions for enterprises then will be difficult to find money for financing the architecture and cultural part of development process. Providing the better conditions for competitiveness success by indirect factors can be seen by focusing on: polycentric development, on demography and social change, and on cultural resources. So, the direct national competitivess factors as domestic economy, management, infrastructure, financial system, internationalisation, government and education are not integrated in the analysis. Regional development research usually ignores the governmental potential and also the financial market success. Competitiveness is

taken from regional research as a socio-economic performance. So, we would like to improve the competitiveness level by regional factors as cultural heritage, demograpfic movements and social change. Because the innovation system is shown separtelly it is logical to have competitiveness research without innovation activity. The national innovation system is analysed alone. The innovation system is understood through innovations, technology development R&D, educational and social change. The overall progress supported by the programme can be explained by creation of more attractive regions and cities. More urbanistic evaluaton of regional competitiveness is logical. Improving the locational attractiveness is important for fostering the investments. The innovative and technological oriented regions calls for higher R&D capacities transfer of technology and on innovation capacities. The accessibility is a very important factor of regional development analysis. We would like to connect different part across EU and provide better conditions for citizens. Transport and information technology development are the main factors. Environment is the last actor of the overall programme goals. We want to have a high quality environment by managing natural resources and heritage. Renewable energy development is supported.

Urban competitiveness can be analysed in light of new programme. The main directions are taken for Ljubljana case. Ljubljana's competitiveness is evaluated compared to new programme. The new programme has an influence on understanding competitiveness concept away from Porter's and Krugman's orientation. The social economic development circumstances in CEE are the basic for understanding determinants of competitiveness strategy. Spatial planning, cultural heritage and demographic changes are part of competitiveness concept. Normally is competitiveness oriented on industrial development, technological progress an on quality of life. The high urbanisation in CEE countries brings the competitiveness concept closer to metropolis. It boasts strong capital regions and numerous medium sized towns, which are carriers of economic growth. Improving the competitiveness level with preserving the cultural heritage is logical goal. Cultural heritage is defined as a totality of material and immaterial cultural assets like libraries, archives and museums, buildings (churches, castles, monasteries) as well as the manifestation and expression of the folk culture, the scientific perception and so on. The immaterial cultural assets are passed down from one generation to the other. They are formulated by communities and groups depending on their particular milieus, their interactions with nature and their history, and are part of the identity and continuity. Cultural heritage contributes to cultural diversity and creativity and is part of a regional identity. Competitiveness in the programme is not only understood in terms of pure economic performance, but rather as a more complex concept, which embraces soft factors that influence economic performance positively. (quality of life, sustainability, gender equality). However competitiveness is also regarded as essential precondition for achieving economic wealth a high quality of life. In this light competitiveness is not only about strategically utilising and developing economic strengths and dynamics but also about the ability to develop territorial, cultural and social capital among individuals, firms and institutions. In economic and territorial terms, competitiveness implies the capability to compete on European single market.

It is strange to show competitiveness without national innovation system. But fostering innovation activity and the circumstances are part of the programme. Innovation is a systemic rather than a linear process, involving many different players and often happening over an extended period of time. Well-functioning innovation systems ensure the free flow of information across the interfaces between researchers, entrepreneurs, investors, public authorities and many other actors. Such systems may have technical components but are, above all, networks of individuals. For this reason, proximity is an important feature of most innovation systems. In the context of the programme, innovation is considered as one of the most important driving forces for economic wealth. It is not just related to a few high-tech industries but a major factor of any industry or economic sector. It is more than simply the initial 'big idea' or a product or services that result from the idea. Innovation is more accurately described as a process through which knowledge is created and translated into new products, services or processes of the private and the public sector. To improve the climate for innovation in all regions and to enable them to make better use of their innovation potential by addressing their specific needs and areas of weakness and fostering the areas of strength. On a general note, transnational cooperation should not omit the fact that regional and national innovation policies are of a highly competitive nature. For this reason, transnational cooperation in the field of innovation will have to address existing limitations to the willingness to freely exchange insights and knowledge. The common goal is to overcome thinking in terms of national/regional competitiveness in order to strive for a more competitive and innovative Central Europe area as a whole. In jointly striving for innovation, the driving force should be learning from Central Europe's diversity. The common goal should be to complement national/regional policies in those areas where it proves to be most effective.

If we analyse competitiveness through urban and regional research than we can put more weight on polycentric development process. Central Europe is characterized by a high degree of urbanisation, with 73% of the population living in cities or urban areas. It boasts strong capital regions and numerous medium sized towns, which are carriers of economic growth. So, the spatial planning and urban development has an important influence on competitiveness. Cities as Berlin, Krakow, Katowize, Poznan, Ljubljana, Budapest, Prag, Milan, Venice or Munchen has a very important economic weight on the whole region. Well connections with towns in surrounding can increase the investments circumstances. In the new Member States, due to the very selective influx of foreign direct investments in urban areas, a mono-centric development at national levels threatens to reinforce disparities between their capital and other regions. The more polycentric development can contribute to avoiding such disparities. Promoting urban and regional cooperation of relevant actors can help to overcome the core-periphery pattern and lead to higher growth and competitiveness. The spatial development concerning urban agglomerations is determined by several distinct factors. Urban areas are confronted with increasing suburbanization processes with negative environmental impacts due to higher traffic and increasing land use. National and international migration flows are mostly concentrated in the cities. For several urban areas, this is the most important factor for the demographic growth and the change of their demographic structure (age, regional origin). The uneven territorial development of Central Europe is reflected in increasing economic and social disparities between urban and rural areas, as well as within urban areas due to social and spatial segregation. The territorial effects of such trends can threaten the competitiveness of the cooperation area. The settlement structure of Central Europe is characterised by a few highly populated urban agglomerations and numerous small and medium-sized towns, which play an important role as regional economic and cultural centres. The development of functional relations between cities and between cities and their hinterland are essential for exploiting the competitive advantage and for the improving of a complementary development. This Area of Intervention aims at achieving a more balanced territorial development by improved urban and urban-regional cooperation. In this sense, the strategic economic and social development of cities and regions will be enhanced by:

-implementing integrated urban and regional development strategies and improved conditions for investments
-establishing durable cooperation of metropolitan areas as well as small and medium-sized cities or agglomerations and their associations on mutually relevant topics of transnational importance
-taking actions for urban-rural relationships with optimised material flows and with sustainable urban development patterns (example, solutions for urban sprawl)
-cooperating on new approaches in the field of rehabilitation and conversion issues of urban and peri-urban functional areas
-putting transnational urban-regional cooperation networks for optimising the joint use of infrastructure, leisure services and recreational facilities into practice
-implementing strategic actions to optimise the urban centre structure and to improve functional linkages between urban centres
-promoting actions to enhance the quality of the environment and open space in cities.

Central Europe is facing demographic trends such as an ageing society and migration, which have economic, social and cultural implications on urban and regional development in the Cooperation Area. Therefore, urban and regional development needs to find solutions and increase the capacity to react effectively to the changing needs of society in Central Europe. Reactions are needed in the sense of ensuring the service provision for all population groups, in sparsely populated areas in particular, but also in urban agglomerations. Housing and services generally need to be adapted closer to demographic and social trends and it will be necessary to work

against social and spatial segregation in urban areas. Consequently, these activities will help to raise the quality of life for citizens in Central Europe and contribute to achieving better social integration and reduced segregation. This Area of Intervention seeks to reduce negative effects of the demographic and social change on urban and regional development by:

-putting innovative solutions for service-provision and for the adaptation and provision of key services and infrastructures (health system, water, housing etc.) into practice
-promoting actions for adapting cities and regions to the needs of specific groups of population (example, elderly people, single households, handicapped people etc.)
-implementing transnational strategies to counter-balance social and spatial segregation and to integrate aspects of citizens' participation at an early stage of planning
-promoting actions for the provision of public services in the proximity of residential quarters
-developing and applying innovative solutions for addressing bottlenecks in urban development (example, housing, service infrastructure, congestions, investment barriers, limited areas for housing and industrial development)
-using new urban technologies to bring innovative and effective solutions to public services
-applying cross-sectoral actions to adapt the housing stock to current needs (example, regeneration of housing areas.) and to integrate housing into urban and regional development policies.

Central Europe is rich in cultural resources, understood as sites, structured landscapes and objects of importance to a culture. However, this richness is threatened by lacking investments or excessive pressure of investments risking destroying them. Cultural resources in Central Europe represent an important factor for its attractiveness, and play a major role for its identity. The programme will therefore develop its cultural resources for the benefits of the citizens and generate an economic base for cities and regions. This will lead to higher income-generation and stronger regional identities, while at the same time ensuring preservation of the cultural heritage. This Area of Intervention aims at fostering sustainable use of cultural resources and heritage. To capitalise on cultural resources will be supported by: building capacities of innovative management strategies for the protection, preservation and sustainable exploitation of cultural resources, promoting valorisation of traditional activities and knowledge, implementing strategic actions to generate income and employment through integrated cultural and economic concepts, putting strategies to enhance the cultural aspect of the regions into practice, using and protecting traditional knowledge and expertise related to cultural heritage, applying new forms of management of urban/cultural heritages with particular attention to natural and social capacity and possible side effects on environment and population in a long-term view.

Public private partnership

Public private Partnership is an important instrument for fostering business investments in the inner city. So, we would like to increase the possibilities for business investments. In Ljubljana can be seen the unfavourable conditions for SMEs development. So, by public private partnership we normally improve the investments opportunities for SMEs. Business conditions can be improved by PPP instruments. Public-private partnership describes a government service or private business venture which is funded and operated through a partnership of government and one or more private sector companies. These schemes are sometimes referred to as PPP. In some types of PPP, the government uses tax revenue to provide capital for investment, with operations run jointly with the private sector or under contract. In other types (notably the Private Finance Initiative), capital investment is made by the private sector on the strength of a contract with government to provide agreed services. Government contributions to a PPP may also be in kind (notably the transfer of existing assets). In projects that are aimed at creating public goods like in the infrastructure sector, the government may provide a capital subsidy in the form of a one-time grant, so as to make it more attractive to the private investors. In some other cases, the government may support the project by providing revenue subsidies, including tax breaks or by providing guaranteed annual revenues for a fixed period. The first attempt of public sector privatization was in the Republic of Slovenia in 1991, when the law on institutes was introduced. This law enabled the participation of private sector in non-commercial public services (example, education, culture, research, etc.). For the first time the possibility of concessions was introduced. The first sectors with concessions were culture, education and health. In 1993 the law on economic public services was introduced (for waste management, telecommunications, electricity, etc.). This law also introduced concessions and two types of possible public private partnerships: public holdings and via investment of public money in private companies to provide public services. Both laws gave only the basic legal framework. How certain public service should be "produced" it should be regulated by each specific law for each type of service. These laws were accepted very slowly because there was a lack of legal knowledge in the field of concessions and it resulted in some "strange" solutions: concession acts and concessions agreements are very short so they are unclear and in practice created and are still creating a lot of troubles; concessions in some fields (e.g. health) were given for eternity; prices went up or the quality of service falls (because there were no given standards what is expected quality). The process of entering in the EU, lack of public finance and the increased demand for public services led in the Republic

of Slovenia at the end of 2006 to the introduction of the law on Public Private Partnerships. This law became fully operable in the middle of 2007 when all the necessary by laws were adopted. The Public Private Partnership Act was published in the official journal of the Republic of Slovenia no. 127/2006 on 7/12-2006. Public-private partner relationships may be operated as: Relationships of contractual partnership in the forms of: (1) a concession; that is a bilateral legal relationship between the state or self-governing local community or other person of public law as the awarding authority and a legal or natural person as a concessionaire, in which the awarding authority awards to the concessionaire the special or exclusive right to perform a commercial public service or other activity in the public interest, which may include the construction of structures and facilities that are in part or entirely in the public interest (hereinafter: concession partnership), or (2) a public procurement relationship; i.e. a payment relationship between the client and supplier of goods, contractor of works or provider of services, of which the subject is the procurement of goods or the performance of works or services (hereinafter: public procurement partnership). (3) Relationships of institutional or equity partnership: by establishing a legal person under the conditions provided by this law, through the sale of an interest by the public partner in a public company or other entity of public or private law; by purchasing an interest in an entity of public or private law, recapitalization or in another manner in comparative terms legally and actually similar and comparable to the aforementioned forms, and through the transfer of the exercising of rights and obligations proceeding from the public-private partnership to such person (for instance performing commercial public services). This law establishes also the minimum requirement for concession contract as: the form and purpose of the works concession, the type, amount and form of joint funds or funds provided through co financing or of invested private funds, the relationships in connection with possible funds invested by the public partner and on the manner of refunding or purchasing invested public funds, a timetable of the use of public funds, the method of supervising the appropriated spending of funds, a timetable and method of carrying out investments in structures and facilities and fulfilling other obligations, the model of ownership right to structures and facilities, the conditions for awarding business to subcontractors, changes in the concessionaire company for which it must obtain the consent of the public partner, the possibilities of entering into a concession relationship in place of the existing concessionaire ("step in"), contractual penalties and other reasons for cancellation, annulment or rescission of the contract and the rights and obligations of contracting parties in such cases. the above mentioned law does not cover all the possible types of public private partnerships (e.g. agency, service contracts, profit sharing contracts, etc.); there are no manuals for operating public private partnerships; state and local communities look at public private partnerships as a magical stick to resolve all the problems in public sector but there are no ideas what are expected standards of provided service, how to protect public interest, how to promote the use of public service etc.; there is no real political wish for public private partnerships; there is strong people's opposition against public private partnerships as a way of public service privatization.

Yet there are some quasi PPP projects going on: Emonika (main railway and bus station in Ljubljana), sport facility in Ljubljana, considerations about modernization of Slovenian railways. Sports Hall Stožice is a well case of Public Private Partnership in Slovenia. The investment was big for Slovenian circumstances. Concept of the area integrates structures (a football stadium, university sports hall, shopping centre, underground parking) and a landscaped park into a coherent whole. In this area sport, nature and culture are intertwined and together they form an interactive social space which facilitates development of numerous events. The park is Ljubljana's new recreational space, a generator of new urban spaces. It is an artificial landscape which connects with the natural landscape on the east. It retains the flatness of the space along the path, and thus also the spatial proportions between the large landscape features now merged with the hall and stadium. The grassy plane, as the central landscaping feature of the wider area, protrudes into the park from the side and rises on the roof of the stadium, where the stadium becomes a part of the park, in the visual and programme sense. In the atriums in the middle of the park it sinks into the shopping centre and it reaches to the parking level. The thick technical slab is pierced with devices that enable operation of the levels below the park. This net of vertical structural connections – vents, sun tunnels, stair-cases designed as circular concrete shafts – gives the park its character and it forms the base for distribution of diverse programmes. The new football stadium with 16,000 seats will be the landmark of the new Ljubljana. With the roof structure in the shape of a green arch it represents the visual icon of the Stožice sports park. It provides optimum conditions for sporting events and also promises its spectators the real sports experience, as well as satisfies the highest safety requirements. The university sports hall will be the central building for national and city sporting and other events. Saddle-shaped construction of the hall ensures the maximal required volume for the arrangement of flexible sports areas and bleachers for 12,000 spectators. Construction of Potniški center Ljubljana (Travelling Centre Ljubljana) – Emonika will start next year. The total cost of the project exceeds EUR 220 million and it will bring numerous advantages for all participants. Emonika is a project of significant scale and importance and will therefore meet with a wide response of experts and general public of Ljubljana as well as of the whole Slovenia. The role and vision of individual subjects that play key part in its realization will also be assessed according to the success of the centre. The combined action of the city, Slovenske Železnice (Slovenian Railways) and as well as of the State, is a preliminary condition to effectively realize a project of this size. However, the interests of cooperating partners are certainly different and limited according to their funds. The main aim of Slovenske Železnice, besides financial considerations, is to ensure a pleasant and well-regulated environment for railway passengers. That would increase their number and assure at least the same standards of facilities, equipment and employees in this area. Here the company does not accept any financial obligations for the realization of the project with the exception of investment in kind. With the Project, the city of Ljubljana will gain greater connection between the north and south parts of the city and a new bus station. Moreover, the new town-planning scheme will provide the space for expansion of the Masarykova cesta into four-lane boulevard at the east section of the station. The city centre will surely revive after construction of Emonika and last but not least, the city will assure itself an annuity on the account of land tax. Initial activities considering Emonika go back to the year 2001 when the public company Slovenske Železnice (now Holding Slovenske Železnice) and Mestna občina Ljubljana (the municipality of Ljubljana) signed an agreement on the project. This deal anticipated an urban design of the railway station of Ljubljana area, connection of the north and south parts of the city, construction of an underground passenger hall with appropriate equipment, moving the bus station and construction of business facilities with attractive city programs that should enliven the struggling city centre and make the railway station more appealing for rail passengers. The aim should be attained with a conclusion of a public-private partnership with the chosen strategic investor. The conclusion was to be made through a project company for funding, planning, constructing, trading and administrating Emonika. In the end of 2004, the newspapers published an invitation to tender for strategic partnership and participation in funds in the construction of Emonika. The urban – architecture solution of the project company Real Engineering from Ljubljana won the international competition in 2002 and was therefore a basis for the public-private partnership. Furthermore, the readiness of the local partners, Slovenske železnice and Mestna občina Ljubljana, to contribute premises and to arrange the communal infrastructure at the site was of crucial importance. They would invest the whole or a part of the funds in kind, whereas the strategic partner would invest financial resources, acquire the majority share in the project company and take control over its operation.

Sustainable orientation in Ljubljana

The comprehensive approach demands dealing with cities in the wider, regional sense. The main aim is the SD development, since activities tied to urban processes impose the greatest changes and burdens on the environment (respect for the principles of Agenda 21 and Habitat Agenda). Good planning and design of settlements can reduce resource inputs and pollution outputs. Thus environmental protection strategies have to be tied to social, economic and other policies (connecting economic development, environmental protection, transports, housing and planning etc.). Model of regional city oriented towards sustainability include two strategies:

A. Development of the central built-up urban area and its historical core Central urban places demand renewal, revitalisation and transformation of urban surfaces.
B. In suburbanised areas decentralised densening, with smaller concentration centres and good network connection between them.

An important principle of the decentralised concentration model is to connect regional structures of urban growth to public transport routes and their stations. The principle enables regeneration of these areas, which need new economic investments, with restructuring and new urban functions. The basic principle is obvious: to put into force a decentralised scheme on the regional level. The construction is concentrated in the subcentres where mixed use of land prevails (housing and the corresponding public use of surfaces, shops, and services) on strategic points, along the routes of the regional public transport system. The key aspect of the concept is to create a lively urban community within walking distances. Towards the end of the 20th century the way of life and work has changed essentially. The differences between the city and the countryside with regard to lifestyle and access to information have been diminished, not only due to traffic connections but also, because of new information and communication technologies. The operational area of work is not limited only to a compact industrial production. Most workplaces can be found in the service field and remain within the living environment. In the spirit of planning for sustainability, close links between living and working is a priority. A star-like shape is typical of the regional development: almost densely built-up city area stretches up to the round by-pass. From the by-pass outwards, the city has been expanding in the shape of five branches. Along those directions, dispersed housing of one-family houses prevails, frequently as dormitories that need the concentration of functions and upgrading in the sense of creating new job opportunities. There are about 270.000 inhabitants within the municipal boundary, but inclusion of the outlying districts (in the functional urban region) increases the total to more than 500.000 inhabitants. The level of motorization is high (1 car per 2, 2 inhabitants) and the mobility (per day) is already 2,4 travels per inhabitant. The increase of private car traffic and the decrease of public transport represent one of the main problems in transportation system and a threat for the environment. Densely built-up city within the circle created by the by-pass has possibilities of development by rehabilitating degraded areas (»grey zones«), by renovating older urban areas and by improving the local pattern. Taking into consideration the SD aspects of the city development and the problems caused by the motor traffic in the inner city, the solution to this issue is to discharge the pressure on the centre by applying the decentralised settlement model. This model gives priority to the development of several urban sub-centres or densely built-up settlements (providing housing, services, employment opportunities, recreation) that would function almost independently along public transport lines. In such a way, the dispersed suburban housing pattern of mainly detached one-family houses would become more densely built-up and improved by a better supply. The city would grow along densely built-up axes with centres linked to a rapid public transportation system. The green intermediary spaces would enable transversal communication between landscape elements and would preserve the integrity of urban units. In designing new or upgraded communities, the existing construction should be taken into consideration as well as the existing central surfaces in the smaller suburban agglomerations. At the same time the dispersed built-up area in the suburbs should become more densely built-up. New or improved central surfaces would represent the central part of the development areas and settling around them should be designed as an autonomous unit within walking distances where functions are intermixed (shops, services, public use of space, housing, etc.) Within such a framework, new job programs would be feasible, as well as new residential areas.

In Ljubljana the demand for building land is very high, especially for housing. We can establish that in the last years the scope of complex housing development has been diminishing, but because of the growing demand prices of land and homes have correspondingly been growing. Besides, in the wider area of Ljubljana dispersed housing is rather extensive. These are unorganised low-density areas (mostly detached single-family houses), often with deficient utilities and low environmental standards. The prevalent circumstances demand sanation, suitable densening in well-accessible areas and the creation of complementary structures with mixed uses, such as: businesses and commercial programmes, services, crafts and manufacturing programmes, but above all, denser housing patterns with better use of building land. Thus we could alleviate the issues caused by dispersed housing and provide these areas with missing contents, which would also benefit their economic revitalisation. Besides urbanistic and architectural planning, solving of technical-technological issues, one of the key conditions for implementing such a project is the adequate use of land policy instruments (land readjustment etc.). Important is also a well-prepared investment programme, which is based on the assessment of economic feasibility (preparation of the building land and construction, the communal infrastructure and the buildings themselves). Because of its vicinity to the city centre and green hinterland of Golovec Hill and the Ljubljansko Barje (Ljubljana Marsh), the area has a beneficial position. With the completion of the southern ring road its accessibility significantly improved. Its setting enables good connections to the business and shopping centre Rudnik, as well as the nearby commercial, health care and cultural centre Rakovnik. Towards the East, the Rudnik sport's park is planned, which articulates the development area's edge. According to the Spatial development concept of Ljubljana (MOL 2001) this is also the green park prospect connecting the two entities of Golovec and Barje. Nearby, towards the West, lies the interesting waterfront area of the Ljubljanica River, while towards the North lies the hilly Golovec. Both are easily accessible from the proposed new neighbourhood. Appeals against the plans prepared in the 80s consisted of objections about the area's scope and possible number of new residents in the area (according to the proposal from 1987, more than 20.000, and slightly less – 15.000, in 1988). Despite the area's size, this number of new residents would be too high and a serious ecological burden. Therefore it was necessary to reconsider the relationship between built and un-built surfaces, number of inhabitants and building economics. The morphological concept of Ljubljana (MOL 2001) suggested low and medium density building amidst greenery. In the analytical phase of the research the following was included:

- Analysis and critique of ongoing planning in the area,
- Specific issues and weaknesses in the area (building on marshy ground, issues of dispersed settlement and other extant developments, deficient utilities infrastructure, hydrological problems, need for dry water retention surfaces),
- Advantages and qualities in the area (living quality, structural and visual qualities.),
- Possibilities and obstacles concerning use of land policy instruments, with respect for the new planning laws (the new Spatial Planning Act and revised Construction Act), Etc.
- Based on these findings a first draft of the layout and programme scheme was prepared. In the second phase of the project, which is presented in this article, for the chosen area Ilovica we further elaborated the following:
- Building proposal with programme concepts and phases of development,
- Proposal for drainage and accumulating water in the area,
- Test case of re-plotting building land with stated spatial measures needed for implementation of the planned development,
- Approximate calculation of land preparation costs with consolidation and costs of equipment: clearing the land, construction of the traffic and utilities infrastructure and preparation costs,
- Estimate of economic feasibility of the investment, which answered the following questions:
- What is the value of investment for purchasing the land

needed for construction of the utilities infrastructure and public programmes?
- How much starting capital does the municipality need to enter the process as an active player in the project?
- How soon the municipality investment will return?

The analyses and estimates concerning spatial qualities of the wider and immediate area showed that that area can offer good residential quality and a healthy environment. From the landscape design aspect the Ilovica area, as part of the Ljubljana marsh (Barje) is rather degraded. Because of rapid urbanisation in the last decade (dispersed, often illegal developments) it is steadily losing its typical character of marsh-land cultivation and colonisation. Despite these increments of dispersed development the area has still preserved some structural and visual qualities, which were seriously considered during planning. The water management study, done for the area, defined areas susceptible to flooding and gave calculations of high water. The findings were used when positioning and calculating necessary retention surfaces, which were dealt with in detail in the proposal for drainage and water retention. Because of the findings from research concerning noise and air pollution because of motorised traffic, but also those concerning flooding, we kept the southern part of the area empty or as a reserve surface for development (combination of manufacturing and housing programmes. The advantage was given to preservation of green surfaces, which could help in easier water management and provide the neighbourhood with an additional green recreation space. Our proposal for developing the particular blocks follows directives concerning sustainability of residential neighbourhoods. Particular quarters are organised as entities where various programmes intertwine, we enforced mixed use, mainly along the more important communication routes and varied building typology. The mix of compatible activities is also important. The predominant land use is housing, which also includes complementary activities (schools, kindergartens, shops for elementary supply, personal services, health-care institutions, parks, sports and children's playgrounds). Jobs will be found in areas intertwined with housing, thus the area will not be zoned into separate units. However areas for businesses, supply, various services, catering etc. lie adjacent to the public and easily accessible surfaces. Smaller production or manufacturing facilities are positioned in a manner that doesn't hinder the housing functions. Moving towards sustainable development on the business level is very important for the government. Company strategy and public policy are alike concerned to match supposed international challenges. This also increasingly affects individuals, who are also required to become competitive in the way they conduct their lives, these demands going under the headings of being flexible, innovative, imaginative entrepreneurial, etc. Slovenian enterprises are now under the European environmental regulation framework. In this article, the correlations among main determinants of Slovenian system of SD indicators will be analysed. The current economic development does not have a perfect balance with environment. Our global civilisation today is also on an economic path that is environmentally unsustainable, a path that is leading us towards economic decline and collapse. For some time, environmental scientists have been claiming that the global economy is slowly being undermined by the trends of environmental destruction and disruption, including shrinking forests, expanding deserts, falling water tables, eroding soils, collapsing fisheries, rising temperatures, melting ice, rising seas, and increasingly destructive storms. Business sector can increase the sustainable position and competitiveness through eco-efficiency. The development of the eco-efficiency concept and its promotion and implementation across business, including industrial companies, services, and the financial sector is another example of responsible entrepreneurship. This concept emerged as an innovative business strategy combining both environmental and economic efficiency to create more value with less environmental impact. It has helped companies understand the challenges of sustainable development, and let them increase efficiency in their processes and create new and better products, for example reducing material and energy intensity, decreasing the use of non renewable resources and toxic substances, enhancing material recyclability and product durability and increasing the service intensity of their goods and services. The need to take into account a life cycle approach and to address the impact across the entire product chain shows these companies that they are able to influence their suppliers and customers and spread the concept across the supply chain. They are also starting a dialogue and co-operation with all their stakeholders and developing measurement and reporting mechanisms to monitor progress, such as eco-efficiency indicators and benchmarks. The relationship between competitiveness and environmental policy can be seen through Porter's hypothesis. The revisionist argument is that well designed environmental policy can stimulate innovation and thus competitiveness, and is called the 'Porter hypothesis', after Michael Porter and Claas van der Linde's article. By environmental regulation, we can foster the modernisation process. Newer machines are more productive and less polluting than older machines, but are more expensive to buy and to install in the capital stock. Stricter environmental regulation, in the form of an increase in the emission tax, will reduce the number of machines of all ages and therefore the size of the firm.

Competitiveness as a new paradigm

Competitiveness is a concept which connects the macroeconomic and microeconomic view of social-economic development. By comparison of European countries I recognized the main differences on micro level (labour market, entrepreneurship, knowledge creation). European governments have traditionally been ambivalent about competitive sub national initiatives because of their uncertain net contribution to the national economy. Some have become more supportive over time, hoping to shape them to serve national purposes and for political expedience when macro economic policies have been more constrained. Indeed local development has increasingly replaced traditional equity based regional policies in some countries (Anyadike-Danes et al., 2001). These sought to reduce spatial disparities by guiding investment away from congested areas to lagging regions with underused resources. Such carrot and stick policies have been scaled back because of concerns about their cost effectiveness and fears about firms being diverted out of the country through growth restrictions in buoyant areas (Turok, 2003). There is in fact an increasing tendency to explain regional growth and development in terms of soft externalities. In particular, considerable emphasis is given to local knowledge, learning and creativity. The argument is that in a globalized economy, the key resources for regional and urban competitiveness depend on localized processes of knowledge creation, in which people and firms learn about new technology, learn to trust each other and share and exchange information (Malecki, 2004). At its simplest, regional competitiveness might be defined as the success with which regions and cities compete with one another in some way. This might be over shares of (national and especially international) export markets. Or it might be over attracting capital or workers. Such notions would seem to underpin Michael Storper's definition of place competitiveness as the ability of an urban economy to attract and maintain firms with stable or rising market shares in an activity while maintaining or increasing standards of living for those who participate in it. Similarly in recent work on regional competitiveness (Porter, 2001) has emphasized the key role of the export oriented clusters as the basis for a high regional standard of living. Economic geographers have been eager to embrace the regional competitiveness concept because it promised to bring back the relevance of geography into economics. Concepts like industrial districts (Becattini, 1990) innovative milieus (Camagni, 1991), learning regions (Asheim, 1996) and regional innovation systems (Cooke, 2001) have described crucial importance of externalities in maintaining competitiveness that extend or cross the boundaries of individual firms but which operate within the boundaries of a territory. In the European Union can be seen the increasing importance of regional competitiveness. While there are many theories about competitiveness and related interdisciplinary fields of strategy, operations, policies, organizations, they are not used widely by practitioners in their decisions for enhancing or sustaining competitiveness. Research efforts have brought many interesting perspectives and frameworks at the country, industry, and firm level. The popularity of the competitiveness benchmarking at the country level such as Global Competitiveness Reports (WEF),

World Competitiveness Yearbooks (IMD), and National Competitiveness Reports is an indicator of growing interest in comprehensive frameworks and data for competetiveness related decision-making. We can measure the competitive position of countries in the context of the Lisbon's goals, and to shed light on where attention should be focused.

Location and the importance of specialization process

Over the last decade, Slovenia has achieved clear and positive macro-economic results that have placed the country among the most successful transitional countries. The basic indicators reveal it has been integrating and catching up with the European Union member countries at an ever increasing pace. Despite this, the challenges of a global economy, where only innovation and entrepreneurship can compete successfully, and the relative lag in the competitive capacity of our economy behind numerous other countries in the world rankings, require drastic changes to be made to Slovenia's economical structure to adopt as much as possible to the demands of the knowledge-based economy. That means the transformation from an economy with low-added value whose competitiveness is based on low-operative costs into an economy based on production and service activities whose competitive advantages are high-added value, quality, innovation, and entrepreneurship. The Ireland has a more than 40% high-tech in manufactured export. The world competition has become especially fierce in high-tech sectors like microelectronics, biotechnology, new materials, telecommunications, robotics, computers and aerospace.

Hungary ranks highest in terms of high-tech. The reason for such a high ranking is the presence of a large amount of foreign capital and multinational companies. Slovenia's weakness from the view of competitiveness is high-tech position. No advanced economy can maintain high wages and living standards, and hold its own in global markets, by producing standard products using standard methods. In addition to human resources, a strong national innovation infrastructure includes the ability of funding for innovation-related investments. There are some reasons why small countries as Slovenia do not display the same thrust towards high-tech industries as do larger countries. High-tech industries are closely associated with high risk. Losers as well as winners are to be expected, as the selection of superior products is essentially based on trial and error (Carter 1994). The differences are presumably not due to disparities in the supply of entrepreneurial talent, but are certainly affected by the obstacles experienced in small countries in obtaining a sufficient market for a specialised and proficient venture capital sector (DeBresson and Lampel 1985).The lack of venture capital will constrain the economic ability of entrepreneurial efforts in small countries. The firms which are operating with close proximity to a set of related firms

and supporting institutions are often more competitive than firms which operate in an isolated manner. This is due to both competition and co-operation. Competition at a local level is usually much less abstract, and often involves personified rivalries, thus creating a stronger pressure than the anonymous mechanism of the invisible hand. Co-operation does not necessarily mean formal alliances, even though even competitors have shown an increasing tendency to enter into arrangements such as strategic technology alliances. Co-operation at the local level often involves activities like informal communication between firms along the value chain, or information about innovation being exchanged over or through employees, which move from one firm to another. Over time this tends to lead to the evolution of strong business associations. In Slovenia we expect the stronger specialisation of industry after EU enlargement. Herindahl index of specialisation of manufacturing is calculated:

$$HI = \sum_{i=1}^{n} S_i^2$$

Where:
S = share of the industry in manufacturing
n = number of industries

Globalization process and European integration process have changed the competitive environment for manufacturing activities. Foreign direct investment flows in new EU countries have fostered the specialization process. If foreign investors have invested in car industry, in electro, and chemical industry then we can see the higher specialisation of industrial sector (Table 1).

According on herfindahl index ranks Hungary well in all period 1993 - 2005. Reason is the high concentration of FDIs in some industrial sectors. Slovakian industry has increased the tare of specialization in period 1993 - 2005, while the rate of specialization stated on the same level by Chech R. Slovenian industry have reached higher specialization after joining EU. In Slovenian case is hard to differ between local, regional and national economy, because country has only two million people. In the literature the clusters are usually connected with regional economy. Clusters and networks provide the context and the spillovers. Free riders do not exist, nor do free lunches, in the sense of complete knowledge transfers. Certain items of knowledge may flow relatively freely, but other types need to be more localised in their transfer, and these spillovers can raise the innovation of localised partner firms (Cantwell, 1999). Business enterprises operate within a regional production system which is constituted by principles of production and organization. Regions that enjoy a high per capita income are generally regions with a critical mass of business enterprises with the capacity to add value to the resources they use. The idea of regional specialization implies that firms do not compete alone in the global marketplace but as members of networked groups of firms sharing and building on distinct

Table 1. Industrial specialization of new EU countries.

Herfindahl index	1993	1998	2002	2005
Hungary	0,131679	0,124759	0,157162	0,209965
Czech R.	0,109993	0,110084	0,101873	0,107449
Slovakia	0,108632	0,103052	0,110916	0,113589
Slovenia	0,091609	0,093109	0,095783	0,103212

Source: Eurostat, own calculation.

regional capabilities. A region's capacity to initiate and sustain high value added production depends upon its capability to foster and reproduce entrepreneurial firms (Best, 2001). Specialization process is very important for new EU member states. European internal market will foster specialization process in all EU members in the next years. The competitive position of each EU country depends on specialization of domestic industry. In an open economy, the competitiveness of firms will be enhanced by the feedback loops with the localised capabilities. Firms of a certain kind find some localised capabilities more valuable than others. The originally chosen location of an industry might have been basically accidental. But once in place, the specialised locational demands from the firm will influence the future development of the localised capabilities, making it advantageous for the industry to remain in the area, and for outlying firms to relocate (Enright, 1994). Some firms deliberately incorporate specific parts of the localised capabilities in constructing a consolidated strategy, by acquiring resources primarily from the local factor market and by subsequently building unique competencies on these resources (Collins, 1991). This makes good sense. From while the firm specific strategies might be imitated by a clever competitor located elsewhere, it is a lot more difficult for even the best competitors to confront the abstruseness of the combined strategy, and to disentangle the ambiguity created when integrating various elements of the localised capabilities (Reed and DeFillippi, 1990).

Regional competitiveness

Because the Slovenia is a small country with two million habitants, it is regional competitiveness also useful for explaining the economic position. The regional factors influence the competitiveness of firm or industry. In a competitive economy, valuable localised capabilities will primarily be those which increase the ability of firms to create; acquire; accumulate; and utilise knowledge a little faster than their competitors. No firm can create the strategies that entirely disregard the quality and character of the capabilities in the region. In Slovenian case is hard to differ between local, regional and national economy, because country has only two millions people. The modern industry is strong connected with local supplies, with regional universities, with technological institutes and service providers, and also by competitors. Enterprises ope-

rate within a regional production system which is constituted by principles of production and organization. Regions that enjoy a high per capita income are generally regions with a critical mass of enterprises with the capacity to add value to the resources they use. As there exists no superior or optimal model one has to think over the consequences for policy making. This is especially relevant because regions pursue to an increasing extent a collective policy strategy to enhance the competitiveness of local firms (Begg, 2002). As noticed above, in advanced countries, sources of territorial competitiveness are constantly undermined, and regions have to cope with this. We have to make a difference among strong and weak competition (Storper, 1997). This partly represents a distinction among competition on hard factors (through the means of relative wages or tax levels) and competition on soft factors (identity, culture, institutions). Weak competition means static price competition. Regions can pursue a strategy that concentrates on relative low labour costs, or they may exploit institutional differences between regions (such as differences in subsidies or labour regulation systems) that affect price competition among firm directly. However, a strategy of strong competition based primarily on exploiting the soft intangible, region specific assets described above is likely to be more effective in the long run (Foss, 1996). The creation of European regions in Slovenia will foster the competitiveness of enterprises. European regions support the specialization process and the internationalization of domestic industry. The idea of regional specialization implies that firms do not compete alone in the global marketplace but as members of networked groups of firms sharing and building on valuable regional capabilities. Today is competitiveness evaluated by different methodologies. Government want to have right answers about policy directions. Different competitveness studies have shown that regions play an important role in European union. Regional specialization process increases the national competitiveness. If the regions in the country are competitive then is also the country competitive. While Slovenia lags in creation of European regions it has also the negative impact on competitiveness of economy. In European Union can be national competitiveness seen as a sum of the success of different regions. While the regional factors are now more important we can search for the reasons in the view of differences in GDP, productivity and in employment. Differences are the consequences of struc-

STATE

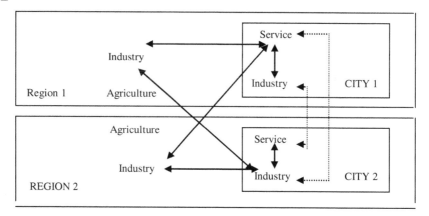

Picture 1. Connections among urban, regional and national competitiveness.
Source: own model.

tural differences in key determinants as physical, human capital, infrastructure, research capacities, quality of business environment. The European integration process gives the more power to some regions. Regions as a geographic units can economically, culturally and tradelly easier interact in enlarged EU. The lower role of national states has created well conditions to European regions for balancing with geographic, cultural, social and economical characteristics of geographic area and with more globalized European Union.

There is a serious risk that the ideal circumstances for regional policy-making are accompanied with a situation of institutional lock-in, with adverse impacts on regional competitiveness in the long run. Or, as Cheshire and Gordon (1996) have put it: a relatively specialized urban economy, with a high degree of integration among long established businesses may be the most promising economic base for the organisation of competitive activity, but the activity will tend to reflect the perceptions and interests of those particular businesses rather than a strategic view of current competitive prospects. One could also argue that since the local environment exercises only a minor influence on the location of new industries subject to increasing returns, there is room for human agency to act effectively and to contribute to the build up of a favourable environment. According on Camagni (2002), in such a world of increasing returns, regional competitiveness should reside in dynamic factors that are all artificial or created advantages, open to the proactive, voluntary action of local communities and their governments. Geographic area where enterprises do a business does not maintain just natural sources, but also play an important role in knowledge accumulation, in models of cooperation and decisions that support the innovative progress of local enterprise. Process and collective learning are connected with characteristics and capacities on specific geographic area. Local labour market, internal culture in enterprises and past experiences has an influence on

progress (Camagni, 2002). The success of enterprises on specific geographic area does not depend just on public sector and social capital, but also on specific external capital and specific sources, that are difficult to find on market. Enterprises are in interaction with other enterprises and with public administration for getting an important external object as building infrastructure (Picture 1).

The strong correlation among urban and regional competitiveness can be see in European union. Regions with rich cities usually rank high in regional competitiveness. In urban centres we have strong service sector that make a business with the industry. Industrial production outside the city in common, while in the city we have financial and trade activities. If region doesn't have a strong city, is the existing industry mare a connection with services outside the region that can be seen in the model. It is normal that service activities exist also outside the cities, but it doesn't have so strong weight as in urban centres. The agriculture activities have a connection with the food industry, but that can't be seen from the model. Globalization progress gives cities the main role in world economy. This is the reason why is the city competitiveness the important challenge not only for local but also for regional competitiveness. The quality of life is the important determinant of city competitiveness, while cities are also a living area. The progress of information connections has increased the role of the cities in national and global networks. Existed studies of urban centres have ignored the unseen aspect of information technological networks, while the studies has focused on physical and unseen aspect of urban development 'market of houses, social research, differences in employment, transport. In new member countries can be seen that competitiveness have increased the urban regions and also the border regions. Border regions that are close to old EU countries have scored the fast integration into EU, while the investments in infrastructure are lower, important markets are closer, foreign direct investments are higher and turistical inflow is the important source of income. Such regions are usually in better competitiveness position. The competitiveness has decreased in the regions that have the decreased industry and regions with high agriculture share. The development of specific competitiveness determinants as infrastructure, human capital, health, regional institutional framework have to follow the needs of regional population and less the needs of national states. The higher possibilities of regional specialization allow the higher competitiveness and easier integration in European area. The interest of European regionalisation is not just in lowering the differences, but also in the fact that institutional frameworks have follow the needs of specific geographic area. Specialization of regions and geographic concentration of selected industries can be measured by comparition of production structures (Aiginger et al, 1999). Process of learning call for non-material and nonformal exchange inside the enterprises. The collective process of learning include the local labour market, chain of professional upgrading, mobility of educated labour force, and density of interaction with local suppliers and buyers (Capello, 1999). Geographical areas compete with each others by creation of competitive advantages. This is good for all economy. Regional studies have shown that competitiveness have increased the regions with capital city and regions with the border on old European member countries.

Globalization process gave cities the key role in world economy. European integration process forced the cities to change according o new challenges and opportunities that came from the European integration. In non integrated Europe was the competition among two cities from the side of the state unlogical. After in new circumstances I can see the strong competition among regions and cities, in the field of opening new jobs, FDIs and tourism. Regions with capital cities usually have a strong concentration of high educated experts, high level of investments, good infrastructure.

Cities are competitive if they can o flexible and efficient way decrease the negative impact of economic growth, that can be seen in high prices of land and business spaces, in density of city traffic, in environmental damage and in increasing the social differences. Important is the competition with services, that must achieve the higher quality compared to other cities. Urban regions in new EU member countries have increased competitiveness in the last years. Ljubljana as a capital with Central Slovenian region is such a case. The movement of employment from industrial to service sector give to Ljubljana a specific place. Cities compete differently with each other, compared to states. Some policy responses have been overtly competitive in a defensive sense, including attempts to protect vulnerable industries or to discourage business relocation by offering subsidies in some form (Cheshire, Gordon 1996). Others have been proactive, including place marketing and incentives to attract mobile private investment. City boosterism reflects more aggressive

competition to promote flagship events, build iconic projects and attract tourism, skilled mobile population and public investment, using both price and the quality of environment. It follows a tradition of policies that were less explicitly competitive, including increasing the business formation rate and strengthening the managerial and technical capabilities of local firms to help them enhance their market position and grow. Resent initiatives seek to exploit novel "urban assets" such as specialized labour pools, university research, institutional networks and even the lifestyle, cultural amenities and tolerant social milieu of cities (Landry, 2000) (Graph 1).

Regional competitiveness can increase in the way that regions specialize in important activities. Herindahl's index allows us to calculate the specialization in Slovenian regions. Specialization of Slovenian regions can be measured by structure of employment. From the graph can be seen that employed in knowledge-based activities and employed with university degree have a low herindahl index. I can say that these activities are not concentrated in some regions. On the other side can be seen, that employed in innovative enterprises are more concentrated. Innovative enterprises are concentrated around Ljubljana. The strong correlation among urban and regional competitiveness can be see in European Union. Regions with rich cities usually rank high in regional competitiveness. In urban centres we have strong service sector that make a business with the industry. Industrial production outside the city in common, while in the city we have financial and trade activities. If region doesn't have a strong city, is the existing industry mare a connection with services outside the region that can be seen in the model. It is normal that service activities exist also outside the cities, but it doesn't have so strong weight as in urban centres. The agriculture activities have a connection with the food industry, but that can't be seen from the model. Globalization progress gives cities the main role in world economy. This is the reason why is the city competitiveness the important challenge not only for local but also for regional competitiveness. The quality of life is the important determinant of city competitiveness, while cities are also a living area. The progress of information connections has increased the role of the cities in national and global networks. Existed studies of urban centres have ignored the unseen aspect of information technological networks, while the studies have focused on physical and unseen aspect of urban development 'market of houses, social research, differences in employment, transport

Conclusion

In new member countries can be seen that competitiveness has increased the urban regions and also the border regions. Border regions that are close to old EU countries have scored the fast integration into EU, while the investments in infrastructure are lower, important markets are closer, foreign direct investments are higher

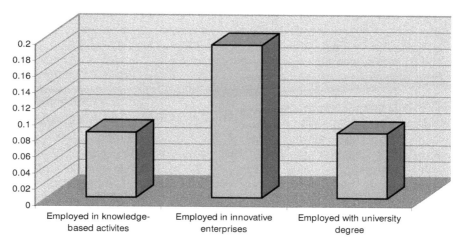

Graph 1. Specialization of Slovenian regions (Herindahl index).
Source: own calculation.

and turistical inflow is the important source of income. This region is usually in better competitiveness position. The competitiveness has decreased in the regions that have the decreased industry and regions with high agriculture share. The development of specific competitiveness determinants as infrastructure, human capital, health, regional institutional framework have to follow the needs of regional population and less the needs of national states. The higher possibilities of regional specialization allow the higher competitiveness and easier integration in European area. The interest of European regionalisation is not just in lowering the differences, but also in the fact that institutional frameworks have follow the needs of specific geographic area. Specialization of regions and geographic concentration of selected industries can be measured by comparition of production structures (Aiginger et al, 1999). Analysed region is specialised in the case, that just some industries have an important share of production on regional level. Analysed industry (car industry: is geographical concentrated, while the important share of production is seen in just some regions. Theoretical and empirical studies have shown that nominal and relative wages became lower by increasing the distance to industrial and capital centres (Krugman and Livas, 1996). Industrial centres have concentrated the capital and knowledge in the era of industrialization. After merchant liberalization is the access to key markets one of the reasons, while industrial and services activities often migrate to border regions. After enlargement of EU can be seen growing importance of regional competitiveness. Regional competitiveness can increase in the way that regions specialize in important activities. Herindahl's index allows us to calculate the specialization in Slovenian regions. Specialization of Slovenian regions can be measured by structure of employment. From the graph can be seen that employed in knowledge-based activities and employed with university degree have a low herindahl index. I can say that these activities are not concen-

trated in some regions. On the other side can be seen, that employed in innovative enterprises are more concentrated. Innovative enterprises are concentrated around Ljubljana. Like in the case of Slovenia, the competitive advantage of the some new member countries lies mainly in the labour-intensive and resource-intensive industries. The conclusion to be drawn here is that an open economy and foreign investment do not lead to an automatic change of the structure of the industry towards greater knowledge and skill intensity: rather than that, it is the other way round. After joining the EU it is more important to build a competitive business environment. If we want to attract foreign companies, we must do more for business environment in the near future. Enterprise reforms are also part of these processes. The Lisbon's strategy has changed the competitiveness evaluation in Slovenia. The microeconomic progress is now more important like ten years ago.

REFERENCES

Anyadike-Danes M, Fothergill S, Glyn A, Smith JG, Kitson M, Martin R, Rowthorn R, Turok I, Tyler P, Webster D (2001). Labor's new Regional Policy: An Assessment, Regional Studies Association: Seaford.

Asheim BT (1996). Industrial districts as learning regions: a condition for prosperity, Euro. Planning Stud. 4: 379-400.

Becattini G (1990). The Marshallian industrial district as a social-economic notion, in Pyke, F. Industrial Districts and inter firm Co-operation in Italy, International Institute for labour Studies: Geneva pp. 37-51.

Begg I (2002). Urban Competitiveness: Policies for Dynamic Cities, Policy press: Bristol.

Best M (1990). The New Competition: Institutions of Industrial Restructuring, Cambridge. Policy Press

Camagni R (1991). Innovation Networks, Spatial Perspectives, Bellhaven: London.

Camagni R (2002). On the concept of territorial competitiveness, Sound of misleading? Urban studies 39: 2395-2411.

Capello R (1999). Spatial transfer of knowledge in high technology milieux: learning versus collective learning processes, Reg. Stud. 33: 353-365.

Carter AP (1994). Measuring the Performance of a Knowledge-based Economy, working paper no. 337, OECD Paris.

Castells M (1996). The Rise of the Network Society, Oxford, Blackwells.

Chesire P, Gordon I (1996). Territorial competition and the predictability of collective action. Int. J. Urban Reg. Res. 20: 383-399.

Cooke P (2001). Regional innovation system, clusters, and the knowledge economy, Industrial and Cooperate Change 10: 945-974.

Daniels PW (1996): The Global Economy in Transition, Longman, London

DeBresson C, Lampel J (1985). Bombardier's mass production of the snow mobile: the Canadian exception?, Scientia Canadensis 29: 133-149.

Dore R (1973). British Factory-Japanese Factory, London: Allen and Unwin

Drnovsek M, Kovačič A (2003). Why Slovenia Lags in National Competitiveness Development, Econ. Bus. Rev. 5(3): 183-201.

Dunning JH (1993). The Globalization of Business: The Challenge of the 1990s, Routledge New York.

EC (2002) European Competitiveness Report, Brussels.

Enright MJ (1994). Regional Clusters and Firm Strategy in The Dynamic Firm 12-14 June, Stockholm.

Esping-Andersen G (1999). Social Foundations of Post-industrial Economies, Oxford University Press.

European Commission (2004). The 2004 Update of the Broad economic policy guidelines for the period 2003-2005, EC Luxemburg.

Fagerberg J (1988). International Competitiveness. Econ. J. 98: 355-374.

Foss NJ (1996). Higher order industrial capabilities and competitive advantage. J. Industrial Stud. 3: 1-20.

Grant RM (1991). Contemporary Strategy Analysis: Concepts, Techniques and Applications, Blackwell Ltd.

Grupp H (1995). Science high technology and the competitiveness of the EU countries, Cambridge J. Econ. 19: 209-223.

Hall G, Johnson R (1970). Transfer of united aerospace technology to Japan, in R. Vernon: The Technology Factor in International Trade, New York, Columbia University Press

Hallin G, Malmberg A (1996) Attraction, competition and regional development in Europe, Euro. Urban Reg. Stud. 3(4):323-337.

IMAD (2001). Strategy for the Economic Development of Slovenia 2001-2006,

IMD (2002). The World Competitiveness Yearbook, IMD Lausanne,

IMD (2003). The World Competitiveness Yearbook, IMD Lausanne,

Young G (1981). The New Export Marketer, London, Kogan Page,

Kavaš D, Pečar J (2004). Reforma "reforme" nacionalne regionalne strukturne politike, Ljubljana: IER,

Kotler P, Jatusripitak S, Maesincee S (1997). The Marketing of Nations, Free Press New York,

Kovacic A (2002). The Global Competitiveness of Slovenia and the Importance of Financial Market, Bank. Rev. (1-2):30-35,

Kovacic A (2002). New Economy Changes the Factors of the Competitiveness, Banking Rev. 4: 13-17.

Kovacic A (2004). Global Competitiveness of Slovenian economy in the time of EU Enlargement, doctoral dissertation, EF Ljubljana.

Kovacic A (2005). Competitiveness as a source of development. Working paper no.28, IER Ljubljana.

Krugman P (1994). Competitiveness: A Dangerous obsession, Foreign Affairs 73(2):28-44

Landry C (2000). The creative City, Earthscan: London.

Malecki EJ (2004). Jockeying for Position, Reg. Stud. 38: 1093-1112.

Maskell P, Eskelinen H, Hannibalsson I, Malmberg A, Vatne E (1998). Competitiveness, Localised Learning and Regional Development, Routledge London.

National Competitiveness Council: Annual Competitiveness Report 2003

Nelson RR, Winter SG (1985). Evolutionary Theory of Economic Change, Belknap Press.

OECD (1997). Industrial Competitiveness in the Knowledge-based Economy, The New Role of Governments, Paris OECD.

Petrin T (2003). Ministry of the Economy's Entrepreneurship and Competitiveness Policy, Ljubljana.

Porter ME (1980). Competitive Strategy; Free Press.

Porter ME (1998). The Competitive Advantage of the Nations, Macmillan Press.

Porter ME (2000). Human Development and Global Competitiveness, World Bank.

Ray JE (1995). Managing official Export Credits: Washington DC, Institute for International Economics.

Reed R, DeFillippi RJ (1990). Causal ambiguity, barriers to imitation and sustainable competitive advantage, Acad. Manag. Rev. 15:88-102.

Reich R (1990). Who is US? Harvard Business Review, 68: 53-64

Rodrigues MJ (2002). The New Knowledge Economy in Europe, Edward Elgar.

Rosenthal D (1993). Some Conceptual Considerations on the Nature of Technological Capability Build-Up, Berkeley California.

Solow RM (1956). A contribution to the theory of economic growth, Quarterly J. Econ. 70(Str):65-94.

Sternberg, R (1999). Innovative Linkages and Proximity, Reg. Stud. 33(6):529-540.

Storper M (1997). The Regional World: Territorial Development in Global Economy, Guildford: New York.

Turok I (2003). Cities, clusters and creative industries: The case of film and television in Scotland, Euro. Planning Stud. 11: 549-565

Zanakis SH, Becerra-Fernandez I (2005). Competitiveness of nations, A knowledge discovery examination. Eur. J. Oper. Res. pp 185-211

WEF (2003). Global Competitiveness Report, WEF Geneva

WEF (2004). The Lisbon Review, WEF Geneva.

## 23

In silico identification of miRNAs and their target prediction from *Japanese encephalitis*

Vijay Laxmi Saxena* and Alka Dwivedi

National Bioinformatics Infrastructure Facility Centre of (DBT) Ministry of Science and Technology (Govt. of India), D.G (PG) College civil lines Kanpur (u.p).

MicroRNA is a family of small non-coding RNAs that regulate gene expression in a sequence-specific manner. miRNAs are a class of post-transcriptional regulators. miRNAs are a family of 19 to 25 small nucleotide RNAs. Since miRNAs have been discovered and their role in gene regulation established, it has been theorized that viruses could generate miRNAs as well and that these viral encoded miRNAs could regulate cellular mechanisms and viral replication. There are several lines of evidence to support this theory. *Japanese encephalitis* is a viral disease (Flavivirus) but its geographic strains differ by RNA sequencing neurotropic virus that primarily affects the central nervous system. That is why this work mainly focuses on finding out its function. An oligonucleotide drug candidate can be designed against this virus. Computational prediction is analyzed and estimation of evolutionary relationship among types of organism is done in this project. 25 precursors and eight potential miRNAs were found, and these miRNAs target 123 target sites in 13 genes in human.

Key words: miRNA, pre-miRNA, pri-miRNA, *Japanese encephalitis,* precursor potential miRNA, +target prediction.

INTRODUCTION

Mature microRNAs (miRNAs) are a class of naturally occurring small non-coding RNA molecules; about 21 to 25 nucleotides in length. MicroRNAs are partially complementary to one or more messenger RNA (mRNA) molecules, and their main function is to down- regulate gene expression in a variety of manners, including translational repression, mRNA cleavage and deadenylation. They were first described by Lee Y et al., 2003, 2004) and the term microRNA was coined in 2001. The genes encoding miRNAs are much longer than the processed mature miRNA molecule (Carthew et al., 2009). Based on the biogenesis of miRNA, many miRNAs are known to reside in introns of their pre-mRNA host genes and share their regulatory elements, primary transcript and have a similar expression profile (Chen, 2005).

MicroRNAs are transcribed by RNA polymerase II as large RNA precursors called pri-miRNAs and comprise a 5' cap and poly-A tail (Erlanger et al., 2009). The pri-miRNAs are processed in the nucleus by the microprocessor complex, consisting of the RNase III enzyme Drosha and the double-stranded-RNA-binding protein, Pasha/DGCR8. The resulting pre-miRNAs are approximately 70-nucleotides in length and are folded into imperfect stem-loop structures (Hammond, 2000). The pre-miRNAs are then exported into the cytoplasm by the karyopherin exportin 5 (Exp5) and Ran-GTP complex Ran (ras-related nuclear protein), a small GTP binding protein belonging to the RNA superfamily that is essential for the translocation of RNA and proteins through the nuclear pore complex (Krek et al., 2005). The Ran GTPase binds Exp5 and forms a nuclear heterotrimer with pre-miRNAs; once in the cytoplasm, the pre-miRNAs undergo an additional processing step by the RNAse III enzyme dicer generating the miRNA, a double-stranded RNA approximately 22 nucleotides in length. Also, Japanese *encephalitis* virus (JEV), a neurotropic mosquito-borne flavivirus mainly prevalent in Asia,

---
*Corresponding author. E-mail: vijaykanpur@rediffmail.com or alkabioinfo964@gmail.com.

.

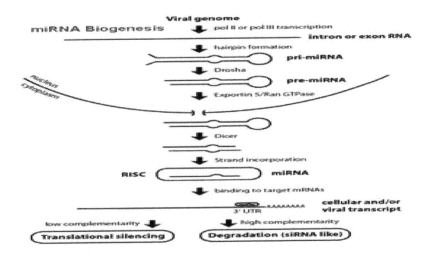

Figure 1. Biogenesis of miRNA.

is the most important causative agent of acute viral encephalitis in humans. JEV is also one of the main causes of infectious reproductive failure in swine,(Murkami et al.,2005), resulting in significant economic losses in the pig industry; this virus has a normal zootomic transmission cycle between swine or birds and mosquitoes. Swine are the main amplifier hosts, from which infected mosquitoes transmit the virus to human (Figure 1).

METHODOLOGY

The genome sequences of J. encephalitis were retrieved from NCBI (www.ncbi.nlm.nihgov).Precursor predicting tools, Mireval (http://tagc.univ mrs.fr/mireval) and MiRPARA (http://www.whiov.ac.cn/bioinformatics/mirpara) were used to find out the precursor sequences; and then the secondary structure with optimal minimum free energy was found out with the help of different types of web servers such as Mfold web server (http://mfold.rit.albany.edu/doc/mfold-manual/), RNA fold web server (http://rna.tbi.univie.ac.at) and DINA melt web server (http://www.microrna.gr/microT). For validating the energy values, miRBASE (mirbase@manchester.ac.uk) was checked, where we browsed all the mature virus sequences and stem loop structure sequences in FASTA format. These sequences were already experimentally identified. Then we find out the optimal minimum energy value of viruses in the miRBASE (only precursors), based on multiple sequence alignment, and then find out the conserved regions for miRNA. This miRNA predicted the target sites, and the target prediction was completed with the help of DIANA tar web server (http://www.microrna.gr); it predicted the different types of target sites.

RESULTS AND DISCUSSION

Precursor analysis

miRNA was the first to be discovered, a class of non-coding RNAs involved in gene regulation, transcribed as

~70 nucleotide precursors and subsequently processed by the dicer enzyme to give a 21 nucleotide product (Moore,1993). The extents of the hairpin precursors are not generally known and are estimated based on hairpin prediction (Ruykum, 1993; Siolas et al., 2005; Sui et al., 2002). This study is exclusively based on *in silico* firstly to find out the precursors from Japanese encephalitis having 1 to 25 precursors in a single whole genome (NC_001437.1); and then this sequence is submitted in miRevaluator and mirPARA software for precursor prediction (Table 1).

Potential miRNA analysis

Prediction of potential miRNA was based on (MSA) multiple sequence alignment (pair wise) and its alignment was completed with the help of EBI clastal-W and mirpara miRNA predicting software. The sequence was submitted in EBI which is retrieved from miRBases; and pair wise alignment was done with precursors of viruses and precursors of Japanese encephalitis (Kozomara et al., 2011). Mainly, MSA focused on conserved regions for miRNA (Table 2).

Target prediction analysis

Based on observation, potential miRNA predicted the different types of target sites in a human gene. Then it predicted the different type of genes and those involved in different type of target sites with conserved information (Tables 3, 4 and 5).

All the tables explain the different types of analyses related to *in silico* prediction only, and the whole information of targeted genes in humans and targeted miRNA of Japanese encephalitis. Table 5 gives important

Table 1. Predicted precursor miRNA from miREvaluator, mirPARA.

S.NO	Annotated precursor name	Precursors (sequences)	Length (nt)	Optimal secondary structure (MFE) value
1	>MIR _JE_P1	ATGCTGAAACGCGGCCTACCCCGCGTATTCCCACTAGTGG AGTGAAGAGGGTAGTAATGAGCTTGTTGGACGGCAGAGGG CAGTACGTTTCGTGCTGGCTCTTATCACGTTCTTCAAGTTTA CAGCATTAGCCCCGAC	140	-65.46
2	>MIR_JE_P2	GGAGGAAATGAAGGCTCAATCATGTGGCTCGCAAGCTTGG CAGTTGTCATAGCTTACGCAGGAGCAATGAAGTTGTCAA	80	-22.75
3	>MIR_JE_P3	TAGCTGCTTGACAATCATGGCAAACGACAAACCAACATTGG ACGTCCGCATGATTAACATCGAAGCTAGCCAACTTGCTG	80	-18.25
4	>MIR_JE_P4	GCTCTCCCCTGGACGTCCCCTTCGAGCACAGCGTGGAGAA ACAGAGAACTCCTCATGGAATTTGAAGAGGCGCACGCCAC	80	-20.28
5	>MIR_JE_P5	GCATGCTGACACTGGATGTGCCATTGACATCACAAGAAAAG AGATGATGTGGAAGTGGCATCTTTGTGCACAACGACG	78	-21.14
6	>MIR_JE_P6	ACACACCCTTTGGGGAGATGGTGTTGAGGAAAGTGAACTCA TCATTCCGCATACCATAGCCGGACCAAAAAGCAAGCACA	80	-21.93
7	>MIR_JE_P7	CTGCTGGTACGGAATGGAAATCAGACCTGTCAGGCATGAAA CAACACTCGTTAGATCACAGGTTGATGCTTTCAATGGTGAA ATGGTTGACCCTTTTCAGCTGGGCCTTCTGGTGATGTTTCT GGCCACCCAGGAGGTCCTTCGCAAGAGGTGGACG	160	-53.83
8	>MIR_JE_P8	TTGATGTTTGCCATCGTAGGTGGCTTGGCCGAGTTGGATAT TGAATCCATGTCAATACCCTTCATGCTGGCAGGTCTCAT	80	-25.91
9	>MIR_JE_P9	CGAGGAACATCCGGCTCACCCATTCTGGATTCTAATGGAGA CATCATAGGCCTATACGGCAATGGAGTTGAGCTTGGCGA	80	-25.13
10	>MIR_JE_P10	CTGGCGGTGTTTCTCATCTGCGTCTTGACCGTGGTTGGAGT GGTGGCAGCAAACGAGTACGGGATGCTAGAGAAAACCAA	80	-26.73
11	>MIR_JE_P11	GCAGCGTTCCTCGTCAACCCTAATGTCACCACTGTGAGAGA AGCAGGGGTATTGGTGACGGCGGCTACGCTCACTTTGT	79	-26.50
12	>MIR_JE_P12	TGAAAACAACATAGTGGGAGGACATCCGGTTTCGCGAGGC TCAGCAAAACTCCGTTGGCTCGTGGAGAAAGGATTTGTCTC GCCAATAGG	90	-31.52
13	>MIR_JE_p13	TCGGAGGTGGGCTAGTGCGTCTCCCCCTGTCCCGGAACTC CAATCACGAGATGTATTGGGTTAGTGGAGCCGCTGGCAATT GGTGCACG	90	-29.76
14	>MIR_JE_p14	GCTGGATGGAATGTGAAGGACACAGCTTGTCTGGCCAAAG CATATGCACAGATGTGGCTACTCCTATACTTCCATCGTAG	80	-28.10
15	>MIR_JE_p15	CTTCTGCTCTATCTCAACATCAGCTACTAGGCACAGAGCGC CGAAGTATGTAGCTGGTGGTGAGGAAGAACACAGGATCT	80	-31.85
16	>MIR_JE_p16	TAGTAATGAGCTTGTTGGACGGCAGAGGGCCAGTACGTTTC GTGCTGGCTCTTATCACGTTCTTCAAGTTTACAGC	76	-35.60
17	>MIR_JE_p17	AGGAGGAAATGAAGGCTCAATCATGTGGCTCGCAAGCTTG GCAGTTGTCATAGCTTACGCAGGAGCAATGAAGTTGTCGA	81	-21.75
18	>MIR_JE_p18	TCACAGGAAGGAGGCCTCCATCAGGCGTTGGCAGGAGCCA CAAGCTCAGTGAAGTTAACA	60	-21.80
19	>MIR_JE_p19	TGGTTGACCCTTTTCAGCTGGGCCTTCTGGTGATGTTTCTG GCCACCCAGGAGGTCCTTCGCAAGAGGTGGACGGCCA	78	-32.90
20	>MIR_JE_p20	ACTATAGCTGCCGGACTAATGGTCTGCAACCCAAACAAGAA GAGAGGGTGGCCAGCCACTGAGTTTTTGTCGGCAGTT	78	-26.72
21	>MIR_JE_p21	GCGGTGTTTCTCATCTGCGTCTTGACCGTGGTTGGAGTGG GCAGCAAACGAGTACGGGATGCTAGAGAAAACCAAAGCA	80	-36.70
22	>MIR_JE_p22	AATGGTCGCCACTGATGTGCCTGAACTGGAAAGGACCACC CTCTGATGCAAAAGAAAGTCGGACAGGTGCTCCTCATAGG GGTAAGCGTAGCAGCGTTCC	100	- 24.10

Table 1. Contd.

23	>MIR_JE_p23	AGGACATCCGGTTTCGCGAGGCTCAGCAAAACTCCGTTGG CTCGTGGAGAAAGGATTTGTCT	62	-25.90
24.	>MIR_JE_p24	GGAGTGGTGAAGCTCATGAGCAAACCTTGGGACGCCATTG CCAACGTCACCACCATGGCCATGACTGACACCAC	78	-29.30
25.	>MIR_JE_25	CTGCTCTATCTCAACATCAGCTACTAGGCACAGAGCGCCGA GTATGTAGCTGGTGGTGAGGAAGAACACAGGATCAC	78	-28.30

Table 2. Precursor and sequence of pre-miRNA and sequence of potential miRNA.

S.NO	Annotated precursors name	Precursor (seq) pre-miRNA (precursor-microRNA)	Potential (miRNA) seq (microRNA)
1	>MIR _JE_P1	AUGCUGAAACGCGGCCUACCCCGCGUAUUCCCACUA GUGGGAGUGAAGAGGGUAGUAAUGAGCUUGUUGGA CGGCAGAGGGCCAGUACGUUUCGUGCUGGCUCUUA UCACGUUCUUCAAGUUUACAGCAUUAGCCCCGAC	AUGCUGAAACGCGGCCUAC CCC
2	>MIR_JE_P2	GGAGGAAAUGAAGGCUCAAUCAUGUGGCUCGCAAGC UUGGCAGUUGUCAUAGCUUACGCAGGAGCAAUGAAG UUGUCGAA	GGAGGAAAUGAAGGCUCAA UCAUG
3	>MIR_JE_P6	ACACACCCUUUGGGGAGAUGGUGUUGAGGAAAGUGA ACUCAUCAUUCCGCAUACCAUAGCCGGACCAAAAAGC AAGCACA	ACACACCCUUUGGGGAGAU GGUGUU
4	>MIR_JE_P8	UUGAUGUUUGCCAUCGUAGGUGGCUUGGCCGAGUU GGAUUUGAAUCCAUGUCAAUACCCUUCAUGCUGGCA GGUCUCAU	UUGAUGUUUGCCAUCGUA GGUGGC
5	>MIR_JE_p16	UAGUAAUGAGCUUGUUGGACGGCAGAGGGCAGUACG UUCGUGCUGGCUCUUAUCACGUUCUUCAAGUUUACA GC	CUUGUUGGACGGCAGAGG GCCA
6	>MIR_JE_p18	UCACAGGAAGGAGGCCUCCAUCAGGCGUUGGAGGAG CCAUCGUGGUGGAGUACUCAAGCUCAGUGAAGUUAA CA	GUGGUGGAGUACUCAAGC UCAGU
7	>MIR_JE_p19	UGGUUGACCCUUUUCAGCUGGGCCUUCUGGUGAUG UUUCUGGCCACCCAGGAGGUCCUUCGCAAGAGGUG GACGGCCA	UUUCAGCUGGGCCUUCUG GU
8	>MIR_JE_p20	ACUAUAGCUGCCGGACUAAUGGUCUGCAACCAACAA GAAGAGAGGGUGGCCAGCCACUGAGUUUUUGUCGG CAGUU	GCCAGCCACUGAGUUUUU GUCG

information of genes for easy understanding of targeted genes by miRNA of Japanese encephalitis.

Conclusion

Finally in this study, eight potential miRNAs were predicted *in silico* and 123 target sites were found in 13 genes. Out of these thirteen genes, VPS13B, NAV1, IQSEC2 and NTRK3 played an important role in the regulation of the central nervous system and its activity in human brain and body; it is shown that if it is damaged it could lead to brain fever and ultimately, death. So, if we can control the malfunction protein at the transcription level, we would be able to save patients suffering from

Table 3. Annotated name of miRNA and sequence of potential miRNA and their genes and number of targets.

S.NO	Annotated miRNA name	miRNA nucleotide sequence	Target site	Name and number of genes
1.	>miR_JEV_1	AUGCUGAAACGCGGCCUACCCC	7	1gene (VPS 13B)
2.	>miR_JEV_2	GGAGGAAAUGAAGGCUCAAUCAUG	10	1gene(LRRc27)
3.	>miR_JEV_3	ACACACCCUUUGGGGAGAUGGUGUU	11	1gene (UPS36)
4.	>miR_JEV_4	UUGAUGUUUGCCAUCGUAGGUGGC	11	1gene (CDH23)
5.	>miR_JEV_5	CUUGUUGGACGGCAGAGGGCCA	7	1 gene (NAV1)
6.	>miR_JEV_6	GUGGUGGAGUACUCAAGCUCAGU	34	3genes(SIRPA),(NKD2),(IQSEC2)
7.	>miR_JEV_7	UUUCAGCUGGGCCUUCUGGU	19	2 genes (NTRK3),(PCNT)
8.	>miR_JEV_8	GCCAGCCACUGAGUUUUUGUCG	24	3 genes(TOM1),(KLF13),(SLIT1)

Table 4. Name of gene and position on chromosomes and target involved in protein codes.

S.NO	Name of genes	Position on Chromosome	3'UTR	Target sites involved in (conservation information)
1.	VPS 13B(7 target sites)vacuolar protein sorting-associated protein 13B	100899004-100899032	3998 - 4026	rn4, bosTau2, canFam2, dasNov1, loxAfr1, echTel1, galGal2
		100860285-100860313	3472 - 3500	bosTau2, canFam2, loxAfr1, echTel1
		100592670-100592698	243 - 271	oryCun1, bosTau2, canFam2
		100935514-100935542	6550 - 6578	rn4, mm8, bosTau2, canFam2, echTel1, galGal2, xenTro1, tetNig1
		100723348-100723376	1205 - 1233	anFam2, dasNov1, monDom4
		100890901-100890929	3905 - 3933	oryCun1, dasNov1, galGal2
		100949767-100949795	7116 - 7144	mm8, bosTau2, dasNov1
2.	LRR LRRc27(10target sites)LRRC27leucine rich repeat containing 27	134039555-134039583	1350 - 1378	Not conserved
		134042269-134042297	4064 - 4092	rn4, mm8, oryCun1, bosTau2, canFam2, dasNov1, loxAfr1, echTel1, monDom4, xenTro1
		134042479-134042507	4274 - 4302	Not conserved
		134042545-134042573	4340 - 4368	Not conserved
		134042611-134042639	4406 - 4434	Not conserved
		134042677-134042705	4472 - 4500	Not conserved
		134042743-134042771	4538 - 4566	Not conserved
		134042809-134042837	4604 - 4632	Not conserved
		134042875-134042903	4670 - 4698	Not conserved
		134042941-134042969	4736 - 4764	Not conserved
3.	USP.36 Ubiquitin carboxyl-terminal hydrolase 36	74306034-74306062	35 - 63	Not conserved
		74306007-74306035	62 - 90	Not conserved
		74305997-74306025	72 - 100	Not conserved

Table 4. Continued.

		74305939- 74305967	130 - 158	rn4
		74305913- 74305941	156 - 184	rn4
		74305886- 74305914	183 - 211	Not conserved
		74305857- 74305885	212 - 240	Not conserved
		74305828- 74305856	241 - 269	Not conserved
		74305808- 74305836	261 - 289	Not conserved
		74305801- 74305829	268 - 296	Not conserved
		74305741- 74305769	328 - 356	Not conserved
4	CDH.23 Cadherin-23 precursor (Otocadherin).	73239812;73240235 - 73239839;73240236	5629 - 5657	rn4, mm8, oryCun1, bosTau2, canFam2, dasNov1, loxAfr1, echTel1, galGal2, tetNig1
		73209039- 73209067	1894 - 1922	rn4, mm8, bosTau2, canFam2, echTel1, galGal2, xenTro1
		73214671- 73214699	2215 - 2243	rn4, mm8, oryCun1, loxAfr1, monDom4, galGal2, tetNig1
		73237491- 73237519	5200 - 5228	rn4, mm8, oryCun1, bosTau2, echTel1, monDom4, tetNig1
		73214809- 73214837	2353 - 2381	rn4, mm8, oryCun1, bosTau2, canFam2, tetNig1
		73223185- 73223213	3184 - 3212	rn4, mm8, bosTau2, dasNov1, echTel1, monDom4
		73229000- 73229028	3868 - 3896	bosTau2, dasNov1, loxAfr1, echTel1, monDom4, galGal2
		73214713 - 73214741	2257 - 2285	rn4, canFam2, loxAfr1, galGal2
		73170638- 73170666	1243 - 1271	bosTau2, loxAfr1
		73220154;73220895 - 73220176;73220901	2719 - 2747	canFam2, loxAfr1
5	NAV1 Neuron navigator 1	200048219 - 200048247	1393 - 1421	oryCun1, bosTau2, canFam2, dasNov1, loxAfr1, echTel1, monDom4, galGal2
		200048300 – 200048328	1474 - 1502	oryCun1, canFam2, dasNov1, loxAfr1, echTel1, monDom4, galGal2
		200052901 - 200052929	1766 - 1794	mm8, bosTau2, canFam2
		200056148 - 200056176	2461 - 2489	rn4, mm8
		200056360 - 200056388	2673 - 2701	Not Conserved
		200059007 - 200059035	5320 - 5348	monDom4
		200060973 - 200061001	7286 - 7314	Not Conserved
	SIRPA (Signal- regulatory protein alpha-1) Brain Ig-like molecule with ty	1866596 - 1866624	381 - 409	Not Conserved
		1866605 - 1866633	390 - 418	Not Conserved
		1866608 - 1866636	393 - 421	Not Conserved
		1866611 - 1866639	396 - 424	Not Conserved
		1866614 - 1866642	399 - 427	Not Conserved
		1866617 - 186664	402 - 430	Not Conserved
		1866620 - 1866648	405 - 433	Not Conserved
		1866623 - 1866651	408 - 436	Not Conserved
		1866626 - 1866654	411 - 439	Not Conserved
		1866629 - 1866657	414 - 442	loxAfr1
		1866638 - 1866666	423 - 451	Not Conserved
		1866641 - 1866669	426 - 454	Not Conserved
		1867457 - 1867485	1242 - 1270	Not Conserved

Table 4. Continued.

	1091218 - 1091246	327 - 355	rn4, mm8, canFam2
	1091410 - 1091438	519 - 547	canFam2
	1091413 - 1091441	522 - 550	bosTau2, canFam2, dasNov1, monDom4
	1091416 - 1091444	525 - 553	bosTau2, canFam2, dasNov1, monDom4
6. NKD2 : (naked cuticle homolog 2)	1091428 - 1091456	537 – 565	rn4, mm8, bosTau2, canFam2, monDom4, tetNig1
	1091431 - 1091459	540 - 568	canFam2, monDom4
	1091434 - 1091462	543 - 571	canFam2, monDom4
	1091437 - 1091465	546 - 574	canFam2, monDom4
	1091440 - 1091468	549 - 577	rn4, mm8, dasNov1
	1091443 - 1091471	552 - 580	rn4, mm8
	1091446 - 1091474	555 - 583	rn4, mm8, canFam2, tetNig1
	53280926 - 53280954	123 - 151	rn4, mm8
	53280870 - 53280898	179 - 207	mm8, bosTau2
	53280867 - 53280895	182 - 210	bosTau2, canFam2
	53280864 - 53280892	185 - 213	bosTau2, canFam2
	53280861 - 53280889	188 - 216	bosTau2, canFam2
IQSEC2 (IQ motif and Sec7 domain-containing protein 2)	53280858 - 53280886	191 – 219	mm8, bosTau2, canFam2
	53280668 - 53280696	381 - 409	Not Conserved
	53280414 - 53280442	635 - 663	bosTau2, canFam2
	53280333 - 53280361	716 - 744	bosTau2
	53278970 - 53278998	2079 - 2107	oryCun1, dasNov1
	86212921 - 86212949	8220 - 8248	loxAfr1, echTel1
	86220308 - 86220336	833 - 861	Not Conserved
	86219395 - 86219423	1746 - 1774	Not Conserved
7. NTRK3 (Neurotrophic tyrosine kinase receptor type 3)	86219348 - 86219376	1793 - 1821	Not Conserved
	86219358 - 86219386	1783 - 1811	Not Conserved
	86215541 - 86215569	5600 - 5628	Not Conserved
	86212564 - 86212592	8577 - 8605	Not Conserved
	86211976 - 86212004	9165 - 9193	Not Conserved
	86207707 - 86207735	13434 - 13462	dasNov1
	46655555 - 46655583	2875 - 2903	rn4, mm8
	46608026 - 46608054	107 – 135	oryCun1
	46626163;46630175 46626183;46630183	1039 - 1067	bosTau2, loxAfr1
	46608115 - 46608143	196 - 224	mm8, bosTau2, loxAfr1, echTel1
PCNT Pericentrin (Pericentrin B) (Kendrin).	46633611 - 46633639	1421 - 1449	canFam2
	46674569;46674849 46674574;46674872	5635 - 5663	Not Conserved
	46674877 - 46674905	5668 - 5696	rn4, mm8
	46676187 - 46676215	6106 - 6134	rn4, mm8, oryCun1
	46681390 - 46681418	6790 - 6818	rn4, mm8
	46682554 – 46682582	6871 - 6899	Not Conserved
	34073331 - 34073359	128 - 156	Not Conserved
TOM1 Target of Myb protein 1	34073461 - 34073489	258 - 286	echTel1
	34073465 - 34073493	262 - 290	Not Conserved
	34073469 - 34073497	266 - 294	Not Conserved

Table 4. Continued.

	34073473 - 34073501	270 – 298	Not Conserved
	34073577 - 34073605	374 – 402	Not Conserved
	34073584 - 34073612	381 – 409	Not Conserved
	34073657 - 34073685	454 – 482	Not Conserved
	29452170 – 29452198	375 – 403	Not Conserved
	29452174 - 29452202	379 – 407	Not Conserved
	29452312 - 29452340	517 - 545	canFam2
KLF13 Krueppel-like factor 13	29452379 - 29452407	584 - 612	Not Conserved
	29453220 - 29453248	1425 - 1453	Not Conserved
	29453605 - 29453633	1810 - 1838	Not Conserved
8	29454155 - 29454183	2360 - 2388	Not Conserved
	29455533 - 29455561	3738 - 3766	Not Conserved
	98798838;98806068 98798865;98806069	- 111 - 139	mm8, oryCun1, bosTau2, canFam2, dasNov1, loxAfr1, echTel1, monDom4, xenTro1, tetNig1
	98792773 - 98792801	815 - 843	Not Conserved
SLIT1 Slit homolog 1 protein	98752506 - 98752534	2860 - 2888	rn4, mm8
precursor (Slit-1) (Multiple	98752502 - 98752530	2864 - 2892	rn4, mm8, galGal2
epidermal growth factor-like	98750456 - 98750484	3767 – 3795	mm8, oryCun1
domains 4).	98749228 - 98749256	4995 - 5023	Not Conserved
	98748667 - 98748695	5556 - 5584	Not Conserved
	98748567 - 98748595	5656 - 5684	Not Conserved

Table 5. Information of genes.

S.No	Gene name	Precision	Ensemble ID	m iTG score	SNR
1.	VPS 13B	0.71	ENSGOOOOO135249	22.31	1.06
2.	LRR c27	0.88	ENSGOOOOO148814	25.00	2.85
3.	USP 36	1	ENSGOOOO055483	29.00	2.32
4.	CDH 23	0.98	ENSGOOOOO107730	29.50	1.45
5.	NAV1	0.78	ENSOOOOO134369	19.80	0.94
	SIRPA	0.96	ENSGOOOOO198053	30.0	2.5
6.	NKD2	0.84	ENSGOOOOO145506	22.0	2.5
	IQSEC2	0.84	ENSGOOOOO124313	20.0	2.5
7.	NTRK3	0.96	ENSGOOOOO140538	24.66	2.01
	PCNT	0.96	ENSGOOOOO160299	23.26	2.01
	TOM1	0.41	ENSGOOOOO100284	21.00	1.18
8.	KLF13	0.41	ENSGOOOOO169926	19.00	1.18
	SLIT1	0.41	ENSGOOOOO187122	19.00	1.18

attack of *J. encephalitis*. Since this is a prediction based method, it has to be proved experimentally.

ACKNOWLEDGEMENT

The authors wish to thank Prof. PP Mathur, Vice-chancellor of KIIT University, Bhubaneswar for Critically examining the manuscript and giving of valuable guidance.And we also thank DBT for giving us this plate form for scientific computational work.

REFERENCES

Amarzguioui M, Rossi JJ, Kim D (2005). Approaches for chemically

Amarzguioui M, Rossi JJ, Kim D (2005). Approaches for chemically synthesized siRNA and vector-mediated RNAi. FEBS Lett. 579:5974-5981.

Carthew RW, Sontheimer EJ, (2009). Origins and Mechanisms of miRNAs and siRNAs. Cell., 136:642–655.

Chen W, Yan W, Du Q, Fei L, Liu M (2008). RNA interference targeting VP1 inhibits foot-and-mouth disease virus replication in BHK-21 cells

and sucklingmice. J. Virol. 78:6900–6907

Cullen BR, (2004). Transcription and processing of human microRNA precursors. Mol Cell. 16:861-865.

Elbashir SM, Harborth J, Lendeckel W, Yalcin A, Weber K, (2001). Duplexes of 21-nucleotide RNAs mediate RNA interference in cultured mammalian cells. Nat. 411:494-498.

Erlanger TE, Weiss S, Keiser J, Utzinger J, Wiedenmayer K, (2009). Past present and future of Japanese encephalitis. Emerg Infect Dis. 15:1-7.

Gregory RI, Yan KP, Amuthan G, Chendrimada T, Doratotaj B, Cooch N, Shiekhattar R, (2004). The Microprocessor complex mediates the genesis of microRNAs. Nat. 432(7014):235-240.

Griffiths-Jones S, (2004). The microRNA Registry. Nucleic Acids Res. 32:D109-D111.

Hammond SM (2000). An RNA-directed nuclease mediates post-transcriptional gene silencing in Drosophila cells. Nat. 404:293-296.

Hammond SM (2005). Dicing and slicing: The core machinery of the RNA interference pathway. FEBS Lett. 579: 5822–5829.

Hammond SM, Caudy AA, Hannon GJ, (2001). Post-transcriptional gene silencing by double-stranded RNA. Nat Rev Genet. 2:110-119.

Krek A, Grün D, Poy MN, (2005).Combinatorial microRNA target predictions. Nat. Genet. 5:495–500.

Kumar P, Wu H, McBride JL, Jung KE, Kim MH (2007). Transvascular delivery of small interfering RNA to the central nervous system. Nat. 448: 39-43.

Lee Y, (2003). the nuclear RNase III Drosha initiates microRNA processing. Natur. 425:415-419.

Lee Y, KM, Han J, Yeom KH, Lee S, Baek SH, Kim VN, (2004). MicroRNA genes are transcribed by RNA polymerase II. EMBO J. 23(20):4051-4060. Please verify the year in the main text with that in the reference section.

Liu YP, Haasnoot J, ter Brake O, Berkhout B, Konstantinova P (2008).Inhibition of HIV-1 by multiple siRNAs expressed from a single microRNA polycistron. Nucleic Acids Res. 36: 2811–2824.

Mathews DH, Sabina J, Zucker M (1999). Turner H, Expanded Sequence Dependence of Thermodynamic Parameters Provides Robust Prediction of RNASecondary Structure. J. Mol. Biol. 288(5):911-940.

Moore MS (1993). The GTP-binding protein Ran/TC4 is required for protein import into the nucleus. Nat. 365:661-663.

Murakami M, Ota T, Nukuzuma S, Takegami T (2005). Inhibitory effect of RNAi on Japanese encephalitis virus replication in vitro and in vivo. Microbiol. Immuno. 49:1047-1056.

Ruvkun G (2001). Molecular Biology: Glimpses of a Tiny RNA World. Sci. 294:797-799.

Siolas D, Lerner C, Burchard J, Linsley PS, (2005). Synthetic shRNAs as potent RNAi triggers. Nat. Biotechnol. 23:227-231.

Sui G, Soohoo C, Affar B, Gay F, Shi Y (2002). A DNA vector-based RNAi technology to suppress gene expression in mammalian cells. Proc. Natl. Acad. Sci. USA, 99:5515-5520.

Watanabe T, Umehara T, Kohara M (2007). Therapeutic application of RNA interference for hepatitis C virus. Adv Drug Deliv Rev. 59:1263-1276.

Zuker M (2003). Mfold web server for nucleic acid folding and hybridization prediction, Nucleic Acids Res. 13:3406-3415.

## 24

Prediction of MHC Class II binders/non-binders using negative selection algorithm in vaccine designing

S. S. Soam[1]*, Feroz Khan[2], Bharat Bhasker[3] and B. N. Mishra[4]

[1]Department of Computer Science and Engineering, Institute of Engineering and Technology Gautam Buddh Technical University, Lucknow, India.
[2]Department of Metabolic and Structural Biology, CSIR-Central Institute of Medicinal and Aromatic Plants, Lucknow, India.
[3]Department of Information Technology and System, Indian Institute of Management, Lucknow, India.
[4]Department of Biotechnology, Institute of Engineering and Technology, Gautam Buddh Technical University, Lucknow, India.

The identification of major histocompatibility complex (MHC) class-II restricted peptides is an important goal in human immunological research leading to peptide based vaccine designing. These MHC class II peptides are predominantly recognized by CD4+ T-helper cells, which when turned on, have profound immune regulatory effects. Thus, prediction of such MHC class-II binding peptide is very helpful towards epitope based vaccine designing. HLA-DR proteins were found to be associated with autoimmune diseases e.g. HLA-DRB1*0401 with rheumatoid arthritis. It is important for the treatment of autoimmune diseases to determine, which peptides bind to MHC class II molecules. The experimental methods for identification of these peptides are both time consuming and cost intensive. Therefore, computational methods have been found helpful in classifying these peptides as binders or non-binders. We have applied negative selection algorithm, an artificial immune system approach to predict MHC class-II binders and non-binders. For the evaluation of the NSA algorithm, five fold cross validation has been used and six MHC class-II alleles have been taken. The average area under ROC curve for HLA-DRB1*0301, DRB1*0401, DRB1*0701, DRB1*1101, DRB1*1501, DRB1*1301 have been found to be 0.75, 0.77, 0.71, 0.72, 0.69, and 0.84, respectively indicating good predictive performance for the small training set.

Key words: Negative selection algorithm, MHC class-II peptides, artificial immune system, epitope, vaccine designing, human immunology.

INTRODUCTION

The CD8+ cytotoxic T-cells (CTL) immune response and CD4+ T-helper (Th) immune response is stimulated by binding of peptides to major histocompatibility complex (MHC) Class I and MHC Class II molecules, respectively (Jacques and Steinman, 1998; De Groot et al., 2002). Intracellular antigens, cut into peptides in the cytosol of the antigen processing cell (APC), bind to MHC Class I molecules and are recognized by CD8+ cytotoxic T-cells (CTLs), which once activated, can directly kill a target cell (that is, an infected cell). Extra cellular antigens that have

entered the endocytic pathway of the APC are processed there. These are generally presented by MHC class II molecules to T-helper cells, which, when turned on, have profound immune regulatory effects. In humans, HLA -A, -B, and -C are the MHC class I type molecules and HLA-DR, -DP and -DQ are the MHC class II type molecules. There are known to be 2DRA, 126DRB, 12DQA, 22DQB, 6DBA and 56 different expressed DPB. HLA-DR proteins were found to be associated with autoimmune diseases e.g. HLA-DRB1*0401 with rheumatoid arthritis. The identification of class II binding peptide epitopes from autoimmune disease-related antigens is an essential step in the development of antigen-specific immune modulation therapy. In the case of type 1 diabetes, two

---

*Corresponding author. E-mail: sssoam@gmail.com.

DRB1*0401-restricted T cell epitopes from human GAD65, 274-286, and 115-127 are immunogenic in transgenic mice expressing functional DRB1*0401 MHC class II molecules but not in non-transgenic littermates.

The presentation of these two T-cell epitopes in the islets of DRB1*0401individuals who are at risk for type 1 diabetes may allow for antigen-specific recruitment of regulatory cells to the islets following peptide immunization. Common allelic variants at the class II HLA-DRB1, DQA1 and DQB1 loci are primarily and jointly associated with the disease (Linda et al., 1996; Christopher and Diane, 2001; Grete et al., 2001). It is important to determine which peptides bind to MHC class II molecules that will help in treatment of the diseases (Sette et al., 2007; Lauemoller et al., 2000; Holden et al., 1998; Emma et al., 2003; Erik et al., 1999). Conventional vaccines comprise live-attenuated microbs, killed inactivated micro-organisms, and purified microbial components, polysaccharide-carrier protein conjugates, or recombinant proteins. In many cases the pathogen to be grown in laboratory conditions, which is both time consuming and costly, and allow for the identification of only the most abundant antigens, which can be purified in quantities for vaccine testing. In case of non-cultivable micro-organisms the conventional vaccine designing approach cannot be applied. The genome sequencing of various microbes and viruses allows the design of vaccines starting from the prediction of all antigens using bioinformatics, independently of their abundance and without the need to grow the pathogen in laboratory. The computational methods are used to identify potential vaccine targets in order to save time and cost (Marirosa et al., 2003; Barbara Capecchi et al., 2004). In our study we have considered six different MHC class II molecules: HLA-DRB1*0301, HLA-DRB1*0401, HLA-DRB1*0701, HLA-DRB1*1101, HLA-DRB1*1501, HLA-DRB1*1301.

The establishment of numerous MHC class-II epitope databases such as SYFPEITHI (Rammensee et al., 1999), MHCBN (Bhasin et al., 2003), AntiJen (Toseland et al., 2005), EPIMHC (Pedro et al., 2005) and IEDB (Peters et al., 2005), has facilitated the development of a large number of prediction algorithms. A number of methods have been developed for the prediction of MHC class-II binding peptides from an antigenic sequence, beginning with, early motif based methods (Chicz et al., 1993; Sette et al., 1993; Hammer et al., 1993), to different scoring matrices based methods (Rammensee et al., 1995; Marshal et al., 1995; Southwood et al., 1998; Wang et al., 2008). The artificial neural network has also been applied for the prediction of HLA-DRB1*0401 binding peptides (Brusic et al., 1998; Honeyman et al., 1998). Some complex tools for identifying the HLA-DRB1*0401 binding peptides have also been designed that is an iterative algorithm to optimize MHC class II binding matrix based stepwise discriminant analysis (Bhasin et al., 2004). We have used an artificial immune system based algorithm; the negative selection algorithm

to predict MHC Class II binders and non-binders.

Other computational approaches used for epitope prediction are: genetic algorithm and fuzzy algorithm with artificial neural network, decision tree algorithms, quadratic and linear programming, support vector machine, Gibbs motif sampler, threading methods, structure based methods (Liliana et al., 2003; Soam et al., 2012; Singh and Mishra, 2008; Yael and Hanah, 2004; Ingvar et al., 2004).

METHODS AND MATERIALS

Negative selection algorithm

Artificial immune systems (AIS), a new computational intelligence paradigm be defined as a system of interconnected components, which emulates a particular subset of aspects originating from the natural immune system in order to accomplish a particular task within a particular environment/domain. AIS are concerned with computing while the theoretical immune system models focus on understanding the behavior of immune system. The primary function of immune system is to monitor the organisms in search of malfunctioning from their own body or foreign disease causing elements. Thus the immune system is capable of discriminating between self and non-self recognition with certain affinity. The thymus is responsible for the maturation of T-cells; and is protected by a blood barrier capable of efficiently excluding non-self antigens from the thymic environment. Thus, most elements found within the thymus are representative of self instead of non-self. As a result, the T-cells containing receptors capable of recognizing these self antigens presented in the thymus are eliminated from the repertoire of T-cells through a process called negative selection. All T-cells that leave the thymus to circulate throughout the body are said to be tolerant to self. The negative selection presents alternative paradigm to perform the pattern recognition/classification by storing information about the complement set (non-self). The main concept behind the negative selection algorithm is to generate a set of detectors. The negative selection process is an alternative computational paradigm for pattern recognition by storing information about the complement set (non-self) of the pattern to recognized (self). Therefore, the AIS and NSA are related. Since we have to predict the self/non-self that is, MHC binders and non-binders, an important molecule in activation of immune system, it is better to use AIS as a computational method for prediction. Concept of artificial immune system is based on how lymphocytes (B-cells and T-cells) mature, adapt, react, and learn in response to a foreign antigen. Artificial immune system based models are either population based or network based models. The algorithms on population based model are negative selection algorithm (NSA) (De Castro and Timmis, 2002; Igawa and Ohashi, 2009) and clonal selection algorithm (CSA), focusing mainly on generating initial population of lymphocytes, and improving and refining that population based on techniques emulated from natural immune system. Network models are based on anti-idiaotypic activity within the natural immune system, which consequently regulate the population of lymphocytes. Artificial immune network approach is an example of network based model (Hunt and Denise ,1996).

Support vector machine is an algorithm for maximizing a particular mathematical function with respect to given collection of data. The separating hyper plane, maximum-margin hyper plane, the soft margin and the kernel function are the main concepts behind SVM (William, 2006). With ANN the adjustments of weights and biases is done during the training, and with SVM the

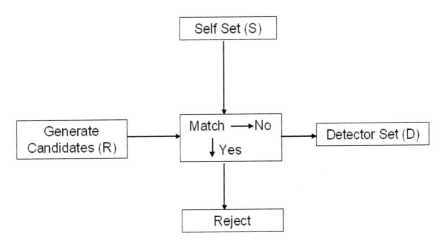

Figure 1. Generating the set of detectors.

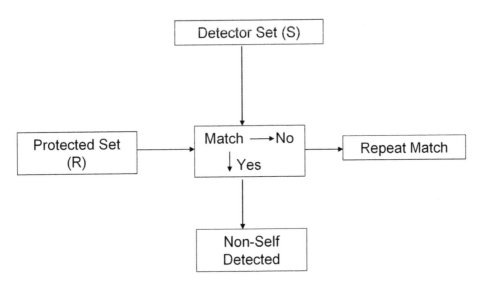

Figure 2. Detecting non-self elements.

parameters of a solved model are difficult to interpret. In case of NSA the appropriate matching function is used to generate a detector set against which the elements of protected set are matched for self and non-self elements. The Negative selection algorithm works as follows:

i. The set of random candidates (generated using any random number generation algorithm) and the self set is given.
ii. Then each element of the randomly generated set is compared with the elements of self set. If a match occurs, then that random element is rejected; else that element is added to the detector set shown in Figure 1.

After generating the detector set, the system is monitored for non-self element. The protected set is compared with the elements of detector set. If match occurs then the non-self is detected otherwise it continue to match as shown in Figure 2. The binding process of MHC class I or MHC class-II molecules with antigenic peptides within the natural immune systems is basically simulated by affinity threshold functions. For a given lymphocyte, x, and an antigen, y, a number of matching rules can be defined to determine whether x

and y match. Some of the commonly used affinity functions are as follows: Hamming distance rule, r-Contiguous bits rule, r-chunks rule. Hamming distance rule have been used to simulate the affinity threshold function in present study.

The detector set for binders (D_b) and non-binders (D_n) generated using the above algorithm. Monitoring the elements of the set C_x (x is replaced by either b or n depending upon the protected set for binders and non-binders) to test the resultant population of artificial lymphocytes against detector set D_{bn} (D_{bn} is union of D_b and D_n). In case of match, value 1 is stored; otherwise value 0 is stored in the set R_x. The values in sets R_b and R_n are used to obtain the values of evaluation parameters FP, FN, TP, and TN. The algorithm for generation of detector set is given in Box 1 and algorithm for predicting the element of protected set is given in Box 2.

The MATCH () function has been implemented based on the concept of Hamming distance. The Hamming distance between two binary vectors is the number of corresponding bits that differ. For example, if A = (1, 0, 0, 1) and B = (1, 1, 0, 1) then the Hamming distance between A and B, is 1. Here, the MATCH () function calculates the Hamming distance between the self tolerant artificial lymphocyte, s, and randomly generated self tolerant artificial lym-

Box 1. Algorithm for generation of detector set.

1.	Let S is the set of self tolerant artificial lymphocytes to train and ns is the numbers of elements in the set, and, the element s ∈ S.
2.	Let C is the set of self tolerant artificial lymphocytes to monitor that is, to classify and nc is the number of elements in the set, and, the element c ∈ C.
3.	S U C is the set of total number of self tolerant artificial lymphocytes.
4.	Let R is the set of all randomly generated self tolerant artificial lymphocytes and nr is the number of elements in the set and the element r ∈ R.
5.	Let D is initially an empty set of detectors.
6.	While nr ≠ Null
7.	read an element r from set R;
8.	flag = false;
9.	for each self element s ∈ S do
10.	if MATCH (s, r) is greater than the affinity threshold t then
11.	flag = true;
12.	break;
13.	end;
14.	end;
15.	if flag = false
16.	add r to D;
17.	end;
18.	end.

Box 2. Algorithm for predicting the elements of set C.

1.	While nr ≠ Null
2.	read an element c from set C;
3.	flag = false;
4.	for each self element dbn ∈ Dbn do
5.	if MATCH (c, dbn) is less than equal to the affinity threshold t then
6.	flag = true;
7.	break;
8.	end;
9.	end;
10.	if flag = true then add 1 to the set Rx
11.	else add 0 to the set Rx;
12.	end.

phocyte, r. The r and s is the binary vector of 180 bits long since these consists of 9 amino acids and an amino acid is represented by 20 bit vector.

Training and validation dataset

We have assembled dataset of peptide binding and nonbinding affinities for six MHC class II allele's molecules from DRFMLI repository (http://bio.dfci.harvard.edu/DFRMLI/). These dataset of high quality MHC binding and nonbinding peptides were taken from IEDB database [9]. The binding affinities (IC_{50}) of these peptides, quantitatively measured by immunological experiments have been used for binders and non-binders. The IC_{50} values have been scaled to binding scores ranging from 0 to 100 using linear

transformation, where score $IC_{50}>=33$ are taken as binders $IC_{50}<33$ as non-binders. The data sets have been shown in Table 1 after removing the duplication. In order to reduce biasness in prediction, the ratio of binder and non-binders has been kept 1:1 by adding randomly generated non-binders to the non-binders set. The number epitopes in training sets as well as in the prediction set has also shown in the Table 1. Five fold cross validation have been used for prediction. To measure the generalization ability of a computational model i.e. the quality of its inductive bias, the test data has to be outside the training data set. For this the data has to be divided into two parts that is, in training set and validation set. In k-fold cross validation the dataset is divided randomly into k equal parts. To create training and validation sets, one of the k parts is kept as validation set and remaining k-1 parts forms the training set. This is done k times, each time leaving out another one of the k

Table 1. Data sets for various MHC class–II alleles.

Allele Name	Total	Bind>=33	NBind<33	Binders	N_Binders	Final N_B	Train_Set	Pred_Set
DRB1-0301	605	430	175	396	156	396	317	79
DRB1-0401	615	450	165	408	143	408	327	81
DRB1-0701	608	468	140	430	120	430	344	86
DRB1-1101	623	494	129	444	114	444	356	88
DRB1-1301	133	55	78	40	57	40	32	8
DRB1-1501	623	415	208	380	180	380	304	76

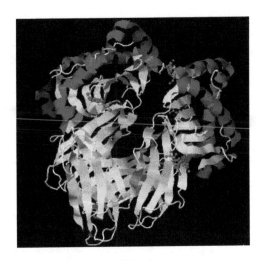

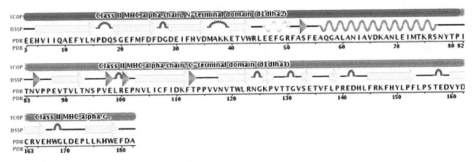

Figure 3. Molecular structure of Class II Histocompatibility antigen (HLA-DR1) (PDB ID: 1DLH) revealing binding domain in beta sheets representation of secondary structure sequence.

parts and combining rest k-1 parts. As k increases the percentage of training instances increases resulting more robust estimators, but validation sets gets smaller and the cost of training increases. The extreme case of k fold cross validation is leave-one-out where given a data set of N instances, only one instance is left out as a validation set and remaining N-1 used as training set. This structure includes the extracellular portion of a class II MHC, with a peptide bound. Figure 3 shows crystal structure of the human class II MHC protein HLA-DRB1 complexed with an influenza virus peptide (PDB ID: 1DLH).

Evaluation parameters

The prediction accuracy of the algorithm for generation of detector set (Box 1) and for predicting the elements of set (Box 2) have been

determined using discrimination between binders and non-binders. In order to, classify peptides into binders (positive data) and non-binders (negative data), a threshold value between 0, 2, 4, 6, 8, 10, 12, 14, 16 and 18 based on the Hamming distance between the binary vectors r and s may be taken. Here, in our study the threshold values 4, 6, 8, 10, 12 have been used. A predicted peptide belongs to one of the four categories, *i.e.* True Positive (TP); an experimentally binding peptide predicted as a binder, False Positive (FP); an experimentally nonbinding peptide predicted as a binder, True Negative (TN); an experimentally nonbinding peptide predicted as a non-binder and False Negative (FN); an experimentally binding peptide predicted as non-binder. A non-parametric performance measure, area under receiver operating characteristic (AROC) curve has been used to evaluate the prediction performance of the applied algorithms. The ROC curve is a plot of the true positive rate TP/(TP+FN) on the vertical axis *vs*

Table 2. HLA-DRB1*0301.

Set #	Sensitivity	Specificity	Accuracy	PPV	NPV	Area ROC
1	0.70	0.72	0.71	0.72	0.71	0.73
2	0.68	0.73	0.70	0.72	0.69	0.73
3	0.72	0.72	0.72	0.72	0.72	0.75
4	0.70	0.72	0.71	0.72	0.71	0.75
5	0.72	0.71	0.72	0.72	0.71	0.79
Average	0.70	0.72	0.71	0.72	0.71	0.75

Table 3. HLA-DRB1*0401.

Set #	Sensitivity	Specificity	Accuracy	PPV	NPV	Area ROC
1	0.70	0.72	0.71	0.71	0.70	0.79
2	0.71	0.70	0.71	0.70	0.71	0.76
3	0.69	0.71	0.70	0.71	0.69	0.75
4	0.68	0.71	0.70	0.71	0.69	0.77
5	0.71	0.70	0.70	0.70	0.70	0.76
Average	0.70	0.71	0.70	0.71	0.70	0.77

false positive rate FP/(TN+FP) on the horizontal axis for the complete range of the decision thresholds.

RESULTS AND DISCUSSION

Predictions of T-cell epitopes have the potential to provide important information for rational research and development of vaccines and immunotherapy. To screen out the binders and non-binders, the experimental methods can be used but this approach is time consuming, as well as, costly. Computational approaches can be applied to predict the binders and non-binders. Various computational methods viz. ANN, SVM etc. have been used for predictions. For a useful prediction, using any machine learning approach, the data in the training set should be sufficient. In case of small training data set the prediction will not be useful. In many cases the numbers of known binders and non-binders for MHC class-II alleles is not sufficient for prediction using the machine leaning approaches. Further, the available HLA-II servers do not match prediction capabilities of HLA-I servers. Currently available HLA-II prediction server offer only limited prediction accuracy and the development of improved predictors is needed for large-scale studies, such as proteome-wide epitope mapping and for the cases where the small data sets are available. Here, in the present study the application of negative selection algorithm (an artificial immune system paradigm) has been applied for the prediction of MHC class-II T-cell epitopes, which has shown useful predictions in case of small data sets also.

Negative selection algorithm is preferred over the other two artificial immune algorithms because it is theoretical simple and also allows any matching function to be employed. Different matching functions have different detecting regions and thus have direct influence on the performance of the algorithm. We have taken a simple matching function based on Hamming distance rule. MATCH () function calculates the Hamming distance between the self tolerant artificial lymphocyte, s, and randomly generated self tolerant artificial lymphocyte, r. Hamming distance 0 indicates that the two strings are perfectly matched with each other. The maximum score is 18 that indicate the strings are fully mismatched. The value of affinity threshold can be between 0, 2, 4, 6, 8, 10, 12, 14, 16 and 18. In our study the values of thresholds 4, 6, 8, 10, 12 are taken. The results for various evaluation parameters viz. sensitivity, specificity, positive predictive value (PPV; PPV = TP / (TP + FP)), negative predictive value (NPV; NPV = TN / (TN + FN)), accuracy and area under ROC curve for five sets are shown in Tables 1 to 5 for various threshold levels. For a predictive performance of an algorithm, the number of training data should be sufficient. Here, in case of negative selection algorithm, a large complementary set of self has to be generated using any random algorithm against the known data set. This leads to better predictive performance. We have used the Hamming distance for matching function. A general rule of thumb is that an AROC value > 0.7 indicates a useful prediction performance and a value > 0.85 indicates a good prediction. The summary of the average area under receiver operating characteristics curve for HLA-DRB1*0301, HLA-DRB1*0401, HLA-DRB1*0701, HLA-DRB1*1101, HLA-DRB1*1501, HLA-DRB1*1301 have

Table 4. HLA-DRB1*0701.

Set #	Sensitivity	Specificity	Accuracy	PPV	NPV	Area ROC
1	0.64	0.69	0.66	0.68	0.65	0.73
2	0.65	0.67	0.66	0.67	0.65	0.71
3	0.66	0.69	0.68	0.68	0.67	0.70
4	0.63	0.69	0.66	0.69	0.64	0.70
5	0.70	0.68	0.69	0.69	0.70	0.73
Average	0.66	0.68	0.67	0.68	0.66	0.71

Table 5. HLA-DRB1*1101.

Set #	Sensitivity	Specificity	Accuracy	PPV	NPV	Area ROC
1	0.65	0.70	0.67	0.69	0.66	0.70
2	0.66	0.68	0.67	0.68	0.66	0.78
3	0.65	0.69	0.67	0.68	0.65	0.70
4	0.67	0.69	0.68	0.69	0.67	0.72
5	0.68	0.66	0.67	0.66	0.68	0.71
Average	0.66	0.69	0.67	0.68	0.66	0.72

Table 6. HLA-DRB1*1301.

Set #	Sensitivity	Specificity	Accuracy	PPV	NPV	Area ROC
1	0.65	0.67	0.66	0.67	0.65	0.78
2	0.63	0.65	0.64	0.65	0.63	0.94
3	0.61	0.71	0.66	0.69	0.64	0.88
4	0.69	0.69	0.69	0.68	0.70	0.78
5	0.67	0.71	0.69	0.70	0.68	0.82
Average	0.65	0.68	0.67	0.68	0.66	0.84

Table 7. HLA-DRB1*1501.

Set #	Sensitivity	Specificity	Accuracy	PPV	NPV	Area ROC
1	0.65	0.66	0.66	0.66	0.66	0.69
2	0.65	0.68	0.67	0.67	0.66	0.60
3	0.68	0.66	0.67	0.67	0.68	0.72
4	0.67	0.69	0.68	0.69	0.68	0.71
5	0.67	0.68	0.67	0.68	0.67	0.71
Average	0.67	0.67	0.67	0.67	0.67	0.69

been shown Tables 2 to 7, respectively. The value of AROC for HLA-DRB1*1501 is 0.84 which has small training set size of 32.

The comparison of AROC for various MHC class–II alleles for different sets has been shown in Figure 4. The average area under ROC curve for HLA-DRB1*0301, DRB1*0401, DRB1*0701, DRB1*1101, DRB1*1501, DRB1*1301 have been found to be 0.75, 0.77, 0.71, 0.72, 0.69, and 0.84, respectively indicating good predictive performance. The above study shows that the negative selection algorithm gives useful predictive performance for MHC class - II binders and non-binders even for small training sets. The above method can be applied for the classification of MHC class – II binders and non-binders even for the small data sets. The negative selection algorithm can be used to implement the servers for

Area Under ROC Curve for various MHC Class II Allels

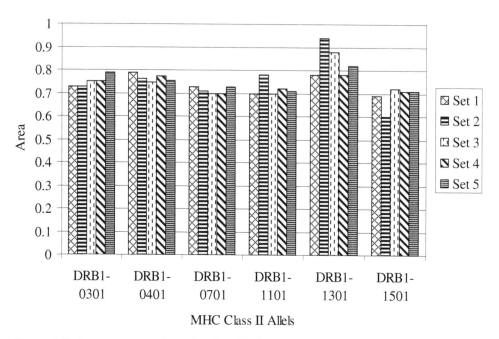

Figure 4. Performance comparison of various MHC Class – II alleles for different sets.

classification of MHC class-II binders and non-binders and help in designing the epitope based vaccine designing.

ACKNOWLEDGEMENT

The authors are thankful to Dr. Satarudra Pratap Singh, Sr. Lecturer, Biotechnology, Amity University, Lucknow, for their kind help in data preparation and analysis.

REFERENCES

Barbara Capecchi, Davide Serruto, Jeannette Adu-Bobie, Rino Rappuoli, Mariagrazia Pizza (2004). The Genome Revolution in Vaccine Research. Curr. Issues Mol Biol. 6:17-28.

Bhasin M, Raghava GPS (2004). SVM based method for prediction DRB*0401 binding peptides in an antigen sequence. Bioinformatics 20:421-423.

Bhasin M, Singh H, Raghava GPS (2003). MHCBN: a comprehensive database of MHC binding and non-binding peptides. Bioinformatics 19:665-666.

Brusic V, Rudy G, Honeyman G, Hammer J, Harrison L (1998). Prediction of MHC class II-binding peptides using an evolutionary algorithm and artificial neural network. Bioinformatics 14:121-30.

Chicz RM, Urban RG, Gorga JC, Vignali DA, Lane WS, Strominger JL (1993). Specificity and promiscuity among naturally processed peptides bound to HLADR alleles. J. Exp. Med. 178:27-47.

Christophe Benoist, Diane Mathis (2001). Autoimmunity provoked by infection: how good is the case for T cell epitope mimicry? Nat. Immunol. 2(9):797-801.

De Castro LN, Timmis J (2002). Artificial Immune Systems: A Novel Paradigm to Pattern Recognition. Artificial Neural Networks in Pattern Recognition (JM Corchado, L Alonso, and C Fyfe (eds.) SOCO-2002, University of Paisley, UK). pp. 67-84.

De Groot AS, Sbai H, Aubin CS, McMurry J, Martin W (2002). Immuno-informatics: Mining Genomes for Vaccine components. Immunol. Cell Biol. 80:255-269.

Erik Novak J, Andrew Liu W, Gerald Nepom T, William Kwok W (1999). MHC Class II tetramers identify peptide-specific human CD4+T cells proliferating in response to influenza A antigens. J. Clin. Investig. 104(12):R63-R67.

Grete Sønderstrup and Hugh O. McDevitt (2001). DR, DQ, and you: MHC alleles and autoimmunity. J. Clin. Investig. 107(7):795-796.

Hammer J, Valsasnini P, Tolba K, Bolin D, Higelin J, Takacs B, Sinigaglia F (1993). Promiscuous and allele-specific anchors in HLA-DR-binding peptides. Cell 74:197-203.

Holden Maecker T, Dale Umetsu T, Rosemarie DeKruyff H, Shoshana Levy (1998). Cytotoxic T Cell Response to DNA vaccination: Dependence on Antigen Presentatiion via Class II MHC. J. Immunol. 161:6532-6536.

Honeyman MC, Brusic V, Stone NL, Harrison LC (1998). Neural network based prediction of candidate T-cell epitopes. Nat. Biotechnol. 16:966-69.

Hunt JE, Denise EC (1996). Learning using an artificial immune system. J. Network Comput. Appl. 19:189-212.

Igawa K, Ohashi H (2009). A negative selection algorithm fro classification and reduction of the noise effect. Appl. Soft Comput. 9:431-438.

Ingvar Eidhammer, Inge Jonassen, William R Taylor (2004). Protein Bioinformatics: An algorithmic approach to sequence and structure analysis. John Wily & Sons Ltd., UK.

Jacques B, Steinman RM (1998). Dendritic cells and the control of immunity. Nature 392:245-252.

Lauemoller SL, Kesmir C, Corbat SL, Fomsgaard A, Holm A, Claesson M H, Brunak S, Buus S. (2000). Identifying cytotoxic T cell epitopes fromn genomic and proteomic information: The human MHC project. Rev. Immunogenet. 2:477-491.

Liliana Florea, Bjarni Halldorsson, Oliver Kohlbacher, Russell Schwartz, Stephen Hoffman, Sorin Istrail (2003). Epitope prediction algorithms for peptide based vaccine design. Proceedings of the Computational Systems Bioinformatics, IEEE Computer Society.

Linda S. Wicker, Shiow-Ling Chen, Gerald T. Nepom, John F. Elliott, Daniel C. Freed, Alka Bansal, Song Zheng, Andrew Herman, Åke Lernmark, Dennis Mhosha. Zaller, Laurence B. Peterson, Jonathan B. Rothbard, Richard Cummings, Phyllis J. Whiteley (1996). Naturally processed T cell epitopes from human glutamic acid decarboxylase identified using mice transgenic for the type 1 diabetes-associated human MHC class II allele, DRB1*0401. J. Clin. Investig. 98(11):2597-2603.

Marirosa Mora, Daniele Veggi, Laura Santini, Mariagrazia Pizza and Rino Rappuoli (2003). Reverse Vaccinology. Drug Discov. Today 8(10):459-465.

Marshal KW, Wilson KJ, Liang J, Woods A, Zaller D, Rothbard JB (1995). Prediction of peptide affinity to HLA-DRB1*0401. J. Immunol. 154:5927-5933.

Pedro A R, Zhang H, Paul J, Ellis G, Reinherz L (2005). EPIMHC: a curated database of MHC-binding peptides for customized computational vaccinology. Bioinforma. 21(9):2140-2141.

Peters B, Sidney J, Bourne P, Bui HH, Buus S (2005). The immune eitope database and analysis resource: From vision to blueprint. PLoS Biol. p. 91.

Rammensee HG, Bachmann J, Emmerich N, Bachor O, Stevanovic S (1999). SYFPEITHI: database for MHC ligands and peptide motifs. Immunogenetics 50:213-219.

Rammensee HG, Friede T, Stevanovic S (1995). MHC ligands and peptide motifs: First listing. Immunogenetics 41:178-228.

Singh SP, BN Mishra (2008). Prediction of MHC binding peptides using Gibbs motif sampler, weight matrix and artificial neural network. Bioinformatics 3(4):150-155

Soam SS, Feroz Khan, Bharat Bhasker, BN Mishra (2012). Classification using Negative Selection Algorithm: Application to MHC Class II Binders / Non-Binders used in Peptide based Vaccine Designing. International Conference on Computer and Automation Engineering"ICCAE2012" Mumbai. Proceedings published by ASME Press.

Sette A, Peters B (2007). Immune epitope mapping in the post-genomic era: Lessons for vaccines development. Curr. Opin. Immunol. 19:106-110.

Sette A, Sidney J, Oseroff C, Del Guercio M F, Southwood S, Arrhenius T, Powell MF, Colon SM, Gaeta FC, Grey HM (1993). HLA DR4w4-binding motifs illustrate the biochemical basis of degeneracy and specificity in peptide-DR interactions. J. Immunol. 151:3163-70.

Southwood S, Sidney J, Kondo A, Del Guercio M F, Appella E, Hoffman S, Kubo R T, Chesnut R W, Grey H M, Sette A (1998). Several common HLA-DR types share largely overlapping peptide binding repertoires. J. Immunol. 160:3363-73.

Toseland CP, Clayton D J, Mc Sparron H, Hemsley S L, Blythe M J, Paine K, Doytchinova I A, Guan P, Hattotuwangama CK, Flower DR (2005). AntiJen: a quantitative immunology database integrating functional, thermodynamic, kinetic, biophysical and cellular data. Immunome Res. 1:4.

Wang P, Sidney J, Dow C, Mothé B, Sette A, Peters B (2008). A systematic assessment of MHC Class II peptide binding predictions and evaluation of a consensus approach. PLoS Comput. Biol. 4(4):e1000048.

William Noble S (2006). What is a support vector machine? Nat. Biotechnol. 24(12):1565-1567.

Yael Altuvia, Hanah Margalit (2004). A structure based approach for prediction of MHC-binding peptides. Elsevier Methods 34:454-459.

## 25

Information fusion and multiple classifiers for haplotype assembly problem from SNP fragments and related genotype

M. Hossein Moeinzadeh[1] and Ehsan Asgarian[2]*

[1]Department of Computer Science, University of Tehran, Iran.
[2]Department of Computer Engineering, Sharif University of Technology, Tehran, Iran.

Most positions of the human genome are typically invariant (99%) and only some positions (1%) are commonly invariant which are associated with complex genetic diseases. Haplotype information has become increasingly important in analyzing fine-scale molecular genetics data, due to the mutated form in human genome. Haplotype assembly is to divide aligned single nucleotide polymorphism (SNP) fragments, which is the most frequent form of difference to address genetic diseases, into two classes, and thus inferring a pair of haplotypes from them. Minimum error correction (MEC) is an important model for this problem but only effective when the error rate of the fragments is low. MEC/GI as an extension to MEC, employs the related genotype information besides the SNP fragments and so results in a more accurate inference. The haplotyping problem, due to its NP-hardness, may have no efficient algorithm for exact solution. In this paper, we focus to design serial and parallel classifiers with two classifiers. Genetic algorithm and K-means were two components of our approaches. This combination helps us to cover the single classifier's weaknesses.

Key words: Multiple classifier systems, parallel classifiers, serial classifiers, haplotype, SNP fragments, genotype information, classification, reconstruction rate.

INTRODUCTION

The availability of complete genome sequence for human beings (Venter, 2001) makes it possible to investigate genetic differences and to associate genetic variations with complex diseases (Zhang, 2006). It is generally accepted that all human share about 99% identity at the deoxyribonucleic acid (DNA) level and only some regions of differences in DNA sequences are responsible for genetic diseases (Terwilliger et al., 1998; Chakravarti, 1998). Single nucleotide polymorphisms

(SNPs), a single DNA base varying from one individual to another, are believed to be the most frequent form responsible for genetic differences (Wang, 2005) and are found approximately every 1000 base pairs in the human genome and turn to be promising tools for doing disease association study. Every nucleotide in an single nucleotide polymorphisms site is called an allele. Most SNPs have two different alleles, known here as 'A' and 'B'. The SNP sequence information on each copy of a pair of chromosomes in a diploid genome is called a haplotype which is a string over {'A', 'B'}. A genotype is the conflated information of a pair of haplotypes on homologous chromosomes. Although haplotypes have more information for disease association than individual SNPs and also more than genotype information, but it is substantially more difficult to determine haplotypes than to determine genotypes or individual single nucleotide polymorphisms through experiments. Hence, computational methods that can reduce the cost of determining haplotypes become attractive alternatives. Hole and error

*Corresponding author. E-mail: asgarian@alum.sharif.edu

Abbreviations: MEC, Minimum error correction; **MEC/GI,** minimum error correction with genotype information; **MCS,** multiple classifier system; **DNA,** deoxyribonucleic acid; **GA,** genetic algorithm; **RR,** reconstruction rate; **SNP,** single nucleotide polymorphism.

consist in SNP fragments.

One question arising from this discussion is how the distribution of holes and error in the input data affects computational complexity. Minimum error correction (MEC), longest haplotype reconstruction (LHR), minimum error correction with genotype information (MEC/GI) and some other models have been discussed for haplotype assembly (Terwilliger, 1998; Chakravarti, 1998; Wang, 2005, 2007; Zhang, 2006, 2007). MEC and also MEC/GI are two standard models for haplotype reconstruction based on SNP fragments and genotype information as an input data to infer the best pair of haplotypes with the minimum error to be corrected. It is proved that MEC is a NP-hard problem (Bonizzoni, 2003; Zhang, 2006), so heuristic methods are used to reduce running time of this problem (Moeinzadeh et al., 2007). This problem was solved by some classification and heuristic methods. Zhang (2007) introduces a classification algorithm based on two distances (Hamming and a proposed distance) to compare SNP fragments together. An algorithm was implemented to solve MEC model (Zhang, 2007). Real and simulation data sets are available as two standard databases. The input in these databases contains an error rate between 10 and 40%. The method by Zhang (2007) is based on K-means algorithm. Although the result and algorithm's running time were acceptable, it is widely believed that K-means does not work well for noisy inputs. Solving MEC and MEC/GI models for haplotype assembly with genetic algorithm (GA) was published by Wang (2005) and Zhang (2006). The results in haplotyping were not only better than K-means but also it takes more execution time. On the other hand, GA has an adaptive behavior in terms of error rate and it approximately guarantees not to get stuck local minima. A variety of approaches that each of them might have its own strengths and weaknesses made us to combine the classifier's results.

We use information fusion techniques to improve our results. These techniques are information processes dealing with the association, correlation, and combination of data and information from single and multiple classifiers or sources to achieve refined estimation of parameters, characteristics, events, and behaviors. This approach is used to improve the result of the mentioned problem.

In this paper, we design serial and parallel classifiers. Utilizing multiple classifiers would help us to increase reconstruction rate (RR), which is described in the following sections, and also using error rate for the first time. In our research, we concentrate on K-means and GA properties and use them together. K.G (K-means.GA), G.K (GA.K-means) as two serial classifiers was implemented. In these two approaches, first classifier's answers and main input are fused to form the second classifier's inputs. We also implement K.G.K and G.K.G to study the results. In parallel classification, result

```
---ABA--AA          Class1
BBBBBB--AA          Class2
B-BBBBB--B          Class2
AABAAAAAAA          Class1
BAA--AAAA-          Class1
BBB--B---A-         Class2
AABAAAAAAA          Class1
BABBBBBBAB          Class2
A---A--A--          Class1
-BB--BBA-B          Class2
AAAAA-A-BA          Class1
```

Figure 1. Classification of the SNP fragments.

combiner, as an information fusion function, was the

Formulation and problem definition

Suppose that there are m SNP fragments from a pair of chromosomes, corresponding to two haplotypes with the length of n, defined $(M = m_{ij})$ as a matrix of SNP fragments, whose every entry m_{ij} has value 'A', 'B' or '-' ('-' is missing or skipped SNP site which is called gap). Each row of the matrix M is one SNP fragment and each column corresponds to one SNP site. The length of SNP fragments including their gaps is the same as its own haplotype. We use partition P (C1, C2), class C1 and class C2, to formulate the problem. P as an exact algorithm or classification method divides SNP fragments into two classes, C1 and C2. The SNP fragments in each class must combine with their own class members to reconstruct the haplotypes. We call this operation voting and define it completely in the following parts (Figure 1). Each genotype is the conflation of two haplotypes, depending on their sites. We define genotype as a string of 'A', 'B' and '-'. 'A' ('B') denotes that both haplotypes are the 'A' ('B') and '-'when they are heterozygous. Reconstruction rate (shortly RR) is a very simple and popular way for comparing the results of designed algorithms in existing databases with each other. RR which is based on Hamming distance is the degree of similarity between the original haplotypes ($h = (h_1, h_2)$) and the reconstructed ones ($h' = (h'_1, h'_2)$). It is defined as:

$$r_{ij} = HD\ (h_i, h'_j), i, j = \{1, 2\}$$

$$RR\ (h, h') = 1 - \frac{\min(\ r_{11} + r_{22}, r_{12} + r_{21})}{2n}$$

And also Hamming distance is based on the distance between two SNP fragments which we call it $d(x, y)$, and which is in turn, defined by the following formula:

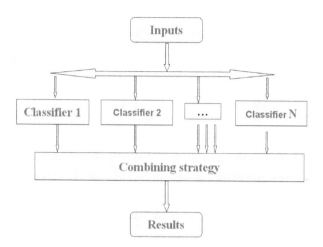

Figure 2. Parallel classifier.

$$HD\ (h_i, h_k) = \sum_{j=1}^{n} d\ (h_{ij}, h_{kj}),$$

$$d\ (m_{ij}, m_{kj}) = \begin{cases} 1 & (m_{ij} \neq m_{kj} \neq -) \\ 0 & otherwise \end{cases}$$

And the usage of a second distance becomes necessary when the hamming distance between one and two other fragments are equal, which is defined as follows:

$$D'_{mm}(m_i, m_k) = \sum_{j=1}^{n} d'(m_{ij}, m_{kj}),$$

$$d'(m_{ij}, m_{kj}) = \begin{cases} -1 & (m_{ij} = m_{kj} \neq -) \\ +1 & (m_{ij} \neq m_{kj} \neq -) \\ 0 & otherwise \end{cases}$$

In this paper, we study MEC (Minimum Error Correction) model. In this model, a matrix of SNP fragments is available as an input. We try to decrease the number of haplotype errors in comparison with corresponding real haplotypes. For doing so, all the aforementioned algorithms in MEC/GI (Minimum error correction with genotype information) model were implemented.

METHODOLOGY

Haplotypes assembly is considered as a multiple classifier system (MCS) which consists of a set of individual classifiers like genetic algorithm (GA) and K-means. For this system, we define a fusion or selection method to combine simple classifiers outputs and make the final decision.

$$MCS = \{W(H), W(E), ..., W(C)\}$$

In this paper, we try to design special composition of classifiers based on our problem models. In the following section, some serial and parallel designs are explained.

Serial classifiers

A serial classifier has two main components; classifiers and information fusion function. In our problem model, information fusion functions are designed based on classifiers properties. In the following section, we describe our serial classifier methods.

K-means – GA

Good initial population can greatly affect the results of genetic algorithm. Our first approach is based on classification SNP fragments by K-means to generate an individual with acceptable fitness. The result of K-means is used for generating initial population for genetic algorithm. The initial population of GA is consisted of K-means answers combined with a predetermined error rate in input and also random individuals to escape from local minima. Genetic algorithm starts to optimize the result of the K-means method. For generating the initial population, we used error information. This combination produces good initial population. The algorithm for MEC (the changes needed for MEC/GI model) is shown in Algorithm 1. The results of this algorithm are discussed in experimental results section.

GA - K-means

For serial MCS information fusion techniques, K-means properties were the center of attention. In haplotype assembly problem, K-means heuristic method needs two centers to start classification procedure. So good initial centers can help the algorithm to converge to better results. In our approach, genetic algorithm was used to find these centers and K-means tries to change the results location towards the real centers. The GA- K-means designed algorithm for MEC model is shown in Figure 2. Here, we designed an algorithm for MEC/GI model with the same fusion function along with some modifications. It was predictable that the result of GA- K-means would be better than the results obtained by applying them individually (Tables 1 and 2).

KGK and GKG

We defined two different information fusion functions in the last two sections (K-means to GA (KG) and GA to K-means (GK). In the same manner, two more algorithms were designed (KGK and GKG) and also their result is discussed in experimental results section (Algorithm 2).

Parallel classifier

Using a single classifier and designing efficient algorithms were not enough to solve MEC and MEC/GI models. The best classifiers are not necessarily the ideal choice in this problem due to noisy and incomplete inputs, so we implement parallel classifier (Figure 3).

K-means and GA

A parallel classifier is proposed which combines K-means and GA. Information fusion combiner function decides according to the majority of classifier decisions. Information fusion function was designed based on ignoring noisy input data. Here is the function:

$$Fragment_i = \begin{cases} 1^{st}\ Class & 1^{st}\ Classifier = 2^{nd}\ Classifier = 1^{st}\ Class \\ 2^{nd}\ Class & 1^{st}\ Classifier = 2^{nd}\ Classifier = 2^{nd}\ Class \\ omitted & otherwise \end{cases}$$

$$i = 1...m$$

Table 1. The comparison of reconstruction rate of multiple classifiers algorithms for MEC model.

		Daly database –MEC model						
Gap rate	Error rate	Single classifier		Serial classifier			Parallel classifier	
		K-Means(k)	G.A. (G)	K.G	G.K	G.K.G	K.G.K	G.K.G and K.G.K
0.25	0.1	0.999	1.000	1.000	0.999	1.000	0.999	0.997
	0.2	0.993	0.993	0.993	0.994	0.994	0.994	0.989
	0.3	0.931	0.933	0.933	0.920	0.929	0.932	0.875
	0.4	0.716	0.718	0.718	0.712	0.713	0.717	0.696
0.5	0.1	0.998	0.998	0.998	0.997	0.997	0.998	0.995
	0.2	0.972	0.973	0.973	0.994	0.973	0.975	0.972
	0.3	0.861	0.869	0.869	0.867	0.868	0.869	0.819
	0.4	0.691	0.694	0.694	0.689	0.690	0.690	0.677
0.75	0.1	0.977	0.977	0.977	0.978	0.976	0.978	0.978
	0.2	0.896	0.898	0.898	0.889	0.892	0.901	0.897
	0.3	0.772	0.774	0.774	0.770	0.765	0.768	0.762
	0.4	0.663	0.665	0.665	0.660	0.653	0.661	0.678

Table 2. The comparison of reconstruction rate of multiple classifiers algorithms for MEC/GI model.

		Daly database –MEC model						
Gap rate	Error rate	Single classifier		Serial classifier			Parallel classifier	
		K-Means(k)	G.A. (G)	K.G	G.K	G.K.G	K.G.K	G.K.G and K.G.K
0.25	0.1	1.000	1.000	1.000	1.000	1.000	1.000	0.924
	0.2	0.999	0.999	0.999	1.000	1.000	1.000	0.928
	0.3	0.993	0.974	0.993	0.994	0.994	0.992	0.925
	0.4	0.904	0.897	0.908	0.896	0.903	0.896	0.894
0.5	0.1	1.000	0.999	1.000	1.000	1.000	1.000	0.934
	0.2	0.999	0.993	0.999	0.999	1.000	0.999	0.926
	0.3	0.972	0.956	0.977	0.975	0.978	0.977	0.926
	0.4	0.881	0.882	0.884	0.881	0.882	0.884	0.876
0.75	0.1	0.998	0.992	0.998	0.998	0.998	0. 997	0.925
	0.2	0.977	0.973	0.981	0.978	0.983	0.980	0.928
	0.3	0.914	0.901	0.925	0.907	0.921	0.915	0.898
	0.4	0.872	0.869	0.871	0.868	0.873	0.870	0.875

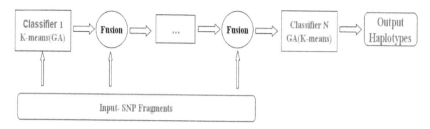

Figure 3. Serial classifier.

Table 3. Information fusion for parallel classifier.

SNP F.	1st classifier	2nd classifier	Parallel fusion function
1	Class 1	Class 1	Class 1
2	Class 1	Class 2	Eliminated
3	Class 2	Class 2	Class 2
-	-	-	-
-	-	-	-
-	-	-	-
n	Class 2	Class 1	Eliminated

For example, as can be seen in Table 3, some haplotypes (which might be useful for reconstruction of final haplotypes) are eliminated. The explanation behind this is to eliminate those noisy haplotypes, on which the two classifiers decisions do not match. So Algorithm 3 was designed. The results of this multiple parallel classifier were worse than serial ones due to probable elimination of some useful haplotypes. To modify the fusion function to avoid elimination of haplotypes, we must increase the number of different classifiers. It is predictable that if other classifiers be added to our MCS, a new fusion function be designed with three or more classifiers, we can improve the results. By doing this, a more number of haplotypes are kept and this can lead us to better results.

EXPERIMENTAL RESULTS

There are real biological datasets and also simulation datasets available for haplotyping problem like ACE, DALY, SIM0 and SIM50. We chose DALY dataset which includes 4 different subsets. Each subset has a different error rate (10, 20, 30 and 40%) and includes 384 different test cases. The results of the experiments on DALY set for MEC model, is shown in Table 1. In Figures 4a, b and c, the comparison of result methodology is focused in each model. Also we implemented all algorithms for MEC/GI model and the results are shown in Table 2 and methods are compared in Figure 4d, e and f.

Conclusion

In this paper, we focus on MCS (multiple classifier system)

to solve MEC and MEC/GI model. The components which were used in our research were genetic and K-means algorithms. First, for MEC model, we designed four serial classifiers (GK, KG, KGK and GKG). Then one parallel classifier which is a combination of GA and K-means is designed. The information fusion function proposed for our MCS is described. Then all of the aforementioned methods are implemented and tested on MEC/GI model problem which are intended to infer haplotypes with high accuracy by employing genotype information. We compare the results of all methods in terms of RR. In both MEC and MEC/GI models, KGK and GK outperform the other approaches due to the fact that GA finds near optimal solutions in search space and K-means acts as a local heuristic classifier to find the real answer.

REFERENCES

Venter JC, Adams MD, Myers EW, Li PW, Mural RJ, Sutton GG, Smith HO, Yandell M, Evans CA, Holt RA, Gocayne JD, Amanatides P, Ballew RM, Huson DH, Wortman JR, Zhang Q, Kodira CD, Zheng XH, Chen L, Skupski M, Subramanian G, Thomas PD, Zhang J, Gabor Miklos GL, Nelson C, Broder S, Clark AG, Nadeau J, McKusick VA, Zinder N, Levine AJ, Roberts RJ, Simon M, Slayman C, Hunkapiller M, Bolanos R, Delcher A, Dew I, Fasulo D, Flanigan M, Florea L, Halpern A, Hannenhalli S, Kravitz S, Levy S, Mobarry C, Reinert K, Remington K, Abu-Threideh J, Beasley E, Biddick K, Bonazzi V, Brandon R, Cargill M, Chandramouliswaran I, Charlab R, Chaturvedi K, Deng Z, Di Francesco V, Dunn P, Eilbeck K, Evangelista C, Gabrielian AE, Gan W, Ge W, Gong F, Gu Z, Guan P, Heiman TJ, Higgins ME, Ji RR, Ke Z, Ketchum KA, Lai Z, Lei Y, Li Z, Li J, Liang Y, Lin X, Lu F, Merkulov GV, Milshina N, Moore HM, Naik AK, Narayan VA, Neelam B, Nusskern D, Rusch DB, Salzberg S, Shao W, Shue B, Sun J, Wang Z, Wang A, Wang X,

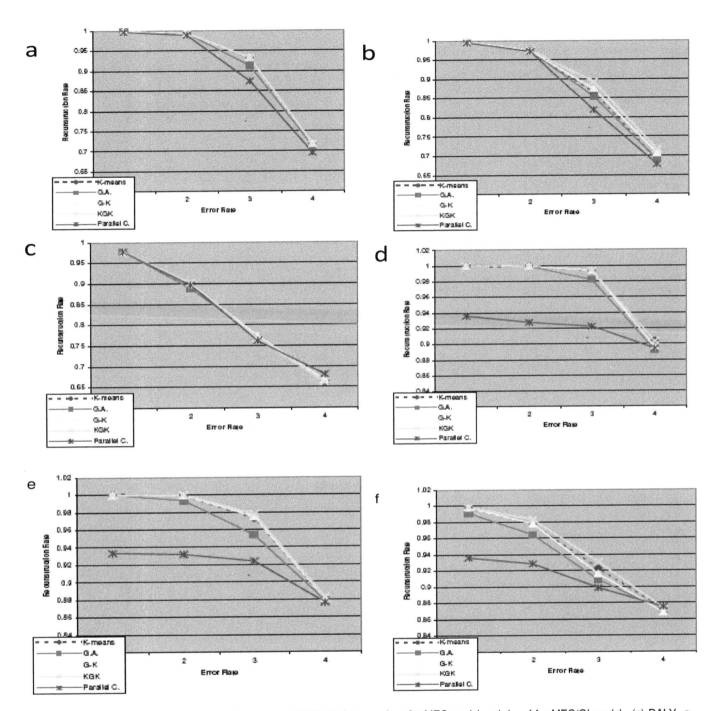

Figure 4. Comparison results of the algorithms using DALY database. a, b, c for MEC model and d, c, f for MEC/GI model . (a) DALY, $g = 0.25$; (b) DALY, $g = 0.5$; (c) DALY, $g = 0.75$; (d) DALY, $g = 0.25$; (e) DALY, $g = 0.5$; (f) DALY, $g = 0.75$.

Wang J, Wei M, Wides R, Xiao C, Yan C, Yao A, Ye J, Zhan M, Zhang W, Zhang H, Zhao Q, Zheng L, Zhong F, Zhong W, Zhu S, Zhao S, Gilbert D, Baumhueter S, Spier G, Carter C, Cravchik A, Woodage T, Ali F, An H, Awe A, Baldwin D, Baden H, Barnstead M, Barrow I, Beeson K, Busam D, Carver A, Center A, Cheng ML, Curry L, Danaher S, Davenport L, Desilets R, Dietz S, Dodson K, Doup L, Ferriera S, Garg N, Glueeksmann A, Hart B, Haynes J, Haynes C, Heiner C, Hladun S, Hostin D, Houck J, Howland T, Ibegwam C, Johnson J, Kalush F, Kline L, Koduru S, Love A, Mann F, May D, McCawley S, McIntosh T, McMullen I, Moy M, Moy L, Murphy B, Nelson K, Pfannkoch C, Pratts E, Puri V, Qureshi H, Reardon M, Rodriguez R, Rogers YH, Romblad D, Ruhfel B, Scott R, Sitter C, Smallwood M, Stewart E, Strong R, Suh E, Thomas R, Tint NN, Tse S, Vech C, Wang G, Wetter J, Williams S, Williams M, Windsor S, Winn-Deen E, Wolfe K, Zaveri J, Zaveri K, Abril JF, Guigó R, Campbell MJ, Sjolander KV, Karlak B, Kejariwal A, Mi H, Lazareva B, Hatton T, Narechania A, Diemer K, Muruganujan A, Guo N, Sato S, Bafna V, Istrail S, Lippert R, Schwartz R, Walenz B, Yooseph S, Allen D, Basu A, Baxendale J, Blick L, Caminha M, Carnes-Stine J, Caulk P, Chiang YH, Coyne M, Dahlke C, Mays A, Dombroski M, Donnelly M, Ely D, Esparham S, Fosler C, Gire H, Glanowski S, Glasser K, Glodek A, Gorokhov M, Graham K, Gropman B, Harris M, Heil J, Henderson S, Hoover J, Jennings D,

Jordan C, Jordan J, Kasha J, Kagan L, Kraft C, Levitsky A, Lewis M, Liu X, Lopez J, Ma D, Majoros W, McDaniel J, Murphy S, Newman M, Nguyen T, Nguyen N, Nodell M, Pan S, Peck J, Peterson M, Rowe W, Sanders R, Scott J, Simpson M, Smith T, Sprague A, Stockwell T, Turner R, Venter E, Wang M, Wen M, Wu D, Wu M, Xia A, Zandieh A, Zhu X (2001). The sequence of the human genome. Sci., 291(5507):1304–1351.

Terwilliger J, Weiss K (1998). Linkage disequilibrium mapping of complex disease: Fantasy and reality? Curr. Opin. Biotechnol., pp. 579–594.

Chakravarti A (1998). It's raining, hallelujah? Nat. Genet., 19: 216–217.

Wang R, Wu L, Li Z, Zhang X (2005). Haplotype reconstruction from SNP fragments by Minimum Error Correction. Bioinformatics, 21(10):2456–2462.

Zhang X, Wang R, Wu L, Zhang W (2006). Minimum conflict individual Haplotyping from SNP fragments and related Genotype. Bioinformatics, pp. 271-280.

Zhang X, Wang R, Wu L, Zhang W (2007). A clustering algorithm based on two distance functions for MEC model. Computational Bio. Chem., 148-150.

Moeinzadeh MH, Asgarian E, Mohammadzadeh J, Ghazinezhad A, Najafi-A A (2007). Three Heuristic Clustering Methods for Haplotype Reconstruction Problem with Genotype Information. The 4th IEEE

International Conference on Innovations in Information Technology, pp. 404-406.

Bonizzoni P, Vedova GD, Dondi R, Li J (2003). The Haplotyping Problem: A review of Computational Models and Solutions. J. Comp. Sci. Tech., 18(6): 675-688.

Panconesi and Sozio M (2004). Fast Hare: A Fast Heuristic for Single Individual SNP Haplotype Reconstruction. Proceedings of 4th Workshop on Algorithms in Bioinformatics (WABI), LNCS Springer-Verlag, pp. 266-277.

Greenberg HJ, Hart EW, Lancia G (2004). Opportunities for Combinatorial Optimization in Computational Biology. INFORMS J. Comp., 16(3): 211-231.

Rieder M, Taylor S, Clark A, Nickerson D (1999). Sequence variation n the human angiotensin converting enzyme. Nat. Genet., 22:59–62.

Wang Y, Feng E, Wang R, Zhang D (2007). The haplotype assembly model with genotype information and iterative local-exhaustive search algorithm. Comput. Bio. Chem., 31: 288–293.

Algorithm 1. Pseudo code serial KG.

Algorithm	Series k –means-GA for MEC (MEC/GI) with gap
Input	SNP fragments (Genotype)
Output	Two haplotypes
Step0	Initialize parameters
Step 1	Executing K –means for MEC (MEC/GI) to find two haplotypes as the class centre (c_1 and c_2).
Step2	Generating initial population for GA using k- means decision, making error them and random generation
Step3	Executing GA to find the two classes (c_1 and c_2).
Step4	Obtain two haplotypes from GA classes.

Algorithm 2. Pseudo code serial GK.

Alogorithm	Series GA k –means- for MEC (MEC/GI) with gap
Input	SNP fragments (Genotype)
Output	Two haplotypes
Step 0	Initialize parameters
Step 1	Executing GA for MEC (MEC/GI)to find the clusters (c_1 and c_2).
Step 2	Obtain to centers from the classes (c_1 and c_2).
Step 3	Set k-means intials centers (c_1 and c_2).
Step 4	Executing k- means for MEC (MEC/GI) to find two haplotypes as its centers

Algorithm 3. Pseudo code parallel classifier.

Algorithm	Series k –means-GA for MEC (MEC/GI) with gap
Input	SNP fragments (Genotype
Output	Two haplotypes
Step 0	Initialize parameters
Parallel steps	
Step 1	Executing GA for MEC (MEC/GI)to find the two classes (c1 and c2).
Step 1	Executing k-means for MEC (MEC/GI) to find the clusters fragments
Step 2	Voting on classifiers decision to eliminate noisy fragments
Step 3	Obtain two haplotypes from new classification

## 26

Toxicogenomics

S. Amala

Department of Biotechnology and Bioinformatics, Dhanalakshmi Srinivasan, College of Arts and Science for Women, Perambalur-621212, Tamil Nadu, India. E-mail:amala.santhanam@gmail.com.

The field of toxicology is defined as the study of stressors and their adverse effects. One discipline should deals with hazard identification, mechanistic toxicology, and risk assessment. Thus emerge a new field called toxicogenomics. Toxicogenomics is a rapidly developing discipline that promises to aid scientists in understanding the molecular and cellular effects of chemicals in biological systems. This is a comparatively new field of biological inquiry now providing insights into the toxic effects of chemicals on biological systems and helping investigators to predict risks associated with exposure to these agents. This field encompasses global assessment of biological effects using technologies such as DNA micro arrays or high throuput NMR and protein expression analysis.

Key words: Genomics, toxicogenomics, toxicology.

INTRODUCTION

The rapid evolution of genome-based technologies has greatly accelerated the application of gene expression profiling in toxicology studies. These technological advances have led to the development of the field of toxicogenomics, which proposes to apply mRNA expression technologies to study effects of hazards in biological sys-tems. Application of genomics to toxicology, toxicogeno-mics, yield a number of substantial dividends, including assisting predevelopment toxicology by facilitating more rapid screens for compound toxicity, allowing compound selection decisions to be based on safety as well as efficacy, the provision of new research leads; a more detailed appreciation of molecular mechanisms of toxicity, and an enhanced ability to extrapolate accurately between experimental animals and humans in the context of risk assessment.

Toxicogenomics combines traditional toxicology using appropriate pharmacological and toxicological models with global "omics" technologies to provide a comprehensive view of the functioning of the genetic and biochemical machinery in organisms under stress. Applications of these technologies help in predicting the potential toxicity of a drug or chemical be-fore functional damages are recognized, in classification of toxicants, and in screening human susceptibility to diseases, drugs or environmental hazards.

WHAT IS TOXICOGENOMICS?

Toxicogenomics is a field of science that deals with the collection, interpretation, and storage of information about gene and protein activity within particular cell or tissue of an organism in response to toxic substances. Toxicogenomics combines toxicology with genomics or other high throughput molecular profiling technologies such as transcriptomics, proteomics and metabolomics. Toxicogenomics endeavors to elucidate molecular mechanisms evolved in the expression of toxicity, and to derive molecular expression patterns that predict toxicity or the genetic susceptibility to it. Toxicogenomics is a rapidly developing discipline that promises to aid scientists in understanding the molecular and cellular effects of chemicals in biological systems. This field encompasses global assessment of biological effects using technologies such as DNA micro arrays or high throuput NMR and protein expression analysis.

Toxicogenomics represents the merging of toxicology with technologies that have been developed, together with bioinformatics, to identify and quantify global gene expression changes. It represents a new paradigm in drug development and risk assessment, which promises to generate a wealth of information towards an increased understanding of the molecular mechanisms that lead to drug toxicity and efficacy, and of DNA polymorphisms responsible for individual susceptibility to toxicity. Gene expression profiling, through the use of DNA micro array and proteomic technologies will aid in establishing links between expression profiles, mode of action and traditional toxic endpoints. Such patterns of gene expression, or 'molecular fingerprints' could be used as diagnostic or predictive markers of exposure that is characteristic of a specific mechanism of induction of that toxic or efficacious effect. It is anticipated that toxicogenomics will be increasingly integrated into all phases of the drug development process particularly in mechanistic and predictive toxicology, and biomarker discovery.

DEFINITION OF TOXICOGENOMICS

United States environmental protection agency stating that "the term "genomics" encompasses a broader scope of scientific inquiry and associated technologies than when genomics was initially considered. A genome is the sum total of all an individual organism's genes. Thus, genomics is the study of all the genes of a cell, or tissue, at the DNA (genotype), mRNA (transcriptome), or protein (proteome) levels. Genomics methodologies are expected to provide valuable insights for evaluating how environmental stressors affect cellular/tissue function and how changes in gene expression may relate to adverse effects. However, the relationships between changes in gene expression and adverse effects are unclear at this time and may likely be difficult to elucidate.

In pharmaceutical research, toxicogenomics is more narrowly defined as the study of the structure and function of the genome as it responds to adverse xenobiotic exposure. It is the toxicological sub discipline of pharmacogenomics, which is broadly defined as the study of inter-individual variations in whole-genome or candidate gene single-nucleotide polymorphism maps, haplotype markers, and alterations in gene expression that might correlate with drug responses.

TECHNOLOGIES IN TOXICOGENOMICS

Gene expression profiling

Gene expression changes are associated with signal pathway. Activation can provide compound-specific information on the pharmacological or toxicological effects of a chemical. An advantage of this traditional molecular technique is that it definitively shows the expression level of all transcripts for a particular gene.

Alternate technologies, including DNA microarrays, can measure the expression of tens of thousands of genes in an equivalent amount of time.

There are two basic types of micro arrays used in gene expression analyses:

Oligonucleotide-based arrays and cDNA arrays

For example, one can compare tissue extracted from toxicant treated organism versus that of vehicle exposed animals. In addition, other scenarios may include the analysis of healthy versus diseased tissue or susceptible versus resistant tissue. One can combine micro arrays with quantitative polymerase chain reaction (QPCR) or Taqman and other technologies in development to monitor the expression of hundreds of genes in a high throughput fashion.

Protein expression

Gene expression alone is not adequate to serve the understanding of toxicant action and the disease outcomes they induce. Abnormalities in protein production or function are expected in response to toxicant exposure and the onset of disease states. To understand the complete mechanism of toxicant action, it is necessary to identify the protein alterations associated with that exposure and to understand how these changes affect protein/cellular function. Unlike classical genomic approaches that discover genes related to toxicant induced disease, proteomics can aid to characterize the disease process directly by capturing proteins that participate in the disease. The lack of a direct functional correlation between gene transcripts and their corresponding proteins necessitates the use of proteomics as a tool in toxicology. Proteomics, under the umbrella of toxicogenomics, involves the comprehensive functional annotation and validation of proteins in response to toxicant exposure. Understanding the functional characteristics of proteins and their activity requires a determination of cellular localization and quantization, tissue distribution, post-translational modification state, domain modules and their effect on protein interactions, protein complexes, ligand binding sites and structural representation. Currently, the most commonly used technologies for proteomics research are 2-dimensional (2D) gel electrophoresis for protein separation followed by mass spectrometry analysis of proteins of interest. Matrix-assisted laser desorption mass spectrometry (MALDI-MS) has become a widely used method for determination of biomolecules including peptides.

Metabolite analysis by NMR

Genomic and proteomic methods do not offer the information needed to gain understanding of the resulting output function in a living system. Neither approach addresses the dynamic metabolic status of the whole animal. The metabonomic approach is based on the premise that toxicant-induced pathological or physiological alterations result in changes in relative concentrations of endogenous biochemical. Metabolites in body fluids such as urine, blood, or cerebrospinal fluid (CSF), are in dynamic equilibrium with those inside cells and tissues, thus toxicant-induced cellular abnormalities in tissues should be reflected in altered biofluid compositions.

TOXICOGENOMIC COMPONENTS

Comparative/predictive toxicogenomics

Comparative genomic, proteomic, or metabonomic studies measure the number and types of genes, protein, and metabolites, respectively, that is present in normal and toxicant-exposed cells, tissues, or biofluids. This approach is useful in defining the composition of the assayed samples in terms of genetic, proteomic or metabolic variables. Thus a biological sample derived from toxicant, or sham treated animals can be regarded as an n-dimensional vector in gene expression space with genes as variables along each dimension.

The possibility that a specific group or class of compounds (grouped by toxic endpoint, mechanism, structure, target organ etc.) may induce signature patterns of gene expression changes is the basis for the application of toxicogenomics to predictive toxicology. The use of these technologies to analyze genome-wide changes in mRNA expression following treatment of *in vitro* systems with known reference toxicants may permit the identification of diagnostic gene expression patterns. Pattern recognition allows the design and construction of mini-arrays, customized to detect specific toxicity endpoints or pathways.

Functional toxicogenomics

Functional toxicogenomics is the study of genes and proteins biological activities in the context of compound effects on an organism. Gene and protein expression profiles are analyzed for information that might provide insight into specific mechanistic pathways. Mechanistic inference is complex when the sequence of events following toxicant exposure is viewed in both dose and time space. Gene and protein expression patterns can indeed be highly dependent on the toxicant concentrations furnished at the assessed tissue and the time of exposure to the agent. Expression patterns are only a snapshot in time and dose space. Thus, a comprehensive understanding of potential mechanisms of action of a compound requires establishing patterns at various combinations of time and dose. Studies that target temporal expression of specific genes and protein in response to toxicant exposure will lead to a better under-standing of the sequence of events in complex regulatory networks. An area of study which is of great interest to toxicologists is the mechanistic understanding of toxicant induced pathological endpoints. The premise that perturbations in gene, protein, or metabolite levels are reflective of adverse

phenotypic effects of toxicants offers an opportunity to phenotypically anchor these perturbations.

This is quite challenging due to the fact that phenotypic effects often vary in the time-dose space of the studied agent and may have regional variations in the tissue. Furthermore, very few compounds exist that result in only one phenotypic alteration at a given coordinate in dose and time. Thus, objective assignment of measured variables to multiple phenotypic events is not possible under these circumstances.

APPLICATIONS OF TOXICOGENOMICS

Toxicogenomics in drug safety

New drugs are screened for adverse reactions using a laborious, costly process and still some promising therapeutics is withdrawn from the marketplace because of unforeseen human toxicity. Novel higher throughput methods in toxicology need to be developed. These new approaches should provide more insight into potential human toxicity than current methods. Toxicogenomics, the examination of changes in gene expression following exposure to a toxicant, offers the potential to identify a human toxicant earlier in drug development and to detect human-specific toxicants that cause no adverse reaction in rats.

To understand the mechanisms of drug-induced hepatotoxicity during drug discovery and development

Hepatotoxicity is a common cause of failure in drug discovery and development and is also frequently the source of adverse drug reactions. Therefore, a better prediction, characterization and understanding of drug-induced hepatotoxicity could result in safer drugs and a more efficient drug discovery and development process. Toxicogenomics represents an attractive approach to predict toxicity and to gain a mechanistic understanding of toxic changes.

Ecotoxicogenomics

Rapid progress in the field of genomics (the study of how an individual's entire genetic make-up, the genome, translates into biological functions) is beginning to provide tools that may assist our understanding of how chemicals can impact on human and ecosystem health. Given the parallel implications for ecological (environmental) risk assessment, a term 'ecotoxicoge-nomics' is there to describe the integration of genomics (transcriptomics, proteomics and metabolomics) into ecotoxicology. Ecotoxicogenomics is defined as the study of gene and protein expression in non-target organisms that is important in responses to environmental toxicant exposures.

The potential of ecotoxicogenomic tools in ecological risk assessment seems great. Many phenomenological approaches that are useful for identifying chemicals of potential concern provide little understanding of the mechanism of chemical toxicity. Without this understanding, it will be difficult to address some of the key challenges that currently face aquatic ecotoxicology. Ecotoxicogenomic tools may provide us with a better mechanistic understanding of aquatic ecotoxico-logy (Snape et al., 2004).

In endocrine disruption Toxicogenomics can be expected to be a useful method for detecting the carcinogenic potential of endocrine active substances (EASs) in the short term with the generation of understanding of mode-of-action and mechanisms when a reliable database with information about proteomics and informatics is established. At present, there are no concrete epidemiological data supporting any exogenous EAS contribution to hormone-related organ carcinogenesis in humans. However, with the establishment of appropriate animal models and analysis of genomic-scale gene expression, risk identification and evaluation should be facilitated within a relatively short period, and this approach eventually promises to contribute a great deal of risk management regarding EASs (Tomoyuki and Makoto, 2003).

In assessment of immunotoxicity

Microarray analysis is used for simultaneous measurement of expression of thousands of genes in a given sample and as such extends and deepens our understanding of biological processes. Application of the technique in toxicology is referred to as toxicogenomics. The assessment of immunotoxicity by gene expression profiling show that micro array analysis is able to detect known and novel effects of a wide range of immunomodulating agents. Besides the elucidation of mechanisms of action, toxicogenomics is also applied to predict consequences of exposing biological systems to toxic agents. Successful attempts to classify compounds using signature gene expression profiles have been reported. The application of toxicogenomics in evaluation of immunotoxicity contributes to the understanding of immunotoxic processes and the development of in vitro screening assays, though, and is therefore expected to be of value for mechanistic insight into immunotoxicity and hazard identification of existing and novel compounds (Baken et al., 2007).

TOXICOGENOMICS DATABASE AND RESOURCES

Toxicogenomics studies are generally built on standard toxicology studies generating biological end point data, and as such, one goal of toxicogenomics is to detect relationships between changes in gene expression and in

those biological parameters. These challenges are best addressed through data collection into a well-designed toxicogenomics database (Mattes et al., 2004).

The chemical effects in biological systems (CEBS) knowledge base

The CEBS knowledge base (http://www.niehs.nih.gov/nct/cebs.htm) is under development by the NIEHS NCT as a public toxicogenomics information resource combining data sets from tran-scri-ptomics, proteomics, metabonomics, and conventional toxicology with pathway and network information relevant to environmental toxicology and human disease. The overall goal of CEBS is to support hypothesis-driven and discovery research in environmental toxicology and the research needs of risk assessment. Specific objectives are a) to compare toxicogenomic effects of chemicals/stressors across species yielding signatures of altered molecular expression; b) to phenotypically anchor these changes with conventional toxicology data classifying biological effects as well as disease phenotypes; and c) to delineate global changes as adaptive, pharmacologic, or toxic outcomes defining early biomarkers, the sequence of key events, and mechanisms of toxicant action. CEBS is designed to meet the information needs of systems toxicology and involves study of chemical or stressor perturbations, monitoring changes in molecular expression, and iteratively integrating biological response data to describe the functioning organism.

Comparative toxicogenomics database (CTD)

The NIEHS DERT supports an international public database devoted primarily to comparative toxicogenomics in aquatic and mammalian species, the CTD (http://www.mdibl.org/). The Mount Desert Island Biological Laboratory is developing CTD as a community-supported genomic resource devoted to genes of human toxicological significance. CTD will be the first publicly available database to a) provide annotated associations between genes, references, and toxic agents; b) include nucleotide and protein sequences from diverse species with a focus on aquatic and mammalian organisms; c) offer a range of analytical tools for customized comparative studies; and d) provide information to investigators on available molecular reagents. The primary goals of CTD are to advance the understanding of the effects of environmental chemicals on human health.

DbZach

The Molecular and Genomic Toxicology Laboratory, Michigan State University (East Lansing, MI) has developed the dbZach System (http://dbzach.fst.msu.edu/), a multifacteted toxicogenomics bioinformatics infrastructure. The goal of the dbZach System is to provide a) facilities for the modeling of toxicogenomics data; b) a centralized source of biological knowledge to facilitate data mining and allow full knowledge-based understanding of the toxicological mechanisms; and c) an environment for bioinformatics algorithmic and analysis tools development. DbZach, designed in a modular structure to handle multispecies array-based toxicogen-omics information, is the core database implemented in Oracle.

Array track

The NCTR (http://www.fda.gov/nctr/science/centers/ toxicoinformatics/tools.htm) is developing TIS to integrate genomics, proteomics, and metabonomics data with conventional *in vivo* and *in vitro* toxicology data. TIS is designed to meet the challenge of data management, analysis, and inter-pretation through the integration of toxicogenomics data, gene function, and pathways to enable hypothesis generation.

EDGE

The EDGE database (http://genome.oncology.wisc.edu/edge2/edge.php) was developed at the McArdle Laboratory for Cancer Research, University of Wisconsin (Madison, WI) as a resource for toxicology-related gene expression information. It is based on experiments conducted using custom cDNA micro arrays that include unique ESTs identified as regulated under conditions of toxicity.

Public toxicogenomics projects

- Chemical Effects in Biological Systems (CEBS) - Project hosted by the National Institute of Environmental Health Sciences (NIEHS) is building a knowledgebase of toxicology studies including study design, clinical pathology, and histopathology and toxicogenomics data.
- InnoMed PredTox for assessing the value of combining results from omics technologies together with the results from more conventional toxicology methods in more informed decision making in preclinical safety evaluation.

- Predictive Safety Testing Consortium aimed at identifying and clinically qualifying safety biomarkers for regulatory use as part of the FDA's Critical Path Initiative
- ToxCast program for Predicting Hazard, Characterizing Toxicity Pathways, and Prioritizing the Toxicity Testing of Environmental Chemicals at the United States Environmental Protection Agency

Conclusion

Toxicogenomics is an information- and informatics-intensive field. An important aspect of toxicogenomics research is the development and application of bioinformatics tools and databases in order to facilitate the analysis, mining, visualizing and sharing of the vast amount of biological information being generated in this field. This rapidly growing research area will have a large impact on many other scientific and medical disciplines, including systems biology, as researchers strive to generate complete descriptions of how components of biological systems work together and across organisms to respond to specific stresses, drugs, or toxicants. By establishing associations between the unique genetic makeup of individuals and their responsiveness to specific drugs, we expect to discover better therapies and improve prospects for providing individuals with personalized medicine. And by combining this knowledge with technology for high-throughput screening of candidate drugs early on, we also expect to streamline and enhance the process of drug discovery

REFERENCES

Baken KA, Vandebriel RJ, Pennings JL, Kleinjans JC, van Loveren H (2007). Toxicogenomics in the assessment of immunotoxicity Methods. 41:132-141.

Snape JR, Maund SJ, Pickford DB, Hutchinson TH, (2004) Ecotoxicogenomics: the challenge of integrating genomics into aquatic and terrestrial ecotoxicology. Aquat. Toxicol., 67 :143-54.

Tomoyuki S, Akoto A (2003). Application of toxicogenomics to the endocrine disruption issue *IUPAC*, Pure and Applied Chemistry 75: 2419–2422

Zhou T, Chou J, Watkins PB, Kaufmann WK (2009), Toxicogenomics: transcription profiling for toxicology assessment EXS. 99: 325-66

## 27

MYCOsoft: A mycological database

Ajit Kumar Saxena[1]*, Jyoti Gupta[1], S. Pandey[1], A. N. Gangopadhyay[2] and L. K. Pandey[3]

[1]Human Molecular Cytogenetic Laboratory, Centre of Experimental Medicine and Surgery,
Banaras Hindu University, Varanasi-221005, India.
[2]Department of Obstetrics and Gynecology, Institute of Medical Sciences, Banaras Hindu University,
Varanasi-221005, India.
[3]Department of Pediatric Surgery, Institute of Medical Sciences, Banaras Hindu University, Varanasi-221005, India.

The realization regarding the significance of microorganisms is increasing with the passage of time. In today's scenario of global climate change and increasing threats to biodiversity, the wheel of advanced biotechnologies is revolving around microbes to restore the ecological balance lost in the past few decades. In Pakistan, however, we lack sufficiently reliable biological data to start with and our knowledge of functional importance of the indigenous microbiota is highly fragmentary. Cataloging and preserving of our rich flora is therefore of extreme importance for regional and national resource management, bioprospecting and fundamental scientific research. Some institutes have their own collection but status of preservation is not satisfactory. The present project had helped to initiate the task to develop computerized data software for an easy access to the cumbersome process of identification. The software entitled "MYCOsoft" would be available in the market as well as from FCBP on request.

Key words: MYCOsoft, microbial diversity, biodiversity conservation, microbial germplasm.

INTRODUCTION

The importance of microorganisms in human affairs is well known. All the world's civilizations have used products derived from microorganisms; and human beings have been making microorganisms work for them for a very long time even before knowing that they exist. For example, Egyptians were the first to use yeast to produce leaven bread about 6000 years ago and the Chinese used moldy soybean curd as an antibiotic in 500 B.C. So, the application of microorganisms and their use in service of man are not new. When scientific explanations for these simple processes began to be established, culture collections became the basis of great industries and modern techniques have given us new and far-ranging powers over microorganisms.

The conservation of all kind of living organisms including the microbial gene pool, with the aim of improving human environment and welfare through prudent utilization of the full potentials of living resources,

has been a subject of concern for United Nations Environment Program (UNEP) for quite some time.

In fact, modern biotechnology is enabling scientists to change and manipulate microorganisms in ways that seemed the stuff of science fiction just a few years ago. The developers of these new technologies are eager to see products that kill pests, clean up oil spills and toxic chemicals, fertilize crops, improve human and animal health, and much more. Achieving such a potential will depend on reliable culture collections and effective infrastructure for exploiting full potential of microorganisms. The success and potential of biotechnology relies on the diversity of microorganism and the biodiversity of the molecules they produce as a result of primary and secondary metabolism and on the conservation of genetic resources they provide. However, more than 30 years after Stockholm conference on human environment, we can say that the world community has been concerned for some time about the conservation of diversity in higher plants and vertebrates. Equal attention has not been given to microorganisms irrespective of their importance. There is a need to

*Corresponding author. E-mail: draksaxena1@rediffmail.com.

persuade policy-makers to be more concerned than they currently are about the conservation of diversity in microorganism.

There is a wide variation in the estimates of the number of species in the world. This is due to the lack of sufficiently reliable biological data and the fact that our knowledge of biology of most species is virtually non-existent and our knowledge of knowledge of their functional importance of remains fragmentary. This is compounded by the fact that increasing levels of complexity and new habitats are discovered progressively. We cannot measure satisfactorily the world's microbial diversity and our estimates of the loss of microbial biodiversity are therefore conjectural. In the case of the fungal gene pool, the number of species of fungi currently maintained in culture collection throughout the world represents about 17% of the 80,000 accepted species of fungi, which itself is far short of the total number of fungal species that has long been quoted as 250,000 but is now conservatively estimated at 1.5 million. The same holds true for other groups (Hawksworth, 1995).

Completing the inventory of the world's biodata for microorganisms will clearly be a major task. Culture collections, their associated laboratories and biosystematists have a crucial role in efforts to respond to this problem. Biosystematics has declined; thus, there is a need to emphasize the contributions of taxonomy in successful applications of microorganisms to agriculture, medicine, and industry, in goods production and resource conservation. There is a need to establish internationally agreed priorities, develop identification services and training courses in taxonomy of fungi.

The present effort has therefore been made to convert the data regarding the microbes in to a bioinformatics software by the name of "MYCOsoft". This software would be available to the scientist and researchers enabling them to identify fungi independently. "MYCOsoft" would shorten the lengthy procedure of identification bringing the whole procedure with the reach of just one click without opening massive compendia and identification manuals.

LITERATURE REVIEW

There is an array of microorganisms like algae, bacteria, fungi, protists, and viruses, not normally visible to the naked eye, but are essential components of biological diversity, without which there can be no sustainable ecosystem (Hawksworth, 1991; Hawksworth, 1992; Hawksworth and Colwell 1992; Sly, 1994; Staley et al., 1997). 50% of the living biomass on the earth is microbial consortia and microorganisms provide a major source of genetic information for molecular biology and biotechnology (Bull et al., 1992; Nisbet, 1992). Under accelerating pressures of climate change and human

perturbations, the natural habitats that harbor these undiscovered microorganisms are disappearing rapidly.

Destruction of tropical forests is estimated at between 16.4×10^6 and 20.4×10^6 hectares per year. Only a small percentage of the Earth's temperate forests remain. The amount and quality of the world's natural habitat are declining, and only the deepest parts of the ocean appear to have maintained some degree of pristine quality. Microorganisms, too, are disappearing from the Earth (Lean and Hinrichsen, 1992).

Standard policies, such as the US Endangered Species Act (ESA) and the Convention on International Trade in Endangered Species of Fauna and Flora (CITES) protect individual species but microorganisms, especially those we have not yet discovered, cannot be protected in this way. Habitat protection is a means to protect organisms and their habitats (Eisner et al., 1995), a method that would be more beneficial to protection of microbial biodiversity.

Hawksworth (1995) pointed out that completing worldwide inventory of biota requires additional taxonomic collections, training of people in many different countries to carry out taxonomic studies, and serious international coordination of these efforts. The African Network of Microbiological Resources Centres (MIRCENs) is a step in that direction (DaSilva, 1993). A new MIRCEN, focusing on microorganisms used in biohydrometallurgical processes has been established in Pune, India (Anon, 1995). Not only are culture collections important, but in a world united by electronic communication, computer databases may supply invaluable information to taxonomists and other researchers. A move to link several microbiological databases and add functional data to the genetic data was explored at the recent International Symposium on Microbial Ecology in Santos, Brazil (Wertheim, 1995). There are 521 culture collection centers working in 66 countries worldwide. Some worldwide known culture collection centres are International Mycological Institute (IMI), American Type Culture Collection (ATCC), Belgian Co-ordinated Collections of Micro-organisms (BCCM), Centraalbureau voor Schimmelcultures (CBS). IMI was founded in 1920 and is part of CAB International, an organization supported by 32 Member Governments established by treaty and with international legal status. The IMI culture collection comprises over 16,500 strains of filamentous fungi, yeasts and bacteria of interest in plant pathology, industry, biodeterioration studies, standards testing and specifications, systematic and biochemical research and education. Uses of fungi include biosynthesis of organic compounds, physiological assay, soil analysis, and enzyme production. The institute provides identification, preservation, microbial testing of materials, contract, consultancy, and training, development of preservation protocols, safe deposit and patent deposit services. ATCC was established in 1925 when a committee of scientists recognized a need for a central collection of microorganisms that would serve scientists all over the world. The early years were spent at the McCormick Institute in Chicago until the organization moved to Georgetown University in Washington, D.C., in 1937. As research in the biosciences expanded, ATCC began to diversify its holdings, and as the collections grew ATCC occupied a series of sites, each providing more storage space. ATCC moved to its current state-of-the-art laboratory in 1998. Common Access to Biological Resources and Information (CABRI) provides a unified search interface for a handful of European culture collections. These include BCCM, CABI and CBS, among others CBS is an important center for mycological research in The Netherlands. Their extensive culture collection can be searched on many criteria, including cultural characteristics. CBS also provide access to databases on fungal nomenclature.

Status of microbial conservancy in Pakistan

Until 3 years ago in Pakistan, few research groups (NIBGE and CEMB) were holding small collections. Most of the research was based on foreign microbial cultures. This was creating a huge economic burden also causing unnecessary delays and discontinuity of research due to accidental loss or death of cultures. Mycologists and plant pathologists have been culturing microorganisms specially fungi for a long time but there has been no maintenance of microbial cultures in Pakistan with the result that whenever cultures were needed by researchers, teachers and students, they were not available anywhere in Pakistan.

Under the newly established Department of Mycology and Plant Pathology, First Fungal Culture Bank of Pakistan (FCBP) was established early in 2003. From June 18, 2003, it started functioning with a meager staff, an Incharge with two research associates. FCBP is registered with the following international organizations: The World Data Centre for Microorganisms (WDCM), World Federation of Culture Collection (WFCC) and Microbial Research Centre (MIRCEN). The main activity of FCBP is isolation in pure culture, identification and preservation of fungi of Pakistan. It has already obtained pure culture, identified and preserved over 800 strains of fungi. On excessive demand of researchers for cultures of bacterial species, about six months ago, bank has also initiated isolation and conservation of bacteria as well. Now bank hold inventory of around 62 isolates of bacteria, this activity will also continue. FCBP is providing authentic cultures to researchers, teachers and students on nominal charges. Disease diagnostic services are also being provided.

Many researchers and research students isolate fungi and other microorganism but they cannot identify them. FCBP is providing facility to identify such cultures up to

species level. It has already provided facility to various research organizations and universities all over Pakistan and activity is in progress. It offered internship on isolation, purification, preservation and identification of fungi during last one year since the internship program was started by Pakistani universities and also providing training to students of the Punjab University. FCBP is supervising M.Sc. (Hons.) and Ph.D. research in taxonomy to overcome scarcity of manpower in this field. It provides training to college teachers and researchers in isolation, identification and conservation of microbial flora. FCBP organized a week long workshop on "Identification and Conservation of Micromycetes" from August 23 to 28, 2004 with financial support of HEC. Submitted a program to HEC for holding second workshop and intends to make it an annual feature. MYCONEWS', an official publication of FCBP since June, 2003 has just completed its three years of publications (13 issues). MYCONEWS consists of news, views and research notes. The most important regular feature is a list of updated accessions of cultures of Pakistani fungi in each issue published as "Current Inventory of FCBP" and also disseminates inventory of bacterial isolates. FCBP research work is also published in the form of Research Bulletins. First research bulletin entitled "NEW RECORDS OF FUNGI IMPERFECTI FROM PAKISTAN" was published in April 2005. This research bulletin includes 22 species of fungi imperfecti as new records with descriptions and microphotographs. It includes five species of *Aspergillus*, four species of *Phoma*, two species of *Acremonium*, two species of *Curvularia*, two species of *Fusarium*, two species of *Trichoderma* and one species of *Alternaria*. Second research bulletin entitled "COPROPHILOUS FUNGI OF PAKISTAN" was published in December 2005. This research bulletin includes nineteen species of coprophilous fungi with descriptions and microphotographs. Four species of *Absidia*, one species of *Drechslera*, two species of *Pilobolus*, one species of *Fusarium*, two species of *Acremonium*, one species of *Saccobolus*, two species of *Ascobolus*, one species of *Penicillium*, one species of *Phycomyces*, one species of *Isaria*, one species of *Syncephalastrum*, on species of *Doratomyces*, one species of *Cephaliophora*. Third bulletin by name of "THE GENUS *TRICHODERMA* IN PAKISTAN" was published in 2009. We are preserving our authentic cultures at 4°C in refrigerator, in mineral oil and at -20°C. FCBP has introduced silica gel technique in preserving cultures. It requires regular reculturing. All these methods are laborious, time consuming and expensive, sometimes resulting in loss of culture viability. FCBP has recently acquired cryopreservation system, to facilitate long-term preservation, and is going to equip itself with cleanroom technology, bio-safety cabinets to follow international standards. A project under PSF-US linkage (83 M) has been submitted for further improvement of infrastructure on international standards and its upgradation into

National Microbial Culture Centre (NMCC). At the same time, it was realized that the data so far collected must be digitized and in a form that it would be accessed easily by the scientists. This idea prompted to work for the development of MYCOsoft for which the proposal was submitted to the University of the Punjab in 2008.

METHODOLOGY

Data analysis

The data presented in the form of research bulletin #2 entitled "Coprophilous Fungi of Pakistan" published by First fungal Culture Bank of Pakistan (FCBP) in the year 2005, was analyzed carefully. Care was taken to observe that all the taxonomic parameters were taken into account. This resource is being updated regularly.

Selection of parameters and their hierarchical arrangement

The parameters were then selected in order of descending priority or significance. It means that less important characters were taken at the end, while characters with increasing significance were towards the top portion of the list. The characters were arranged and then the units were discussed and finalized on the basis of which the entries would be made.

Defining ranges or limitations

Each and every character, no matter at what level of priority it was, was discussed at length separately and the extent or limitations were earmarked before the entry of data in terms of real figures or units. For example colony diameter may range from 0.5 to 5.0 cm.

Data uploading

The elaborate and lengthy phase of data entry was carried out after defining the limits. The program was regularly checked by running during this phase of data entry also and any loophole or flaw was removed for a smooth working of the program. Cross check and double check was also done at times to facilitate the working of the program.

Uploading of images (micrographs and line drawings)

The images or line drawings to support the software database were also uploaded along with the dataset. The synchronous working of the two data bases was also ensured carefully.

SOFTWARE SPECIFICATION

Overview

Help to develop the software was taken from IT officials of University of the Punjab.

Scope of project

The system consists of the following modules/features:

Features

The features are as follows:

1. Species group (up to 5 level).
2. Species parameters.
3. Species images.
4. Advance search (using Boolean operator).

Backup and security

1. Username/password protected.
2. Multi client supported.
3. Database backup feature.

Requirements

1. SQL Server 2000.
2. Dot Net Framework 2.0.
3. Microsoft XP Operating system or higher.

Implementation

1. Institute of Agricultural Sciences.

Technical details

Application architecture

Three-tier architecture is used in the development of our application and our application is both web and desktop based. The block diagram of three-tier architecture of our application is given in Figure 1.

Software specification

The following software should be installed:

1. Microsoft XP or Higher.
2. Dot NET Framework.
3. SQL Server 2000.

Tools and technologies: We used the Dot NET framework in the development of this project because our platform for running the software was also Microsoft. Another reason for using the Dot NET framework is that our application is multilingual, so we used localization feature provided by Microsoft Dot Net Framework. Using the feature of localization, our application can support more than 250 languages. It works efficiently on the Microsoft Windows.

SQL server: SQL server is one of the best options to develop a large database. So we used it at the back end of our project.

Context level diagram

The context level diagram is shown in Figure 2.

Future plan

The future plans are place all functionality of the system online, so that users can add/update/search specious information online.

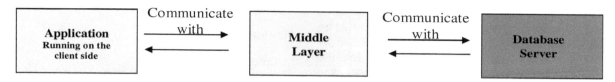

Figure 1. Block diagram of three-tier architecture.

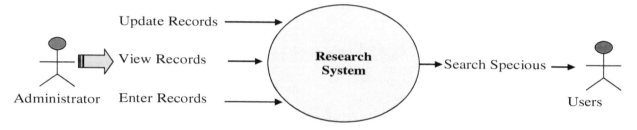

Figure 2. Context level diagram.

Requirements

Hardware required

1. One server machine with Microsoft Windows Server Operating System. This is a basic requirement.
2. Clients machines with Microsoft Operating System. This is a basic requirement.
3. Clients machines should be connected to server through LAN or internet.
4. Scanner for scanning Images.

Software requirements

1. Dot Net Framework 2.0 for client machines.
2. Microsoft Office should be installed on client machine for importing reports.
3. SQL Server 2005 on server machine.

Operators

Training

1. A technical person required to maintain database and able to install the application.
2. Data entry operator: It depends on the collection of specious.

RESULTS

User manual

The first screen is the splash screen followed by login screen and the main screen (Figure 3).

Defining new group

This is shown in Figure 4.

Defining characteristics

This is shown in Figure 5.

Defining specious

This is shown in Figure 6.

Advance search

This is shown in Figure 7.

Change password

This is shown in Figure 8.

Backup data base

Finally, we have a backup data base.

DISCUSSION

The climate of the planet Earth is changing rapidly and this change is creating pressure on the native fungal flora. A number of species are at the verge of extinction due to changing environmental conditions and habitat destruction. Biodiversity is going to face consequences which are irreversible and cascading. The pattern of species distribution is also changing due to such perturbations. As a result of which the organisms are pushed towards extinction while on the other hand intrusions into new geographical areas are also being

Figure 3. Splash screen.

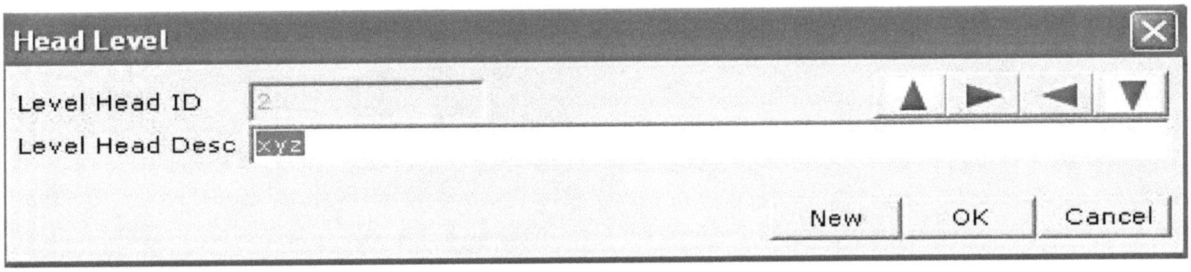

Figure 4. Defining new group.

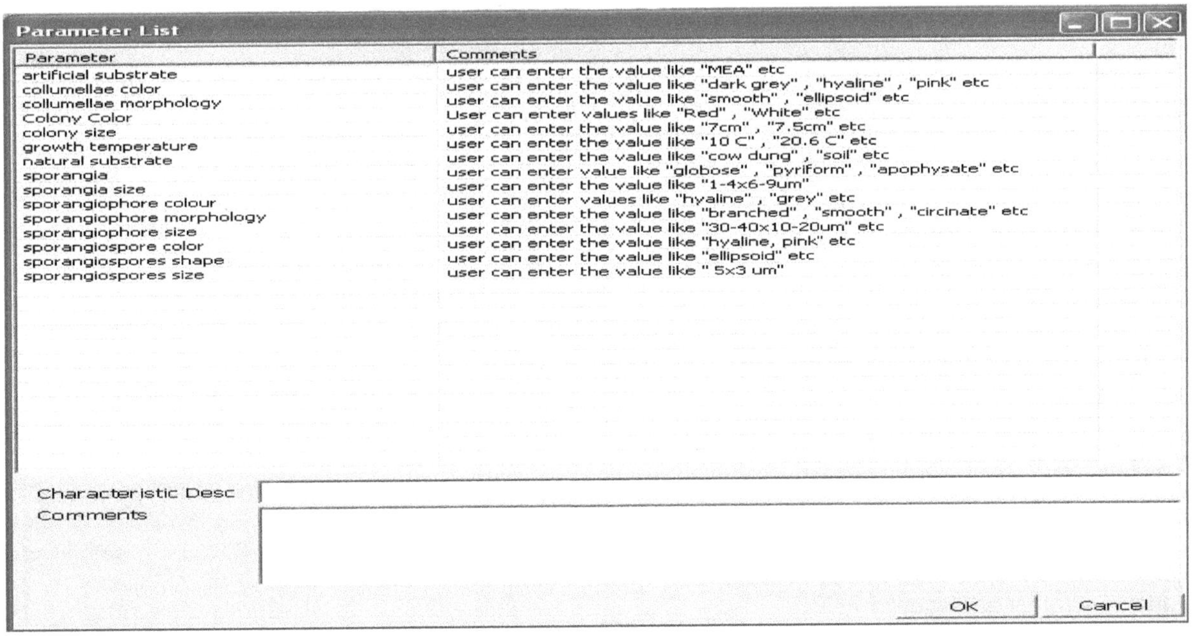

Figure 5. Defining characteristics.

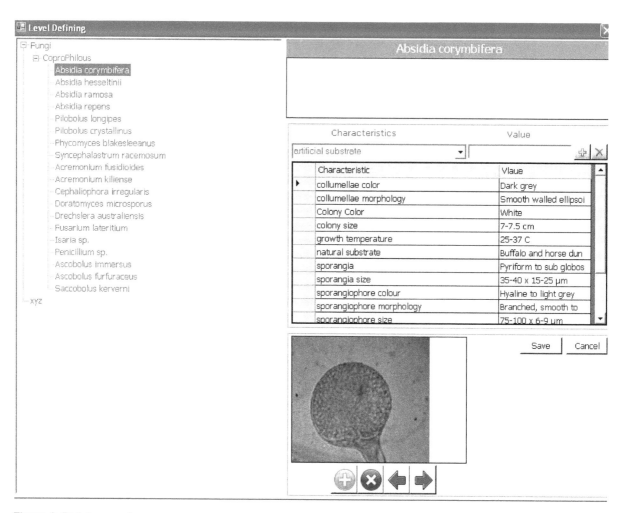

Figure 6. Defining specious.

Figure 7. Changing password.

reported, so it is very important to have the electronic records of the native fungal flora. First, Fungal Culture Bank of Pakistan (FCBP) which was established in 2004 is working as a sole source of microbial collection and information. So, it was necessary to digitize the information of microbial collection at FCBP.

No doubt that the fungi can be identifying by growing them on culture media and recording characters like morphology and colour of the colony and colour, size and microscopic structures of the fungal propagules. Some of the books of fungal taxonomy also offer diagnostic keys to provide help in the process of identification. More importantly, one has to be a good taxonomist to reach to a subtle conclusion or at least rely on an expert fungal systematist. However, all these methods are time consuming and labour intensive. Therefore, it was the

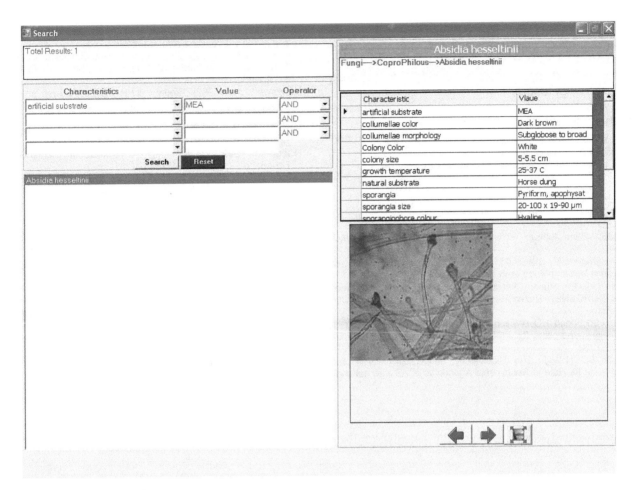

Figure 8. Advance search.

need of the hour to keep the knowledge updated and more reliable for the researchers in the recent scenario of global climate change. So, it was merely important to develop this software to make the way of identification easier and more authentic. It was developed for the cataloging of various groups of fungi. There is need to keep the pace with the world of information technology; so, it is a basic step to give the sense of bioinformatics in mycological studies.

Main features of the software

The following tasks are fulfilled by the software which has been developed by the Institute of Mycology and Plant Pathology in collaboration with a team of IT experts:

1. The electronic record of the fungal collection of FCBP would be maintained.
2. Can identify the specimen used by feeding simple characters.
3. The data is available on CD and online.
4. Others groups of fungi, bacteria, nematodes would be transformed into the same shape.

5. The software is multipurpose and has no limitation of making further entries or improvements.
6. Software requires a password for its operating, this is essential for the protection of the secured data.
7. It has the option to make a data file for a specific organism.
8. We can upload micro and macro features of the fungi additionally with their photographs. The remote users get the updates online or through new versions of MYCOsoft.
9. Software is able to complete search for a particular organism, if we provide just part of the name as key word.
10. Software is also able to do advanced search which is an important tool of it.
11. By the use of this software, we are able to digitalize our herbarium while cataloging the specimen.

Activities done

The following activities were done for the completion of the project:

1. Software development by using languages like C++ and

Oracle.

2. Data regarding characterization of the fungi was uploaded.

3. Initially the software is able to identify Coprophillous (growing on dung) fungi.

4. Data was equipped with macro, micro characters as well as their microphotographs.

5. CDs were also prepared for the dissemination and further presentation of the software.

6. There is an option to upload further fungal groups.

REFERENCES

Anon (1995). Pune Mircen, World J. Microbiol. Biotechnol. IUMS 11(3):4-6.

Bull AT, Goodfellow M, Slater JH, (1992). Biodiversity as a source of innovation in biotechnology. Ann. Rev. Microbiol. 46:219-252.

DaSilva E (1993). African Network of Microbiological Resources Centres [MIRCENS]. Biofertilizer Production and Use. UNESCO, UNDP, Paris.

Eisner TJ, Lubchenco EO, Wilson DS, Bean MJ (1995). Building a scientifically sound policy for protecting endangered species. Science 268:1231-1232.

Hawksworth DL (1991). The Biodiversity of Microorganisms and Invertebrates: Its Role in Sustainable Agriculture. CAB International, UK.

Hawksworth D, Colwell R (1992). Biodiversity amongst microorganisms and its relevance. Biodivers. Conserv. 1:219.

Hawksworth DL (1995). The Convention on Biological Diversity: First Conference of the Parties [COP1]. World J. Microbiol. Biotech. IUMS 11[3]:1-2.

Hawksworth DL (1992). Biodiversity in microorganisms and its role in ecosystem function. IUBS Monograph 8, International Union. Biol. Sci. Paris, pp. 83-93

Lean G, Hinrichsen D (1992). WWF Atlas of the Environment. 2nd edn. Harper Perennial, New York, p. 192.

Nisbet LJ (1992). Useful functions of microbial metabolites. CIBA-Foundation Symp. 171:215-225.

Sly L (1994). Culture collections world-wide. In Kirsop, B. and Hawksworth, D. L. (Eds.). The biodiversity of microorganisms and the role of microbial resource centres. World Federation for Culture Collections. pp. 29-35.

Staley JT, Castenholz RW, Colwell RR, Holt JG, Kane MD, Pace NR, Salyers AA, Tiedje JM (1997). The Microbial World: Foundation of the biosphere. American Academy of Microbiology.

Wertheim M (1995). Call to desegregate microbial databases. Science 269:15-16.

## 28

Identification of unique repeated patterns, location of mutation in DNA finger printing using artificial intelligence technique

B. Mukunthan[1]*, N. Nagaveni[2] and A. Pushpalatha[3]

[1]Department of Master of Computer Applications and Research, SVS College of Engineering, Coimbatore, Tamil Nadu, India- 614030.
[2]Department of Mathematics and Research, Coimbatore Institute of Technology, Coimbatore, Tamil Nadu, India.
[3]Department of Mathematics and Informatics, Government Arts College, Udumalpet, Tamil Nadu, India-642126.

The proposed Neural-Fuzzy pattern recognition (NFPR) system discussed in this paper effectively reduces the complication in precisely analyzing and interpreting human deoxyribonucleic acid (DNA) sample. In this novel approach, the perfect blend made of bioinformatics and a competitive method of neural networks technique, which has the advantage over conventional computation technique, in their ability to solve problem that do not have an algorithmic solution or the available solutions are also too complex to be found, results in efficient DNA pattern analysis algorithm that identifies repeated patterns in the given human DNA sample assisting in generation of unique identification number of an individual, location of occurrence of mutation in the mutated DNA sample with utmost prediction accuracy.

Key words: Neural-Fuzzy resonance mapping, competitive learning, NFPR processor, Input generator, preprocessor, discriminator, DNA profiling, DNA sequence, FASTA format.

INTRODUCTION

The genome (Joe and John, 1999) is the entirety of an organism's hereditary information which is encoded either in deoxyribonucleic acid (DNA) or, for many types of virus, in ribonucleic acid (RNA). The role of DNA sequences has become indispensable for many biological researches. DNA sequencing is applied in various fields such as diagnostic, biotechnology, forensic biology and biological systematic.

The DNA sequences of thousands of organisms have been decoded and stored in databases. A comparison of genes within a species or between different species can show similarities between protein functions, or relations between species. With the growing amount of data, it became impractical to analyze DNA sequences manually. A pattern (Richard et al., 2006; Donald, 2005) is essentially an arrangement or an ordering, in which some organization of underlying structure can be said to exist, that is, a pattern can be referred to as a quantitative or structural description of an object or some item of interest. A set of patterns that share some common properties can be regarded as pattern class (Phipps, 1996) in our case the unique repeated nucleotide sequence from the given human DNA sample.

Neural networks (Advances in Neural Networks issn, 2006) can process information in parallel, at high speed, and in a distributed manner. Neural networks which are simplified models of the biological neuron system, made up of highly interconnected neural computing elements that have the ability to learn and thereby acquire knowledge and make it available for use. Neural networks are capable of learning by examples to solve

*Corresponding author. E-mail: mukunth_bmk@yahoo.co.in, mukunthan.bmk2011@gmail.com .

unknown or untrained instances of the problem, if it's aptly trained.

Neural networks architectures (Stephen et al., 2009; Robert, 2007) can be trained with known examples of a problem before they are tested for their inference. They can, therefore, identify new objects previously untrained. Neural networks (Carpenter and Grossberg, 1987) are robust systems and are fault tolerant. They can therefore, recall full patterns from incomplete, partial or noisy patterns. Network architectures (John et al., 2008) have been classified into various types based on their learning mechanisms and other features.

In Competitive Learning method those neurons which respond strongly to input stimuli have their weights updated, when an input pattern is presented, all neurons in the layer compete and the winning neuron undergoes weight adjustment. Hence it is a "Winner-takes-all" strategy.

Neural networks (Advances in Neural Networks issn, 2006) suitable particularly for pattern classification problems in realistic environment is Neural-Fuzzy resonance mapping (NFRM) (Carpenter and Grossberg, 2010), it is a vast simplification of fuzzy resonance mapping which possess reduced computational overhead and architectural redundancy.

DNA PROFILING AND SEQUENCING

DNA profiling (Stephen and David, 2003) also called DNA testing, DNA typing, or genetic fingerprinting, is a technique employed by forensic (Norah and Keith, 2002; Joe and John, 1999; John and Brent, 2005) scientists to assist in the identification of individuals on the basis of their respective DNA profiles. DNA profiles (David, 2004) are encrypted sets of numbers that reflect a person's DNA makeup (David, 2008; Andreas, 2001), which can also be used as the person's identifier. DNA sequencing theory addresses physical processes related to sequencing DNA .The term DNA sequencing refers to sequencing methods for determining the order of the nucleotide bases—adenine, guanine, cytosine, thymine and uracil (rare case) in a molecule of DNA. Single nucleotide poly-orphisms (Computational Intelligence and Bio inspired Systems, 2005) are a DNA sequence variation occurring when a single nucleotide A, T, C, or G in the genome (Julie, 2001) (or other shared sequence) differs between members of a species (Des and willie, 2000) (or between paired chromosomes in an individual).

For example, two sequenced DNA fragments from different individuals (Michael, 2007), AAGCCTA to AAGCTTA, contain a difference in a single nucleotide. Various DNA sequence formats available are: Plain sequence format, EMBL format, GCG format, GCG-RSF (rich sequence format, Gen Bank format, IG format and given sample is used as an input to neural-fuzzy pattern

recognition (NFPR) processor which is to be interpreted and analysed. Fuzzy representation of nucleotide bases in NFPR processor is Adenine (A)-0.1, Thymine (T)-0.2, Guanine (G)-0.3, Cytosine (C)-0.4, Uracil (U)-0.5.The concept of clustering logical and illogical sequence is shown in Figure 1.

NEURAL-FUZZY PATTERN RECOGNITION PROCESSOR

Learning input generator

The input generator is used for input normalization and it represents the presence of particular feature in the input patterns and its absence. Various cases for generating normalized learning inputs are shown in Table 1.

Learning inputs

$$\text{LIN}_{i, n} = I_1, I_2 ..., I_p \tag{1}$$

Where $\quad 0.1 \le i \le 0.5, 0.1 \le n \le 0.5$

and $p = 4$ (size of learning input, weights of NFPR processor)

Various cases for learning input normalization is given in Table 2.

Activation function generator

When coded input patterns from input generator are presented to NFPR-Processor all output nodes become active to varying degrees. The output activation denoted by activation function (ACFj) for the jth output node. Where LIN is the learning input and LIW_j is the corresponding learning input weights.

Activation unction

$$\text{ACFj} = \frac{\left| \text{LIN} \wedge \text{LI Wj} \right|}{\alpha + \left| \text{LI Wj} \right|} \tag{2}$$

Here α is kept as a small value close to 0 it's about 0.0000001.The node which registers the highest activation function is deemed Winner node, that is:

$$\text{Winner node} = \max(\text{ACFj}) \tag{3}$$

In the event of more than one node emerging as the winner owing to the same activation function value some FASTA format. A sequence file in FASTA format of a

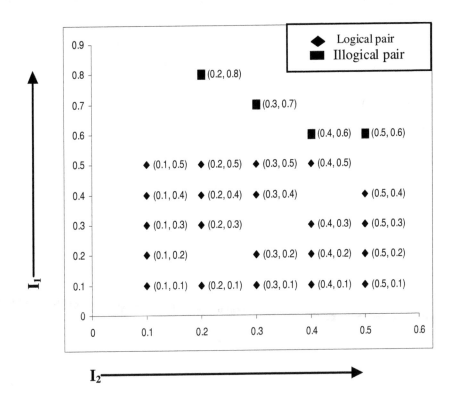

Figure 1. Concept of Clustering Logical and Illogical sequence.

Match function generator

mechanism such as choosing a node with the smallest index may be devised to break the tie.

The match function (MAF) which helps to determine whether the network must adjust its learning parameters is given by:

Matching function

$$\text{MAF}_j = \frac{\left|\text{LIN} \wedge \text{LI W}_j\right|}{\left|\text{LIN}\right|} \qquad (4)$$

The MAF association with the vigilance parameter (ρ) decides on whether a particular output node is good enough to encode a given input pattern or whether a new output node should be opened to encode the same.

The network is said to be in a state of resonance, if the match function value exceeds vigilance parameter. However, for a node to exhibit resonance, it is essential that it not only encodes the given input pattern but should also represent the same category as that of the input pattern. The network is said to be in state of mismatch reset if the vigilance parameter exceeds match function, Such a state only means that the particular output node is not fit enough to learn the given input pattern and thereby cannot update its weights even though the category of the output node may be the same as that of the input pattern. This is so, since the output node has fallen short of the expected encoding granularity indicated by the vigilance parameter. If match function is greater than vigilance parameter and category of input pattern is not same with the learning input, the vigilance parameter is updated and is given by:

$$\rho = \text{MAF} + \delta \qquad (\delta = 0.001) \qquad (5)$$

The weight updating equation of an output node j when it proceeds to learn the given input pattern LIN is given by:

Weight for Inference (WFI)

$$\text{WFI}_j^{\text{new}} = \beta(\text{LIN} \wedge \text{WFI}_j^{\text{old}}) + (1-\beta)\text{WFI}_j^{\text{old}} \qquad (6)$$

where $\quad 0 \leq \beta \leq 1 \qquad (\beta = 1)$

The computation involved in generating WFI and category for Inference (CFI) for some nucleotide pairs is

Table 1. Generating weights for inference (WFI), category for inference (CFI) from learning inputs.

Nucleotide pair		A,A*	A,U*	T,A*	T,T**	T,U*	G,A*	G,G**	G,U*	C,A*	C,C**	C,U*	U,A*	U,U***
Category		L	L	L	ILL	L	L	ILL	L	L	ILL	L	L	ILL
Learning input(LIN)		0.1,0.1, 0.9,0.9	0.1,0.5, 0.9,0.5	0.2,0.1, 0.8,0.9	0.2,0.8, 0.8,0.2	0.2,0.5, 0.8,0.5	0.3,0.1, 0.7,0.9	0.3,0.7, 0.7,0.3	0.3,0.5, 0.7,0.5	0.4,0.1, 0.6,0.9	0.4,0.6, 0.6,0.4	0.4,0.5, 0.6,0.5	0.5,0.1, 0.5,0.9	0.5,0.6, 0.5,0.4
ρ		0.5	0.5	0.5	0.5	0.5	0.5	0.5	0.5	0.5	0.5, 0.600+δ	0.601	0.601	0.601
Learning input weights	LIW(1)	=LIN	0.1,0.1, 0.9,0.9	0.1,0.1, 0.8,0.5	0.1,0.1, 0.8,0.5	0.1,0.1, 0.8,0.5	0.1,0.1, 0.8,0.5	0.1,0.1, 0.7,0.5	0.1,0.1, 0.7,0.5	0.1,0.1, 0.7,0.5	0.1,0.1, 0.6,0.5	0.1,0.1, 0.6,0.5	0.1,0.1, 0.6,0.5	0.1,0.1, 0.6,0.5
	LIW(2)	?	?	?	=LIN	0.2,0.8, 0.8,0.2	0.2,0.8, 0.8,0.2	0.2,0.8, 0.8,0.2	0.2,0.7, 0.7,0.2	0.2,0.7, 0.7,0.2	0.2,0.7, 0.7,0.2	0.2,0.6, 0.6,0.2	0.2,0.6, 0.6,0.2	0.2,0.6, 0.6,0.2
	LIW(3)	?	?	?	?	?	?	?	?	?	?	?	?	0.5,0.1, 0.5,0.9
Activation function	ACF(1)	0.9999	0.7999	0.9375	0.7999	0.9999	0.9333	0.8751	0.9999	0.9285	0.9230	0.9999	0.9230	0.8461
	ACF(2)	?	?	?	?	0.8499	0.5999	0.8999	0.8888	0.6111	0.8888	0.9375	0.6249	0.9375
	ACF(3)	?	?	?	?	?	?	?	?	?	?	?	?	0.7499
Highest Activation Function		ACF(1)	ACF(1)	ACF(1)	ACF(2)	ACF(1)	ACF(1)	ACF(2)	ACF(1)	ACF(1)	ACF(2)	ACF(1)	ACF(1), ACF(2)	ACF(2)
Category Match / Mismatch		Match	Match	Match	Match	Match	Match	Match	Match	Match	Mismatch Match	Match	Match	Match Match
Match Function	MAF(1)	1.0000	0.8000	0.7500	0.6000	0.7500	0.7000	0.6000	0.7000	0.6500	0.6000	0.6500	0.6000	0.5500
	MAF(2)	?	?	?	?	0.8500	0.6000	0.9000	0.8000	0.5500	0.8000	0.7500	0.5000	0.7500
	MAF(3)	?	?	?	?	?	?	?	?	?	?	?	?	0.7500
Weight for inference and category	WFI(1)	0.1,0.1, 0.9,0.9	0.1,0.1, 0.9,0.5	0.1,0.1, 0.8,0.5	0.1,0.1, 0.8,0.5	0.1,0.1, 0.8,0.5	0.1,0.1, 0.7,0.5	0.1,0.1, 0.7,0.5	0.1,0.1, 0.7,0.5	0.1,0.1, 0.6,0.5	0.1,0.1, 0.6,0.5	0.1,0.1, 0.6,0.5	0.1,0.1, 0.6,0.5	**0.1,0.1, 0.6,0.5**
	CFI(1)	L	L	L	L	L	L	L	L	L	L	L	L	**L**
for inference	WFI(2)	?	?	0.2,0.8, 0.8,0.2	0.2,0.8, 0.8,0.2	0.2,0.8, 0.8,0.2	0.2,0.8, 0.8,0.2	0.2,0.7, 0.7,0.2	0.2,0.7, 0.7,0.2	0.2,0.7, 0.7,0.2	0.2,0.6, 0.6,0.2	0.2,0.6, 0.6,0.2	0.2,0.6, 0.6,0.2	**0.2,0.6, 0.5,0.2**

Table 1. Contd.

													ILL
CFI(2)	~	~	~	~	ILL	ILL	ILL	ILL	ILL	ILL	ILL	ILL	**0.5,0.1, 0.5,0.9**
WFI(3)	~	~	~	~	~	~	~	~	~	~	0.5,0.1, 0.5,0.9	0.5,0.1, 0.5,0.9	
CFI(3)	~	~	~	~	~	~	~	~	~	~	L	L	**L**

ρ=VIGILANCE PARAMETER *- CASE1,**-CASE2,***CASE3.

given below and shown in Table 1:

Delta (δ) =0.001; Beta (β) =1; and Alpha (α) =0.0000001,

For nucleotide pair (AA)

Category to be trained: L (Logical)

Fuzzy Equivalent (FE): 0.1(A), 0.1(A)

Learning Input (LIN) =0.1, 0.1, 1-0.1, 1-0.1 = 0.1, 0.1, 0.9, 0.9 (Case1)

Rho (ρ) =0.5, LIW(1)= AI= 0.1,0.1,0.9,0.9

$$ACF(1) = \frac{\left|0.1,0.1,0.\ 9,0.9\ \wedge\ 0.1,0.1,0.\ 9,0.9\right|}{0.0000001\ +\ \left|0.1,0.1,0.1,0.\ 9,0.9\right|}$$

$$= \frac{\left|0.1,0.1,0.\ 9,0.9\right|}{2.0000001} = \frac{\left|2.0\right|}{2.0000001} = 0.9999$$

$$MAF(1) = \frac{\left|0.1,0.1,0.\ 9,0.9\ \wedge\ 0.1,0.1,0.\ 9,0.9\right|}{\left|0.1,0.1,0.\ 9,0.9\right|}$$

$$= \frac{\left|0.1,0.1,0.\ 9,0.9\right|}{2.0} = \frac{\left|2.0\right|}{2.0} = 1.0000$$

As it's the first learning input,

WFI(1) = 0.1,0.1,0. 9,0.9 , CFI(1) = L.

For nucleotide pair (AU)

Category to be trained: L (Logical). Fuzzy Equivalent: 0.1(A), 0.5(U).

Learning Input (LIN) = 0.1, 0.5, 1-0.1, 1-0.5 =0.1, 0.5, 0.9, 0.5 (Case1)

Rho (ρ) =0.5,

LIN = 0.1,0.5,0.9,0.5, LIW(1)= 0.1,0.1,0.9,0.9

$$ACF(1) = \frac{\left|0.1,0.5,0.\ 9,0.5\ \wedge\ 0.1,0.1,0.\ 9,0.9\right|}{0.0000001\ +\ \left|0.1,0.1,0.1,0.\ 9,0.9\right|}$$

$$= \frac{\left|0.1,0.1,0.\ 9,0.\ 5\right|}{2.0000001} = \frac{\left|1.6\right|}{2.0000001} = 0.7999$$

$$ACF(1) = \frac{\left|0.1,0.5,0.\ 9,0.5\ \wedge\ 0.1,0.1,0.\ 9,0.9\right|}{0.0000001\ +\ \left|0.1,0.1,0.1,0.\ 9,0.9\right|}$$

$$= \frac{\left|0.1,0.1,0.\ 9,0.\ 5\right|}{2.0000001} = \frac{\left|1.6\right|}{2.0000001} = 0.7999$$

$$MAF(1) = \frac{\left|0.1,0.5,0.\ 9,0.5\ \wedge\ 0.1,0.1,0.\ 9,0.9\right|}{\left|0.1,0.5,0.\ 9,0.5\right|}$$

$$= \frac{\left|0.1,0.1,0.\ 9,0.5\right|}{2.0} = \frac{\left|1.6\right|}{2.0} = 0.8000$$

ACF (1) has same category as of category of nucleotide pair, MFI (1) is greater than rho, so

WFI(1) =1*(0.1,0.5,0.9,0.5) ∧ (0.1,0.1,0.9,0.9) + (1-1)(0.1,0.1,0.9,0.9) = 0.1,0.1,0.9,0.5

WFI(1)=0.1,0.1,0.9,0.5 , CFI(1) = L.

For nucleotide pair (TT)

Category to be trained: ILL (Illogical)

Fuzzy Equivalent: 0.2(T), 0.2(T)

Learning Input (LIN) = 0.2, 1-0.2, 1-0.2, 0.2 =0.2, 0.8, 0.8, 0.2 (Case2)

Rho (ρ) =0.5, LIW(1)=0.1,0.1,0.8,0.5

Table 2. Various cases for learning input normalization

	Condition	Learning Input	Category
Case 1	$i \neq n$ or $i=n=0.1$ and $n<=0.5$	$LIN_{i,n} = i, n, 1-i, 1-n$ e.g. $LIN_{0.1, 0.1} = 0.1, 0.1, (1-0.1), (1-0.1)$ $LIN_{0.1, 0.1} = 0.1, 0.1, 0.9, 0.9$ $LIN_{0.2, 0.5} = 0.2, 0.5, (1-0.2), (1-0.5)$ $LIN_{0.2, 0.5} = 0.2, 0.5, 0.8, 0.5$	Category=L (logical)
Case 2	$i = n$ and $0.1> i, n <0.5$	$LIN_{i,n} = i, 1-i, 1-n, n$ e.g. $LIN_{0.2, 0.2}= 0.2, (1-0.2), (1-0.2), 0.2$ $LIN_{0.2, 0.2} = 0.2, 0.8, 0.8, 0.2$ $LIN_{0.3, 0.3}= 0.3, (1-0.3), (1-0.3), 0.3$ $LIN_{0.3, 0.3}= 0.3, 0.7, 0.7, 0.3$	Category=ILL (illogical)
Case 3	$i=n=0.5$	$LIN_{i,n} = i, i+0.1, n, n-0.1$ e.g. $LIN_{0.5, 0.5}= 0.5, (0.5+1), 0.5, (0.5-0.1)$ $LIN_{0.5, 0.5}= 0.5, 0.6, 0.5, 0.4$	Category=ILL (illogical)

$$ACF(1) = \frac{\left|0.2,0.8,0.8,0.2 \wedge 0.1,0.1,0.8,0.5\right|}{0.0000001+ \mid 0.1,0.1,0.8,0.5 \mid}$$

$$= \frac{\left|0.1,0.1,0.8,0.2\right|}{1.5000001} = \frac{\left|1.2\right|}{1.5000001} = 0.9999$$

$$MAF(1) = \frac{\left|0.2,0.8,0.8,0.2 \wedge 0.1,0.1,0.8,0.5\right|}{\mid 0.2,0.8,0.8,0.2 \mid}$$

$$= \frac{\left|0.1,0.1,0.8,0.2\right|}{2.0} = \frac{\left|1.2\right|}{2.0} = 0.6000$$

As category of nucleotide pair is the new category to be trained:

$WFI(1)= 0.1,0.1,0.8,0.5$, $WFI(2)= 0.2,0.8,0.8,0.2$.

$CFI(1) = L$, $CFI(2) = ILL$.

For nucleotide pair (CC)

Category to be trained: ILL (Illogical)

Fuzzy Equivalent: 0.4(C), 0.4(C)

Learning Input (LIN): 0.4, 1-0.4, 1-0.4, 0.4
   =0.4, 0.6, 0.6, 0.4(Case2)

Rho (ρ) =0.5

$LIW(1)= 0.1,0.1,0.6,0.5$, $LIW(2) = 0.2,0.7,0.7,0.2$

$$ACF(1) = \frac{\left|0.4,0.6,0.6,0.4 \wedge 0.1,0.1,0.6,0.5\right|}{0.0000001 + \mid 0.1,0.1,0.6,0.5 \mid}$$

$$= \frac{\left|0.1,0.1,0.6,0.4\right|}{1.3000001} = \frac{\left|1.2\right|}{1.3000001} = 0.9230$$

$$ACF(2) = \frac{\left|0.4,0.6,0.6,0.4 \wedge 0.2,0.7,0.7,0.2\right|}{0.0000001 + \mid 0.2,0.7,0.7,0.2 \mid}$$

$$= \frac{\left|0.2,0.6,0.6,0.2\right|}{1.8000001} = \frac{\left|1.6\right|}{1.8000001} = 0.8888$$

$$MAF(1) = \frac{\left|0.4,0.6,0.6,0.4 \wedge 0.1,0.1,0.6,0.5\right|}{\mid 0.4,0.6,0.6,0.4 \mid}$$

$$= \frac{\left|0.1,0.1,0.6,0.4\right|}{2.0} = \frac{\left|1.2\right|}{2.0} = 0.6000$$

$$MAF(2) = \frac{\left|0.4,0.6,0.6,0.4 \wedge 0.2,0.7,0.7,0.2\right|}{\mid 0.4,0.6,0.6,0.4 \mid}$$

$$= \frac{\left|0.2,0.6,0.6,0.2\right|}{2.0} = \frac{\left|1.6\right|}{2.0} = 0.8000$$

ACF (1) has the highest value and its category is Logical

which is not same as the category of input nucleotide pair, update the value of rho, that is, 0.600 (MAF (1)) +0.001(δ) =0.601, find the next highest value which is ACF (2) whose category is same as that of nucleotide pair, so update WIF(2):

$$WFI(1) = 0.1,0.1,06,0.5 \quad CFI(1) = L.$$

$$WFI(2) = 1*(0.4,0.6,06,0.4) \wedge (0.2,0.7,07,0.2)$$

$$+(1-1)(0.2,0.70.7,0.2) = 0.2,0.6,06,0.2,$$

$$CFI(2) = ILL.$$

For nucleotide pair (UA)

Category to be trained: L (Logical)

Fuzzy Equivalent: 0.5(U), 0.1(A)

Learning Input (LIN): 0.5, 0.1, 1-0.5, 1-0.1
=0.5, 0.1, 0.5, 0.9(Case1)

Rho (ρ) =0.601,

$$LIW(1) = 0.1,0.1,0.6,0.5 , LIW(2) = 0.2,0.6,0.6,0.2$$

$$ACF(1) = \frac{|0.5,0.1,0.\ 5,0.9 \wedge 0.1,0.1,0.\ 6,0.5|}{0.0000001 + |0.1,0.1,0.\ 6,0.5|}$$

$$= \frac{|0.1,0.1,0.\ 5,0.5|}{1.3000001} = \frac{|1.2|}{1.3000001} = 0.9230$$

$$ACF(2) = \frac{|0.5,0.1,0.\ 5,0.9 \wedge 0.2,0.6,0.\ 6,0.2|}{0.0000001 + |0.2,0.6,0.\ 6,0.2|}$$

$$= \frac{|0.2,0.1,0.\ 5,0.2|}{1.6000001} = \frac{|1.0|}{1.6000001} = 0.6249$$

$$MAF(1) = \frac{|0.5,0.1,0.\ 5,0.9 \wedge 0.1,0.1,0.\ 6,0.5|}{|0.5,0.1,0.\ 5,0.9|}$$

$$= \frac{|0.1,0.1,0.\ 5,0.5|}{2.0} = \frac{|1.2|}{2.0} = 0.6000$$

$$MAF(2) = \frac{|0.5,0.1,0.\ 5,0.9 \wedge 0.2,0.6,0.\ 6,0.2|}{|0.4,0.6,0.\ 6,0.4|}$$

$$= \frac{|0.2,0.1,0.\ 5,0.2|}{2.0} = \frac{|1.0|}{2.0} = 0.5000$$

ACF (1) has the highest value and MAF (1) is less than rho, find the next highest value which is ACF (2) ,its corresponding MAF (2) is also less than rho, so add new WFI (3), that is, WFI(3)=LIN:

$$WFI(1) = 0.1,0.1,06,0.5, WFI(2) = 0.2,0.6,06,0.2$$

$$WFI(3) = 0.5,0.1,0.5,0.9 , CFI(1) = L ,$$

$$CFI(2) = ILL , CFI(3) = L .$$

For nucleotide pair (UU)

Category to be trained: ILL (Illogical)

Fuzzy Equivalent: 0.5(U), 0.5(U)

Learning Input (AI): 0.5, 0.5+0.1, 0.5, 0.5-0.1
=0.5, 0.6, 0.5, 0.4(Case3)

Rho (ρ) =0.601, LIW(1) = 0.1,0.1,0.6,0.5 ,

$$LIW(2) = 0.2,0.6,0.6,0.2 , LIW(3) = 0.5,0.1,0.5,0.9$$

$$ACF(1) = \frac{|0.5,0.6,0.\ 5,0.4 \wedge 0.1,0.1,0.\ 6,0.5|}{0.0000001 + |0.1,0.1,0.\ 6,0.5|}$$

$$= \frac{|0.1,0.1,0.\ 5,0.\ 4|}{1.3000001} = \frac{|1.1|}{1.3000001} = 0.8461$$

$$ACF(1) = \frac{|0.5,0.6,0.\ 5,0.4 \wedge 0.1,0.1,0.\ 6,0.5|}{0.0000001 + |0.1,0.1,0.\ 6,0.5|}$$

$$= \frac{|0.1,0.1,0.\ 5,0.\ 4|}{1.3000001} = \frac{|1.1|}{1.3000001} = 0.8461$$

$$ACF(2) = \frac{|0.5,0.6,0.\ 5,0.4 \wedge 0.2,0.6,0.\ 6,0.2|}{0.0000001 + |0.2,0.6,0.\ 6,0.2|}$$

$$= \frac{|0.2,0.6,0.\ 5,0.\ 2|}{1.6000001} = \frac{|1.5|}{1.6000001} = 0.9375$$

$$ACF(3) = \frac{|0.5,0.6,0.5,0.4 \wedge 0.5,0.1,0.5,0.9|}{0.0000001 + |0.5,0.1,0.5,0.9|}$$

$$= \frac{|0.5,0.1,0.5,0.4|}{2.0000001} = \frac{|1.5|}{2.0000001} = 0.7499$$

$$MAF(1) = \frac{|0.5,0.6,0.\ 5,0.4 \wedge 0.1,0.1,0.\ 6,0.5|}{|0.5,0.6,0.\ 5,0.4|}$$

$$= \frac{|0.1,0.1,0.\ 5,0.4|}{2.0} = \frac{|1.1|}{2.0} = 0.5500$$

Table 3. Various conditions for generating preprocessor output.

Preprocessor Input	Condition		Preprocessor Output
	1	$i \neq n$ or $i=n=0.1$ and $n<=0.5$	PPO(i, n) = i, n, 1- i, 1-n e.g. PPO(0.1, 0.1) = 0.1, 0.1, (1- 0.1), (1-0.1) PPO(0.1, 0.1) = 0.1, 0.1, 0.9, 0.9 PPO(0.2, 0.5) = 0.2, 0.5, (1- 0.2), (1-0.5) PPO(0.2, 0.5) = 0.2, 0.5, 0.8, 0.5
PPI(i, n)	2	$i = n$ and $0.1> i$, $n <0.5$	PPO(i, n) = i, 1-i, 1-n, n e.g. PPO(0.2, 0.2) = 0.2, (1-0.2), (1- 0.2), 0.2 PPO(0.2, 0.2) = 0.2, 0.8, 0.8, 0.2 PPO(0.3, 0.3) = 0.3, (1-0.3), (1- 0.3), 0.3 PPO(0.3, 0.3) = 0.3, 0.7, 0.7, 0.3
	3	$i=n=0.5$	PPO(i, n) = i, $i+0.1$, n, $n-0.1$ e.g. PPO(0.5, 0.5) = 0.5, (0.5+1), 0.5, (0.5- 0.1) PPO(0.5, 0.5) = 0.5, 0.6, 0.5, 0.4

$$MAF(2) = \frac{\left|0.5,0.6,0.5,0.4 \wedge 0.2,0.6,0.6,0.2\right|}{|0.5,0.6,0.5,0.4|}$$

$$= \frac{\left|0.2,0.6,0.5,0.2\right|}{2.0} = \frac{|1.5|}{2.0} = 0.7500$$

$$MAF(3) = \frac{\left|0.5,0.6,0.5,0.4 \wedge 0.5,0.1,0.5,0.9\right|}{|0.5,0.6,0.5,0.4|}$$

$$= \frac{\left|0.5,0.1,0.5,0.4\right|}{2.0} = \frac{|1.5|}{2.0} = 0.7500$$

ACF (2) has the highest value, whose category is Illogical which is same as the category of input nucleotide pair, update WFI (2):

$$WFI(2) = (0.5,0.6,0.5,0.4) \wedge (0.2,0.6,0.6,0.2)$$

$$= 0.2,0.6,0.5,0.2 \text{ So } WFI(1) = (0.1,0.1,0.6,0.5)$$

$$WFI(3) = 0.5,0.1,0.5,0.9, \; CFI(1) = L,$$

$$CFI(2) = ILL, \; CFI(3) = L.$$

$$WFI(3) = 0.5,0.1,05,0.9.$$

The WFI, CFI generated for various learning input is shown in Table 1.Once the network has been trained; the inference of patterns, logical or illogical, that is, the categories to which the patterns belong may be easily computed. This is accomplished by subjecting DNA input to CIF function through pre-processor. Various conditions for generating pre-processed output are shown in Table 3.

Category inference function (CIF)

$$CIFj = \frac{\left|PPO \wedge WFIj\right|}{\left|WFIj\right|} \tag{7}$$

Computation involved in finding CIF for DNA Input (TG) is shown as:

If CIF (1)/ CIF (3) is greater than CIF (2) then greatest inferred category (GIF) is CIF (1) /CIF (3), so the category inferred is logical, else if CIF (2) is greater than CIF (1) and CIF (3) then greatest inferred category(IC) is illogical.

For DNA input TG

Pre-processor Input (PPI): 0.2(T), 0.3(G)

Pre-processor Output (PPO): 0.2, 0.3, 0.8, 0.7

$$CIF(1) = \frac{\left|0.2,0.3,0. \quad 8,0.7 \wedge 0.1,0.1,0. \quad 6,0.5\right|}{|0.1,0.1,0. \quad 6,0.5|}$$

$$= \frac{\left|0.1,0.1,0. \quad 6,0.5\right|}{1.3} = \frac{|1.3|}{1.3} = 1.0000$$

$$CIF(2) = \frac{|0.2,0.3,0.8,0.7 \wedge 0.2,0.6,0.5,0.2|}{|0.2,0.6,0.5,0.2|}$$

$$= \frac{|0.2,0.3,0.5,0.2|}{1.5} = \frac{|1.2|}{2.0} = 0.6000$$

$$CIF(3) = \frac{|0.2,0.3,08,0.7 \wedge 0.5,0.1,05,0.9|}{|0.5,0.1,05,0.9|}$$

$$= \frac{|0.2,0.1,05,07|}{2.0} = \frac{|1.5|}{2.0} = 0.7500$$

CIF(1) has the highest value whose category is logical so the corresponding seven consecutive nucleotide base from TG in the DNA sample is chosen as single logical sequence i.e.0.2,0.3,0.2,0.3,0.2,0.3,0.1 and DNA inputs whose category is illogical, two consecutive similar nucleotide base is considered as an illogical sequence as shown in Table 4.

Logical sequence (LS):

$$LS_{p,s,k} = Lseq_{p,s,1}, Lseq_{p,s,2},..., Lseq_{p,s,k}$$

$$\text{Where} \quad p,s = 1 \text{ to } \infty \quad \text{(8)}$$
$$\text{and} \quad k = 1 \text{ to } 7$$

The sequence that are logical in their category alone are fed to the discriminator (D1) where unique identification number(0.182464) is computed using the equation 9 as shown in Table 6 and the standard deviation of logical sequence is calculated and plotted using MATLAB (Sivanandam, 2006) to represent unique repeated logical sequence pictorially as in Figure 2.

$$D1_{p,s} = \sum_{k=1}^{7} k(Lseq_{p,s,k})^k \quad \text{(9)}$$
$$p,s = 1 \text{ to } \infty$$

$$e.g. D1_{1,3} = 1(0.4)^1 + 2(0.2)^2 + 3(0.4)^3 + 4(0.1)^4$$
$$+ 5(0.1)^5 + 6(0.1)^6 + 7(0.1)^7 = 0.672457$$

Illogical sequence (IS):

$$IS_{p,s} = ILseq_s, ILseq_s,..., ILseq_\infty \quad \text{(10)}$$

The sequence that are illogical in their category are fed to the discriminator (D2) where identification number is computed as shown in Table 5a and b using the equation:

$$D2_{p,s} = ILseq_s{}^m$$

$$\text{whe re } p, s, m = 1 \text{to } \infty$$

m = Number of times nucleotide base is repeated . (11)

$$e.g. \quad D2_{1,2} = (0.2)^3 = 0.008000$$

The discriminator outputs of both D1, D2 are used to identify the location of mutation in the given sample as thus discussed.

DNA SAMPLE: HUMAN-1 [BASE PAIR =32, SEQUENCE =25]

>AB000263 |acc=AB000263|descr=Homo sapiens mRNA for prepro cortistatin like peptide, complete cds.|len=368
AATGTGTTGTGTGACCCCTCAAAATCTCTCAAATGTG
TTTTTACACTCCGTTGGTAATATGGAATGTGTTAAAGT
TGCTACCCGGGGGTTTTTTAATGTGTCTCT
TGTGACCCCTCAAAATCTCTCAAATGTGTTTTTACACT
CCGTTGGTAATATGGAATGTGTTAAAGTTGCTACCCG
GGGTTTTTTAATGTGTCTCT

IDENTIFCIATION OF MUTATION IN THE SAMPLE

Mutation (Charles, 2007) is a change of DNA sequence within a gene or chromosome of an organism resulting in the creation of a new character or trait not found in the parental type .The mutation (Mark and Marcus, 2007) results when a change occurs in a chromosome, either through an alteration in the nucleotide sequence of the DNA coding for a gene or through a change in the physical arrangement of a chromosome.

Mutations (Graham, 2007) that result in missing DNA are called deletions. These can be small, or longer deletions that affect a large number of genes on the chromosome. Deletions can also cause frame-shift mutations. Mutations (Richard et al., 1998 that result in the addition of extra DNA are called insertions. Insertions can also cause frame-shift mutations, and generally result in a non-functional protein. In an inversion mutation, an entire section of DNA is reversed. A small inversion may involve only a few bases within a gene, while longer inversions involve large regions of a chromosome containing several genes.

Various types of mutation identification in human-1 sample

Before mutation

LS1/RS	LS2	IS1		IS1	IS1
AATGTGT	TGTGTGA	C		C	C

Table 4. Identification of logical and illogical sequence using CIF.

							DNA inputs of *human-1*						
	A,A*	T,G*	C,C**	C,C**	C,C**	C,T*	T,C*	A,A*	T,T**	T,T**	T,T**	T,T*	T,A*
PPI (Preprocessor Input)	**0.1,0.1**	**0.2,0.3**	**0.4,0.4**	**0.4,0.4**	**0.4,0.4**	**0.4,0.2**	**0.2,0.4**	**0.1,0.1**	**0.2,0.2**	**0.2,0.2**	**0.2,0.2**	**0.2,0.2**	**0.2,0.1**
PPO Preprocessor Output	0.1,0.1, 0.9,0.9	0.2,0.3, 0.8,0.7	0.4,0.6, 0.6,0.4	0.4,0.6, 0.6,0.4	0.4,0.6, 0.6,0.4	0.4,0.2, 0.6,0.8	0.2,0.4, 0.8,0.6	0.1,0.1, 0.9,0.9	0.2,0.8, 0.8,0.2	0.2,0.8, 0.8,0.2	0.2,0.8, 0.8,0.2	0.2,0.8, 0.8,0.2	0.2,0.1, 0.8,0.9
WFI WFI(1) / CFI(1)-L	0.1,0.1, 0.6,0.5	0.1,0.1, 0.6,0.5	0.1,0.1, 0.6,0.5	0.1,0.1, 0.6,0.5	0.1,0.1, 0.6,0.5	0.1,0.1, 0.6,0.5	0.1,0.1, 0.6,0.5	0.1,0.1, 0.6,0.5	0.1,0.1, 0.6,0.5	0.1,0.1, 0.6,0.5	0.1,0.1, 0.6,0.5	0.1,0.1, 0.6,0.5	0.1,0.1, 0.6,0.5
WFI(2) / CFI(2)-ILL	0.2,0.6, 0.5,0.2	0.2,0.6, 0.5,0.2	0.2,0.6, 0.5,0.2	0.2,0.6, 0.5,0.2	0.2,0.6, 0.5,0.2	0.2,0.6, 0.5,0.2	0.2,0.6, 0.5,0.2	0.2,0.6, 0.5,0.2	0.2,0.6, 0.5,0.2	0.2,0.6, 0.5,0.2	0.2,0.6, 0.5,0.2	0.2,0.6, 0.5,0.2	0.2,0.6, 0.5,0.2
WFI(3) / CFI(3)-L	0.5,0.1, 0.5,0.9	0.5,0.1, 0.5,0.9	0.5,0.1, 0.5,0.9	0.5,0.1, 0.5,0.9	0.5,0.1, 0.5,0.9	0.5,0.1, 0.5,0.9	0.5,0.1, 0.5,0.9	0.5,0.1, 0.5,0.9	0.5,0.1, 0.5,0.9	0.5,0.1, 0.5,0.9	0.5,0.1, 0.5,0.9	0.5,0.1, 0.5,0.9	0.5,0.1, 0.5,0.9
CIF CIF(1)	1.0000	1.0000	0.9230	0.9230	0.9230	1.0000	1.0000	1.0000	0.7692	0.7692	0.7692	0.7692	1.0000
CIF(2)	0.6000	0.6000	1.0000	1.0000	1.0000	0.7333	0.8666	0.6000	1.0000	1.0000	1.0000	1.0000	0.6666
CIF(3)	0.8000	0.7500	0.7000	0.7000	0.7000	0.9000	0.7000	0.8000	0.5000	0.5000	0.5000	0.5000	0.8500
GIC	CIF(1)	CIF(1)	CIF(2)	CIF(2)	CIF(2)	CIF(1)	CIF(1)	CIF(1)	CIF(2)	CIF(2)	CIF(2)	CIF(2)	CIF(1)
IC LOGICAL / ILLOGICAL	L	L	ILL	ILL	ILL	L	L	L	ILL	ILL	ILL	ILL	L
Categorized Sequence	0.1,0.1,0. 2,0.3,0.2, 0.3,0.2 0.1	0.2,0.3,0.2,0 .3,0.2,0.3, 0.1	0.4,0.4	0.4,0.4	0.4,0.4	0.4,0.2,0.4,0 .4,0.2,0.4, 0.1	0.2,0.4,0.2, 0.4,0.2,0.4, 0.1	0.1,0.1,0.2, 0.3,0.2,0.3, 0.2	0.2,0.2	0.2,0.2	0.2,0.2	0.2,0.2	0.2,0.1,0.4, 0.1,0.4,0.2, 0.4

CIF, Category inference function; *, condition 1; **, condition 2; ***, condition 3; **IC**, inferred category.

Case 1

LS1/RS   LS2   IS1
CTCTXXX AATGTGT IS1

G   GTTTTTTT
LS3   LS4   LS5/RS   IS2 IS2
CTCAAA   TCTCTCA   AATGTGT   T   T
IS2   LS6   LS7   LS8
T   TACACTC   CGTTGGT   AATATGG
LS9/RS   LS10   LS11   IS3 IS3
AATGTGT TAAAGTT   GCTACCC   G   G
IS3   LS12   LS13/RS   LS14

After point mutation in the sample

LS3   LS4   LS5/RS   LS7   IS2
AATGTGT TGTGTGA   C   C
CTCA C AA   TCTCTCA   AATGTG T T
IS2   LS6   LS8
T   TACACTC   CGTTGGT   AATATGG
LS9/RS   LS10   LS11   IS2
AATGTGT   TAAAGTT   GCTACCC   T
IS3   G

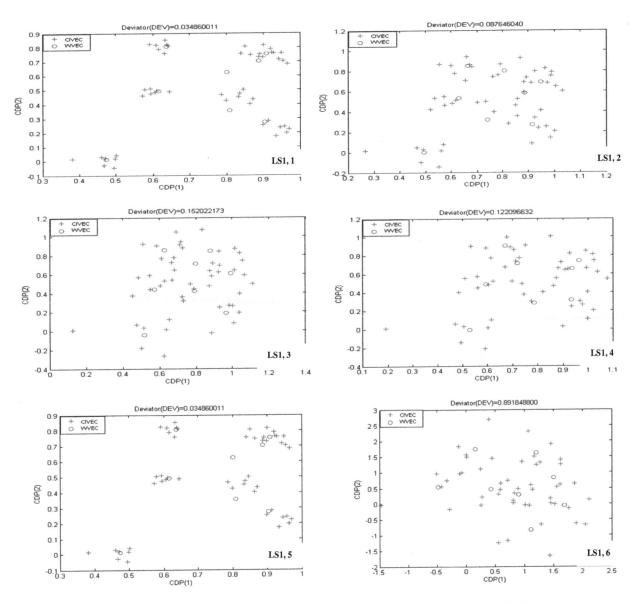

Figure 2. MATLAB output for logical sequence (LS $_{(1, 1)}$-LS $_{(1, 6)}$) showing LS $_{(1, 1)}$ and LS $_{(1, 5)}$ are unique. CDP, Clustered data points; CIVEC, cluster of input vectors; WVEC, weight vectors.

IS3	IS3	LS12	LS13/RS	LS14
G	G	GTTTTTT	AATGTGT	CTCTXXX

In case 1 the point mutation occurred in logical sequence (LS$_{1, 3}$) by the mutant C that can be identified with the change in identification number of LS$_{1, 3}$ where identification number of illogical sequence remains unaltered as in Table 6.

Result

Change in polypeptide sequence might change the shape or function of the protein, depending on where in the sequence occurs.

Case 2

After frame shift mutation [Insertion] in the sample:

LS1/RS	LS2	IS1	IS1	IS1
AATGTGT	TGTGTGA	C	C	C
LS3	**LS4**	**LS5/RS**	**IS2**	**IS2**
CTCAAAA	TCTCTCA	AATGTGT	T	T
IS2	**LS6**	**LS7**	**LS8**	
T	TACACTC	CGTTGGT	AATATGG	

Table 5a. Discriminator (d2) outputs for categorized IS from non-mutated human 1 sample.

Illogical Sequence (IS $_{p,s}$)	Number of time sequence repeated(m)	Human (p)	Sequence (s)	ILseq$_s$	Identification number (D2$_{p,s}$)
IS$_{1,1}$	1	1	1	0.4	0.064000
IS$_{1,1}$	2	1	1	0.4	
IS$_{1,1}$	3	1	1	0.4	
IS$_{1,2}$	1	1	2	0.2	0.008000
IS$_{1,2}$	2	1	2	0.2	
IS$_{1,2}$	3	1	2	0.2	
IS$_{1,3}$	1	1	3	0.3	0.027000
IS$_{1,3}$	2	1	3	0.3	
IS$_{1,3}$	3	1	3	0.3	

Table 5b. Discriminator (d1) outputs for categorized logical sequence from non-mutated human1 sample.

Logical sequence (LS $_{p,s}$)	Human (p)	Sequence (s)	LSeq $_{p,s,k}$							Identification number (D1$_{p,s}$)
			k=1	k=2	k=3	k=4	k=5	k=6	k=7	
LS$_{1,1}$	1	1	0.1	0.1	0.2	0.3	0.2	0.3	0.2	**0.182464**
LS$_{1,2}$	1	2	0.2	0.3	0.2	0.3	0.2	0.3	0.1	0.442375
LS$_{1,3}$	1	3	0.4	0.2	0.4	0.1	0.1	0.1	0.1	0.672457
LS$_{1,4}$	1	4	0.2	0.4	0.2	0.4	0.2	0.4	0.1	0.672577
LS$_{1,5}$	1	5	0.1	0.1	0.2	0.3	0.2	0.3	0.2	**0.182464**
LS$_{1,6}$	1	6	0.2	0.1	0.4	0.1	0.4	0.2	0.4	0.475453
LS$_{1,7}$	1	7	0.4	0.3	0.2	0.2	0.3	0.3	0.2	0.627014
LS$_{1,8}$	1	8	0.1	0.1	0.2	0.1	0.2	0.3	0.3	0.151905
LS$_{1,9}$	1	9	0.1	0.1	0.2	0.3	0.2	0.3	0.2	**0.182464**
LS$_{1,10}$	1	10	0.2	0.1	0.1	0.1	0.3	0.2	0.2	0.236024
LS$_{1,11}$	1	11	0.3	0.4	0.2	0.1	0.4	0.4	0.4	0.731645
LS$_{1,12}$	1	12	0.3	0.2	0.2	0.2	0.2	0.2	0.2	0.412474
LS$_{1,13}$	1	13	0.1	0.1	0.2	0.3	0.2	0.3	0.2	**0.182464**

0.182464 (Unique identification number)

LS9/RS	LS10	LS11	LS12
AATGTGT	TAAAGTT	GCTACCC	G **C** GGGTT
IS3 IS3		IS3	LS13	LS14
T T		T	TAATGTG	TCTCTXX

In case 2 the frame shift mutation (insertion) occurred in one of the IS$_{1,3}$ by the mutant C which alters both the logical sequence (LS$_{1,12}$) and illogical sequence (IS$_{1,3}$) that can be identified by the change in identification number of both logical sequence (LS$_{1,12}$) and illogical sequence (IS$_{1,3}$) as in Table 7.

Result

Change in polypeptide sequence might change the shape or function of the protein, depending on where in the sequence occurs.

Case 3

After point mutation [neutral or silent] in the sample

LS1/RS	LS2	IS1	IS1	IS1
AATGTGT	TGTGTGA	C	C	C
LS3	LS4	LS5/RS	IS2	IS2
CTCAAAA	TCTCTCA	AATGTGT	T	T
IS2	LS6	LS7	LS8	
T	TACACTC	CGTTGGT	AATATGG	
LS9/RS	LS10	LS11		IS3
AATGTGT	TAAAGTT	GCTACCC		G

Table 6. Point mutation.

Logical Sequence (LS)	Identification number (before mutation)	Identificatio number (after mutation)
$LS_{1,1}$	0.182464	0.182464
$LS_{1,2}$	0.442375	0.442375
$LS_{1,3}$	0.672457	**0.723607**
$LS_{1,4}$	0.672577	0.672577
$LS_{1,5}$	0.182464	0.182464
$LS_{1,6}$	0.475453	0.475453
$LS_{1,7}$	0.627014	0.627014
$LS_{1,8}$	0.151905	0.151905
$LS_{1,9}$	0.182464	0.182464
$LS_{1,10}$	0.236024	0.236024
$LS_{1,11}$	0.731645	0.731645
$LS_{1,12}$	0.412474	0.412474
$LS_{1,13}$	0.182464	0.182464
illogical sequence (IS)	**Identification number (before mutation)**	**Identification number (after mutation)**
$IS_{1,1}$	0.064000	0.064000
$IS_{1,2}$	0.008000	0.008000
$IS_{1,3}$	0.027000	0.027000

Table 7. Frame shift mutation (insertion).

Logical Sequence (LS)	Identification number (before mutation)	Identification number (after mutation)
$LS_{1,1}$	0.182464	0.182464
$LS_{1,2}$	0.442375	0.442375
$LS_{1,3}$	0.672457	0.672457
$LS_{1,4}$	0.672577	0.672577
$LS_{1,5}$	0.182464	0.182464
$LS_{1,6}$	0.475453	0.475453
$LS_{1,7}$	0.627014	0.627014
$LS_{1,8}$	0.151905	0.151905
$LS_{1,9}$	0.182464	0.182464
$LS_{1,10}$	0.236024	0.236024
$LS_{1,11}$	0.731645	0.731645
$LS_{1,12}$	0.412474	0.7459736
$LS_{1,13}$	0.182464	0.243464
Illogical sequence (IS)	**Identification number (before mutation)**	**Identification number (after mutation)**
$IS_{1,1}$	0.064000	0.064000
$IS_{1,2}$	0.008000	0.008000
$IS_{1,3}$	0.027000	0.008000

Table 8. point mutation neutral or silent.

Logical sequence (LS)	Identification number (before mutation)	Identification number (after mutation)
$LS_{1,1}$	0.182464	0.182464
$LS_{1,2}$	0.442375	0.442375
$LS_{1,3}$	0.672457	0.672457
$LS_{1,4}$	0.672577	0.672577
$LS_{1,5}$	0.182464	0.182464
$LS_{1,6}$	0.475453	0.475453
$LS_{1,7}$	0.627014	0.627014
$LS_{1,8}$	0.151905	0.151905
$LS_{1,9}$	0.182464	0.182464
$LS_{1,10}$	0.236024	0.236024
$LS_{1,11}$	0.731645	0.731645
$LS_{1,12}$	0.412474	0.412474
$LS_{1,13}$	0.182464	0.182464

Illogical sequence (IS)	Identification number (before mutation)	Identification number (after mutation)
$IS_{1,1}$	0.064000	0.064000
$IS_{1,2}$	0.008000	0.008000
$IS_{1,3}$	0.027000	**0.008100**

IS3	IS3	IS3	LS12	LS13/RS
G	G	G	GTTTTTT	AATGTGT

LS14
CTCTXXX

Result

No change in polypeptide sequence, possible consequence for the organism =none. In case 3, the point mutation is occurred in same $IS_{1,3}$ as case 2 but with mutant G that only alters the illogical sequence ($IS_{1,3}$) and not any of the LS that can be identified only using the change in identification number of illogical sequence ($IS_{1,3}$) Table 8.

Case 4

After Frame shift mutation in the sample

LS1/RS	LS2	IS1	IS1	IS1
AATGTGT	TGTGTGA	C	C	C
LS3	**LS4**	**LS5/RS**	**IS2**	**IS2**
CTCAAAA	TCTCTCA	AATGTGT	T	T
IS2	**LS6**	**LS7**		**LS8**
T	TACACTC	CGTTGGT	AATATGG	
LS9/RS	**LS10**	**LS11**	**IS3**	**IS3**

AATGTGT	TAAAGTT	GCTACCC	G	G
IS3	**LS12**	**LS13/RS**	**LS14**	
GGTTT	TTA	ATGTGTC	TCTXXX	

In case 4 the frame mutation [deletion] occurred in logical sequence ($LS_{1,12}$) by the removal of mutant T and can be identified with the change in identification number of logical sequence ($LS_{1,12}$) with no alteration in any of the illogical sequence as in Table 9 .

Result

Change in polypeptide sequence might change the shape or function of the protein, depending on where in the sequence occurs.

Case 5

In case 5, the inversion mutation occurred in logical sequence ($LS_{1,10}$) by replacing TAAAGTT with mutant TTGAAAT that can be identified with the change in identification number of logical sequence ($LS_{1,10}$) alone with no alteration in any of the IS as in Table 10.

After inversion mutation in the sample

LS1/RS	LS2	IS1	IS1	IS1

Table 9. Frame shift mutation deletion.

Logical sequence (LS)	Identification number (before mutation)	Identification number (after mutation)
$LS_{1,1}$	0.182464	0.182464
$LS_{1,2}$	0.442375	0.442375
$LS_{1,3}$	0.672457	0.672457
$LS_{1,4}$	0.672577	0.672577
$LS_{1,5}$	0.182464	0.182464
$LS_{1,6}$	0.475453	0.475453
$LS_{1,7}$	0.627014	0.627014
$LS_{1,8}$	0.151905	0.151905
$LS_{1,9}$	0.182464	0.182464
$LS_{1,10}$	0.236024	0.236024
$LS_{1,11}$	0.731645	0.731645
$LS_{1,12}$	0.412474	**0.410945**
$LS_{1,13}$	0.182464	**0.291402**
Illogical sequence (IS)	**Identification number (before mutation)**	**Identification number (after mutation)**
$IS_{1,1}$	0.064000	0.064000
$IS_{1,2}$	0.008000	0.008000
$IS_{1,3}$	0.027000	0.027000

Table 10. Inversion mutation.

Logical sequence (LS)	Identification number (before mutation)	Identification number (after mutation)
$LS_{1,1}$	0.182464	0.182464
$LS_{1,2}$	0.442375	0.442375
$LS_{1,3}$	0.672457	0.672457
$LS_{1,4}$	0.672577	0.672577
$LS_{1,5}$	0.182464	0.182464
$LS_{1,6}$	0.475453	0.475453
$LS_{1,7}$	0.627014	0.627014
$LS_{1,8}$	0.151905	0.151905
$LS_{1,9}$	0.182464	0.182464
$LS_{1,10}$	0.236024	0.361546
$LS_{1,11}$	0.731645	0.731645
$LS_{1,12}$	0.412474	0.412474
$LS_{1,13}$	0.182464	0.182464
Ilogical sequence (IS)	**Identification number (before mutation)**	**Identification number (after mutation)**
$IS_{1,1}$	0.064000	0.064000
$IS_{1,2}$	0.008000	0.008000
$IS_{1,3}$	0.027000	0.027000

AATGTGT	TGTGTGA	C		C		C
LS3	**LS4**	**LS5/RS**	**IS2**	**IS2**		
CTCAAAA	TCTCTCA	AATGTGT	T	T		
IS2	**LS6**	**LS7**	**LS8**			
T	TACACTC	CGTTGGT	AATATGG			
LS9/RS	**LS10**	**LS11**	**IS3**			
AATGTGT	**TTGAAAT**	GCTACCC	G			
IS3	**IS3**	**LS12**	**LS13/RS**	**LS14**		
G	G	GTTTTTT	AATGTGT	CTCTXXX		

CONCLUSION

As an attempt to automate the genetic finger printing the Neural-fuzzy pattern recognition system (NFPR) discussed in the above work assists forensic scientists by generating unique identification number for individuals from their DNA sample. The proposed system also helps to identify the location of occurrence mutation in the given mutated DNA sample, for instance, gene mutations which triggers hereditary nonpolyposis colorectal cancer (HNPCC) tumor that could not be detected even by PCR-SSCP can be easily detected by subjecting the sample to gene sequencing process and analyzed using above system.

Further development can be extended by training patterns in DNA protein that can be represented by suitable fuzzy equivalent in order to classify and predict the protein structure in the protein folding problem. The above technique can be used in the areas where feature extraction is to be done in genetic engineering with suitable modification.

ACKNOWLEDGEMENTS

We like to thank Senior Scientist, Dr. K. Thangarasu of Bio-Rad Laborataries, Banaglore, India and Dr. K. Somasundaram of Amirtha University, Coimbatore, India for their assistance in conducting the experiment.

Abbreviations: DNA, DEOXYRIBONUCLEIC acid; **RNA,** ribonucleic acid; **NFPR,** neural-fuzzy pattern recognition; **NFRM,** neural- fuzzy resonance mapping; **A,** adenine; **T,** thymine; **G,** guanine; **C,** cytosine; **U,** uracil; **ACF,** activation function; **MAF,** match function; **CFI,** category for Inference; **CIF,** category inference function; IS, illogical sequence; **CDP,** clustered data points; **CIVEC,** cluster of input vectors; **WVEC,** weight vectors; **HNPCC,** hereditary nonpolyposis colorectal cancer; **SL,** logical sequence.

REFERENCES

Mark D.Evans and Marcus S.Cooke (2007). Oxidative Damage to Nucleic Acids, Springer science press, New York.

Advances in Neural Networks issn (2006). Third international symposium on neural networks, Springer Berlin Heidelberg, New York publications.

Andreas DB (2001). Bioinformatics-A practical Guide to the Analysis of genes and proteins, second edition, A John wiley & sons, Inc., Publication.

Ayala-Gross JA (2001). DNA Analysis: The best method for Human Identifications, National University, San Diego.

Carpenter GA, Grossberg (1987). A Massively Parallel Architecture for a self-organizing Neural Pattern Recognition Machine, Computer Vision, Graphics and Image Processing, 37: 54-115.

Carpenter GA, Grossberg S, Reynolds JH (2010). "ARTMAP: Supervised Real Time Learning and Classification of Non-stationary Data by a Self- organizing Neural Network", 4: 565-588.

Charles LV (2007). New developments in Mutation Research, Nova science publishers Inc New York.

David EN (2008). DNA Evidence and Forensic science- 2008 facts on file, Inc. http://www.factsonfile.com.

David WM (2004). Bioinformatics Sequence and Genome analysis-Second Edition, Cold Spring Harbor Laboratory Press, New York.

Des H, Willie T (2000). Bioinformatics Sequence, Structure and data banks, Oxford University Press.

Donald RT (2005). The Pattern Recognition Basis of Artificial Intelligence", IEEE Press, New York. Computational Intelligence and Bio inspired Systems, 8th international work conference on artificial neural networks, iwann-2005proceedings. Elsevier Inc., p. 117.

Graham RT (2007). Laboratory methods for the detection of mutations and polymorphisms in DNA, CRC Press, 2007 - Science.

Joe N, John FF (1999). Crime Science Methods of Forensic Detection, 1999. University Press of Kentucky.

John H, Anders K, Richard GP (2008). Introduction to the Theory of Neural Computation, Addison Wesley, Redwood City, A.

John OS, Brent ET (2005). Rape Investigation Hand book, 2005,

Michael RB (2007). Bioinformatics for geneticists, Second Edition, John Wiley & Sons Ltd.

Norah R, Keith I (2002). An Introduction forensic DNA Analysis, 2002-CRC Press.

Phipps A, Lawrence J, Geert-De-Soete (1996).. Clustering and Classification, World Scientific, River Edge, NJ.

Richard GHC, Edward E, Sue F (1998). Mutation detection, IRL Press at Oxford University Press.

Richard OD, Peter EH, David GS (2006). Pattern classification-Second Edition, John Wiley and sons.

Robert S (2007). Pattern Recognition: Statistical, Structural and Neural Approaches, 2007, John Wiley and sons.

Sivanandam SN (2006). Introduction to neural networks and MATLAB-6.0", Tata McGraw-Hill publishing company.

Stephen JH, Jack DC, Giles CL (2009). Advances in Neural Information Processing Systems, volume 5, Morgan Kaufmann San Mateo CA.

Stephen K, David DW (2003). Introduction to Bioinformatics A Theoretical and Practical Approach, Human Press Inc.

## 29

Primer designing for PreS region of hepatitis B virus from the most conserved patches of hepatitis B virus genome

Naaz Abbas[1] , Mohammad Ajmal[2] and Talat Afroze[2]

[1]Food and Biotechnology Research Center, PCSIR Laboratories complex Lahore 54600, Pakistan.
[2]Centre of Excellence in Molecular Biology, University of the Punjab, Lahore, Pakistan.

The most conserved regions for 15 hepatitis B virus complete genome of different subtypes were aligned using PCGENE software CLUSTAL to design a new pair of primer that can bind to each subtype of hepatitis B virus (HBV), to amplify PreS region of HBV genome. A pair of primer from these conserved patches was selected using software PRIMER and named as Nhepf1 and Nhepr1. Nhepf1, forward primer bound 2362-2385 nucleotides and Nhepr1, reverse primer bound 260-283 nucleotide amplify 1.12 Kb region of HBV genome that contain PreS sequence. The pair of primer was optimized for PCR. Nhepf1 and Nhepr1 annealed well at 50°C to subtype adw2 (American), adr4 (Japanese) and Pakistanian patient derived HBV DNA without any nonspecific bands. The results were found to be highly reproducible with greater accuracy.

Key words: Hepatitis B virus (HBV) genome, HBV conserved region, polymerase chains reaction (PCR) primers, primer designing.

INTRODUCTION

There is prevalence of hepatitis B virus in an estimated 500 million person in the world, the frequent occurrence of this infection in close contacts of carriers, perinatal vertical transmission from mother to infant and high incidence of insidious chronic liver disease or cancer of the liver among the carriers, signify a major public health problem of worldwide concern (Abbas, 2007). Hepatitis B viral genome (3200 bp) has four known genes, S encoding the viral surface protein, C encoding core protein, P DNA polymerase encoding gene and X gene (Lai et al., 1991). Virus envelope proteins designated PreS1, PreS2 and S carries neutralization epitopes and plays an important role in virus/cell interactions (Wong et al., 2004). At least five epitopes have been mapped within PreS region (Kuroki et al., 1990) and it contains two directly or indirectly binding sites to hepatocytes that constitute the first step in the infection (Dash et al., 1992). Antibodies to PreS region are considered to play a major role in clearance of HBV. Various naturally occurring mutations in the PreS and S genes have been described, including deletions and point mutations leading to subtypic changes (Okamoto et al., 1987 and Lai et al., 1991).

There are at least four subtypes (adw, adr, ayr and ayw) of HBV that can be recognized by antigenic differences in the antigen (Ono et al., 1983; Abbas et al., 2006; Abbas, 2009). HBsAg has distinct geographical, epidemiological and anthropological settings (Courouce-Pauty et al., 1983; Abbas et al., 2008). The considerable number of HBV isolates with divergent nucleotide sequences and the partially double stranded characteristic of HBV impose the need for extreme care in the choice of primers for both full length and fragment amplification (Zhang et al., 2007).

Subtypes provide useful epidemiological marker of HBV. The mutation rate of HBV is estimated to be 100 times higher than that of other DNA viruses. Since HBV infection persists for many decades in patients, base changes can accumulate over time (Drosten et al., 2000). One in every ten HBV isolates is slightly different at the nucleotide level from other all sequenced isolates, that is, >10% sequence heterogeneity in HBV (Lauder et al., 1993; Zhang et al., 2007). It is hence crucial to study sequence variation of envelope protein of Pakistanian HBV isolates and to plan a noval strategy for designing a new set of primers with the anticipated use for clinical diagnosis of HBV after the selection of the most conserved region of HBV genomic DNA of different subtypes. The aim of the current investigation was to design such a pair of primer which could perfectly bind to all different genotypes and subtypes of HBV, and would be helpful in detection and DNA amplification of HBV isolated from areas (as Pakistan) that have no previous HBV sequence data.

MATERIALS AND METHODS

Primer designing

Eight sequences were collected from GenBank and seven were selected and edited from research papers and fed into computer (PCGENE Release 6.5, 1991 Intelligenetics Inc.). Two sets of subfiles, for each of the fifteen sequences, one having 200 nucleotides stretch from 2300/2307 to 2500/2507 positions and other of 300 nucleotides stretch from 155/157 to 455/457 positions, were created using SEQIN (PCGENE). Fifteen subfiles for each portion were compiled in a library file using FILE (PCGENE). These library files were used in CLUSTAL (PCGENE), to align fifteen patches of HBV genome. The most conserved regions found in this way were subjected to biological software PRIMER version 0.5 (MIT USA, 1991) for primer selection.

DNA preparation

An American clone adw2 gifted by Dr. Aleem Siddique (NIH USA)

and a Japanese clone kindly provided by Dr. Okubo (Japan) were prepared as in Sambrook et al. (1989). HBV DNA from sera of HbsAg positive patients were extracted as described in Abbas et al. (2005).

PCR amplification

The cloned DNA as well as patient derived HBV DNA were used for PCR amplification using 1 µM of each Nhepf1 and Nhepr1 with 10 mM Tris-Cl (pH 8.3), 2.5 mM MgCl$_2$, 50 mM KCl, 200 µM each dNTP, 2U *Taq* polymerase per 100 µl reaction (Persing et al., 1993). The mixture was denatured at 95°C for 2 min, annealed at 50°C for 2 min, and elongated at 70°C for 2 min for 35 cycles. PCR product was resolved on 1% agarose gel according to Sambrook et al. (1989).

RESULTS AND DISCUSSION

Fifteen (15) sequences of different genotypes and subtypes were collected and aligned to find conserved regions to design a pair of primer. Eight nucleotide sequences of hepatitis B virus were collected from Genbank with accession numbers were M32138, X75658, X75657, X04615, X75664, X75665, X75663, X75656 and seven selected from research papers (Okamoto et al., 1986; Norder et al., 1994; Tong et al., 1990; Ono et al., 1983). Two regions which were reported to be conserved (Lauder et al., 1993) were selected. The 200 nucleotides conserved patch was from the end of core region overlapping with start of P gene at 2300/2307-2500/2507 position. This patch gave only one region of 37 nucleotides (Figure 1) after alignment of library file through CLUSTAL, which was adopted for forward primer selection.

The 300 nucleotide conserved patch selected for reverse primer was from first hydrophobic region of surface antigen at 155/157-455/457 position. The alignment of library file through CLUSTAL of this patch gave three stretches of 27 nucleotides each (Figure 2). First stretch was chosen for reverse primer selection.

The above two selected regions which were found absolutely conserved and consensus to each other by CLUSTAL were used to select forward and reverse primer respectively by PRIMER selection (Figure 3). After examining 37 forward primers it accepted 9 forward primers, similarly after examining 27 reverse primers, it accepted 10 reverse primers. Finally, one pair of 24-mer each was selected AS given below:

Nhepf1 GTCCCCTAGAAGAAGAACTCCCTC Tm= 62.0°C

Nhepr1 CCCTAGAAAATTGAGAGAAGTCCA Tm= 60.1°C

Forward primer possesses one GC clamp while reverse primer possesses two GC clamps at its 3' end. GC

```
=========================================================================PC/GENE===

* * * * * * * * * * * * * * * * * * * * * * * * * * * * * * * * * * * * * * *
* MULTIPLE SEQUENCE ALIGNMENT forward primer. *
* * * * * * * * * * * * * * * * * * * * * * * * * * * * * * * * * * * * * * *
Setting of computation parameters
=================================

K-tuple value  : 2
Gap penalty    : 5
Window size    : 10
Filtering level: 2.5
Open gap cost  : 10
Unit gap cost  : 10
Transitions are: WEIGHTED twice as likely as tranversions.
Setting of other parameters
===========================

The alignment was done on 15 Nucleic acid sequences.
Character to show that a position in the alignment is perfectly conserved: '*'
Character to show that a position is well conserved: '.'


Alignment
B4          ATGCCCCTATCTTATCAACACTTCCGGAGAATACTGTTGTTAGACGAAG-      49
B8          ATGCCCCTATCTTATCAACACTTCCGGAGAATACTGTTGTTAGACGAAG-      49
B10         ATGCCCCTATCCTATCCACACTTCCGGAAACTACTGTTGTTAGACGACG-      49
B12         ATGCCCCTATCCTATCCACACTTCCGGAAACTACTGTTGTTAGACGACG-      49
B2          ATGCCCCTATCTTATCAACACTTCCGGAAACTACTGTTGTTAGACGACG-      49
B18         ATGCCCCTATCTTATCAACACTTCCGGAAACTACTGTTGTTAGACGACG-      49
B6          ATGCCCCTATCTTATCAACACTTCCGGAAACTACTGTTGTTAGACGAAG-      49
B14         ATGCCCCTATCTTATCAACACTTCCGGAAACTACTGTTGTTAGACGTCG-      49
B24         ATGCCCCTATCTTATCAACACTTCCGGAAACTACTGTTGTTAGACGACG-      49
B26         ATGCCCCTATCTTATCAACACTTCCGGAAACTACTGTTGTTAGACGAAG-      49
B28         ATGCCCCTATCTTATCAACACTTCCGGAAACTACTGTTGTTAGACGACG-      49
B22         ATGCCCCTATCCTATCAACACTTCCGGAGACTACTGTTGTTAGACGACG-      49
B16         ATGCCCCTATCTTATCAACACTTCCGGAGACTACTGTTGTTAGACGACG-      49
B30         ATGCCCCTATCTTATCAACACTTCCGGAGACTACTGTTGTTAGACGACG-      49
B20         ATGCCCCTATCTTATCAACACTTCCGGAAACTACTGTTGTTAGACGACGG      50
            * * * * * * * * * *  * * * *  * * * * * * * * * * .*  * * * * * * * * * * * * * * *.  *


B4          -----AGGCAGGTCCCCTAGAAGAAGAACTCCCTCGCCTCGCAGACGAAG      94
B8          -----AGGCAGGTCCCCTAGAAGAAGAACTCCCTCGCCTCGCAGACGAAG      94
B10         -----AGGCAGGTCCCCTAGAAGAAGAACTCCCTCGCCTCGCCGACGAAG      94
B12         -----AGGCAGGTCCCCTAGAAGAAGAACTCCCTCGCCTCGCAGACGAAG      94
B2          -----AGGCAGGTCCCCTAGAAGAAGAACTCCCTCGCCTCGCAGACGAAG      94
B18         -----AGGCAGGTCCCCTAGAAGAAGAACTCCCTCGCCTCGCAGACGAAG      94
B6          -----AGGCAGGTCCCCTAGAAGAAGAACTCCCTCGCCTCGCAGACGAAG      94
B14         -----AGGCAGGTCCCCTAGAAGAAGAACTCCCTCGCCTCGCAGACGAAG      94
B24         -----AGGCAGGTCCCCTAGAAGAAGAACTCCCTCGCCTCGCAGACGAAG      94
B26         -----AGGCAGGTCCCCTAGAAGAAGAACTCCCTCGCCTCGCAGACGAAG      94
B28         -----AGGCAGGTCCCCTAGAAGAAGAACTCCCTCGCCTCGCAGACGAAG      94
B22         -----AGGCAGGTCCCCTAGAAGAAGAACTCCCTCGCCTCGCAGACGAAG      94
B16         -----AGGCAGGTCCCCTAGAAGAAGAACTCCCTCGCCTCGCAGACGAAG      94
B30         -----AGGCAGGTCCCCTAGAAGAAGAACTCCCTCGCCTCGCAGACGAAG      94
B20         GACCGAGGCAGGTCCCCTAGAAGAAGAACTCCCTCGCCTCGCAGACGCAG     100
                 * * * * * * * * * * * * * * * * * * * * * * * * * * * * * * * * * * *  * * * *  * *
```

Figure 1. Multiple sequence alignment for forward primer.

```
*************************************************
* MULTIPLE SEQUENCE ALIGNMENT FOR REVERSE PRIMER. *
*************************************************
Setting of computation parameters
===================================
K-tuple value  : 2
Gap penalty    : 5
Window size    : 10
Filtering level: 2.5
Open gap cost  : 10
Unit gap cost  : 10
Transitions are: WEIGHTED twice as likely as tranversions.
Setting of other parameters
============================
The alignment was done on 15 Nucleic acid sequences.
Character to show that a position in the alignment is perfectly conserved: '*'
Character to show that a position is well conserved: '.'
Alignment


B1      GGGGTTTTTCTTGTTGACAAGAATCCTCACAATACCACAGAGTCTAGACT    100
B17     GGGGTTTTTCTTGTTGACAAGAATCCTCACAATACCACAGAGTCTAGACT    100
B5      GGGGTTTTTCTTGTTGACAAAAATCCTCACAATACCACAGAGTCTAGACT    100
B13     GGGGTTTTTCTTGTTGACAAGAATCCTCACAATACCACAGAGTCTAGACT    100
B3      GGGGTTTTTCTTGTTGACAAAAATCCTCACAATACCGCAGAGTCTAGACT    100
B7      GGGGTTTTTCTTGTTGACAAAAATCCTCACAATACCGCAGAGTCTAGACT    100
B15     GGGGTTTTTCTTGTTGACAAAAATCCTCACAATACCGAAGAGTCTAGACT    100
B29     GGGGTTTTTCTTGTTGACAAAAATCCTCACAATACCGAAGAGTCTAGACT    100
B21     GGGGTTTTTCTTGTTGACAAGAATCCTCACAATACCGCAGAGTCTAGACT    100
B19     GGGGTTTTTCTTGTTGACAAGAATCCTCACAATACCGCAGAGTCTAGACT    100
B9      GGTGTGTTTCTTGTTGACAAAAATCCTCACAATACCACAGAGTCTAGACT    100
B11     GGTGTGTTTCTTGTTGACAAAAATCCTCACAATACCACAGAGTCTAGACT    100
B23     GGGGTTTTTCTTGTTGACAAAAATCCTCACAATACCACAGAGTCTAGACT    100
B25     GGGGTTTTTCTTGTTGACAAAAATCCTCACAATACCACAGAGTCTAGACT    100
B27     GGGGTTTTTCTCGTTGACAAAAATCCTCACAATACCTCTGAGTCTAGACT    100
        **.**.***** ******* .***************. .**********


B1      CGTGGTGGACTTCTCTCAATTTTCTAGGGGGAGCACCCACGTGTCCTGGC    150
B17     CGTGGTGGACTTCTCTCAATTTTCTAGGGGGAGCACCCACGTGTCCTGGC    150
B5      CGTGGTGGACTTCTCTCAATTTTCTAGGGGGAGCACCCGTGTGTCCTGGC    150
B13     CGGGGTGGACTTCTCTCAATTTTCTAGGGGAAGCACCAAGGTGTCCTGGC    150
B3      CGTGGTGGACTTCTCTCAATTTTCTAGGGGGAGCTCCCGTGTGTCTTGGC    150
B7      CGTGGTGGACTTCTCTCAATTTTCTAGGGGGAGCTCCCGTGTGTCTTGGC    150
B15     CGTGGTGGACTTCTCTCAATTTTCTAGGGGGAACCACCGTGTGTCTTGGC    150
B29     CGTGGTGGACTTCTCTCAATTTTCTAGGGGGAACCACCGTGTGTCTTGGC    150
B21     CGTGGTGGACTTCTCTCAATTTTCTAGGGGGAACTACCGTGTGTCTTGGC    150
B19     CGTGGTGGACTTCTCTCAATTTTCTAGGGGGATCACCCGTGTGTCTTGGC    150
B9      CGTGGTGGACTTCTCTCAATTTTCTAGGGGGACTACCCAGGTGTCCTGGC    150
B11     CGTGGTGGACTTCTCTCAATTTTCTAGGGGGACTACCCGGGTGTCCTGGC    150
B23     CGTGGTGGACTTCTCTCAATTTTCTAGGGGGAACACCCGTGTGTCTTGGC    150
B25     CGTGGTGGACTTCTCTCAATTTTCTAGGGGGAACACCCGTGTGTCTTGGC    150
B27     CGTGGTGGACTTCTCTCAATTTTCTAGGGGAAACACCCGTGTGTCTTGGC    150
        **.************************.* * . ***** ****
```

Figure 2. Multiple sequence alignment for reverse primer.

```
PRIMER PREFERENCES FILE
************************************************************
Analyzing sequence 1 (seq1)
'*' = target, 'X' = restriction site, '?' = N, number = high repeat
homology
            +10        +20        +30        +40
    AGGCAGGTCC CCTAGAAGAA GAACTCCCTC GCCTCGCATG CAGTGGAACT
1   ---------- ---------- ---------- -------*** **********
    TCCGTCCAGG GGATCTTCTT CTTGAGGGAG CGGAGCGTAC GTCACCTTGA
            +10        +20        +30        +40
    CCACAACCTT CCACCAAACT CTGCAAGATC CCAGAGTGAG AGGCCTGTAT
51  ********** ********** ********** ********** **********
    GGTGTTGGAA GGTGGTTTGA GACGTTCTAG GGTCTCACTC TCCGGACATA
            +10        +20        +30        +40
    CTCCCTGCTG GTGGCTCCAG TTCAGGAACA GTAAACCCTG TTCCGACTAC
101 ********** ********** ********** ********** **********
    GAGGGACGAC CACCGAGGTC AAGTCCTTGT CATTTGGGAC AAGGCTGATG
            +10        +20        +30        +40
    TGTCTCTCCC ATATCGTCAA TCTTCTCGAG GATTGGGGAC CCTGCGCTGA
151 ********** ********** ********** ********** **********
    ACAGAGAGGG TATAGCAGTT AGAAGAGCTC CTAACCCCTG GGACGCGACT
            +10        +20        +30        +40
    ACGGTGGACT TCTCTCAATT TTCTAGGGG
201 **-------- ---------- ---------
    TGCCACCTGA AGAGAGTTAA AAGATCCCC
Acceptable regions for a primer:
base 1 to 37
base 203 to 229

Examining 37 forward primers...9 forward primers accepted.
Examining 27 reverse primers...10 reverse primers accepted.
Testing pairs...

Product size range 201-226...
forward primer    7->30  : GTCCCCTAGAAGAAGAACTCCCTC      Tm = 62.0
reverse primer  228->205 : CCCTAGAAAATTGAGAGAAGTCCA      Tm = 60.1
PCR product length:  222, GC = 54%
```

Figure 3. Primer software results.

contents of primers were 54%. Both primers have five self-complementary bases (2.83%), which were not consecutive to each other but occur at irregular intervals. Tm were 62 and 60.8°C, respectively. The annealing temperature of the primers is 10-15° below the Tm of the primers (Desselberger, 1995). Therefore, PCR was tried using newly selected primers at different annealing temperatures ranging from 60-48°C. The optimum temperature selected was 50°C, which was then used for routine PCR. DNA concentrations for cloned adw2 and

adr4 were tried from 10 - 500 ng, 50 ng was found best. MgCl$_2$ concentration found best for these primers was 1,5 mM of tested ranges 1-4 mM. Primer (NhepF1 and NhepR1) amplified a fragment of 1.1 Kb of PreS region both in pSHBV and patient derived HBV DNA (Figure 4). HBV clone pSHBV gave 3.7 Kb as the orientation of the HBV insert, vector was amplified along with insert lane 2 and 4 (Figure 4).

Hepatitis B virus is the smallest known DNA virus that cause infection in man. The genome is partially double

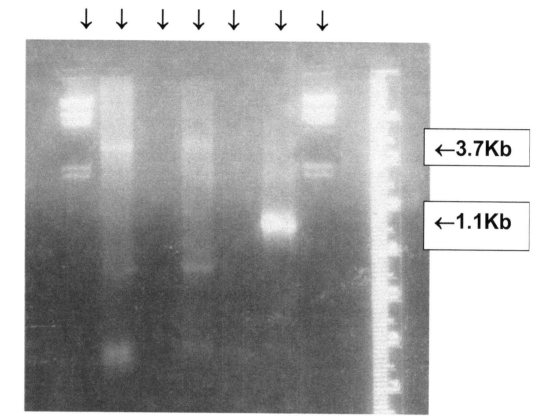

Figure 4. Hepatitis B virus PCR products derived from cloned and patient derived templates using NHepF1 and NhepR1. Lane 1 and 7 (M): λ HindIII marker. Lane 2 and 4 (+C): pSHBV as positive control, Lane 3 (-C): negative control, Lane 5 (P1): patient NA016 PCR, Lane 6 (P2): patient NA012 PCR band.

stranded circular, 3.2 Kb DNA molecule, 0.78 μM in length which corresponds to a molecular weight around 1.6×10^6. HBV genome contains an *Eco*RI site which lies 9 bp downstream from 5'end of PreS2 region. A new set of well conserved primers of 24-mer each were selected from consensus regions (the region encoding hydrophobic region of HBV surface gene and the start of the P gene which overlaps the end of gene C).

It is also imperative that the primers should be greater than 18 or 20 mer, in the range of 20-25 mer, so that they may provide better background. The primers should have at least two to three GC clamps at their 3'end to have a strong grip during the positioning and walking of Taq DNA polymerase to extend the primer for polymerization. In the ideal condition, the F and R primers should not have any intra or/and inter complementary bases, but if there is, they should not be greater than 2.5%. The complementary bases should not be consecutive to each other but present at irregular intervals, because all the complementary bases at one site are consecutive to each

other, more likely have a chance to come close together quickly and complement each other and may have strong grip as compared to the self-complementation at distance intervals.

We look forward with the hope that this pair can be used for routine clinical diagnosis of hepatitis B virus infection in the diversified geographical world of highly variable strains of HBV. This may prove as the reliable primers for obtaining accurate and confident results.

Conflict of Interests

The author(s) have not declared any conflict of interests.

REFERENCES

Abbas N, Abbas S, Afroze T (2008). PCR amplification of Hepatitis B Virus in limiting DNA dilution format. Pak. J. Zool. 40(4):255-260.
Abbas N, Shakoori AR (2007). Hepatitis B virus X gene. A Review: Proceedings Pak Congress Zool. 27:127-136.

Abbas N, Rasool M, Afroze T (2005). PCR based diagnosis of hepatitis B virus. Pak. J. Zool. 37(4):285-288.

Abbas N, Yousra A, Shakoori AR (2006). Mutations in the Hepatitis B virus core gene and its efficacy as a vaccine, A Review: Proceedings Pak Congress Zool. 26:301-319.

Courouce-Pauty AM, Plancon A, Soulier JP (1983). Distribution of HBsAg subtypes in the world. Vox Sang 44:197-211. http://dx.doi.org/10.1111/j.1423-0410.1983.tb01885.x

Dash S, Rao KV, Panda SK (1992). Receptor for pre-S1(21-47) component of hepatitis B virus on the liver cell: role in virus cell interaction. J. Med. Virol. 37(2):116-121. http://dx.doi.org/10.1002/jmv.1890370208

Desselberger U (1995). Medical Virology: A Practical approach. IRL press Oxford University Press New York.

Drosten C, Weber M, Seifried E, Roth WK (2000). Evaluation of a new PCR assay with competitive internal control sequence for blood donor screening. Transfusion 40(6):718-724. http://dx.doi.org/10.1046/j.1537-2995.2000.40060718.x

Kuroki K, Froreani M, Mimms LT, Ganem D (1990). Epitope Mapping of the Pres1 domain of the Hepatitis B virus large surface protein. Virol. 176:620-624. http://dx.doi.org/10.1016/0042-6822(90)90032-M

Lai KE, Melis A, Mazzoleni AP, Farci P, Balestrier A (1991). Sequence analysis of hepatitis B virus genome of new mutant of ayw subtype isolated in Sardinia. NAR, 19:5078. http://dx.doi.org/10.1093/nar/19.18.5078

Lauder IJ, Lin HJ, Lau JYN, Siu TS, Lai CL (1993). The variability of the hepatitis B virus genome: Statistical analysis and biological implications. Mol. Biol. Evol., 10(2):457-470.

Naaz A (2009). Variability anlysis in Immunogenic Region of Hepatitis B virus: Sequence variation in Pakistanian Hepatitis B virus Variability anlysis in Immunogenic Region of Hepatitis B virus: Sequence variation in Pakistanian Hepatitis B virus. VDM Verlag Dr Muller Aktiengesellschaft & Co. KG Dudweiler Landstr. Saarbrucken, Germany. 99:66123. ISBN: 978-3-639-14908-1.

Norder H, Courouce AM, Magnius LO (1994). Complete genomes, phylogenetic relatedness, and strurctural proteins of six strains of the HBV, four of which represent two new genotypes. Virol. 198(2):489-503. http://dx.doi.org/10.1006/viro.1994.1060

Okamoto H, Imai M, Shimozaki M, Hoshi Y, Iizuka H, Gotanda T, Tsuda F, Miyakawa Y, Mayumi M (1986). Nucleotide sequence of a cloned HBV genome, subtype "ayr": Comparison with genomes of the other three subtypes. J. Gen. Virol. 67(11):2305-2314. http://dx.doi.org/10.1099/0022-1317-67-11-2305

Okamoto H, Imai M, Tsuda F, Tanaka T, Miyakawa Y, Mayumi M (1987). Point mutations in the S gene of HBVfor a d/y or w/r subtypic change in two blood donors carring a surface antigen of compound subtype adyr or adwr. J. Virol. 61:3030-3034.

Ono Y, Onda H, Sasada R, Igarashi K, Sugino Y, Nishioka K (1983). The complete nucleotide sequence of the cloned hepatitis B virus DNA: subtype adr and adw. NAR, 11(6):1747-1757. http://dx.doi.org/10.1093/nar/11.6.1747

Persing DH, Smith TF, Tenover FC, White JT (1993). Diagnostic Molecular Biology: Principles and Applications. American Society for Microbiology, Washington D.C.

Sambrook J, Fritsch EF, Maniatis T (1989). Molecular Cloning: a Laboratory Manual, 2nd edn. Cold Spring Harbor, NY: Cold Spring Harbor Laboratory.

Tong SP, LI J, Vitvitski L, Trepo C (1990). Active hepatitis B virus replication in the presence of anti-HBE is associated with viral variants containing an inactive pre-C region. Virol. 176:596-603. http://dx.doi.org/10.1016/0042-6822(90)90030-U

Wong DK, Yuen MF, Tse E, Yuan H, Sum SS, Hui CK, Lai CL (2004). Detection of intrahepatic hepatitis B virus DNA and correlation with hepatic necroinflammation and fibrosis. J. Clin. Microbiol. 42(9):3920-3924. http://dx.doi.org/10.1128/JCM.42.9.3920-3924.2004

Zhang Q, Wu G, Richards E, Jia S, Zeng C (2007). Universal primers for HBV genome DNA amplification across subtypes: a case study for designing more effective viral primers. Virol. J. 4:92. http://dx.doi.org/10.1186/1743-422X-4-92

## 30

A framework for classification of antifreeze proteins in over wintering plants based on their sequence and structural features

J. Muthukumaran[1], P. Manivel[1], M. Kannan[1], J. Jeyakanthan[2] and R. Krishna[1]*

[1]Centre for Bioinformatics, School of Life Sciences, Pondicherry University, Puducherry – 605 014, India.
[2]Department of Bioinformatics, Alagappa University, Karaikudi, 630 003, India.

Overwintering plants produce antifreeze proteins (AFPs) which permits the plant survival in cold condition. Analysis of sequence and structural features of these proteins would help in better understanding of their functions. In this study, we report the analysis of 40 plant AFPs on the basis of sequence and structural based classification scheme (CS). Sequence based CS segregates the AFPs into various categories such as physicochemical properties, transmembrane regions, glycosylation sites, and sub cellular localization. Phylogeny based CS separate the chosen proteins into several groups, in which, the AFP from *Festuca pratensis*, *Pinus monticola*, *Ricinus communis* and *Populus suaveolens* are newly identified leucine rich repeat (LRR), pathogenesis related (PR), hemagglutinin related (HR) and pleckstrin homology (PH) family, respectively. The secondary and 3D structures of 27 AFPs were predicted, whereas the remaining 13 protein structures were reported in different studies. Selected proteins are found to have mixed secondary structural elements and the more coil like content were observed in few of the proteins. The proposed classification scheme in over wintering plants can be useful in searching the newly sequenced plant genome for putative AFPs or designing an engineered construct helpful for several industrial and biomedical applications.

Key words: Antifreeze protein, ice-structuring protein, ice-binding protein, thermal hysteresis proteins, over wintering plants.

INTRODUCTION

Antifreeze proteins (AFPs) have an affinity for ice due to their structural complementarity nature, thereby inhibiting the ice-crystal growth. It protects organisms from deep freezing temperatures and is expressed in vertebrates, invertebrates, plants, bacteria, and fungi (Venketesh and Dayananda, 2008). Adsorption of AFPs onto ice surfaces has two different effects such as thermal hysteresis (TH) and recrystallization inhibition (RI). These two properties of AFPs, which prevents the growth of ice crystals, can be used in the development of transgenic plants with antifreeze properties thereby the yield of important crops can be increased. The activity of AFPs can be quantitatively assayed by measuring the TH activity, and it is also qualitatively assayed by examining the morphology of ice crystals grown in the AFPs. They do not prevent the ice formation, but instead function by changing the morphology of ice crystal and inhibit its further escalation (Griffith and Yaish, 2004). AFPs are used to preserve the cells, tissues and organs for transplant or transfusion in medicine at low temperature. It is also used to improve the production of farm fishes in winter season. There is also rising evidence that AFPs interact with mammalian cell membranes to protect from freezing damage through cold acclimatization (Fletcher et al., 2001).

The interaction of AFPs with ice crystals is a precise process, and it is mediated through non covalent interactions between hydrophilic groups of the AFP and oxygen atoms of ice lattice (Bayer-Giraldi et al., 2010).

AFPs can be classified into five different types in which

---
*Corresponding author. E-mail: krishstrucbio@gmail.com, krishna.bic@pondiuni.edu.in.

Type I, Type I-hyp, II, III and IV are belonging to fishes and type V AFPs are hyperactive (greater TH value), found in insects. Type I AFPs are found in flounder and sculpin, which is amphiphilic and single α- helical structure containing ~30 to 50 residues with putative ice-binding threonine residues, and it is repeated every 11 residues along the length of the helix (Sicheri and Yang, 1995). Type I-hyp AFPs are found in many right eye flounders, which is ~32 kD and it is substantially superior at depressing the freezing temperature than most fish AFPs (Scotter et al., 2006). Type II AFPs from sea raven, smelt and herring is ~125 residues long and cysteine-rich globular proteins containing five disulfide bonds (Ng and Hew, 1992). Type III AFPs are globular proteins of ~65 amino acid residues but with a plane ice-binding surface, and it is isolated from Arctic and Antarctic eel pouts (Sonnichsen et al., 1993). Type IV AFPs are found in longhorn sculpins and they are alpha helical proteins rich in glutamate and glutamine residues (Deng et al., 1997).

The activity of AFPs in over wintering plants was first reported in 1992 (Sidebottom et al., 2000) with low TH activity and high ice RI activity. AFPs prevent plants from the damages caused by cellular dehydration and growth of ice crystals on their surface via the recrystallization inhibition mechanism by inhibiting the formation of extracellular ice. The homologous nature of plant AFPs with PR (β-1, 3-glucanases, chitinases, thaumatin-like protein and polygalacturonase inhibiting protein) protein was evident from their properties of providing a protection to the plants against various psychrophilic pathogens (Davies et al., 2002). The AFPs from plants have been isolated from *Solanum dulcamara, Secale cereale, Daucus carota* and *Lolium perenne* (Kuiper et al., 2001). The antifreeze or ice-recrystallization inhibitory activity is present in overwintering plants only after they have been rendering to low temperatures and only in plants that abide the presence of ice in their tissues. RI activity of AFP has been observed in different parts of over wintering plants such as seeds, stems, flowers, buds, rhizomes, etc. Cold-tolerant plants use a variety of small molecular weight solutes like simple sugars to stabilize the structure of membrane or combat cold-induced osmotic imbalances (Thomashow, 1998). The antifreeze nature of plant AFPs was aided by the presence of characteristic LRR domain in their protein sequences (Meyer et al., 1999).

In the present study, first time, we have developed a sequence and structural based classification scheme for plant AFPs to understand their functions. Some of the classification study was already reported based on extensive phylogenetic analysis (Tyagi et al., 2010). The proposed sequence and structural based classification can be separated into various stages.

At the first stage of the study, various physical and chemical properties of the selected AFPs were computed. At the second stage, we identified the functional domains present in the proteins; however, the functional class of undetermined.

AFPs was identified through comparative sequence analysis. At the third stage, the sub-cellular localization and signal peptide cleavage site was predicted, which helped to explore the functional localization of AFPs in the cell. At the fourth stage, we predicted the topology of the proteins and identified the transmembrane regions present in the proteins. At the fifth stage, the N- and O-linked glycosylation sites were predicted, which is essential for antifreeze activity in some of the plant such as *S. dulcamara*. At the sixth stage, we employed comparative sequence analysis to understand the evolutionary relationship of chosen and their related proteins, which can be helped into identifying the functional classes of undetermined AFPs. At the seventh stage, the secondary and 3D structures of AFPs were predicted and compared with reported structures. Finally, the binding site residues and solvation energy was computed, and it can be useful for further molecular interaction studies of AFPs with ice-crystal. Moreover, from an application point of view, the sequence and structural features described here could be used to search for new class of AFPs and their homology in newly sequenced plant genome.

MATERIALS AND METHODS

Primary sequence analysis

Antifreeze protein sequences were retrieved from two different databases such as UniProt (www.uniprot.org) (Wu et al., 2006), and GenPept (http://www.ncbi.nlm.nih.gov) (Figure 1a and Table 1). These proteins were subjected into ProtParam web server (www.expasy.org/tools) (Wilkins et al., 1999), for computing various physico chemical properties such as amino acid composition, molecular weight, isoelectric point, instability index, aliphatic index, extinction coefficient and grand average of hydropathicity (GRAVY) score. Functional domains present in the given sequences were identified using SMART web server (www.expasy.org/tools) (Letunic et al., 2009). The sub cellular localization of AFPs was predicted using TargetP (www.expasy.org/tools) and prediction of signal peptides presented in the given sequences were identified through SignalP server (www.expasy.org/tools) (Emanuelsson et al., 2007). The web server SOSUI (www.expasy.org/tools) (Hirokawa et al., 1998) was used for the prediction of transmembrane regions and N and O glycosylation sites of AFPs were predicted using two different servers namely NetNGlyc (http://www.cbs.dtu.dk/services/NetNGlyc/) and NetOGlyc (http://www.cbs.dtu.dk/services/NetOGlyc/).

Multiple sequence alignment (MSA) and phylogenetic tree construction

Local MSA was performed using Dialign web server (http://bibiserv.techfak.uni-bielefeld.de/dialign/submission.html) (Brudno et al., 2004) with the default threshold value (T = 0), and it finds the region of local similarity. Based on the MSA results, an unrooted phylogenetic tree was constructed using the neighbor-joining (NJ) method. The statistical significance of NJ method was evaluated by a bootstrap analysis with 1000 iterative tree constructions. The "consense" program of Phylip (Retief, 2008) was used to generate a consensus tree, and it was visualized by Phylodraw 0.82 program(Choi et al., 2000). The rectangular binary

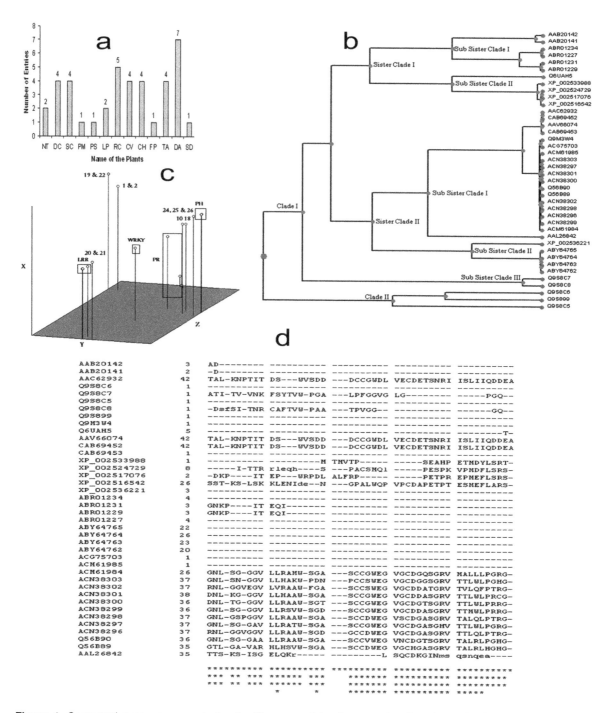

Figure 1. Comparative sequence analysis of antifreeze proteins in over wintering plants. **(a)** Bar diagram showing number of entries present in the protein sequence databases (At the time of study). Species abbreviations followed in the diagram: NT, *Nicotiana tabacum,* DC, *D. carota,* SC, *S. cereale,* PM, *P. monticola,* PS, *P. suaveolens,* LP, *L. perenne,* RC, *R. communis,* CV, *C. vulgaris,* CH, *Chlamydomonas sp. CCMP681,* FP, *F. pratensis,* TA, *T. aestivum,* DA, *D. antarctica,* SD, *S. dulcamara.* **(b)** NJ tree of antifreeze proteins was constructed by importing the numeric output of Dialign web server into Phylip - consense program to generate a consensus tree and it was visualized by Phylodraw Version 0.8. **(c)** The Principal coordinate analysis of antifreeze proteins was performed by NTSYS pc. Expansion of codes in this 3D plot is: 1 & 2 = *N. tabacum,* LRR = Leucine Rich Repeat (*D. carota, F. pratensis, T. aestivum, L. perenne* and *D. antarctica*), PH = Pleckstrin Homology (*R. communis*), PR = Pathogenesis Related (*Secale cereale* & *Pinus monticola*), WRKY = DNA binding protein from *S. dulcamara,* 10 & 18 = *P. suaveolens* and *R. communis,* 19, 22 = *C. vulgaris* and 24, 25 and 26 = *Chlamydomonas sp. CCMP681.* **(d)** A portion of multiple sequence alignment of antifreeze proteins was performed using Dialign web server. "*" indicate the degree of local similarity among the sequences. Residues in the blocks represent sequentially conserved regions (SCRs). Lower-case letters denote residues not belonging to any of these selected diagonals or segment pairs and which are not considered to be aligned by Dialign.

Table 1. List of plant antifreeze protein sequences retrieved from GenPept and UniProt database.

S/No.	Accession number	Protein name	Source	Database
1	AAB20142	Afa5, antifreeze protein	*Nicotiana tabacum*	GenPept
2	AAB20141	Afa3-antifreeze protein	*N. tabacum*	GenPept
3	AAC62932	Antifreeze protein	*Daucus carota*	GenPept
4	Q9S8C6	32 kDa antifreeze protein	*Secale cereale*	UniProt
5	Q9S8C7	25 kDa antifreeze protein	*S. cereale*	UniProt
6	Q9S8C5	35 kDa antifreeze protein	*S.e cereale*	UniProt
7	Q9S8C8	16 kDa antifreeze protein	*S.e cereale*	UniProt
8	Q9S899	18.4 kDa candidate antifreeze protein	*Pinus monticola* (Western white pine)	UniProt
9	Q9M3W4	Ice recrystallisation inhibition protein	*Lolium perenne* (Perennial ryegrass)	UniProt
10	Q6UAH5	Antifreeze protein	*Populus suaveolens*	UniProt
11	AAV66074	Antifreeze protein	*Daucus carota*	GenPept
12	CAB69452	Antifreeze protein	*D. carota*	GenPept
13	CAB69453	Antifreeze protein	*D. carota*	GenPept
14	XP_002533988	Putative ice-binding protein	*Ricinus communis*	GenPept
15	XP_002524729	Putative ice-binding protein	*R.communis*	GenPept
16	XP_002517076	Putative ice-binding protein	*R. communis*	GenPept
17	XP_002516542	Putative ice-binding protein	*R. communis*	GenPept
18	XP_002536221	Putative ice-binding protein	*R. communis*	GenPept
19	ABR01234	Antifreeze protein	*Chlorella vulgaris*	GenPept
20	ABR01231	Antifreeze protein	*C. vulgaris*	GenPept
21	ABR01229	Antifreeze protein	*C. vulgaris*	GenPept
22	ABR01227	Antifreeze protein	*C. vulgaris*	GenPept
23	ABY64765	Ice-binding protein-4	*Chlamydomonas sp. CCMP681*	GenPept
24	ABY64764	Ice-binding protein-3	*Chlamydomonas sp. CCMP681*	GenPept
25	ABY64763	Ice-binding protein-2	*Chlamydomonas sp. CCMP681*	GenPept
26	ABY64762	Ice-binding protein-1	*Chlamydomonas sp. CCMP681*	GenPept
27	ACG75703	Ice recrystallization inhibition protein	*Festuca pratensis*	GenPept
28	ACM61985	Ice recrystallization inhibition protein 4	*Triticum aestivum*	GenPept
29	ACM61984	Ice recrystallization inhibition protein 3	*T. aestivum*	GenPept
30	ACN38303	Ice recrystallization inhibition protein 1	*Lolium perenne*	GenPept
31	ACN38302	Ice recrystallization inhibition protein 7	*Deschampsia antarctica*	GenPept
32	ACN38301	Ice recrystallization inhibition protein 6	*D. antarctica*	GenPept
33	ACN38300	Ice recrystallization inhibition protein 5	*D. antarctica*	GenPept
34	ACN38299	Ice recrystallization inhibition protein 4	*D. antarctica*	GenPept
35	ACN38298	Ice recrystallization inhibition protein 3	*D. antarctica*	GenPept
36	ACN38297	Ice recrystallization inhibition protein 2	*D. antarctica*	GenPept
37	ACN38296	Ice recrystallization inhibition protein 1	*D. antarctica*	GenPept
38	Q56B90	Ice recrystallization inhibition protein 1	*Triticum aestivum*	UniProt
39	Q56B89	Ice recrystallization inhibition protein 2	*T.aestivum*	UniProt
40	AAL26842	Thermal hysteresis protein STHP-64	*Solanum dulcamara*	UniProt

data matrix was created, and all the data analysis was performed by Numerical Taxonomy System, NTSYS-pc ver. 2.02 (Applied Biostatistic, Exeter Software, Setauket, New York, USA). The PCoA analysis of the pair wise genetic distances was also conducted for validating the results of phylogenetic analysis using NTSYS-pc package.

Secondary and three-dimensional structure predictions

Out of 40 AFPs, only 13 proteins have their own structural details. Therefore, the secondary structure of remaining 27 plant AFPs was predicted using GOR web server (www.expasy.org/tools) (Sen et al., 2005). In Homology Modeling, the template sequences were selected from the Protein BLAST search (http://blast.ncbi.nlm.nih.gov/Blast.cgi?PAGE=Proteins) (Altschul et al., 1997) with the help of Protein Data Bank (http://www.rcsb.org). The 3D structure for 13 AFPs showing reasonable sequence similarity with their templates, and their structures were modeled through homology modeling using Modeller 9V4 (Eswar et al., 2008), whereas structures for remaining 14 AFPs were modeled through threading approach using Phyre server (http://www.sbg.bio.ic.ac.uk/~phyre/) (Kelley and Sternberg, 2009). Gromacs 3.3.1(Hess, 2008) was used to refine the 3D models and Molecular dynamic calculations for the generated models soaked in the triclinic single point charge (SPC) water molecule system were carried out for 10 ps and 5000 steps were employed for the calculations. The quality of the generated models was investigated using RamPage (http://mordred.bioc.cam.ac.uk/~rapper/rampage.php) (Lovell et al., 2003) and combinatorial extension (CE) (http://cl.sdsc.edu/ce.html) (Shindyalov and Bourne, 1998). Salvation energy/solvent accessible surface area was predicted through Get Area web server (http://curie.utmb.edu/getarea.html) (Fraczkiewics and Braun, 1998). The binding site analysis of generated protein models were performed using theoretical macroscopic titration curves (Thematics) web server (http://pfweb.chem.neu.edu/thematics/submit.html) (Ondrechen et al., 2001).

RESULTS AND DISCUSSION

Primary sequence analysis

Physicochemical properties

Calculation of physicochemical properties by conventional *invitro* methods besides being expansive, is time consuming and cumbersome. The *insilico* physicochemical property prediction may be enhancing our knowledge for experimental design. The amino acid sequence of plant AFPs revealed that eighteen of the plant AFPs was hydrophobic; twenty one were hydrophilic in nature due to the presence of polar and non-polar amino acid residues in their protein sequence. The AFP from *S. cereale* (Q9S8C5) has an equal number of polar and non-polar residues. The calculated isoelectric point (pI) value of 21 AFPs was less than 7, and it indicated that these were acidic and remaining 19 proteins were basic in nature. This result will be essential for developing buffer systems for purification of proteins by isoelectric focusing and two-dimensional electro-phoresis. Extinction coefficient (EC) value calculated for the given entries revealed that the following four proteins ACG75703, AAB20141, Q9M3W4 and AAB20142 cannot be studied by UV spectral method. Instability index calculations identified twenty seven entries as stable proteins with the values were smaller than 40 and remaining proteins may be unstable. Most of the entries were found to have a good aliphatic index score which indicated that these AFPs were thermodynamically stable over a wide range of temperatures. Calculated GRAVY index values are normally used as a guide to help, predict, with a great measure of uncertainty, the probability

that the protein will produce crystals and therefore, be amendable for X-ray crystallographic analysis. In our study, twenty seven proteins were showing good GRAVY index value where as others were found to have optimum values. The primary sequence analysis of the selected proteins was listed in Tables 2 and 3, respectively.

Prediction of signal peptide cleavage site and sub cellular localization

The regions 14 to 15 of ACM61985, 15 to 16 of ACM61984, 18 of AAB20141, 20 to 21 of ACN38300, ACN38299, Q56B90, Q56B89, 21 to 22 of ACN38303, ACN38302, ACN38298, ACN38297, ACN38296, 22 to 23 of ACN38301, 23 to 24 of ABY64762, 25 to 26 of CAB69453, ABY64765, 26 to 27 of AAC62932, AAV66074, CAB69452, ABY64763, 29 to 30 of ABY64764 and 31 of AAB20142 indicated the presence of N-terminal signal peptides, which implies that these proteins could be targeted through the secretory pathway. The AFP from *N. tabacum, D. carota, T. aestivum, D. antarctica, L. perenne* (ACN38303) *and Chlamydomonas sp. CCMP681* contained putative signal peptide sequences, suggesting that these AFPs were secreted and primarily function in extra cellular space. However, *S. cereale, P. monticola, L. perenne* (Q9M3W4), *R. communis, C. vulgaris, F. pratensis* and *S. dulcamara* have a type of AFP that did not contain putative signal peptide sequence, and it is therefore, likely to remain intracellular.

Analysis of domain

Apart from the signal peptide, sixteen of the plant AFPs has a LRR (and LRRNT), four AFPs have PH and one AFP has WRKY domain. The sequence of *D. carota* - AFP is similar to that of PGIPs and contained LRRs, which exhibit antifreeze activity (Meyer et al., 1999). Similarly, the AFP from *L. perenne, T. aestivum* and *D. antarctica* is also containing LRR domain, which also showed the antifreeze activity. The functional class of undetermined AFPs was identified through comparative sequence analysis.

Analysis of glycosylation sites and transmembrane regions

By using the NetNGlyc and NetOGlyc web servers, the amino acid sequence of AFPs was examined for possible N- and O-linked glycosylation. In our study, the AFPs (Q9S8C6 and Q6UAH5) from *S. cereale* and *P. suaveolens* did not contain glycosylation sites, where as remaining AFPs were found to have several glycosylation sites (N-Linked: 24, O-Linked: 34 and Both N and O Linked: 20). Glycosylation, a post translational modification,

Table 2. Various physicochemical parameters of plant antifreeze proteins computed using ProtParam web server.

S/No.	Accession number	Molecular weight	Isoelectric point	Instability index	Aliphatic index	Extinction coefficient	Grand average of hydropathicity (GRAVY)
1	AAB20142	5109.6	3.56	8.04	96.13	-	1.134
2	AAB20141	3359.6	4.43	1.131	81.05	-	0.563
3	AAC62932	36742.1	5.02	42.12	99.00	23210	-0.064
4	Q9S8C6	2093.3	5.83	51.87	116.50	1490	0.395
5	Q9S8C7	2934.3	8.63	26.58	87.24	6990	0.514
6	Q9S8C5	1549.6	4.00	43.18	36.88	125	-0.588
7	Q9S8C8	2482.7	5.83	34.14	52.92	5500	0.100
8	Q9S899	2419.6	4.79	77.00	79.55	5500	-0.368
9	Q9M3W4	11766.1	5.17	11.54	61.61	-	-0.679
10	Q6UAH5	17548.1	10.02	55.42	67.15	19605	-0.550
11	AAV66074	36825.1	4.87	43.21	97.83	23210	-0.087
12	CAB69452	36845.3	4.99	43.35	98.70	23210	-0.056
13	CAB69453	21785.9	5.78	37.91	93.55	4720	-0.104
14	XP_002533988	39792.6	5.87	31.19	82.19	43930	-0.185
15	XP_002524729	51873.7	9.22	46.69	78.17	34085	-0.298
16	XP_002517076	51022.9	9.27	41.75	81.66	44710	-0.286
17	XP_002516542	45915.0	9.06	44.94	77.14	47940	-0.423
18	XP_002536221	30830.4	4.58	3.45	82.65	8940	0.247
19	ABR01234	18682.6	8.68	21.27	62.81	1490	-0.810
20	ABR01231	10803.7	6.07	21.99	52.88	5500	-0.903
21	ABR01229	10775.7	6.07	23.44	51.06	5500	-0.926
22	ABR01227	18710.6	8.68	21.11	63.88	1490	-0.796
23	ABY64765	36814.1	4.48	32.85	73.58	28960	0.147
24	ABY64764	36975.7	4.66	33.12	85.40	42815	0.254
25	ABY64763	36507.0	4.48	34.32	81.69	41325	0.209
26	ABY64762	36523.8	4.46	41.36	69.72	35950	0.011
27	ACG75703	11555.1	7.54	11.62	65.74	-	-0.492
28	ACM61985	18245.8	9.23	20.05	78.29	8480	-0.491
29	ACM61984	19046.2	9.65	41.16	106.74	18240	0.188
30	ACN38303	29135.7	9.04	25.83	93.51	30855	-0.070
31	ACN38302	22803.1	9.04	29.49	79.37	16750	-0.192
32	ACN38301	29252.9	9.12	38.14	93.24	27875	-0.040
33	ACN38300	29195.7	8.56	35.31	89.32	23865	-0.071
34	ACN38299	23021.3	5.72	32.89	82.06	18490	-0.166

Table 2. Cont'd

35	ACN38298	22011.1	9.01	30.78	78.99	18240	-0.162
36	ACN38297	30514.0	9.58	36.94	89.80	30855	-0.158
37	ACN38296	22560.0	9.86	27.25	83.38	11250	-0.125
38	Q56B90	29104.1	8.23	25.37	99.96	27305	0.114
39	Q56B89	42886.5	8.60	29.46	102.69	26845	0.051
40	AAL26842	64757.9	6.27	52.77	63.11	29255	-0.969

Table 3. Primary sequence analysis of plant antifreeze proteins was predicted by using various web servers [Domain: SMART, signal peptide: Signal P, sub cellular localization: Target P, transmembrane region: SOSUI and glycosylation sites: NetNGlyc and NetOGlyc] and expansion of domains [LRR: Leucine rich repeat, PH: Pleckstrin homology, ND: Not determined, *: Domain are identified through comparative sequence analysis].

Accession number	Domain Name	Domain Position	Signal Peptide cleavage site position	Sub cellular localization	Transmembrane region Number	Transmembrane region position	Glycosylation N-linked	Glycosylation O-linked
AAB20142	ND	ND	31	Secretory pathway	No	No	No	Yes
AAB20141	ND	ND	18	Secretory pathway	No	No	No	Yes
AAC62932	LRR-1, LRRNT-2	30-68, 266-288	26,27	Secretory pathway	1	4-26	Yes	No
Q9S8C6	ND	ND	No	Other	No	No	No	No
Q9S8C7	ND	ND	No	Other	No	No	No	Yes
Q9S8C5	ND	ND	No	Other	No	No	No	Yes
Q9S8C8	ND	ND	No	Other	No	No	No	Yes
Q9S899	ND	ND	No	Other	No	No	No	Yes
Q9M3W4	ND	ND	No	Chloroplast	No	No	No	Yes
Q6UAH5	PH*	ND	No	Mitochondrion	No	No	No	No
AAV66074	LRRNT-2, LRR-1, LRR-1, LRR-1	30-68, 147-169, 171-193, 266-268	26,27	Secretory pathway	1	4-26	No	No
CAB69452	LRRNT-2, LRR-1, LRR-1, LRR-1	30-68, 147-169, 171-193, 266-268	26,27	Secretory pathway	1	4-26	Yes	No

Table 3. Cont'd

CAB69453	LRR-1	131-153	25,26	Secretory pathway	No	No	Yes	No
XP_002533988	PH-2	244-350	No	Other	No	No	Yes	Yes
XP_002524729	PH-2	364-474	No	Other	No	No	Yes	Yes
XP_002517076	PH-2	362-472	No	Other	No	No	Yes	Yes
XP_002516542	PH-2	297-406	No	Chloroplast	No	No	Yes	Yes
XP_002536221	ND	ND	No	Other	No	No	Yes	Yes
ABR01234	ND	ND	No	Chloroplast	No	No	No	Yes
ABR01231	ND	ND	No	Other	No	No	No	Yes
ABR01229	ND	ND	No	Other	No	No	No	Yes
ABR01227	ND	ND	No	Chloroplast	No	No	No	Yes
ABY64765	ND	ND	25,26	Secretory pathway	No	No	Yes	Yes
ABY64764	ND	ND	29,30	Secretory pathway	2	15-37, 43-65	Yes	Yes
ABY64763	ND	ND	26,27	Secretory pathway	2	11-33, 41-63	Yes	Yes
ABY64762	ND	ND	23,24	Secretory pathway	No	No	Yes	Yes
ACG75703	LRR*	ND	No	Chloroplast	No	No	Yes	Yes
ACM61985	LRR-1	13-35	14,15	Secretory pathway	No	No	Yes	Yes
ACM61984	LRRNT-2 LRR-1	14-53 83-105	15,16	Secretory pathway	No	No	Yes	Yes
ACN38303	LRRNT-2 LRR-1	25-64 65-93	21,22	Secretory pathway	1	8-28	Yes	Yes
ACN38302	LRRNT-2	25-65	21,22	Secretory pathway	2	6-27, 40-62	No	Yes
ACN38301	LRRNT-2 LRR-1	25-65 95-117	22,23	Secretory pathway	3	2-23, 45-67, 75-97	No	Yes
ACN38300	LRRNT-2 LRR-1	24-63 93-115	20,21	Secretory pathway	2	1-22, 39-60	Yes	Yes
ACN38299	LRRNT-2	24-63	20,21	Secretory pathway	No	No	Yes	Yes
ACN38298	LRRNT-2	25-65	21,22	Secretory pathway	1	5-26	No	Yes
ACN38297	LRRNT-2	25-64	21,22	Secretory pathway	2	5-26, 41-63	Yes	Yes
ACN38296	LRRNT-2	25-65	21,22	Secretory pathway	No	No	Yes	Yes

Table 3. Cont'd

Q56B90	LRRNT-2	24-63	secretory pathway	3	20,21	2-23, 38-60, 75-97	Yes	Yes
	LRR-1	93-115						
	LRR-1	117-139						
Q56B89	LRR-1	90-114	Secretory pathway	1	20,21	1-22	Yes	Yes
	LRR-1	138-162						
	LRR-1	187-211						
	LRR-1	212-235						
	LRR-1	236-260						
	LRR-1	262-284						
AAL26842	WRKY	182-250	other	No	No	No	Yes	Yes

is not essential for antifreeze activity in some cases such as *D. carota* (Worrall et al., 1998). However, the AFP from *S. dulcamara* lost the activity after the removal of their glycan moiety (Huang and Duman, 2002). Therefore, the analysis of glycosylation sites is also one of the important parameter to understand the mechanism of ice-recrystallization inhibition. From the results of SOSUI web server, it was concluded that the thirteen of the given entries were classified as membrane proteins and the remaining were classified as soluble proteins.

Comparative sequence analysis

In this study, we have used comparative sequence analysis approach to categorize the AFPs based on sequence level similarity, identity and pair wise distances, which provide information about the homology of particular AFP. It includes multiple sequence alignment followed by phylo-genetic analysis. The PCoA was used to validate the results for phylogenetic analysis of all AFPs.

Multiple sequence alignment, phylogenetic analysis and principal coordinate analysis

Dialign web server constructed the local alignment from the gap free pairs of segments of the protein sequences. The results for MSA (Figure 1d) of plant AFPs explore that, there was a considerable variation among the proteins (Number of variable sites: 804), with extensive variation in both amino and carboxy terminals. Remarkably, 198 conserved sites were observed in the amino acid residues of the plant AFPs and they were interspersed throughout the alignment. The overall mean distance of fourty AFPs from various plants was 1.589. In order to determine the evolutionary relationship of these AFPs, the phylogenetic tree was constructed from various plants such as *N. tabacum, D. carota, S. cereale, P. monticola, L. perenne, P. suaveolens, R. communis, C. vulgaris, Chlamydomonas sp. CCMP681, F. pratensis, T. aestivum, D. antarctica* and *S. dulcamara*. NJ phylogenetic analysis of the plant AFP sequences resulted in the clustering of two major clades (Figure 1b) and their details were

given as follows.

Clade I: This is strongly supported group, and it composed of numerous sister cades (SC) such as SC1, SC2 and SC3. The SC1 has two sub sister clades (SSC) namely SSC1 [AAB20142, AAB20141 (*N. tabacum*), ABR01234, ABR01227, ABR01231, ABR01229 (*C. vulgaris*)] and SSC2 [Q6UAH5 (*P. suaveolens*) and PH domain: XP_002533988, XP_002524729, XP_002517076, XP_002516542 (*R. communis*)]. SC2 also has two SSCs and they are SSC1 [AAC62932, AAV66074, CAB69452, CAB69453 (*D. carota*), Q9M3W4 (*L. perenne*), ACG75703 (*F. pratensis*), ACM61985 (*T. aestivum*), ACN38303 (*L. perenne*), ACN38297, ACN38301, ACN38300 (*D. Antarctica*), Q56B90, Q56B89 (*T. aestivum*), ACN38302, ACN38298, ACN38296, ACN38299 (*D. antarctica*), ACM61984 (*T. aestivum*), AAL26842 (*S. dulcamara*)], in which eighteen AFPs are belonging to LRR domain and a AFP belongs to WRKY DNA binding domain and SSC2 [XP_002536221 (*R. communis*), ABY64765, ABY64764, ABY64763, ABY64762

(*Chlamydomonas sp. CCMP681*)]. In addition, the SC3 contained PR related AFPs such as Q9S8C7 and Q9S8C8 (*S. cereale*). Homogenous (Same taxas: SC3) andheterogeneous (Different taxas: SC1 and SC2 with its Sub Clades) sister clades were obtained by the aforementioned observation. In addition to this, five mono taxas were also observed (Q6UAH5, XP_002533988, ACM61985, AAL26842, XP_002536221), which are closely related to SC1 and SC2. Based on above observation, the AFP from *F. pratensis* is newly identified LRR domain containing protein, which is closely related to AFP of *D. antarctica, D. carota, T. aestivum* and *L. perenne*. The AFP from *P. suaveolens* (Q6UAH5) exists as mono taxa, and it is closely related to PH domain containing proteins, which revealed that this protein mighthave PH like activity. The AFP – domains of *C. vulgaris* (ABR01231, ABR01229, ABR01227, and ABR01234) and *R. communis* (XP_002536221) are undetermined. More detailed comparative sequence analysis was performed on the above mentioned proteins. The AFPs from *N. tabacum* resemble type III *Winter flounder* AFP. One of the undetermined AFP (XP_002536221) from *R. communis* is similar with hemagglutinin-related protein from *Granulibacter bethesdensis CGDNIH1* (YP_744956 and YP_745229) and remaining proteins are belonging to PH family. *C. vulgaris* AFPs are similar with some of the hypothetical proteins from *Desulfovibrio piger ATCC 29098* (ZP_03311955), *Rhodobacter sphaeroides 2.4.1* (YP_352443), *Rhodobacter sphaeroides KD131* (YP_02525057). Similarity, the AFPs from *Chlamydomonas sp. CCMP681* showed similarity with some of the hypothetical proteins from bacteria (Raymond et al., 2009).

Clade II: This is a very small clade compared to clade I, which comprised of Q9S8C6 (*S. cereale*), Q9S899 (*P. monticola*) and Q9S8C5 (*S. cereale*). It has no further sub divisions. *S. cereale* AFPs are homologous to PR proteins, which also found in clade II (Q9S8C6 and Q9S8C5), and it has both antifreeze as well as enzymatic activities. It provides a protection against psychrophilic pathogens. The AFPs from *S. cereale* is similar to the member of three classes of PR related proteins such as endochitinases, endo-β-1, 3 glucanases and thaumatin like proteins (Hon et al., 1995). The domain sequence of Q9S899 (*P. monticola*) was undetermined and however, it was found to be closely related to *S. cereale* - AFP. The pair wise distance between *S. cereale* and *P. monticola* was 0.673 (sequence identity: 57.1% and sequence similarity: 71.4%), which was very low in comparison with others indicating that less divergence has occurred. Based on the aforementioned observation, it was concluded that, the *P. monticola* – AFP is a newly identified PR family protein. All the AFPs were well supported in bootstrap analysis (100%).

The 3D plot (Figure 1c) of PCoA is a diverse combination of various AFP data. Several closely related plant groups were observed through this three-dimensional plot such as LRR (*D. carota*: AAC62932, AAV66074, CAB69452, CAB69453, *L. perenne*: Q9M3W4, ACN38303, *T. aestivum*: ACM61985, ACM61984, Q56B90, Q56B89, *D. antarctica*: ACN38302, ACN38301, ACN38300, ACN38299, ACN38298, ACN38297, ACN38296 and *F. pratensis*: ACG75703), PH (*R. communis*: XP_002533988, XP_002524729, XP_002517076 and XP_002516542) and PR (*S. cereale*: Q9S8C6, Q9S8C7, Q9S8C5, Q9S8C8 and *P. monticola*: Q9S899). Both phylogenetic and PCoA analysis revealed that, the newly identified *F. pratensis* and *P. monticola* – AFPs are belonging to LRR and PR family, respectively. WRKY domain containing AFP from *S. dulcamara* was deviated significantly from other Plant AFPs, which is located in the central position of Mod3D plot. In addition, some of the plant - AFPs are existing as mono taxa as phylogenetic analysis such as *P. monticola, P. suaveolens, R. communis*, etc. Hence, PcoA agreed well with the results of phylogenetic analysis.

Secondary structure prediction

Secondary structural study is significant as it provides direct imminent into the functional role of a protein, and it can be a preliminary step in the direction towards the prediction of 3D structures by fold recognition or threading. Secondary and 3D structure of AFPs from *L. perenne*, (Kuiper et al., 2001) *D. antarctica* (John et al., 2009) and *D. carota* (Zhang et al., 2004) were reported previously. Various secondary structural classes (alpha: 8, beta: 11 and alpha + beta: 8) of AFPs were observed from the results of ProClass web server (Raghava, 1999), in which, most of the LRR domain containing proteins are exist as Alpha + Beta class. Alpha helices are dominated in some of the AFPs such as *N. tabacum* and *C. vulgaris*. The secondary structure of *S. cereale* AFPs looks coil like structure, which is similar to the PR proteins and posses, both antifreeze as well as antifungal activity. The composition of secondary structural elements from the various AFPs was represented in Table 4. The secondary structure of four AFPs (XP_002533988, XP_002524729, XP_002517076 and XP_002516542) from *R. communis* belongs to beta class, which contained PH domain, and it may be essential for intracellular signaling. A newly identified LRR domain containing AFP from *F. pratensis* contain only beta pleated sheets, which is closely related to AFP of *D. antarctica, D. carota, T. aestivum* and *L. perenne*. The secondary structure composition of this protein is Ee: 38.26% and Cc: 61.74%, which is more similar to the reported AFP structure (Kuiper et al., 2001) from *L. perenne* (E: 36.44% and C: 63.56%). The secondary structural class of AFP from R. *communis* (XP_002536221) is beta as hemagglutinin-related proteins from several bacteria. The coil composition of

Table 4. Secondary structural classes and their composition of plant antifreeze proteins.

Accession number	Secondary structural class	Secondary structure composition (%)							
		Hh	Gg	Ii	Bb	Ee	Tt	Ss	Cc
AAB20142	Alpha	90.32	-	-	-	-	-	-	9.68
AAB20141	Alpha	84.21	-	-	-	-	-	-	15.79
Q9S8C6	Beta	-	-	-	-	35	-	-	65
Q9S8C7	Beta	-	-	-	-	48.28	-	-	51.72
Q9S8C5	Beta	-	-	-	-	12.50	-	-	57.50
Q9S8C8	Beta	-	-	-	-	33.33	-	-	66.67
Q9S899	Alpha	50	-	-	-	9.09	-	-	40.91
Q6UAH5	Alpha + Beta	37.75	-	-	-	19.87	-	-	42.38
XP_002533988	Beta	24.17	-	-	-	33.33	-	-	42.50
XP_002524729	Beta	13.37	-	-	-	38.48	-	-	48.15
XP_002517076	Beta	10.90	-	-	-	43.61	-	-	45.49
XP_002516542	Beta	8.29	-	-	-	52.37	-	-	39.34
XP_002536221	Beta	1.81	-	-	-	39.76	-	-	58.43
ABR01234	Alpha	74.16	-	-	-	4.49	-	-	21.35
ABR01231	Alpha	68.27	-	-	-	4.81	-	-	26.92
ABR01229	Alpha	70.19	-	-	-	4.81	-	-	25
ABR01227	Alpha	71.35	-	-	-	4.49	-	-	24.16
ABY64765	Beta	9.22	-	-	-	31.28	-	-	59.5
ABY64764	Beta	13.09	-	-	-	25.07	-	-	61.84
ABY64763	Beta	10.96	-	-	-	27.25	-	-	61.80
ABY64762	Beta	7.93	-	-	-	30.31	-	-	61.76
ACG75703	Beta	-	-	-	-	38.26	-	-	61.74
ACM61985	Beta	13.14	-	-	-	25.14	-	-	61.71
ACM61984	Alpha+Beta	29.28	-	-	-	19.89	-	-	50.83
Q56B90	Alpha+Beta	18.93	-	-	-	28.27	-	-	52.86
Q56B89	Alpha+Beta	30.32	-	-	-	19.56	-	-	50.12
AAL26842	Alpha+Beta	18.78	-	-	-	19.80	-	-	61.42

Hh: Alpha helix, Gg: 3_{10} helix, Ii: Pi helix, Bb: Beta bridge, Ee: Extended strand, Tt: Beta turn, Ss: Bend region, Cc: Coil.

AFP from *P. suaveolens* is nearly similar to PH domain containing AFP of *R. communis*. The predicted secondary structure class of *C. vulgaris* and *Chlamydomonas sp. CCMP681* AFPs is alpha and beta, which is generally consistent with their predicted models. The secondary structure elements of *S. dulcamara* AFP contained five beta pleated sheets, which is similar to the experimental structure of *A. thaliana* WRKY DNA binding domain (Yamasaki et al., 2005) and it belongs to beta class.

Three-dimensional structure prediction and binding site analysis

In the result of BLAST$_P$ search, only 13 AFPs were showing reasonable identity (> = 40%) with their templates. So, the 3D structures for these proteins were predicted using Modeller 9V4 based on homology modeling approach. A threading method was also adopted for predicting the 3D structure of the remaining 14 AFPs using Phyre server, because BLAST$_P$ provided the low sequence identity (Less than 40%) structural homologs or templates. To eliminate the distortion in geometry, the predicted homology models (Figure 2) were refined by consecutive iterations of MD simulation followed by energy minimization using Gromacs 3.3.1. MD simulation was carried out on all the predicted models in an aqueous environment (SPC water molecules). During the MD simulation process, the root mean square deviation (RMSD) of the predicted models and their corresponding templates were studied, which are less than 2. MD simulation results indicated that our predicted models were more stable and they will make good interaction with ice crystal. In this step, the quality of the predicted models was also improved. The optimized models were subjected into internal assessment of self-consistency checks such as stereo chemical quality to locate the divergences from normal bond lengths, dihedrals and non-bonded atom-atom distances. No spurious angle to

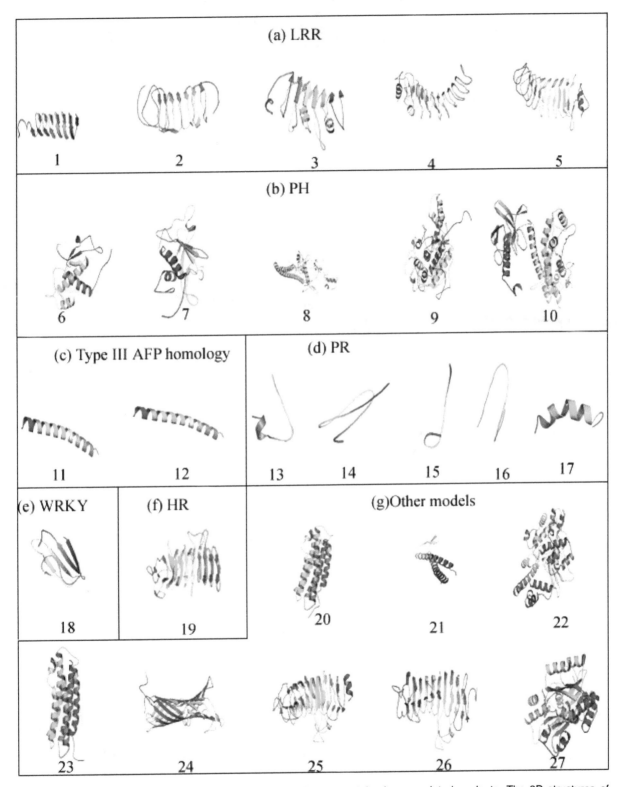

Figure 2. Snap shots of three-dimensional models of antifreeze proteins in over wintering plants. The 3D structures of antifreeze proteins were predicted through homology modeling and threading approaches. The structures were displayed by PyMOL visualization tool (http:// http://www.pymol.org/). Numerical order indicates: (a) Leucine rich repeat: (1) ACG75703, (2) ACM61985, (3) ACM61984, (4) Q56B90 and (5) Q56B89; (b) Pleckstrin homology: (6) Q6UAH5, (7) XP_002533988, (8) XP_002524729, (9) XP_002517076 and (10) XP_002516542; (c) Type III AFP homology: (11) AAB20142 and (12) AAB20141, (d) Pathogenesis related: (13) Q9S8C6, (14) Q9S8C7, (15) Q9S8C5, (16) Q9S8C8 and (17) Q9S899; (e) WRKY: (18) AAL26842, (f) Hemagglutinin related: (19) XP_002536221, and (g) Other models: (20) ABR01234, (21) ABR01231, (22) ABR01229, (23) ABR01227, (24) ABY64765, (25) ABY64764, (26) ABY64763 and (27) ABY64762.

Table 5. Model validation results of plant antifreeze proteins.

Accession number	Template ID	Identity (%)	Approach used	Rampage - Ramachandran plot (%)			CE, RMSD (A°)	PMDB ID
				Favored	Allowed	Outlier		
AAB20142	1WFA	100	Homology modeling	100	0	0	0.1	PM0076159
AAB20141	1WFA	100	Homology modeling	100	0	0	0.1	PM0076158
Q9S8C6	1GHS	100	Homology modeling	100	0	0	0.5	PM0076160
Q9S8C7	1Z3Q	59	Homology modeling	96.3	0	3.7	0.5	PM0076161
Q9S8C5	2DKV	85	Homology modeling	85.7	14.3	0	0.2	PM0076162
Q9S8C8	1DU5	61	Homology modeling	95.5	4.5	0	0.5	PM0076163
Q9S899	2GRV	54	Homology modeling	100	0	0	0.2	PM0076164
Q6UAH5	1GD8	LT 40	Threading	88.6	9.4	2	0.9	PM0076165
XP_002533988	1MAI	42	Homology modeling	89.2	8.7	2.1	1.4	PM0076166
XP_002524729	1IEX, 1IH7, 1MAI, 1TXD, 2DA0, 2H94	LT 40	Threading	81.0	14.5	4.5	1.2	PM0076167
XP_002517076	1PLS, 1N4C, 1D0V	LT 40	Threading	85.4	14.6	0	1.8	PM0076168
XP_002516542	1PLS, 1BTN, 1DRO, 1QQG, 1MR5	LT 40	Threading	82.8	14.2	3	1.9	PM0076169
XP_002536221	1RWR	LT 40	Threading	89.7	7.3	3	0.8	PM0076170
ABR01234	1EQ1	LT 40	Threading	90.3	6.8	2.9	0.7	PM0076171
ABR01231	2ZDI	45	Homology modeling	96.1	2.9	1	1.1	PM0076172
ABR01229	1RQU, 1Y79	LT 40	Threading	88	10.3	1.7	1.8	*
ABR01227	1EQ1	LT 40	Threading	91.5	5.7	2.8	0.7	PM0076173
ABY64765	1I78	LT 40	Threading	88.5	8.7	2.8	1.3	PM0076174
ABY64764	1HG8	LT 40	Threading	82.9	12.6	4.5	0.8	PM0076175
ABY64763	1HG8	LT 40	Threading	83.9	10.5	5.6	0.8	PM0076176
ABY64762	1JX6	40	Homology modeling	94.9	4.3	0.8	1.7	PM0076177
ACG75703	1P9H	LT 40	Threading	88.5	10.6	0.9	0.3	PM0076178
ACM61985	1OGQ	41	Homology modeling	86.1	11	2.9	0.4	PM0076179
ACM61984	2Z82	40	Homology modeling	91.6	7.8	0.6	1.8	PM0076180
Q56B90	1OGQ	LT 40	Threading	85.3	11.9	2.8	0.9	PM0076181
Q56B89	1OGQ	LT 40	Threading	85.3	11.9	2.8	0.9	*
AAL26842	2AYD	71	Homology modeling	100	0	0	0.2	PM0076182

List of chosen templates with identity are mentioned. Twenty five refined models have been deposited into PMDB and accession codes are given. * indicates coordinates are also deposited and codes are pending for processing.

or bond length was detected in our refined models. Ramachandran Plot analysis revealed that, all the models were with good structural quality. The structural details and the refined three dimensional models of 27 AFPs have been deposited into the protein model data base (PMDB, http://mi.caspur.it/PMDB/) and their accession numbers are displayed in Table 5.

LRR/IRI – AFPs

LRR/IRI domain containing AFP models (*T. aestivum*: ACM61985, ACM61984, Q56B89, Q56B90 and *F. pratensis*: ACG75703) are conserved with already reported AFPs of *L. perenne and D. Antarctica*. As LRR, IRI domain is also involved in ice-recrystallization inhibitory activity. The 3D structure of AFP from *F. pratensis* is closely related to *L. perenne* - AFP, because the secondary structural identity of both the protein is 78%. Though LRR domain present in the AFPs, the predominant ice-binding region is predicted to be the IRI domain, and it contained two ice-binding surfaces, on either side of the β roll domain. The concave side of the predicted models is made up of continuous beta sheets and the convex side showed a variety of secondary structural elements such as helices and coil. Ascending and descending loops of predicted models made the connection between alpha helices and beta sheets as experimental LRR domain containing proteins. The structure classification of both experimental and most of the predicted LRR domain containing proteins is alpha + beta, which explains the reliability of the predicted models.

PH - AFPs

The PH domain contains 100 amino acid residues that occur in a broad range of proteins concerned in signal transduction mechanism or as constituents of the cytoskeleton. Several PH domain containing protein structures are solved with high resolution such as pleckstrin (N-terminal), β-spectrin, dynamin, phospholipase C-δ_1 (PLC- δ_1), Son of sevenless (Sos) and Bruton's tyrosine kinase (Btk) (Rebecchi and Scarlata, 1998). PH domains consist of two perpendicular anti-parallel beta sheets, followed by a C-terminal amphipathic helix. In our study, the four AFPs from *R. communis* are belonging to PH family (XP_002533988, XP_002524729, XP_002517076 and XP_002516542). However, the remaining protein (XP_002536221) was beta class, which is similar to hemagglutinin-related protein from *Granulibacter bethesdensis CGDNIH1*. The secondary structural class of our predicted PH domain containing AFP models is beta as experimental structure (Yoon et al., 1994). The PH domain containing proteins is not directly involved in ice-recrystallization inhibitory activity;

however, it may be involved in intracellular signaling during the cold condition.

WRKY - AFPs

The WRKY proteins comprise major family of a transcription factor that is essential for plant disease resistance, abiotic stress, senescence and some developmental processes in plants. This kind of protein is also named as thermal hysteresis proteins (THP). Crystal structure of *Arabidopsis thaliana* WRKY1-C (C-terminal) domain is composed of five β- strands (β1: 294–300, β2: 312–318, β3: 327–332, β4: 340–345 and β 5, 352–358), which forms the antiparallel β- sheet. The zinc-binding site is located at one end of the β- sheet, between strands β4 and β5 (Yamasaki et al., 2005). WRKY domain containing AFP model from *S. dulcamara* is also consisted of five β- strands as experimental structure. The secondary structure of *At*WRKY1-C is beta. Our predicted WRKY AFP model is also coming under the same class. The function of *S. dulcamara* – AFP is intracellular, because it does not contain putative signal peptide sequence in N-terminal region. The main function for this protein is DNA-binding activity.

Other AFPs

The 3D structure of two AFPs (AAB20142 and AAB20141) from *N. tabacum* contain only alpha helices, which is exactly similar to the *Winter flounder* - antifreeze protein Isoform HPLC6 (1WFA). *S. cereale* – AFPs (Q9S8C6, Q9S8C7, Q9S8C5 and Q9S8C8) are generally termed as PR (Glucan endo-1, 3-beta-glucosidase, Thaumatin-like protein and Endochitinase) proteins, in which, their predominant secondary structural composition is predicted to be coil rather than helices and sheets. The composition of alpha helices (ABR01234: 74.16%, ABR01231: 68.27%, ABR01229: 70.19% and ABR01227: 71.35%) is high in *C. vulgaris* - AFPs, where as coil content (ABY64765: 59.5%, ABY64764: 61.84%, ABY64763: 61.80% and ABY64762: 61.76%) is high in *Chlamydomonas sp. CCMP681*- AFPs.

Binding site analysis

Get area was used to calculate the solvent accessible surface area/solvation energy, number of surface atoms and buried atoms of the refined models. The very high value of the solvation energy resulted in a better interaction with ice. Thematics web server was used to identify the potential binding site residues from the predicted models. This analysis can be used to study the surface features and functional regions of the refined models. The probable binding sites residues of all AFPs

Table 6. Solvent accessibility and predicted binding site residues of plant antifreeze proteins.

S/No.	Accession number	Solvent accessibility			Probable binding residues of plant antifreeze proteins
		Solvation energy/SASA	No. of surface atoms	No. of buried atoms	
1	AAB20142	2839.67	162	44	ASP 4, THR 5, ALA 6, ASP 8, ALA 9
2	AAB20141	2839.67	178	48	ASP 2 , ASP 6
3	Q9S8C6	2287.83	126	20	TYR 5 , ARG 15
4	Q9S8C7	2643.65	168	41	LYS 8
5	Q9S8C5	1681.51	90	16	CYS 3 , CYS 12
6	Q9S8C8	2640.72	152	23	CYS 9
7	Q9S899	2536.12	141	29	VAL 1,GLU 9
8	Q6UAH5	10477.17	786	450	ARG 14 , LYS 18 , LYS 40 , CYS 41 , TYR 136 , HIS 138 , LYS 114 , ARG 112, ASP 129
9	XP_002533988	11507.00	921	616	GLU 46, ASP 53 , ASP 63 , GLU 95 , ASP 88, HIS 139 , ASP 179 , HIS 185
10	XP_002524729	31224.04	2532	1099	ALA 420, TRP 421, PRO 422, THR 460, ASN 461, VAL 463, SER 464, LEU 479, GLN 482
11	XP_002517076	20398.54	1710	1868	GLU 356 , TYR 381 , LYS 404 , LYS 405 , ARG 432
12	XP_002516542	22593.60	2002	1212	LYS 263 , TYR 270, LYS 305 , CYS 346 , CYS 386 , LYS 376 , LYS 392 , TYR 372
13	XP_002536221	13973.67	1309	852	ASP 57 , ASP 77, HIS 93 , HIS 219, ASP 321
14	ABR01234	9800.32	804	503	ARG 12 , ARG 19 , GLU 128 , ASP 159, GLU 52 , ASP 53 , LYS 55 , ASP 56 , ASP 104 , GLU 174 , LYS 59, ASP 92
15	ABR01231	7765.63	555	234	ASP 50 , ASP 61, GLU 78, GLU 90 , HIS 93 , GLU 97 , ASP 96
16	ABR01229	25524.65	2273	1305	GLU 196 , GLU 267 , HIS 268 , LYS 233 , CYS 255 , GLU 257, LYS 303 , LYS 391 , GLU 445 , ASP 455 , ARG 384 , ARG 441, ARG 305, GLU 346, ARG 431
17	ABR01227	9901.57	808	501	GLU 52 , LYS 55 , ASP 56 , LYS 59 , ASP 96 , ASP 92, GLU 174
18	ABY64765	19232.02	1669	900	TYR 71 , CYS 147 , LYS 205 , TYR 277 , ARG 78 , ARG 292 , ARG 131, ASP 195 , ASP 241, LYS 27 , CYS 328
19	ABY64764	15650.82	1496	1087	ASP 71 , GLU 92 , GLU 117, ASP 310 , GLU 317 , CYS 339 , CYS 350

Table 6. Cont'd.

20	ABY64763	15923.20	1505	1044	ASP 91 , GLU 114, ASP 263 , GLU 302 , HIS 339 , CYS 303 , CYS 309 , TYR 312 , CYS 336 , CYS 347
21	ABY64762	17157.43	1590	955	GLU 54 , GLU 106, ASP 88, GLU 155 , ASP 286 , ASP 287 , ASP 238 , CYS 322 , LYS 334, LYS 296 , CYS 300
22.	ACG75703	6069.71	488	324	HIS 54 , HIS 61 , ASP 65 , ASP 74 , ASP 73
23.	ACM61985	9148.36	859	423	HIS 13, ARG 60 , ARG 61, ASP 91 , ASP 114, HIS 129, HIS 150 , HIS 171 , GLY 175,
24.	ACM61984	11132.72	954	377	CYS 45, LYS 93, TYR 110 , ARG 152 , ARG 155 , LYS 130 , ARG 176
25.	Q56B90	13709.62	1269	772	ARG 19, ARG 68 , ARG 93 , HIS 117 , GLU 95 , CYS 119 , LYS 140 , TYR 120 , ASP 168 , ASP 122 , GLU 169 , HIS 147, ASP 235
26	Q56B89	13709.62	1269	772	ARG 19, ARG 68 , ARG 93 , HIS 117 , GLU 95 , CYS 119 , LYS 140 , TYR 120 , ASP 168 , ASP 122 , GLU 169 , HIS 147, ASP 235
27	AAL26842	5119.16	389	205	ASP 368, LYS 378, GLN 381, ASN 389, PRO 390, SER 392, TYR 394, VAL 407, GLU 408, VAL 417

were mentioned in Table 6. Based on the results of protein modeling and binding site analysis, these sites were chosen as the most favorable binding sites for further molecular docking studies of AFPs with ice. All the sequence and structural analysis helped into classifying the AFPs in over wintering plants (Figure 3), and it is essential information for further experimental studies.

Conclusion

The present study involving analysis of various sequence and structural features of AFPs in over wintering plants has provided insight into the ice-recrystallization inhibition process. The dataset of 40 plant AFPs was retrieved from UniProt and GenPept databases and classify the AFPs into different categories. Primary structure analysis shows that most of AFPs are hydrophilic in nature. Computed pI value revealed that 21 AFPs posses the acidic property, whereas remaining to have basic property. The AFPs ACG75703, AAB20141, Q9M3W4

and AAB20142 cannot be used for UV spectrometry studies due to the absence of EC value. GRAVY index computes the possible crystallization propensity of all the AFPs, in which, twenty seven are more chances to get the crystal due to their high GRAVY score, whereas remaining were found to be optimum chances.

Molecular phylogenetic tree segregated the AFPs into various groups based on the sequence similarity and distances. The AFP from *F. pratensis* does not show any significant similarity with PGIPs. Moreover, transmembrane domains are observed in some of AFPs. *S. ceareale* and *P. suaveolens* AFPs (Q9S8C6 and Q6UAH5) do not contain glycosylation sites, whereas remaining AFPs were found to have several glycosylation sites. Presence of N-terminal signal peptide in AFPs suggests that these proteins would participate in the secretory pathway. In our study, 22 AFPs are targeted into extra cellular space and remaining is targeted into mitochondria, chloroplast and other locations. Our secondary structure results suggested that 7 AFPs are belonging to alpha, 15 is beta and 5 are alpha + beta

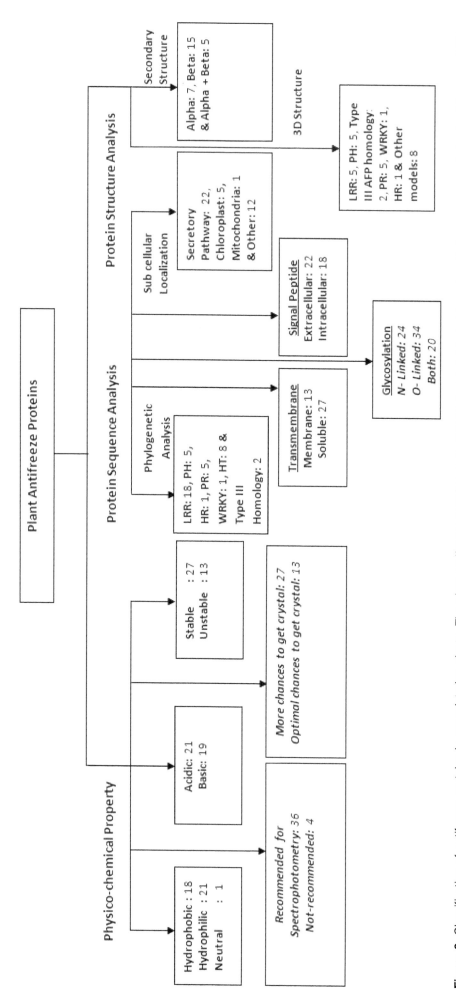

Figure 3. Classification of antifreeze proteins in overwintering plants. The plant antifreeze proteins were classified and distributed based on their sequence and structural features (LRR: Leucine rich repeat, PH: Pleckstrin homology, PR: Pathogenesis related, HR: Hemagglutinin related and HT: Hypothetical).

classes, respectively.

Ongoing efforts are directed towards the development of molecular docking and dynamics based CS towards plant AFPs to understand the mechanism of an ice-recrystallization inhibiton. Newly identified LRR, PR and HR AFPs can be validated by employing the molecular interactions studies with their interacting partners. The proposed classification scheme allowed us to identify the binding sites of AFP and design an engineered construct of potential AFP with superior ice-recrystallization inhibitory activity or in production of fusion protein, which will protect the plants from freezing conditions and psychrophilic pathogens. Multigene transformation could be necessary to transfer these characteristics to other plants. This type of research will eventually permit evaluation of the effectiveness of the AFPs for the enhancement of frost resistance of commercially important crops.

ACKNOWLEDGEMENTS

J. Muthukumaran thanks Council for Scientific and Industrial Research (CSIR) for Senior Research Fellowship (SRF). P. Manivel thanks University Grant Commission (UGC), Government of India for providing financial assistance to carry out the research work. M. Kannan thanks UGC for Rajiv Gandhi National Fellowship to pursue his Ph.D degree. R. Krishna thanks Centre of Excellence in Bioinformatics, Pondicherry University funded by Department of Biotechnology and Department of Information technology, Government of India, New Delhi for providing the essential computational resources for carrying out the research work.

Abbreviations: AFP, Antifreeze proteins; **LRR,** Leucine rich repeat; **PH,** Pleckstrin homology; **PR,** Pathogenesis related; **PGIP,** Polygalatouronase inhibiting protein; **SMART,** Simple modular architecture research tool; **MSA,** Multiple sequence alignment; **LRRNT,** Leucine rich repeat N-terminal; **RI,** Recrystallization inhibition; **TH,** thermal hysteresis; **GRAVY,** grand average of hydropathicity; **PCoA,** principal coordinate analysis; **PDB,** protein data bank; **SPC,** single point charge; **CE,** combinatorial extension; **THEMATICS,** Theoretical macroscopic titration curves; **EC,** extinction coefficient; **pI,** isoelectric point; **NJ,** neighbor-joining; **RMSD,** root mean square deviation; **PMDB,** protein model data base.

REFERENCES

Altschul SF, Madden TL, Schaffer AA, Zhang J, Zhang Z, Miller W and Lipman DJ (1997). Gapped BLAST and PSI-BLAST: a new generation of protein database search programs. Nucleic Acids Res. 25: 3389-3402.

Bayer-Giraldi M, Uhlig C, John U, Mock T and Valentin K (2010). Antifreeze proteins in polar sea ice diatoms: diversity and gene expression in the genus Fragilariopsis. Environ. Microbiol. 12: 1041-52.

Brudno M, Steinkamp R, Morgenstern B (2004). The CHAOS/DIALIGN WWW server for multiple alignment of genomic sequences. Nucleic Acids Res. 32: W41-44.

Choi JH, Jung HY, Kim HS, Cho HG (2000). PhyloDraw: a phylogenetic tree drawing system. Bioinformatics 16: 1056-1058.

Davies PL, Baardsnes J, Kuiper MJ, Walker VK (2002). Structure and function of antifreeze proteins. Philos. Trans. R. Soc. Lond. B. Biol. Sci. 357: 927-935.

Deng G, Andrews DW, Laursen RA (1997). Amino acid sequence of a new type of antifreeze protein, from the longhorn sculpin Myoxocephalus octodecimspinosis. FEBS Lett. 402: 17-20.

Emanuelsson O, Brunak S, von Heijne G, Nielsen H (2007). Locating proteins in the cell using TargetP, SignalP and related tools. Nat. Protoc. 2: 953-971.

Eswar N, Eramian D, Webb B, Shen MY, Sali A (2008). Protein structure modeling with MODELLER. Methods Mol. Biol. 426: 145-159.

Fletcher GL, Hew CL, Davies PL (2001). Antifreeze proteins of teleost fishes. Annu. Rev. Physiol. 63: 359-390.

Fraczkiewics RB, Braun W (1998). Exact and efficient analytical calculation of the accessible surface areas and their Gradients for Macromolecules. J. Comp. Chem 19: 319-333.

Raghava GPS (1999). Proclass: A computer program for predicting the protein structural classes. J. Biosciences 24: 176.

Griffith M, Yaish MW (2004). Antifreeze proteins in overwintering plants: a tale of two activities. Trends Plant Sci. 9: 399-405.

Hess B (2008). GROMACS 4: Algorithms for Highly Efficient, Load-Balanced, and Scalable Molecular Simulation. J. Chem. Theory. Comput 4: 435-447.

Hirokawa T, Boon-Chieng S, Mitaku S (1998). SOSUI: classification and secondary structure prediction system for membrane proteins. Bioinformatics 14: 378-379.

Hon WC, Griffith M, Mlynarz A, Kwok YC, Yang DS (1995). Antifreeze proteins in winter rye are similar to pathogenesis-related proteins. Plant Physiol. 109: 879-889.

Huang T, Duman JG (2002). Cloning and characterization of a thermal hysteresis (antifreeze) protein with DNA-binding activity from winter bittersweet nightshade, Solanum dulcamara. Plant Mol. Biol. 48: 339-350.

John UP, Polotnianka RM, Sivakumaran KA, Chew O, Mackin L, Kuiper MJ, Talbot JP, Nugent GD, Mautord J, Schrauf GE, Spangenberg GC (2009). Ice recrystallization inhibition proteins (IRIPs) and freeze tolerance in the cryophilic Antarctic hair grass Deschampsia antarctica E. Desv. Plant Cell Environ. 32: 336-348.

Kelley LA, Sternberg MJ (2009). Protein structure prediction on the Web: a case study using the Phyre server. Nat. Protoc. 4: 363-371.

Kuiper MJ, Davies PL, Walker VK (2001). A theoretical model of a plant antifreeze protein from Lolium perenne. Biophys. J. 81: 3560-3565.

Letunic I, Doerks T, Bork P (2009). SMART 6: recent updates and new developments. Nucleic Acids Res. 37: D229-232.

Lovell SC, Davis IW, Arendall WB 3rd, de Bakker PI, Word JM, Prisant MG, Richardson JS, Richardson DC (2003). Structure validation by Calpha geometry: phi,psi and Cbeta deviation. Proteins 50: 437-450.

Meyer K, Keil M, Naldrett MJ (1999). A leucine-rich repeat protein of carrot that exhibits antifreeze activity. FEBS Lett. 447: 171-178.

Ng NF, Hew CL (1992). Structure of an antifreeze polypeptide from the sea raven. Disulfide bonds and similarity to lectin-binding proteins. J. Biol. Chem. 267: 16069-16075.

Ondrechen MJ, Clifton JG, Ringe D (2001). THEMATICS: a simple computational predictor of enzyme function from structure. Proc. Natl. Acad. Sci. USA 98: 12473-12478.

Raymond JA, Janech MG, Fritsen CH (2009). Novel ice-binding proteins from a psychorophilic antarctic alga (Chlamydomonadaceae, Chlorophyceae). J. Phycol. 45: 130-136.

Rebecchi MJ, Scarlata S (1998). Pleckstrin homology domains: a common fold with diverse functions. Ann. Rev. Biophys. Biomol. Struct. 27: 503-528.

Retief JD (2008). Phylogenetic Analysis using PHYLIP. In: Krawetz, S.M.a.S.A. (Ed.), Bioinformatics Methods and Protocols, Humana Press, pp. 243-258.

Scotter AJ, Marshall CB, Graham LA, Gilbert JA, Garnham CP, Davies PL (2006). The basis for hyperactivity of antifreeze proteins.

Cryobiology 53: 229-239.

Sen TZ, Jernigan RL, Garnier J, Kloczkowski A (2005). GOR V server for protein secondary structure prediction. Bioinformatics 21: 2787-2788.

Shindyalov IN, Bourne PE (1998). Protein structure alignment by incremental combinatorial extension (CE) of the optimal path. Protein Eng. 11: 739-747.

Sicheri F, Yang DS (1995). Ice-binding structure and mechanism of an antifreeze protein from winter flounder. Nature 375: 427-431.

Sidebottom C, Buckley S, Pudney P, Twigg S, Jarman C, Holt C, Telford J, McArthur A, Worrall D, Hubbard R, Lillford P (2000). Heat-stable antifreeze protein from grass. Nature 406: 256.

Sonnichsen FD, Sykes BD, Chao H, Davies PL (1993). The nonhelical structure of antifreeze protein type III. Science 259: 1154-1157.

Thomashow MF (1998). Role of cold-responsive genes in plant freezing tolerance. Plant Physiol. 118: 1-8.

Tyagi N, Anamika K, Srinivasan N (2010). A framework for classification of prokaryotic protein kinases. PLoS One. 26: e10608.

Venketesh S, Dayananda C (2008). Properties, potentials, and prospects of antifreeze proteins. Crit. Rev. Biotechnol. 28: 57-82.

Wilkins MR, Gasteiger E, Bairoch A, Sanchez JC, Williams KL, Appel RD, Hochstrasser DF(1999). Protein identification and analysis tools in the ExPASy server. Methods Mol. Biol. 112: 531-552.

Worrall D, Elias L, Ashford D, Smallwood M, Sidebottom C, Lillford P, Telford J, Holt C, Bowles D (1998). A carrot leucine-rich-repeat protein that inhibits ice recrystallization. Science 282: 115-117.

Wu CH, Apweiler R, Bairoch A, Natale DA, Barker WC, Boeckmann B, Ferro S, Gasteiger E, Huang H, Lopez R, Magrane M, Martin MJ, Mazumder R, O'Donovan C, Redaschi N, Suzek B (2006). The Universal Protein Resource (UniProt): an expanding universe of protein information. Nucleic Acids Res. 34: D187-191.

Yamasaki K, Kigawa T, Inoue M, Tateno M, Yamasaki T, Yabuki T, Aoki M, Seki E, Matsuda T, Tomo Y, Hayami N, Terada T, Shirouzu M, Tanaka A, Seki M, Shinozaki K, Yokoyama S (2005). Solution structure of an Arabidopsis WRKY DNA binding domain. Plant Cell 17: 944-956.

Yoon HS, Hajduk PJ, Petros AM, Olejniczak ET, Meadows RP, Fesik SW (1994). Solution structure of a pleckstrin-homology domain. Nature 369: 672-675.

Zhang DQ, Liu B, Feng DR, He YM, Wang SQ, Wang HB, Wang JF (2004). Significance of conservative asparagine residues in the thermal hysteresis activity of carrot antifreeze protein. Biochem. J. 377: 589-595.

## 31

SEALI: A sequence alignment tool

Manoj Giri[1]*, **Dipti Jindal**[2], **Savita Kumari**[2], **Sarla Kumari**[3], **Devender Singh**[4], **Jawahar Lal**[5] and **Neena Jaggi**[6]

[1]Department of Applied Sciences, Haryana College of Technology and Management, Kaithal-136 027, India.
[2]Department of Bioinformatics, Chaudhary Charan Singh Haryana Agricultural University, Hisar- 125 004, India.
[3]Deparmtnet of Electronics and Communication Engineering, Haryana College of Technology and Management, Kaithal-136 027, India.
[4]Department of Applied Sciences, Dayal Singh College, Karnal-132 001, India.
[5]Department of Applied Sciences, Markanda National College, Sahabad (M) 136 135, India.
[6]Department of Applied Sciences, National Institute of Technology, Kurukshetra-136 199, India.

In this paper we propose a novel program for sequence alignment. This program has been developed in PERL. The web interface uses CGI and front end for data input and viewing the result has also been developed. This program counts the length of two sequences, aligns the two sequences, counts the number of matches, mismatches, gaps and score and displays the possible alignment.

Key words: Sequnce alignment, SEALI tool, PERL, dynamic programming, DNA, adenine (A), guanine (G), cytosine (C), thymine (T).

INTRODUCTION

Sequence alignment is by far the most common task in Bioinformatics. A sequence alignment is a way of arranging the primary sequences of DNA, RNA, or protein to identify regions of similarity that may be a consequence of functional, structural, or evolutionary relationships between the sequences [Mount, 2004]. Sequence alignments are useful in bioinformatics for identifying sequence similarity, producing phylogenetic trees, and developing homology models of protein structures. Alignments are often assumed to reflect a degree of evolutionary change between sequences descended from a common ancestor [HTTP//www.wikipedia.org/sequence_alignment//.].

There are three primary methods of producing pairwise alignments namely dynamic programming, dotplot and word method. The Needleman and Wunsch algorithm was the first rapid method in the biological literature for determining sequence homology (Needleman and Wunsch, 1970). It was based on dynamic programming

and was used to align sequences globally. Smith and Waterman algorithm yields local alignment (Smith and Waterman, 1981). There are various tools for the sequence analysis available in the public domain such as FASTA, LALIGN and PRSS, BLAST, PipMaker, LAGAN, ParAlign, BLAT, YASS and Nigila, etc (Lipman and Pearson, 1985; Pearson, 1990; Altschul et al., 1990; Schwartz et al., 2000; Brudno et al., 2003; Rognes, 2001; Kent, 2002; Noe and Kucherov, 2004; Noe and Kucherov, 2005; Cartwright, 2007; Wang and Jiang, 1994).

The present research has been carried out to develop a simple sequence alignment tool using dynamic programming which counts the length of two sequences, aligns the two sequences, counts the number of matches, mismatches, gaps and score and displays the possible alignment.

METHODS AND IMPLEMENTATION

The SEALI program has been implemented in Perl script. The web interface uses common gateway interfaces (CGI) and a front end for data input and viewing the results has also been developed. The script for web interfaces has been written in html. The hypertext

---

*Corresponding author. E-mail: manojgiri1@rediffmail.com.

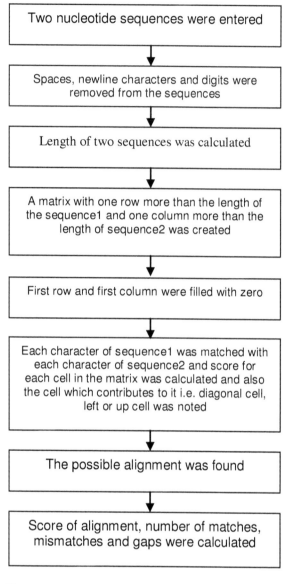

Figure 1. Pictorial representation of the steps followed during workflow of SEALI.

letter other than the four (A, G, C, and T).
4. The length of the two sequences was counted.
5. Alignment of two sequences was done.
6. Number of matches, mismatches, gaps and score were counted.
7. Results were displayed.

Pictorial presentation

The pictorial presentation for the SEALI has been shown in the Figure 1.

Program code

The program code has been written in PERL language. With the help of the coding, the SEALI tool runs and it takes the two nucleotide sequences as input through web interface and counts the length of two sequences, align the two sequences, counts the number of matches, mismatches, gaps and score and display the possible alignment. In this program there are two library files namely;

```perl
global.lib and local.lib.
#!/usr/bin/perl
require "global.lib";
require "local.lib";
print"Content-type: text/html\n\n";
print"<html>";
print"<body>";
read(STDIN,$buffer,$ENV{'CONTENT_LENGTH'});
$a = $buffer;
#get the name and value for each form input
@array= split(/&/,$a);
foreach $array(@array)
{
#separate the name and value
($key,$value) =split(/=/,$array);
#convert +signs to space
$value =~tr/+/ /;
#convert hexadecimal to ASCII characters
$value=~ s/%([a-fA-F0-9][a-fA-F0-9])/pack("C",hex($1))/eg;
#store values in a hash called %form
$form{$key}=$value;
}
#print the algo  you have selected
print"$form{'algo'}\t";
$b =$form{'algo'};
if($b eq 'needle')
{
 &global($form{'text1'} ,$form{'text2'});
}
else
{
&local($form{'text1'} ,$form{'text2'});
}
print"</body>";
print"</html>";
```

Coding of library files

```perl
global.lib
sub need1
{
$seq1 = $_[0];
$seq2 =$_[1];
my $match =2;
```

transport protocol (HTTP) is used for data transport. The main function of the program developed in the present work is to count the length of two sequences, align the two sequences, count the number of matches, mismatches, gaps, and score and display the possible alignment. The nucleotide or gene sequence (DNA) contains four nucleotide bases adenine (A), guanine (G), cytosine (C) and thymine (T). The sequence of these bases comprises genetic information. The complete nucleotide sequence is taken as a single string. Two nucleotide sequences are taken as two strings. The sequence of characters was given to computer program as input for manipulating for the required purpose. The methods followed for the functioning of the program is summarized as:

1. In the first step, two nucleotide sequences were given as input to the program.
2. The program for alignment either global or local was chosen.
3. It was checked whether the entered sequences were correct or not, that is the correct sequence should not contain any spaces or

```perl
my $mismatch =-1;
my $gap =-2;
print"(global alignment)<br>";
my @best_score;
$seq1 =~s/\n|\s*|\d*//gi;
print"$seq1<br>";
$seq2 =~s/\n|\s*|\d*//gi;
 print"$seq2<br>";
my $size1=length($seq1);
print"length of seq1 is : $size1<br>";
my $size2 = length($seq2);
print"length of seq2 is : $size2<br>";
print"<br>";
# initialization
my @matrix;
$matrix[0][0] = 0;
for(my $j = 1; $j <= $size1; $j++) {
$matrix[0][$j]   =0;
}
for(my $i = 1; $i <=$size2; $i++) {
$matrix[$i][0]   = 0;
 for(my $j = 1; $j <=$size1; $j++) {
my ($diagonal_score, $left_score, $up_score);
# calculate match score
my $letter1 = substr($seq1, $j-1, 1);
my $letter2 = substr($seq2, $i-1, 1);
if ($letter1 eq $letter2) {
$diagonal_score = $matrix[$i-1][$j-1] + $match;
}
else {
$diagonal_score = $matrix[$i-1][$j-1] + $mismatch;
}
# calculate gap scores
$up_score   = $matrix[$i-1][$j] + $gap;
$left_score = $matrix[$i][$j-1] + $gap;
# choose best score
if ($diagonal_score >= $up_score)
{
if ($diagonal_score >= $left_score)
{
$matrix[$i][$j]  = $diagonal_score;
$best_score[$i][$j] = "diagonal";
}
else
{
$matrix[$i][$j]   = $left_score;
$best_score[$i][$j] = "left";
}
}
else {
if ($up_score >= $left_score) {
$matrix[$i][$j]   = $up_score;
$matrix[$i][$j]   = $up_score;
$best_score[$i][$j] = "up";
}
else {
$matrix[$i][$j]   = $left_score;
             $best_score[$i][$j] = "left";
}
}

}
}

# trace-back
 my $align1 = "";
 my $align2 = "";
 # start at last cell of matrix
```

```perl
my $j = $size1;

my $i = $size2;
while($i!=0 || $j!=0) {
if ($best_score[$i][$j] eq "diagonal") {
$align1 .= substr($seq1, $j-1, 1);
$align2 .= substr($seq2, $i-1, 1);
$i--;
$j--;
}
elsif ($best_score[$i][$j] eq "left") {
$align1 .= substr($seq1, $j-1, 1);
$align2 .= "_";
$j--;
}
elsif ($best_score[$i][$j] eq "up") {
$align1 .= "_";
$align2 .= substr($seq2, $i-1, 1);
$i--;
}
elsif($j==0)
{
$align1.="_";
$align2 .= substr($seq2,$i-1,1);
$i--;
}
elsif($i == 0)
{
$align1 .=substr($seq1,$j-1,1);
$align2 .="_";
$j--;
}
}
$align1 = reverse $align1;
$align2 = reverse $align2;
#score
@a =split(//,$align1);
@b = split(//,$align2);
$len= @a;
$sum=0;
$j=0;
$nomatch = 0;
$nomismatch = 0;
$nogap = 0;
for($i=0;$i<$len;$i++)
{
while($i==$j)
{
if($a[$i] eq $b[$i])
{
$sum =$sum+ $match;
$nomatch = $nomatch + 1;
}

elsif(($a[$i] eq "_")||($b[$i] eq "_"))
{
$sum = $sum + $gap;
$nogap = $nogap +1;
}
else
{
$sum = $sum+ $mismatch;
$nomismatch = $nomismatch +1;
}
$j++;
}
}
print" score: $sum<br>";
```

```perl
print" matches: $nomatch<br>";
print" mismatches: $nomismatch<br>";
print" gaps: $nogap<br>";
$l1 = length($align1);
$l2 = length($align2);
print"<b>The possible alignment is:</b><br>";
$i=1;
for($i=1;$i<=$l1;$i++)
{
if($l1 >60)
{
$align1=~m/.{60}/;
print"$&<br>";
$align1= $';
$l1 = length($align1);
$align2=~m/.{60}/;
print"$&<br><br>";
$align2= $';
}
if($l1<=60)
{
print"$align1<br>";
print"$align2<br><br>";
last
}
}
}
1;


Coding of local.lib

sub water1
{
print"(local alignment)<br>";
$seq1= $_[0];
$seq2= $_[1];
my $match    = 2;
my $mismatch = -1;
my $gap      = -2;
# initialization
my @matrix;
my @best_score;
$seq1 =~s/\n|\s*|\d*//gi;
print"$seq1<br>";
$seq2 =~s/\n|\s*|\d*//gi;
print"$seq2<br>";
$len1= length($seq1);
$len2= length($seq2);
print"length of sequence1 is $len1 <br>";
print"length of sequence2 is $len2 <br>";
$matrix[0][0]   = 0;

for(my $j = 1; $j <= length($seq1); $j++) {
$matrix[0][$j]   = 0;
}
for (my $i = 1; $i <= length($seq2); $i++) {
$matrix[$i][0]   = 0;
# fill
for(my $j = 1; $j <= length($seq1); $j++) {
my ($diagonal_score, $left_score, $up_score);
# calculate match score

my $letter1 = substr($seq1, $j-1, 1);
my $letter2 = substr($seq2, $i-1, 1);
if ($letter1 eq $letter2) {
$diagonal_score = $matrix[$i-1][$j-1] + $match;
}
```

```perl
else {
$diagonal_score = $matrix[$i-1][$j-1]+ $mismatch;

}
# calculate gap scores
$up_score   = $matrix[$i-1][$j] + $gap;
$left_score = $matrix[$i][$j-1] + $gap;
if ($diagonal_score <= 0 and $up_score <= 0 and $left_score <= 0)
{
$matrix[$i][$j]   = 0;
}
# choose best score
else{
if($diagonal_score >= $up_score) {
if ($diagonal_score >= $left_score) {
$matrix[$i][$j]   = $diagonal_score;
$best_score[$i][$j]="diagonal";
}
else {
$matrix[$i][$j]    = $left_score;
$best_score[$i][$j]="left";
}
} else {
if ($up_score >= $left_score) {
$matrix[$i][$j] = $up_score;
$best_score[$i][$j]= "up";
}
else{
$matrix[$i][$j]= $left_score;
$best_score[$i][$j]= "left";
}
}
}
}
}
my $max_score = 0;
my $min_score = 99;
my $s=0;
my $t=0;
my $u=0;
my @index1;
my @index2;
for(my $i=1;$i<=length($seq2);$i++)
{
for(my $j=1;$j<=length($seq1);$j++)
{
if($matrix[$i][$j]>= $max_score){
$max_score = $matrix[$i][$j];

$index1[$s] =$i;
$index2[$t] = $j;
$s++;
$t++;
}
if($matrix[$i][$j]< $min_score){
$min_score= $matrix[$i][$j] ;
}
$maxscore[$u] = $matrix[$i][$j];
$u++;
}
}
print"<br>";
for(my $i=1;$i<=length($seq2);$i++)
{
for(my $j=1;$j<=length($seq1);$j++)
{
if($matrix[$i][$j]== $max_score){
$ind1[$r] = $i;
```

```perl
$ind2[$s] = $j;
$r++;
$s++;
}
}
}

#trace back
my $m=0;
my $n=0;
foreach $i(@ind1)
{
foreach$j(@ind2)
{
while(!($matrix[$i][$j] == 0))
{
 if($best_score[$i][$j] eq "diagonal")
 {
$align1[$m] .= substr($seq1, $j-1,1);
$align2[$n] .= substr($seq2, $i-1,1);
$i--;
$j--;
}
 elsif($best_score[$i][$j] eq "left")
 {
$align1[$m] .= substr($seq1,$j-1,1);
$align2[$n] .= "_";
$j--;
}
 elsif($best_score[$i][$j] eq "up")
 {
$align1[$m] .="_";
$align2[$n] .=substr($seq2 ,$i-1,1);
$i--;
}
}
}
}
$align1[$m]= reverse $align1[$m];
$align2[$n] = reverse $align2[$n];
$m++;
$n++;
}
#score
$p=0;
$o=0;
foreach $a(@align1)
{
@c =split(//,$a);
$len=@c;
foreach $b(@align2)
{
while($o==$p)
{
@d=split(//,$b);
$j=0;
$sum=0;
$nomatch=0;
$nomismatch=0;
$nogap=0;
for($i=0;$i<$len;$i++)
{
while($j==$i)
{
if($c[$j] eq $d[$j])
{
$sum =$sum+ $match;
$nomatch = $nomatch +1;
}
elsif(($c[$i] eq'_')||($d[$i] eq'_'))
{
$sum += $gap;
$nogap= $nogap+1;
}
else
{
$sum += $mismatch;
$nomismatch = $nomismatch+1;
}
$j++;
}
}
print"score: $sum<br>";
print"matches: $nomatch<br>";
print"mismatches: $nomismatch<br>";
print"gaps: $nogap<br>";
last;
}
$p++;
}
$p=0;
$o=$o+1;

$length = @align1;
for($j=0;$j<$length;$j++)
{
$align1[$j]=$align1[$j];
$align2[$j]=$align2[$j];
$l1= length($align1[$j]);
for($i=1;$i<=$l1;$i++)
{
if($l1 >60)
{
$align1[$j]=~m/.{60}/;
print"$&<br>";
$align1[$j]= $';
$l1 = length($align1[$j]);
$align2[$j]=~m/.{60}/;
print"$&<br><br>";
$align2[$j]= $';
}
if($l1<60)
{
print"$align1[$j]<br>";
print"$align2[$j]<br><br>";
last;
}
}
}
}
1;
```

DISCUSSION

A sequence alignment is a way of arranging the primary sequences of DNA, RNA, or protein. Alignment provides a powerful tool to compare related sequences, and the alignment of two residues could reflect a common evolutionary origin, or could represent common structural and/or catalytic roles, not always reflecting an evolutionary process. If two sequences in an alignment share a common ancestor, mismatches can be interpreted as point mutations and gaps as indels introduced in one or both lineages in the time since they diverged from one another [HTTP//www.wikipedia.org/sequence_alignment//.].

Pairwise sequence alignment methods are used to find the best-matching piecewise (local) or global alignments of two query sequences. Pairwise alignments can only be used between two sequences at a time. Multiple sequence alignment is an extension of pairwise alignment to incorporate more than two sequences at a time. Multiple alignment methods try to align all of the sequences in a given query set. Multiple alignments are often used in identifying conserved sequence regions across a group of sequences hypothesized to be evolutionarily related (Wang and Jiang, 1994). Computational approaches to sequence alignment generally fall into two categories: global alignments and local alignments. So SEALI is a tool which aligns the two sequences globally and locally. For the tool development the code was written in perl and script for front end was written in html. Two nucleotide sequences were given as input to the program. In this tool, sequences can be aligned either locally or globally by selecting one option. It was checked whether the entered sequences were correct or not, that is the correct sequence should not contain any spaces or letter other than the four (A, G, C, and T). The length of the two sequences was counted. Alignment of two sequences was done. Number of matches, mismatches, gaps and score were counted. Results were found.

ACKNOWLEDGMENTS

The authors are thankful to Dr. Sudhir Kumar, Associate Professor and Head of the Bioinformatics Section, at CCSHAU, Hisar for his inspiration to the present work.

REFERENCES

Altschul SF, Gish W, Miller W, Myers EW, Lipman DJ (1990). Basic local alignment search tool. J. Mol. Biol., 215: 403-410.

Brudno M, Do CB, Cooper GM, Kim MF, Davydov E, Green ED, Sidow A, Batzoglou S (2003). LAGAN and Multi-LAGAN: Efficient Tools for Large-Scale Multiple Alignment of Genomic DNA. Genome Res., 13: 721-731.

Cartwright AR (2007). Ngila: global pairwise alignments with logarithmic and affine gap costs. Bioinform, 23: 1427-1428.

Kent WJ (2002). BLAT-The BLAST-like alignment tool. Genome Res., 12: 656-664.

Mount DW (2004). Bioinformatics: Sequence and Genome Analysis (2nd ed), Cold Spring Harbour Laboratory Press: Cold Spring Harbour,HTTP//www.wikipedia.org/sequence_alignment//.

Needleman SB, Wunsch CD (1970). A general method applicable to the search for similarities in the amino acid sequence of two proteins. J. Mol. Biol., 48: 443-453.

Noe L, Kucherov G (2004). Improved hit criteria for DNA local alignment. BMC Bioinform., 5: 149.

Noe L, Kucherov G (2005). YASS: enhancing the sensitivity of DNA similarity search. Nucleic Acid Res., 33: 540-543.

Pearson WR (1990). Rapid and sensitive sequence comparison with FASTP and FASTA. Methods Enzymol., 183: 63–98.

Pearson WR, Lipman DJ (1985). Rapid and sensitive protein similarity searches. Science, 227(4693): 1435-1441.

Rognes T (2001). ParAlign: a parallel sequence alignment algorithm for rapid and sensitive database searches. Nucleic Acids Res., 29: 1647-1652.

Schwartz S, Zhangf Z, Frazer KA, Smit A, Riemer C, Bouck J, Gibbs R, Hardison R, Miller W (2000). PipMaker-A web server for aligning two genomic DNA sequences. Genome Res., 10: 577-586.

Smith T, Waterman M (1981). Identification of common molecular subsequences. J. Mol. Biol., 147: 195-197.

Wang L, Jiang T (1994). On the complexity of multiple sequence alignment. J. Comput. Biol., 1: 337-348.

Permissions

All chapters in this book were first published in JBSA, by Academic Journals; hereby published with permission under the Creative Commons Attribution License or equivalent. Every chapter published in this book has been scrutinized by our experts. Their significance has been extensively debated. The topics covered herein carry significant findings which will fuel the growth of the discipline. They may even be implemented as practical applications or may be referred to as a beginning point for another development.

The contributors of this book come from diverse backgrounds, making this book a truly international effort. This book will bring forth new frontiers with its revolutionizing research information and detailed analysis of the nascent developments around the world.

We would like to thank all the contributing authors for lending their expertise to make the book truly unique. They have played a crucial role in the development of this book. Without their invaluable contributions this book wouldn't have been possible. They have made vital efforts to compile up to date information on the varied aspects of this subject to make this book a valuable addition to the collection of many professionals and students.

This book was conceptualized with the vision of imparting up-to-date information and advanced data in this field. To ensure the same, a matchless editorial board was set up. Every individual on the board went through rigorous rounds of assessment to prove their worth. After which they invested a large part of their time researching and compiling the most relevant data for our readers.

The editorial board has been involved in producing this book since its inception. They have spent rigorous hours researching and exploring the diverse topics which have resulted in the successful publishing of this book. They have passed on their knowledge of decades through this book. To expedite this challenging task, the publisher supported the team at every step. A small team of assistant editors was also appointed to further simplify the editing procedure and attain best results for the readers.

Apart from the editorial board, the designing team has also invested a significant amount of their time in understanding the subject and creating the most relevant covers. They scrutinized every image to scout for the most suitable representation of the subject and create an appropriate cover for the book.

The publishing team has been an ardent support to the editorial, designing and production team. Their endless efforts to recruit the best for this project, has resulted in the accomplishment of this book. They are a veteran in the field of academics and their pool of knowledge is as vast as their experience in printing. Their expertise and guidance has proved useful at every step. Their uncompromising quality standards have made this book an exceptional effort. Their encouragement from time to time has been an inspiration for everyone.

The publisher and the editorial board hope that this book will prove to be a valuable piece of knowledge for researchers, students, practitioners and scholars across the globe.

List of Contributors

Q. M. Alfred
University Institute of Technology, University of Burdwan, West Bengal, India 713104

K. Bishayee
University Institute of Technology, University of Burdwan, West Bengal, India 713104

P. Roy
Department of Biotechnology, University of Burdwan, West Bengal, India, 713104

T. Ghosh
Burdwan Medical College and Hospital, West Bengal, India

D. Gowsia
DBT-Bioiformatics Facility Center, Department of Biochemistry, S.K. University, Anantapur-515055, India

B. Babajan
DBT-Bioiformatics Facility Center, Department of Biochemistry, S.K. University, Anantapur-515055, India

M. Chaitanya
DBT-Bioiformatics Facility Center, Department of Biochemistry, S.K. University, Anantapur-515055, India

C. Rajasekhar
DBT-Bioiformatics Facility Center, Department of Biochemistry, S.K. University, Anantapur-515055, India

P. Madhusudana
DBT-Bioiformatics Facility Center, Department of Biochemistry, S.K. University, Anantapur-515055, India

C. M. Anuradha
DBT-Bioiformatics Facility Center, Department of Biochemistry, S.K. University, Anantapur-515055, India

G. Ramakrishna
Department of Microbiology, Government College (for Boys), Anantapur-515055, India

K. R. S. Sambasiva Rao
DBT-Bioiformatics Facility Center, Department of Biochemistry, S.K. University, Anantapur-515055, India

Chitta Suresh Kumar
DBT-Bioiformatics Facility Center, Department of Biochemistry, S.K. University, Anantapur-515055, India

Aditi Sharma
Department of Biochemical Engineering and Biotechnology, Indian Institute of Technology (IIT) Delhi, Hauz Khas, New Delhi 110016, India

Ankita Punetha
Department of Biochemical Engineering and Biotechnology, Indian Institute of Technology (IIT) Delhi, Hauz Khas, New Delhi 110016, India

Abhinav Grover
Department of Biochemical Engineering and Biotechnology, Indian Institute of Technology (IIT) Delhi, Hauz Khas, New Delhi 110016, India

Durai Sundar
Department of Biochemical Engineering and Biotechnology, Indian Institute of Technology (IIT) Delhi, Hauz Khas, New Delhi 110016, India

Gopal Ramesh Kumar
Bioinformatics Lab, AU-KBC Research Centre, MIT Campus, Anna University, Chennai-600 044, India

Ganesan Aravindhan
Bioinformatics Lab, AU-KBC Research Centre, MIT Campus, Anna University, Chennai-600 044, India

Thankaswamy Kosalai Subazini
Bioinformatics Lab, AU-KBC Research Centre, MIT Campus, Anna University, Chennai-600 044, India

Radhakrishnan Sathish Kumar
NRCFOSS, AU-KBC Research Centre, MIT Campus, Anna University, Chennai-600 044, India

Pankaj Koparde
Institute of Bioinformatics and Biotechnology, University of Pune, Pune -411007, India

Shailza Singh
National Centre for Cell Science, Pune University Campus, Pune -411007, India

Vibhu Ranjan Prasad
School of Bioscience and Technology, Vellore Institute of Technology, Vellore, Tamil Nadu – 632014, India

Soumya Chaurasia
School of Bioscience and Technology, Vellore Institute of Technology, Vellore, Tamil Nadu – 632014, India

Rao Sethumadhavan
School of Bioscience and Technology, Vellore Institute of Technology, Vellore, Tamil Nadu – 632014, India

Xiang-Long Li
College of Animal Science and Technology, Hebei Agricultural University, Baoding 071001, China

Fu-Jun Feng
College of Animal Science and Technology, Hebei Agricultural University, Baoding 071001, China

Rong-Yan Zhou
College of Animal Science and Technology, Hebei Agricultural University, Baoding 071001, China

Lan-Hui Li
College of Animal Science and Technology, Hebei Agricultural University, Baoding 071001, China

Hui-qin Zheng
College of Animal Science and Technology, Hebei Agricultural University, Baoding 071001, China

Gui-ru Zheng
College of Animal Science and Technology, Hebei Agricultural University, Baoding 071001, China

Marc Girondot
Laboratoire d'Écologie, Systématique et Évolution, UMR 8079 Centre National de la Recherche Scientifique, Université Paris Sud et ENGREF, 91405 Orsay cedex 05, France
Département de Systématique et Evolution, Muséum National d'Histoire Naturelle de Paris, 25 rue Cuvier, 75005 Paris, France

Jean-Yves Sire
Université Pierre and Marie Curie-Paris 6, UMR 7138 "Systématique, Adaptation, Evolution", 7 quai St-Bernard, 75005 Paris, France

Oladele Peter Kolawole
Federal university of Technology Akure, Nigeria
International Institute of Tropical Agriculture, Ibadan, Nigeria

Leo Ayodeji Sunday Agbetoye
Federal university of Technology Akure, Nigeria

Agboola Simeon Ogunlowo
Federal university of Technology Akure, Nigeria

Uma Maheshwari
Department of Bioinformatics, Aloysius Institute of Management and Information Technology, St. Aloysius College
(Autonomous), 2nd Cross, Sharada Nagar, Beeri, Kotekar Post, Madoor, Mangalore -575022, Karnataka, India

Hasan Bilal Mirza
Department of Biosciences, COMSATS Institute of Information Technology, Chak Shehzad Campus, Islamabad, Pakistan

Maryam Anwar
Department of Biosciences, COMSATS Institute of Information Technology, Chak Shehzad Campus, Islamabad, Pakistan

S. Habib Bokhari
Department of Biosciences, COMSATS Institute of Information Technology, Chak Shehzad Campus, Islamabad, Pakistan

Satya vani Guttula
Department, Biotechnology, Al-Ameer College of Engineering and IT, Visakhapatam, Andhra Pradesh, India

Allam Appa Rao
Jawaharlal Nehru Technological University, Kakinada, Andhra Pradesh, India

G. R. Sridhar
Endocrine and Diabetes Centre, Visakhapatnam, Andhra Pradesh, India

M. S. Chakravarthy
Department of Marine Living Resources, Andhra University, Andhra Pradesh, India

Tabish Qidwai
Department of Biochemistry, University of Allahabad, Allahabad, U. P., India

Prabhash K. Pandey
Department of Biochemistry, Dr. Ram Manohar Lohia Avadh University, Faizabad-224001, U.P., India

Sangram Singh
Department of Biochemistry, Dr. Ram Manohar Lohia Avadh University, Faizabad-224001, U.P., India

Farrukh Jamal
Department of Biochemistry, Dr. Ram Manohar Lohia Avadh University, Faizabad-224001, U.P., India

G. Jhansi Rani
Department of Biochemistry and Bioinformatics, Hindustan College of Arts and Science, Chennai, India

M. Vinoth
Department of Biochemistry and Bioinformatics, Hindustan College of Arts and Science, Chennai, India

P. Anitha
Department of Biochemistry and Bioinformatics, Hindustan College of Arts and Science, Chennai, India

V. Srinivasa Rao
Department of Computer Science and Engineering, V.R Siddhartha Engineering College, Kanuru, Vijayawada-520 007, India

K. Srinivas
Department of Computer Science and Engineering, V.R Siddhartha Engineering College, Kanuru, Vijayawada-520 007, India

Shailza Singh
Institute of Bioinformatics and Biotechnology, University of Pune, Pune-411007, India

Priyanka Joshi
Institute of Bioinformatics and Biotechnology, University of Pune, Pune-411007, India

Balu Ananda Chopade
Institute of Bioinformatics and Biotechnology, University of Pune, Pune-411007, India

Mohammad Arjmand
Department of Biochemistry, Pasteur Institute of Iran, Pasteur Ave, Tehran 13164, Iran

Fatemeh Darvizeh
Department of Chemistry, Sharif University of Technology, Tehran 11155-9516, Iran

Ziba Akbari
Department of Biochemistry, Pasteur Institute of Iran, Pasteur Ave, Tehran 13164, Iran

Reyhaneh Mohabati
Department of Biochemistry, Pasteur Institute of Iran, Pasteur Ave, Tehran 13164, Iran

Zahra Zamani
Department of Biochemistry, Pasteur Institute of Iran, Pasteur Ave, Tehran 13164, Iran

Naresh Kumar
Department of Biotechnology, Himachal Pradesh University (HPU), Summer Hill, Shimla, Himachal Pradesh-171005, India

T. C. Bhalla
Department of Biotechnology, Himachal Pradesh University (HPU), Summer Hill, Shimla, Himachal Pradesh-171005, India

Samina Bilal
Department of Computer Sciences and Bioinformatics, Mohammad Ali Jinnah University Islamabad Sihala Road, Pakistan

Shumaila Barkat Ali
Department of Computer Sciences and Bioinformatics, Mohammad Ali Jinnah University Islamabad Sihala Road, Pakistan

Sahar Fazal
Department of Computer Sciences and Bioinformatics, Mohammad Ali Jinnah University Islamabad Sihala Road, Pakistan

Asif Mir
Department of Computer Sciences and Bioinformatics, Mohammad Ali Jinnah University Islamabad Sihala Road, Pakistan

Morad Rostami
Biochemistry Department, Faculty of Medicine, Ahvaz Jundishapur University of Medical Sciences, Iran

Mohammad Aberomand
Biochemistry Department, Faculty of Medicine, Ahvaz Jundishapur University of Medical Sciences, Iran

Alireza Khirollah
Biochemistry Department, Faculty of Medicine, Ahvaz Jundishapur University of Medical Sciences, Iran

Masoomeh Jorfi
Microbiology Department, Faculty of Medicine, Ahvaz Jundishapur University of Medical Sciences, Iran

Manoranjan Kumar Singh
Department of Mathematics, Magadh University, Bodhagaya, Gaya, Bihar, India-823001

L. Rakesh
Magadh University, Bodhgaya, Gaya, India-823001

Aniket Ranjan
Department of Computer-Science, SCT Institute of Technology, Bangalore, India-560075

Art Kovačič
Institute for Economic Research, Kardeljeva pl. Ljubljana, Slovenia

Vijay Laxmi Saxena
National Bioinformatics Infrastructure Facility Centre of (DBT) Ministry of Science and Technology (Govt. of India), D.G (PG) College civil lines Kanpur (u.p)

Alka Dwivedi
National Bioinformatics Infrastructure Facility Centre of (DBT) Ministry of Science and Technology (Govt. of India), D.G (PG) College civil lines Kanpur (u.p)

S. S. Soam
Department of Computer Science and Engineering, Institute of Engineering and Technology Gautam Buddh Technical University, Lucknow, India

Feroz Khan
Department of Metabolic and Structural Biology, CSIR-Central Institute of Medicinal and Aromatic Plants, Lucknow, India

Bharat Bhasker
Department of Information Technology and System, Indian Institute of Management, Lucknow, India

B. N. Mishra
Department of Biotechnology, Institute of Engineering and Technology, Gautam Buddh Technical University, Lucknow, India

M. Hossein Moeinzadeh
Department of Computer Science, University of Tehran, Iran

Ehsan Asgarian
Department of Computer Engineering, Sharif University of Technology, Tehran, Iran

S. Amala
Department of Biotechnology and Bioinformatics, Dhanalakshmi Srinivasan, College of Arts and Science for Women, Perambalur-621212, Tamil Nadu, India

Ajit Kumar Saxena
Human Molecular Cytogenetic Laboratory, Centre of Experimental Medicine and Surgery, Banaras Hindu University, Varanasi-221005, India

Jyoti Gupta
Human Molecular Cytogenetic Laboratory, Centre of Experimental Medicine and Surgery, Banaras Hindu University, Varanasi-221005, India

S. Pandey
Human Molecular Cytogenetic Laboratory, Centre of Experimental Medicine and Surgery, Banaras Hindu University, Varanasi-221005, India

A.N. Gangopadhyay
Department of Obstetrics and Gynecology, Institute of Medical Sciences, Banaras Hindu University, Varanasi-221005, India

L. K. Pandey
Department of Pediatric Surgery, Institute of Medical Sciences, Banaras Hindu University, Varanasi-221005, India

B. Mukunthan
Department of Master of Computer Applications and Research, SVS College of Engineering, Coimbatore, Tamil Nadu, India- 614030

N. Nagaveni
Department of Mathematics and Research, Coimbatore Institute of Technology, Coimbatore, Tamil Nadu, India

A.Pushpalatha
Department of Mathematics and Research, Coimbatore Institute of Technology, Coimbatore, Tamil Nadu, India

Naaz Abbas
Food and Biotechnology Research Center, PCSIR Laboratories complex Lahore 54600, Pakistan

Mohammad Ajmal
Centre of Excellence in Molecular Biology, University of the Punjab, Lahore, Pakistan

Talat Afroze
Centre of Excellence in Molecular Biology, University of the Punjab, Lahore, Pakistan

J. Muthukumaran
Centre for Bioinformatics, School of Life Sciences, Pondicherry University, Puducherry – 605 014, India

P. Manivel
Centre for Bioinformatics, School of Life Sciences, Pondicherry University, Puducherry – 605 014, India

M. Kannan
Centre for Bioinformatics, School of Life Sciences, Pondicherry University, Puducherry – 605 014, India

J. Jeyakanthan
Department of Bioinformatics, Alagappa University, Karaikudi, 630 003, India

R. Krishna
Centre for Bioinformatics, School of Life Sciences, Pondicherry University, Puducherry – 605 014, India

Manoj Giri
Department of Applied Sciences, Haryana College of Technology and Management, Kaithal-136 027, India

Dipti Jindal
Department of Bioinformatics, Chaudhary Charan Singh Haryana Agricultural University, Hisar- 125 004, India

Savita Kumari
Department of Bioinformatics, Chaudhary Charan Singh Haryana Agricultural University, Hisar- 125 004, India

Sarla Kumari
Deparmtnet of Electronics and Communication Engineering, Haryana College of Technology and Management, Kaithal-136 027, India

Devender Singh
Department of Applied Sciences, Dayal Singh College, Karnal-132 001, India

Jawahar Lal
Department of Applied Sciences, Markanda National College, Sahabad (M) 136 135, India

Neena Jaggi
Department of Applied Sciences, National Institute of Technology, Kurukshetra-136 199, India

Printed in the USA
CPSIA information can be obtained
at www.ICGtesting.com
JSHW051428221024
72173JS00006B/1410